THE
BIBLE
CHAPTER
BY
CHAPTER

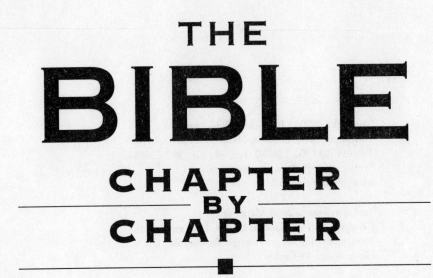

BY MARK WATER

John Hunt
Publishing Limited

Copyright © 2003 John Hunt Publishing Ltd
46A West Street, Alresford, Hants SO24 9AU, U.K.
Tel: +44 (0) 1962 736880 Fax: +44 (0) 1962 736881
E-mail: office@johnhunt-publishing.com
www.johnhunt-publishing.com

Text copyright © 2003 Mark Water
Cover illustration: Nautilus Design, Basingstoke, UK
Typography: Jim Weaver Design. Basingstoke, UK
Cover images by Corbis

ISBN 1 84298 058 0

A CIP catalogue record for this book is available from the British
Library.

Printed by W S Bookwell, Finland

Contents

Introduction

One of the most difficult problems facing Christendom is that the world's most widely translated, most widely distributed, and best-selling book is, often, an unopened book. And even when it is opened, most Christians remain ignorant of 90 per cent of its contents. Many rarely stray beyond the Psalms in the Old Testament and the Gospels in the New Testament. *The Bible Chapter by Chapter* seeks to remedy this. The reader who studies this encyclopedic volume will have a bird's-eye view of every chapter of the Bible. Here the 929 chapters of the Old Testament and the 260 chapters of the New Testament are outlined and analyzed.

The chapter divisions and verse divisions in our Bible are not part of the original Bible. Archbishop Stephen Langton, in 1551, divided the Bible into chapters. The Geneva Bible of 1560 was the first Bible to divide the Scriptures into verses, following the divisions worked out by the Parisian printer of Greek New Testaments, Robert Estienne. Many people, including another Frenchman, John Calvin, have criticized some of these verse and chapter divisions. However, in *The Bible Chapter by Chapter* the chapter divisions as printed in our Bibles today are followed.

Ten keys

In *The Bible Chapter by Chapter* ten "keys" are used to unlock each chapter. By means of these keys each group of verses within a chapter is linked up with the rest of its own chapter, and each chapter of the Bible is linked to the book from which it comes, and each Bible book is linked to the whole Bible.

1. ### Before and after this chapter
   This places the chapter being studied in the context of the preceding and following chapters.

2. ### Analysis of chapter
   This breaks down the chapter into sections. The headings used to indicate the theme of each section are an edited version of those chosen by Matthew Henry.

3. ### Key verse in chapter
   There is often more than just one key verse in a chapter. It is also true that

no two people would select the same key verses from all 1,189 chapters of the Bible. But thinking about someone else's choice engages our own minds. We may agree with that choice, or prefer to substitute a verse of our own choosing.

The Bible version used throughout is the New International Version, except for the key verses in chapter sections in the Old Testament, and in quotations from Psalms and Proverbs under the heading key "Quotable Quote," when the King James Version is used.

4. Key word /key phrase in chapter

As we consider the word chosen here, we can compare it with the word we would have selected as the key word for each chapter, and in this way be helped to think about the chapter carefully.

5. Key event / key person / key theme

It is surprisingly easy to miss the significant happening in a chapter of the Bible, just because we are familiar with it, and because we think we know all about it. By forcing ourselves to note the key event, and the key person in a chapter, the content of the chapter comes more clearly into focus.

6. Key thought in chapter

This section highlights one important thought from each chapter in the Bible.

7. Key thing/s to look out for in chapter

In this section one important question is raised.

8. Key biblical cross-reference to chapter

These cross-references enable the Bible student to engage in one of the most profitable aspects of Bible study: comparing scripture with scripture.

9. Key "by way of explanation"

There are scores of background details which, once explained, give greater understanding of the chapter of the Bible being studied. Sometimes these have an important bearing on leading theological issues.

10. Key "Quotable Quote"

These quotations, often taken from expert Bible expositors, leading theologians, and experienced pastors, give an illuminating comment on the chapter, or one verse from the chapter.

The urgent need for Bible study

William Tyndale (c. 1492-1536) was forced to flee from England to Germany to work on his translation of the New Testament. When published on the continent in 1526 it was smuggled back and distributed in England. It became the most important translation of the Bible in English in its day. Because Tyndale was a close friend of Martin Luther the Roman Catholic authorities attempted to stop his translation work, but by 1535 Tyndale had completed translations of the Pentateuch and Jonah. However British agents, with the permission of King Henry VIII, and on the orders of Cardinal Wolsey, were sent to arrest Tyndale. He was tracked down and seized in the Belgium town of Antwerp and confined, awaiting trial, in Vilvorde Castle, near Brussels. Before he was strangled and burned at the stake he wrote the following letter as he languished in prison in Vilvorde Castle.

> I believe, right worshipful, that you are not ignorant of what has been determined concerning me [by the Council of Brabant]; therefore I entreat your Lordship, and that by the Lord Jesus, that if I am to remain here [in Vilvorde] during the winter, you will request the Procurer to be kind enough to send me from my goods, which he has in his possession, a warmer cap, for I suffer extremely from cold in the head, being afflicted with a perpetual catarrh, which is considerably increased in the cell. . . .
>
> But above all, I entreat and beseech your clemency to be urgent with the Procurer that he may kindly permit me to have my Hebrew Bible, Hebrew Grammar, and Hebrew Dictionary, that I may spend my time with that study. And in return, may you obtain your dearest wish, provided always it be consistent with the salvation of your soul. But if any other resolutions have been come to concerning me, before the conclusion of the winter, I shall be patient, abiding the will of God to the glory of the grace of my Lord Jesus Christ, whose spirit, I pray, may ever direct your heart. Amen.
>
> W. Tindalus (William Tyndale)

Tyndale's passion for Bible study is in urgent need of being replicated today. The former slave-trader, John Newton, said of the Bible, "Some books are copper, some are silver, and some few are gold; but the Bible alone is like a book all made up of bank notes." We need to study the Bible for ourselves, both for our own spiritual health and so that we may make an effective and authentic spiritual contribution to our Christian fellowship and wider community.

John R.W. Stott has written, "The secrets of Christian maturity are to be found in Scripture by all who seek them. There is a breadth to God's Word which few of us ever encompass, a depth which we seldom plumb. The Bible is the portrait of Jesus Christ. We need to gaze upon him with such intensity of desire that (by the gracious work of the Holy Spirit) he comes alive to us, meets with us, and fills us with himself." As Augustine put it, "Ignorance of Scripture is ignorance of Christ."

The Bible Chapter by Chapter enables the reader to explore the unfamiliar books of the Bible as well as the Bible books which are already treasured and well known. The contents of each page can be used in both personal and group Bible study. The aim of *The Bible Chapter by Chapter* is to help us to carry out for ourselves the command of Paul the apostle: "Study to shew thyself approved unto God, a workman that needeth not to be ashamed, rightly dividing the word of truth" (2 Timothy 2:15 KJV).

THE OLD TESTAMENT

Genesis

Genesis chapter 1

1. ### Following chapter

    Chapter 2: A second account of creation

2. ### Analysis of chapter

    God creates heaven and earth. (1,2)
    The creation of light. (3-5)
    God separates the earth from the waters, and makes it fruitful. (6-13)
    God forms the sun, moon, and stars. (14-19)
    Animals created. (20-25)
    Man created in the image of God. (26-28)
    Food is given. (29,30)
    The work of creation ended and approved. (31)

3. ### Key verse

    Verse 1: "In the beginning God created the heaven and the earth."

4. ### Key word / key phrase

    Verse 1, "beginning."

5. ### Key event / key person / key theme

    God's creation explains the origin of the earth and the heavens.

6. ### Key thought

    Everything that God created was good. Note how this is repeatedly stated in this chapter.

7. ### Key thing to look out for

    Man was made in the image of God, verses 26,27.

8. ### Key Bible cross-reference

    Read the opening chapter of John's Gospel alongside this chapter.

9. ### Key "by way of explanation"

    The Bible never attempts to explain, justify, or defend God as the Creator of the universe. The truth is boldly stated as a fact and is affirmed by Bible poetry, Psalm 102:25, and Bible prophecy, Isaiah 40:21.

10. ### Key "Quotable Quote"

    "Whatever view is taken of the relationship of the two accounts of creation, in chapters 1 and 2, it is clear that the former is written from God's standpoint, while man is the center of the latter."
    H. L. Ellison

Genesis chapter 2

1. *Before and after*

Previous chapter: Chapter 1: The first account of creation
Following chapter: Chapter 3: The record of the fall of humankind

2. *Analysis of chapter*

The first Sabbath. (1-3)
Details about the creation. (4-7)
The planting of the garden of Eden. (8-14)
Man is placed in it. (15)
God's command. (16,17)
The animals named, the making of woman, the divine institution of marriage. (18-25)

3. *Key verse*

Verse 1: "Thus the heavens and the earth were finished, and all the host of them."

4. *Key word / key phrase*

Verse 1, "The heavens and the earth."

5. *Key event / key person / key theme*

God completed his creation.

6. *Key thought*

Verse 2. The "seventh day" was special, and was especially blessed by God.

7. *Key thing to look out for*

Verse 15. What responsibilities have been given to humankind?

8. *Key Bible cross-reference*

Verse 9, "Tree of life." See 3:22; Revelation 2:7; 22:2,14.

9. *Key "by way of explanation"*

Verse 7, "And the Lord God formed man from the dust of the ground." The Hebrew word translated "formed" is used of a potter and his work: Isaiah 45:9; Jeremiah 18:6. God "formed" humans and animals: verse 19; 1:21,25.

10. *Key "Quotable Quote"*

"If man is the head, she [woman] is the crown, a crown to her husband, the crown of visible creation. The man was dust refined, but the woman was dust double-refined."
Matthew Henry's *Commentary on the Bible* (on Genesis 2:21-25).

Genesis chapter 3

1. *Before and after*

Previous chapter: Chapter 2: A second account of creation
Following chapter: Chapter 4: Cain and Abel

2. *Analysis of chapter*

The serpent deceives Eve. (1-5)
Adam and Eve break the divine command, and fall into sin and misery. (6-8)
God calls upon Adam and Eve to answer. (9-13)
The serpent cursed, and the promised Seed. (14,15)
The punishment of humankind. (16-19)
The first clothing of humankind. (20,21)
Adam and Eve are driven out of paradise. (22-24)

3. *Key verse*

Verse 6: "And when the woman saw that the tree was good for food, and that it was pleasant to the eyes, and a tree to be desired to make one wise, she took of the fruit thereof, and did eat, and gave also unto her husband with her; and he did eat."

4. *Key word / key phrase*

Verse 17, "cursed."

5. *Key event / key person / key theme*

The Fall

6. *Key thought*

Both Adam and Eve gave way to temptation. "Many a dangerous temptation comes to us in fine gay colors, that are but skin-deep." Matthew Henry

7. *Key thing to look out for*

"There is a kind of foreshadowing of the whole gospel in Genesis 3:15." D. Martyn Lloyd-Jones

8. *Key Bible cross-reference*

Verse 6 shows three aspects of temptation: see 1 John 2:16; Luke 4:3,5,9.

9. *Key "by way of explanation"*

Verse 1. The "serpent" is a reference to the devil. He is also described as "that ancient serpent" Revelation 12:9.

10. *Key "Quotable Quote"*

"Jesus assumes the thorns, that he may cancel the sentence; for this cause also was he buried in the earth, that the earth which had been cursed might receive the blessing instead of a curse."
Cyril of Jerusalem, *Catechetical Lectures*

Genesis chapter 4

1. Before and after

Previous chapter: Chapter 3: The record of the fall of humankind
Following chapter: Chapter 5: Potted histories: Adam to Noah

2. Analysis of chapter

The birth, work, and religion of Cain and Abel. (1-7)
Cain murders Abel, and the curse of Cain. (8-15)
The behavior of Cain, his family. (16-18)
Lamech and his wives, and the skill of Cain's descendants. (19-24)
The birth of another son and grandson of Adam. (25,26)

3. Key verse

Verse 8: "And Cain talked with Abel his brother: and it came to pass, when they were in the field, that Cain rose up against Abel his brother, and slew him."

4. Key word / key phrase

Verse 5, "anger."

5. Key event / key person / key theme

The first murder recorded in the Bible.

6. Key thought

Verse 8. Cain was deliberately deceitful.

7. Key thing to look out for

Verse 24. The extent of personal revenge can be contrasted with Jesus' teaching about the extent of our forgiving, see Matthew 18:21,22.

8. Key Bible cross-reference

Verse 10. See Luke 11:50,51; Hebrews 11:4; 12:24.

9. Key "by way of explanation"

Verse 7, "sin is crouching at your door." Sin is pictured here, crouching, and waiting to pounce on Cain.

10. Key "Quotable Quote"

"Original sin may be defined as hereditary corruption and depravity of our nature, extending to all the parts of the soul, which first makes us obnoxious to the wrath of God, and then produces in us works which in Scripture are termed works of the flesh."
John Calvin, *The Institutes of Christian Religion*

Genesis chapter 5

1. **Before and after**

   Previous chapter: Chapter 4: Cain and Abel
   Following chapter: Chapter 6: The judgment of the Flood

2. **Analysis of chapter**

   Adam and Seth. (1-5)
   The patriarchs from Seth to Enoch. (6-20)
   Enoch. (21-24)
   Methuselah to Noah. (25-32)

3. **Key verse**

   Verse 5: "This is the book of the generations of Adam."

4. **Key word / key phrase**

   Verse 23, "walked."

5. **Key event / key person / key theme**

   Account of Adam's descendants

6. **Key thought**

   Verse 3. Adam was made in God's perfect image, but because of the Fall,
   Adam's son was born with Adam's fallen nature.

7. **Key thing to look out for**

   If the number of years each person lived for is taken literally, then Methuselah
   died in the same year as the flood. The figures in verses 27 and 25,28, and 7:6
   make 969.

8. **Key Bible cross-reference**

   Verse 23. The only other person whom the Bible records as being translated
   directly to heaven without dying is Elijah. See 2 Kings 2:10; Hebrews 11:5.

9. **Key "by way of explanation"**

   Verse 31, "777." Lamech is said to have lived for 777 years. Seven stands for
   completeness, so 777 would be a number emphasizing completeness.

10. **Key "Quotable Quote"**

    "Someone once quipped that the doctrine of original sin is the only
    philosophy empirically validated by thirty-five centuries of recorded human
    history."
    Charles Colson

Genesis chapter 6

1. Before and after

Previous chapter: Chapter 5: Potted histories: Adam to Noah
Following chapter: Chapter 7: Entering the ark and the flooded earth

2. Analysis of chapter

The wickedness of the world, which provoked God's wrath. (1-7)
Noah finds grace. (8-11)
Noah warned of the flood, and the directions about the ark. (12-21)
Noah's faith and obedience. (22)

3. Key verse

Verse 8: "But Noah found grace in the eyes of the LORD."

4. Key word / key phrase

Verse 5, "wickedness."

5. Key event / key person / key theme

The Flood

6. Key thought

Verses 11,12. The Flood event pictures God's wrath and attitude to human sin.

7. Key thing to look out for

Verse 9. Noah's character.

8. Key Bible cross-reference

Verse 18. God rescuing Noah from the flood is a picture of God's salvation.
See Hebrews 11:7; 2 Peter 2:5.

9. Key "by way of explanation"

Verse 17, "Destroy all life." From this some argue that the flood was universal.
Others, however, argue that such universal language is also used elsewhere,
such as 41:54,57, where it was not intended to be interpreted as having a global
dimension.

10. Key "Quotable Quote"

"Noah was the first of many individuals who, apparently single-handed, have
been used by God to carry out his purpose and to make a crucial difference
to the world. Even today people famous and people unknown are making a
difference in the world simply by trying to obey God. They have refused to be
bullied into believing that what they do makes no difference."
Stephen Travis

Genesis chapter 7

1. Before and after

Previous chapter: Chapter 6: The judgment of the Flood
Following chapter: Chapter 8: The Flood recedes

2. Analysis of chapter

Noah, his family, and the living creatures enter the ark, and the flood begins. (1-12)
Noah shut in the ark. (13-16)
The flood rises for forty days. (17-20)
All flesh is destroyed by the flood. (21-24)

3. Key verse

Verse 5: "And Noah did according unto all that the LORD commanded him."

4. Key word / key phrase

Verse 5, "commanded."

5. Key event / key person / key theme

Noah obeys God.

6. Key thought

Verse 16, "God . . . commanded . . . the Lord shut." This verse illustrates how God takes the initiative in salvation, how humankind should obey, and how God acts.

7. Key thing to look out for

Verse 4, "Forty days and forty nights." This period of time is mentioned at other key moments in the Bible: see Deuteronomy 9:11; Matthew 4:1-11.

8. Key Bible cross-reference

Verse 13. See 1 Peter 3:20 and 2 Peter 2:5.

9. Key "by way of explanation"

Verse 2, "Take with you seven of every kind of clean animal, a male and its mate, and two of every kind of unclean animal." The ceremonially clean animals would be needed as sacrifices after the Flood.

10. Key "Quotable Quote"

"God, if he has freely justified you by faith in his Son, and given you his Spirit, has sealed you to be his; and has secured you, as surely as he secured Noah, when he locked him in the ark."
George Whitefield

Genesis chapter 8

1. *Before and after*

Previous chapter: Chapter 7: Entering the ark and the flooded earth
Following chapter: Chapter 9: God's covenant with Noah

2. *Analysis of chapter*

God remembers Noah, and dries up the waters. (1-3)
The ark rests on Ararat. Noah sends out a raven and a dove. (4-12)
Noah being commanded, goes out of the ark. (13-19)
Noah offers sacrifices, God promises never again to destroy all living creatures. (20-22)

3. *Key verse*

Verse 1: "And God remembered Noah."

4. *Key word / key phrase*

Verse 20, "sacrificed."

5. *Key event / key person / key theme*

Noah leaves the ark.

6. *Key thought*

Worship is the appropriate way to acknowledge God's goodness.

7. *Key thing to look out for*

Verse 14. The length of time Noah and his family were in the ark, even after the rain had stopped.

8. *Key Bible cross-reference*

Verse 8. Note how God remembers his people on this occasion, and, "with favor," on other occasions: see Nehemiah 5:19; 13:31.

9. *Key "by way of explanation"*

Verse 11, "olive leaf." Olives do not grow at the tops of mountains, but at lower altitudes. So the waters must have receded.

10. *Key "Quotable Quote"*

"Nature is God's tongue."
Henry Ward Beecher

Genesis chapter 9
God's covenant with Noah

1. *Before and after*

    Previous chapter: Chapter 8: The Flood is over; a new beginning
    Following chapter: Chapter 10: Family lines after the Flood

2. *Analysis of chapter*

    God blesses Noah, and grants flesh for food. (1-3)
    Murder forbidden. (4-7)
    God's covenant and the sign of the rainbow. (8-17)
    Noah plants a vineyard gets drunk and is mocked by Ham. (18-23)
    Noah curses Canaan, blesses Shem, and prays for Japheth. Noah's death. (24-29)

3. *Key verse*

    Verse 13: "I do set my bow in the cloud, and it shall be for a token of a covenant between me and the earth."

4. *Key word / key phrase*

    Verse 15, "never again."

5. *Key event / key person / key theme*

    God's covenant with Noah

6. *Key thought*

    Verse 12. The covenant "sign" pointed to God's love in making the covenant.

7. *Key thing to look out for*

    Noah's first actions on leaving the ark.

8. *Key Bible cross-reference*

    Verse 6. See Exodus 21:12-14; Numbers 35:16-32; Romans 13:3,4; 1 Peter 2:13,14.

9. *Key "by way of explanation"*

    Verse 12, "Rainbow." There is no suggestion that rainbows did not exist before the Flood. But now they have been given special significance.

10. *Key "Quotable Quote"*

    "If you say, 'Would there were no wine' because of the drunkards, then you must say, going on by degrees, 'Would there were no steel,' because of the murderers, 'Would there were no night,' because of the thieves, 'Would there were no light,' because of the informers, and 'Would there were no women,' because of adultery."
    John Chrysostom, *Homilies*

Genesis chapter 10
Descendants of Noah's sons

1. **Before and after**

   Previous chapter: Chapter 9: God's covenant with Noah
   Following chapter: Chapter 11: The tower of Babel

2. **Analysis of chapter**

   The sons of Noah, of Japheth, of Ham. (1-7)
   Nimrod the first ruler. (8-14)
   The descendants of Canaan, and the sons of Shem. (15-32)

3. **Key verse**

   Verse 1: "Now these are the generations of the sons of Noah, Shem, Ham, and Japheth: and unto them were sons born after the flood."

4. **Key word / key phrase**

   Verse 32, "flood."

5. **Key event / key person / key theme**

   The record of family trees

6. **Key thought**

   God is the Author of all human life.

7. **Key thing to look out for**

   The Bible is full of history, not fairy tales.

8. **Key Bible cross-reference**

   Verse 12. The "great city" here is most probably Nineveh, see Jonah 1:2; 3:2; 4:11.

9. **Key "by way of explanation"**

   Verse 29, "Ophir." Much of Solomon's gold came from here, 1 Kings 9:28.

10. **Key "Quotable Quote"**

    "Peace in society depends upon peace in the family."
    Augustine of Hippo

Genesis chapter 11

1. *Before and after*

Previous chapter: Chapter 10: Family lines after the Flood
Following chapter: Chapter 12: God calls Abraham

2. *Analysis of chapter*

One language in the world, and the building of Babel. (1-4)
The confusion of tongues, and the builders of Babel scattered. (5-9)
The descendants of Shem. (10-26)
Terah, father of Abram, grandfather of Lot, they move to Haran. (27-32)

3. *Key verse*

Verse 4: "And they said, Go to, let us build us a city and a tower, whose top may reach unto heaven; and let us make us a name, lest we be scattered abroad upon the face of the whole earth."

4. *Key word / key phrase*

Verse 4, "scattered."

5. *Key event / key person / key theme*

Building the tower of Babel

6. *Key thought*

Abram is introduced.

7. *Key thing to look out for*

God sees everything, even hidden motives.

8. *Key Bible cross-reference*

Verse 30. Sarah being barren was a most important event: 15:2-3; 17:5, 17.

9. *Key "by way of explanation"*

Verse 3, "brick instead of stone." As stones were so scarce in Mesopotamia, bricks made of mud and bitumen were used as building materials.

10. *Key "Quotable Quote"*

"The only Bible-honoring conclusion is, of course, that Genesis 1-11 is actual historical truth, regardless of any scientific or chronological problems thereby entailed."
Dr Henry Morris, President ICR, 1972

Genesis chapter 12

1. Before and after

Previous chapter: Chapter 11: The tower of Babel
Following chapter: Chapter 13: Abraham and Lot separate

2. Analysis of chapter

God calls Abram, and blesses him with a promise about Christ. (1-3)
Abram departs from Haran. (4,5)
He travels through Canaan, and worships God in that land. (6-9)
Abram is driven by a famine into Egypt, he pretends that his wife is his sister. (10-20)

3. Key verse

Verse 1: "Now the LORD had said unto Abram, Get thee out of thy country, and from thy kindred, and from thy father's house, unto a land that I will show thee."

4. Key word / key phrase

Verse 2, "bless."

5. Key event / key person / key theme

The call of Abram

6. Key thought

From one person, God chose a great people who would be his followers.

7. Key thing to look out for

Verse 7. The Lord often appeared to Abram, even though he did not appear in all his glory.

8. Key Bible cross-reference

Verses 2-3. See verses 7; 15:2-21; 17:4-8; 18:18,19; 22:17,18.

9. Key "by way of explanation"

Verses 2-3. God reaffirmed his covenant and blessing to Isaac, 26:2-4, and to Jacob, 28:13-15, and to Moses, Exodus 3:6-8.

10. Key "Quotable Quote"

"Election is God's eternal choice of some persons unto everlasting life – not because of foreseen merit in them, but of his sheer mercy in Christ – in consequence of which choice they are called, justified, and glorified."
James Boyce

Genesis chapter 13

1. *Before and after*

> Previous chapter: Chapter 12: God calls Abraham
> Following chapter: Chapter 14: Abram rescues Lot

2. *Analysis of chapter*

> Abram returns from of Egypt with great riches. (1-4)
> Strife between the herdsmen of Abram and Lot. Abram gives Lot his choice of the country. (5-9)
> Lot chooses to live at Sodom. (10-13)
> God renews his promise to Abram, who moves to Hebron. (14-18)

3. *Key verse*

> Verse 7: "And there was a strife between the herdmen of Abram's cattle and the herdmen of Lot's cattle: and the Canaanite and the Perizzite dwelled then in the land."

4. *Key word / key phrase*

> Verse 8, "quarrelling."

5. *Key event / key person / key theme*

> Abram and Lot separate.

6. *Key thought*

> Lot was asking for trouble by going close to the wicked people of Sodom.

7. *Key thing to look out for*

> Abram shows his generous nature to Lot in allowing him to choose first where to live.

8. *Key Bible cross-reference*

> Verse 16. See 28:14; 2 Chronicles 1:9.

9. *Key "by way of explanation"*

> Verse 10, "well watered." Archaeological findings show that this area, which is now desert, was indeed once full of people who had good water supplies.

10. *Key "Quotable Quote"*

> "God judged it better to bring good out of evil than to suffer no evil to exist."
> Augustine of Hippo

Genesis chapter 14

1. **Before and after**

   Previous chapter: Chapter 13: Abraham and Lot separate
   Following chapter: Chapter 15: God's promise of children

2. **Analysis of chapter**

   The battle of the kings, Lot is taken prisoner. (1-12)
   Abram rescues Lot. (13-16)
   Melchizedek blesses Abram. (17-20)
   Abram restores the spoil. (21-24)

3. **Key verse**

   Verse 18: "And Melchizedek king of Salem brought forth bread and wine: and he was the priest of the most high God."

4. **Key word / key phrase**

   Verse 18, "Melchizedek."

5. **Key event / key person / key theme**

   Abram rescues Lot.

6. **Key thought**

   In the Bible, God is frequently identified as the Creator, see verse 19.

7. **Key thing to look out for**

   Abraham's great wealth is indicated in many ways. See verse 14.

8. **Key Bible cross-reference**

   Verse 18. See Psalm 110:4; Hebrews 7:11

9. **Key "by way of explanation"**

   Verse 20. A tenth was the amount given to a king. See 1 Samuel 8: 15,17.

10. **Key "Quotable Quote"**

    "By faith we are convinced that the signs of permanence, order, progress, which we observe in nature are true."
    B.F. Westcott

Genesis chapter 15

1. Before and after

Previous chapter: Chapter 14: Abram rescues Lot
Following chapter: Chapter 16: Hagar and Ishmael

2. Analysis of chapter

God encourages Abram. (1)
The divine promise, Abraham is justified by faith. (2-6)
God promises Canaan to Abraham for an inheritance. (7-11)
The promise confirmed in a vision. (12-16)
The promise confirmed by a sign. (17-21)

3. Key verse

Verse 6: "And he believed in the LORD; and he counted it to him for righteousness."

4. Key word / key phrase

Verse 8, "Sovereign."

5. Key event / key person / key theme

God's covenant with Abram

6. Key thought

The first reference to anyone exercising faith in God's promises comes in verse 6.

7. Key thing to look out for

The greatness of God is seen in the number of stars. 8,000 stars can be seen in a clear Near-Eastern night sky.

8. Key Bible cross-reference

Verse 17. This symbolizes God's presence: see Exodus 3:2; 14:24; 19:18; 1 Kings 18: 38: Acts 2:3,4.

9. Key "by way of explanation"

Verse 9, "three years old." This was the specified age of most sacrificial animals, 1 Samuel 1:24.

10. Key "Quotable Quote"

"Our faith was prefigured in Abraham. He was the patriarch of our faith, and, as it were, the prophet of it, as the apostle very fully taught, when he says in the epistle to the Galatians: 'Even as Abraham believed God, and it was accounted unto him for righteousness. Know ye therefore, that they which are of faith, the same are the children of Abraham.' [Abraham's] faith and ours are one and the same."
Irenaeus

Genesis chapter 16

1. *Before and after*
Previous chapter: Chapter 15: God's promise of children
Following chapter: Chapter 17: Circumcision

2. *Analysis of chapter*
Sarai gives Hagar to Abram. (1-3)
Hagar's misbehavior towards Sarai. (4-6)
The Angel commands Hagar to return, and the promise about the birth of Ishmael. (7-16)

3. *Key verse*
Verse 1: "Now Sarai Abram's wife bare him no children: and she had an handmaid, an Egyptian, whose name was Hagar."

4. *Key word / key phrase*
Verse 5, "despises."

5. *Key event / key person / key theme*
Hagar and Ishmael

6. *Key thought*
God cares for people, especially rejects of society.

7. *Key thing to look out for*
Sara's infertility illustrates that even in the most trying of situations God watches over his people.

8. *Key Bible cross-reference*
Angels are the Lord's messengers. See 19:1, 21; 31:11; Zechariah 3:1-6.

9. *Key "by way of explanation"*
Verse 5, "May the Lord judge between you and me," was a saying that indicated hatred, hostility, or suspicion. See 31:53.

10. *Key "Quotable Quote"*
"Afflictions make the heart more deep, more experimental, more knowing and profound, and so, more able to hold, to contain, and bear more."
John Bunyan

Genesis chapter 17

1. Before and after

Previous chapter: Chapter 16: Hagar and Ishmael
Following chapter: Chapter 18: Sarah and Abraham's tested

2. Analysis of chapter

God renews the covenant with Abram. (1-6)
Circumcision instituted. (7-14)
Sarai's name changed, Isaac promised. (15-22)
Abraham and his family are circumcised. (23-27)

3. Key verse

Verse 10: "This is my covenant, which ye shall keep, between me and you and thy seed after thee; Every man child among you shall be circumcised."

4. Key word / key phrase

Verse 11, "circumcision."

5. Key event / key person / key theme

The giving of circumcision as the sign of the covenant

6. Key thought

Verse 7. While we may break God's covenant, it still remains an everlasting covenant.

7. Key thing to look out for

God always requires his people to respond to his love: see verse 9.

8. Key Bible cross-reference

Verse 7. See Jeremiah 24:7; Ezekiel 24:30,31; Hosea 2:23 and Zechariah 8:8.

9. Key "by way of explanation"

Verse 19, God is referred to as "God Almighty." The Hebrew word here is "El-Shaddai," referring to God's power, and was the special name through which God revealed himself to the patriarchs.

10. Key "Quotable Quote"

"God defined: 'The One who loves.'"
Karl Barth

Genesis chapter 18

1. **Before and after**

   Previous chapter: Chapter 17: Circumcision
   Following chapter: Chapter 19: Destruction of Sodom and Gomorrah

2. **Analysis of chapter**

   The Lord appears to Abraham. (1-8)
   Sarah's unbelief reproved. (9-15)
   God reveals to Abraham the destruction of Sodom. (16-22)
   Abraham's intercession for Sodom. (23-33)

3. **Key verse**

   Verse 32: "And he said, Oh let not the Lord be angry, and I will speak yet but this once: Peradventure ten shall be found there. And he said, I will not destroy it for ten's sake."

4. **Key word / key phrase**

   Verse 25, "Judge."

5. **Key event / key person / key theme**

   Abraham entertains three visitors.

6. **Key thought**

   God's followers should always pray, no matter how bad the circumstances are.

7. **Key thing to look out for**

   Abraham's persistence in many things, and here, his persistence in prayer.

8. **Key Bible cross-reference**

   Verse 17. Abraham is said to have been God's friend: see 2 Chronicles 20:7; James 2:23.

9. **Key "by way of explanation"**

   Verse 2 says there were "three men." At least two of these "men" were angels, see 19:1. That the third "man" was the Lord himself is supported by verse 18:19.

10. **Key "Quotable Quote"**

    "Our valleys may be filled with foes and tears; but we can lift our eyes to the hills to see God and the angels, heaven's spectators, who support us according to God's infinite wisdom as they prepare our welcome home."
    Billy Graham

Genesis chapter 19

1. **Before and after**

   Previous chapter: Chapter 18: Sarah and Abraham's
   Following chapter: Chapter 20: Abimelech is tested

2. **Analysis of chapter**

   The destruction of Sodom, and the deliverance of Lot. (1-29)
   The sin and disgrace of Lot. (30-38)

3. **Key verse**

   Verse 26: "But his wife looked back from behind him, and she became a pillar of salt."

4. **Key word / key phrase**

   Verse 13, "destroy."

5. **Key event / key person / key theme**

   The destruction of Sodom

6. **Key thought**

   The blatant wickedness of the people of Sodom comes under God's judgment.

7. **Key thing to look out for**

   Lot's initial reaction to the angel's command to flee was one of hesitation, verses 16-18.

8. **Key Bible cross-reference**

   Lot's wife "looking back" became proverbial: see Luke 17:32.

9. **Key "by way of explanation"**

   Verse 26, "a pillar of salt." Strange shapes from dried salt are seen to this day at the southern end of the Dead Sea.

10. **Key "Quotable Quote"**

    "Moses here records the wonderful judgment of God, by which the wife of Lot was transformed into a statue of salt."
    John Calvin

Genesis chapter 20

1. Before and after

Previous chapter: Chapter 19: Destruction of Sodom and Gomorrah
Following chapter: Chapter 21: The birth of Isaac

2. Analysis of chapter

Abraham's stay at Gerar, Sarah is taken by Abimelech. (1-8)
Abimelech's rebuke to Abraham. (9-13)
Abimelech restores Sarah. (14-18)

3. Key verse

Verse 17: "So Abraham prayed unto God: and God healed Abimelech, and his wife, and his maidservants; and they bare children."

4. Key word / key phrase

Verse 5, "clear conscience."

5. Key event / key person / key theme

Abraham visits Abimelech.

6. Key thought

Sometimes God's followers are less righteous than those who do not profess to know God.

7. Key thing to look out for

The Bible's portraits of people includes "warts and all."

8. Key Bible cross-reference

In the Old Testament God often used dreams to reveal his will. See Numbers 12:6; Judges 7:13; Daniel 2:3.

9. Key "by way of explanation"

Verse 7. Abraham is the first person in the Bible to be given the title of prophet.

10. Key "Quotable Quote"

"It is profitable for the pious to be unsettled on earth, lest, by setting their minds on a commodious and quiet habitation, they should lose the inheritance of heaven."
John Calvin, commentating on Genesis 20:1

Genesis chapter 21

1. *Before and after*

> Previous chapter: Chapter 20: Abimelech is tested
> Following chapter: Chapter 22: Abraham's severe test

2. *Analysis of chapter*

> Birth of Isaac, Sarah's joy. (1-8)
> Ishmael mocks Isaac. (9-13)
> Hagar and Ishmael are ejected, and they are comforted by an angel. (14-21)
> Abimelech's covenant with Abraham. (22-34)

3. *Key verse*

> Verse 2: "For Sarah conceived, and bare Abraham a son in his old age, at the set time of which God had spoken to him."

4. *Key word / key phrase*

> Verse 1, "promised."

5. *Key event / key person / key theme*

> The birth of Isaac

6. *Key thought*

> God very often works "against all the odds."

7. *Key thing to look out for*

> Behind what may be read as a story or historical event, the Bible writers expect us to detect God's providential hand.

8. *Key Bible cross-reference*

> Verse 23, "kindness" is seen as an act of friendship. See verse 27; 20:14.

9. *Key "by way of explanation"*

> Verse 8. It was quite normal for toddlers in the ancient Near East, as it is in Africa today, not to be weaned before they were two or three years old.

10. *Key "Quotable Quote"*

> "The family should be a place where each new human being can have an early atmosphere conducive to the development of constructive creativity."
> Edith Schaeffer

Genesis chapter 22

1. *Before and after*

    Previous chapter: Chapter 21: The birth of Isaac
    Following chapter: Chapter 23: Abraham buries Sarah

2. *Analysis of chapter*

    God commands Abraham to sacrifice Isaac. (1,2)
    Abraham's faith and obedience to the divine command. (3-10)
    Another sacrifice is provided in the place of Isaac. (11-14)
    The covenant with Abraham renewed. (15-19)
    The family of Nahor. (20-24)

3. *Key verse*

    Verse 2: "And he said, Take now thy son, thine only son Isaac, whom thou lovest, and get thee into the land of Moriah; and offer him there for a burnt offering upon one of the mountains which I will tell thee of."

4. *Key word / key phrase*

    Verse 8, "God himself will provide."

5. *Key event / key person / key theme*

    Abraham's faith is tested.

6. *Key thought*

    God asks Abraham to give up his most prized possession.

7. *Key thing to look out for*

    Note how this event depicts the resurrection.

8. *Key Bible cross-reference*

    Verse 8 says God provided a ram. Jesus was God's sacrificial lamb. See John 1:29, 36.

9. *Key "by way of explanation"*

    Verse 13, "He went over and took the ram and sacrificed it as a burnt offering instead of his son." This is the first time that the concept of substitutionary sacrifice is mentioned in the Bible. See Mark 10:45.

10. *Key "Quotable Quote"*

    "For family devotions, Martin Luther once read the account of Abraham offering Isaac on the altar in Genesis 22. His wife, Katie, said, 'I do not believe it. God would not have treated his son like that!' 'But, Katie,' Luther replied, 'he did.'"
    Warren Wiersbe

Genesis chapter 23

1. Before and after

Previous chapter: Chapter 22: Abraham's severe test
Following chapter: Chapter 24: Finding a wife for Isaac

2. Analysis of chapter

The death of Sarah, Abraham buys a burial place. (1-13)
Sarah's burial place. (14-20)

3. Key verse

Verse 2: "And Sarah died in Kirjatharba."

4. Key word / key phrase

Verse 6, "tomb/s."

5. Key event / key person / key theme

Sarah's death

6. Key thought

Abraham bought land in "the land of Canaan," verse 19, and so showed his faith in God's promise that Canaan would be his new homeland.

7. Key thing to look out for

The purchase of the cave of Machpelah, verse 9, became important later on. See 25:8-10; 49:30,31; 50:12,13.

8. Key Bible cross-reference

Verse 4. The patriarchs often referred to themselves as "aliens" or "strangers." See 1 Chronicles 29:15; Psalm 39:12.

9. Key "by way of explanation"

Verses 10-16. Abraham was coaxed into paying a high price for the land. But Abraham did not mind, as this land became the first part of a great inheritance.

10. Key "Quotable Quote"

"Faith has to do with things that are not seen, and hope with things that are not in hand."
Thomas Aquinas

Genesis chapter 24

1. *Before and after*

Previous chapter: Chapter 23: Abraham buries Sarah
Following chapter: Chapter 25: Abraham dies

2. *Analysis of chapter*

Abraham's concern for Isaac's marriage. (1-9)
The journey of Abraham's servant to Mesopotamia, his meeting with Rebekah. (10-28)
Rebekah and her relatives consent to her marriage. (29-53)
The happy meeting and marriage of Isaac and Rebekah. (54-67)

3. *Key verse*

Verse 3: "And I will make thee swear by the LORD, the God of heaven, and the God of the earth, that thou shalt not take a wife unto my son of the daughters of the Canaanites, among whom I dwell."

4. *Key word / key phrase*

Verse 7, "promised."

5. *Key event / key person / key theme*

Rebekah becomes Isaac's wife.

6. *Key thought*

This chapter revolves around the faith and faithfulness of an unnamed servant.

7. *Key thing to look out for*

The unnamed servant was not ashamed to acknowledge God. "I praised the Lord," verse 48.

8. *Key Bible cross-reference*

Verse 40. See 5:22; 6:8,9; 17:1.

9. *Key "by way of explanation"*

Verse 11. Women went out to wells "towards evening," as that was the coolest part of the day.

10. *Key "Quotable Quote"*

"Faithfulness in little things is a big thing."
John Chrysostom

Genesis chapter 25

1. *Before and after*

> Previous chapter: Chapter 24: Finding a wife for Isaac
> Following chapter: Chapter 26: Isaac in Philistine country

2. *Analysis of chapter*

> Abraham's family by Keturah, his death and burial. (1-10)
> God blesses Isaac, and the descendants of Ishmael. (11-18)
> The birth of Esau and Jacob. (19-26)
> The different characters of Esau and Jacob. (27,28)
> Esau despises and sells his birthright. (29-34)

3. *Key verse*

> Verse 8: "Then Abraham gave up the ghost, and died in a good old age, an old man, and full of years; and was gathered to his people."

4. *Key word / key phrase*

> Verse 24, "birth."

5. *Key event / key person / key theme*

> Abraham's death

6. *Key thought*

> When Rebekah was barren "Isaac prayed to the Lord," verse 21.

7. *Key thing to look out for*

> Verse 23 states that the elder will serve the younger and this illustrates God's love in his election of anyone for salvation.

8. *Key Bible cross-reference*

> "Esau despised his birthright," verse 34, thus showing his godlessness. See Hebrews 12:16.

9. *Key "by way of explanation"*

> Verse 26, "Jacob." This name means "he grasps the heel." Figuratively speaking it means "to deceive." Jacob became a proverbial name for a deceptive person.

10. *Key "Quotable Quote"*

> "Dare to be true:
> Nothing can need a lie;
> A fault, which needs it most, grows two thereby."
> George Herbert

Genesis chapter 26

1. Before and after

Previous chapter: Chapter 25: Abraham dies
Following chapter: Chapter 27: Jacob gains Esau's blessing

2. Analysis of chapter

Isaac, because of famine, goes to Gerar. (1-5)
He denies his wife and is reproved by Abimelech. (6-11)
Isaac grows rich, and the Philistines envy him. (12-17)
Isaac digs wells and God blesses him. (18-25)
Abimelech makes a covenant with Isaac. (26-33)
Esau's wives. (34,35)

3. Key verse

Verse 2: "And the LORD appeared unto him, and said, Go not down into Egypt; dwell in the land which I shall tell thee of."

4. Key word / key phrase

Verse 3, "bless."

5. Key event / key person / key theme

Isaac meets Abimelech.

6. Key thought

God's promises are always spiritually reviving. See verse 3.

7. Key thing to look out for

Esau showed his godlessness by marrying a Hittite, that is, Canaanite woman, verse 34.

8. Key Bible cross-reference

Verse 20. There were frequent disputes about wells and water rights where water was so scarce. See 13:6-11; 21:25; 36:7.

9. Key "by way of explanation"

Verse 30, "feast." Covenant agreements often concluded with a feast or shared meal, which was a further token of friendship between the two parties. See 31:54; Exodus 24:11.

10. Key "Quotable Quote"

"The Christian's faith is strengthened as he keeps the promises of God before him and considers, not the difficulties in the way of the things promised, but the character and resources of God who has made the promise."
Paul Little

Genesis chapter 27

1. Before and after

Previous chapter: Chapter 26: Isaac in Philistine country
Following chapter: Chapter 28: Jacob's dream

2. Analysis of chapter

Isaac sends Esau for venison. (1-5)
Rebekah tells Jacob how to obtain the blessing. (6-17)
Jacob, pretending to be Esau, obtains the blessing. (18-29)
Isaac's fear, Esau's importunity. (30-40)
Esau threatens Jacob's life, Rebekah sends Jacob away. (41-46)

3. Key verse

Verse 3: "Now therefore take, I pray thee, thy weapons, thy quiver and thy bow, and go out to the field, and take me some venison."

4. Key word / key phrase

"Bless" or "blessing" come twenty-four times in this chapter.

5. Key event / key person / key theme

Jacob obtains Isaac's blessing through deceit.

6. Key thought

To live by deception brings people down.

7. Key thing to look out for

Rebekah's favoritism among her children reaped a terrible harvest. See 25:28.

8. Key Bible cross-reference

Verse 27. Jesus was also betrayed with a kiss. See Matthew 26:48,49.

9. Key "by way of explanation"

Verse 1. Blindness among old people was even more common then than now. See 48:10; 1 Samuel 4:15.

10. Key "Quotable Quote"

"We are experts at deceiving others and ourselves too!"
Erwin W. Lutzer

Genesis chapter 28

1. Before and after

Previous chapter: Chapter 27: Jacob gains Esau's blessing
Following chapter: Chapter 29: Jacob's marriages

2. Analysis of chapter

Isaac sends Jacob to Padan-aram. (1-5)
Esau marries the daughter of Ishmael. (6-9)
Jacob's vision. (10-15)
The stone of Bethel. (16-19)
Jacob's vow. (20-22)

3. Key verse

Verse 5: "And Isaac sent away Jacob: and he went to Padanaram unto Laban, son of Bethuel the Syrian, the brother of Rebekah, Jacob's and Esau's mother."

4. Key word / key phrase

Verse 12, "dream."

5. Key event / key person / key theme

Jacob's famous dream

6. Key thought

Verse 15. God promises to bless us, despite our failings.

7. Key thing to look out for

Verse 20. Jacob, despite his past deception, now seeks to honor God.

8. Key Bible cross-reference

Verse 12. See what Jesus had to say about this: John 1:51. Also see John 14:6 and 1 Timothy 2:5.

9. Key "by way of explanation"

Verse 4. Paul applied this verse to Christians. See Galatians 3:14.

10. Key "Quotable Quote"

"What greater insult . . . can there be to God, than not to believe his promises?"
Martin Luther

Genesis chapter 29

1. Before and after

> Previous chapter: Chapter 28: Jacob's dream
> Following chapter: Chapter 30: Jacob's bargain with Laban

2. Analysis of chapter

> Jacob comes to the well of Haran. (1-8)
> Jacob meets Rachel, Laban entertains him. (9-14)
> Jacob's covenant for Rachel, Laban's deceit. (15-30)
> Leah's sons. (31-35)

3. Key verse

> Verse 6: "Rachel his daughter cometh with the sheep."

4. Key word / key phrase

> Verse 20, "love."

5. Key event / key person / key theme

> Jacob marries Leah before he can marry Rachel.

6. Key thought

> The great deceiver is himself deceived.

7. Key thing to look out for

> Through the many ups and downs of his life Jacob experienced God's providential care.

8. Key Bible cross-reference

> Verse 22. It was not uncommon for feasts to last up to seven days: see verses 27,28; Judges 14:10,12.

9. Key "by way of explanation"

> Verse 9. Rachel is called a "shepherdess" as the work of shepherding flocks was done by both men and women then.

10. Key "Quotable Quote"

> "Many times divine providence intervenes in our matters, to make us correct ourselves."
> Basil the Great

Genesis chapter 30

1. Before and after

Previous chapter: Chapter 29: Jacob's marriages
Following chapter: Chapter 31: Jacob flees from Laban

2. Analysis of chapter

A further account of Jacob's family. (1-13)
Rachel bears Joseph. (14-24)
Jacob's new agreement with Laban to serve him for cattle. (25-43)

3. Key verse

Verse 1: "And when Rachel saw that she bare Jacob no children, Rachel envied her sister; and said unto Jacob, Give me children, or else I die."

4. Key word / key phrase

Verse 31, "flocks."

5. Key event / key person / key theme

Jacob's flocks increase, and so his wealth.

6. Key thought

Although Jacob was one of the patriarchs, he continued to live by deception.

7. Key thing to look out for

God does not withhold his blessings just because we are unholy.

8. Key Bible cross-reference

Verse 27, "divinination." See Ezekiel 21:21; Acts 16:16; Leviticus 19:26; Deuteronomy 18:10,14.

9. Key "by way of explanation"

Verse 23. Barrenness was thought to be a disgrace and a sign of God's disfavor.

10. Key "Quotable Quote"

"We all bow down before wealth. It is a homage resulting from a profound faith that with wealth we may do all things."
Augustine of Hippo

Genesis chapter 31

1. Before and after

Previous chapter: Chapter 30: Jacob's bargain with Laban
Following chapter: Chapter 32: Jacob fights with an angel

2. Analysis of chapter

Jacob leaves secretly. (1-21)
Laban pursues Jacob. (23-35)
Jacob's complaint and Laban's response. (36-42)
Their covenant at Galeed. (43-55)

3. Key verse

Verse 3: "And the LORD said unto Jacob, Return unto the land of thy fathers, and to thy kindred; and I will be with thee."

4. Key word / key phrase

Verse 11, "dream."

5. Key event / key person / key theme

Jacob leaves Laban.

6. Key thought

God does not always tell people to do things they do not want to do.

7. Key thing to look out for

God frequently promises that his presence will go with his servants.

8. Key Bible cross-reference

Verse 48. See Joshua 22:10-12, 34.

9. Key "by way of explanation"

Verse 19. "Household gods" belonged to a pagan belief that these small, portable, gods could bring "good luck" to their owners.

10. Key "Quotable Quote"

"The best of all is, God is with us."
John Wesley

Genesis chapter 32

1. **Before and after**

   Previous chapter: Chapter 31: Jacob flees from Laban
   Following chapter: Chapter 33: Jacob makes peace with Esau

2. **Analysis of chapter**

   Jacob's vision at Mahanaim, his fear of Esau. (1-8)
   Jacob's earnest prayer for deliverance, he prepares a present for Esau. (9-23)
   He wrestles with the angel. (24-32)

3. **Key verse**

   Verse 25: "And when he saw that he prevailed not against him, he touched the hollow of his thigh; and the hollow of Jacob's thigh was out of joint, as he wrestled with him."

4. **Key word / key phrase**

   Verse 26, "bless."

5. **Key event / key person / key theme**

   Jacob wrestles with God.

6. **Key thought**

   God met Jacob at the critical points in his life.

7. **Key thing to look out for**

   Jacob had something physically wrong with him to remind him of God's presence.

8. **Key Bible cross-reference**

   Verse 12. See 28:14; 22:17.

9. **Key "by way of explanation"**

   Verse 30. It was thought that if you saw God you would die. That is why, in a symbolic sense, only God's "back" Exodus 33:23, or "feet" Exodus 24:10 might be seen.

10. **Key "Quotable Quote"**

    "Fear imprisons, faith liberates;
    fear paralyzes, faith empowers;
    fear disheartens, faith encourages;
    fear sickens, faith heals;
    fear makes useless, faith makes serviceable;
    most of all, fear puts hopelessness at the heart of life,
    while faith rejoices in its God."
    H.E. Fosdick

Genesis chapter 33

1. Before and after

> Previous chapter: Chapter 32: Jacob fights with an angel
> Following chapter: Chapter 34: Dinah is raped

2. Analysis of chapter

> The friendly meeting between Jacob and Esau. (1-16)
> Jacob comes to Succoth and Schechem, he builds an altar. (17-20)

3. Key verse

> Verse 1: "And Jacob lifted up his eyes, and looked, and, behold, Esau came, and with him four hundred men"

4. Key word / key phrase

> Verse 3, "bowed down."

5. Key event / key person / key theme

> Jacob meets Esau.

6. Key thought

> Reconciliation should never be ruled out.

7. Key thing to look out for

> Jacob took great pains to make amends for his previous evil behavior.

8. Key Bible cross-reference

> Verse 18, "Shechem." See 12:6; John 4:5-6. There is a well to this day at Shechem.

9. Key "by way of explanation"

> Verse 3. Bowing down seven times is documented in the texts discovered at Tell el-Amarna in Egypt, and indicates total submission.

10. Key "Quotable Quote"

> "All who strive for reconciliation seek to listen rather than to convince, to understand rather than to impose themselves."
> Brother Roger of Taizé

Genesis chapter 34

1. **Before and after**

    Previous chapter: Chapter 33: Jacob makes peace with Esau
    Following chapter: Chapter 35: Jacob returns to Bethel

2. **Analysis of chapter**

    Dinah defiled by Shechem. (1-19)
    The Shechemites murdered by Simeon and Levi. (20-31)

3. **Key verse**

    Verse 5: "And Jacob heard that he had defiled Dinah his daughter."

4. **Key word / key phrase**

    Verse 2, "raped."

5. **Key event / key person / key theme**

    Dinah is raped.

6. **Key thought**

    The name of God comes in the last verse of chapter 33, and it starts chapter 35, but it is absent from this horrific chapter.

7. **Key thing to look out for**

    Sin leads to sin. The revenge exacted for Shechem's evil deed seems disproportionate. See verses 25-31.

8. **Key Bible cross-reference**

    Verse 2, "Shechem." The person was probably named after the city of that name. See 33:19.

9. **Key "by way of explanation"**

    Verse 20, "the gate of their city." The gate of a city acted as a meeting place for business and as an open-air courtroom.

10. **Key "Quotable Quote"**

    "Man must evolve for all human conflict a method which rejects revenge, aggression and retaliation. The foundation of such a method is love."
    Martin Luther King, Jr.

Genesis chapter 35

1. *Before and after*

Previous chapter: Chapter 34: Dinah is raped
Following chapter: Chapter 36: The history of Esau

2. *Analysis of chapter*

God commands Jacob to go to Bethel, he puts away idols from his family. (1-5)
Jacob builds an altar, the death of Deborah. God blesses Jacob. (6-15)
Death of Rachel. (16-20)
Reuben's crime, and the death of Isaac. (21-29)

3. *Key verse*

Verse 1: "And God said unto Jacob, Arise, go up to Bethel, and dwell there: and make there an altar unto God, that appeared unto thee when thou fleddest from the face of Esau thy brother."

4. *Key word / key phrase*

Verse 1, "Bethel."

5. *Key event / key person / key theme*

Rachel and Isaac die.

6. *Key thought*

Jacob insists that the people be pure before God.

7. *Key thing to look out for*

Once again God reassures Jacob of his presence.

8. *Key Bible cross-reference*

Verse 4, "rings." See Hosea 2:13. Rings here were worn as pagan charms.

9. *Key "by way of explanation"*

Verse 10. To the name "Jacob" is now added "Israel." See 32:28. For other instances of name-changing compare 21:31 with 26:33, and 28:19 with 35:15.

10. *Key "Quotable Quote"*

"You will never be able to pray everywhere all the time until you have learned to pray somewhere some of the time."
Dalrymple

Genesis chapter 36

1. *Before and after*

Previous chapter: Chapter 35: Jacob returns to Bethel
Following chapter: Chapter 37: Joseph's dreams

2. *Analysis of chapter*

Esau and his descendants. (1-43)

3. *Key verse*

Verse 1: "Now these are the generations of Esau, who is Edom."

4. *Key word / key phrase*

Verse 1, "Esau."

5. *Key event / key person / key theme*

Esau's descendants

6. *Key thought*

Our times are in God's hands.

7. *Key thing to look out for*

Christians are supposed to care for their close family.

8. *Key Bible cross-reference*

As Eliphaz, verse 11, was also the name of one of Job's so-called comforters, and since Job was from the land of Uz, Job 1:1, it has been thought that Job may have lived in Edom. See verses 28,34.

9. *Key "by way of explanation"*

Verses 10-14 and verses 15-19 have a list of identical names in them. The first list is of Esau's descendants and the second is a list of the tribal chiefs.

10. *Key "Quotable Quote"*

"He who loves not his wife and children feeds a lioness at home and broods a nest of sorrows."
Jeremy Taylor

Genesis chapter 37

1. Before and after

Previous chapter: Chapter 36: The history of Esau
Following chapter: Chapter 38: Judah and Tamar

2. Analysis of chapter

Joseph is loved by Jacob, but hated by his brothers. (1-4)
Joseph's dreams. (5-11)
Jacob sends Joseph to visit his brothers, and they plot to kill him. (12-22)
Joseph's brothers sell him. (23-10)
Jacob deceived, and Joseph sold to Potiphar. (31-36)

3. Key verse

Verse 5: "And Joseph dreamed a dream."

4. Key word / key phrase

Verse 5, "dream," which comes nine times in this chapter.

5. Key event / key person / key theme

Joseph the dreamer

6. Key thought

There is no suggestion in this chapter that Joseph was showing off.

7. Key thing to look out for

Joseph knew, with hindsight, that God was looking after him. See verse 36.

8. Key Bible cross-reference

Verse 3. There have been many suggestions about the meaning of the Hebrew word, translated in the *King James Version* as "of many colors." The coat was certainly a mark of his father's favoritism. See 2 Samuel 13:18.

9. Key "by way of explanation"

Verse 1, "Canaan." Jacob made his home in Canaan, the promised land, and was buried there, 49:29-30; 50:13. Joseph also ensured that he was buried there, 50:24,25.

10. Key "Quotable Quote"

"Every Christian family ought to be, as it were, a little church consecrated to Christ, and wholly influenced and governed by his rules."
Jonathan Edwards

Genesis chapter 38

1. ### *Before and after*
   Previous chapter: Chapter 37: Joseph's dreams
   Following chapter: Chapter 39: Joseph and Potiphar's wife

2. ### *Analysis of chapter*
   The profligate behavior of Judah and his family. (1-30)

3. ### *Key verse*
   Verse 1: "And it came to pass at that time, that Judah went down from his brethren."

4. ### *Key word / key phrase*
   Verse 18, "seal."

5. ### *Key event / key person / key theme*
   Judah treats his daughter-in-law, Tamar, as a prostitute.

6. ### *Key thought*
   Judge not and you will not be judged.

7. ### *Key thing to look out for*
   Jesus spoke out strongly against hypocrites.

8. ### *Key Bible cross-reference*
   Verse 8 refers to levirate marriage. See Deuteronomy 25:5,6; Matthew 22:24; Ruth 4:5.

9. ### *Key "by way of explanation"*
   Verse 14. Prostitutes often positioned themselves along a roadside. See Jeremiah 3:2.

10. ### *Key "Quotable Quote"*
    "The knowledge of God, and the remembrance of his all-seeing presence, are the most powerful means against hypocrisy."
    Richard Baxter

Genesis chapter 39

1. Before and after

Previous chapter: Chapter 38: Judah and Tamar
Following chapter: Chapter 40: Joseph in prison

2. Analysis of chapter

Joseph is chosen by Potiphar. (1-6)
Joseph resists temptation. (7-12)
Joseph is falsely accused by his master's wife. (13-18)
He is thrown into prison, God is with him there. (19-23)

3. Key verse

Verse 1: "And Joseph was brought down to Egypt."

4. Key word / key phrase

Verse 19, "prison."

5. Key event / key person / key theme

Joseph resists Potiphar's wife's advances.

6. Key thought

Doing right does not always seem to pay.

7. Key thing to look out for

Verse 21. Even in prison Joseph experienced the Lord's kindness.

8. Key Bible cross-reference

Verse 6. Joseph is said to have been given full responsibility on two other occasions. See verses 22,23 and 41:41.

9. Key "by way of explanation"

Verse 2. In the account of Joseph it is often stressed that the Lord was with him. See verses 3, 21, 23, and 26:3, and Acts 7:9.

10. Key "Quotable Quote"

"The one and only infallible way to go safely through all the difficulties, trials, temptations, dryness, or opposition of our own evil tempers is this: It is to expect nothing from ourselves, to trust to nothing in ourselves, but in everything to expect and depend upon God for relief."
William Law

Genesis chapter 40

1. Before and after

Previous chapter: Chapter 39: Joseph and Potiphar's wife
Following chapter: Chapter 41: Joseph interprets Pharaoh's dreams

2. Analysis of chapter

Pharaoh's chief butler and baker in prison, and their dreams interpreted by Joseph. (1-19)
The ingratitude of the chief butler. (20-23)

3. Key verse

Verse 23: "Yet did not the chief butler remember Joseph, but forgat him."

4. Key word / key phrase

Verse 16, "interpretation."

5. Key event / key person / key theme

The cupbearer and the baker

6. Key thought

Waiting is not easy for anyone. The cupbearer forgot about Joseph for two years.

7. Key thing to look out for

Verse 15. Joseph was more than once a victim of injustice.

8. Key Bible cross-reference

Verse 8 states that only God can correctly interpret dreams. See 41:16,25,28; Daniel 2:28.

9. Key "by way of explanation"

Verse 5. People in the ancient Near East believed that dreams had meanings.

10. Key "Quotable Quote"

"The dungeon became to me as it were a palace."
Perpetua, the Christian martyr

Genesis chapter 41

1. Before and after

Previous chapter: Chapter 40: Joseph in prison
Following chapter: Chapter 42: Joseph's brothers seek food in Egypt

2. Analysis of chapter

Pharaoh's dreams. (1-8)
Joseph interprets Pharaoh's dreams. (9-32)
Joseph's counsel, and his promotion. (33-45)
Joseph's children, and the beginning of the famine. (46-57)

3. Key verse

Verse 14: "Then Pharaoh sent and called Joseph, and they brought him hastily out of the dungeon: and he shaved himself, and changed his raiment, and came in unto Pharaoh."

4. Key word / key phrase

Verse 8, "dreams," mentioned thirteen times in this chapter.

5. Key event / key person / key theme

Joseph is released from prison.

6. Key thought

Verse 38. Pharaoh recognized God's Spirit at work in Joseph.

7. Key thing to look out for

Verse 16. Joseph made sure that Pharaoh knew that his ability to interpret dreams was God-given.

8. Key Bible cross-reference

Verse 16. See 40:4; Daniel 2:27,28, 30; 2 Corinthians 3:5.

9. Key "by way of explanation"

Verse 40. Pharaoh ordered that people should "submit" to Joseph. Literally this means to kiss his hands and feet, as a sign of giving him homage. See Psalm 2:12.

10. Key "Quotable Quote"

"Someone defined responsibility as 'our response to God's ability.'"
Warren Wiersbe

Genesis chapter 42

1. Before and after

Previous chapter: Chapter 41: Joseph interprets Pharaoh's dreams
Following chapter: Chapter 43: Joseph's brothers return to Egypt with Benjamin

2. Analysis of chapter

Jacob sends ten sons to buy corn. (1-6)
Joseph's treatment of his brothers. (7-20)
Their remorse, Simeon detained. (21-24)
The rest return with corn. (25-28)
Jacob refuses to send Benjamin to Egypt. (29-38)

3. Key verse

Verse 2: "And he said, Behold, I have heard that there is corn in Egypt: get you down thither, and buy for us from thence; that we may live, and not die."

4. Key word / key phrase

Verse 5, "famine."

5. Key event / key person / key theme

Joseph's brothers go to Egypt in search of food.

6. Key thought

The circumstances in which Joseph's first dreams would come true were taking shape.

7. Key thing to look out for

Verse 21. The brothers' sense of guilt.

8. Key Bible cross-reference

Verse 15, "As surely as Pharaoh lives." It was common for solemn oaths to be taken in the name of rulers, Psalm 16:4, or of the Lord himself, Judges 8:19; 1 Samuel 14:39,45.

9. Key "by way of explanation"

Verse 4. Jacob would "not send Benjamin." Rachel was dead, 35:19, Jacob thought that Joseph was dead, 37:33. Jacob could not bear to be parted from the only other son of his beloved Rachel.

10. Key "Quotable Quote"

"If you can't change circumstances, change the way you respond to them."
Tim Hansel

Genesis chapter 43

1. *Before and after*

Previous chapter: Chapter 42: Joseph's brothers seek food in Egypt
Following chapter: Chapter 44: Joseph's cup goes missing

2. *Analysis of chapter*

Jacob is persuaded to send Benjamin into Egypt. (1-14)
Joseph's reception of his brothers, their fears. (15-25)
Joseph makes a feast for his brothers. (26-34)

3. *Key verse*

Verse 2: "And it came to pass, when they had eaten up the corn which they had brought out of Egypt, their father said unto them, Go again, buy us a little food."

4. *Key word / key phrase*

Verse 34, "Benjamin."

5. *Key event / key person / key theme*

Joseph's brothers go to Egypt a second time.

6. *Key thought*

Joseph's determination to ensure that his father comes to Egypt is clear.

7. *Key thing to look out for*

Verse 30. There are a number of pointers to Joseph's great love for his family.

8. *Key Bible cross-reference*

Verse 11, "a gift." See 1 Samuel 16:20; 17:18; 2 Kings 5:15.

9. *Key "by way of explanation"*

Verse 3, "Judah said." Judah acted as the leader and spokesman of the remaining brothers, 8-10; 44:14-34; 46:28; and he became Jesus' ancestor, Matthew 1:2,17; Luke 3:23,33.

10. *Key "Quotable Quote"*

"I believe the family was established long before the Church, and my duty is to my family first."
D.L. Moody

Genesis chapter 44

1. **Before and after**

   Previous chapter: Chapter 43: Joseph's brothers return to Egypt with Benjamin
   Following chapter: Chapter 45: Joseph reveals himself to his brothers

2. **Analysis of chapter**

   Joseph's plan to detain his brothers, and test their affection for Benjamin. (1-17)
   Judah's plea to Joseph. (18-34)

3. **Key verse**

   Verse 2: "And put my cup, the silver cup, in the sack's mouth of the youngest, and his corn money."

4. **Key word / key phrase**

   Verse 12, "cup."

5. **Key event / key person / key theme**

   Joseph's silver cup is found in Benjamin's sack.

6. **Key thought**

   Verse 34. The brothers now show concern for their father.

7. **Key thing to look out for**

   Joseph's plan to keep Benjamin and so bring Jacob to Egypt.

8. **Key Bible cross-reference**

   Verse 14. See 37:7,9; 42:6; 43:26,28.

9. **Key "by way of explanation"**

   Verse 30. In 1 Samuel 18:1 a similar statement is made about David and Jonathan's close friendship.

10. **Key "Quotable Quote"**

    "You don't choose your family. They are God's gift to you, as you are to them."
    Desmond Tutu

Genesis chapter 45

1. Before and after

Previous chapter: Chapter 44: Joseph's cup goes missing
Following chapter: Chapter 46: Jacob and his family go to Egypt

2. Analysis of chapter

Joseph comforts his brothers, and sends for his father. (1-15)
Pharaoh confirms Joseph's invitation, Joseph's gifts to his brothers. (16-24)
Jacob receives the news of Joseph being alive. (25-28)

3. Key verse

Verse 1: "And there stood no man with him, while Joseph made himself known unto his brethren."

4. Key word / key phrase

Verse 26, "alive."

5. Key event / key person / key theme

Joseph reveals himself to his brothers.

6. Key thought

Verse 5 summarizes Joseph's response to all the harm his brothers had done to him.

7. Key thing to look out for

Joseph's genuine love for his family is clearly illustrated in this chapter.

8. Key Bible cross-reference

Verse 14. See 42:23.

9. Key "by way of explanation"

Verse 5. See Acts 7:9; 2:23; 4:28.

10. Key "Quotable Quote"

"God is the first object of our love. Its next office is to bear the defects of others. And we should begin the practice of this amid our own household."
John Wesley

Genesis chapter 46

1. Before and after

Previous chapter: Chapter 45: Joseph reveals himself to his brothers
Following chapter: Chapter 47: Jacob's family safe in Egypt

2. Analysis of chapter

God's promises to Jacob. (1-4)
Jacob and his family go to Egypt. (5-27)
Joseph meets his father and his brothers. (28-34)

3. Key verse

Verse 1: "And Israel took his journey with all that he had, and came to Beersheba, and offered sacrifices unto the God of his father Isaac."

4. Key word / key phrase

Verse 1, "Israel."

5. Key event / key person / key theme

Jacob goes to Egypt.

6. Key thought

Jacob could hardly take it in that Joseph was really still alive.

7. Key thing to look out for

Joseph took great pains to ensure that his large family would be very well cared for in Egypt.

8. Key Bible cross-reference

Verse 1. See 21:33; 26:23-25.

9. Key "by way of explanation"

Verse 4. Jacob knew from experience that the Lord himself went with him on his journeys. See 28:15; 15:6; 48:21.

10. Key "Quotable Quote"

"If your father and mother, your sister and brother, if the very cat and dog in the house, are not happier for your being Christian, it is a question whether you really are."
James Hudson Taylor

Genesis chapter 47

1. Before and after

Previous chapter: Chapter 46: Jacob and his family go to Egypt
Following chapter: Chapter 48: Jacob blesses Ephraim and Manasseh

2. Analysis of chapter

Joseph presents his brothers to Pharaoh. (1-6)
Jacob blesses Pharaoh. (7-12)
Joseph's dealings with the Egyptians during the famine. (13-26)
Jacob's age. His desire to be buried in Canaan. (27-31)

3. Key verse

Verse 14: "And Joseph gathered up all the money that was found in the land of Egypt, and in the land of Canaan, for the corn which they bought: and Joseph brought the money into Pharaoh's house."

4. Key word / key phrase

Verse 13, "famine."

5. Key event / key person / key theme

Joseph's role in providing food for Egypt

6. Key thought

Without Joseph's administrative skills Egypt would have starved.

7. Key thing to look out for

The relationship of respect between Pharaoh and Jacob.

8. Key Bible cross-reference

Verse 27. See 35:11,12; 46:3.

9. Key "by way of explanation"

Verse 13. Joseph ensured that Egypt had food, but the price the people had to pay for this involved their money, their livestock, their land, and themselves. See 14,15,16,17, 20,21.

10. Key "Quotable Quote"

"He that respects not is not respected."
George Herbert

Genesis chapter 48

1. **Before and after**

   Previous chapter: Chapter 47: Jacob's family safe in Egypt
   Following chapter: Chapter 49: Jacob's last words and death

2. **Analysis of chapter**

   Joseph visits his dying father. (1-7)
   Jacob blesses Joseph's sons. (8-22)

3. **Key verse**

   Verse 21: "And Israel said unto Joseph, Behold, I die: but God shall be with you, and bring you again unto the land of your fathers"

4. **Key word / key phrase**

   Verse 3, "blessed."

5. **Key event / key person / key theme**

   Jacob blesses Manasseh and Ephraim.

6. **Key thought**

   God's grace is illustrated in the way Jacob puts Manasseh and Ephraim on a par with his own two firstborn.

7. **Key thing to look out for**

   God's deliverance includes physical deliverance as well as forgiveness of sins.

8. **Key Bible cross-reference**

   Verse 15. See Psalm 23:1; 49:24.

9. **Key "by way of explanation"**

   Verse 20. Joseph enables the younger son of Joseph, Ephraim, to take precedence over the elder son, Manasseh.

10. **Key "Quotable Quote**

    "There is a famine in America. Not a famine of food, but of love, of truth, of life."
    Mother Teresa of Calcutta

Genesis chapter 49

1. *Before and after*

Previous chapter: Chapter 48: Jacob blesses Ephraim and Manasseh
Following chapter: Chapter 50: The death of Joseph

2. *Analysis of chapter*

Jacob calls his sons to bless them. (1,2)
Reuben, Simeon, Levi. (3-7)
Judah. (8-12)
Zebulun, Issachar, Dan. (13-18)
Gad, Asher, Naphtali. (19-21)
Joseph and Benjamin. (22-27)
Jacob's charge about his burial, his death. (28-33)

3. *Key verse*

Verse 1: "And Jacob called unto his sons, and said, Gather yourselves together, that I may tell you that which shall befall you in the last days."

4. *Key word / key phrase*

Verse 26, "blessings."

5. *Key event / key person / key theme*

Jacob blesses his sons.

6. *Key thought*

In fulfillment of his dreams, Joseph is referred to as "the prince among his brothers," verse 26.

7. *Key thing to look out for*

God does not bestow the same blessings on everyone.

8. *Key Bible cross-reference*

Verses 2-27. See further poetic blessings in Genesis in 9:26,27; 14:19,20; 27:27-29; 27:39,40; 48:15,16; 48:20.

9. *Key "by way of explanation"*

Verses 2-27 is the longest poem in Genesis. Jacob's blessings were intended for the descendants of the twelve brothers and not just for the twelve themselves

10. *Key "Quotable Quote"*

"Justice – When you get what you deserve.
Mercy – When you don't get what you deserve.
Grace – When you get what you don't deserve."
Author unknown

Genesis chapter 50

1. *Previous chapter*

   Chapter 49: Jacob's last words and death

2. *Analysis of chapter*

   The mourning for Jacob. (1-6)
   His funeral. (7-14)
   Joseph's brothers beg for his pardon, he comforts them. (15-21)
   Joseph's instructions about his bones, his death. (22-26)

3. *Key verse*

   Verse 26: "So Joseph died, being an hundred and ten years old: and they embalmed him, and he was put in a coffin in Egypt."

4. *Key word / key phrase*

   Verse 17, "forgive."

5. *Key event / key person / key theme*

   Joseph dies.

6. *Key thought*

   Verse 17. The brothers show that they still do not fully believe that Joseph's love for them is total and genuine.

7. *Key thing to look out for*

   How God provided for a slave in a foreign country.

8. *Key Bible cross-reference*

   Verse 25. See Exodus 13:19; Joshua 24:32; Genesis 33:19.

9. *Key "by way of explanation"*

   Verse 20. This summarizes God's grace in Joseph's heart, despite all the ill will his brothers had shown him.

10. *Key "Quotable Quote"*

    "Our blessed Lord reveals himself to his people more in the valleys, in the shades, in the deeps, than he does anywhere else."
    C.H. Spurgeon

Exodus

Exodus chapter 1

1. **Following chapter**

   Chapter 2: The birth of Moses

2. **Analysis of chapter**

   The children of Israel increase in Egypt after the death of Joseph. (8-14)
   They are oppressed, but multiply exceedingly. (1-7)
   The baby boys destroyed. (15-22)

3. **Key verse**

   Verse 8: "Now there arose up a new king over Egypt, which knew not Joseph."

4. **Key word / key phrase**

   Verse 15, "Hebrew."

5. **Key event / key person / key theme**

   A new Pharaoh

6. **Key thought**

   When is it right to obey God and disobey men?

7. **Key thing to look out for**

   The history of the Israelites and Pharaoh's motives.

8. **Key Bible cross-reference**

   Verse 7. See Acts 7:17; Genesis 1:28; Genesis 8:17; Genesis 17:2,6; Genesis 26:4 and 48:4.

9. **Key "by way of explanation"**

   Verse 1, "Israel." Jacob had been given this additional name by God. See Genesis 32:28; 35:10.

10. **Key "Quotable Quote"**

    "History is a story written by the finger of God."
    C.S. Lewis

Exodus chapter 2

1. **Before and after**

    Previous chapter: Chapter 1: A new king in Egypt
    Following chapter: Chapter 3: Moses and the burning bush

2. **Analysis of chapter**

    Moses is born, and exposed on the river. (1-4)
    He is found, and brought up by Pharaoh's daughter. (5-10)
    Moses kills an Egyptian, and flees to Midian. (11-15)
    Moses marries the daughter of Jethro. (16-22)
    God hears the Israelites. (23-25)

3. **Key verse**

    Verse 3: "And when she could not longer hide him, she took for him an ark of
    bulrushes, and daubed it with slime and with pitch, and put the child therein;
    and she laid it in the flags by the river's brink."

4. **Key word / key phrase**

    Verse 10, "Moses."

5. **Key event / key person / key theme**

    Moses is born.

6. **Key thought**

    A mother's love and a princess' compassion combine to save one baby.

7. **Key thing to look out for**

    God's greatest leaders are frequently misunderstood.

8. **Key Bible cross-reference**

    Verse 2. See Acts 7:20; Hebrews 11:23.

9. **Key "by way of explanation"**

    Verse 3, "papyrus basket." Moses' waterproof cradle was a tiny version of a
    papyrus boat. See Isaiah 18:2.

10. **Key "Quotable Quote"**

    "The Church does not need brilliant personalities but faithful servants of
    Jesus and the brethren."
    Dietrich Bonhoeffer

Exodus chapter 3

1. Before and after

Previous chapter: Chapter 2: The birth of Moses
Following chapter: Chapter 4: Moses returns to Egypt

2. Analysis of chapter

God appears to Moses in a burning bush. (1-6)
God sends Moses to deliver Israel. (7-10)
The name of God. (11-15)
The deliverance of the Israelites promised. (16-22)

3. Key verse

Verse 2: "And the angel of the LORD appeared unto him in a flame of fire out of the midst of a bush: and he looked, and, behold, the bush burned with fire, and the bush was not consumed."

4. Key word / key phrase

Verse 3, "bush."

5. Key event / key person / key theme

The burning bush

6. Key thought

Moses learns about God's holiness.

7. Key thing to look out for

Initially, Moses shows himself to be a most reluctant leader.

8. Key Bible cross-reference

Verse 4. See 1 Samuel 3:4; Isaiah 6:8; Jeremiah 1:4,5; Ezekiel 2:1-8.

9. Key "by way of explanation"

Verse 8. God is also said to come down in judgment in Genesis 11:5-9; 18:21.

10. Key "Quotable Quote"

"How beautiful, how beautiful
The sight of thee must be,
Thine endless wisdom, boundless power,
And awful purity!"
F.W. Faber

Exodus chapter 4

1. Before and after

Previous chapter: Chapter 3: Moses and the burning bush
Following chapter: Chapter 5: Moses in conflict with Pharaoh

2. Analysis of chapter

God gives Moses power to work miracles. (1-9)
Moses does not want to be sent, Aaron is to assist him. (10-17)
Moses leaves Midian, God's message to Pharaoh. (18-23)
God's displeasure with Moses, Aaron meets him, and the people believe them. (24-31)

3. Key verse

Verse 18: "And Moses went and returned to Jethro his father in law, and said unto him, Let me go, I pray thee, and return unto my brethren which are in Egypt, and see whether they be yet alive."

4. Key word / key phrase

Verse 30, "signs."

5. Key event / key person / key theme

Moses goes back to Egypt.

6. Key thought

God's plans are not thwarted by anyone.

7. Key thing to look out for

The excuses made by Moses.

8. Key Bible cross-reference

Verse 21. See 7:3; 9:12; 10:1,20,27; 11:10; 14:4,8; Romans 9:17,18.

9. Key "by way of explanation"

Verse 22, "firstborn son." This phrase is a figure of speech used to show Israel's unique relationship with God. See Jeremiah 31:9; Hosea 11:1.

10. Key "Quotable Quote"

"Evidence of our hardness is that we are more concerned about our sufferings than our sins."
Matthew Henry

Exodus chapter 5

1. *Before and after*

Previous chapter: Chapter 4: Moses returns to Egypt
Following chapter: Chapter 6: The family of Moses and Aaron

2. *Analysis of chapter*

Pharaoh's displeasure, he increases the tasks of the Israelites. (1-9)
The sufferings of the Israelites, Moses' complaint to God. (10-23)

3. *Key verse*

Verse 18: "Go therefore now, and work; for there shall no straw be given you, yet shall ye deliver the tale of bricks."

4. *Key word / key phrase*

Verse 7, "bricks."

5. *Key event / key person / key theme*

Bricks but no straw

6. *Key thought*

Moses has a most unpromising start as Israel's great leader and deliverer.

7. *Key thing to look out for*

Strong criticism from his own people was part of the price Moses had to pay for being a leader.

8. *Key Bible cross-reference*

Verse 21. See Genesis 16:5; 31:49.

9. *Key "by way of explanation"*

Verse 7. Straw was essential in making bricks as it helped to bind the clay together and so give the bricks strength.

10. *Key "Quotable Quote"*

"A man would do nothing, if he waited until he could do it so that no one would find fault with what he has done."
John Henry Newman

Exodus chapter 6

1. *Before and after*

Previous chapter: Chapter 5: Moses in conflict with Pharaoh
Following chapter: Chapter 7: The River Nile is turned to blood

2. *Analysis of chapter*

God renews his promise. (1-9)
Moses and Aaron again sent to Pharaoh. (10-13)
The parentage of Moses and Aaron. (14-30)

3. *Key verse*

Verse 1: "Then the LORD said unto Moses, Now shalt thou see what I will do to Pharaoh: for with a strong hand shall he let them go, and with a strong hand shall he drive them out of his land."

4. *Key word / key phrase*

Verse 5, "covenant."

5. *Key event / key person / key theme*

Aaron

6. *Key thought*

Aaron had totally different gifts from Moses, but was essential to God's plan.

7. *Key thing to look out for*

Moses' whole ministry is underpinned with God's promises.

8. *Key Bible cross-reference*

Verse 7. See 19:5,6; Jeremiah 31:33.

9. *Key "by way of explanation"*

Verse 6. Redemption included deliverance for Israel, but judgment for Egypt.

10. *Key "Quotable Quote"*

"I will not glory because I am righteous but because I am redeemed, not because I am clear of sin, but because my sins are forgiven."
Ambrose

Exodus chapter 7

1. *Before and after*

Previous chapter: Chapter 6: The family of Moses and Aaron
Following chapter: Chapter 8: Frogs, gnats, and flies

2. *Analysis of chapter*

Moses and Aaron encouraged. (1-7)
The staffs turned into serpents, Pharaoh's heart is hardened. (8-13)
The river is turned into blood, and the distress of the Egyptians. (14-25)

3. *Key verse*

Verse 20: "And Moses and Aaron did so, as the LORD commanded; and he lifted up the rod, and smote the waters that were in the river, in the sight of Pharaoh, and in the sight of his servants; and all the waters that were in the river were turned to blood."

4. *Key word / key phrase*

Verse 9, "miracle."

5. *Key event / key person / key theme*

Aaron's ministry

6. *Key thought*

Nothing is so hard as the human heart.

7. *Key thing to look out for*

The greatest miracle is someone turning to God in repentance.

8. *Key Bible cross-reference*

Verse 17. See Psalm 78:44; 105:29.

9. *Key "by way of explanation"*

Verse 14. One way of viewing the first nine plagues is to put them into three groups, with three plagues in each group: 7:14–8:19; 8:20–9:12; 9:13–10:29.

10. *Key "Quotable Quote"*

"I never have any difficulty believing in miracles, since I experienced the miracle of a change in my own heart."
Augustine of Hippo

Exodus chapter 8

1. *Before and after*

Previous chapter: Chapter 7: The River Nile is turned to blood
Following chapter: Chapter 9: Death of animals, boils, and hail

2. *Analysis of chapter*

The plague of frogs. (1-15)
The plague of lice. (16-19)
The plague of flies. (20-32)

3. *Key verse*

Verse 16: "And the LORD said unto Moses, Say unto Aaron, Stretch out thy rod, and smite the dust of the land, that it may become lice throughout all the land of Egypt."

4. *Key word / key phrase*

Verse 5, "frogs."

5. *Key event / key person / key theme*

Plagues

6. *Key thought*

Hardness of heart is not limited to a Pharaoh.

7. *Key thing to look out for*

Moses and his prayer life.

8. *Key Bible cross-reference*

Verse 19, "finger of God." See 31:18; Psalm 83; Luke 11:20.

9. *Key "by way of explanation"*

Verse 22, "deal differently." God made a distinction between the Egyptians and the Israelites in most of the plagues, illustrating how he preserves some people and judges other people.

10. *Key "Quotable Quote"*

"Prayer is the highest activity of the human soul, and therefore it is at the same time the ultimate test of a man's true spiritual condition."
D. Martyn Lloyd-Jones

Exodus chapter 9

1. Before and after

Previous chapter: Chapter 8: Frogs, gnats, and flies
Following chapter: Chapter 10: Locusts and darkness

2. Analysis of chapter

The plague on the livestock. (1-7)
The plague of boils. (8-12)
The plague of hail threatened. (13-21)
The plague of hail inflicted. (22-35)

3. Key verse

Verse 23: "And Moses stretched forth his rod toward heaven: and the LORD sent thunder and hail, and the fire ran along upon the ground; and the LORD rained hail upon the land of Egypt."

4. Key word / key phrase

Verse 18, "hailstorm."

5. Key event / key person / key theme

More plagues

6. Key thought

God is never seen to be in a hurry.

7. Key thing to look out for

The plague on the livestock would be seen as an attack on Egyptian religion, in which bull-gods were worshiped.

8. Key Bible cross-reference

Verse 29. See 1 Kings 8:22,38,54; 2 Chronicles 6:12,13,29; Ezra 9:5.

9. Key "by way of explanation"

Verse 16. The apostle Paul used this verse to illustrate God's sovereignty. See Romans 9:17.

10. Key "Quotable Quote"

"Of all the doctrines of the Bible, none is so offensive to human nature as the doctrine of God's sovereignty."
J.C. Ryle

Exodus chapter 10

1. Before and after

Previous chapter: Chapter 9: Death of animals, the boils, and hail
Following chapter: Chapter 11: The death of the firstborn is announced

2. Analysis of chapter

The plague of locusts threatened, Pharaoh, moved by his servants, inclines to let the Israelites go. (1-11)
The plague of locusts. (12-20)
The plague of thick darkness. (21-29)

3. Key verse

Verse 13: "And Moses stretched forth his rod over the land of Egypt, and the LORD brought an east wind upon the land all that day, and all that night; and when it was morning, the east wind brought the locusts."

4. Key word / key phrase

Verse 13, "locusts."

5. Key event / key person / key theme

More plagues

6. Key thought

It is not hard to be half-hearted.

7. Key thing to look out for

The last verse of this chapter points to a momentous event.

8. Key Bible cross-reference

Verse 4. See Joel 1:4-7; 2:1-11; Amos 7:1-3.

9. Key "by way of explanation"

Verse 2. God ensured that his acts would never be forgotten. See 12:26,27; 13:8,14,15; Deuteronomy 4:9; Psalm 77:11-20.

10. Key "Quotable Quote"

"Half-hearted Christianity is worse than no Christianity."
Johann Heinrich Arnold

Exodus chapter 11

1. Before and after

Previous chapter: Chapter 10: Locusts and darkness
Following chapter: Chapter 12: The Passover and the Exodus

2. Analysis of chapter

God's last instructions to Moses about Pharaoh and the Egyptians. (1-3)
The death of the firstborn threatened. (4-10)

3. Key verse

Verse 5: "And all the firstborn in the land of Egypt shall die."

4. Key word / key phrase

Verse 5, "firstborn."

5. Key event / key person / key theme

Death of Egypt's firstborn

6. Key thought

God's judgments may appear to be harsh, but what about human sin?

7. Key thing to look out for

Verse 9. God is in control all the time.

8. Key Bible cross-reference

Verse 5. See Psalm 78:51; 105:36; 135:8.

9. Key "by way of explanation"

Verse 5, "firstborn." When God's judgment fell on the firstborn, it was judgment on whole families and the whole Egyptian community.

10. Key "Quotable Quote"

"God examines both rich and poor, not according to their lands and houses, but according to the riches of their hearts."
Augustine of Hippo

Exodus chapter 12

1. **Before and after**

    Previous chapter: Chapter 11: The death of the firstborn is announced
    Following chapter: Chapter 13: The festival of unleavened bread

2. **Analysis of chapter**

    The beginning of the year changed, and the Passover instituted. (1-20)
    The people instructed how to observe the Passover. (21-28)
    The death of the firstborn of the Egyptians. The Israelites urged to leave the land of Egypt. (29-36)
    The Israelites' first journey to Succoth. (37-42)
    Ordinance about the Passover. (43-51)

3. **Key verse**

    Verse 17: "And ye shall observe the feast of unleavened bread; for in this selfsame day have I brought your armies out of the land of Egypt: therefore shall ye observe this day in your generations by an ordinance for ever."

4. **Key word / key phrase**

    Verse 21, "Passover."

5. **Key event / key person / key theme**

    The initiation of the Passover

6. **Key thought**

    The idea of the Passover is central to the Lord's Supper.

7. **Key thing to look out for**

    God explained profound spiritual truth through ordinary things everyone knew about.

8. **Key Bible cross-reference**

    Verse 22 and sprinkling. See Leviticus 14:4,6,49,51,52; Hebrews 9:19.

9. **Key "by way of explanation"**

    Verse 21. For Christians, the "Passover lamb" is Jesus, 1 Corinthians 5:7, who died once for all according to Hebrews 7:27.

10. **Key "Quotable Quote"**

    "He was condemned, that thou mightest be justified, and was killed, that thou mightest live."
    John Bunyan

Exodus chapter 13

1. **Before and after**

   Previous chapter: Chapter 12: The Passover and the Exodus
   Following chapter: Chapter 14: Crossing the Red Sea

2. **Analysis of chapter**

   The firstborn sanctified to God. The Passover must be commemorated. (1-10)
   The firstborn of beasts set apart. (11-16)
   Joseph's bones carried with the Israelites, and they come to Etham. (17-20)
   God guides the Israelites by a pillar of cloud and a pillar of fire. (21,22)

3. **Key verse**

   Verse 21: "And the LORD went before them by day in a pillar of a cloud, to lead
   them the way; and by night in a pillar of fire, to give them light; to go by day
   and night."

4. **Key word / key phrase**

   Verse 7, "unleavened."

5. **Key event / key person / key theme**

   The pillar of cloud and the pillar of fire

6. **Key thought**

   The meal of unleavened bread was never meant to be a mere empty ritual. See
   verse 14.

7. **Key thing to look out for**

   God never leaves his people without the guidance they need.

8. **Key Bible cross-reference**

   Verse 13 and redemption. See Genesis 22:12; Numbers 3:39-51; Romans 12:1.

9. **Key "by way of explanation"**

   Verse 21. God often spoke to his people from a cloud. See Numbers 12:5,6;
   Deuteronomy 31:15,16; Psalm 99:6,7.

10. **Key "Quotable Quote"**

    "One drop of Christ's blood is worth more than heaven and earth."
    Martin Luther

Exodus chapter 14

1. *Before and after*

   > Previous chapter: Chapter 13: The festival of unleavened bread
   > Following chapter: Chapter 15: The Song of Moses

2. *Analysis of chapter*

   > God directs the Israelites to Pihahiroth, Pharaoh pursues them. (1-9)
   > The Israelites murmur, Moses comforts them. (10-14)
   > God instructs Moses, and the cloud between the Israelites and the Egyptians. (15-20)
   > The Israelites pass through the Red Sea, which drowns the Egyptians. (21-31)

3. *Key verse*

   > Verse 29: "But the children of Israel walked upon dry land in the midst of the sea; and the waters were a wall unto them on their right hand, and on their left."

4. *Key word / key phrase*

   > Verse 17, "glory."

5. *Key event / key person / key theme*

   > Crossing the Red Sea

6. *Key thought*

   > God is the God of the impossible.

7. *Key thing to look out for*

   > God is Judge.

8. *Key Bible cross-reference*

   > Verse 31. See Joshua 24:29; 1 Samuel 3:10; 2 Samuel 3:18.

9. *Key "by way of explanation"*

   > Verse 22. This event was never to be forgotten, and was frequently spoken of in the Psalms. See Psalm 66:6; 106:9; 136:13,24.

10. *Key "Quotable Quote"*

    > "What have we our time and strength for, but to lay them out for God? What is a candle made for, but to be burned?"
    > Richard Baxter

Exodus chapter 15

1. *Before and after*

Previous chapter: Chapter 14: Crossing the Red Sea
Following chapter: Chapter 16: Food miraculously provided

2. *Analysis of chapter*

The song of Moses for the deliverance of Israel. (1-21)
The bitter waters at Marah, and the Israelites come to Elim. (22-27)

3. *Key verse*

Verse 1: "Then sang Moses and the children of Israel this song unto the LORD, and spake, saying, I will sing unto the LORD, for he hath triumphed gloriously: the horse and his rider hath he thrown into the sea."

4. *Key word / key phrase*

Verse 2, "sing."

5. *Key event / key person / key theme*

The Song of Moses

6. *Key thought*

Thanksgiving is essential.

7. *Key thing to look out for*

Much of the Bible is taken up with recalling God's goodness.

8. *Key Bible cross-reference*

Verse 1. See Judges 5:3; Psalm 89:1; 101:1; 108:1.

9. *Key "by way of explanation"*

Verse 20. Prophetesses were not unknown in the Bible. See Numbers 12:1,2; Judges 4:4; 2 Kings 22:14; Nehemiah 6:14; Luke 2:36, Acts 21:9.

10. *Key "Quotable Quote"*

"No duty is more urgent than that of returning thanks."
Ambrose

Exodus chapter 16

1. **Before and after**

   Previous chapter: Chapter 15: The Song of Moses
   Following chapter: Chapter 17: Water from a rock

2. **Analysis of chapter**

   The Israelites come to the desert of Sin. They murmur for food, God promises bread from heaven. (1-12)
   God sends quails and manna. (13-21)
   Details about the manna. (22-31)
   An omer of manna to be preserved. (32-36)

3. **Key verse**

   Verse 15: "And when the children of Israel saw it, they said one to another, It is manna: for they wist not what it was. And Moses said unto them, This is the bread which the LORD hath given you to eat."

4. **Key word / key phrase**

   Verse 12, "grumbling."

5. **Key event / key person / key theme**

   God's provision through manna and quail

6. **Key thought**

   God shows his kindness despite human failures and sins.

7. **Key thing to look out for**

   God's commands are given for our benefit.

8. **Key Bible cross-reference**

   Verse 34. See 31:18; 32:15; 34:29; Hebrews 9:4.

9. **Key "by way of explanation"**

   Verse 4. For Christians Jesus is the "bread from heaven." See John 6:32,33,35,48.

10. **Key "Quotable Quote"**

    "All plenty which is not my God is poverty to me."
    Augustine of Hippo

Exodus chapter 17

1. Before and after

Previous chapter: Chapter 16: Food miraculously provided
Following chapter: Chapter 18: Jethro meets the Israelites

2. Analysis of chapter

The Israelites murmur for water at Rephidim, God provides it from the rock.
(1-7)
Amalek overcome, and the prayers of Moses. (8-16)

3. Key verse

Verse 6: "Behold, I will stand before thee there upon the rock in Horeb; and
thou shalt smite the rock, and there shall come water out of it, that the people
may drink. And Moses did so in the sight of the elders of Israel."

4. Key word / key phrase

Verse 7, "quarreled."

5. Key event / key person / key theme

Water from the rock

6. Key thought

God hates grumblers.

7. Key thing to look out for

Wars in the Bible can be seen as an illustration of the spiritual battle every
Christian faces.

8. Key Bible cross-reference

Verse 6. See 1 Corinthians 10:4; Hebrews 11:24-26.

9. Key "by way of explanation"

Verse 11. Hands were held up as a symbol of appealing to God for his help. See
9:22; 10:12.

10. Key "Quotable Quote"

"When afflicted, love can allow thee to groan, but not to grumble."
William Gurnall

Exodus chapter 18

1. Before and after

Previous chapter: Chapter 17: Water from a rock
Following chapter: Chapter 19: The Israelites at Mount Sinai

2. Analysis of chapter

Jethro brings to Moses his wife and two sons. (1-6)
Moses entertains Jethro. (7-12)
Jethro's counsel to Moses. (13-27)

3. Key verse

Verse 5: "And Jethro, Moses' father in law, came with his sons and his wife unto Moses into the desert, where he encamped at the mount of God."

4. Key word / key phrase

Verse 1, "Jethro."

5. Key event / key person / key theme

Jethro visits Moses.

6. Key thought

Jethro is delighted to hear all that God did, verse 9.

7. Key thing to look out for

Shared leadership and delegation are essential in Christian work.

8. Key Bible cross-reference

Verse 11. See 2 Kings 5:15.

9. Key "by way of explanation"

Verse 15. God's will was sought by going to a place of worship, Genesis 25:22, and by visiting a prophet, 1 Samuel 9:9.

10. Key "Quotable Quote"

"We never find a presbyter in the singular in the New Testament. He is always a member of a team."
E.M.B. Green

Exodus chapter 19

1. Before and after

Previous chapter: Chapter 18: Jethro meets the Israelites
Following chapter: Chapter 20: The Ten Commandments

2. Analysis of chapter

The people come to Sinai, God's message to them, and their answer. (1-8)
The people told to prepare to hear the law. (9-15)
The presence of God on Sinai. (16-25)

3. Key verse

Verse 20: "And the LORD came down upon mount Sinai, on the top of the mount: and the LORD called Moses up to the top of the mount; and Moses went up."

4. Key word / key phrase

Verse 10, "consecrate."

5. Key event / key person / key theme

Moses meets the Lord on top of Mount Sinai.

6. Key thought

God's holiness should never be forgotten.

7. Key thing to look out for

Moses was content to do what God ordered.

8. Key Bible cross-reference

Verse 6. See Deuteronomy 7:6; 14:2; 26:18; Psalm 135:4.

9. Key "by way of explanation"

Verse 6. The point about priests is that they are meant to be wholly consecrated to the service of God. See Isaiah 61:6; 1 Peter 2:5.

10. Key "Quotable Quote"

"Nothing shall be lost that is done for God or in obedience to him."
John Owen

Exodus chapter 20

1. Before and after

Previous chapter: Chapter 19: The Israelites at Mount Sinai
Following chapter: Chapter 21: Laws about the rights of people

2. Analysis of chapter

The preface to the Ten Commandments. (1,2)
Commandments 1 to 4: our duty to God. (3-11)
Commandments 5-10: our relationship with others. (12-17)
The fear of the people. (18-21)
Idolatry again forbidden. (22-26)

3. Key verse

Verse 1: "And God spake all these words, saying, I am the LORD thy God, which have brought thee out of the land of Egypt, out of the house of bondage."

4. Key word / key phrase

Verse 1, "spoke."

5. Key event / key person / key theme

God gives the Ten Commandments.

6. Key thought

The Ten Commandments never go out of date.

7. Key thing to look out for

The Ten Commandments explain how we are to love God and our fellow human beings in our daily lives.

8. Key Bible cross-reference

Verses 1-17. See Deuteronomy 5:6-21; Matthew 5:21,27; 19:17-19.

9. Key "by way of explanation"

Verse 4, "idol." The problem with idols is that they aim to represent God, yet God has no visible form. So all idols misrepresent God. See Deuteronomy 4:12,15-18.

10. Key "Quotable Quote"

"The only things which ought to be painted or sculptured, are things which can be presented to the eye; the majesty of God, which is far beyond the reach of any eye, must not be dishonored by unbecoming representations."
John Calvin

Exodus chapter 21

1. Before and after

Previous chapter: Chapter 20: The Ten Commandments
Following chapter: Chapter 22: Laws about repayment, and moral and religious laws

2. Analysis of chapter

Laws about servants. (1-11)
Laws about personal injuries. (12-36)

3. Key verse

Verse 1: "Now these are the judgments which thou shalt set before them."

4. Key word / key phrase

Verse 2, "servant."

5. Key event / key person / key theme

How to treat slaves

6. Key thought

God's kindness extends to everyone.

7. Key thing to look out for

Laws are meant to benefit the wronged.

8. Key Bible cross-reference

Verses 12-15. See Numbers 35:16-34; Deuteronomy 19:1-13.

9. Key "by way of explanation"

Verse 32. The price of a slave was the same as the payment Judas received for betraying Jesus, see Matthew 26:14,15.

10. Key "Quotable Quote"

"Lex mala, lex nulla. An evil law, is no law."
Thomas Aquinas

Exodus chapter 22

1. Before and after

Previous chapter: Chapter 21: Laws about the rights of people
Following chapter: Chapter 23: The seventh day and the seventh year, and three national festivals

2. Analysis of chapter

Laws about protection of property. (1-15)
Laws about social responsibility. (16-31)

3. Key verse

Verse 31: "And ye shall be holy men unto me."

4. Key word / key phrase

Verse 7, "pay back."

5. Key event / key person / key theme

Moral and religious laws

6. Key thought

God's laws extend to every area of life.

7. Key thing to look out for

God's laws come from a compassionate heart, verse 27.

8. Key Bible cross-reference

Verses 21-27. See Psalm 10:14,17,18; 68:5; 82:3; 146:9.

9. Key "by way of explanation"

Verse 20. Total destruction of idols and those who worshiped idols was commanded by God. See Numbers 21:2.

10. Key "Quotable Quote"

"One has not only a legal but a moral responsibility to obey just laws . Conversely, one has a moral responsibility to disobey unjust laws."
Martin Luther King, Jr.

Exodus chapter 23

1. *Before and after*

Previous chapter: Chapter 22: Laws about repayment, and moral and religious laws
Following chapter: Chapter 24: The covenant is ratified

2. *Analysis of chapter*

Laws against falsehood and injustice. (1-9)
The year of rest, and the Sabbath, and the three festivals. (10-19)
God promises to take the Israelites to Canaan. (20-33)

3. *Key verse*

Verse 32: "Thou shalt make no covenant with them, nor with their gods."

4. *Key word / key phrase*

Verse 2, "crowd."

5. *Key event / key person / key theme*

Laws about justice and mercy

6. *Key thought*

Following the crowd very often means following evil.

7. *Key thing to look out for*

Righteousness exalts a nation.

8. *Key Bible cross-reference*

Verse 1. See Leviticus 19:16; Deuteronomy 23:13-19.

9. *Key "by way of explanation"*

Verse 7. This verse is often illustrated in the Bible. See 1 Kings 21:10-13.

10. *Key "Quotable Quote"*

"Justice is truth in action."
Joseph Joubert

Exodus chapter 24

1. Before and after

Previous chapter: Chapter 23: The seventh day and the seventh year, and three national festivals

Following chapter: Chapter 25: The covenant box, the special table, and the lampstand

2. Analysis of chapter

Moses is called up into the mountain, and the people promise obedience. (1-8)

The glory of the Lord appears. (9-11)

Moses goes up into the mountain. (12-18)

3. Key verse

Verse 7: "And he took the book of the covenant, and read in the audience of the people: and they said, All that the LORD hath said will we do, and be obedient."

4. Key word / key phrase

Verse 17, "glory."

5. Key event / key person / key theme

The covenant is confirmed.

6. Key thought

Moses alone was allowed to approach God, as he was the mediator of the covenant.

7. Key thing to look out for

Jesus' new covenant was sealed with his own blood. See Matthew 26:28.

8. Key Bible cross-reference

Verse 7. See 20:22–23:19; 20:2-17; 23:20-33.

9. Key "by way of explanation"

Verse 17. Every glimpse of God's glory is like a blinding light. During Jesus' transfiguration his clothes looked like the most brilliant white.

10. Key "Quotable Quote"

"Grace is but glory begun, and glory is but grace perfected."
Jonathan Edwards

Exodus chapter 25

1. Before and after

> Previous chapter: Chapter 24: The covenant is ratified
> Following chapter: Chapter 26: The tent of the Lord's presence

2. Analysis of chapter

> What the Israelites were to offer for making the tabernacle. (1-9)
> The ark. (10-22)
> The table, with its furniture. (23-30)
> The candlestick. (31-40)

3. Key verse

> Verse 10: "And they shall make an ark of shittim [acacia] wood."

4. Key word / key phrase

> Verse 21, "ark."

5. Key event / key person / key theme

> The ark

6. Key thought

> Nothing is more important than worshiping God.

7. Key thing to look out for

> Verses 8,22. The purpose of the ark.

8. Key Bible cross-reference

> Verse 30. See 33:14,15; Isaiah 63:9.

9. Key "by way of explanation"

> The ark was a wooden box covered with gold. Its lid (KJV "mercy seat") was
> made of pure gold. At either end of the lid was a golden cherubim.

10. Key "Quotable Quote"

> "'Divine service' is not a thing of a few hours and a few places, but when all
> life becomes holiness unto the Lord, and every place and thing, as
> consecrated as the tabernacle."
> C.H. Spurgeon

Exodus chapter 26

1. Before and after

Previous chapter: Chapter 25: The covenant box, the special table, and the lampstand
Following chapter: Chapter 27: The altar and tabernacle enclosure

2. Analysis of chapter

The curtains of the tabernacle. (1-6)
The curtains of goats' hair. (7-14)
The boards, sockets, and bars. (15-30)
The curtain (veil) in front of the holy of holies, and for the entrance. (31-37)

3. Key verse

Verse 1: "Moreover thou shalt make the tabernacle with ten curtains of fine twined linen, and blue, and purple, and scarlet: with cherubims of cunning work shalt thou make them."

4. Key word / key phrase

Verse 1, "tabernacle."

5. Key event / key person / key theme

Instructions for making the tabernacle

6. Key thought

Is it not amazing that humans can have fellowship with God?

7. Key thing to look out for

God wishes humans to worship him.

8. Key Bible cross-reference

Verse 1. In John 1:14 John says that Jesus "made his dwelling among us." The word used here means "tabernacled," or, "pitched his tent" among us.

9. Key "by way of explanation"

Verse 31. This curtain was dramatically torn from top to bottom at Jesus' crucifixion, Mark 15:38, indicating that access to God was now possible.

10. Key "Quotable Quote"

"What God chooses, he cleanses.
What God cleanses, he molds.
What God molds, he fills.
What God fills, he uses."
J.S. Baxter

Exodus chapter 27

1. *Before and after*

Previous chapter: Chapter 26: The tent of the Lord's presence
Following chapter: Chapter 28: The clothes for the priests and the breastpiece

2. *Analysis of chapter*

The altar of burnt offerings. (1-8)
The court of the tabernacle. (9-19)
The oil for the lamps. (20,21)

3. *Key verse*

Verse 20: "And thou shalt command the children of Israel, that they bring thee
pure oil olive beaten for the light, to cause the lamp to burn always."

4. *Key word / key phrase*

Verse 1, "altar."

5. *Key event / key person / key theme*

Some of the furniture for the temple

6. *Key thought*

Every item of "furniture" in the temple was full of significant symbolism.

7. *Key thing to look out for*

Nothing was thought to be too costly if needed in God's service.

8. *Key Bible cross-reference*

Verse 21. See 29:42,43.

9. *Key "by way of explanation"*

Verse 2. The "horns" at each corner of the altar were symbols of help and
refuge. See 1 Kings 1:50.

10. *Key "Quotable Quote"*

"Often, what passes for religious experience is a communal emotion felt in
church services, in meetings, in singing or contrived fellowship. Few
Christians would know God on their own."
Os Guinness

Exodus chapter 28

1. Before and after

Previous chapter: Chapter 27: The altar and tabernacle enclosure
Following chapter: Chapter 29: Instructions for Aaron's ordination and the daily offerings

2. Analysis of chapter

Aaron and his sons set apart for the priest's office, and their garments. (1-5)
The ephod. (6-14)
The breastpiece, and the Urim and Thummim. (15-30)
The robe of the ephod (a sleeveless garment), and the plate of gold. (31-39)
The garments for Aaron's sons. (40-43)

3. Key verse

Verse 15: "And thou shalt make the breastplate of judgment with cunning work."

4. Key word / key phrase

Verse 15, "breastpiece."

5. Key event / key person / key theme

Clothes for the priests

6. Key thought

The garments the priests wore were to reflect the special work they were engaged in.

7. Key thing to look out for

If worship does not emphasize God's holiness, verse 36, there is something wrong with it.

8. Key Bible cross-reference

Verse 6. See Judges 8:27; 18:17; Hosea 3:4.

9. Key "by way of explanation"

Verse 30, "Urim and Thummim," were sacred lots which were cast in order to discover God's will. See Numbers 27:21.

10. Key "Quotable Quote"

"He humbled himself for us; let us glorify him."
Augustine of Hippo

Exodus chapter 29

1. Before and after

Previous chapter: Chapter 28: The clothes for the priests and the breastpiece
Following chapter: Chapter 30: Instructions for using the tabernacle

2. Analysis of chapter

The sacrifice and ceremony for the consecration of the priests. (1-37)
The continual burnt offerings, God's promise to live among the Israelites. (38-46)

3. Key verse

Verse 44: "And I will sanctify the tabernacle of the congregation, and the altar: I will sanctify also both Aaron and his sons, to minister to me in the priest's office."

4. Key word / key phrase

Verse 43, "glory."

5. Key event / key person / key theme

The consecration of the priests

6. Key thought

Worship and God's glory should always be linked. See verse 43.

7. Key thing to look out for

God's presence was never restricted to the tabernacle. See verse 45.

8. Key Bible cross-reference

Verse 14. See Hebrews 13:11-13.

9. Key "by way of explanation"

Verse 20. The right ears symbolize listening to God; the right hands and right feet symbolize serving others for God's sake.

10. Key "Quotable Quote"

"There are few individuals in this life, and perhaps even none, who sufficiently understand how much we hinder and keep God from doing what he desires in our souls."
Ignatius of Loyola

Exodus chapter 30

1. ### Before and after

   Previous chapter: Chapter 29: Instructions for Aaron's ordination and the daily offerings
   Following chapter: Chapter 31: Instructions for building the tabernacle, and the sign of the covenant

2. ### Analysis of chapter

   The altar of incense. (1-10)
   The ransom of souls. (11-16)
   The bronze laver. (17-21)
   The holy anointing oil, and the perfume. (22-38)

3. ### Key verse

   Verse 16: "And thou shalt take the atonement money of the children of Israel, and shalt appoint it for the service of the tabernacle of the congregation; that it may be a memorial unto the children of Israel before the LORD, to make an atonement for your souls."

4. ### Key word / key phrase

   Verse 15, "atone."

5. ### Key event / key person / key theme

   More furniture for the temple

6. ### Key thought

   Washing with water is often used in the Bible to symbolize God washing away our sins.

7. ### Key thing to look out for

   When a person or object was anointed with oil he, she, or it, was set apart for God's use.

8. ### Key Bible cross-reference

   Verse 12. See Numbers 1:2; 26:2.

9. ### Key "by way of explanation"

   Verse 1. Incense stood for prayers. See Psalm 141:2; Luke 1:10; Revelation 5:8.

10. ### Key "Quotable Quote"

    "If you are talking of atonement, the means by which we sinners can be reconciled to the God of holy love, why then, yes, I don't think we can escape the truth of the divine substitution."
    John R.W. Stott

Exodus chapter 31

1. Before and after

Previous chapter: Chapter 30: Instructions for using the tabernacle
Following chapter: Chapter 32: Moses prays for Israel's salvation

2. Analysis of chapter

Bezalel and Oholiab are appointed and qualified for the work of the tabernacle. (1-11)
The observance of the Sabbath. (12-17)
Moses receives the tablets of the law. (18)

3. Key verse

Verse 14: "Ye shall keep the Sabbath therefore; for it is holy unto you."

4. Key word / key phrase

Verse 3, "skill."

5. Key event / key person / key theme

Bezalel and Oholiab

6. Key thought

Every talent can be used in God's service.

7. Key thing to look out for

The Sabbath was God's gift to humankind.

8. Key Bible cross-reference

Verse 18, "two tablets." See 25:21.

9. Key "by way of explanation"

Verse 18. The covenant came from God with his instructions, so it was said to be inscribed with God's finger.

10. Key "Quotable Quote"

"I feel as if God had, by giving the Sabbath, given fifty-two springs in every year."
Samuel Taylor Coleridge

Exodus chapter 32

1. Before and after

Previous chapter: Chapter 31: Instructions for building the tabernacle, and the sign of the covenant

Following chapter: Chapter 33: God shows Moses his glory

2. Analysis of chapter

The people tell Aaron to make a golden calf. (1-6)

God's displeasure, and the intercession of Moses. (7-14)

Moses breaks the tablets of the law. He destroys the golden calf. (15-20)

Aaron's excuse, and the idolaters killed. (21-29)

Moses prays for the people. (30-35)

3. Key verse

Verse 4: "And he received them at their hand, and fashioned it with a graving tool, after he had made it a molten calf: and they said, These be thy gods, O Israel, which brought thee up out of the land of Egypt."

4. Key word / key phrase

Verse 4, "idol."

5. Key event / key person / key theme

Making an idol in the shape of a golden calf

6. Key thought

Idleness led to idolatry.

7. Key thing to look out for

None of God's people are exempt from being tempted to sin against God.

8. Key Bible cross-reference

Verse 14. See Psalm 106:45; Amos 7:1-6; James 5:16.

9. Key "by way of explanation"

Verse 9. To be "stiff-necked" was to behave like some unbending and unresponsive ox which would not go the way it was being directed. See Jeremiah 27:11,12.

10. Key "Quotable Quote"

"We think it unlawful to give a visible shape to God, because God himself has forbidden it, and because it cannot be done without, in some degree, tarnishing his glory."

John Calvin, *The Institutes of Christian Religion*

Exodus chapter 33

1. Before and after

Previous chapter: Chapter 32: Moses prays for Israel's salvation
Following chapter: Chapter 34: The second set of stone tablets, and the renewal of the covenant

2. Analysis of chapter

The Lord refuses to go with Israel. (1-6)
The "tent of meeting" set up outside the camp. (7-11)
Moses desires to see the glory of God. (12-23)

3. Key verse

Verse 14: "And he said, My presence shall go with thee, and I will give thee rest."

4. Key word / key phrase

Verse 18, "glory."

5. Key event / key person / key theme

God's people are told to move on from Mount Sinai.

6. Key thought

No one deserves God's mercy.

7. Key thing to look out for

God is compassionate and so showers his love on everyone.

8. Key Bible cross-reference

Verse 17. See Matthew 17:5; Hebrews 3:1-6.

9. Key "by way of explanation"

The tabernacle was in the midst of the camp; the tent of meeting was a temporary structure until the tabernacle was finished.

10. Key "Quotable Quote"

"Man may dismiss compassion from his heart, but God never will."
William Cowper

Exodus chapter 34

1. Before and after

Previous chapter: Chapter 33: God shows Moses his glory
Following chapter: Chapter 35: Rules for the Sabbath, and the craftsmen for the tabernacle.

2. Analysis of chapter

The tablets of the law renewed. (1-4)
The name of the Lord proclaimed, and the entreaty of Moses. (5-9)
God's covenant. (10-17)
The festivals. (18-27)
The veil of Moses. (28-35)

3. Key verse

Verse 4: "And he hewed two tables of stone like unto the first; and Moses rose up early in the morning, and went up unto mount Sinai, as the LORD had commanded him, and took in his hand the two tables of stone."

4. Key word / key phrase

Verse 6, "faithfulness."

5. Key event / key person / key theme

A replacement set of stone tablets

6. Key thought

It is not possible to hide the fact that one has been in God's presence.

7. Key thing to look out for

The revelation which the Bible gives about God's character.

8. Key Bible cross-reference

Verses 6,7. See Numbers 14:18; Nehemiah 9:17; Jonah 4:2.

9. Key "by way of explanation"

Verse 13. "Asherah poles" were erected in honor of Asherah, the partner of the main Canaanite god, El.

10. Key "Quotable Quote"

"The infinite-personal God, the God who is Trinity, has spoken. He is there, and he is not silent."
Francis A. Schaeffer

Exodus chapter 35

1. *Before and after*

Previous chapter: Chapter 34: The second set of stone tablets, and the renewal of the covenant
Following chapter: Chapter 36: Making the tabernacle.

2. *Analysis of chapter*

The Sabbath to be observed. (1-3)
The free gifts for the tabernacle. (4-19)
The willingness of the people to present offerings. (20-29)
Bezaleol and Oholiab called to the work. (30-35)

3. *Key verse*

Verse 31: "And he hath filled him with the spirit of God, in wisdom, in understanding, and in knowledge, and in all manner of workmanship."

4. *Key word / key phrase*

Verse 5, "offering."

5. *Key event / key person / key theme*

More items for the tabernacle

6. *Key thought*

God loves a generous heart.

7. *Key thing to look out for*

All service for God is meant to be carried out willingly.

8. *Key Bible cross-reference*

35:4–39:43. See 25–28; 30:1-5; 31:1-11.

9. *Key "by way of explanation"*

Verse 5 emphasizes the voluntary nature of serving God. See verses 21,26,29; 36:2,3.

10. *Key "Quotable Quote"*

"Everybody can be great . . . because anybody can serve."
Martin Luther King, Jr.

Exodus chapter 36

1. Before and after

Previous chapter: Chapter 35: Rules for the Sabbath, and the craftsmen for the tabernacle

Following chapter: Chapter 37: Making the furniture for the tabernacle

2. Analysis of chapter

The making of the tabernacle. The liberality of the people restrained. (1-38)

3. Key verse

Verse 8: "And every wise hearted man among them that wrought the work of the tabernacle made ten curtains of fine twined linen, and blue, and purple, and scarlet: with cherubims of cunning work made he them."

4. Key word / key phrase

Verse 8, "tabernacle."

5. Key event / key person / key theme

Items made for the tabernacle.

6. Key thought

Any service for God is honorable.

7. Key thing to look out for

God calls specific people to serve him in specific ways.

8. Key Bible cross-reference

Verses 1-38. See 35:4–39:43.

9. Key "by way of explanation"

Verse 7. The enthusiasm of God's people was so great that Moses had to ask them not to bring in anything more for the sanctuary.

10. Key "Quotable Quote"

"Dislike of enthusiasm is to quench the Spirit."
D. Martyn Lloyd-Jones

Exodus chapter 37

1. Before and after

Previous chapter: Chapter 36: Making the tabernacle
Following chapter: Chapter 38: Making the altar and bronze basin, and the materials used

2. Analysis of chapter

The making of the ark, and the furniture of the tabernacle. (1-29)

3. Key verse

Verse 1: "And Bezalel made the ark of shittim [acacia] wood: two cubits and a half was the length of it, and a cubit and a half the breadth of it, and a cubit and a half the height of it."

4. Key word / key phrase

Verse 1, "ark."

5. Key event / key person / key theme

Making the furniture for the tabernacle

6. Key thought

The design of the ark, with all its gold, would have emphasized God's holiness.

7. Key thing to look out for

All the tabernacle furnishings in some way reflected an aspect of God's greatness.

8. Key Bible cross-reference

Verses 1-9. See Exodus 25:10-20.

9. Key "by way of explanation"

Verse 1. As Bezalel was the chief craftsman he was given the privilege of making the most sacred object for the tabernacle, the ark.

10. Key "Quotable Quote"

"Now, if you will prove that your ceremonies proceed from faith, and do please God, you must prove that God in expressed words has commanded them; or else you shall never prove that they proceed from faith, nor yet that they please God; but they are sin, and do displease him, according to the words of the apostle, 'Whatsoever is not of faith is sin.'"
John Knox

Exodus chapter 38

1. Before and after

Previous chapter: Chapter 37: Making the furniture for the tabernacle
Following chapter: Chapter 39: Clothes for the priests

2. Analysis of chapter

The bronze altar and basin. (1-8)
The courtyard. (9-20)
The offerings of the people. (21-31)

3. Key verse

Verse 1: "And he made the altar of burnt offering of shittim [acacia] wood: five cubits was the length thereof, and five cubits the breadth thereof; it was foursquare; and three cubits the height thereof."

4. Key word / key phrase

Verse 1, "altar of burnt offering."

5. Key event / key person / key theme

Making the altar for the burnt offerings

6. Key thought

Everyone contributed financially to the cost of building the tabernacle.

7. Key thing to look out for

The tabernacle was constructed so it could be dismantled, transported, and then erected again.

8. Key Bible cross-reference

Verse 26, "603,550 men." See Numbers 1:21-43; 2:4-31.

9. Key "by way of explanation"

Verse 8. Mirrors were not made of glass in ancient times, but a reflection was obtained by looking into bronze mirrors.

10. Key "Quotable Quote"

"Act wisely, as a good steward, holding everything as lent to you who have been made God's steward."
Catherine of Siena

Exodus chapter 39

1. *Before and after*

Previous chapter: Chapter 38: Making the altar and bronze basin, and the materials used

Following chapter: Chapter 40: The tent is put up and filled with God's glory

2. *Analysis of chapter*

The priests' garments. (1-31)
The tabernacle completed. (32-43)

3. *Key verse*

Verse 2: "And he made the ephod of gold, blue, and purple, and scarlet, and fine twined linen."

4. *Key word / key phrase*

Verse 8, "breastpiece."

5. *Key event / key person / key theme*

Making the special clothes for the priests

6. *Key thought*

Nothing but the best was good enough for God. So pure gold was always used.

7. *Key thing to look out for*

The Israelites, verse 32, were most conscientious in the way they carried out God's orders for building the tabernacle.

8. *Key Bible cross-reference*

Verse 32. See Genesis 2:1-3.

9. *Key "by way of explanation"*

Verse 30. The plate on the turbans worn by the priests was given the name of the "sacred diadem."

10. *Key "Quotable Quote"*

"By perseverance the snail reached the ark."
C.H. Spurgeon

Exodus chapter 40

1. Previous chapter

> Chapter 39: Clothes for the priests

2. Analysis of chapter

> The tabernacle is to be set up, Aaron and his sons to be sanctified. (1-15)
> Moses performs all as directed. (16-33)
> The glory of the Lord fills the tabernacle. (34-38)

3. Key verse

> Verse 34: "Then a cloud covered the tent of the congregation, and the glory of the LORD filled the tabernacle."

4. Key word / key phrase

> Verse 34, "glory."

5. Key event / key person / key theme

> Setting up and dedicating the tabernacle

6. Key thought

> The whole of the tabernacle cried out, "Glory to God."

7. Key thing to look out for

> God's presence and glory so filled the tabernacle that Moses was unable to enter.

8. Key Bible cross-reference

> Verse 16. See Matthew 7:21.

9. Key "by way of explanation"

> Verse 34. The climax to the book of Exodus is the glory of the Lord filling the tabernacle.

10. Key "Quotable Quote"

> "Afflictions are light when compared with what we really deserve. They are light when compared with the sufferings of the Lord Jesus. But perhaps their real lightness is best seen by comparing them with the weight of glory which is awaiting us."
> Arthur W. Pink

Leviticus

Leviticus chapter 1

1. **Following chapter**

    Chapter 2: Cereal offerings

2. **Analysis of chapter**

    The offerings. (1,2)
    From the herds. (3-9)
    From the flocks, and birds. (10-17)

3. **Key verse**

    Verse 1: "And the LORD called unto Moses, and spake unto him out of the tabernacle of the congregation."

4. **Key word / key phrase**

    Verse 4, "burnt offering."

5. **Key event / key person / key theme**

    Offering sacrifices which were burnt whole

6. **Key thought**

    Verse 1. God is the speaker in the book of Leviticus.

7. **Key thing to look out for**

    The offerings, which are "without defect," verse 3, are types of Jesus' offering of himself. See Hebrews 9:14; 1 Peter 1:19.

8. **Key Bible cross-reference**

    Verse 9, "aroma pleasing to the LORD." See Ephesians 5:2; Philippians 4:18.

9. **Key "by way of explanation"**

    Jews called the book of Leviticus the "priests law." It consists of laws connected with the worship and ritual of the tabernacle, and so gives a background to the other books in the Bible.

10. **Key "Quotable Quote"**

    "Read the Old Testament, and to get re-acquainted with the character of God."
    R.C. Sproul

Leviticus chapter 2

1. *Before and after*

Previous chapter: Chapter 1: Burnt offerings
Following chapter: Chapter 3: Peace offerings

2. *Analysis of chapter*

The meat offering of flour. (1-11)
The offering of first fruits. (12-16)

3. *Key verse*

Verse 4: "And if thou bring an oblation of a meat offering baken in the oven, it shall be unleavened cakes of fine flour mingled with oil, or unleavened wafers anointed with oil."

4. *Key word / key phrase*

Verse 4, "flour."

5. *Key event / key person / key theme*

Grain offerings

6. *Key thought*

Each offering symbolized a reason for coming to worship God.

7. *Key thing to look out for*

All the offerings detailed in the Old Testament express the worshiper's devotion to God.

8. *Key Bible cross-reference*

Verse 1. See 6:14-23; 7:9,10.

9. *Key "by way of explanation"*

Verse 4. Grain offerings were made to thank God for his provision.

10. *Key "Quotable Quote"*

"Worship is our occupation with God himself, with the greatness of his being."
Ray Stedman

Leviticus chapter 3

1. **Before and after**

    Previous chapter: Chapter 2: Cereal offerings
    Following chapter: Chapter 4: Sin offerings

2. **Analysis of chapter**

    The peace offering of the herd. (1-5)
    The peace offering of the flock. (6-17)

3. **Key verse**

    Verse 1: "And if his oblation be a sacrifice of peace offering, if he offer it of the herd; whether it be a male or female, he shall offer it without blemish before the LORD."

4. **Key word / key phrase**

    Verse 6, "fellowship offering."

5. **Key event / key person / key theme**

    Fellowship offerings

6. **Key thought**

    The traditional name for this fellowship offering was "peace offering." This came from the Hebrew word for peace, *shalom*, which also means wholeness.

7. **Key thing to look out for**

    God is the focal point of all the Old Testament offerings.

8. **Key Bible cross-reference**

    Verse 1. See 7:11-21, 28-34

9. **Key "by way of explanation"**

    Verse 6. Fellowship offerings were motivated by the desire to give thanks to God.

10. **Key "Quotable Quote"**

    "One act of thanksgiving when things go wrong with us is worth a thousand thanks when things are agreeable to our inclination."
    John Jewell

Leviticus chapter 4

1. Before and after

Previous chapter: Chapter 3: Peace offerings
Following chapter: Chapter 5: Guilt offerings

2. Analysis of chapter

The sin offering of ignorance for the priest. (1-12)
For the whole congregation. (13-21)
For a ruler. (22-26)
For any of the people. (27-35)

3. Key verse

Verse 2: "Speak unto the children of Israel, saying, If a soul shall sin through ignorance against any of the commandments of the LORD concerning things which ought not to be done, and shall do against any of them."

4. Key word / key phrase

Verse 20, "atonement."

5. Key event / key person / key theme

Offerings for unintentional sins

6. Key thought

Note "will be forgiven" which comes nine times in chapter 4, 5, and 6.

7. Key thing to look out for

There are two types of sin offering to note. See verses 3-21 for the first one, and 4:22–5:13 for the second one.

8. Key Bible cross-reference

Verse 20. See Exodus 29:36; 32:30; Romans 3:25.

9. Key "by way of explanation"

Verse 3. Sin offerings had to be made for specific unintentional sins. Unlike fellowship offerings they were not voluntary.

10. Key "Quotable Quote"

"What can I give him,
     Poor as I am?
If I were a shepherd,
     I would bring a lamb,
If I were a Wise Man,
     I would do my part –
Yet what can I give him?
     Give my heart."
Christina Rossetti

Leviticus chapter 5

1. Before and after

Previous chapter: Chapter 4: Sin offerings
Following chapter: Chapter 6: Laws for administering offerings

2. Analysis of chapter

Various trespasses. (1-13)
Trespasses against the Lord. (14-19)

3. Key verse

Verse 16: "And he shall make amends for the harm that he hath done in the holy thing."

4. Key word / key phrase

Verse 15, "guilt offering."

5. Key event / key person / key theme

Repayment offerings

6. Key thought

"There is a way back to God from the dark path of sin."

7. Key thing to look out for

Verse 5, "he must confess." The guilty person had to confess his sin before he could be forgiven.

8. Key Bible cross-reference

Verse 15. See Isaiah 53:10.

9. Key "by way of explanation"

The sin offering and guilt offering were similar, but the former related more to the sinner's relationship to God; the latter involved making compensation for damage done.

10. Key "Quotable Quote"

"The confession of evil works is the first beginning of good works."
Augustine of Hippo

Leviticus chapter 6

1. Before and after

Previous chapter: Chapter 5: Guilt offerings

Following chapter: Chapter 7: Laws for administering guilt and peace offerings

2. Analysis of chapter

Trespasses against our neighbor. (1-7)

The burnt offering. (8-13)

The meat offering. (14-23)

The sin offering. (24-30)

3. Key verse

Verses 24,25: "And the LORD spake unto Moses, saying, Speak unto Aaron and to his sons, saying, This is the law of the sin offering."

4. Key word / key phrase

Verse 5, "offering."

5. Key event / key person / key theme

More regulations about offerings

6. Key thought

These offerings catered for the whole range of sins.

7. Key thing to look out for

Dealing with personal sin is essential for any kind of spiritual life.

8. Key Bible cross-reference

Verse 25, "sin offering." See 4:1–5:13.

9. Key "by way of explanation"

Verses 9,12. As well as the private offerings made by the people, a public burnt offering was made every morning and evening.

10. Key "Quotable Quote"

"The deadliest sin were the consciousness of no sin."
Thomas Carlyle

Leviticus chapter 7

1. Before and after

Previous chapter: Chapter 6: Laws for administering offerings
Following chapter: Chapter 8: Consecration of priests

2. Analysis of chapter

The trespass offering. (1-10)
The peace offering. (11-27)
The fellowship offering. (28-34)
The conclusion of these institutions. (35-38)

3. Key verse

Verse 11: "And this is the law of the sacrifice of peace offerings, which he shall offer unto the LORD."

4. Key word / key phrase

Verse 11, "fellowship offering."

5. Key event / key person / key theme

Further regulations about the three types of fellowship offerings.

6. Key thought

Every worship service should include thanksgiving.

7. Key thing to look out for

Note how seriously the Bible takes sin.

8. Key Bible cross-reference

Verse 26. Not eating the blood. See 3:17; 19:26; Ezekiel 33:25.

9. Key "by way of explanation"

Verse 20. Some people were in danger of being cut off from God's covenant.

10. Key "Quotable Quote"

"Not to think of God is grievously to offend him. Not to praise him day by day for all he is and has done is in itself terrible sin."
D. Martyn Lloyd-Jones

Leviticus chapter 8

1. Before and after

Previous chapter: Chapter 7: Laws for administering guilt and peace offerings

Following chapter: Chapter 9: Sacrifices are offered

2. Analysis of chapter

The consecration of Aaron and his sons. (1-13)

The offerings of consecration. (14-36)

3. Key verse

Verse 2: "Take Aaron and his sons with him, and the garments, and the anointing oil, and a bullock for the sin offering, and two rams, and a basket of unleavened bread."

4. Key word / key phrase

Verse 12, "anointing."

5. Key event / key person / key theme

Ordination of Aaron and his sons

6. Key thought

Aaron had a special work to do for God and so was anointed with oil.

7. Key thing to look out for

Aaron and his sons were happy to obey God, even though their instructions came through Moses.

8. Key Bible cross-reference

Verse 2. See Exodus 39:1-31; 40:12-16.

9. Key "by way of explanation"

Verse 14. During Aaron's consecration service a sin offering for atonement was offered.

10. Key "Quotable Quote"

"There is need of a great revival of spiritual life, of truly fervent devotion to our Lord Jesus, of entire consecration to his service."
Andrew Murray

Leviticus chapter 9

1. Before and after

> Previous chapter: Chapter 8: Consecration of priests
> Following chapter: Chapter 10: Rules for the priests

2. Analysis of chapter

> The first offerings of Aaron for himself and the people. (1-21)
> Moses and Aaron bless the people. Fire comes on the altar from the Lord. (22-24)

3. Key verse

> Verse 22: "And Aaron lifted up his hand toward the people, and blessed them, and came down from offering of the sin offering, and the burnt offering, and peace offerings."

4. Key word / key phrase

> Verse 4, "sacrifice."

5. Key event / key person / key theme

> Aaron offers sacrifices.

6. Key thought

> Only those blessed by God are capable of passing on any blessing from God.

7. Key thing to look out for

> Aaron's threefold blessing.

8. Key Bible cross-reference

> Verse 24, "fire." See 10:2; 1 Kings 18:38.

9. Key "by way of explanation"

> Verse 23. The "glory of the Lord" is seen again, as it was when the tabernacle was erected, Exodus 40:34,35.

10. Key "Quotable Quote"

> "*Soli Deo Gloria*," (Only to God be the glory).
> J.S. Bach, often wrote these words at the end of his musical compositions.

Leviticus chapter 10

1. **Before and after**

   Previous chapter: Chapter 9: Sacrifices are offered
   Following chapter: Chapter 11: Animals that may and may not be eaten

2. **Analysis of chapter**

   The sin and death of Nadab and Abihu. (1,2)
   Aaron and his sons forbidden to mourn for Nadab and Abihu. (3-7)
   Priests are forbidden to drink when serving in the tabernacle. (8-11)
   Eating the holy things. (12-20)

3. **Key verse**

   Verse 2: "And there went out fire from the LORD, and devoured them, and they died before the LORD."

4. **Key word / key phrase**

   Verse 13, "holy."

5. **Key event / key person / key theme**

   Nadab and Abihu die as a result of their sin.

6. **Key thought**

   We cannot over-emphasize the importance of God's holiness.

7. **Key thing to look out for**

   God's teaching must be passed on to the next generation.

8. **Key Bible cross-reference**

   Verse 2. See a comparable incident in Acts 5:1-11.

9. **Key "by way of explanation"**

   Verse 2, "died before the Lord." While this incident may seem harsh, one lesson it teaches is that God's people had to remember that they existed for God's glory.

10. **Key "Quotable Quote"**

    "God, being infinitely holy, has an infinite hatred of sin."
    Jerry Bridges

Leviticus chapter 11

1. *Before and after*

Previous chapter: Chapter 10: Rules for the priests
Following chapter: Chapter 12: Cleansing after childbirth

2. *Analysis of chapter*

What animals were clean (i.e. could be sacrificed, and could be eaten) and
unclean. (1-47)

3. *Key verse*

Verse 2: "These are the beasts which ye shall eat among all the beasts that are
on the earth."

4. *Key word / key phrase*

Verse 4, "unclean."

5. *Key event / key person / key theme*

Animals which may and may not be eaten.

6. *Key thought*

Verse 45. This refrain, "brought . . . out of Egypt" comes 18 times in this book.

7. *Key thing to look out for*

The word "holiness" appears more frequently in the book of Leviticus than in
any other book of the Bible.

8. *Key Bible cross-reference*

Verse 2. See Deuteronomy 14:3-21.

9. *Key "by way of explanation"*

Verse 44. "Be holy." Holiness, the most important theme in Leviticus, hinges
on God's own holiness.

10. *Key "Quotable Quote"*

"There is a danger of forgetting that the Bible reveals, not first the love of God,
but the intense, blazing holiness of God, with his love as the center of that
holiness."
Oswald Chambers

Leviticus chapter 12

1. **Before and after**

   Previous chapter: Chapter 11: Animals that may and may not be eaten
   Following chapter: Chapter 13: Cases of skin disease

2. **Analysis of chapter**

   Ceremonial purification. (1-8)

3. **Key verse**

   Verse 8: "And if she be not able to bring a lamb, then she shall bring two turtles, or two young pigeons."

4. **Key word / key phrase**

   Verse 2, "ceremonially unclean."

5. **Key event / key person / key theme**

   Purifying women after childbirth

6. **Key thought**

   Being ceremonially unclean underlines the importance of remembering God's holiness.

7. **Key thing to look out for**

   It would appear that Mary and Joseph were poor, or else they would have offered a lamb.

8. **Key Bible cross-reference**

   Verse 8. See 1:14-17; 5:7-10; Luke 2:24.

9. **Key "by way of explanation"**

   Verse 2. The uncleanness was not due to the birth of the baby, but to the bleeding. The word translated leprosy refers to a wide variety of skin disorders, not all malignant, and also to mildew in clothing and houses.

10. **Key "Quotable Quote"**

    "The will of God is the purification and sanctification of the heart that comes about through fully experienced and conscious participation in the perfect and divine Spirit."
    Makarios of Egypt

Leviticus chapter 13

1. **Before and after**

   Previous chapter: Chapter 12: Cleansing after childbirth
   Following chapter: Chapter 14: Cleansing if skin disease is cured

2. **Analysis of chapter**

   Directions to the priest to judge concerning leprosy. (1-17)
   Further directions. (18-44)
   How the leper must be treated. (45,46)
   The mildew in garments. (47-59)

3. **Key verse**

   Verse 46: "All the days wherein the plague shall be in him he shall be defiled;
   he is unclean: he shall dwell alone; without the camp shall his habitation be."

4. **Key word / key phrase**

   Verse 2, "infectious skin disease."

5. **Key event / key person / key theme**

   Regulations about infectious skin diseases

6. **Key thought**

   These regulations were intended to provide a way for a healed person to be
   officially declared "clean."

7. **Key thing to look out for**

   Just as some people needed physical healing, everyone needs spiritual
   healing.

8. **Key Bible cross-reference**

   Verse 2. See 22:4; Numbers 5:2.

9. **Key "by way of explanation"**

   Verses 45,46. Nobody who was ceremonially unclean was allowed into the
   Israelite camp, as God's presence was there.

10. **Key "Quotable Quote"**

   "God heals, and the doctor takes the fee."
   George Herbert

Leviticus chapter 14

1. Before and after

Previous chapter: Chapter 13: Cases of skin disease
Following chapter: Chapter 15: Uncleanliness from discharges

2. Analysis of chapter

Of declaring the leper to be clean. (1-9)
The sacrifices to be offered by him. (10-32)
The mildew in a house. (33-53)
Summary of the law about leprosy. (54-57)

3. Key verse

Verse 3: "And the priest shall go forth out of the camp."

4. Key word / key phrase

Verse 57, "unclean."

5. Key event / key person / key theme

Purification after having a skin disease

6. Key thought

Disease was often used as a picture of sin.

7. Key thing to look out for

The pains that were taken to declare that a person was physically cured.

8. Key Bible cross-reference

Verse 7. See Psalm 51:7.

9. Key "by way of explanation"

Verse 45. A house with mildew had to be "torn down" or it would continue to
be a serious health risk.

10. Key "Quotable Quote"

"There is a great market for religious experience in our world . . . there is little
inclination to sign up for the long apprenticeship in what earlier generations
of Christians called holiness."
Eugene H. Peterson

Leviticus chapter 15

1. **Before and after**

   Previous chapter: Chapter 14: Cleansing if skin disease is cured
   Following chapter: Chapter 16: The Day of Atonement

2. **Analysis of chapter**

   Laws about ceremonial uncleanness. (1-33)

3. **Key verse**

   Verse 31: "Thus shall ye separate the children of Israel from their uncleanness;
   that they die not in their uncleanness, when they defile my tabernacle that is
   among them."

4. **Key word / key phrase**

   Verse 2, "bodily discharge."

5. **Key event / key person / key theme**

   Unclean bodily discharges

6. **Key thought**

   Spiritual purity is even more important that physical purity.

7. **Key thing to look out for**

   God has provided the solution to the worst impurity.

8. **Key Bible cross-reference**

   Verse 25. See Matthew 9:20.

9. **Key "by way of explanation"**

   Verse 31. This verse summarizes the teaching about the need to keep unclean
   people and objects away from God. It prepares the way for the teaching about
   atonement (chapter 16).

10. **Key "Quotable Quote"**

   "Religion that is merely ritual and ceremonial can never satisfy. Neither can
   we be satisfied by a religion that is merely humanitarian or serviceable to
   mankind. Man's craving is for the spiritual."
   Samuel M. Shoemaker

Leviticus chapter 16

1. Before and after

Previous chapter: Chapter 15: Uncleanliness from discharges
Following chapter: Chapter 17: Blood is sacred

2. Analysis of chapter

The great Day of Atonement. (1-14)
The sacrifices on it, and the scapegoat. (15-34)

3. Key verse

Verse 6: "And Aaron shall offer his bullock of the sin offering, which is for himself, and make an atonement for himself, and for his house."

4. Key word / key phrase

Verse 6, "atonement."

5. Key event / key person / key theme

The Day of Atonement

6. Key thought

Without atonement we remain dead in our sins.

7. Key thing to look out for

The different elements which make up the Day of Atonement as they are detailed in this chapter.

8. Key Bible cross-reference

Verses 20-22 describe substitutionary atonement. See Leviticus 1:4; 3:8; 4:4.

9. Key "by way of explanation"

According to verse 34 atonement was made once a year. Jesus' atonement was made once and for all time. See Hebrews 9:11–10:14.

10. Key "Quotable Quote"

"I must die or get somebody to die for me. If the Bible doesn't teach that, it doesn't teach anything. And that is where the atonement of Jesus Christ comes in."
D.L. Moody

Leviticus chapter 17

1. *Before and after*

Previous chapter: Chapter 16: The Day of Atonement
Following chapter: Chapter 18: Forbidden relationships

2. *Analysis of chapter*

All sacrifices to be offered at the tabernacle. (1-9)
Eating of blood, or of animals which died a natural death, forbidden. (10-16)

3. *Key verse*

Verse 11: "For the life of the flesh is in the blood: and I have given it to you upon the altar to make an atonement for your souls: for it is the blood that maketh an atonement for the soul."

4. *Key word / key phrase*

Verse 6, "blood."

5. *Key event / key person / key theme*

Animals offered in sacrifice.

6. *Key thought*

Do not eat blood.

7. *Key thing to look out for*

The central role of blood in the sacrifices.

8. *Key Bible cross-reference*

Verse 11. For teaching on substitutionary atonement, see verse 6; 1:5; 3:2; 4:6,25; 7:2.

9. *Key "by way of explanation"*

Verse 11, "the life of a creature is in the blood." As blood symbolized life it had to be treated with great respect, especially in all the sacrifices.

10. *Key "Quotable Quote"*

"An atonement that does not regenerate is not an atonement in which men can be asked to believe."
James Denney

Leviticus chapter 18

1. **Before and after**

   Previous chapter: Chapter 17: Blood is sacred
   Following chapter: Chapter 19: Rules for life: love your neighbor

2. **Analysis of chapter**

   Unlawful marriages and unlawful sexual relations. (1-30)

3. **Key verse**

   Verse 3: "After the doings of the land of Egypt, wherein ye dwelt, shall ye not do: and after the doings of the land of Canaan, whither I bring you, shall ye not do: neither shall ye walk in their ordinances."

4. **Key word / key phrase**

   Verse 4, "obey."

5. **Key event / key person / key theme**

   Forbidden sexual relations

6. **Key thought**

   Sex is a gift from God.

7. **Key thing to look out for**

   As God is the Creator he knows best about every aspect of our behavior.

8. **Key Bible cross-reference**

   Verse 18 "live." See Ezekiel 20:11,13,21; Romans 10:5; Galatians 3:12.

9. **Key "by way of explanation"**

   Verse 2. The phrase "I am the Lord," coming 42 times in chapters 18–26, underlines the fact that it is God and his authority that stands behind these instructions.

10. **Key "Quotable Quote"**

    "No country can be happy while the walls may still be standing but the morals are collapsing."
    Augustine of Hippo

Leviticus chapter 19

1. Before and after

Previous chapter: Chapter 18: Forbidden relationships
Following chapter: Chapter 20: Laws of penalties

2. Analysis of chapter

Various laws, dealing with many aspects of daily life. (1-17)

3. Key verse

Verse 2: "Ye shall be holy: for I the LORD your God am holy."

4. Key word / key phrase

Verse 32, "revere."

5. Key event / key person / key theme

Detailed expansion of some of the Ten Commandments

6. Key thought

A prohibition can be very positive.

7. Key thing to look out for

How happy a society would be if it followed these commands.

8. Key Bible cross-reference

Verse 26, "sorcery." See Exodus 22:18; Deuteronomy 18:14; 1 Samuel 28:9; Isaiah 47:12-14.

9. Key "by way of explanation"

Verse 35, "dishonest standards." Dishonesty in business was a way of life. See Deuteronomy 25:13-16.

10. Key "Quotable Quote"

"It is the perfection of holiness to do what God loves, and to love what God does."
William Bates, Puritan

Leviticus chapter 20

1. *Before and after*

   Previous chapter: Chapter 19: Rules for life: love your neighbor
   Following chapter: Chapter 21: Rules for godly living for priests

2. *Analysis of chapter*

   Law against sacrificing children to Moloch. Children who curse their parents.
   (1-9)
   Laws repeated. Holiness commanded. (10-27)

3. *Key verse*

   Verse 7: "Sanctify yourselves therefore, and be ye holy: for I am the LORD your
   God."

4. *Key word / key phrase*

   Verse 13, "detestable."

5. *Key event / key person / key theme*

   Penalties for going against God's morality

6. *Key thought*

   In God's book evil will be punished.

7. *Key thing to look out for*

   The distinction between right and wrong is not at all blurred.

8. *Key Bible cross-reference*

   Verse 5. See 17:7.

9. *Key "by way of explanation"*

   Verse 6. It was sinful to be a medium, and it was also sinful to consult one.

10. *Key "Quotable Quote"*

    "Moral collapse follows upon spiritual collapse."
    C.S. Lewis

Leviticus chapter 21

1. *Before and after*

    Previous chapter: Chapter 20: Laws of penalties
    Following chapter: Chapter 22: Holiness of the offerings

2. *Analysis of chapter*

    Laws about the priests. (1-24)

3. *Key verse*

    Verse 8: "Thou shalt sanctify him therefore; for he offereth the bread of thy God: he shall be holy unto thee: for I the LORD, which sanctify you, am holy."

4. *Key word / key phrase*

    Verse 1, "priests."

5. *Key event / key person / key theme*

    The holiness of priests

6. *Key thought*

    God's servants should be holy.

7. *Key thing to look out for*

    Priests had to be separate from any kind of ceremonial uncleanness.

8. *Key Bible cross-reference*

    Verse 1. See Numbers 19:11;14.

9. *Key "by way of explanation"*

    Verse 5. In pagan religions worshipers disfigured their bodies in an effort to gain the attention of their deities. See 1 Kings 18:28.

10. *Key "Quotable Quote"*

    "God makes me pure in heart; I must make myself pure in conduct."
    Oswald Chambers

Leviticus chapter 22

1. **Before and after**

   Previous chapter: Chapter 21: Rules for godly living for priests
   Following chapter: Chapter 23: The religious calendar

2. **Analysis of chapter**

   Laws about the priests and sacrifices. (1-33)

3. **Key verse**

   Verse 32: "Neither shall ye profane my holy name."

4. **Key word / key phrase**

   Verse 2, "offerings."

5. **Key event / key person / key theme**

   The holiness of the offerings

6. **Key thought**

   The idea of restitution is promoted.

7. **Key thing to look out for**

   God's name must be acknowledged among the ungodly.

8. **Key Bible cross-reference**

   Verse 9. See 10:1-3; Malachi 1:6–2:9.

9. **Key "by way of explanation"**

   Verse 3. Being cut off from the Lord's presence and being excluded from the fellowship with God's people are almost identical.

10. **Key "Quotable Quote"**

    "He does not believe that does not live according to his belief."
    Thomas Fuller

Leviticus chapter 23

1. *Before and after*

Previous chapter: Chapter 22: Holiness of the offerings
Following chapter: Chapter 24: An example of sin and punishment

2. *Analysis of chapter*

The feasts of the Lord, and the Sabbath. (1-3)
The Passover, and the offering of first-fruits. (4-14)
The feast of Pentecost. (15-22)
The feast of Trumpets, and the Day of Atonement. (23-32)
The feast of Tabernacles. (33-44)

3. *Key verse*

Verse 6: "And on the fifteenth day of the same month is the feast of unleavened bread unto the LORD: seven days ye must eat unleavened bread."

4. *Key word / key phrase*

Verse 27, "Day of Atonement."

5. *Key event / key person / key theme*

The religious festivals

6. *Key thought*

Should we observe more Christian festivals?

7. *Key thing to look out for*

God's followers spent a great deal of time in worshiping the Lord.

8. *Key Bible cross-reference*

Verse 27. See Hebrews 9:7; 13:11,12.

9. *Key "by way of explanation"*

Verse 27. The Jewish *Yom Kippur*, Day of Atonement, comes from the Hebrew words *yom* (day) and *kipper* (to atone).

10. *Key "Quotable Quote"*

"Worship is celebration."
Clement of Alexander

Leviticus chapter 24

1. **Before and after**

   Previous chapter: Chapter 23: The religious calendar
   Following chapter: Chapter 25: The seventh year, and restorations

2. **Analysis of chapter**

   Oil for the lamps, and the shew-bread. (1-9)
   The law of blasphemy, blasphemer is stoned. (10-23)

3. **Key verse**

   Verse 17: "And he that killeth any man shall surely be put to death."

4. **Key word / key phrase**

   Verse 2, "light."

5. **Key event / key person / key theme**

   Taking care of the lamps

6. **Key thought**

   An eye for an eye limited retribution.

7. **Key thing to look out for**

   The seriousness of blasphemy could not be plainer.

8. **Key Bible cross-reference**

   Verse 20. See Exodus 21:23-25; Matthew 5:38-42.

9. **Key "by way of explanation"**

   Verse 8. The bread represented a gift from all the twelve tribes of Israel and so
   symbolized God sustaining them.

10. **Key "Quotable Quote"**

    "Special vengeance will be executed on those who have taken the name of
    God in vain."
    John Calvin

Leviticus chapter 25

1. *Before and after*

Previous chapter: Chapter 24: An example of sin and punishment
Following chapter: Chapter 26: Reward and punishment

2. *Analysis of chapter*

The Sabbath of rest for the land in the seventh year. (1-7)
The jubilee of the fiftieth year. Oppression forbidden. (8-22)
Redemption of the land and houses. (23-34)
Compassion toward the poor. (35-38)
Laws about the poor. Oppression forbidden. (39-55)

3. *Key verse*

Verse 8: "And thou shalt number seven Sabbaths of years unto thee, seven
times seven years; and the space of the seven Sabbaths of years shall be unto
thee forty and nine years."

4. *Key word / key phrase*

Verse 4, "seventh year."

5. *Key event / key person / key theme*

The Sabbath year

6. *Key thought*

God's commands extend to the business world.

7. *Key thing to look out for*

God, as a God of justice and kindness, wants his followers to be just and kind.

8. *Key Bible cross-reference*

Verse 10. See Isaiah 61:1,2; Luke 4:16-21.

9. *Key "by way of explanation"*

Verse 13. The principle here is that the Lord did not allow the poor to be
exploited as an individual accumulated property.

10. *Key "Quotable Quote"*

"As a fresh start, the Church should give away all her endowments to the poor
and needy."
Dietrich Bonhoeffer

Leviticus chapter 26

1. ### Before and after
   Previous chapter: Chapter 25: The seventh years, and restorations
   Following chapter: Chapter 27: Rules about vows and tithes

2. ### Analysis of chapter
   Promises on keeping the precepts. (1-13)
   Warnings against disobedience. (14-39)
   God promises to remember those who repent. (40-46)

3. ### Key verse
   Verse 45: "But I will for their sakes remember the covenant of their ancestors, whom I brought forth out of the land of Egypt in the sight of the heathen, that I might be their God: I am the LORD."

4. ### Key word / key phrase
   Verse 14, "commands."

5. ### Key event / key person / key theme
   Obedience and disobedience are contrasted

6. ### Key thought
   Obedience brings blessing.

7. ### Key thing to look out for
   Disobedience brings punishment.

8. ### Key Bible cross-reference
   Verse 14. See Deuteronomy 28:15-29.

9. ### Key "by way of explanation"
   Verse 30. The word "high places" at first meant a hill-top, and later an idolatrous shrine built on a hill-top.

10. ### Key "Quotable Quote"
    "Disobedience and sin are the same thing, for there is no sin but disobedience."
    Theologia Germanica

Leviticus chapter 27

1. Previous chapter

Chapter 26: Reward and punishment

2. Analysis of chapter

The law about vows. About people and animals. (1-13)
Vows about houses and land. (14-25)
Devoted things not to be redeemed. (26-33)
Conclusion. (34)

3. Key verse

Verse 34: "These are the commandments, which the LORD commanded Moses for the children of Israel in mount Sinai."

4. Key word / key phrase

Verse 9, "acceptable."

5. Key event / key person / key theme

Law about gifts given to the Lord

6. Key thought

Servants, houses and land were given to the Lord.

7. Key thing to look out for

Money was also given to the Lord.

8. Key Bible cross-reference

Verse 30. See Numbers 18:21-29; Deuteronomy 12:6-18.

9. Key "by way of explanation"

Verse 34 is taken to support Moses' authorship of this book, as well as its divine origin.

10. Key "Quotable Quote"

"The tithe can be a beginning way to acknowledge God as the owner of all things, but it is only a beginning and not an ending."
Richard J. Foster

Numbers

Numbers chapter 1

1. *Following chapter*

   Chapter 2: The arrangement of the camp

2. *Analysis of chapter*

   The numbering of the Israelites. (1-43)
   The number of the people. (44-46)
   The Levites not numbered with the rest. (47-54)

3. *Key verse*

   Verse 2: "Take ye the sum of all the congregation of the children of Israel, after their families, by the house of their fathers, with the number of their names, every male by their poll."

4. *Key word / key phrase*

   Verse 2, "census."

5. *Key event / key person / key theme*

   The first census of Israel

6. *Key thought*

   God's people came from one man who was childless.

7. *Key thing to look out for*

   The Exodus was so important to God's people that events were cited in relation to it.

8. *Key Bible cross-reference*

   Verse 46. See Exodus 12:27; 38:26.

9. *Key "by way of explanation"*

   In the book of Leviticus we are told over one hundred times in twenty different ways that God spoke to and through Moses.

10. *Key "Quotable Quote"*

    "O God, give me the grace to be faithful in my actions, but indifferent to success."
    François Fénelon

Numbers chapter 2

1. *Before and after*

   Previous chapter: Chapter 1: The first census
   Following chapter: Chapter 3: The census of the Levites

2. *Analysis of chapter*

   The arrangement of the tribes in their tents. (1-34)

3. *Key verse*

   Verse 2: "Every man of the children of Israel shall pitch by his own standard, with the ensign of their father's house: far off about the tabernacle of the congregation shall they pitch."

4. *Key word / key phrase*

   Verse 2, "camp."

5. *Key event / key person / key theme*

   The arrangement of the tribes in camp

6. *Key thought*

   There is nothing wrong with things being done decently and in order.

7. *Key thing to look out for*

   Worship is central for the followers of God.

8. *Key Bible cross-reference*

   Verse 2. See Ezekiel 1:10; Revelation 4:7.

9. *Key "by way of explanation"*

   Verse 17. The tabernacle, representing God's presence, is at the center of the camp.

10. *Key "Quotable Quote"*

    "The humblest and the most unseen activity in the world can be the true worship of God."
    William Barclay

Numbers chapter 3

1. *Before and after*

Previous chapter: Chapter 2: The arrangement of the camp
Following chapter: Chapter 4: The ministry of the Levites

2. *Analysis of chapter*

The sons of Aaron, and the Levites taken instead of the firstborn. (1-13)
The Levites numbered by their families, and their duties. (14-39)
The firstborn are numbered. (40-51)

3. *Key verse*

Verse 6: "Bring the tribe of Levi near, and present them before Aaron the priest, that they may minister unto him."

4. *Key word / key phrase*

Verse 2, "Aaron's sons."

5. *Key event / key person / key theme*

The Levites are appointed to serve the priests.

6. *Key thought*

God has a special work for each of his followers to do.

7. *Key thing to look out for*

Money is important in God's work.

8. *Key Bible cross-reference*

Verse 4. See 1 Samuel 2:12-17,22-25,27-36; 3:11-14.

9. *Key "by way of explanation"*

Verse 1. Aaron precedes Moses in this verse because it is Aaron's sons who are about to be given directions.

10. *Key "Quotable Quote"*

"The living Church ought to be dependent on its living members."
Thomas Barnardo

Numbers chapter 4

1. **Before and after**

   Previous chapter: Chapter 3: The census of the Levites
   Following chapter: Chapter 5: The law of jealousy

2. **Analysis of chapter**

   The Levites' service. (1-3)
   The duties of the Kohathites. (4-20)
   The duties of the Gershonites and Merarites. (21-33)
   The numbers of the serviceable Levites. (34-49)

3. **Key verse**

   Verse 46: "All those that were numbered of the Levites, whom Moses and
   Aaron and the chief of Israel numbered, after their families, and after the
   house of their fathers."

4. **Key word / key phrase**

   Verse 2, "Kohathite."

5. **Key event / key person / key theme**

   The duties of the Levite clan of Kohath

6. **Key thought**

   Purity is essential in God's holy eyes.

7. **Key thing to look out for**

   Jesus taught that inner purity is vital.

8. **Key Bible cross-reference**

   Verse 16. See 3:12; 6:8.

9. **Key "by way of explanation"**

   Verse 4. God's own holiness is underlined here as the Kohathites were not
   allowed even to look on the holy things, let alone touch them.

10. **Key "Quotable Quote"**

    "Purity of heart and simplicity are of great force with Almighty God, who is
    in purity most singular, and of nature most simple."
    Gregory the Great

Numbers chapter 5

1. *Before and after*

Previous chapter: Chapter 4: The ministry of the Levites
Following chapter: Chapter 6: The Nazirite vows

2. *Analysis of chapter*

The unclean to be taken out of the camp.
Restitution to be made for trespasses. (1-10)
The trial of jealousy. (11-31)

3. *Key verse*

Verse 6: "When a man or woman shall commit any sin that men commit, to
do a trespass against the LORD, and that person be guilty."

4. *Key word / key phrase*

Verse 3, "defile."

5. *Key event / key person / key theme*

Purity among God's people

6. *Key thought*

Wrongs need to be put right.

7. *Key thing to look out for*

Faithfulness to God and in relationships is commanded by God.

8. *Key Bible cross-reference*

Verse 2. See Leviticus 13:2; Luke 5:12-16.

9. *Key "by way of explanation"*

Verse 2. Anything that made a person ceremonially "unclean" such as contact
with a dead body, meant that the person was separated from the community
until he was cleansed.

10. *Key "Quotable Quote"*

"To be true to ourselves, we must be true to others."
Jimmy Carter

Numbers chapter 6

1. **Before and after**

   Previous chapter: Chapter 5: The law of jealousy
   Following chapter: Chapter 7: The offerings of the leaders

2. **Analysis of chapter**

   The law about the Nazirites. (1-21)
   The form of blessing the people. (22-27)

3. **Key verse**

   Verse 25: "The LORD make his face shine upon thee, and be gracious unto thee."

4. **Key word / key phrase**

   Verse 2, "Nazirite."

5. **Key event / key person / key theme**

   Rules for Nazirites

6. **Key thought**

   These vows were made to God, not for show.

7. **Key thing to look out for**

   God's blessings are to be sought daily.

8. **Key Bible cross-reference**

   Verse 6. See 5:2; Leviticus 21:1-3.

9. **Key "by way of explanation"**

   Verses 24-26. Note how Aaron's blessing calls on God's name three times, and how each verse mentions two blessings.

10. **Key "Quotable Quote"**

    "Moody did not have a monopoly on God, God had a monopoly on Moody."
    Author unknown

Numbers chapter 7

1. *Before and after*

Previous chapter: Chapter 6: The Nazirite vows
Following chapter: Chapter 8: The consecration of the Levites

2. *Analysis of chapter*

The offerings of the princes at the dedication of the tabernacle. (1-9)
The offerings of the princes at the dedication of the altar. (10-89)

3. *Key verse*

Verse 1: "And it came to pass on the day that Moses had fully set up the tabernacle, and had anointed it, and sanctified it, and all the instruments thereof, both the altar and all the vessels thereof, and had anointed them, and sanctified them."

4. *Key word / key phrase*

Verse 1, "finished."

5. *Key event / key person / key theme*

The offerings at the dedication of the tabernacle

6. *Key thought*

The people are blessed and they respond by giving back to God.

7. *Key thing to look out for*

We have nothing that God did not give us.

8. *Key Bible cross-reference*

Verses 12-78. See 1:5-15; 2:3-32.

9. *Key "by way of explanation"*

Verses 84-88 act as a summary, giving the totals of all the twelve sets of gifts.

10. *Key "Quotable Quote"*

"Gratitude is the fairest blossom which springs from the soul."
Henry Ward Beecher

Numbers chapter 8

1. *Before and after*

    Previous chapter: Chapter 7: The offerings of the leaders
    Following chapter: Chapter 9: The second Passover, and the fiery cloud

2. *Analysis of chapter*

    The lamps of the sanctuary. (1-4)
    Consecration of the Levites, and their service. (5-26)

3. *Key verse*

    Verse 6: "Take the Levites from among the children of Israel, and cleanse them."

4. *Key word / key phrase*

    Verse 5, "Levites."

5. *Key event / key person / key theme*

    Purification and dedication of the Levites

6. *Key thought*

    Everyone needs to be dedicated to God.

7. *Key thing to look out for*

    God gives special responsibilities to some of his followers.

8. *Key Bible cross-reference*

    Verse 2. See Exodus 25:37; 27:21.

9. *Key "by way of explanation"*

    Verses 5-26. There is a striking similarity between the cleansing of the Levites and the ordination of Aaron's sons. See Leviticus 8.

10. *Key "Quotable Quote"*

    "If I can stop one heart from breaking,
    I shall not live in vain;
    If I can ease one life the aching,
    Or cool one pain,
    Or help one fainting robin
    Unto his nest again,
    I shall not live in vain."
    Emily Dickinson

Numbers chapter 9

1. *Before and after*

Previous chapter: Chapter 8: The consecration of the Levites
Following chapter: Chapter 10: Israel leaves Mount Sinai

2. *Analysis of chapter*

The Passover. (1-14)
The cloud about the tabernacle. (15-23)

3. *Key verse*

Verse 2: "Let the children of Israel also keep the Passover at his appointed season."

4. *Key word / key phrase*

Verse 2, "Passover."

5. *Key event / key person / key theme*

The second Passover

6. *Key thought*

The Lord knows how we suffer from lapse of memory.

7. *Key thing to look out for*

All that the Passover continues to stand for.

8. *Key Bible cross-reference*

Verse 13. See 1 Corinthians 11:28-30.

9. *Key "by way of explanation"*

Verse 12. Jesus is our Passover Lamb and his bones were not broken. See 1 Corinthians 5:7.

10. *Key "Quotable Quote"*

"Here, O my Lord, I see thee face to face."
Horatius Bonar

Numbers chapter 10

1. *Before and after*

Previous chapter: Chapter 9: The second Passover, and the fiery cloud
Following chapter: Chapter 11: Moses complains, and the quails

2. *Analysis of chapter*

The silver trumpets. (1-10)
The Israelites move from Sinai to Paran. (11-28)
Hobab entreated by Moses to continue. (29-32)
The blessing pronounced by Moses. (33-36)

3. *Key verse*

Verse 13: "And they first took their journey according to the commandment of the LORD by the hand of Moses."

4. *Key word / key phrase*

Verse 13, "set out."

5. *Key event / key person / key theme*

The Israelites leave their camp

6. *Key thought*

God always leads his people onwards.

7. *Key thing to look out for*

Trumpets alert us to God himself and his actions.

8. *Key Bible cross-reference*

Verses 14-27. See 1:5-15; 2:3-31; 7:12-83.

9. *Key "by way of explanation"*

Verse 35. This verse starts Psalm 68's celebration of God's march from Sinai to Jerusalem.

10. *Key "Quotable Quote"*

"Unfurl the sails, and let God steer us where God will."
Bede

Numbers chapter 11

1. *Before and after*

Previous chapter: Chapter 10: Israel leaves Mount Sinai
Following chapter: Chapter 12: Miriam and Aaron complain

2. *Analysis of chapter*

The burning at Taberah. (1-3)
The people long for meat, and loathe the manna. (4-9)
Moses complains about his charge. (10-15)
Elders appointed to divide the charge. Meat promised. (16-23)
The Spirit rests on the elders. (24-30)
Quails are given. (31-35)

3. *Key verse*

Verse 1: ". . . the fire of the LORD burnt among them, and consumed them that
were in the uttermost parts of the camp."

4. *Key word / key phrase*

Verse 16, "seventy."

5. *Key event / key person / key theme*

Moses chooses seventy leaders.

6. *Key thought*

Complaining is one of our besetting sins.

7. *Key thing to look out for*

God's goodness is clear for all to see.

8. *Key Bible cross-reference*

Verse 25. See 1 Samuel 10:5,6; 18:10; 19:20-24.

9. *Key "by way of explanation"*

Verse 21. It appears from this verse that there were over two million Israelites
on the march.

10. *Key "Quotable Quote"*

"God is so good that he only awaits our desire to overwhelm us with the gift
of himself."
François Fénelon

Numbers chapter 12

1. *Before and after*

   Previous chapter: Chapter 11: Moses complains, and the quails
   Following chapter: Chapter 13: The mission and report of the spies

2. *Analysis of chapter*

   God rebukes the murmuring of Aaron and Miriam. (1-9)
   Miriam struck with leprosy, and healed by the prayer of Moses. (10-16)

3. *Key verse*

   Verse 1: "And Miriam and Aaron spake against Moses because of the
   Ethiopian woman whom he had married: for he had married an Ethiopian
   woman."

4. *Key word / key phrase*

   Verse 1, "Miriam."

5. *Key event / key person / key theme*

   Miriam is punished.

6. *Key thought*

   Casting doubt on what God has said was the trick the serpent played on Eve.

7. *Key thing to look out for*

   Punishment for wrongdoing can bring about most positive results.

8. *Key Bible cross-reference*

   Verse 4. See Job 22:10; Isaiah 47:11; Jeremiah 4:20.

9. *Key "by way of explanation"*

   Verse 5. The words "came down" are often used in connection with God
   making himself known.

10. *Key "Quotable Quote"*

   "Man punishes the action, but God the intention."
   Thomas Fuller

Numbers chapter 13

1. Before and after

Previous chapter: Chapter 12: Miriam and Aaron complain
Following chapter: Chapter 14: Rebellion and judgment in the camp

2. Analysis of chapter

Twelve men sent to search the land of Canaan, and their instructions. (1-20)
Their exploration of the land. (21-25)
Their account of the land. (26-33)

3. Key verse

Verse 2: "Send thou men, that they may search the land of Canaan, which I
give unto the children of Israel."

4. Key word / key phrase

Verse 1, "explore."

5. Key event / key person / key theme

The spies

6. Key thought

There is much land still to be captured.

7. Key thing to look out for

God's gifts are always totally satisfying.

8. Key Bible cross-reference

Verse 22. See Genesis 13:14-18; 14:13; 23:2; 25:9; 50:13.

9. Key "by way of explanation"

Verse 16. This verse paves the way for the later importance of Joshua.

10. Key "Quotable Quote"

"He who blesses most is blest."
John Greenleaf Whittier

Numbers chapter 14

1. Before and after

> Previous chapter: Chapter 13: The mission and report of the spies
> Following chapter: Chapter 15: Rules for the priests

2. Analysis of chapter

> The people murmur at the report of the spies. (1-4)
> Joshua and Caleb attempt to calm the people. (5-10)
> The divine warnings, and the intercession of Moses. (11-19)
> The murmurers forbidden to enter the promised land. (20-35)
> Death of the evil spies. (36-39)
> Defeat of the people, who now want to invade the land. (40-45)

3. Key verse

> Verse 44: "But they presumed to go up unto the hill top: nevertheless the ark of the covenant of the LORD, and Moses, departed not out of the camp."

4. Key word / key phrase

> Verse 2, "grumbled."

5. Key event / key person / key theme

> More complaints from God's people

6. Key thought

> When things go wrong some will immediately grumble.

7. Key thing to look out for

> Christian leaders need to know how to deal with grumblers.

8. Key Bible cross-reference

> Verse 22. See Exodus 14 – 17; 32; Numbers 11 and 14.

9. Key "by way of explanation"

> Verse 10. This was undoubtedly a theophany, a manifestation of God's glory.

10. Key "Quotable Quote"

> "Murmur at nothing."
> C.C. Colton

Numbers chapter 15

1. Before and after

Previous chapter: Chapter 14: Rebellion and judgment in the camp
Following chapter: Chapter 16: Rebellion against Moses and Aaron

2. Analysis of chapter

The law of the meat-offering and the drink-offering. The stranger under the same law. (1-21)
The sacrifice for the sin of ignorance. (22-29)
The punishment of presumption The Sabbath-breaker stoned. (30-36)
The law for tassels on garments. (37-41)

3. Key verse

Verse 27: "And if any soul sin through ignorance, then he shall bring a she goat of the first year for a sin offering."

4. Key word / key phrase

Verse 6, "offering."

5. Key event / key person / key theme

Laws about sacrifice

6. Key thought

God gave things to help his people to obey him.

7. Key thing to look out for

Whenever we read about God punishing sin we should take heed.

8. Key Bible cross-reference

Verse 38. See Deuteronomy 6:4-9.

9. Key "by way of explanation"

Verse 2. God's punishments and God's grace should always be held in balance.

10. Key "Quotable Quote"

"Punishment is justice for the unjust."
Augustine of Hippo

Numbers chapter 16

1. **Before and after**

   Previous chapter: Chapter 15: Rules for the priests
   Following chapter: Chapter 17: Aaron's blossoming rod

2. **Analysis of chapter**

   The rebellion of Korah, Dathan, and Abiram. Korah contends for the priesthood. (1-11)
   Disobedience of Dathan and Abiram. (12-15)
   The glory of the Lord appears. The intercession of Moses and Aaron. (16-22)
   The earth swallows up Dathan and Abiram. (23-34)
   The company of Korah consumed. (35-40)
   The people murmur. A plague sent. (41-50)

3. **Key verse**

   Verse 1: "Now Korah, the son of Izhar, the son of Kohath, the son of Levi, and Dathan and Abiram, the sons of Eliab, and On, the son of Peleth, sons of Reuben, took me."

4. **Key word / key phrase**

   Verse 2, "rose up against."

5. **Key event / key person / key theme**

   Rebellion against Moses' leadership

6. **Key thought**

   It is easier to rebel than to remain faithful.

7. **Key thing to look out for**

   God does not take rebellion lightly.

8. **Key Bible cross-reference**

   Verse 1. See Jude 11.

9. **Key "by way of explanation"**

   Verse 49. The census lists in Numbers are huge, so 14,700 people dying is quite possible.

10. **Key "Quotable Quote"**

    "The curse of infidelity is sensuality."
    Richard Cecil

Numbers chapter 17

1. Before and after

Previous chapter: Chapter 16: Rebellion against Moses and Aaron
Following chapter: Chapter 18: Rules for the priests and Levites

2. Analysis of chapter

Twelve staffs laid up before the Lord. (1-7)
Aaron's staff buds, and is kept for a memorial. (8-13)

3. Key verse

Verse 8: ". . . the rod of Aaron for the house of Levi was budded, and brought
forth buds, and bloomed blossoms, and yielded almonds."

4. Key word / key phrase

Verse 8, "almonds."

5. Key event / key person / key theme

Aaron's rod produces ripe almonds

6. Key thought

Nothing is too hard for the Lord.

7. Key thing to look out for

Yet again Moses' obedience to God is highlighted.

8. Key Bible cross-reference

Verse 10. See Exodus 16:33,34; Hebrews 9:4.

9. Key "by way of explanation"

Verse 10. Aaron's staff is given a place of special honor and this contrasts with
the dreadful grumbling of the Israelites.

10. Key "Quotable Quote"

"Become a good manager of those things given you by God."
John Chrysostom

Numbers chapter 18

1. Before and after

Previous chapter: Chapter 17: Aaron's blossoming rod
Following chapter: Chapter 19: Purification of the red heifer

2. Analysis of chapter

The charge of the priests and Levites. (1-7)
The priests' portion. (8-19)
The Levites' portion. (20-32)

3. Key verse

Verse 18: "And I, behold, I have taken your brethren the Levites from among the children of Israel: to you they are given as a gift for the LORD, to do the service of the tabernacle of the congregation."

4. Key word / key phrase

Verse 2, "Levites."

5. Key event / key person / key theme

The duties of the priests and Levites

6. Key thought

All service for God is a privilege and responsibility.

7. Key thing to look out for

There is a right way and a wrong way to act in God's service.

8. Key Bible cross-reference

Verses 1-7. See Psalm 99:6-8.

9. Key "by way of explanation"

Verse 7. Serving in the priesthood is specifically said to be God's gift.

10. Key "Quotable Quote"

"Love God, serve God; everything is in that."
Clare of Assisi

Numbers chapter 19

1. *Before and after*

> Previous chapter: Chapter 18: Rules for the priests and Levites
> Following chapter: Chapter 20: The people complain, and the death of Aaron

2. *Analysis of chapter*

> The ashes of a heifer. (1-10)
> Used to purify the unclean. (11-22)

3. *Key verse*

> Verse 9: "And a man that is clean shall gather up the ashes of the heifer, and lay them up without the camp in a clean place, and it shall be kept for the congregation of the children of Israel for a water of separation: it is a purification for sin."

4. *Key word / key phrase*

> Verse 2, "red heifer."

5. *Key event / key person / key theme*

> Ashes of the red cow

6. *Key thought*

> God has provided a way for us to be presented clean before him.

7. *Key thing to look out for*

> No matter how unclean a person may have become in God's sight, there is a way back to God.

8. *Key Bible cross-reference*

> Verse 9. See Hebrews 9:13.

9. *Key "by way of explanation"*

> Verse 18. The idea behind sprinkling with a hyssop branch is explained here.

10. *Key "Quotable Quote"*

> "The Church should be the Society of the Forgiven and Forgiving."
> William George Spencer

Numbers chapter 20

1. Before and after

Previous chapter: Chapter 19: Purification of the red heifer
Following chapter: Chapter 21: The bronze serpent

2. Analysis of chapter

The people come to Zin, and they grumble about the lack of water. Moses is told to hit the rock, and the infirmity of Moses and Aaron. (1-13)
The Israelites are refused a route through Edom. (14-21)
Aaron hands on the priest's office to Eleazar, and dies on Mount Hor. (22-29)

3. Key verse

Verse 11: "And Moses lifted up his hand, and with his rod he smote the rock twice: and the water came out abundantly, and the congregation drank, and their beasts also."

4. Key word / key phrase

Verse 1, "Kadesh."

5. Key event / key person / key theme

Events at Kadesh

6. Key thought

Water from a rock illustrates God's power to do the impossible.

7. Key thing to look out for

God's people have always met with opposition.

8. Key Bible cross-reference

Verse 28. See Exodus 29:29; Numbers 33:38.

9. Key "by way of explanation"

Verse 24. "Gathered to his people," was a euphemistic way of referring to death.

10. Key "Quotable Quote"

"Lord, grant that my last hour may be my best hour."
Author unknown, Old English prayer

Numbers chapter 21

1. *Before and after*

Previous chapter: Chapter 20: The people complain, and the death of Aaron
Following chapter: Chapter 22: Balak, Balaam and his talking donkey

2. *Analysis of chapter*

The Canaanites of Arad destroyed. (1-3)
The people murmur. The plague of poisonous snakes. The people repent and
are healed through the bronze snake. (4-9)
Further journeys of the Israelites. (10-20)
Sihon and Og overcome, and their land possessed. (21-35)

3. *Key verse*

Verse 8: "And the LORD said unto Moses, Make thee a fiery serpent, and set it
upon a pole: and it shall come to pass, that every one that is bitten, when he
looketh upon it, shall live."

4. *Key word / key phrase*

Verse 8, "snake."

5. *Key event / key person / key theme*

Making a bronze snake

6. *Key thought*

God's way of dealing with sin may look strange to outsiders.

7. *Key thing to look out for*

The principle of looking in faith to the bronze snake illustrates repentance
and faith in God.

8. *Key Bible cross-reference*

Verse 9. See John 3:14.

9. *Key "by way of explanation"*

Verse 7. Moses only ordered the bronze snake to be made after the people had
confessed their sins.

10. *Key "Quotable Quote"*

"Confession of sin;
Shame for sin;
Hatred for sin;
Turning from sin."
Thomas Watson

Numbers chapter 22

1. Before and after

Previous chapter: Chapter 21: The bronze serpent
Following chapter: Chapter 23: Balaam's first prophecies

2. Analysis of chapter

Balak's fear of Israel. He sends for Balaam. (1-14)
Balaam goes to Balak. (15-21)
Balaam's donkey. (22-35)
Balaam and Balak meet. (36-41)

3. Key verse

Verse 28: "And the LORD opened the mouth of the ass, and she said unto Balaam, What have I done unto thee, that thou hast smitten me these three times?"

4. Key word / key phrase

Verse 8, "the answer the Lord gives me."

5. Key event / key person / key theme

Balaam is sent for by the king of Moab

6. Key thought

God uses all kinds of means to direct us along his paths.

7. Key thing to look out for

It seems hard to believe that a dumb animal should speak. Is it not harder to believe that humans should be so brute-like in their disobedience?

8. Key Bible cross-reference

Verse 35. See 23:12,20,26.

9. Key "by way of explanation"

Verse 23. Balaam's donkey could see more spiritual reality than Balaam.

10. Key "Quotable Quote"

"Only he who believes is obedient. Only he who is obedient, believes."
Dietrich Bonhoeffer

Numbers chapter 23

1. *Before and after*

   Previous chapter: Chapter 22: Balak, Balaam and his talking donkey
   Following chapter: Chapter 24: Balaam's third and fourth prophecies

2. *Analysis of chapter*

   Balak's sacrifice. Balaam pronounces a blessing instead of a curse. (1-10)
   Balak's disappointment, and second sacrifice. Balaam again blesses Israel. (11-30)

3. *Key verse*

   Verse 12: "Must I not take heed to speak that which the LORD hath put in my mouth?"

4. *Key word / key phrase*

   Verse 1, "Balaam."

5. *Key event / key person / key theme*

   Balaam's three prophesies

6. *Key thought*

   Obedience to God is never easy.

7. *Key thing to look out for*

   Following the crowd and pleasing men is easy.

8. *Key Bible cross-reference*

   Verse 21. See Psalm 32;2,5; 85:2.

9. *Key "by way of explanation"*

   Verse 8. God prevented Balaam from cursing God's people, even though he had been hired for that purpose.

10. *Key "Quotable Quote"*

    "A truly intelligent man has only one care – wholeheartedly to obey Almighty God and to please him."
    Antony the Great

Numbers chapter 24

1. Before and after

Previous chapter: Chapter 23: Balaam's first prophecies
Following chapter: Chapter 25: Moab seduces Israel

2. Analysis of chapter

Balaam, abandoning sorcery, prophesies the happiness of Israel. (1-9)
Balak dismisses Balaam in anger. (10-14)
Balaam's prophesies. (15-25)

3. Key verse

Verse 1: "And when Balaam saw that it pleased the LORD to bless Israel, he went not, as at other times, to seek for enchantments, but he set his face toward the desert."

4. Key word / key phrase

Verse 2, "the Spirit of God."

5. Key event / key person / key theme

Balaam's final prophesies

6. Key thought

Balaam was now determined to carry out God's will.

7. Key thing to look out for

The graphic imagery Balaam uses in his oracles.

8. Key Bible cross-reference

Verse 9. See Genesis 12:3; 49:9.

9. Key "by way of explanation"

Verse 1. Balaam had come a long way from the times when he had indulged in sorcery.

10. Key "Quotable Quote"

"Absolutely reject all divination, fortune-telling, sacrifices to the dead, prophecies in groves or by fountains, amulets, incantations, sorcery (i.e.: evil spells), and all those sacrilegious practices that used to go on in your country."
Gregory III

Numbers chapter 25

1. *Before and after*

Previous chapter: Chapter 24: Balaam's third and fourth prophecies
Following chapter: Chapter 26: The second census

2. *Analysis of chapter*

The Israelites enticed by the daughters of Moab and Midian. (1-5)
Phinehas puts Zimri and Cozbi to death. (6-15)
The Midianites to be punished. (16-18)

3. *Key verse*

Verse 2: "And they called the people unto the sacrifices of their gods: and the people did eat, and bowed down to their gods."

4. *Key word / key phrase*

Verse 3, "Baal of Peor."

5. *Key event / key person / key theme*

The people of Israel at Peor

6. *Key thought*

Nobody is beyond temptation.

7. *Key thing to look out for*

The same temptations kept on defeating God's people.

8. *Key Bible cross-reference*

Verse 11. See Exodus 20:4-6; Leviticus 10:1-3.

9. *Key "by way of explanation"*

Verses 1-18. It only becomes clear in 31:8,16 who is behind this temptation of God's people: Balaam.

10. *Key "Quotable Quote"*

"The devil's snare does not catch you unless you are first caught by the devil's bait."
St. Ambrose

Numbers chapter 26

1. **Before and after**

    Previous chapter: Chapter 25: Moab seduces Israel
    Following chapter: Chapter 27: Joshua is to succeed Moses

2. **Analysis of chapter**

    Numbering of Israel in the plains of Moab. (1-51)
    The division of the land. (52-56)
    Number of the Levites. (57-62)
    None remaining of the first numbering. (63-65)

3. **Key verse**

    Verse 2: "Take the sum of all the congregation of the children of Israel, from twenty years old and upward, throughout their fathers' house, all that are able to go to war in Israel."

4. **Key word / key phrase**

    Verse 2, "census."

5. **Key event / key person / key theme**

    The second census

6. **Key thought**

    God provides against all the odds.

7. **Key thing to look out for**

    God uses his followers, even though they have let him down in the past.

8. **Key Bible cross-reference**

    Verses 1-51. See 1:1-46.

9. **Key "by way of explanation"**

    Verse 51, "601,730" is very close to the number in the first census. That God's people had not been greatly reduced in size was due to his mercy.

10. **Key "Quotable Quote"**

    "The house of my soul is too small for you to come to it. May it be enlarged by you. It is in ruins; restore it."
    Augustine of Hippo

Numbers chapter 27

1. Before and after

Previous chapter: Chapter 26: The second census
Following chapter: Chapter 28: Seasonal offerings

2. Analysis of chapter

The daughters of Zelophehad ask for an inheritance, and the law of inheritances. (1-11)
Moses warned of his death. (12-14)
Joshua appointed to succeed Moses. (15-23)

3. Key verse

Verse 18: "And the LORD said unto Moses, Take thee Joshua the son of Nun, a man in whom is the spirit, and lay thine hand upon him."

4. Key word / key phrase

Verse 22, "Joshua."

5. Key event / key person / key theme

Joshua is chosen to succeed Moses

6. Key thought

God is never tied to one leader.

7. Key thing to look out for

God provides leadership in every generation.

8. Key Bible cross-reference

Verse 18. See Exodus 17:9-14; 24:13; 32:17.

9. Key "by way of explanation"

Verse 16. After Moses is reminded of his own sin he is very positive and prayerfully asks about his successor.

10. Key "Quotable Quote"

"No man safely rules but he who loves to be subject. No man safely commands but he who loves to obey."
Thomas à Kempis

Numbers chapter 28

1. *Before and after*

Previous chapter: Chapter 27: Joshua is to succeed Moses
Following chapter: Chapter 29: Offering for New Year, Day of Atonement, and Festival of Shelters

2. *Analysis of chapter*

Offerings, and the daily sacrifice. (1-8)
The offering on the Sabbath and new moons. (9-15)
Offerings at the Passover, and on the day of firstfruits. (16-31)

3. *Key verse*

Verses 16,17: "And in the fourteenth day of the first month is the Passover of the LORD. And in the fifteenth day of this month is the feast: seven days shall unleavened bread be eaten."

4. *Key word / key phrase*

Verse 16, "the Lord's Passover."

5. *Key event / key person / key theme*

Differing offerings

6. *Key thought*

The Day of Atonement is given pride of place.

7. *Key thing to look out for*

Compare the Day of Atonement with the death of Jesus.

8. *Key Bible cross-reference*

Verses 1-8. See Exodus 29:38-41; Leviticus 1-7.

9. *Key "by way of explanation"*

Verses 1-31. These verses illustrate the centrality of sacrifice and the work of the priests to the life of the Israelites.

10. *Key "Quotable Quote"*

"Christ died for all men; I am a man: therefore, Christ died for me."
John Owen

Numbers chapter 29

1. *Before and after*

Previous chapter: Chapter 28: Seasonal offerings
Following chapter: Chapter 30: Laws about vows

2. *Analysis of chapter*

The offering at the Feats of Trumpets, and on the Day of Atonement. (1-11)
Offerings at the Feast of Tabernacles. (12-40)

3. *Key verse*

Verse 11: "One kid of the goats for a sin offering; beside the sin offering of atonement, and the continual burnt offering, and the meat offering of it, and their drink offerings."

4. *Key word / key phrase*

Verse 2, "offering."

5. *Key event / key person / key theme*

Offerings made to God

6. *Key thought*

Moses thought of himself as the Lord's messenger.

7. *Key thing to look out for*

Doing what God commands always pleases him. See verse 6.

8. *Key Bible cross-reference*

Verses 1-6. See Leviticus 23:23-25.

9. *Key "by way of explanation"*

Verses 7-11. The Feast of Trumpets led into the Day of Atonement with its confession of sin and celebration of God's redemption.

10. *Key "Quotable Quote"*

"Put aside your own will so as to go to war under Christ the Lord, the real King, picking up the keen and glittering weapons of obedience."
Benedict

Numbers chapter 30

1. Before and after

Previous chapter: Chapter 29: New Year, Day of Atonement, and Festival of Shelters offerings

Following chapter: Chapter 31: Judgment on Midian

2. Analysis of chapter

Vows to be kept. (1,2)

The reasons why vows might be waived. (3-16)

3. Key verse

Verse 2: "If a man vow a vow unto the LORD, or swear an oath to bind his soul with a bond; he shall not break his word, he shall do according to all that proceedeth out of his mouth."

4. Key word / key phrase

Verse 2, "vow."

5. Key event / key person / key theme

Rules about vows

6. Key thought

Vows made to God should not be broken.

7. Key thing to look out for

Vows should not be entered into lightly. See Ecclesiastes 5:1-7.

8. Key Bible cross-reference

Verses 10-15. See 27:1-11; Matthew 5:33-37.

9. Key "by way of explanation"

Verses 1-16. This is the main biblical passage on taking vows. See also Deuteronomy 23:21-23.

10. Key "Quotable Quote"

"We ought not to be weary of doing little things for the love of God, who regards not the greatness of the work, but the love with which it is performed."

Brother Lawrence

Numbers chapter 31

1. *Before and after*

Previous chapter: Chapter 30: Laws about vows
Following chapter: Chapter 32: Division of the land east of Jordan

2. *Analysis of chapter*

War with Midian. (1-6)
Balaam killed. (7-12)
Those killed who caused sin. (13-38)
Purification of the Israelites. (39-24)
Division of the spoil. (25-47)
Offerings. (48-54)

3. *Key verse*

Verses 1,2: "And the LORD spake unto Moses, saying, Avenge the children of
Israel of the Midianites: afterward shalt thou be gathered unto thy people."

4. *Key word / key phrase*

Verse 2, "Midianites."

5. *Key event / key person / key theme*

God's war against Midian

6. *Key thought*

Personal revenge is forbidden.

7. *Key thing to look out for*

Human attributes like petulant anger should never be attributed to God.

8. *Key Bible cross-reference*

Verses 19-24. Because this was a holy war everything had to be cleansed. See
19:11-13.

9. *Key "by way of explanation"*

Verses 1-24. Moses engaged in this war, not out of personal anger, but because
it was "the Lord's vengeance," verse 3, since the Midianites has led the
Israelites into idolatry.

10. *Key "Quotable Quote"*

"God's wrath is God's punishment of sin and evil. It is a mighty declaration
that God has done what he has always said he would do, namely, that he
would punish sin, and the wages of sin is death."
D. Martyn Lloyd-Jones

Numbers chapter 32

1. **Before and after**

   Previous chapter: Chapter 31: Judgment on Midian
   Following chapter: Chapter 33: Summary of Israel's journeys

2. **Analysis of chapter**

   The tribes of Reuben and Gad request an inheritance on the east of Jordan. (1-5)
   Moses reproves the Reubenites and Gadites. (6-15)
   They explain their views. Moses consents. (16-27)
   They take possession of the land to the east of Jordan. (28-42)

3. **Key verse**

   Verse 1: "Now the children of Reuben and the children of Gad had a very great multitude of cattle: and when they saw the land of Jazer, and the land of Gilead, that, behold, the place was a place for cattle."

4. **Key word / key phrase**

   Verse 5, "Jordan."

5. **Key event / key person / key theme**

   The tribes east of the Jordan

6. **Key thought**

   Wholeheartedness in following God is held up as the ideal.

7. **Key thing to look out for**

   Moses could listen to reasonable arguments and change his mind.

8. **Key Bible cross-reference**

   Verses 8-9. See Numbers 13:17-33.

9. **Key "by way of explanation"**

   Verse 2. Moses did not want the tribes to be separated as that might encourage rebellion.

10. **Key "Quotable Quote"**

    "God will put up with a great many things in the human heart, but there is one thing he will not put up with – a second place."
    John Ruskin

Numbers chapter 33

1. Before and after

Previous chapter: Chapter 32: Division of the land east of Jordan
Following chapter: Chapter 34: The boundaries of the land

2. Analysis of chapter

Stages in Israel's journey. (1-49)
The Canaanites to be destroyed. (50-56)

3. Key verse

Verse 2: "And Moses wrote their goings out according to their journeys by the commandment of the LORD: and these are their journeys according to their goings out."

4. Key word / key phrase

Verse 1, "stages in the journey."

5. Key event / key person / key theme

The Israelites' journey from Egypt to Moab

6. Key thought

After the great victory of escaping from Egypt the Israelites just wandered in the desert.

7. Key thing to look out for

After some spiritual victory in the Christian life Christians are most vulnerable to temptation.

8. Key Bible cross-reference

Verse 38. See Numbers 20:22-28.

9. Key "by way of explanation"

Verses 1-49. The Israelites wandered in the desert for forty years. These verses list forty places visited by the Israelites during this time.

10. Key "Quotable Quote"

"Faithfulness in little things is a big thing."
John Chrysostom

Numbers chapter 34

1. ## Before and after

   Previous chapter: Chapter 33: Summary of Israel's journeys
   Following chapter: Chapter 35: Levitical cities and cities of refuge

2. ## Analysis of chapter

   The boundaries of the promised land. (1-15)
   Those appointed to divide the land. (16-29)

3. ## Key verse

   Verse 2: "Command the children of Israel, and say unto them, When ye come into the land of Canaan; (this is the land that shall fall unto you for an inheritance, even the land of Canaan with the coasts thereof:)"

4. ## Key word / key phrase

   Verse 1, "Canaan."

5. ## Key event / key person / key theme

   The boundaries of the land in Canaan

6. ## Key thought

   The earth and all its land belongs to God.

7. ## Key thing to look out for

   As one leader from each tribe is chosen to divide the land, impartiality is ensured.

8. ## Key Bible cross-reference

   Verses 16-29. See 1:5-16.

9. ## Key "by way of explanation"

   Verses 3-12. The size of the land listed underlines God's great generosity.

10. ## Key "Quotable Quote"

    "Seek to distinguish yourself from others only in your generosity."
    Clement

Numbers chapter 35

1. Before and after

Previous chapter: Chapter 34: The boundaries of the land
Following chapter: Chapter 36: Inheritance of married women

2. Analysis of chapter

The cities of the Levites. (1-8)
The cities of refuge, and the laws about murder. (9-34)

3. Key verse

Verse 6: "And among the cities which ye shall give unto the Levites there shall be six cities for refuge, which ye shall appoint for the manslayer, that he may flee thither: and to them ye shall add forty and two cities."

4. Key word / key phrase

Verse 6, "cities of refuge."

5. Key event / key person / key theme

Cities of refuge

6. Key thought

The psalmist thought of God as his refuge.

7. Key thing to look out for

The existence of these cities of refuge curbed angry revenge and promoted justice.

8. Key Bible cross-reference

Verses 9-34. See Deuteronomy 19:1-13; Joshua 20:1-9.

9. Key "by way of explanation"

Verse 33. The land is held to be sacred. So murder pollutes the land.

10. Key "Quotable Quote"

"God's freedom from bias does not mean that he maintains neutrality in the struggle for justice."
Ronald J. Sider

Numbers chapter 36

1. **Previous chapter**

   Chapter 35: Levitical cities and cities of refuge

2. **Analysis of chapter**

   The inheritance of the daughters of Zelophehad. (1-4)
   The daughters of Zelophehad are to marry in their own tribe. (5-12)
   Conclusion. (13)

3. **Key verse**

   Verse 13: "These are the commandments and the judgments, which the LORD commanded by the hand of Moses unto the children of Israel in the plains of Moab by Jordan near Jericho."

4. **Key word / key phrase**

   Verse 2, "inheritance."

5. **Key event / key person / key theme**

   The inheritance of married women

6. **Key thought**

   These women were more concerned about the Lord's good name than their own welfare.

7. **Key thing to look out for**

   The choice of a marriage partner has been called the "second most important decision we ever make."

8. **Key Bible cross-reference**

   Verses 1-13. See 27:1-11.

9. **Key "by way of explanation"**

   Verse 10: Much in this book is about rebellion, but it ends on a positive note, since "Zelophehad's daughters did as the LORD commanded Moses."

10. **Key "Quotable Quote"**

    "Christianity has glorified marriage more than any other religion."
    C.S. Lewis

Deuteronomy

Deuteronomy chapter 1

1. *Following chapter*

    Chapter 2: Wandering in the desert for thirty-eight years

2. *Analysis of chapter*

    The words Moses spoke to Israel in the plains of Moab, and the promise of Canaan. (1-8)
    Judges provided for the people. (9-18)
    The spies are sent. God's anger over their unbelief and disobedience. (19-46)

3. *Key verse*

    Verse 1: "These be the words which Moses spake unto all Israel on this side Jordan in the wilderness, in the plain over against the Red sea, between Paran, and Tophel, and Laban, and Hazeroth, and Dizahab."

4. *Key word / key phrase*

    Verse 22, "spy."

5. *Key event / key person / key theme*

    Spies sent out

6. *Key thought*

    Caleb's devotion to God is most instructive, verse 36.

7. *Key thing to look out for*

    Even a great leader like Moses had clay feet.

8. *Key Bible cross-reference*

    Verse 31. See Isaiah 40:11; Jeremiah 31:10; Ezekiel 34:11-16.

9. *Key "by way of explanation"*

    Verse 10. God is the prime mover in Israel's history.

10. *Key "Quotable Quote"*

    "It is very difficult to be humble if you are always successful, so God chastises us with failure at times in order to humble us, to keep us in a state of humility."
    D. Martyn Lloyd-Jones

Deuteronomy chapter 2

1. *Before and after*

Previous chapter: Chapter 1: Judges appointed, spies sent out
Following chapter: Chapter 3: Land east of Jordan conquered

2. *Analysis of chapter*

The Edomites to be spared. (1-7)
The Moabites and Ammonites to be spared. (8-23)
The Amorites to be destroyed. (24-37)

3. *Key verse*

Verse 1: "Then we turned, and took our journey into the wilderness by the way of the Red sea, as the LORD spake unto me: and we compassed mount Seir many days."

4. *Key word / key phrase*

Verse 1, "desert."

5. *Key event / key person / key theme*

Wandering in the desert

6. *Key thought*

All victories in the Christian life should be attributed to God.

7. *Key thing to look out for*

God's plans are never permanently thwarted by human disobedience.

8. *Key Bible cross-reference*

Verse 34. See 3:7; Joshua 8:2.

9. *Key "by way of explanation"*

Verse 5. The tribes of Lot and Esau were given land, just as the Israelites were.

10. *Key "Quotable Quote"*

"Let no man think to kill sin with few, easy, or gentle strokes."
John Owen

Deuteronomy chapter 3

1. Before and after

Previous chapter: Chapter 2: Wandering in the desert for thirty-eight years
Following chapter: Chapter 4: Summary of God's covenant

2. Analysis of chapter

The conquest of Og king of Bashan. (1-11)
The land of Gilead and Bashan. (12-20)
Moses encourages Joshua. (21-29)

3. Key verse

Verse 18: "And I commanded you at that time, saying, The LORD your God hath given you this land to possess it: ye shall pass over armed before your brethren the children of Israel, all that are meet for the war."

4. Key word / key phrase

Verse 12, "land."

5. Key event / key person / key theme

The land is divided up

6. Key thought

Moses' single sin had unforeseen consequences.

7. Key thing to look out for

All kinds of rest, verse 20, come from the Lord's hand.

8. Key Bible cross-reference

Verses 23-25. See 1:37; 31:2.

9. Key "by way of explanation"

Verse 22. These events are recorded in such a way that it is clear that God himself lay behind each advance and victory.

10. Key "Quotable Quote"

"Thou hast made us for thyself, O Lord, and our hearts are restless until they find their rest in thee."
Augustine of Hippo

Deuteronomy chapter 4

1. **Before and after**

   Previous chapter: Chapter 3: Land east of Jordan conquered
   Following chapter: Chapter 5: The Ten Commandments

2. **Analysis of chapter**

   Earnest exhortations to obedience, and warnings against idolatry. (1-23)
   Warnings against disobedience, and promises of mercy. (24-40)
   Cities of refuge appointed. (41-49)

3. **Key verse**

   Verse 34: "Or hath God assayed to go and take him a nation from the midst of
   another nation, by temptations, by signs, and by wonders, and by war, and by
   a mighty hand, and by a stretched out arm, and by great terrors, according to
   all that the LORD your God did for you in Egypt before your eyes?"

4. **Key word / key phrase**

   Verse 16, "idol."

5. **Key event / key person / key theme**

   The sin of idolatry

6. **Key thought**

   God's faithful followers learn from their failures.

7. **Key thing to look out for**

   Out of God's kindness the cities of refuge are set up.

8. **Key Bible cross-reference**

   Verse 20. See 1 Kings 8:51; Jeremiah 11:4; Isaiah 48:10.

9. **Key "by way of explanation"**

   Verse 25. This verse shows a pattern of events repeated in this book: rebellion,
   expulsion, repentance, and restoration.

10. **Key "Quotable Quote"**

    "The purpose of revelation is restoration, the renewal in us of that likeness to
    God which man lost by sin."
    Stephen Neill

Deuteronomy chapter 5

1. **Before and after**

   Previous chapter: Chapter 4: Summary of God's covenant
   Following chapter: Chapter 6: Command to teach the law

2. **Analysis of chapter**

   The covenant in Horeb. (1-5)
   The Ten Commandments repeated. (6-22)
   The request of the people that the law might be delivered through Moses. (23-33)

3. **Key verse**

   Verse 4: "The LORD talked with you face to face in the mount out of the midst of the fire."

4. **Key word / key phrase**

   Verse 22, "commandments."

5. **Key event / key person / key theme**

   The Ten Commandments

6. **Key thought**

   The Ten Commandments have not dated.

7. **Key thing to look out for**

   Prosperity follows from obedience.

8. **Key Bible cross-reference**

   Verse 2. See Jeremiah 31:31-34.

9. **Key "by way of explanation"**

   Verses 16-21. The Ten Commandments form the basis of God's relationship with his people.

10. **Key "Quotable Quote"**

    "If men will not be governed by the Ten Commandments, they shall be governed by the ten thousand commandments."
    G.K. Chesterton

Deuteronomy chapter 6

1. Before and after

Previous chapter: Chapter 5: The Ten Commandments
Following chapter: Chapter 7: Command to conquer Canaan

2. Analysis of chapter

A persuasive to obedience. (1-3)
An exhortation to obedience. (4,5)
Obedience taught. (6-16)
General precepts. Instructions to be given to their children. (17-25)

3. Key verse

Verse 6: "And thou shalt love the LORD thy God with all thine heart, and with all thy soul, and with all thy might."

4. Key word / key phrase

Verse 5, "love."

5. Key event / key person / key theme

Loving God

6. Key thought

Keeping God's commandments involves fearing God, loving God, but not putting God to the test.

7. Key thing to look out for

Obedience is essential in the Christian life.

8. Key Bible cross-reference

Verse 2. See 4:40; 5:16,33.

9. Key "by way of explanation"

Verse 6. One of the characteristics of the new covenant was to be having God's laws in the heart, not just on stone tablets.

10. Key "Quotable Quote"

"There are no disappointments to those whose wills are buried in the will of God."
F.W. Faber

Deuteronomy chapter 7

1. *Before and after*

Previous chapter: Chapter 6: Command to teach the Law
Following chapter: Chapter 8: Command to remember the Lord

2. *Analysis of chapter*

Driving out the nations. (1-11)
The promises of obedience. (12-26)

3. *Key verse*

Verse 1: "When the LORD thy God shall bring thee into the land whither thou goest to possess it, and hath cast out many nations before thee."

4. *Key word / key phrase*

Verse 7, "choose."

5. *Key event / key person / key theme*

Taking possession of the land

6. *Key thought*

God does not love us on account of any merit on our part.

7. *Key thing to look out for*

Spiritual power comes from obeying God, verse 24.

8. *Key Bible cross-reference*

Verse 9. See Psalm 103:3.

9. *Key "by way of explanation"*

Verse 4. God did not forbid mixed marriages on racial grounds, but on religious grounds. He wanted to avoid apostasy.

10. *Key "Quotable Quote"*

"Though Christians be not kept altogether from falling, yet they are kept from falling altogether."
William Secker

Deuteronomy chapter 8

1. Before and after

Previous chapter: Chapter 7: Command to conquer Canaan
Following chapter: Chapter 9: Israel's disobedience to God

2. Analysis of chapter

Exhortations and warnings, enforced by the Lord's former dealings with Israel, and his promises. (1-9)
Exhortations and warnings further enforced. (10-20)

3. Key verse

Verse 19: "And it shall be, if thou do at all forget the LORD thy God, and walk after other gods, and serve them, and worship them, I testify against you this day that ye shall surely perish."

4. Key word / key phrase

Verse 2, "remember."

5. Key event / key person / key theme

Do not forget the Lord.

6. Key thought

God's discipline should be welcomed.

7. Key thing to look out for

God's goodness is to be recalled.

8. Key Bible cross-reference

Verse 3. See Matthew 4:4; Luke 4:4.

9. Key "by way of explanation"

Verses 7-9. These verses give a good description of the land that God's followers were about to enter.

10. Key "Quotable Quote"

"The purpose of Christ's redeeming work was to make it possible for bad men to become good – deeply, radically, and finally."
A.W. Tozer

Deuteronomy chapter 9

1. **Before and after**

   Previous chapter: Chapter 8: Command to remember the Lord
   Following chapter: Chapter 10: The covenant is renewed

2. **Analysis of chapter**

   The Israelites should not think their success came by their own merit. (1-6)
   Moses reminds the Israelites of their rebellions. (7-29)

3. **Key verse**

   Verse 16: "And I looked, and, behold, ye had sinned against the LORD your God, and had made you a molten calf: ye had turned aside quickly out of the way which the LORD had commanded you."

4. **Key word / key phrase**

   Verse 16, "an idol cast in the shape of a calf."

5. **Key event / key person / key theme**

   The golden calf

6. **Key thought**

   No group of God's people are beyond falling into temptation.

7. **Key thing to look out for**

   The body is willing but the spirit is weak.

8. **Key Bible cross-reference**

   Verse 6. See 10:16; 31:27.

9. **Key "by way of explanation"**

   Verse 19. Moses' prayer resulted in the survival of the Israelites.

10. **Key "Quotable Quote"**

    "Apostasy begins in the closet. No man ever backslid from the life and power of Christianity who continued constant and fervent in private prayer. He who prays without ceasing is likely to rejoice evermore."
    Adam Clark

Deuteronomy chapter 10

1. Before and after

Previous chapter: Chapter 9: Israel's disobedience to God
Following chapter: Chapter 11: Victory is dependent on obedience

2. Analysis of chapter

God's mercies to Israel after their rebellion. (1-11)
An exhortation to obedience. (12-22)

3. Key verse

Verse 1: "At that time the LORD said unto me, Hew thee two tables of stone like unto the first, and come up unto me into the mount, and make thee an ark of wood."

4. Key word / key phrase

Verse 4, "Ten Commandments."

5. Key event / key person / key theme

Moses receives the Ten Commandments again

6. Key thought

Moses is given a clear command by the Lord about what he has to do, verse 11.

7. Key thing to look out for

The correct reaction to seeing God's greatness is humility in his presence.

8. Key Bible cross-reference

Verse 16. See 9:6,13; 31:27.

9. Key "by way of explanation"

Verses 1-3. Different Bible versions use a variety of words such as "box," or "chest,"for what was traditionally translated as "ark."

10. Key "Quotable Quote"

"Wherever the fear of God rules in the heart, it will appear both in works of charity and piety, and neither will excuse us from the other."
Matthew Henry

Deuteronomy chapter 11

1. *Before and after*

Previous chapter: Chapter 10: The covenant is renewed
Following chapter: Chapter 12: Detailed instructions for worship

2. *Analysis of chapter*

The great work God performed for Israel. (1-7)
Promises and warnings. (8-17)
Careful study of God's word is necessary. (18-25)
The blessings and the curse are set out. (26-32)

3. *Key verse*

Verse 26: "Behold, I set before you this day a blessing and a curse."

4. *Key word / key phrase*

Verse 9, "milk and honey."

5. *Key event / key person / key theme*

The blessings of the promised land

6. *Key thought*

The more the Lord is loved the more he will be obeyed.

7. *Key thing to look out for*

God's promises and blessings are more than we can imagine.

8. *Key Bible cross-reference*

Verse 28. See 13:2,6,13; 28:64.

9. *Key "by way of explanation"*

Verse 14. The main season for rain in Palestine is between October and April.

10. *Key "Quotable Quote"*

"Fear the Lord and you will do everything well."
Shepherd of Hermas

Deuteronomy chapter 12

1. **Before and after**

   Previous chapter: Chapter 11: Victory is dependent on obedience
   Following chapter: Chapter 13: Warning against idolatry

2. **Analysis of chapter**

   Monuments of idolatry to be destroyed. (1-4)
   The place of God's service to be kept. (5-32)

3. **Key verse**

   Verse 2: "Ye shall utterly destroy all the places, wherein the nations which ye shall possess served their gods, upon the high mountains, and upon the hills, and under every green tree."

4. **Key word / key phrase**

   Verse 2, "worship."

5. **Key event / key person / key theme**

   The one place for worship

6. **Key thought**

   Idolatry remains a temptation for God's followers.

7. **Key thing to look out for**

   The Lord tolerates no rivals.

8. **Key Bible cross-reference**

   Verse 5. See 14:23,24; 16:2.

9. **Key "by way of explanation"**

   Verse 12. Joy was meant to characterize God's followers.

10. **Key "Quotable Quote"**

   "Joy is the great note all through the Bible."
   Oswald Chambers

Deuteronomy chapter 13

1. *Before and after*

   Previous chapter: Chapter 12: Detailed instructions for worship
   Following chapter: Chapter 14: Laws about food and tithes

2. *Analysis of chapter*

   People who entice others to idolatry to be put to death. (1-5)
   Relatives who entice to idolatry not to be spared. (6-11)
   Idolatrous cities not to be spared. (12-18)

3. *Key verse*

   Verse 5: "So shalt thou put the evil away from the midst of thee."

4. *Key word / key phrase*

   Verse 6, "other gods."

5. *Key event / key person / key theme*

   Warning against idolatry

6. *Key thought*

   Evil and goodness do not mix.

7. *Key thing to look out for*

   Idolatry requires drastic action if it is to be eliminated.

8. *Key Bible cross-reference*

   Verse 13. See 1 Samuel 1:16; 2:12; 25:17.

9. *Key "by way of explanation"*

   Verse 5. Evil as well as those who promoted evil had to be thrown out of the
   land.

10. *Key "Quotable Quote"*

    "You don't have to go to heathen lands today to find false gods. America is full
    of them. Whatever you love more than God is your idol."
    D.L. Moody

Deuteronomy chapter 14

1. **Before and after**

   Previous chapter: Chapter 13: Warning against idolatry
   Following chapter: Chapter 15: Laws about debts, slaves, and the firstborn

2. **Analysis of chapter**

   The Israelites to be different from other nations. (1-21)
   About making tithes. (22-29)

3. **Key verse**

   Verse 3: "Thou shalt not eat any abominable thing."

4. **Key word / key phrase**

   Verse 4, "animals."

5. **Key event / key person / key theme**

   Clean and unclean animals

6. **Key thought**

   God's regulations are for our benefit.

7. **Key thing to look out for**

   God is concerned about every aspect of life, including health and hygiene.

8. **Key Bible cross-reference**

   Verses 22-29. See Numbers 18:21-29.

9. **Key "by way of explanation"**

   Verse 2. The Israelites had to separate themselves from anything that was ceremonially unclean.

10. **Key "Quotable Quote"**

    "If you do not give the tenth part to God, he will take the nine parts."
    Ambrose

Deuteronomy chapter 15

1. *Before and after*

Previous chapter: Chapter 14: Laws about food and tithes
Following chapter: Chapter 16: Laws about feasts

2. *Analysis of chapter*

The year of release. (1-11)
The release of servants. (12-18)
About the firstborn of cattle. (19-23)

3. *Key verse*

Verse 1: "At the end of every seven years thou shalt make a release."

4. *Key word / key phrase*

Verse 1, "debts."

5. *Key event / key person / key theme*

The year for canceling debts

6. *Key thought*

Money matters are constantly taught in the Bible.

7. *Key thing to look out for*

The importance of a generous heart is underlined in verse 10.

8. *Key Bible cross-reference*

Verse 1. See Exodus 23:10,11; Leviticus 25:1-7.

9. *Key "by way of explanation"*

Verse 4. If the Israelites followed the orders of God that are set out in this chapter then there would be no poor people in their number.

10. *Key "Quotable Quote"*

"God prizes generosity, especially joyful generosity."
Charles R. Swindoll

Deuteronomy chapter 16

1. **Before and after**

   Previous chapter: Chapter 15: Laws about debts, slaves, and the firstborn
   Following chapter: Chapter 17: Instructions for a king

2. **Analysis of chapter**

   The yearly feasts. (1-17)
   About judges. Sacred stones and images forbidden. (18-22)

3. **Key verse**

   Verse 1: "Observe the month of Abib, and keep the Passover unto the LORD thy
   God: for in the month of Abib the LORD thy God brought thee forth out of
   Egypt by night."

4. **Key word / key phrase**

   Verse 1, "Passover."

5. **Key event / key person / key theme**

   The Passover and other festivals

6. **Key thought**

   Celebrating these festivals was meant to help the Israelites never to forget the
   Lord.

7. **Key thing to look out for**

   Different festivals emphasized different aspects of God's character.

8. **Key Bible cross-reference**

   Verses 1-8. See Exodus 12:1-28; 13:1-16.

9. **Key "by way of explanation"**

   Verse 16. The Israelites were ordered to attend these three festivals each year.

10. **Key "Quotable Quote"**

    "The life of man consists in beholding God."
    Irenaeus

Deuteronomy chapter 17

1. *Before and after*

Previous chapter: Chapter 16: Laws about feasts
Following chapter: Chapter 18: Laws about prophecy

2. *Analysis of chapter*

All sacrifices to be perfect. Idolaters must be killed. (1-7)
Difficult controversies. (8-13)
The choice of a king. His duties. (14-20)

3. *Key verse*

Verse 8: "If there arise a matter too hard for thee in judgment, between blood and blood, between plea and plea, and between stroke and stroke, being matters of controversy within thy gates: then shalt thou arise, and get thee up into the place which the LORD thy God shall choose."

4. *Key word / key phrase*

Verse 11, "do not turn aside."

5. *Key event / key person / key theme*

Law courts

6. *Key thought*

Contempt should not be part of the character of God's followers.

7. *Key thing to look out for*

The importance of having leaders who obey God.

8. *Key Bible cross-reference*

Verse 6. See Numbers 35:30.

9. *Key "by way of explanation"*

Verse 14. Although the Lord did not want the Israelites to have a king, Moses is here anticipating a time when they will seek one.

10. *Key "Quotable Quote"*

"Dost thou wish to rise? Begin by descending."
Augustine of Hippo

Deuteronomy chapter 18

1. **Before and after**

   Previous chapter: Chapter 17: Instructions for a king
   Following chapter: Chapter 19: Cities of refuge, and laws of witnesses

2. **Analysis of chapter**

   A provision about Levites. (1-8)
   The abominations of the Canaanites to be avoided. (9-14)
   Christ the great Prophet. (15-22)

3. **Key verse**

   Verse 15: "The LORD thy God will raise up unto thee a Prophet from the midst of thee, of thy brethren, like unto me; unto him ye shall hearken."

4. **Key word / key phrase**

   Verse 9, "detestable ways."

5. **Key event / key person / key theme**

   Warning against pagan practices

6. **Key thought**

   Our society is so godless that it is hardly possible to escape being influenced by it.

7. **Key thing to look out for**

   Sorcery is out for God's followers.

8. **Key Bible cross-reference**

   Verse 4. See Exodus 23:19; 34:26.

9. **Key "by way of explanation"**

   Verse 9. This verse gives the Bible's most detailed list of magical things forbidden by the Bible.

10. **Key "Quotable Quote"**

    "Magic is not mere superstition. It can corrupt people."
    Andrew Murray

Deuteronomy chapter 19

1. ***Before and after***

> Previous chapter: Chapter 18: Laws about prophecy
> Following chapter: Chapter 20: Laws about war

2. ***Analysis of chapter***

> The cities of refuge, the man-slayer, and the murderer. (1-13)
> Landmarks not to be removed. (14)
> The punishment of false witnesses. (15-21)

3. ***Key verse***

> Verse 15: "One witness shall not rise up against a man for any iniquity, or for any sin, in any sin that he sinneth: at the mouth of two witnesses, or at the mouth of three witnesses, shall the matter be established."

4. ***Key word / key phrase***

> Verse 4, "flees."

5. ***Key event / key person / key theme***

> The cities of refuge

6. ***Key thought***

> God is deeply concerned about us, especially when things go wrong.

7. ***Key thing to look out for***

> God is a God of justice.

8. ***Key Bible cross-reference***

> Verses 1-13. See 4:41-43; Numbers 35:9-28.

9. ***Key "by way of explanation"***

> Verse 14. To move a boundary stone was to rob someone of part of their property.

10. ***Key "Quotable Quote"***

> "The Bible tells us to love our neighbors, and also to love our enemies; probably because they are generally the same people."
> G.K. Chesterton

Deuteronomy chapter 20

1. Before and after

Previous chapter: Chapter 19: Cities of refuge, and laws of witnesses
Following chapter: Chapter 21: Laws about unsolved murders, and other laws

2. Analysis of chapter

Exhortation and proclamation about those who went to war. (1-9)
Peace to be offered. Which cities were to be devoted. (10-20)

3. Key verse

Verse 1: "When thou goest out to battle against thine enemies, and seest horses, and chariots, and a people more than thou, be not afraid of them: for the LORD thy God is with thee, which brought thee up out of the land of Egypt."

4. Key word / key phrase

Verse 1, "war."

5. Key event / key person / key theme

Going to war

6. Key thought

Marriage is placed above war.

7. Key thing to look out for

Evil has to be destroyed or else it takes us over.

8. Key Bible cross-reference

Verse 11. See Genesis 9:25.

9. Key "by way of explanation"

Verses 5-8. Israelites were not to rely on the size of their army but on the Lord.

10. Key "Quotable Quote"

"All that is necessary for the triumph of evil is that good men do nothing."
Edmund Burke

Deuteronomy chapter 21

1. Before and after

Previous chapter: Chapter 20: Laws about war
Following chapter: Chapter 22: Laws about sexual purity

2. Analysis of chapter

The expiation of uncertain murder. (1-9)
Marrying a captive woman. (10-14)
The firstborn not to be disinherited for private affection. (15-17)
A stubborn son to be stoned. (18-21)
Bodies of criminals not to be left hanging on a tree all night. (22,23)

3. Key verse

Verse 8: "Be merciful, O LORD, unto thy people Israel, whom thou hast redeemed, and lay not innocent blood unto thy people of Israel's charge. And the blood shall be forgiven them."

4. Key word / key phrase

Verse 22, "capital offence."

5. Key event / key person / key theme

Justice

6. Key thought

The death penalty was given for a capital offence.

7. Key thing to look out for

To be hung on a tree was thought to be a total disgrace.

8. Key Bible cross-reference

Verse 22. See Genesis 40:19.

9. Key "by way of explanation"

Verse 23. A body hung on a tree was under God's condemnation. Hence the significance of Jesus' death by crucifixion on a tree. See Galatians 3:13.

10. Key "Quotable Quote"

"He was condemned, that thou mightest be justified, and was killed, that thou mightest live."
John Bunyan

Deuteronomy chapter 22

1. Before and after

Previous chapter: Chapter 21: Laws about unsolved murders, and other laws
Following chapter: Chapter 23: Laws about exclusion from God's people

2. Analysis of chapter

Humility towards brethren. (1-4)
Various precepts. (5-12)
Against impurity. (13-30)

3. Key verse

Verse 4: "Thou shalt not see thy brother's ass or his ox fall down by the way, and hide thyself from them: thou shalt surely help him to lift them up again"

4. Key word / key phrase

Verse 4, "donkey."

5. Key event / key person / key theme

Further laws to ensure a humanitarian and just society.

6. Key thought

We are not meant to pass by on the other side.

7. Key thing to look out for

We are meant to be on the look-out for the safety of other people.

8. Key Bible cross-reference

Verse 15. See 25:7.

9. Key "by way of explanation"

Verse 5. God made men and women and it is his intention that the differences between the sexes should be maintained.

10. Key "Quotable Quote"

"Faith and works should travel side by side, step answering to step, like the legs of men walking. First faith, and then works; and then faith again, and then works again – until you can scarcely distinguish which is the one and which is the other."
William Booth

Deuteronomy chapter 23

1. *Before and after*

Previous chapter: Chapter 22: Laws about sexual purity
Following chapter: Chapter 24: Divorce and remarriage

2. *Analysis of chapter*

Who are excluded from the congregation. (1-8)
Cleanliness commanded. (15-25)
About fugitive servants. Usury, and other precepts. (9-14)

3. *Key verse*

Verse 24: "When thou comest into thy neighbor's vineyard, then thou mayest eat grapes thy fill at thine own pleasure; but thou shalt not put any in thy vessel."

4. *Key word / key phrase*

Verse 24 "vineyard."

5. *Key event / key person / key theme*

The just society

6. *Key thought*

We are never meant to take advantage of our neighbor.

7. *Key thing to look out for*

God is the one who protects us.

8. *Key Bible cross-reference*

Verse 6. See Ezekiel 25:1-11; Zephaniah 2:8-11.

9. *Key "by way of explanation"*

Verses 9-14. Rules about hygiene were crucial, especially during a war.

10. *Key "Quotable Quote"*

"Divine love not only repeatedly commands us to love our neighbors, but also itself produces this love and pours it out into our hearts."
Francis de Sales

Deuteronomy chapter 24

1. *Before and after*

Previous chapter: Chapter 23: Laws about exclusion from God's people
Following chapter: Chapter 25: Duty to a dead brother

2. *Analysis of chapter*

About divorce. (1-4)
About newly-weds, thieves, and pledges. (5-13)
Justice and generosity. (14-22)

3. *Key verse*

Verse 22: "And thou shalt remember that thou wast a bondman in the land of Egypt: therefore I command thee to do this thing."

4. *Key word / key phrase*

Verse 1, "marries."

5. *Key event / key person / key theme*

Divorce and remarriage

6. *Key thought*

The importance of helping newly-weds is clear from verse 5.

7. *Key thing to look out for*

Kindness should extend to people who are in debt to us.

8. *Key Bible cross-reference*

Verses 1-4. See Leviticus 21:7,14; Matthew 5:31,32; 19:3-9.

9. *Key "by way of explanation"*

Verses 1-4. Although divorce was allowed in the books of Moses, it was severely restricted.

10. *Key "Quotable Quote"*

"Kindness is an essential part of God's work and ours here on earth."
Billy Graham

Deuteronomy chapter 25

1. *Before and after*

Previous chapter: Chapter 24: Divorce and remarriage
Following chapter: Chapter 26: Laws about tithes, and Israel's vows

2. *Analysis of chapter*

Extent of punishment. (1-3)
The ox that treads the corn. (4)
Marriage of a brother's wife. (5-12)
Dishonest weights. (13-16)
War against Amalek. (17-19)

3. *Key verse*

Verse 1: "If there be a controversy between men, and they come unto judgment, that the judges may judge them; then they shall justify the righteous, and condemn the wicked."

4. *Key word / key phrase*

Verse 5, "brothers."

5. *Key event / key person / key theme*

Duty to a dead brother

6. *Key thought*

Cruelty must never be part of punishment.

7. *Key thing to look out for*

Duty to family should take a very high priority.

8. *Key Bible cross-reference*

Verse 4. See 1 Corinthians 9:9,10; 1 Timothy 5:17,18.

9. *Key "by way of explanation"*

Verse 23. A limit was put on corporal punishment.

10. *Key "Quotable Quote"*

"The foundations of civilization are no stronger and no more enduring than the corporate integrity of the homes on which they rest. If the home deteriorates, civilization will crumble and fall."
Billy Graham

Deuteronomy chapter 26

1. *Before and after*

   Previous chapter: Chapter 25: Duty to a dead brother
   Following chapter: Chapter 27: The curse of disobedience

2. *Analysis of chapter*

   Confession in offering the first-fruits. (1-11)
   The prayer after disposal of the third year's tithe. (12-15)
   The covenant between God and the people. (16-19)

3. *Key verse*

   Verse 12: "When thou hast made an end of tithing all the tithes of thine increase the third year, which is the year of tithing, and hast given it unto the Levite, the stranger, the fatherless, and the widow, that they may eat within thy gates, and be filled."

4. *Key word / key phrase*

   Verse 2, "firstfruits."

5. *Key event / key person / key theme*

   Harvest offerings

6. *Key thought*

   We are meant to show our gratitude to God.

7. *Key thing to look out for*

   Rejoicing in God's goodness should be our daily delight. See verse 11.

8. *Key Bible cross-reference*

   Verse 2. See 18:4.

9. *Key "by way of explanation"*

   Verse 5. The "wandering Aramean" refers to Jacob and his journeys.

10. *Key "Quotable Quote"*

    "Whether God gives us something or withholds it from us, he acts for our good, even if we, like children, are not aware of this."
    Peter of Damaskos

Deuteronomy chapter 27

1. **Before and after**

   Previous chapter: Chapter 26: Laws about tithes, and Israel's vows
   Following chapter: Chapter 28: Warnings of the covenant

2. **Analysis of chapter**

   The law to be written on stones in the promised land. (1-10)
   The curses to be pronounced on Mount Ebal. (11-26)

3. **Key verse**

   Verse 15: "Cursed be the man that maketh any graven or molten image, an abomination unto the LORD, the work of the hands of the craftsman, and putteth it in a secret place. And all the people shall answer and say, Amen."

4. **Key word / key phrase**

   Verse 15, "cursed."

5. **Key event / key person / key theme**

   God's curses on disobedience

6. **Key thought**

   Obedience to God is not an optional extra.

7. **Key thing to look out for**

   As we sow, so shall we reap.

8. **Key Bible cross-reference**

   Verse 15. See 4:28; 5:6-10; 31:29.

9. **Key "by way of explanation"**

   Verse 26. Galatians 3:10 quotes this verse to show that no one can keep all of God's laws.

10. **Key "Quotable Quote"**

    "We are God's glory, when we follow his ways."
    Florence Nightingale

Deuteronomy chapter 28

1. *Before and after*

   Previous chapter: Chapter 27: The curse of disobedience
   Following chapter: Chapter 29: The Lord's covenant in the land of Moab

2. *Analysis of chapter*

   The blessings for obedience. (1-14)
   The curses for disobedience. (15-44)
   Their ruin, if disobedient. (45-68)

3. *Key verse*

   Verse 9: "The LORD shall establish thee an holy people unto himself, as he hath sworn unto thee, if thou shalt keep the commandments of the LORD thy God, and walk in his ways."

4. *Key word / key phrase*

   Verse 1, "obey."

5. *Key event / key person / key theme*

   Blessings for obedience

6. *Key thought*

   God gave us his laws for our good.

7. *Key thing to look out for*

   Obeying God may seem tough but that does not mean that we should disobey God.

8. *Key Bible cross-reference*

   Verse 12. See Job 38:22; Psalm 135:7.

9. *Key "by way of explanation"*

   Compare verses 3-6 with 16-19 to see how blessings are the opposite of curses.

10. *Key "Quotable Quote"*

    "Our first resurrection begins when we first show obedience to God."
    Baldwin of Canterbury

Deuteronomy chapter 29

1. *Before and after*

Previous chapter: Chapter 28: Warnings of the covenant
Following chapter: Chapter 30: Promise of repentance and forgiveness

2. *Analysis of chapter*

Moses recalls Israel's mercies. (1-9)
The divine wrath on those who bask in their wickedness. (10-21)
The ruin of the Jewish nation. (22-28)
Secret things belong to God. (29)

3. *Key verse*

Verse 4: "Yet the LORD hath not given you an heart to perceive, and eyes to see, and ears to hear, unto this day."

4. *Key word / key phrase*

Verse 1, "covenant."

5. *Key event / key person / key theme*

God's covenant in the land of Moab

6. *Key thought*

Time taken to reflect on God's past blessings is time well spent.

7. *Key thing to look out for*

We are meant to take great care in following God's commands.

8. *Key Bible cross-reference*

Verse 23. See Genesis 19:24,25.

9. *Key "by way of explanation"*

God has revealed to us what we need to know. This does not mean to say that God has revealed everything to us. See verse 29.

10. *Key "Quotable Quote"*

"The essence of obedience lies in the hearty love which prompts the deed rather than in the deed itself."
C.H. Spurgeon

Deuteronomy chapter 30

1. **Before and after**

   Previous chapter: Chapter 29: The Lord's covenant in the land of Moab
   Following chapter: Chapter 31: Joshua to succeed Moses and the Lord's last instructions to Moses

2. **Analysis of chapter**

   Mercies promised to the repentant. (1-10)
   The commandment is clear. (11-14)
   The choice between death and life. (15-20)

3. **Key verse**

   Verse 9: ". . . for the LORD will again rejoice over thee for good, as he rejoiced over thy fathers."

4. **Key word / key phrase**

   Verse 16, "walk in his ways."

5. **Key event / key person / key theme**

   Choosing between life and death

6. **Key thought**

   Every day we face a choice in how we follow God.

7. **Key thing to look out for**

   Hearts can grow cold.

8. **Key Bible cross-reference**

   Verse 19. See 31:28; 32:1.

9. **Key "by way of explanation"**

   Verse 20. To choose the Lord is to choose life.

10. **Key "Quotable Quote"**

    "Good and evil both increase at compound interest. That is why the little decisions you and I make every day are of such infinite importance."
    C.S. Lewis

Deuteronomy chapter 31

1. *Before and after*

Previous chapter: Chapter 30: Promise of repentance and forgiveness
Following chapter: Chapter 32: The Song of Moses

2. *Analysis of chapter*

Moses encourages the people, and Joshua. (1-8)
The Law to be read every seventh year. (9-13)
The Israelites' apostasy foretold. A song given to be witness against them. (14-22)
The Law given to the Levites. (22-30)

3. *Key verse*

Verse 7: "And Moses called unto Joshua, and said unto him in the sight of all Israel, Be strong and of a good courage: for thou must go with this people unto the land which the LORD hath sworn unto their fathers to give them; and thou shalt cause them to inherit it."

4. *Key word / key phrase*

Verse 7, "Joshua."

5. *Key event / key person / key theme*

Joshua will succeed Moses

6. *Key thought*

We need to pray for the Lord's strength if we are to be strong.

7. *Key thing to look out for*

Moses reminds Joshua that his most important asset will be the Lord's presence.

8. *Key Bible cross-reference*

Verse 6. See Joshua 1:6,7,9,18.

9. *Key "by way of explanation"*

Verse 2. Moses' age did not stop him being Israel's leader, but his sin did. See 1:37; 3:23-27.

10. *Key "Quotable Quote"*

"When God is our strength, it is strength indeed; when our strength is our own, it is only weakness."
Augustine of Hippo

Deuteronomy chapter 32

1. **Before and after**

    Previous chapter: Chapter 31: Joshua to succeed Moses and the Lord's last
    instructions to Moses
    Following chapter: Chapter 33: Moses blesses Israel

2. **Analysis of chapter**

    The song of Moses. (1,2)
    The character of God, and the character of Israel. (3-6)
    The great things God had done for Israel. (7-14)
    The wickedness of Israel. (19-25)
    The judgments which would come on them because of their sins. (15-18)
    Deserved vengeance withheld. (26-38)
    God's deliverance for his people. (39-43)
    The exhortation with which the song was delivered. (44-47)
    Moses to go up Mount Nebo to die. (48-52)

3. **Key verse**

    Verse 9: "For the LORD'S portion is his people; Jacob is the lot of his
    inheritance."

4. **Key word / key phrase**

    Verse 1, "I will speak."

5. **Key event / key person / key theme**

    The Song of Moses

6. **Key thought**

    Recalling God's goodness is the most positive thing we can do today.

7. **Key thing to look out for**

    Using a prayer like this can be our way of sharing in Moses' delight in the
    Lord.

8. **Key Bible cross-reference**

    Verse 4. See verses 15,18,30,31.

9. **Key "by way of explanation"**

    Verse 10. This refers to God's protection of us, just as the pupil is kept safe by
    the rest of the eye.

10. **Key "Quotable Quote"**

    "Just the word thanksgiving prompts the spirit of humility."
    Charles R. Swindoll

Deuteronomy chapter 33

1. *Before and after*

Previous chapter: Chapter 32: The Song of Moses
Following chapter: Chapter 34: The death of Moses

2. *Analysis of chapter*

The glorious majesty of God. (1-5)
The blessings of the twelve tribes. (6-23)
Strength to believers. (24,25)
The excellency of Israel. (26-29)

3. *Key verse*

Verse 1: "And this is the blessing, wherewith Moses the man of God blessed the children of Israel before his death."

4. *Key word / key phrase*

Verse 1, "blessing."

5. *Key event / key person / key theme*

Moses blesses the tribes

6. *Key thought*

Moses starts his blessings by recalling God's great love.

7. *Key thing to look out for*

Everyone may not be blessed in the same way, but each has his or her special blessing from the Lord.

8. *Key Bible cross-reference*

Verse 16. See Exodus 3:1-6.

9. *Key "by way of explanation"*

Verse 9. The book of the Law was kept in the ark. The ark was kept in the tabernacle. The Levites looked after the tabernacle, and so are said to watch over the Lord's word.

10. *Key "Quotable Quote"*

"God is more anxious to bestow his blessings on us than we are to receive them."
Augustine of Hippo

Deuteronomy chapter 34

1. **Previous chapter**

   Chapter 33: Moses blesses Israel

2. **Analysis of chapter**

   Moses views the promised land from Mount Nebo. (1-4)
   The death and burial of Moses. The people mourn. (5-8)
   Joshua succeeds Moses, and the praise of Moses. (9-12)

3. **Key verse**

   Verse 5: "So Moses the servant of the LORD died there in the land of Moab, according to the word of the LORD."

4. **Key word / key phrase**

   Verse 5, "died."

5. **Key event / key person / key theme**

   The death of Moses

6. **Key thought**

   No greater prophet than Moses ever came.

7. **Key thing to look out for**

   Moses' greatness lay in the fact that he experienced God face to face.

8. **Key Bible cross-reference**

   Verse 10. See Numbers 12:8.

9. **Key "by way of explanation"**

   Verse 5. The words "servant of the Lord" refer to someone the Lord has taken into his service.

10. **Key "Quotable Quote"**

    "One drop of water helps to swell the ocean; a spark of fire helps to give light to the world. None are too small, too feeble, too poor to be of service. Think of this and act."
    Hannah More

Joshua

Joshua chapter 1

1. **Following chapter**

   Chapter 2: The spies are sent out

2. **Analysis of chapter**

   The Lord appoints Joshua to succeed Moses. (1-4)
   God promises to assist Joshua. (5-9)
   Preparation to cross over Jordan. (10-15)
   The people promise to obey Joshua. (16-18)

3. **Key verse**

   Verse 7: "Only be thou strong and very courageous, that thou mayest observe to do according to all the law, which Moses my servant commanded thee: turn not from it to the right hand or to the left, that thou mayest prosper whithersoever thou goest."

4. **Key word / key phrase**

   Verse 2, "cross the Jordan River"

5. **Key event / key person / key theme**

   Joshua is told to conquer Canaan.

6. **Key thought**

   Conquering the promised land was not Joshua's idea.

7. **Key thing to look out for**

   The Book of the Law was to be in Joshua's mind all the time.

8. **Key Bible cross-reference**

   Verse 1. See Exodus 24:13; 33:11; Deuteronomy 1:38.

9. **Key "by way of explanation"**

   Verse 8, the "Book of the Law." This must have been made up of some of the laws given at Mount Sinai that had already been written down.

10. **Key "Quotable Quote"**

    "Listen less to your own thoughts and more to God's thoughts."
    François Fénelon

Joshua chapter 2

1. Before and after

Previous chapter: Chapter 1: Joshua is commissioned to be Israel's leader
Following chapter: Chapter 3: Crossing the River Jordan

2. Analysis of chapter

Rahab receives and hides two Israelites. (1-7)
Rahab and the spies. (8-21)
The return of the spies. (22-24)

3. Key verse

Verse 1: "And Joshua the son of Nun sent out of Shittim two men to spy secretly, saying, Go view the land, even Jericho."

4. Key word / key phrase

Verse 1, "Rahab."

5. Key event / key person / key theme

Rahab and the spies

6. Key thought

God cares for individuals.

7. Key thing to look out for

There is no greater privilege than to serve God.

8. Key Bible cross-reference

Verse 1. See Judges 7:10,11; 1 Samuel 26:16.

9. Key "by way of explanation"

Verse 18. The scarlet cord acted as a marker, just as the blood on doorposts did at the first Passover.

10. Key "Quotable Quote"

"The most eloquent prayer is the prayer through hands that heal and bless. The highest form of worship is the worship of unselfish Christian service. The greatest form of praise is the sound of consecrated feet seeking out the lost and helpless."
Billy Graham

Joshua chapter 3

1. Before and after

Previous chapter: Chapter 2: The spies are sent out
Following chapter: Chapter 4: Erecting a memorial

2. Analysis of chapter

The Israelites come to Jordan. (1-6)
The Lord encourages Joshua. Joshua encourages the people. (7-13)
The Israelites pass over the River Jordan on dry land. (14-17)

3. Key verse

Verse 5: "And Joshua said unto the people, Sanctify yourselves: for to morrow the LORD will do wonders among you."

4. Key word / key phrase

Verse 14, "Jordan."

5. Key event / key person / key theme

The Israelites cross over the River Jordan

6. Key thought

Consecration to God should take place before engaging on any important action.

7. Key thing to look out for

It is crucial to listen to God's word and God's words, verse 9.

8. Key Bible cross-reference

Verse 3. See Numbers 10:33-36.

9. Key "by way of explanation"

Verse 7. Through God's miracle at the River Jordan Joshua's leadership was vindicated.

10. Key "Quotable Quote"

"Hear the true Word of God; lay hold of it, and spend your days not in raising hard questions, but in feasting upon precious truth."
C.H. Spurgeon

Joshua chapter 4

1. **Before and after**

   Previous chapter: Chapter 3: Crossing the River Jordan
   Following chapter: Chapter 5: Joshua prepares Israel spiritually

2. **Analysis of chapter**

   Stones taken out of Jordan. (1-9)
   The people pass through Jordan. (10-19)
   The twelve stones placed in Gilgal. (20-24)

3. **Key verse**

   Verse 8: "And the children of Israel did so as Joshua commanded, and took up twelve stones out of the midst of Jordan, as the LORD spake unto Joshua, according to the number of the tribes of the children of Israel, and carried them with them unto the place where they lodged, and laid them down there."

4. **Key word / key phrase**

   Verse 2, "twelve stones."

5. **Key event / key person / key theme**

   Memorial stones are set up.

6. **Key thought**

   Without the faithful obedience of countless unnamed Israelites God's plans would not have been carried out.

7. **Key thing to look out for**

   God's nature is seen to be powerful. The people should therefore reverence him.

8. **Key Bible cross-reference**

   Verse 6. See 24:26; 1 Samuel 7:12.

9. **Key "by way of explanation"**

   Verse 6. These stones were to act as a reminder to future generations of God's actions.

10. **Key "Quotable Quote"**

    "Every man naturally desires knowledge; but what good is knowledge without fear of God?"
    Thomas à Kempis

Joshua chapter 5

1. *Before and after*

    Previous chapter: Chapter 4: Erecting a memorial
    Following chapter: Chapter 6: Victory at Jericho

2. *Analysis of chapter*

    The Canaanites are afraid. Circumcision renewed. (1-9)
    The Passover at Gilgal. The manna ceases. (10-12)
    The Captain of the Lord's host appears to Joshua. (13-15)

3. *Key verse*

    Verse 15: "And the captain of the LORD's host said unto Joshua, Loose thy shoe
    from off thy foot; for the place whereon thou standest is holy. And Joshua did
    so."

4. *Key word / key phrase*

    Verse 2, "circumcise."

5. *Key event / key person / key theme*

    Circumcision at Gilgal

6. *Key thought*

    God's people are meant to be marked out by holy lives.

7. *Key thing to look out for*

    God's provision of manna lasted until they could eat food from Canaan.

8. *Key Bible cross-reference*

    Verse 11. See Exodus 12:15; Leviticus 23:6.

9. *Key "by way of explanation"*

    Verse 2. Circumcision was given as a way of showing that people belonged to
    God. See Genesis 17:10,11.

10. *Key "Quotable Quote"*

    "Baptized, re-baptized, circumcised, confirmed, fed upon sacraments, and
    buried in consecrated ground – you shall all perish except you believe in
    Christ."
    C.H. Spurgeon

Joshua chapter 6

1. *Before and after*

Previous chapter: Chapter 5: Joshua prepares Israel spiritually
Following chapter: Chapter 7: Defeat at Ai

2. *Analysis of chapter*

The siege of Jericho. (1-5)
The city is surrounded. (6-16)
Jericho is taken, Rahab and her family are saved. (17-27)

3. *Key verse*

Verse 2: "And the LORD said unto Joshua, See, I have given into thine hand Jericho, and the king thereof, and the mighty men of valor."

4. *Key word / key phrase*

Verse 1, "Jericho."

5. *Key event / key person / key theme*

Jericho is captured.

6. *Key thought*

God's people had to exercise faith in him before Jericho would fall.

7. *Key thing to look out for*

Spiritual victories are impossible without the help of God's Spirit.

8. *Key Bible cross-reference*

Verse 25. See Hebrews 11:31; James 2:25.

9. *Key "by way of explanation"*

Verse 4. The blowing of "rams' horns" announced God's presence.

10. *Key "Quotable Quote"*

"In God We Trust."
This motto first appeared on U.S. 2-cent coins after April 22, 1864. On July 30, 1956, it became the national motto.

Joshua chapter 7

1. *Before and after*

Previous chapter: Chapter 6: Victory at Jericho
Following chapter: Chapter 8: Victory at Ai

2. *Analysis of chapter*

The Israelites defeated at Ai. (1-5)
Joshua's humiliation and prayer. (6-9)
God instructs Joshua what to do. (10-5)
Achan is detected, and is destroyed. (16-26)

3. *Key verse*

Verse 6: "And Joshua rent his clothes, and fell to the earth upon his face before the ark of the LORD until the eventide, he and the elders of Israel, and put dust upon their heads."

4. *Key word / key phrase*

Verse 1, "acted unfaithfully."

5. *Key event / key person / key theme*

Achan's sin

6. *Key thought*

God demands wholehearted obedience from his followers.

7. *Key thing to look out for*

It is never difficult to rationalize about taking a different course of action from the one we know God has chosen.

8. *Key Bible cross-reference*

Verse 15. See Deuteronomy 22:21; 2 Samuel 13:12.

9. *Key "by way of explanation"*

Verse 11. One person's sin can affect the whole fellowship.

10. *Key "Quotable Quote"*

"The deceitfulness of sin is seen in that it is modest in its first proposals but when it prevails it hardens men's hearts, and brings them to ruin."
John Owen

Joshua chapter 8

1. *Before and after*

    Previous chapter: Chapter 7: Defeat at Ai
    Following chapter: Chapter 9: Failure with the Gibeonites

2. *Analysis of chapter*

    God encourages Joshua. (1,2)
    The taking of Ai. (3-22)
    The destruction of Ai and its king. (23-29)
    The law read on Ebal and Gerizim. (30-35)

3. *Key verse*

    Verse 34: "And afterward he read all the words of the law, the blessings and cursings, according to all that is written in the book of the law."

4. *Key word / key phrase*

    Verse 1, "do not be discouraged."

5. *Key event / key person / key theme*

    Ai is destroyed.

6. *Key thought*

    After failure God issues fresh orders.

7. *Key thing to look out for*

    Recovery from failure is always possible with God's help.

8. *Key Bible cross-reference*

    Verse 1. See 1:3-5; 3:11-13.

9. *Key "by way of explanation"*

    Verse 34. Joshua promoted God's word among God's people.

10. *Key "Quotable Quote"*

    "Emulate the tiny ant; be an ant of God. Listen to the word of God and hide it in your heart. Collect plenty of food during the happy days of your spiritual summers."
    Augustine of Hippo

Joshua chapter 9

1. Before and after

> Previous chapter: Chapter 8: Victory at Ai
> Following chapter: Chapter 10: Victory over the Amorites

2. Analysis of chapter

> The kings unite against Israel. (1,2)
> The Gibeonites ask for peace. (3-13)
> They obtain peace, but are soon detected. (14-21)
> The Gibeonites are to be servants. (22-27)

3. Key verse

> Verse 15: "And Joshua made peace with them, and made a league with them, to let them live: and the princes of the congregation sware unto them."

4. Key word / key phrase

> Verse 14, "did not enquire of the Lord."

5. Key event / key person / key theme

> The Gibeonites deceive Joshua.

6. Key thought

> Godless standards common in the world are not to be followed.

7. Key thing to look out for

> Deceit is no small matter.

8. Key Bible cross-reference

> Verse 15. See Exodus 20:7; Leviticus 19:12.

9. Key "by way of explanation"

> Verse 4. If the Gibeonites had trusted God they would not have needed to resort to this deception.

10. Key "Quotable Quote"

> "The commandment of absolute truthfulness is really only another name for the fullness of discipleship."
> Dietrich Bonhoeffer

Joshua chapter 10

1. **Before and after**

   Previous chapter: Chapter 9: Failure with the Gibeonites
   Following chapter: Chapter 11: Conquering northern Canaan, and summary of conquests

2. **Analysis of chapter**

   Five kings fight against Gibeon. (1-6)
   Joshua succors Gibeon. The sun and moon stand still. (7-14)
   The kings are taken, their armies defeated, and they are put to death. (15-27)
   Seven other kings defeated and killed. (28-43)

3. **Key verse**

   Verse 13: "And the sun stood still, and the moon stayed, until the people had avenged themselves upon their enemies."

4. **Key word / key phrase**

   Verse 12, "sun."

5. **Key event / key person / key theme**

   The day the sun stood still.

6. **Key thought**

   Conversion is the greatest miracle.

7. **Key thing to look out for**

   The different ways in which God revealed his mighty power.

8. **Key Bible cross-reference**

   Verse 11. See Judges 5:20; Job 38:22.

9. **Key "by way of explanation"**

   Verse 13. There are a number of history books mentioned in the Old Testament, such as the "Book of Jashar" which we no longer have.

10. **Key "Quotable Quote"**

    "True conversion will involve the mind, the affection, and the will."
    Billy Graham

Joshua chapter 11

1. *Before and after*

Previous chapter: Chapter 10: Victory over the Amorites
Following chapter: Chapter 12: Kings conquered by Moses and Joshua

2. *Analysis of chapter*

Various kings overcome at the Waters of Merom. (1-9)
Hazor is taken and burned. (10-14)
All that country subdued, and the Anakites cut off. (15-23)

3. *Key verse*

Verse 6: "And the LORD said unto Joshua, Be not afraid because of them: for to
morrow about this time will I deliver them up all slain before Israel: thou shalt
hough their horses, and burn their chariots with fire."

4. *Key word / key phrase*

Verse 8, "defeated."

5. *Key event / key person / key theme*

Northern kings defeated.

6. *Key thought*

The battle belongs to the Lord.

7. *Key thing to look out for*

If we experience peace that is God's gift.

8. *Key Bible cross-reference*

Verse 20. See Exodus 8:32; 9:12.

9. *Key "by way of explanation"*

Verse 13. "Mounds" were formed by successive towns being built on one site.

10. *Key "Quotable Quote"*

"We rest on thee, our shield and our defender!
Thine is the battle, thine shall be the praise;
When passing through the gates of pearly splendor,
Victors, we rest with thee, through endless days."
Edith Gilling Cherry

Joshua chapter 12

1. **Before and after**

   Previous chapter: Chapter 11: Conquering northern Canaan, and summary of
   conquests
   Following chapter: Chapter 13: Tribal boundaries

2. **Analysis of chapter**

   The two kings conquered by Moses. (1-6)
   The kings whom Joshua defeated. (7-24)

3. **Key verse**

   Verse 1: "Now these are the kings of the land, which the children of Israel
   smote"

4. **Key word / key phrase**

   Verse 1, "kings."

5. **Key event / key person / key theme**

   Kings defeated by Moses and Joshua.

6. **Key thought**

   Paul often pictured the Christian life as one long battle.

7. **Key thing to look out for**

   Count your blessings, name them one by one.

8. **Key Bible cross-reference**

   Verse 4. See Nehemiah 9:22; Psalm 135:11.

9. **Key "by way of explanation"**

   Verse 1 gives the boundaries of the conquered territories.

10. **Key "Quotable Quote"**

    "Christians have overcome, but they are still fighting."
    D. Martyn Lloyd-Jones

Joshua chapter 13

1. Before and after

Previous chapter: Chapter 12: Kings conquered by Moses and Joshua
Following chapter: Chapter 14: Land for Caleb

2. Analysis of chapter

Boundaries of the land not yet conquered. (1-6)
Inheritance of Reuben. (7-33)

3. Key verse

Verse 1: "Now Joshua was old and stricken in years; and the LORD said unto him, Thou art old and stricken in years, and there remaineth yet very much land to be possessed."

4. Key word / key phrase

Verse 1, "land."

5. Key event / key person / key theme

Land still to be taken

6. Key thought

Paul pressed on even at the end of his life.

7. Key thing to look out for

Jesus told his followers to aim for perfection.

8. Key Bible cross-reference

Verse 33. See Deuteronomy 18:1-8.

9. Key "by way of explanation"

Verse 1. Joshua was between ninety and a hundred years old. For Caleb's age, see 14.10.

10. Key "Quotable Quote"

"We ought to persevere to the end in good works."
Anselm

Joshua chapter 14

1. **Before and after**

    Previous chapter: Chapter 13: Tribal boundaries
    Following chapter: Chapter 15: Land for Judah

2. **Analysis of chapter**

    The inheritance of the nine and a half tribes. (1-5)
    Caleb is given Hebron. (6-15)

3. **Key verse**

    Verse 1: "And these are the countries which the children of Israel inherited in
    the land of Canaan, which Eleazar the priest, and Joshua the son of Nun, and
    the heads of the fathers of the tribes of the children of Israel, distributed for
    inheritance to them."

4. **Key word / key phrase**

    Verse 614 "inheritance."

5. **Key event / key person / key theme**

    Hebron is given to Caleb.

6. **Key thought**

    God's promises never fail.

7. **Key thing to look out for**

    Experienced Christians should be valued for their wisdom.

8. **Key Bible cross-reference**

    Verse 6. See Numbers 13:30; Deuteronomy 1:34-36.

9. **Key "by way of explanation"**

    Verse 1. Eleazar was in charge of casting lots.

10. **Key "Quotable Quote"**

    "The next best thing to being wise oneself is to live in a circle of those who
    are."
    C.S. Lewis

Joshua chapter 15

1. Before and after

Previous chapter: Chapter 14: Land for Caleb
Following chapter: Chapter 16: Boundaries of Joseph and Ephraim

2. Analysis of chapter

The boundaries of the lot of Judah. (1-12)
Caleb's portion. His daughter's blessing. (13-19)
The cities of Judah. (20-63)

3. Key verse

Verse 1: "This then was the lot of the tribe of the children of Judah by their families; even to the border of Edom the wilderness of Zin southward was the uttermost part of the south coast."

4. Key word / key phrase

Verse 2, "boundary."

5. Key event / key person / key theme

Caleb's daughter

6. Key thought

All possessions are given from God.

7. Key thing to look out for

We are tenants not owners.

8. Key Bible cross-reference

Verse 1. See Genesis 49:8-12; 2 Kings 17:18.

9. Key "by way of explanation"

Verse 17. Othniel's work as judge is recorded in Judges 3:7-11.

10. Key "Quotable Quote"

"A Church of comfort, property, privilege, and position stands in sharp contrast with the Bible which describes the people of God as aliens, exiles, pilgrims and strangers."
Jim Wallis

Joshua chapter 16

1. **Before and after**

   Previous chapter: Chapter 15: Land for Judah
   Following chapter: Chapter 17: Boundaries of the half tribe of Manasseh

2. **Analysis of chapter**

   The territory given to Ephraim. (1-10)

3. **Key verse**

   Verse 4: "So the children of Joseph, Manasseh and Ephraim, took their inheritance."

4. **Key word / key phrase**

   Verse 10, "Canaanites."

5. **Key event / key person / key theme**

   Territory for Ephraim and Manasseh

6. **Key thought**

   A failure is recorded in verse 10.

7. **Key thing to look out for**

   What matters is how we are viewed in God's eyes.

8. **Key Bible cross-reference**

   Verse 10. See 1 Kings 9:15,16; 2 Samuel 5:25.

9. **Key "by way of explanation"**

   Verse 1. After Judah; Joseph's tribes (the tribes of his two sons) are given priority.

10. **Key "Quotable Quote"**

    "Your reputation is what people say about you. Your character is what God and your wife know about you."
    William Ashley (Billy) Sunday

Joshua chapter 17

1. Before and after

Previous chapter: Chapter 16: Boundaries of Joseph and Ephraim
Following chapter: Chapter 18: Boundaries of Benjamin

2. Analysis of chapter

The lot of Manasseh. (1-6)
The boundaries of Manasseh, and the Canaanites not driven out. (7-13)
Joseph desires a larger portion. (14-18)

3. Key verse

Verse 1: "There was also a lot for the tribe of Manasseh; for he was the firstborn of Joseph; to wit, for Machir the firstborn of Manasseh, the father of Gilead: because he was a man of war, therefore he had Gilead and Bashan."

4. Key word / key phrase

Verse 14, "only one allotment."

5. Key event / key person / key theme

A request for more land

6. Key thought

Our inheritance comes from God.

7. Key thing to look out for

Our inheritance is God himself.

8. Key Bible cross-reference

Verse 1. See Genesis 48:14,19.

9. Key "by way of explanation"

Verse 16. Anybody who had an iron chariot had the latest in weapons and would be feared.

10. Key "Quotable Quote"

"A conscience void of offence before God and man is an inheritance for eternity."
Daniel Webster

Joshua chapter 18

1. Before and after

Previous chapter: Chapter 17: Boundaries of the half tribe of Manasseh
Following chapter: Chapter 19: Boundaries of seven tribes

2. Analysis of chapter

The tabernacle set up at Shiloh. (1)
The remainder of the land described and divided. (2-10)
The boundaries of Benjamin. (11-28)

3. Key verse

Verse 3: "And Joshua said unto the children of Israel, How long are ye slack to go to possess the land, which the LORD God of your fathers hath given you?"

4. Key word / key phrase

Verse 2, "inheritance."

5. Key event / key person / key theme

Division of the rest of the land

6. Key thought

An inheritance gained from this world may be valueless.

7. Key thing to look out for

God keeps our inheritance for us in heaven.

8. Key Bible cross-reference

Verse 7. See Deuteronomy 18:1-8.

9. Key "by way of explanation"

Verse 3. After victory, the people had to settle in the land before they would experience it as theirs.

10. Key "Quotable Quote"

"It does not take great men to do great things; it only takes consecrated men."
Phillips Brooks

Joshua chapter 19

1. *Before and after*

Previous chapter: Chapter 18: Boundaries of Benjamin
Following chapter: Chapter 20: Six cities of refuge

2. *Analysis of chapter*

The lot of Simeon. (1-9)
The lot of Zebulun. (10-16)
The lot of Issachar, Asher, Naphtali, and Dan. (17-51)

3. *Key verse*

Verse 1: "And the second lot came forth to Simeon, even for the tribe of the children of Simeon according to their families: and their inheritance was within the inheritance of the children of Judah."

4. *Key word / key phrase*

Verse 49, "allotted portions."

5. *Key event / key person / key theme*

More territory assigned

6. *Key thought*

All our faculties are God's gifts.

7. *Key thing to look out for*

Any influence we have comes from God.

8. *Key Bible cross-reference*

Verse 49. See Numbers 13:30; 14:6.

9. *Key "by way of explanation"*

Verse 49. Joshua is the last one to receive any inheritance, which is most fitting for a servant of God.

10. *Key "Quotable Quote"*

"Make it a rule, and pray to God to help you to keep it, never, if possible, to lie down at night without being able to say: 'I have made one human being at least a little wiser, or a little happier, or at least a little better this day.'"
Charles Kingsley

Joshua chapter 20

1. *Before and after*

    Previous chapter: Chapter 19: Boundaries of seven tribes
    Following chapter: Chapter 21: The levitical cities selected

2. *Analysis of chapter*

    The law about the cities of refuge. (1-6)
    The cities appointed as refuges. (7-9)

3. *Key verse*

    Verse 2: "Speak to the children of Israel, saying, Appoint out for you cities of refuge, whereof I spake unto you by the hand of Moses."

4. *Key word / key phrase*

    Verse 2, "cities of refuge."

5. *Key event / key person / key theme*

    Cities of refuge

6. *Key thought*

    Revenge is never to be indulged in.

7. *Key thing to look out for*

    God cared for his people in countless different ways.

8. *Key Bible cross-reference*

    Verse 3. See Ruth 3:9; Psalm 19:14.

9. *Key "by way of explanation"*

    Verse 9. Foreigners were looked after by the people of Israel.

10. *Key "Quotable Quote"*

    "The more familiar we are with sickness or hunger, the greater will be our compassion for others who are sick or hungry."
    Bernard of Clairvaux

Joshua chapter 21

1. **Before and after**

   Previous chapter: Chapter 20: Six cities of refuge
   Following chapter: Chapter 22: The altar of witness

2. **Analysis of chapter**

   Cities for the Levites. (1-8)
   The cities allotted to the Levites. (9-42)
   God gave the land and rest to the Israelites, according to his promise. (43-45)

3. **Key verse**

   Verse 4: "And the lot came out for the families of the Kohathites"

4. **Key word / key phrase**

   Verse 8, "Levites."

5. **Key event / key person / key theme**

   Towns for the Levites

6. **Key thought**

   God never breaks any of his promises.

7. **Key thing to look out for**

   We need to appropriate God's promises.

8. **Key Bible cross-reference**

   Verses 43-45. See Genesis 15:18-21.

9. **Key "by way of explanation"**

   Verse 43-45. These verses are a summary of how God fulfilled his promise and
   provided land for the Israelites.

10. **Key "Quotable Quote"**

   "The stars may fall, but God's promises will stand and be fulfilled."
   J.I. Packer

Joshua chapter 22

1. *Before and after*

   Previous chapter: Chapter 21: Selecting the levitical cities
   Following chapter: Chapter 23: Reminders from history

2. *Analysis of chapter*

   Reuben and Gad, with the half tribe of Manasseh, dismissed to their homes. (1-9)
   They build an altar of testimony. (10-20)
   The answer of the Reubenites. (21-29)
   The children of Israel satisfied. (30-34)

3. *Key verse* ·

   Verse 1: "Then Joshua called the Reubenites, and the Gadites, and the half tribe of Manasseh . . ."

4. *Key word / key phrase*

   Verse 6, "sent them away."

5. *Key event / key person / key theme*

   Joshua sends the eastern tribes home

6. *Key thought*

   Nobody is beyond benefiting from a warning.

7. *Key thing to look out for*

   Experiencing God's presence is the greatest possible daily blessing.

8. *Key Bible cross-reference*

   Verse 12. See Deuteronomy 13:12-18; Judges 20.

9. *Key "by way of explanation"*

   Verse 5. Like Moses, Joshua knew that God needed to be loved from the heart.

10. *Key "Quotable Quote"*

    "I longed to be a flame of fire continually glowing in the divine service and building up of Christ's kingdom to my last and dying breath."
    David Brainerd

Joshua chapter 23

1. *Before and after*

Previous chapter: Chapter 22: The altar of witness
Following chapter: Chapter 24: Renewing the covenant, and deaths of Joshua and Eleazar

2. *Analysis of chapter*

Joshua's exhortation before his death. (1-10)
Joshua warns the people of idolatry. (11-16)

3. *Key verse*

Verse 2: "I am old and stricken in age . . ."

4. *Key word / key phrase*

Verse 2, "leaders."

5. *Key event / key person / key theme*

Joshua's farewell words to the leaders

6. *Key thought*

Leaders need leadership.

7. *Key thing to look out for*

The advice to rely on God's strength.

8. *Key Bible cross-reference*

Verse 6. See 1:7,8; 22:5.

9. *Key "by way of explanation"*

Verse 12. Joshua includes a severe warning in his encouraging last words.

10. *Key "Quotable Quote"*

"No gift is more precious than good advice."
Desiderius Erasmus

Joshua chapter 24

1. *Previous chapter*

Chapter 23: Reminders from history

2. *Analysis of chapter*

God's benefits to their fathers. (1-13)
Joshua renews the covenant between the people and God. (14-28)
Joshua's death, Joseph's bones buried, and the state of Israel. (29-33)

3. *Key verse*

Verse 29: "And it came to pass after these things, that Joshua the son of Nun, the servant of the LORD, died, being an hundred and ten years old."

4. *Key word / key phrase*

Verse 29, "died."

5. *Key event / key person / key theme*

Joshua is buried in the promised land

6. *Key thought*

View your life from the day after you are dead.

7. *Key thing to look out for*

We have only one life to live.

8. *Key Bible cross-reference*

Verse 22. See Deuteronomy 30:19.

9. *Key "by way of explanation"*

Verse 19. Joshua contrasts the people's inability to serve God in their own strength with God's wonderful character.

10. *Key "Quotable Quote"*

"A life spent in communion with God, is the pleasantest life in the world."
Matthew Henry, his last words

Judges

Judges chapter 1

1. **Following chapter**

   Chapter 2: God's judgment for not completing the conquest

2. **Analysis of chapter**

   Events among the tribes of Judah and Simeon. (1-8)
   Hebron and other cities taken. (9-20)
   The events among the other tribes. (21-36)

3. **Key verse**

   Verse 1: "Now after the death of Joshua it came to pass, that the children of Israel asked the LORD, saying, Who shall go up for us against the Canaanites first, to fight against them?"

4. **Key word / key phrase**

   Verse 8, "Jerusalem."

5. **Key event / key person / key theme**

   Jerusalem and Hebron conquered

6. **Key thought**

   God's people should have nothing to do with brutal practices.

7. **Key thing to look out for**

   Some of the practices of God's people are recorded as examples for us, others as warnings for us to heed.

8. **Key Bible cross-reference**

   Verse 20. See Numbers 14:24; Joshua 14:9-14.

9. **Key "by way of explanation"**

   Verse 8. Jerusalem was conquered but the Israelites did not occupy it until David reconquered it.

10. **Key "Quotable Quote"**

    "We can do nothing unless divine aid support us."
    Bonaventure

Judges chapter 2

1. **Before and after**

   Previous chapter: Chapter 1: Israel fails to complete the conquest
   Following chapter: Chapter 3: The southern campaign

2. **Analysis of chapter**

   The angel of the Lord rebukes the people. (1-5)
   The wickedness of the new generation after Joshua. (6-23)

3. **Key verse**

   Verse 4: "And it came to pass, when the angel of the LORD spake these words unto all the children of Israel, that the people lifted up their voice, and wept."

4. **Key word / key phrase**

   Verse 2, "yet you have disobeyed me."

5. **Key event / key person / key theme**

   The death of Joshua

6. **Key thought**

   There is no higher station in life than being God's servant.

7. **Key thing to look out for**

   The Israelites were constantly violating God's covenant, yet God never gave up on them.

8. **Key Bible cross-reference**

   Verse 8. See Isaiah 41:8,9; 42:1.

9. **Key "by way of explanation"**

   The judges were tribal leaders. Some of them led the people to victory over their enemies.

10. **Key "Quotable Quote"**

    "Beware of Christian activities instead of Christian being."
    Oswald Chambers

Judges chapter 3

1. Before and after

Previous chapter: Chapter 2: God's judgment for not completing the conquest

Following chapter: Chapter 4: The northern campaign

2. Analysis of chapter

The nations left to test Israel. (1-7)

Othniel delivers Israel. (8-11)

Ehud delivers Israel from Eglon. (12-30)

Shamgar delivers and judges Israel. (31)

3. Key verse

Verse 12: "And the children of Israel did evil again in the sight of the LORD: and the LORD strengthened Eglon the king of Moab against Israel, because they had done evil in the sight of the LORD."

4. Key word / key phrase

Verse 9,15 "they cried to the LORD."

5. Key event / key person / key theme

Othniel, Ehud

6. Key thought

God's people slowly settled down in the promised land, thanks to God's charismatic leaders.

7. Key thing to look out for

The results of doing evil.

8. Key Bible cross-reference

Verse 10. See 6:34; 1 Samuel 16:13.

9. Key "by way of explanation"

Verse 15. Because Ehud was left-handed he was able to conceal his dagger without anyone suspecting him of carrying his lethal weapon.

10. Key "Quotable Quote"

"We are each born into a world in which it is easy for us to do evil and hard for us to do good."

Bishop Kallistos Ware

Judges chapter 4

1. Before and after

Previous chapter: Chapter 3: The southern campaign
Following chapter: Chapter 5: Song of Deborah and Barak

2. Analysis of chapter

Israel again rebels, and is oppressed by Jabin. (1-3)
Deborah plans their deliverance with Barak. (4-9)
Sisera defeated. (10-16)
Sisera put to death by Jael. (17-24)

3. Key verse

Verse 4: "And Deborah, a prophetess, the wife of Lapidoth, she judged Israel at that time."

4. Key word / key phrase

Verse 6, "the Lord commands you."

5. Key event / key person / key theme

Judge Deborah

6. Key thought

God used men and women judges.

7. Key thing to look out for

God spoke through prophets and prophetesses.

8. Key Bible cross-reference

Verse 14. See 1 Samuel 8:20; Exodus 15:3.

9. Key "by way of explanation"

Chapter 4 celebrates victory over Sisera in prose and chapter 5 celebrates the same victory, but in a poem.

10. Key "Quotable Quote"

"I expect to pass through the world but once. Any good therefore that I can do, or any kindness or abilities that I can show to any fellow creature, let me do it now. Let me not defer or neglect it, for I shall not pass this way again."
William Penn

Judges chapter 5

1. Before and after

Previous chapter: Chapter 4: The northern campaign
Following chapter: Chapter 6: Gideon is called

2. Analysis of chapter

Praise and glory given to God. (1-5)
The distress and deliverance of Israel. (6-11)
Some commended, others censured. (12-23)
Sisera's mother disappointed. (24-31)

3. Key verse

Verse 1: "Then sang Deborah and Barak the son of Abinoam on that day . . ."

4. Key word / key phrase

Verse 31, "the land had peace."

5. Key event / key person / key theme

Victory

6. Key thought

Praise is given to the Lord, rather than to the people who fought.

7. Key thing to look out for

Singing God's praises gives an added dimension to saying God's praises.

8. Key Bible cross-reference

Verses 4-5. See Deuteronomy 33:2; Psalm 68:7,8.

9. Key "by way of explanation"

Verses 1-31. The Israelites frequently celebrated their victories in song. See
Exodus 15:1-18; Numbers 21:27-30.

10. Key "Quotable Quote"

"Sing lustily and with a good courage. Beware of singing as if you were half
dead, or half asleep; but lift up your voice with strength."
John Wesley

Judges chapter 6

1. Before and after

Previous chapter: Chapter 5: Song of Deborah and Barak
Following chapter: Chapter 7: Defeat of the Midianites

2. Analysis of chapter

Israel oppressed by Midianites. (1-6)
Israel rebuked by a prophet. (7-10)
Gideon told to deliver Israel. (11-24)
Gideon destroys Baal's altar. (25-32)
Signs given him. (33-40)

3. Key verse

Verse 11: "And there came an angel of the LORD, and sat under an oak which was in Ophrah, that pertained unto Joash the Abiezrite: and his son Gideon threshed wheat by the winepress, to hide it from the Midianites."

4. Key word / key phrase

Verse 14, "Go in the strength you have."

5. Key event / key person / key theme

After the Israelites had ignored God, he raised up a new leader to guide them back into his ways.

6. Key thought

God looks on the heart, not on outward appearances.

7. Key thing to look out for

Sometimes things have to be torn down before anything can be built up.

8. Key Bible cross-reference

Verse 25. See Exodus 34:13; Deuteronomy 7:5.

9. Key "by way of explanation"

Verse 15. God often called the lowly to serve him. See Genesis 25:23; 1 Samuel 9:21.

10. Key "Quotable Quote"

"The curse of much modern Christian work is its determination to preserve itself."
Oswald Chambers

Judges chapter 7

1. *Before and after*

Previous chapter: Chapter 6: Gideon is called
Following chapter: Chapter 8: Gideon as judge, and his death

2. *Analysis of chapter*

Gideon's army reduced. (1-8)
Gideon is encouraged. (9-15)
The defeat of the Midianites. (16-22)
The Ephraimites take Oreb and Zeeb. (23-25)

3. *Key verse*

Verse 8: "So the people took victuals in their hand, and their trumpets: and he sent all the rest of Israel every man unto his tent, and retained those three hundred men: and the host of Midian was beneath him in the valley."

4. *Key word / key phrase*

Verse 2, "that Israel may not boast."

5. *Key event / key person / key theme*

The Midianites are defeated by Gideon.

6. *Key thought*

Numbers do not have the final say in God's kingdom.

7. *Key thing to look out for*

One plus God is a majority.

8. *Key Bible cross-reference*

Verse 13. See 2 Kings 7:1.

9. *Key "by way of explanation"*

Verse 6. The point about the numbers being reduced to 300 is that this made it clear that the battle was won by God and not by the power of a vast army of Israelites.

10. *Key "Quotable Quote"*

"God's part is to put forth power; our part is to put forth faith."
Andrew A. Bonar

Judges chapter 8

1. Before and after

Previous chapter: Chapter 7: Defeat of the Midianites
Following chapter: Chapter 9: Abimelech

2. Analysis of chapter

Gideon pacifies the Ephraimites. (1-3)
Succoth and Penuel refuse to relieve Gideon. (4-12)
Succoth and Penuel punished. (13-17)
Gideon avenges his brethren. (18-21)
Gideon declines to govern, but allows idolatry. (22-28)
Gideon's death, Israel's ingratitude. (29-35)

3. Key verse

Verse 32: "And Gideon the son of Joash died in a good old age, and was buried in the sepulcher of Joash his father, in Ophrah of the Abiezrites."

4. Key word / key phrase

Verse 23, "The LORD will rule over you."

5. Key event / key person / key theme

The final defeat of the Midianites.

6. Key thought

Victories often come in stages.

7. Key thing to look out for

There are no spiritual victories where God is not given the glory.

8. Key Bible cross-reference

Verse 3. See Proverbs 15:1.

9. Key "by way of explanation"

Verse 28, "forty years" often represents a round number in the Bible, such as a generation.

10. Key "Quotable Quote"

"Be thou therefore ready for the conflict, if thou wilt have the victory."
Thomas à Kempis

Judges chapter 9

1. ### Before and after

    Previous chapter: Chapter 8: Gideon as judge, and his death
    Following chapter: Chapter 10: Israel sins

2. ### Analysis of chapter

    Abimelech murders his brethren, and is made king. (1-6)
    Jotham rebukes the Shechemites. (7-21)
    The Shechemites conspire against Abimelech. (22-29)
    Abimelech destroys Shechem. (30-49)
    Abimelech is killed. (50-57)

3. ### Key verse

    Verse 56: "Thus God rendered the wickedness of Abimelech, which he did unto his father, in slaying his seventy brethren."

4. ### Key word / key phrase

    Verse 56. "God repaid the wickedness."

5. ### Key event / key person / key theme

    Abimelech received God's punishment for his wicked ways in his lifetime.

6. ### Key thought

    Many evil people become rulers.

7. ### Key thing to look out for

    God does not abdicate just because an ungodly person is in power.

8. ### Key Bible cross-reference

    Verse 15. See Isaiah 30:2,3; Lamentations 4:20.

9. ### Key "by way of explanation"

    Verse 1-57. Abimelech and Gideon can be studied together as they are such contrasting characters.

10. ### Key "Quotable Quote"

    "Those who will not be governed by God, will be ruled by tyrants."
    William Penn

Judges chapter 10

1. Before and after

Previous chapter: Chapter 9: Abimelech
Following chapter: Chapter 11: Jephthah and his daughter

2. Analysis of chapter

Tola and Jair judge Israel. (1-5)
The Philistines and Ammonites oppress Israel. (6-9)
Israel's repentance. (10-18)

3. Key verse

Verse 6: "And the children of Israel did evil again in the sight of the LORD, and
served Baalim, and Ashtaroth, and the gods of Syria, and the gods of Zidon,
and the gods of Moab, and the gods of the children of Ammon, and the gods
of the Philistines, and forsook the LORD, and served not him."

4. Key word / key phrase

Verse 16, "foreign gods."

5. Key event / key person / key theme

More judges

6. Key thought

Rulers come and go, but God reigns forever.

7. Key thing to look out for

Evangelism needs to take place in times of war as well as in times of peace.

8. Key Bible cross-reference

Verse 6. See 1 Kings 11:7; Leviticus 18:21.

9. Key "by way of explanation"

Verse 11. The Lord is always aware of any unfaithfulness.

10. Key "Quotable Quote"

"When the sovereign God brings us to nothing, it is to reroute our lives, not
to end them."
Charles R. Swindoll

Judges chapter 11

1. ### Before and after

   Previous chapter: Chapter 10: Israel sins
   Following chapter: Chapter 12: Ibzan, Elon, and Abdon

2. ### Analysis of chapter

   Jephtah and the Gileadites. (1-11)
   He attempts to make peace. (12-28)
   Jephthah's vow. He vanquishes the Ammonites. (29-40)

3. ### Key verse

   Verse 1: "Now Jephthah the Gileadite was a mighty man of valor."

4. ### Key word / key phrase

   Verse 130 "vow."

5. ### Key event / key person / key theme

   Jephthah

6. ### Key thought

   Righteousness exalts a nation.

7. ### Key thing to look out for

   Evil never has the last word.

8. ### Key Bible cross-reference

   Verse 11. See 1 Samuel 11:15; Rehoboam, 1 Kings s12:1.

9. ### Key "by way of explanation"

   Verse 34. Dancing women often greeted successful armies as they returned
   home. See Exodus 15:20.

10. ### Key "Quotable Quote"

    "Suppose a nation in some distant region should take the Bible for their only
    Law Book, and every member should regulate his conduct by the precepts
    there exhibited . . . What a paradise would this region be!"
    John Adams

Judges chapter 12

1. Before and after

Previous chapter: Chapter 11: Jephthah and his daughter
Following chapter: Chapter 13: Samson's miraculous birth

2. Analysis of chapter

Ephraimites quarrel with Jephthah. (1-7)
Ibzan, Elon, and Abdon judge Israel. (8-15)

3. Key verse

Verse 7: "And Jephthah judged Israel six years. Then died Jephthah the Gileadite, and was buried in one of the cities of Gilead."

4. Key word / key phrase

Verse 1, "men of Ephraim."

5. Key event / key person / key theme

Jephthah and the Ephraimites

6. Key thought

Peter was told that his accent gave him away and that it showed that he was a friend of Jesus.

7. Key thing to look out for

How we speak can bring glory to God.

8. Key Bible cross-reference

Verse 1. See 14:15; 20:48.

9. Key "by way of explanation"

Verse 6. By listening to how people pronounced the word "Shibboleth" you could tell which region they came from.

10. Key "Quotable Quote"

"Happy the man whose words come from the Holy Spirit and not from himself!"
Anthony of Padua

Judges chapter 13

1. ### Before and after

    Previous chapter: Chapter 12: Ibzan, Elon, and Abdon
    Following chapter: Chapter 14: Samson's sinful marriage

2. ### Analysis of chapter

    The Philistines, Samson announced. (1-7)
    The angel appears to Manoah. (8-14)
    Manoah's sacrifice. (15-23)
    Birth of Samson. (24,25)

3. ### Key verse

    Verse 24: "And the woman bare a son, and called his name Samson: and the child grew, and the LORD blessed him."

4. ### Key word / key phrase

    Verse 1, "Philistines."

5. ### Key event / key person / key theme

    The birth of Samson

6. ### Key thought

    Every birth is a miracle.

7. ### Key thing to look out for

    God has loved us from before we were born.

8. ### Key Bible cross-reference

    Verse 5. See 1 Samuel 7:10-14; 2 Samuel 5:17-25; 8:1.

9. ### Key "by way of explanation"

    Verse 5. "Nazirite" comes from a word meaning "dedicated." Samon's Nazirite calling differed from the vow described in Numbers 6:1-21 in that his was not voluntary, and was to be for a lifetime.

10. ### Key "Quotable Quote"

    "The good pleasure of God is an act of the divine will freely and effectively determining all things."
    William Ames

Judges chapter 14

1. *Before and after*

   Previous chapter: Chapter 13: Samson's miraculous birth
   Following chapter: Chapter 15: Samson as judge

2. *Analysis of chapter*

   Samson desires a wife of the Philistines. (1-4)
   Samson kills a lion. (5-9)
   Samson's riddle. (10-20)

3. *Key verse*

   Verse 1: "And Samson went down to Timnath, and saw a woman in Timnath of the daughters of the Philistines."

4. *Key word / key phrase*

   Verse 2, "wife."

5. *Key event / key person / key theme*

   Samson's marriage

6. *Key thought*

   Marriages need a better foundation than this one.

7. *Key thing to look out for*

   Countless marriages between Christians also break up.

8. *Key Bible cross-reference*

   Verse 6. See 13:25; 14:19; 15:14.

9. *Key "by way of explanation"*

   Verse 12. Riddles were often posed at feasts as part of the entertainment.

10. *Key "Quotable Quote"*

    "Temptations, when we meet them at first, are as the lion that reared upon Samson; but if we overcome them, the next time we see them we shall find a nest of honey within them."
    John Bunyan

Judges chapter 15

1. **Before and after**

   Previous chapter: Chapter 14: Samson's sinful marriage
   Following chapter: Chapter 16: Samson's decline and fall

2. **Analysis of chapter**

   Samson is denied his wife. He kills the Philistines. (1-8)
   Samson kills a thousand of the Philistines with a jaw-bone. (9-17)
   His distress from thirst. (18-20)

3. **Key verse**

   Verse 16: "And Samson said, With the jawbone of an ass, heaps upon heaps, with the jaw of an ass have I slain a thousand men."

4. **Key word / key phrase**

   Verse 3, "get even with."

5. **Key event / key person / key theme**

   Samson takes his revenge on the Philistines.

6. **Key thought**

   Revenge never succeeds in pleasing God.

7. **Key thing to look out for**

   Taking revenge usually only increases hatred between the opposing factions.

8. **Key Bible cross-reference**

   Verse 15. See 3:31.

9. **Key "by way of explanation"**

   Verse 19. God provided water for Samson just as he had for the Israelites in the desert.

10. **Key "Quotable Quote"**

   "Let us learn humility from Christ, humiliation from David, and from Peter to cry over what has happened; but let us also learn to avoid the despair of Samson, Judas, and the wisest of men, Solomon."
   Hesychois of Sinai

Judges chapter 16

1. *Before and after*

Previous chapter: Chapter 15: Samson as judge
Following chapter: Chapter 17: An example of personal idolatry

2. *Analysis of chapter*

Samson's escape from Gaza. (1-3)
Samson enticed to reveal the source of his strength. (4-17)
The Philistines take Samson, and put out his eyes. (18-21)
Samson's strength is renewed. (22-24)
He destroys many of the Philistines. (25-31)

3. *Key verse*

Verse 4: "And it came to pass afterward, that he loved a woman in the valley of Sorek, whose name was Delilah."

4. *Key word / key phrase*

Verse 15, "day after day."

5. *Key event / key person / key theme*

Samson and Delilah

6. *Key thought*

Not to know that God's Spirit had left Samson was a terrible state to have arrived at.

7. *Key thing to look out for*

Samson had great strengths and great weaknesses.

8. *Key Bible cross-reference*

Verse 21. See 1 Samuel 11:2; 2 Kings 25:7.

9. *Key "by way of explanation"*

Verses 19,20. From these verses it is clear that God was the source of Samson's strength.

10. *Key "Quotable Quote"*

"As Samson fell asleep in Delilah's lap, so many have fallen so fast asleep in the lap of prosperity, that they have never awaked till they have been in hell."
Thomas Watson

Judges chapter 17

1. **Before and after**

    Previous chapter: Chapter 16: Samson's decline and fall
    Following chapter: Chapter 18: An example of tribal idolatry

2. **Analysis of chapter**

    The beginning of idolatry in Israel, Micah and his mother. (1-6)
    Micah hires a Levite to be his priest. (7-13)

3. **Key verse**

    Verse 5: "And the man Micah had an house of gods, and made an ephod, and teraphim, and consecrated one of his sons, who became his priest."

4. **Key word / key phrase**

    Verse 6, "everyone did as he saw fit."

5. **Key event / key person / key theme**

    Micah

6. **Key thought**

    Modern forms of idolatry are easy to take on board.

7. **Key thing to look out for**

    John told his readers, in the last verse of the last chapter of his first letter, to beware of idols.

8. **Key Bible cross-reference**

    Verse 6. See 18:1; 19:1; 21:25.

9. **Key "by way of explanation"**

    Verse 5. This verse indicates how low the Israelites had sunk. They made and worshiped idols.

10. **Key "Quotable Quote"**

    "I confess Jesus Christ, the son of God, with my whole being. Those whom you call gods are idols; they are made by hands."
    Alban, first British martyr

Judges chapter 18

1. Before and after

Previous chapter: Chapter 17: An example of personal idolatry
Following chapter: Chapter 19: Personal and tribal immorality

2. Analysis of chapter

The Danites seek to enlarge their inheritance, and rob Micah. (1-31)

3. Key verse

Verse 31: "And they set them up Micah's graven image, which he made, all the time that the house of God was in Shiloh."

4. Key word / key phrase

Verse 1, "had no king."

5. Key event / key person / key theme

Micah and the tribe of Dan

6. Key thought

If a man is essentially evil he will do little good no matter how highly he is promoted.

7. Key thing to look out for

Evil can rule individuals as well as groups.

8. Key Bible cross-reference

Verse 31. See Joshua 18:1.

9. Key "by way of explanation"

Verse 31. Shiloh was eventually destroyed: see Psalm 78:60; Jeremiah 7:12,14; 26:6.

10. Key "Quotable Quote"

"Someone once asked Billy Graham, 'If Christianity is valid, why is there so much evil in the world?' Billy Graham replied, 'With so much soap, why are there so many dirty people in the world? Christianity, like soap, must be personally applied if it is to make a difference in our lives.'"
Billy Graham

Judges chapter 19

1. **Before and after**

   Previous chapter: Chapter 18: An example of tribal idolatry
   Following chapter: Chapter 20: War between Israel and Dan

2. **Analysis of chapter**

   The wickedness of the men of Gibeah. (1-30)

3. **Key verse**

   Verse 1: "And it came to pass in those days, when there was no king in Israel, that there was a certain Levite sojourning on the side of mount Ephraim, who took to him a concubine out of Bethlehemjudah."

4. **Key word / key phrase**

   Verse 23, "vile."

5. **Key event / key person / key theme**

   A Levite and his concubine

6. **Key thought**

   If God is left out of any society it is doomed.

7. **Key thing to look out for**

   Without God men live like the animals in the jungle.

8. **Key Bible cross-reference**

   Verse 14. See Hosea 9:9; 10:9.

9. **Key "by way of explanation"**

   This chapter illustrates the moral degradation to which the Israelites had sunk.

10. **Key "Quotable Quote"**

    "Back to the Bible or back to the jungle."
    Luis Palau

Judges chapter 20

1. *Before and after*

Previous chapter: Chapter 19: Personal and tribal immorality
Following chapter: Chapter 21: The need for a king

2. *Analysis of chapter*

The tribe of Benjamin nearly wiped out. (1-48)

3. *Key verse*

Verse 1: "Then all the children of Israel went out, and the congregation was gathered together as one man, from Dan even to Beersheba, with the land of Gilead, unto the LORD in Mizpeh."

4. *Key word / key phrase*

Verse 18, "enquired of God."

5. *Key event / key person / key theme*

War against the Benjamites

6. *Key thought*

All wrongs may not be put right in our lifetime.

7. *Key thing to look out for*

In heaven there will not be room for any injustice.

8. *Key Bible cross-reference*

Verse 16. See 3:15; 1 Samuel 17:49.

9. *Key "by way of explanation"*

Verse 1. Speaking about "Dan to Beersheba" was a way of referring to the whole of the country, from its northern tip to its most southerly point.

10. *Key "Quotable Quote"*

"Christianity is a warfare, and Christians are spiritual soldiers."
Robert Southwell

Judges chapter 21

1. **Previous chapter**

   Chapter 20: War between Israel and Dan

2. **Analysis of chapter**

   The Israelites mourn for the Benjamites. (1-25)

3. **Key verse**

   Verse 25: "In those days there was no king in Israel: every man did that which was right in his own eyes."

4. **Key word / key phrase**

   Verse 25, "as he saw fit."

5. **Key event / key person / key theme**

   Wives for the tribe of Benjamin

6. **Key thought**

   Evil may be eradicated but it often leaves a terrible legacy.

7. **Key thing to look out for**

   The fight against evil never stops.

8. **Key Bible cross-reference**

   Verse 2. See 20:18,26,27.

9. **Key "by way of explanation"**

   Verse 25. The last verse of this book shows how rudderless the Israelites were. They should have been satisfied with God as their ruler.

10. **Key "Quotable Quote"**

    "Christianity introduced no new forms of government, but a new spirit, which totally transformed the old ones."
    John E.E D. Acton

Ruth

Ruth chapter 1

1. **Following chapter**

   Chapter 2: Ruth meets Boaz

2. **Analysis of chapter**

   Elimelech and his sons die in the land of Moab. (1-5)
   Naomi returns home. (6-14)
   Orpah stays behind, but Ruth goes with Naomi. (15-18)
   They come to Bethlehem. (19-22)

3. **Key verse**

   Verse 16: "And Ruth said, Entreat me not to leave thee, or to return from following after thee: for whither thou goest, I will go; and where thou lodgest, I will lodge: thy people shall be my people, and thy God my God."

4. **Key word / key phrase**

   Verse 2, "Naomi."

5. **Key event / key person / key theme**

   Tragedy wiping out Naomi's family

6. **Key thought**

   Ruth was not an Israelite.

7. **Key thing to look out for**

   Ruth's selflessness was amazing.

8. **Key Bible cross-reference**

   Verse 22. See 2:2,6,21; 4:5,10.

9. **Key "by way of explanation"**

   Verse 1. This account of Ruth's life is set in the time of the judges.

10. **Key "Quotable Quote"**

    "Set a high value on spontaneous kindness."
    Samuel Johnson

Ruth chapter 2

1. Before and after

Previous chapter: Chapter 1: Ruth comes to Bethlehem
Following chapter: Chapter 3: Ruth claims the protection of the kinsmen

2. Analysis of chapter

Ruth gleans in the field of Boaz. (1-3)
The kindness of Boaz to Ruth. (4-16)
Ruth returns to her mother-in-law. (17-23)

3. Key verse

Verse 12: "The LORD recompense thy work, and a full reward be given thee of the LORD God of Israel, under whose wings thou art come to trust."

4. Key word / key phrase

Verse 20, "kindness."

5. Key event / key person / key theme

Ruth works in Boaz's field

6. Key thought

There is no such thing as a "chance" meeting.

7. Key thing to look out for

God can bring hope out of every desperate situation.

8. Key Bible cross-reference

Verse 1. See Matthew 1:5; Luke 3:32.

9. Key "by way of explanation"

Verse 20, "kinsman-redeemers." Such people could redeem a slave who had been sold into slavery or redeem land that a poor relative had been forced to sell.

10. Key "Quotable Quote"

"No creature that deserved redemption would need to be redeemed."
C.S. Lewis

Ruth chapter 3

1. *Before and after*

Previous chapter: Chapter 2: Ruth meets Boaz
Following chapter: Chapter 4: Boaz marries Ruth

2. *Analysis of chapter*

The directions given to Ruth by Naomi. (1-5)
Boaz acknowledges the duty of a kinsman. (6-13)
Ruth's return to her mother-in-law. (14-18)

3. *Key verse*

Verse 13: "Tarry this night, and it shall be in the morning, that if he will perform unto thee the part of a kinsman, well; let him do the kinsman's part: but if he will not do the part of a kinsman to thee, then will I do the part of a kinsman to thee, as the LORD liveth: lie down until the morning."

4. *Key word / key phrase*

Verse 9, "kinsman-redeemer."

5. *Key event / key person / key theme*

Ruth finds a husband.

6. *Key thought*

Ruth had never dreamed that she would find a husband in the foreign land of her mother-in-law.

7. *Key thing to look out for*

God's loving care for those who trust him.

8. *Key Bible cross-reference*

Verse 3. See Isaiah 9:3; 16:9,10.

9. *Key "by way of explanation"*

Verse 9. This was probably an indirect way of asking someone to marry you. See Ezekiel 38:13-30.

10. *Key "Quotable Quote"*

"God moves in a mysterious way
   his wonders to perform;
he plants his footsteps in the sea
   And rides upon the storm."
William Cowper

Ruth chapter 4

1. **Previous chapter**

   Chapter 3: Ruth claims the protection of the kinsmen

2. **Analysis of chapter**

   The kinsman refuses to redeem Ruth's inheritance. (1-8)
   Boaz marries Ruth. (9-12)
   Birth of Obed. (13-22)

3. **Key verse**

   Verse 22: "And Obed begat Jesse, and Jesse begat David."

4. **Key word / key phrase**

   Verse 13, "wife."

5. **Key event / key person / key theme**

   Boaz marries Ruth.

6. **Key thought**

   God's providence is clear throughout these chapters.

7. **Key thing to look out for**

   The book ends with the most amazing genealogy.

8. **Key Bible cross-reference**

   Verses 18-22. See Matthew 1:3-6; Luke 3:31-33.

9. **Key "by way of explanation"**

   Verses 18-22. Business was conducted at the town gate.

10. **Key "Quotable Quote"**

    "Man proposes, but God disposes."
    Thomas à Kempis

1 Samuel and 2 Samuel

1 Samuel chapter 1

1. ### Following chapter

   Chapter 2: Eli and his family

2. ### Analysis of chapter

   Elkanah and his family. (1-8)
   Hannah's prayer. (9-18)
   Samuel, Hannah presents him to the Lord. (19-28)

3. ### Key verse

   Verse 11: "And she vowed a vow, and said, O LORD of hosts, if thou wilt indeed look on the affliction of thine handmaid, and remember me, and not forget thine handmaid, but wilt give unto thine handmaid a man child, then I will give him unto the LORD all the days of his life, and there shall no razor come upon his head."

4. ### Key word / key phrase

   Verse 10, "Hannah wept and prayed."

5. ### Key event / key person / key theme

   The birth of Samuel

6. ### Key thought

   Here is another example of God's power to do the seemingly impossible.

7. ### Key thing to look out for

   Hannah's response to suffering and to blessing.

8. ### Key Bible cross-reference

   Verse 21. See Leviticus 7:16; Psalm 50:14.

9. ### Key "by way of explanation"

   Verse 3. At "Shiloh" the ark of the covenant was kept. See Joshua 18:1; Judges 21:19.

10. ### Key "Quotable Quote"

    "*Nil sine Numine*, Nothing without providence."
    Motto of the State of Colorado

1 Samuel chapter 2

1. *Before and after*

> Previous chapter: Chapter 1: Hannah's prayer and the birth of Samuel
> Following chapter: Chapter 3: The call of Samuel

2. *Analysis of chapter*

> Hannah's song of thanksgiving. (1-10)
> The wickedness of Eli's sons, Samuel's ministry. (11-26)
> The prophecy against Eli's family. (27-36)

3. *Key verse*

> Verse 1: "And Hannah prayed, and said, My heart rejoiceth in the LORD, mine horn is exalted in the LORD: my mouth is enlarged over mine enemies; because I rejoice in thy salvation."

4. *Key word / key phrase*

> Verse 1, "prayed."

5. *Key event / key person / key theme*

> Hannah's prayer

6. *Key thought*

> Hannah began her prayer by rejoicing in the Lord.

7. *Key thing to look out for*

> Hannah's reasons for praising God.

8. *Key Bible cross-reference*

> Verse 1. See Psalm 72:20.

9. *Key "by way of explanation"*

> Verse 1. As there are a number of similarities between this prayer and that of Mary's, see Luke 1:46-55, it is unsurprising that it has been called the "Magnificat of the Old Testament."

10. *Key "Quotable Quote"*

> "You can do more than pray after you've prayed, but you cannot do more than pray until you have prayed."
> John Bunyan

1 Samuel chapter 3

1. *Before and after*

Previous chapter: Chapter 2: Eli and his family
Following chapter: Chapter 4: The Philistines capture the covenant box (the ark)

2. *Analysis of chapter*

The word of the Lord first revealed to Samuel. (1-10)
God tells Samuel about the destruction of Eli's house. (11-18)
Samuel established to be a prophet. (19-21)

3. *Key verse*

Verse 10: "And the LORD came, and stood, and called as at other times, Samuel, Samuel. Then Samuel answered, Speak; for thy servant heareth."

4. *Key word / key phrase*

Verse 1, "the word of the Lord was rare."

5. *Key event / key person / key theme*

Samuel's call

6. *Key thought*

God's call often goes unrecognized and is more often recognized, than followed.

7. *Key thing to look out for*

Verses 12,13. The judgment against Eli's family did not come without prior warning.

8. *Key Bible cross-reference*

Verse 3. See Exodus 27:20,21; 30:7,8.

9. *Key "by way of explanation"*

Verse 1. Throughout the period of the judges the word of the Lord did appear to be "rare" as we only know of two prophets. See Judges 4:4; 6:8.

10. *Key "Quotable Quote"*

"Christian spirituality begins with listening to God call us, heal us, forgive us."
Eugene H. Peterson

1 Samuel chapter 4

1. Before and after

Previous chapter: Chapter 3: The call of Samuel
Following chapter: Chapter 5: The covenant box in the land of the Philistines

2. Analysis of chapter

The Israelites overcome by the Philistines. (1-9)
The ark taken. (10,11)
The death of Eli. (12-18)
The birth of Ichabod. (19-22)

3. Key verse

Verse 11: "And the ark of God was taken."

4. Key word / key phrase

Verse 2, "defeated."

5. Key event / key person / key theme

The death of Eli

6. Key thought

Eli's children did not follow in the ways of their godly father.

7. Key thing to look out for

Eli must take some of the blame for his wayward children.

8. Key Bible cross-reference

Verse 12. This describes signs of grief and mourning. See Joshua 7:6;
2 Samuel 1:2.

9. Key "by way of explanation"

Verse 18. The death of Eli brings an era to a close. See Joshua 24:29,31;
2 Samuel 7:11.

10. Key "Quotable Quote"

"People who really want help may attack you if you help them. Help them
anyway."
Mother Teresa of Calcutta

1 Samuel chapter 5

1. *Before and after*

Previous chapter: Chapter 4: The Philistines capture the covenant box
Following chapter: Chapter 6: The return of the covenant box

2. *Analysis of chapter*

Dagon is broken before the ark. (1-5)
The Philistine killed. (6-12)

3. *Key verse*

Verse 4: "Dagon was fallen upon his face to the ground before the ark of the
LORD."

4. *Key word / key phrase*

Verse 1, "ark."

5. *Key event / key person / key theme*

The ark with the Philistines

6. *Key thought*

God is stronger than evil.

7. *Key thing to look out for*

If God is against us it does not matter who is for us.

8. *Key Bible cross-reference*

Verse 2. See Judges 16:21,23,26.

9. *Key "by way of explanation"*

Verse 6. God would not allow the Philistines to think that their capture of the
ark meant that they had power over the Israelites.

10. *Key "Quotable Quote"*

"Power is never good, unless the one who has it is good."
King Alfred

1 Samuel chapter 6

1. *Before and after*

Previous chapter: Chapter 5: The covenant box in the land of the Philistines
Following chapter: Chapter 7: Samuel judges Israel

2. *Analysis of chapter*

The Philistines decide to send back the ark. (1-9)
They bring it to Bethshemesh. (10-18)
The people killed for looking into the ark. (19-21)

3. *Key verse*

Verse 1: "And the ark of the LORD was in the country of the Philistines seven months."

4. *Key word / key phrase*

Verse 20, "the presence of the Lord."

5. *Key event / key person / key theme*

The ark is returned to Israel

6. *Key thought*

What if God still punished us today for our irreverence, as he did in verse 19?

7. *Key thing to look out for*

Even non-believers have consciences and often know when they have done wrong.

8. *Key Bible cross-reference*

Verse 2. See Deuteronomy 18:10; Isaiah 2:6; Ezekiel 21:21.

9. *Key "by way of explanation"*

Verse 6. God's action among the Egyptians was known about far and wide.

10. *Key "Quotable Quote"*

"God's created beings cannot help without him, but he can help without them."
Matthew Henry

1 Samuel chapter 7

1. *Before and after*

    Previous chapter: Chapter 6: The return of the covenant box
    Following chapter: Chapter 8: The people demand a king

2. *Analysis of chapter*

    The ark moved to Kiriath Jearim. (1-4)
    The Israelites solemnly repent. (5,6)
    The Lord defeats the Philistines. (7-12)
    They are subdued, Samuel judges Israel. (13-17)

3. *Key verse*

    Verse 1: "And the men of Kirjathjearim came, and fetched up the ark of the
    LORD"

4. *Key word / key phrase*

    Verse 2, "mourned."

5. *Key event / key person / key theme*

    Samuel rules Israel.

6. *Key thought*

    Samuel gives a clear choice in verse 4.

7. *Key thing to look out for*

    The Israelites were so fearful that they asked Samuel to pray for them.

8. *Key Bible cross-reference*

    Verse 3. See 12:10; Judges 2:13; 3:7.

9. *Key "by way of explanation"*

    Verse 6. This was a symbolic way of showing deep repentance.

10. *Key "Quotable Quote"*

    "The desire to rule is the mother of heresies."
    John Chrysostom

1 Samuel chapter 8

1. Before and after

Previous chapter: Chapter 7: Samuel judges Israel
Following chapter: Chapter 9: Saul is chosen and anointed king

2. Analysis of chapter

The evil government of Samuel's sons. (1-3)
The Israelites ask for a king. (4-9)
The behavior of their future king. (10-22)

3. Key verse

Verse 6: "Give us a king to judge us."

4. Key word / key phrase

Verse 6, "king."

5. Key event / key person / key theme

To choose a king means to choose trouble.

6. Key thought

It is clear that asking for a king meant that the Israelites were rejecting God.

7. Key thing to look out for

Rejecting good advice is most unwise.

8. Key Bible cross-reference

Verse 18. See 1 Kings 12:4; Jeremiah 22:13-17.

9. Key "by way of explanation"

Verse 5. The Israelites longed to be like the surrounding nations. This motivated their request for a king.

10. Key "Quotable Quote"

"God considers not the action, but the spirit of the action."
Peter Abelard

1 Samuel chapter 9

1. Before and after

> Previous chapter: Chapter 8: The people demand a king
> Following chapter: Chapter 10: Saul is acclaimed as king

2. Analysis of chapter

> Saul is brought to Samuel. (1-10)
> Samuel is told about Saul. (11-17)
> Samuel's treatment of Saul. (18-27)

3. Key verse

> Verse 2: "And he had a son, whose name was Saul, a choice young man, and a goodly: and there was not among the children of Israel a goodlier person than he: from his shoulders and upward he was higher than any of the people."

4. Key word / key phrase

> Verse 2, "an impressive young man."

5. Key event / key person / key theme

> Samuel anoints Saul.

6. Key thought

> Samuel was known as "the man of God."

7. Key thing to look out for

> Who would have thought that Saul could end up being such an evil person?

8. Key Bible cross-reference

> Verse 12. See Leviticus 26:30.

9. Key "by way of explanation"

> Verse 16. Although priests were also anointed the phase "the anointed of the Lord" now referred to the king.

10. Key "Quotable Quote"

> "It is evidently a falling away from the faith, and a proof of great presumption, to neglect any part of what is written, or to introduce anything that is not written in the Scriptures."
> Basil

1 Samuel chapter 10

1. Before and after

Previous chapter: Chapter 9: Saul is chosen and anointed king
Following chapter: Chapter 11: Saul defeats the Ammonites

2. Analysis of chapter

Samuel anoints Saul. (1-8)
Saul prophesies. (9-16)
Saul chosen king. (17-27)

3. Key verse

Verse 1: "Then Samuel took a vial of oil, and poured it upon his head."

4. Key word / key phrase

Verse 9, "God changed Saul's heart."

5. Key event / key person / key theme

Saul is made king.

6. Key thought

Settling for second best is never a good idea.

7. Key thing to look out for

Some people, verse 27, can never be satisfied.

8. Key Bible cross-reference

Verse 24. See 2 Samuel 16:16.

9. Key "by way of explanation"

Verse 25. Samuel tried to ensure that Saul's reign would not be incompatible with God's rule over his people.

10. Key "Quotable Quote"

"I have never met a soul who has set out to satisfy the Lord and has not been satisfied himself."
Watchman Nee

1 Samuel chapter 11

1. *Before and after*

Previous chapter: Chapter 10: Saul is acclaimed as king
Following chapter: Chapter 12: Samuel speaks to the people

2. *Analysis of chapter*

Jabesh Gilead delivered. (1-11)
Saul confirmed in his kingdom. (12-15)

3. *Key verse*

Verse 15: "And all the people went to Gilgal; and there they made Saul king before the LORD in Gilgal."

4. *Key word / key phrase*

Verse 14, "reaffirm the kingship."

5. *Key event / key person / key theme*

Saul is confirmed as king.

6. *Key thought*

Spiritual power only comes from the Lord.

7. *Key thing to look out for*

Without the Spirit there is no spiritual life.

8. *Key Bible cross-reference*

Verse 6. See 10:6,10; Judges 14:6.

9. *Key "by way of explanation"*

Verses 14,15. Samuel is affirming the Lord's rule over Saul.

10. *Key "Quotable Quote"*

"The means by which we live have outdistanced the ends for which we live. Our scientific power has outrun our spiritual power. We have guided missiles and misguided men."
Martin Luther King, Jr.

1 Samuel chapter 12

1. **Before and after**

   Previous chapter: Chapter 11: Saul defeats the Ammonites
   Following chapter: Chapter 13: War against the Philistines

2. **Analysis of chapter**

   Samuel testifies his integrity. (1-5)
   Samuel reproves the people. (6-15)
   Thunder sent in harvest time. (16-25)

3. **Key verse**

   Verse 1: "And Samuel said unto all Israel, Behold, I have hearkened unto your voice in all that ye said unto me, and have made a king over you."

4. **Key word / key phrase**

   Verse 7, "Confront."

5. **Key event / key person / key theme**

   Samuel's farewell speech

6. **Key thought**

   Breaking God's covenant always brings down God's judgment.

7. **Key thing to look out for**

   The people were in no mood to listen to Samuel's timely warnings.

8. **Key Bible cross-reference**

   Verse 14. See Exodus 19:5,6; Joshua 24:20.

9. **Key "by way of explanation"**

   Verse 25. Samuel warned the people that if they broke God's covenant they themselves would be broken by God.

10. **Key "Quotable Quote"**

   "Where there is charity and wisdom, there is neither fear nor ignorance."
   Francis of Assisi

1 Samuel chapter 13

1. Before and after

Previous chapter: Chapter 12: Samuel speaks to the people
Following chapter: Chapter 14: Jonathan and the Philistine defeat

2. Analysis of chapter

The invasion of the Philistines. (1-7)
Saul sacrifices. He is reproved by Samuel. (8-14)
The policy of the Philistines. (15-23)

3. Key verse

Verse 9: "And Saul said, Bring hither a burnt offering to me, and peace offerings. And he offered the burnt offering."

4. Key word / key phrase

Verse 19, "blacksmith."

5. Key event / key person / key theme

War against the Philistines

6. Key thought

Saul and Jonathan make a great team.

7. Key thing to look out for

Saul knew that he had acted wrongly, but showed no sign of repentance.

8. Key Bible cross-reference

Verse 13. See 2 Samuel 24:10.

9. Key "by way of explanation"

Verse 19. If you had a blacksmith it meant you had the great advantage of knowing about how to make weapons of war from iron.

10. Key "Quotable Quote"

"Whoever delays his repentance does in effect pawn his soul with the devil."
Thomas Manton

1 Samuel chapter 14

1. **Before and after**

    Previous chapter: Chapter 13: War against the Philistines
    Following chapter: Chapter 15: War against Amalek, and rejection of Saul as king

2. **Analysis of chapter**

    Jonathan attacks the Philistines. (1-15)
    Their defeat. (16-23)
    Saul forbids the people to eat until evening. (24-35)
    Jonathan pointed out by lot. (36-46)
    Saul's family. (47-52)

3. **Key verse**

    Verse 13: "And Jonathan climbed up upon his hands and upon his feet, and his armor bearer after him: and they fell before Jonathan; and his armor bearer slew after him."

4. **Key word / key phrase**

    Verse 13, "climbed."

5. **Key event / key person / key theme**

    Jonathan acts courageously.

6. **Key thought**

    Saul is motivated by a personal vendetta more than by the glory of God.

7. **Key thing to look out for**

    Saul reveals that he does not have the right character to be a good king.

8. **Key Bible cross-reference**

    Verse 41. See 10:20,21; Joshua 7:14-18.

9. **Key "by way of explanation"**

    Verse 24. Saul's order that his men should fast before a battle only weakened them for the fight.

10. **Key "Quotable Quote"**

    "If I take care of my character, my reputation will take care of itself."
    Dwight Moody

1 Samuel chapter 15

1. *Before and after*

Previous chapter: Chapter 14: Jonathan and the Philistine defeat
Following chapter: Chapter 16: God anoints David as king

2. *Analysis of chapter*

Saul sent to destroy Amalek. (1-9)
Saul excuses and commends himself. (10-23)
Saul's imperfect confession. (24-31)
Agag put to death, Samuel and Saul part. (32-35)

3. *Key verse*

Verse 3: "Now go and smite Amalek, and utterly destroy all that they have."

4. *Key word / key phrase*

Verse 22, "obey."

5. *Key event / key person / key theme*

The Lord rejects Saul as king.

6. *Key thought*

If we reject God's word God rejects us.

7. *Key thing to look out for*

Rebellion and divination are put on the same level.

8. *Key Bible cross-reference*

Verse 29. See Psalm 89:17; Isaiah 13:19.

9. *Key "by way of explanation"*

Verse 22. Samuel is not speaking against making sacrifices, but points out how useless they are if they are not accompanied by devotion in the heart.

10. *Key "Quotable Quote"*

"Obey God in the thing he is at present showing you, and instantly the next thing is opened up."
Oswald Chambers

1 Samuel chapter 16

1. Before and after

Previous chapter: Chapter 15: War against Amalek, and rejection of Saul as king

Following chapter: Chapter 17: God confirms David over Saul

2. Analysis of chapter

Samuel sent to Bethlehem to Jesse. (1-5)
David is anointed. (6-13)
Saul troubled with an evil spirit, is calmed by David. (14-23)

3. Key verse

Verse 13: "Then Samuel took the horn of oil, and anointed him in the midst of his brethren: and the Spirit of the LORD came upon David from that day forward."

4. Key word / key phrase

Verse 13, "David."

5. Key event / key person / key theme

David is anointed by Samuel.

6. Key thought

God's plans are never tied to one person if he or she should prove unfaithful.

7. Key thing to look out for

David has many God-given talents.

8. Key Bible cross-reference

Verse 11. See 2 Samuel 7:7,8; Psalm 78:71,72.

9. Key "by way of explanation"

Verse 14. On whom God's Spirit stayed became the critical point in the history of Israel.

10. Key "Quotable Quote"

"When the Spirit leaves me, I am like dry gunpowder. Oh for a sense of this!"
Robert Murray M'Cheyne

1 Samuel chapter 17

1. *Before and after*

Previous chapter: Chapter 16: God anoints David as king
Following chapter: Chapter 18: Saul attempts to kill David

2. *Analysis of chapter*

Goliath's challenge. (1-11)
David comes to the camp. (12-30)
David undertakes to fight Goliath. (31-39)
and goes to meet him. (40-47)
He kills Goliath. (48-58)

3. *Key verse*

Verse 4: "And there went out a champion out of the camp of the Philistines, named Goliath, of Gath, whose height was six cubits and a span."

4. *Key word / key phrase*

Verse 45, "the Lord Almighty."

5. *Key event / key person / key theme*

David defeats Goliath.

6. *Key thought*

The power of the world is puny against Almighty God.

7. *Key thing to look out for*

David's quiet confidence came from his trust in God.

8. *Key Bible cross-reference*

Verse 46. See Exodus 7:17; 9:14,16,29; Joshua 2:10,11.

9. *Key "by way of explanation"*

The stones for the sling were about the size of a base ball ball.

10. *Key "Quotable Quote"*

"When a man has no strength, if he leans on God, he becomes powerful."
D.L. Moody

1 Samuel chapter 18

1. **Before and after**

   Previous chapter: Chapter 17: God confirms David over Saul
   Following chapter: Chapter 19: Saul continues to try to kill David

2. **Analysis of chapter**

   Jonathan's friendship with David. (1-5)
   Saul seeks to kill David. (6-11)
   Saul's fear of David. (12-30)

3. **Key verse**

   Verse 1: "And it came to pass, when he had made an end of speaking unto Saul, that the soul of Jonathan was knit with the soul of David, and Jonathan loved him as his own soul."

4. **Key word / key phrase**

   Verse 8, "galled him."

5. **Key event / key person / key theme**

   Saul becomes jealous of David

6. **Key thought**

   Jealousy can ruin relationships.

7. **Key thing to look out for**

   The contrast between the characters of Saul and David.

8. **Key Bible cross-reference**

   Verse 4. See 20:14,15,31; 23:17.

9. **Key "by way of explanation"**

   Verse 7. When women sang about David killing "tens of thousands" it was a poetic way of referring to thousands. See Deuteronomy 32:30; Psalm 91:7.

10. **Key "Quotable Quote"**

    "In jealousy there is more self-love than love."
    François duc de La Rochefoucauld

1 Samuel chapter 19

1. *Before and after*

Previous chapter: Chapter 18: Saul attempts to kill David
Following chapter: Chapter 20: David flees, but Jonathan remains his friend

2. *Analysis of chapter*

Jonathan reconciles his father to David, Saul again tries to kill him. (1-10)
David flees to Samuel. (11-24)

3. *Key verse*

Verse 2: "But Jonathan Saul's son delighted much in David: and Jonathan told David, saying, Saul my father seeketh to kill thee"

4. *Key word / key phrase*

Verse 9, "spear."

5. *Key event / key person / key theme*

Saul attempts to kill David.

6. *Key thought*

It can be a short step from jealousy and anger to murder.

7. *Key thing to look out for*

Contrast Jonathan's character with that of his father Saul.

8. *Key Bible cross-reference*

Verse 1. See 18:13,17,25.

9. *Key "by way of explanation"*

Verse 9. The phrase "An evil spirit from the Lord" indicates that even evil spirits are not out of God's control. See Judges 9:23; 1 Kings 22:19-23.

10. *Key "Quotable Quote"*

"Sow a thought and you reap an act;
Sow an act and you reap a habit;
Sow a habit and you reap a character;
Sow a character and you reap a destiny."
Samuel Smiles

1 Samuel chapter 20

1. *Before and after*

Previous chapter: Chapter 19: Saul continues to try to kill David
Following chapter: Chapter 21: David is protected by Achish at Gath

2. *Analysis of chapter*

David consults Jonathan. (1-10)
Jonathan's covenant with David. (11-23)
Saul seeks to kill Jonathan. (24-34)
Jonathan and David part. (35-42)

3. *Key verse*

Verse 4: "Then said Jonathan unto David, Whatsoever thy soul desireth, I will even do it for thee."

4. *Key word / key phrase*

Verse 41, "wept together."

5. *Key event / key person / key theme*

David and Jonathan's friendship

6. *Key thought*

Jonathan had to choose between his friend and his father.

7. *Key thing to look out for*

Jonathan and David's friendship was profound.

8. *Key Bible cross-reference*

Verse 5. See Leviticus 23:24,25; Numbers 29:1-6.

9. *Key "by way of explanation"*

Verse 31. Saul tries to turn Jonathan against David by saying that David will take the throne from him.

10. *Key "Quotable Quote"*

"No medicine is more valuable, none more efficacious, none better suited to the cure of all our temporal ills than a friend to whom we may turn for consolation in time of trouble, and with whom we may share our happiness in times of joy."
Aelred Rievaulx

1 Samuel chapter 21

1. **Before and after**

   Previous chapter: Chapter 20: David flees, but Jonathan remains his friend
   Following chapter: Chapter 22: Saul kills God's priests

2. **Analysis of chapter**

   David with Ahimelech. (1-9)
   David at Gath pretends to be mad. (10-15)

3. **Key verse**

   Verse 1: "Then came David to Nob to Ahimelech the priest."

4. **Key word / key phrase**

   Verse 1, "trembled."

5. **Key event / key person / key theme**

   David at Nob and Gath

6. **Key thought**

   David was a fugitive on the run.

7. **Key thing to look out for**

   Note how Doeg, verse 7, plays a key role in the next chapter.

8. **Key Bible cross-reference**

   Verse 1. See 22:10.15.

9. **Key "by way of explanation"**

   Verse 4. Jesus referred to this verse and taught that ceremonial law should not
   be viewed in a legalistic way. See Matthew 12:3,4.

10. **Key "Quotable Quote"**

    "When I am in the cellar of affliction, I look for the Lord's choicest wines."
    Samuel Rutherford

1 Samuel chapter 22

1. Before and after

Previous chapter: Chapter 21: David is protected by Achish at Gath
Following chapter: Chapter 23: Saul chases David

2. Analysis of chapter

David at Adullam. Many come to him. (1-5)
Saul destroys the priests of Nob. (6-19)
Abiathar escapes to David. (20-23)

3. Key verse

Verse 1: "David therefore departed thence, and escaped to the cave Adullam."

4. Key word / key phrase

Verse 18, "struck them down."

5. Key event / key person / key theme

Saul slaughters the priests.

6. Key thought

A Doeg type of a person and a tyrant go together.

7. Key thing to look out for

Saul's evil now knows no bounds.

8. Key Bible cross-reference

Verse 7. See 8:14.

9. Key "by way of explanation"

Verse 7. As Saul was himself a Benjamite he hoped for tribal loyalty from his officials from the same tribe.

10. Key "Quotable Quote"

"My child, flee from every evil and everything that resembles it."
Didache

1 Samuel chapter 23

1. Before and after

Previous chapter: Chapter 22: Saul kills God's priests
Following chapter: Chapter 24: David spares Saul's life

2. Analysis of chapter

David rescues Keilah. (1-6)
God warns him to escape from Keilah. (7-13)
Jonathan comforts David. (14-18)
He is rescued from Saul by an invasion of the Philistines. (19-29)

3. Key verse

Verse 16: "And Jonathan Saul's son arose, and went to David into the wood, and strengthened his hand in God."

4. Key word / key phrase

Verse 8, "besiege."

5. Key event / key person / key theme

Saul pursues David

6. Key thought

Jonathan does not resent David' ascendancy.

7. Key thing to look out for

Evil, once let loose, overtakes people and situations.

8. Key Bible cross-reference

Verse 17. See 18:8.

9. Key "by way of explanation"

Verse 2. David used Urim and Thummim to discover the Lord's will. See verses 6,9.

10. Key "Quotable Quote"

"The perfect person does not only try to avoid evil. Nor does he do good for fear of punishment, still less in order to qualify for the hope of a promised reward. The perfect person does good through love."
Clement of Alexandria

1 Samuel chapter 24

1. *Before and after*

    Previous chapter: Chapter 23: Saul chases David
    Following chapter: Chapter 25: David marries Abigail

2. *Analysis of chapter*

    David spares Saul's life. (1-7)
    David shows his innocence. (8-15)
    Saul acknowledges his fault. (16-22)

3. *Key verse*

    Verse 4: "Then David arose, and cut off the skirt of Saul's robe privily."

4. *Key word / key phrase*

    Verse 5, "conscience-stricken."

5. *Key event / key person / key theme*

    David spares Saul's life.

6. *Key thought*

    Even though he was being hounded David followed his conscience.

7. *Key thing to look out for*

    Saul showed remorse but not repentance.

8. *Key Bible cross-reference*

    Verse 16. See 26:21.

9. *Key "by way of explanation"*

    Verse 6. David was determined not to act as if he, rather than the Lord, controlled everything.

10. *Key "Quotable Quote"*

    "Conscience is the perfect interpreter of life."
    Karl Barth

1 Samuel chapter 25

1. Before and after

Previous chapter: Chapter 24: David spares Saul's life
Following chapter: Chapter 26: Saul admits his guilt

2. Analysis of chapter

Death of Samuel. (1)
David's request; Nabal's churlish refusal. (2-11)
David's intention to kill Nabal. (12-17)
Abigail takes a present to David. (18-31)
He is pacified. Nabal dies. (32-39)
David takes Abigail as his wife. (39-44)

3. Key verse

Verse 1: "And Samuel died."

4. Key word / key phrase

Verse 11, "Why should I?"

5. Key event / key person / key theme

David and Abigail

6. Key thought

Nabal and Abigail show how different they are.

7. Key thing to look out for

David shows that he was open to changing his mind.

8. Key Bible cross-reference

Verse 3. See 24:12,14,15.

9. Key "by way of explanation"

Verse 25, "Fool." In this instance the meaning of Nabal's name exactly reflected his character. Names were often chosen to do this in ancient times.

10. Key "Quotable Quote"

"The greatest thing a man can do for his heavenly Father is to be kind to some of his other children."
Henry Drummond

1 Samuel chapter 26

1. **Before and after**

    Previous chapter: Chapter 25: David marries Abigail
    Following chapter: Chapter 27: David joins the Philistines

2. **Analysis of chapter**

    Saul goes after David, who again spares Saul's life. (1-12)
    David exhorts Saul. (13-20)
    Saul acknowledges his sin. (21-25)

3. **Key verse**

    Verse 2: "Then Saul arose, and went down to the wilderness of Ziph, having three thousand chosen men of Israel with him, to seek David in the wilderness of Ziph."

4. **Key word / key phrase**

    Verse 21, "acted like a boy."

5. **Key event / key person / key theme**

    David spares Saul's life again.

6. **Key thought**

    Verses 10,23, David's actions are based on his knowledge of God's character.

7. **Key thing to look out for**

    Saul ignores another opportunity to repent.

8. **Key Bible cross-reference**

    Verse 20. See 24:14.

9. **Key "by way of explanation"**

    Verse 12. By taking his spear and water jug David thought that Saul would realize that he did not seek to kill him.

10. **Key "Quotable Quote"**

    "If we hope for mercy we must show mercy."
    Peter Chrysologus

1 Samuel chapter 27

1. Before and after

Previous chapter: Chapter 26: Saul admits his guilt
Following chapter: Chapter 28: Saul visits a medium

2. Analysis of chapter

David retires to Gath. (1-7)
David deceives Achish. (8-12)

3. Key verse

Verse 1: "And David said in his heart, I shall now perish one day by the hand of Saul: there is nothing better for me than that I should speedily escape into the land of the Philistines; and Saul shall despair of me, to seek me any more in any coast of Israel: so shall I escape out of his hand."

4. Key word / key phrase

Verse 1, "escape."

5. Key event / key person / key theme

David among the Philistines

6. Key thought

David feels that Saul gave him no option but to go over to the Philistines.

7. Key thing to look out for

Some of David's most moving psalms were written in times of despair.

8. Key Bible cross-reference

Verse 7. See 2 Samuel 1:1; 2:1-3.

9. Key "by way of explanation"

Verse 1. The verse probably shows that David was beginning to doubt his own faith in the Lord.

10. Key "Quotable Quote"

"The kingdom of God is not attained by enduring one or two troubles, but many!"
Elder Anthony of Optina

1 Samuel chapter 28

1. *Before and after*

    Previous chapter: Chapter 27: David joins the Philistines
    Following chapter: Chapter 29: David is spared from fighting Saul

2. *Analysis of chapter*

    Achish puts confidence in David, Saul's fear. (1-6)
    Saul consults a witch at Endor. (7-19)
    Saul's terror. (20-25)

3. *Key verse*

    Verse 3: "Now Samuel was dead, and all Israel had lamented him, and buried him in Ramah, even in his own city."

4. *Key word / key phrase*

    Verse 7, "medium."

5. *Key event / key person / key theme*

    Saul consults a medium.

6. *Key thought*

    Going against God's commands leads to evil.

7. *Key thing to look out for*

    The Bible is categorical in its condemnation of mediums.

8. *Key Bible cross-reference*

    Verse 7. See verse 3; Leviticus 19:26.

9. *Key "by way of explanation"*

    Verse 14. Saul recalls that this description fits the kind of clothes Samuel used to wear.

10. *Key "Quotable Quote"*

    "How absurd would it be that in satisfying men you should incur the displeasure of him for whose sake you obey men themselves!"
    John Calvin

1 Samuel chapter 29

1. **Before and after**

   Previous chapter: Chapter 28: Saul visits a medium
   Following chapter: Chapter 30: David fights against the Amalekites

2. **Analysis of chapter**

   The Philistines object to having David with them. (1-5)
   He is dismissed by Achish. (6-11)

3. **Key verse**

   Verse 3: "Then said the princes of the Philistines, What do these Hebrews here? And Achish said unto the princes of the Philistines, Is not this David, the servant of Saul the king of Israel, which hath been with me these days, or these years, and I have found no fault in him since he fell unto me unto this day?"

4. **Key word / key phrase**

   Verse 3, "what about these Hebrews?"

5. **Key event / key person / key theme**

   David is rejected by the Philistines.

6. **Key thought**

   David could not have forever stayed with the Philistines.

7. **Key thing to look out for**

   The events of this chapter help David to be free of the Philistines.

8. **Key Bible cross-reference**

   Verse 4. See 27:6.

9. **Key "by way of explanation"**

   Verse 3. David was an accomplished tactician and fighter.

10. **Key "Quotable Quote"**

   "God never does anything to you that isn't for you."
   Elizabeth Elliott

1 Samuel chapter 30

1. Before and after

Previous chapter: Chapter 29: David is spared from fighting Saul
Following chapter: Chapter 31: Saul and Jonathan are killed

2. Analysis of chapter

Ziklag defeated by the Amalekites. (1-6)
David overtakes the Amalekites. (7-15)
He recovers what had been lost. (16-20)
David's distribution of the spoil. (21-31)

3. Key verse

Verse 10: "But David pursued, he and four hundred men: for two hundred abode behind, which were so faint that they could not go over the brook Besor."

4. Key word / key phrase

Verse 24, "all shall share alike."

5. Key event / key person / key theme

David destroys the Amalekites.

6. Key thought

The Lord knows about every part of our lives.

7. Key thing to look out for

A great deal of David's life was full of danger.

8. Key Bible cross-reference

Verse 1. See 27:8.

9. Key "by way of explanation"

Verse 23. David attributes their success to the Lord.

10. Key "Quotable Quote"

"How often has providence convinced believers, upon a sober recollection of the events of their lives, that if the Lord had left them to their own counsels they had as often been their own tormentors, if not executioners!"
John Flavel

1 Samuel chapter 31

1. **Previous chapter**

    Chapter 30: David fights against the Amalekites

2. **Analysis of chapter**

    Saul's defeat and death. (1-7)
    Saul's body rescued by the men of Jabesh Gilead. (8-13)

3. **Key verse**

    Verse 6: "So Saul died, and his three sons, and his armor bearer, and all his men, that same day together."

4. **Key word / key phrase**

    Verse 1, "slain."

5. **Key event / key person / key theme**

    Saul's death

6. **Key thought**

    Death-bed repentances are rare.

7. **Key thing to look out for**

    Saul's life failed to live up to its early promise.

8. **Key Bible cross-reference**

    Verse 13. See 2 Samuel 21:12-14.

9. **Key "by way of explanation"**

    Verse 4, "abuse me." It was common practice for captured prisoners to be mutilated. See Judges 16:23-25.

10. **Key "Quotable Quote"**

    "The divine providence, which is sufficient to deliver us in our utmost, is equally necessary to our preservation in the most peaceful situation."
    John Newton

2 Samuel chapter 1

1. *Following chapter*

   Chapter 2: War between Israel and Judah

2. *Analysis of chapter*

   News brought to David of the death of Saul. (1-10)
   The Amalekite is put to death. (11-16)
   David's lamentation for Saul and Jonathan. (17-27)

3. *Key verse*

   Verse 11: "Then David took hold on his clothes, and rent them; and likewise all the men that were with him."

4. *Key word / key phrase*

   Verse 17, "lament."

5. *Key event / key person / key theme*

   David mourns for Saul and Jonathan.

6. *Key thought*

   Saul may have hounded David but David still genuinely mourned his passing.

7. *Key thing to look out for*

   David's love for Jonathan is openly expressed, verse 26.

8. *Key Bible cross-reference*

   Verse 1. See Joshua 1:1; Judges 1:1.

9. *Key "by way of explanation"*

   Verse 28. When well-known people died or were killed it was normal for a lament to be written for them.

10. *Key "Quotable Quote"*

   "Grief is itself a medicine."
   William Cowper

2 Samuel chapter 2

1. ### Before and after
    Previous chapter: Chapter 1: The death of King Saul
    Following chapter: Chapter 3: Abner's murder

2. ### Analysis of chapter
    David made king in Hebron. (1-7)
    Abner makes Ish-Bosheth king. Battle between Abner's men and those of Joab. (8-17)
    Both parties retreat. (18-24)
    Asahel killed by Abner. (25-32.)

3. ### Key verse
    Verse 4: "And the men of Judah came, and there they anointed David king over the house of Judah."

4. ### Key word / key phrase
    Verse 1, "enquired of the LORD."

5. ### Key event / key person / key theme
    David is made king of Judah

6. ### Key thought
    The Lord raises the humble.

7. ### Key thing to look out for
    Qualities such as kindness and faithfulness need fostering.

8. ### Key Bible cross-reference
    Verse 3. See 1 Samuel 22:2; 23:13; 30:3,9.

9. ### Key "by way of explanation"
    Verse 28. "Joab blew the trumpet." The trumpet was the main means of communication between troops and their leader in a battle situation.

10. ### Key "Quotable Quote"
    "Conquer evil men by your gentle kindness."
    Isaac from Syria

2 Samuel chapter 3

1. ### Before and after

   Previous chapter: Chapter 2: War between Israel and Judah
   Following chapter: Chapter 4: Ish-Bosheth's murder

2. ### Analysis of chapter

   David's power increases his family. (1-6)
   Abner goes over to David. (7-21)
   Joab kills Abner. David mourns for him. (22-39)

3. ### Key verse

   Verse 1: "Now there was long war between the house of Saul and the house of
   David: but David waxed stronger and stronger, and the house of Saul waxed
   weaker and weaker."

4. ### Key word / key phrase

   Verse 9, "what the LORD promised him."

5. ### Key event / key person / key theme

   Abner's death

6. ### Key thought

   Hatred kills.

7. ### Key thing to look out for

   Verse 32. David, who was not yet king of all Israel, felt that his position was
   insecure.

8. ### Key Bible cross-reference

   Verse 25. See 2:18,23; 3:27.

9. ### Key "by way of explanation"

   Verse 17. The "elders of Israel" were the leaders of Israel who ruled their
   nation. See 1 Samuel 8:4; 2 Samuel 5:3.

10. ### Key "Quotable Quote"

    "The devil does not care who you hate, even if it's himself."
    Metropolitan Anthony

2 Samuel chapter 4

1. *Before and after*

   Previous chapter: Chapter 3: Abner's murder
   Following chapter: Chapter 5: David's reign in Jerusalem

2. *Analysis of chapter*

   Ish-Bosheth murdered. (1-7)
   David puts to death the murderers. (8-12)

3. *Key verse*

   Verse 6: "And they came thither into the midst of the house, as though they would have fetched wheat; and they smote him under the fifth rib."

4. *Key word / key phrase*

   Verse 1, "lost courage."

5. *Key event / key person / key theme*

   Ish-Bosheth is murdered.

6. *Key thought*

   Man's inhumanity to man appears in every generation.

7. *Key thing to look out for*

   Verse 40. What happened to Jonathan's son.

8. *Key Bible cross-reference*

   Verse 4. See 9:1-13; 16:1-4; 19:24-30.

9. *Key "by way of explanation"*

   Verse 8. The murderers of Ish-Bosheth couched their deed in pious language but that did not please David.

10. *Key "Quotable Quote"*

   "Anger is a weed. Hate is the tree."
   Augustine of Hippo

2 Samuel chapter 5

1. Before and after

Previous chapter: Chapter 4: Ish-Bosheth's murder
Following chapter: Chapter 6: The covenant box comes to Jerusalem

2. Analysis of chapter

David king over all Israel. (1-5)
He captures Jerusalem. (6-10)
David's kingdom established. (11-16)
He defeats the Philistines. (17-25)

3. Key verse

Verse 3: "So all the elders of Israel came to the king to Hebron; and king David made a league with them in Hebron before the LORD: and they anointed David king over Israel."

4. Key word / key phrase

Verse 6, "Jebusites."

5. Key event / key person / key theme

Seven years after the death of Saul, the northern tribes invite David to be their king.

6. Key thought

Rulers are meant to be like shepherds.

7. Key thing to look out for

David's success is attributed to the Lord Almighty.

8. Key Bible cross-reference

Verse 2. See 1 Samuel 13:13,14; 16:1,13.

9. Key "by way of explanation"

Verse 6. The "Jebusites" lived in the region of Jerusalem and were a Canaanite people. See Genesis 10:15,16. Since Jerusalem had been controlled neither by the northern nor southern tribes it made a perfect capital city for David.

10. Key "Quotable Quote"

"The United States was founded upon a Christian consensus. We today should bring Judeo-Christian principles into play in regard to government." Francis A. Schaeffer

2 Samuel chapter 6

1. **Before and after**

   Previous chapter: Chapter 5: David's reign in Jerusalem
   Following chapter: Chapter 7: David's covenant

2. **Analysis of chapter**

   The ark moved from Kirjath Jearim. (1-5)
   Uzzah killed for touching the ark. Obed-Edom blessed. (6-11)
   David brings the ark to Zion. (12-19)
   Michal's evil behavior. (20-23)

3. **Key verse**

   Verse 7: "And the anger of the LORD was kindled against Uzzah; and God smote him there for his error; and there he died by the ark of God."

4. **Key word / key phrase**

   Verse 2, "ark."

5. **Key event / key person / key theme**

   The ark is brought to Jerusalem.

6. **Key thought**

   God's holiness cannot be ign ed.

7. **Key thing to look out for**

   Michal's and David's charact s are set in great contrast to each other.

8. **Key Bible cross-reference**

   Verse 7. See Exodus 25:15; Numbers 4:5,6;15.

9. **Key "by way of explanation"**

   Verse 7. The death of Uzzah would have brought home to the Israelites that they must serve the Lord with all their hearts.

10. **Key "Quotable Quote"**

    "If I hate or despise any one man in the world, I hate something which God cannot hate, and despise that which he loves."
    William Law

2 Samuel chapter 7

1. *Before and after*

Previous chapter: Chapter 6: The covenant box comes to Jerusalem
Following chapter: Chapter 8: David's military triumphs

2. *Analysis of chapter*

David's care for the ark. (1-3)
God's covenant with David. (4-17)
His prayer and thanksgiving. (18-29)

3. *Key verse*

Verse 3: "And Nathan said to the king, Go, do all that is in thine heart; for the LORD is with thee."

4. *Key word / key phrase*

Verses 12,13, "house."

5. *Key event / key person / key theme*

Nathan's message to David

6. *Key thought*

David reveals his trust in God in his prayer.

7. *Key thing to look out for*

God's promises to David.

8. *Key Bible cross-reference*

Verse 2. See 12:1-14; 1 Kings 1.

9. *Key "by way of explanation"*

Verse 3. David may have acted rightly in consulting Nathan the prophet, but the prophet did not consult the Lord before pronouncing the Lord's will.

10. *Key "Quotable Quote"*

"Where God finds charity with its loving concern, there he recognizes the reflection of his own fatherly care."
Leo the Great

2 Samuel chapter 8

1. **Before and after**

   Previous chapter: Chapter 7: David's covenant
   Following chapter: Chapter 9: David's kindness to Mephibosheth

2. **Analysis of chapter**

   David subdues the Philistines, the Moabites, and the Syrians. (1-8)
   The spoil dedicated. (9-14)
   David's government and officers. (15-18)

3. **Key verse**

   Verse 1: "And after this it came to pass, that David smote the Philistines, and subdued them."

4. **Key word / key phrase**

   Verse 1, "subdued."

5. **Key event / key person / key theme**

   David's military victories

6. **Key thought**

   You don't have to be king to promote justice and right living.

7. **Key thing to look out for**

   Everything we have should be dedicated to the Lord.

8. **Key Bible cross-reference**

   Verse 2. See Genesis 19:37; 1 Samuel 14:47.

9. **Key "by way of explanation"**

   Verse 15. Justice and right actions are two characteristics of a godly king.

10. **Key "Quotable Quote"**

    "God does not desire "something" from us – he desires us, ourselves; not our works, but our personality, our will, our heart."
    Emil Brunner

2 Samuel chapter 9

1. *Before and after*

Previous chapter: Chapter 8: David's military triumphs
Following chapter: Chapter 10: David triumphs over Ammon and Syria

2. *Analysis of chapter*

David sends for Mephibosheth. (1-8)
And provides for him. (9-13)

3. *Key verse*

Verse 7: "And David said unto him, Fear not: for I will surely show thee kindness for Jonathan thy father's sake, and will restore thee all the land of Saul thy father; and thou shalt eat bread at my table continually."

4. *Key word / key phrase*

Verse 1, "for Jonathan's sake."

5. *Key event / key person / key theme*

David shows kindness to Mephibosheth.

6. *Key thought*

David deliberately sets out to be kind.

7. *Key thing to look out for*

Should our society show positive discrimination toward the disabled?

8. *Key Bible cross-reference*

Verse 1. See 1 Samuel 20:15,42.

9. *Key "by way of explanation"*

Verse 8. Mephibosheth shows his genuine humility before David by calling himself a "dead dog."

10. *Key "Quotable Quote"*

"I thank God for my handicaps for, through them, I have found myself, my work, and my God."
Helen Keller

2 Samuel chapter 10

1. *Before and after*

Previous chapter: Chapter 9: David's kindness to Mephibosheth
Following chapter: Chapter 11: David, Bathsheba, and Uriah

2. *Analysis of chapter*

David's messengers ill-treated by Hanun. (1-5)
The Ammonites defeated. (6-14)
The Syrians defeated. (15-19)

3. *Key verse*

Verse 5: "When they told it unto David, he sent to meet them, because the men were greatly ashamed: and the king said, Tarry at Jericho until your beards be grown, and then return."

4. *Key word / key phrase*

Verse 2, "I will show kindness."

5. *Key event / key person / key theme*

David defeats the Ammonites and Arameans.

6. *Key thought*

Verse 3. The Ammonite nobles created a problem. It could have been solved if the king had listened to David's men. How often wars and feuds are caused by suspicion and misunderstanding.

7. *Key thing to look out for*

Joab's courage and trust in God.

8. *Key Bible cross-reference*

Verse 4. See Isaiah 20:4.

9. *Key "by way of explanation"*

Verse 4. To shave off his beard was one of the most insulting things you could do to a man.

10. *Key "Quotable Quote"*

"Your actions in passing, pass not away, for every good work is a grain of seed for eternal life."
Bernard of Clairvaux

2 Samuel chapter 11

1. *Before and after*

Previous chapter: Chapter 10: David triumphs over Ammon and Syria
Following chapter: Chapter 12: Nathan rebukes David

2. *Analysis of chapter*

David's adultery. (1-5)
He tries to conceal his sin. (6-13)
Uriah murdered. (14-27)

3. *Key verse*

Verse 4: "And David sent messengers, and took her; and she came in unto him, and he lay with her."

4. *Key word / key phrase*

Verse 1, "David remained in Jerusalem."

5. *Key event / key person / key theme*

David and Bathsheba

6. *Key thought*

Thou shalt not commit adultery.

7. *Key thing to look out for*

One evil leads on to another evil.

8. *Key Bible cross-reference*

Verse 5. See Leviticus 20:10; Deuteronomy 22:22.

9. *Key "by way of explanation"*

Verse 15. David arranged for Uriah to be killed in battle so he could then marry Bathsheba.

10. *Key "Quotable Quote"*

"I've committed adultery in my heart many times. This is something that God recognizes I do and I have done it and God forgives me for it."
Jimmy Carter

2 Samuel chapter 12

1. **Before and after**

   Previous chapter: Chapter 11: David, Bathsheba, and Uriah
   Following chapter: Chapter 13: Tamar is raped: Absalom's revenge on Amnon

2. **Analysis of chapter**

   Nathan's parable. David confesses his sin. (1-14)
   The birth of Solomon. (15-25)
   David's severity to the Ammonites. (26-31)

3. **Key verse**

   Verse 1: "And the LORD sent Nathan unto David."

4. **Key word / key phrase**

   Verse 7, "You are the man."

5. **Key event / key person / key theme**

   Nathan rebukes David.

6. **Key thought**

   Parables can be most effective in conveying truth.

7. **Key thing to look out for**

   David repented.

8. **Key Bible cross-reference**

   Verse 13. See Psalm 51:8,12.

9. **Key "by way of explanation"**

   Verse 20. David shows his willingness to accept whatever punishment God would give him as a result of his sin.

10. **Key "Quotable Quote"**

    "True repentance brings an urge to be different."
    Florence Allshorn

2 Samuel chapter 13

1. **Before and after**

   Previous chapter: Chapter 12: Nathan rebukes David
   Following chapter: Chapter 14: Joab arranges for Absalom's restoration

2. **Analysis of chapter**

   Amnon's violence to his sister. (1-20)
   Absalom murders his brother Ammon. (21-29)
   David's grief. Absalom flees to Geshur. (30-39)

3. **Key verse**

   Verse 14: "Howbeit he would not hearken unto her voice: but, being stronger than she, forced her, and lay with her."

4. **Key word / key phrase**

   Verse 1, "Tamar."

5. **Key event / key person / key theme**

   Amnon and Tamar

6. **Key thought**

   Uncontrolled lust ruins lives.

7. **Key thing to look out for**

   Revenge solves nothing.

8. **Key Bible cross-reference**

   Verse 19. See Jeremiah 2:37.

9. **Key "by way of explanation"**

   Verse 15. This verse proves that Amnon never loved Tamar in the first place.

10. **Key "Quotable Quote"**

    "Lust is felt even by fleas and lice."
    Martin Luther

2 Samuel chapter 14

1. Before and after

Previous chapter: Chapter 13: Tamar is raped: Absalom's revenge on Amnon
Following chapter: Chapter 15: Absalom rebels, and David flees Jerusalem

2. Analysis of chapter

Joab procures Absalom's recall. (1-20)
Absalom recalled. (21-24)
His personal beauty. (25-27)
He is admitted to his father's presence. (28-33)

3. Key verse

Verse 1: "Now Joab the son of Zeruiah perceived that the king's heart was toward Absalom."

4. Key word / key phrase

Verse 1, "longed for."

5. Key event / key person / key theme

Joab arranges for Absalom to return.

6. Key thought

Absalom reveals his nasty character.

7. Key thing to look out for

David shows weakness in not seeking justice or Absalom's repentance and apology.

8. Key Bible cross-reference

Verse 8. See Deuteronomy 19:4-6.

9. Key "by way of explanation"

Verse 32. There is nothing here to indicate that Absalom was repentant for what he had done.

10. Key "Quotable Quote"

"A stiff apology is a second insult."
G.K. Chesterton

2 Samuel chapter 15

1. ***Before and after***

   Previous chapter: Chapter 14: Joab arranges for Absalom's restoration
   Following chapter: Chapter 16: David, Ziba, and Shimei

2. ***Analysis of chapter***

   Absalom's ambition. (1-6)
   His conspiracy. (7-12)
   David leaves Jerusalem. (13-23)
   David sends back the ark. (24-30)
   He prays against Ahithophel's counsel. (31-37)

3. ***Key verse***

   Verse 12: "And the conspiracy was strong; for the people increased continually with Absalom."

4. ***Key word / key phrase***

   Verse 14, "we must flee."

5. ***Key event / key person / key theme***

   Absalom's conspiracy

6. ***Key thought***

   Absalom was a thief.

7. ***Key thing to look out for***

   David had so many ups and downs in his life. Here he is on the run again.

8. ***Key Bible cross-reference***

   Verse 21. See Ruth 1:16,17.

9. ***Key "by way of explanation"***

   Verse 31. In deep trouble, David turns to the Lord in prayer.

10. ***Key "Quotable Quote"***

    "Prayer and helplessness are inseparable. Only he who is helpless can truly pray."
    O. Hallesby

2 Samuel chapter 16

1. **Before and after**

   Previous chapter: Chapter 15: Absalom rebels, and David flees Jerusalem
   Following chapter: Chapter 17: Absalom's reign

2. **Analysis of chapter**

   Ziba's falsehood. (1-4)
   David cursed by Shimei. (5-14)
   Ahithophel's counsel. (15-23)

3. **Key verse**

   Verse 1: "And when David was a little past the top of the hill, behold, Ziba the servant of Mephibosheth met him."

4. **Key word / key phrase**

   Verse 20, "your advice."

5. **Key event / key person / key theme**

   Treachery

6. **Key thought**

   Why did David believe Ziba's lies?

7. **Key thing to look out for**

   It takes a wise person to know which advice to take.

8. **Key Bible cross-reference**

   Verse 2. See 9:7-10.

9. **Key "by way of explanation"**

   Verses 20,21. By following Ahithopheh's advice Absalom announced his open rebellion on David.

10. **Key "Quotable Quote"**

    "Knowledge without wisdom may be soon discerned; it is usually curious and censorious."
    Thomas Manton

2 Samuel chapter 17

1. **Before and after**

   Previous chapter: Chapter 16: David, Ziba, and Shimei
   Following chapter: Chapter 18: Absalom's murder

2. **Analysis of chapter**

   Ahithophel's counsel overthrown. (1-21)
   He hangs himself. Absalom pursues David. (22-29)

3. **Key verse**

   Verse 4: "And the saying pleased Absalom well, and all the elders of Israel."

4. **Key word / key phrase**

   Verse 5, "Summon also Hushai the Arkite."

5. **Key event / key person / key theme**

   Hushai, the mole in Absalom's court

6. **Key thought**

   Absalom failed to take God into account as he made his plans.

7. **Key thing to look out for**

   The courage and loyalty of David's friends.

8. **Key Bible cross-reference**

   Verse 5. See 16:16-19.

9. **Key "by way of explanation"**

   Verse 14. This verse indicates that David's prayer was answered. See 15:31.

10. **Key "Quotable Quote"**

    "Catastrophe can be a means of grace."
    Eugune H. Peterson

2 Samuel chapter 18

1. *Before and after*

Previous chapter: Chapter 17: Absalom's reign
Following chapter: Chapter 19: David returns to Jerusalem

2. *Analysis of chapter*

Absalom's army defeated. (1-8)
He is killed. (9-18)
David's great sorrow. (19-33)

3. *Key verse*

Verse 14: "Then said Joab, I may not tarry thus with thee. And he took three
darts in his hand, and thrust them through the heart of Absalom, while he
was yet alive in the midst of the oak."

4. *Key word / key phrase*

Verse 53, "Oh my son Absalom!"

5. *Key event / key person / key theme*

Absalom's death

6. *Key thought*

David loved his wicked son to the end.

7. *Key thing to look out for*

David's great sadness was brought on him by his own inaction and sin, as well
as by Absalom's rebellion.

8. *Key Bible cross-reference*

Verse 6. See 15:13; 16:15.

9. *Key "by way of explanation"*

Verse 5. David could not bear the thought that Absalom would come to any
harm.

10. *Key "Quotable Quote"*

"We never know the love of the parent until we become parents ourselves."
Henry Ward Beecher

2 Samuel chapter 19

1. **Before and after**

   Previous chapter: Chapter 18: Absalom's murder
   Following chapter: Chapter 20: Sheba's rebellion|

2. **Analysis of chapter**

   Joab helps David to stop mourning. (1-8)
   At David's instigation the elders of Judah invite him back. (9-15)
   He pardons Shimei. (16-23)
   David withholds judgment on Mephibosheth. (24-30)
   David's parting with Barzillai. (31-40)
   David's homecoming; the leaders of Israel quarrel with the leaders of Judah.
   (41-43)

3. **Key verse**

   Verse 8: "Then the king arose, and sat in the gate. And they told unto all the
   people, saying, Behold, the king doth sit in the gate. And all the people came
   before the king: for Israel had fled every man to his tent."

4. **Key word / key phrase**

   Verse 14, "return."

5. **Key event / key person / key theme**

   David returns to Jerusalem

6. **Key thought**

   Mephibosheth is a picture of loyalty.

7. **Key thing to look out for**

   People in places of responsibility can be guilty of betraying people.

8. **Key Bible cross-reference**

   Verse 24. See 9:6-13.

9. **Key "by way of explanation"**

   Verse 20. The "house of Joseph" refers to the northern tribes, whose most
   important parts were Ephraim and Manasseh.

10. **Key "Quotable Quote"**

    "Our loyalty is due not to our species but to God . . . it is spiritual, not
    biological, kinship that counts."
    C.S. Lewis

2 Samuel chapter 20

1. *Before and after*

Previous chapter: Chapter 19: David returns to Jerusalem
Following chapter: Chapter 21: Famine, and war with Philistia

2. *Analysis of chapter*

Sheba's rebellion. (1-3)
Amasa killed by Joab. (4-13)
Sheba takes refuge in Abel Beth Maacah where he is killed. (14-22)
David's officers. (23-26)

3. *Key verse*

Verse 2: "So every man of Israel went up from after David, and followed Sheba."

4. *Key word / key phrase*

Verse 1, "troublemaker."

5. *Key event / key person / key theme*

Sheba rebels against David

6. *Key thought*

Joab was no stranger to committing murder in order to secure his own position.

7. *Key thing to look out for*

The part played by the wise woman.

8. *Key Bible cross-reference*

Verse 19. See Jeremiah 50:12; Galatians 4:26.

9. *Key "by way of explanation"*

Verse 19. The phrase "a mother in Israel" refers to a city that produced people who became faithful Israelites.

10. *Key "Quotable Quote"*

"The least-used words by an unselfish person are I, me, my, and mine."
Charles R. Swindoll

2 Samuel chapter 21

1. *Before and after*

Previous chapter: Chapter 20: Sheba's rebellion|
Following chapter: Chapter 22: Psalms of thanksgiving

2. *Analysis of chapter*

The Gibeonites avenged. (1-9)
Rizpah's care for the bodies of Saul's descendants. (10-14)
Battles with the Philistines. (15-22)

3. *Key verse*

Verse 7: "But the king spared Mephibosheth, the son of Jonathan the son of
Saul, because of the LORD'S oath that was between them, between David and
Jonathan the son of Saul."

4. *Key word / key phrase*

Verse 1, "famine."

5. *Key event / key person / key theme*

Saul's descendants are killed

6. *Key thought*

Trials drive us to the Lord as times of ease do not.

7. *Key thing to look out for*

Verse 1. When trouble came, what was David's purpose in praying?

8. *Key Bible cross-reference*

Verse 4. See Exodus 22:21; Leviticus 19:34.

9. *Key "by way of explanation"*

Verse 12. David shows his respect for King Saul and his love for Jonathan by
taking charge of their bones.

10. *Key "Quotable Quote"*

"Troubles are often the tools by which God fashions us for better things."
Henry Ward Beecher

2 Samuel chapter 22

1. Before and after

Previous chapter: Chapter 21: Famine, and war with Philistia
Following chapter: Chapter 23: Deeds of David's mighty men

2. Analysis of chapter

David's psalm of thanksgiving. (1-51)

3. Key verse

Verse 1: "And David spake unto the LORD the words of this song in the day that the LORD had delivered him out of the hand of all his enemies, and out of the hand of Saul."

4. Key word / key phrase

Verse 1, "sang."

5. Key event / key person / key theme

David's song of praise

6. Key thought

David's heart is full of thanksgiving.

7. Key thing to look out for

For a man who suffered so much it is noteworthy that he can give thanks to the Lord so much.

8. Key Bible cross-reference

Verse 1. See Psalm 18.

9. Key "by way of explanation"

Verse 2. It is most instructive to see the first name David gives to his Lord in this psalm: it is "rock."

10. Key "Quotable Quote"

"Praise focuses our hearts on God. The problem or need about which we pray may seem overwhelming, but we must see God infinitely greater than our problem, able to meet all our need."
Wesley Duewel

2 Samuel chapter 23

1. Before and after

Previous chapter: Chapter 22: Psalms of thanksgiving
Following chapter: Chapter 24: The census and the plague

2. Analysis of chapter

David's last words. (1-7)
David's mighty men. (8-39)

3. Key verse

Verse 1: "Now these be the last words of David."

4. Key word / key phrase

Verse 10, "the LORD brought about."

5. Key event / key person / key theme

David's last words

6. Key thought

David saw how much righteousness means to the Lord.

7. Key thing to look out for

The different ways in which people can be "mighty."

8. Key Bible cross-reference

Verse 1. See 1 Kings 2:1-10.

9. Key "by way of explanation"

David's mighty men are subdivided into the Three and Thirty.

10. Key "Quotable Quote"

"We should not give the impression in our practice that, just because they are expressed in traditional Christian terminology, all religious concepts are on a graduated, quantitative spectrum – that, in regard to central doctrine, no chasm exists between right and wrong."
Francis A. Schaeffer

2 Samuel chapter 24

1. **Previous chapter**

   Chapter 23: Deeds of David's mighty men

2. **Analysis of chapter**

   David numbers the people. (1-9)
   He chooses the plague. (10-15)
   The plague is stopped. (16,17)
   David's sacrifice, and the plague lifted. (18-25)

3. **Key verse**

   Verse 1: "And again the anger of the LORD was kindled against Israel, and he moved David against them to say, Go, number Israel and Judah."

4. **Key word / key phrase**

   Verse 1, "census."

5. **Key event / key person / key theme**

   David takes a census

6. **Key thought**

   David is quick to take the blame.

7. **Key thing to look out for**

   David's humility and confession of sin before the Lord rectifies the situation.

8. **Key Bible cross-reference**

   Verse 1. See 24:1.

9. **Key "by way of explanation"**

   Verse 1. It appears that the taking of this particular census showed that David was trusting in human power rather than in God's power.

10. **Key "Quotable Quote"**

    "There is nothing morbid about the confession of sins, so long as we go on to give thanks for the forgiveness of sins."
    John R.W. Stott

1 Kings and 2 Kings

1 Kings chapter 1

1. **Following chapter**

   Chapter 2: Solomon is established as king

2. **Analysis of chapter**

   David's old age. (1-4)
   Adonijah aspires to the throne. (5-10)
   David makes Solomon king. (11-31)
   Solomon is anointed king, and Adonijah's usurpation stopped. (32-53)

3. **Key verse**

   Verse 1: "Now king David was old and stricken in years; and they covered him with clothes, but he gat no heat."

4. **Key word / key phrase**

   Verse 30, "Carry out."

5. **Key event / key person / key theme**

   David appoints Solomon to succeed him as king.

6. **Key thought**

   David never seemed to be far from some rebellion against him.

7. **Key thing to look out for**

   Solomon shows his wisdom in a difficult situation.

8. **Key Bible cross-reference**

   Verse 31. See Nehemiah 2:3; Daniel 2:4; 3:9; 5:10.

9. **Key "by way of explanation"**

   Verse 5. David's fourth son, Adonijah, attempts to ensure that he will succeed to David's throne.

10. **Key "Quotable Quote"**

    "He will not be a wise man who does not study the human heart. "
    C.H. Spurgeon

1 Kings chapter 2

1. **Before and after**

   Previous chapter: Chapter 1: Solomon is appointed king
   Following chapter: Chapter 3: Solomon asks for wisdom

2. **Analysis of chapter**

   David's dying charge to Solomon. (1-4)
   David's charge to Joab and others. (5-11)
   Solomon reigns. Adonijah aspiring to the throne is put to death. (12-25)
   Abiathar banished. Joab put to death. (26-34)
   Shimei is put to death. (35-46)

3. **Key verse**

   Verse 1: "Now the days of David drew nigh that he should die; and he charged
   Solomon his son . . ."

4. **Key word / key phrase**

   Verse 1, "die."

5. **Key event / key person / key theme**

   David's last instructions to Solomon

6. **Key thought**

   Solomon knew that David's overriding concern was that he should be faithful
   to God.

7. **Key thing to look out for**

   Solomon was also told to whom he should show kindness.

8. **Key Bible cross-reference**

   Verse 4. See Deuteronomy 4:29; 6:5.

9. **Key "by way of explanation"**

   Verse 22. Solomon saw that this request was a thinly disguised attempt to take
   the throne away from him.

10. **Key "Quotable Quote"**

    "I do not pray for success, I ask for faithfulness."
    Mother Teresa of Calcutta

1 Kings chapter 3

1. **Before and after**

   Previous chapter: Chapter 2: Solomon is established as king
   Following chapter: Chapter 4: Solomon's rule over Israel

2. **Analysis of chapter**

   Solomon's marriage. (1-4)
   His vision. His prayer for wisdom. (5-15)
   The judgment of Solomon. (16-28)

3. **Key verse**

   Verse 9: "Give therefore thy servant an understanding heart to judge thy people, that I may discern between good and bad: for who is able to judge this thy so great a people?"

4. **Key word / key phrase**

   Verse 9, "discerning heart."

5. **Key event / key person / key theme**

   Solomon asks for wisdom

6. **Key thought**

   God reads our hearts.

7. **Key thing to look out for**

   Wisdom comes from God.

8. **Key Bible cross-reference**

   Verse 13. See Luke 12:31.

9. **Key "by way of explanation"**

   Verse 9, "discerning." This comes from the Hebrew word meaning "listen" – "a listening heart."

10. **Key "Quotable Quote"**

    "Knowledge is horizontal. Wisdom is vertical – it comes down from above."
    Billy Graham

1 Kings chapter 4

1. *Before and after*

Previous chapter: Chapter 3: Solomon asks for wisdom
Following chapter: Chapter 5: The materials and laborers used to build the temple

2. *Analysis of chapter*

Solomon's court. (1-19)
Solomon's dominions. His daily provision. (20-28)
The wisdom of Solomon. (29-34)

3. *Key verse*

Verse 29: "And God gave Solomon wisdom and understanding exceeding much, and largeness of heart, even as the sand that is on the sea shore."

4. *Key word / key phrase*

Verse 22, "daily provisions."

5. *Key event / key person / key theme*

Solomon's prosperous reign

6. *Key thought*

Material prosperity is a gift from God.

7. *Key thing to look out for*

In what ways did Solomon reveal his wisdom?

8. *Key Bible cross-reference*

Verse 1. See 2 Samuel 8:15.

9. *Key "by way of explanation"*

Verse 32. Some of the "three thousand proverbs" of Solomon have been preserved in the Old Testament book of Proverbs.

10. *Key "Quotable Quote"*

"A wise man cares not for what he cannot have."
George Herbert

1 Kings chapter 5

1. *Before and after*

Previous chapter: Chapter 4: Solomon's rule over Israel
Following chapter: Chapter 6: The completion of the temple

2. *Analysis of chapter*

Solomon's agreement with Hiram. (1-9)
Solomon's workmen for the temple. (10-18)

3. *Key verse*

Verse 1: "And Hiram king of Tyre sent his servants unto Solomon; for he had heard that they had anointed him king in the room of his father: for Hiram was ever a lover of David."

4. *Key word / key phrase*

Verse 5, "build a temple."

5. *Key event / key person / key theme*

Preparations are made to build the temple

6. *Key thought*

Friendship between nations can be mutually beneficial.

7. *Key thing to look out for*

Skilled craftsmen were used at each stage of the temple's building.

8. *Key Bible cross-reference*

Verse 3. See 1 Chronicles 22:2-5.

9. *Key "by way of explanation"*

Verse 13. This forced labor eventually resulted in rebellion after Solomon died.

10. *Key "Quotable Quote"*

"We can express our worship to God in many ways. But if we love the Lord and are led by his Holy Spirit, our worship will always bring a delighted sense of admiring awe and a sincere humility on our part."
A.W. Tozer

1 Kings chapter 6

1. **Before and after**

   Previous chapter: Chapter 5: The materials and laborers used to build the temple
   Following chapter: Chapter 7: Solomon's house and the temple's furniture

2. **Analysis of chapter**

   The building of Solomon's temple. (1-10)
   Promise given about the temple. (11-14)
   Details about the temple. (15-38)

3. **Key verse**

   Verse 2: "And the house which king Solomon built for the LORD, the length thereof was threescore cubits, and the breadth thereof twenty cubits, and the height thereof thirty cubits."

4. **Key word / key phrase**

   Verse 1, "build."

5. **Key event / key person / key theme**

   Solomon builds the temple

6. **Key thought**

   Solomon is reassured that his own family will succeed him.

7. **Key thing to look out for**

   The building materials used indicate the great care that was taken to ensure that the temple was fit to be "the house of the Lord."

8. **Key Bible cross-reference**

   Verse 19. See Exodus 25:16,21.

9. **Key "by way of explanation"**

   Verse 14. Much more attention is paid to Solomon building the temple, and completing it, than to the buildings he erected for himself.

10. **Key "Quotable Quote"**

   "We should dedicate ourselves to becoming in this life the most perfect worshipers of God we can possibly be, as we hope to be through all eternity."
   Brother Lawrence

1 Kings chapter 7

1. *Before and after*

Previous chapter: Chapter 6: The completion of the temple
Following chapter: Chapter 8: Dedication of the temple

2. *Analysis of chapter*

Solomon's buildings. (1-12)
Furniture of the temple. (13-47)
Furniture made from gold. (48-51)

3. *Key verse*

Verse 1: "But Solomon was building his own house thirteen years, and he finished all his house."

4. *Key word / key phrase*

Verse 14, "craftsman."

5. *Key event / key person / key theme*

The furniture for the temple

6. *Key thought*

From this chapter what can we learn about our own lives and service for God?

7. *Key thing to look out for*

The beauty of the temple must have been mind-blowing.

8. *Key Bible cross-reference*

Verse 23. See Exodus 30:17-21.

9. *Key "by way of explanation"*

Verse 13, "Huram." Huram, a half-Israelite, was indeed highly skilled. While his expertise is not directly attributed to God's Spirit, he nevertheless reminds one of Bezalel. See Exodus 31:4.

10. *Key "Quotable Quote"*

"We have lost our spirit of worship and our ability to withdraw inwardly to meet God in adoring silence."
A.W. Tozer

1 Kings chapter 8

1. Before and after

Previous chapter: Chapter 7: Solomon's house and the temple's furniture
Following chapter: Chapter 9: The Lord appears to Solomon again

2. Analysis of chapter

The ark is brought into the temple. (1-11)
The occasion. (12-21)
Solomon's prayer. (22-53)
His blessing and exhortation. (54-61)
Solomon's peace-offerings. (62-66)

3. Key verse

Verse 10: "And it came to pass, when the priests were come out of the holy place, that the cloud filled the house of the LORD."

4. Key word / key phrase

Verse 1, "ark."

5. Key event / key person / key theme

The ark is brought to the temple.

6. Key thought

The symbol of God's presence arriving in "God's city" must have been a most memorable day.

7. Key thing to look out for

The requests that Solomon made in his prayer of dedication.

8. Key Bible cross-reference

Verse 40. See Deuteronomy 5:29; 6:1-2.

9. Key "by way of explanation"

The ark symbolized God's presence.

10. Key "Quotable Quote"

"To my God a heart of flame;
To my fellow men a heart of love;
To myself a heart of steel."
Augustine of Hippo

1 Kings chapter 9

1. *Before and after*

   Previous chapter: Chapter 8: Dedication of the temple
   Following chapter: Chapter 10: Visit from the Queen of Sheba

2. *Analysis of chapter*

   God's answer to Solomon. (1-9)
   The presents of Solomon and Hiram. (10-14)
   Solomon's buildings. His trade. (15-28)

3. *Key verse*

   Verse 4: "And if thou wilt walk before me, as David thy father walked, in integrity of heart, and in uprightness, to do according to all that I have commanded thee, and wilt keep my statutes and my judgments."

4. *Key word / key phrase*

   Verse 2, "appeared."

5. *Key event / key person / key theme*

   The Lord appears to Solomon.

6. *Key thought*

   The Lord reminds Solomon about the need to stay faithful to him.

7. *Key thing to look out for*

   Solomon ensured that all the temple regulations for correct worship and all the sacrifices were carried out.

8. *Key Bible cross-reference*

   Verse 28. See 2 Chronicles 8:18; Job 28.

9. *Key "by way of explanation"*

   Verse 4,5. With the coming of prosperity this warning not to break God's covenant was especially timely.

10. *Key "Quotable Quote"*

   "We do the works, but God works in us the doing of the works."
   Augustine of Hippo

1 Kings chapter 10

1. **Before and after**

   Previous chapter: Chapter 9: The Lord appears to Solomon again
   Following chapter: Chapter 11: Solomon's unfaithfulness and his death

2. **Analysis of chapter**

   The Queen of Sheba's visit to Solomon. (1-13)
   Solomon's wealth. (14-29)

3. **Key verse**

   Verse 1: "And when the queen of Sheba heard of the fame of Solomon concerning the name of the LORD, she came to prove him with hard questions."

4. **Key word / key phrase**

   Verse 1, "queen of Sheba."

5. **Key event / key person / key theme**

   The Queen of Sheba visits Solomon.

6. **Key thought**

   The Queen of Sheba appreciated both Solomon's possessions and his wisdom.

7. **Key thing to look out for**

   The Queen of Sheba attributed all that Solomon had to the eternal love of the Lord.

8. **Key Bible cross-reference**

   Verse 22. See verse 11; 9:26-28.

9. **Key "by way of explanation"**

   It has been suggested that the Queen of Sheba came on a trade mission because Solomon's sea trade was in competition with the lucrative overland trade routes which brought prosperity to the little kingdom of Sheba.

10. **Key "Quotable Quote"**

    "Wealth is like a viper that is harmless if a man knows how to take hold of it; but if he does not, it will twine round his hand and bite him."
    Clement

1 Kings chapter 11

1. *Before and after*

Previous chapter: Chapter 10: Visit from the Queen of Sheba
Following chapter: Chapter 12: The cause of the kingdom's division

2. *Analysis of chapter*

Solomon's wives and concubines. His idolatry. (1-8)
God's anger. (9-13)
Solomon's adversaries. (14-25)
Jeroboam's promotion. (26-40)
The death of Solomon. (41-43)

3. *Key verse*

Verse 3: "And he had seven hundred wives, princesses, and three hundred concubines: and his wives turned away his heart."

4. *Key word / key phrase*

Verse 1, "foreign women."

5. *Key event / key person / key theme*

Solomon's wives

6. *Key thought*

Solomon's unfaithfulness in marrying non-Israelites was his undoing.

7. *Key thing to look out for*

Verse 4 categorically states that Solomon's heart was turned away from the Lord by his foreign wives.

8. *Key Bible cross-reference*

Verse 4. See 8:61.

9. *Key "by way of explanation"*

Verse 5. Worshiping the pagan deities of Molech and Milcom sometimes involved the evil practice of child sacrifice.

10. *Key "Quotable Quote"*

"Collapse in the Christian life is rarely a blow out. It's usually a slow leak."
George Sweeting

1 Kings chapter 12

1. Before and after

Previous chapter: Chapter 11: Solomon's unfaithfulness and his death
Following chapter: Chapter 13: Jeroboam's evil ways

2. Analysis of chapter

Rehoboam's accession, and the people's request. His rough answer. (1-15)
Ten tribes rebel. (16-24)
Jeroboam's idolatry. (25-33)

3. Key verse

Verse 1: "And Rehoboam went to Shechem: for all Israel were come to Shechem to make him king."

4. Key word / key phrase

Verse 4, "a heavy yoke."

5. Key event / key person / key theme

The northern tribes revolt

6. Key thought

Rehoboam, Solomon's son and successor, made an unwise choice in the advice he accepted.

7. Key thing to look out for

Verse 28. the disastrous spiritual consequences of the revolt.

8. Key Bible cross-reference

Verse 29. See Genesis 12:8; Judges 20:26-28.

9. Key "by way of explanation"

From now on the nation is divided into two: Israel, comprising the ten northern tribes; and Judah and Benjamin, centered on Jerusalem.

10. Key "Quotable Quote"

"Like many political leaders he tried to harness the power of religion to bolster his own regime."
Stephen Travis

1 Kings chapter 13

1. *Before and after*

   Previous chapter: Chapter 12: The cause of the kingdom's division
   Following chapter: Chapter 14: Judgment on Jeroboam

2. *Analysis of chapter*

   Jeroboam's sin reproved. (1-10)
   The prophet deceived. (11-22)
   The disobedient prophet is killed. Jeroboam's obstinacy. (23-34)

3. *Key verse*

   Verse 1: "And, behold, there came a man of God out of Judah by the word of the LORD unto Bethel: and Jeroboam stood by the altar to burn incense."

4. *Key word / key phrase*

   Verse 1, "Bethel."

5. *Key event / key person / key theme*

   The elderly prophet of Bethel

6. *Key thought*

   Age is of little consequence in God's service.

7. *Key thing to look out for*

   Some people seem to be so intent on evil that they are impossible to change.

8. *Key Bible cross-reference*

   Verse 6. See 2:3; Genesis 27:20.

9. *Key "by way of explanation"*

   Verse 3. A "sign" meant the immediate fulfillment of a prophecy.

10. *Key "Quotable Quote"*

   "God does not so much need people to do extraordinary things as he needs people who do ordinary things extraordinarily well."
   William Barclay

1 Kings chapter 14

1. *Before and after*

   Previous chapter: Chapter 13: Jeroboam's evil ways
   Following chapter: Chapter 15: Reigns of Abijam and Asa in Judah

2. *Analysis of chapter*

   Abijah being sick, his mother consults Ahijah. (1-6)
   The destruction of Jeroboam's family. (7-20)
   Rehoboam's wicked reign. (21-31)

3. *Key verse*

   Verse 1: "At that time Abijah the son of Jeroboam fell sick."

4. *Key word / key phrase*

   Verse 6, "Why this pretence?"

5. *Key event / key person / key theme*

   King Rehoboam of Judah

6. *Key thought*

   Some kind of idolatry seems to have been the besetting sin of God's people in nearly every generation.

7. *Key thing to look out for*

   The reasons why Rehoboam was condemned.

8. *Key Bible cross-reference*

   Verse 22. See 2 Chronicles 11-12.

9. *Key "by way of explanation"*

   Verses 23,24. Moses had warned God's people to have nothing at all to do with the "male shrine-prostitutes" but his voice was not heeded now.

10. *Key "Quotable Quote"*

    "All sin is a kind of lying."
    Augustine of Hippo

1 Kings chapter 15

1. *Before and after*

Previous chapter: Chapter 14: Judgment on Jeroboam
Following chapter: Chapter 16: Five kings of Israel: Baasha, Elah, Zimri, Omri, and Ahab

2. *Analysis of chapter*

Wicked reign of Abijam, king of Judah. (1-8)
Good reign of Asa, king of Judah. (9-24)
The evil reigns of Nadab and Baasha in Israel. (25-34)

3. *Key verse*

Verse 1: "Now in the eighteenth year of king Jeroboam the son of Nebat reigned Abijam over Judah."

4. *Key word / key phrase*

Verse 1, "Abijah."

5. *Key event / key person / key theme*

King Abijah of Judah

6. *Key thought*

Life father like son . . .

7. *Key thing to look out for*

Lack of wholeheartedness in following the Lord ends in disaster.

8. *Key Bible cross-reference*

Verse 7. See 2 Chronicles 13.

9. *Key "by way of explanation"*

Verse 3. David may have sinned in dreadful ways. But his heart was not divided between serving the Lord and worshiping pagan idols.

10. *Key "Quotable Quote"*

"What God asks is a will which will no longer be divided between him and any creature."
François Fénelon

1 Kings chapter 16

1. **Before and after**

   Previous chapter: Chapter 15: Reigns of Abijam and Asa in Judah
   Following chapter: Chapter 17: Elijah's ministry in the drought

2. **Analysis of chapter**

   The reigns of Baasha and Elah in Israel. (1-14)
   Reigns of Zimri and Omri in Israel. (15-28)
   Ahab's wickedness, Hiel rebuilds Jericho. (29-34)

3. **Key verse**

   Verse 8: "In the twenty and sixth year of Asa king of Judah began Elah the son
   of Baasha to reign over Israel in Tirzah, two years."

4. **Key word / key phrase**

   Verse 1, "Baasha."

5. **Key event / key person / key theme**

   Kings of Israel

6. **Key thought**

   The end does not justify the means.

7. **Key thing to look out for**

   A series of evil rulers does not mean that God is no longer in ultimate control
   in the world.

8. **Key Bible cross-reference**

   Verse 3. See 14:10; 21:21.

9. **Key "by way of explanation"**

   Verse 7. Baasha did kill off the house of Jeroboam, but in an evil way.

10. **Key "Quotable Quote"**

    "Order your soul; reduce your wants; live in charity; associate in Christian
    community; obey the laws; trust in providence."
    Augustine of Hippo

1 Kings chapter 17

1. Before and after

Previous chapter: Chapter 16: Five kings of Israel: Baasha, Elah, Zimri, Omri, and Ahab

Following chapter: Chapter 18: Miracle of fire on Mount Carmel

2. Analysis of chapter

Elijah fed by ravens. (1-7)
Elijah sent to Zarephath. (8-16)
Elijah raises the widow's son to life. (17-24)

3. Key verse

Verse 6: "And the ravens brought him bread and flesh in the morning, and bread and flesh in the evening; and he drank of the brook."

4. Key word / key phrase

Verse 1, "the Lord whom I serve."

5. Key event / key person / key theme

Elijah and the drought

6. Key thought

God provides by one means or another.

7. Key thing to look out for

God is on the side of the poor.

8. Key Bible cross-reference

Verse 21. See Romans 4:17; Hebrews 11:19.

9. Key "by way of explanation"

Verse 16. A non-Israelite was prepared to risk her life for Elijah.

10. Key "Quotable Quote"

"The cruse of oil and the barrel of meal overflow because the widow has firm faith."
Agathias Scholasticus

1 Kings chapter 18

1. ### Before and after

   Previous chapter: Chapter 17: Elijah's ministry in the drought
   Following chapter: Chapter 19: God's help for the depressed Elijah

2. ### Analysis of chapter

   Elijah sends Ahab notice of his coming. (1-16)
   Elijah meets Ahab. (17-20)
   Elijah's trial with the false prophets. (21-40)
   Elijah, by prayer, obtains rain. (41-46)

3. ### Key verse

   Verse 1: "And it came to pass after many days, that the word of the LORD came to Elijah in the third year, saying, Go, show thyself unto Ahab; and I will send rain upon the earth."

4. ### Key word / key phrase

   Verse 17, "You troubler of Israel."

5. ### Key event / key person / key theme

   God sends down fire.

6. ### Key thought

   Elijah prayed and God answered.

7. ### Key thing to look out for

   Elijah had God's glory at the forefront of his thinking.

8. ### Key Bible cross-reference

   Verse 24. See Psalm 104:3; 29:3-9.

9. ### Key "by way of explanation"

   Verse 21. Elijah made the people choose between good and evil, between following the Lord God and following Baal.

10. ### Key "Quotable Quote"

    "God has not always answered my prayers. If he had, I would have married the wrong man – several times!"
    Ruth Bell Graham

1 Kings chapter 19

1. *Before and after*

Previous chapter: Chapter 18: Miracle of fire on Mount Carmel
Following chapter: Chapter 20: War with Syria

2. *Analysis of chapter*

Elijah flees to the desert. (1-8)
God manifests himself to Elijah. (9-13)
God's answer to Elijah. (14-18)
The call of Elisha. (19-21)

3. *Key verse*

Verse 8: "And he arose, and did eat and drink, and went in the strength of that meat forty days and forty nights unto Horeb the mount of God."

4. *Key word / key phrase*

Verse 4, "I have had enough, Lord."

5. *Key event / key person / key theme*

Elijah on Mount Sinai hears God in a gentle whisper.

6. *Key thought*

Elijah felt like committing suicide.

7. *Key thing to look out for*

Elijah was revived with very ordinary physical things.

8. *Key Bible cross-reference*

Verse 4. See Jonah 4:3,8.

9. *Key "by way of explanation"*

Verse 10. Elijah felt that he was the only faithful follower of the Lord left on earth.

10. *Key "Quotable Quote"*

"The ultimate cause of all spiritual depression is unbelief. For if it were not for unbelief even the devil could do nothing. It is because we listen to the devil instead of listening to God that we go down before him and fall before his attacks."
D. Martyn Lloyd-Jones

1 Kings chapter 20

1. *Before and after*

Previous chapter: Chapter 19: God's help for the depressed Elijah
Following chapter: Chapter 21: Ahab murders Naboth for his vineyard

2. *Analysis of chapter*

Benhadad besieges Samaria. (1-11)
Benhadad's defeat. (12-21)
The Syrians again defeated. (22-30)
Ahab makes peace with Benhadad. (31-43)

3. *Key verse*

Verse 1: "And Benhadad the king of Syria gathered all his host together: and there were thirty and two kings with him, and horses, and chariots: and he went up and besieged Samaria, and warred against it."

4. *Key word / key phrase*

Verses 13,28, "You will know that I am the Lord."

5. *Key event / key person / key theme*

Ben-Hadad attacks Samaria

6. *Key thought*

God sends his blessings pressed down and running over.

7. *Key thing to look out for*

Our God is in charge, no matter what is happening on the world stage.

8. *Key Bible cross-reference*

Verse 35, "sons of the prophets." See 2 Kings 2:3,5,7,15.

9. *Key "by way of explanation"*

Verse 30. Not only did Israel's army beat the Assyrians, but the Lord inflicted further disaster on twenty-seven thousand of them.

10. *Key "Quotable Quote"*

"All history is incomprehensible without Christ."
Joseph Ernest Renan

1 Kings chapter 21

1. Before and after

Previous chapter: Chapter 20: War with Syria
Following chapter: Chapter 22: Defeat by Syria, and death of Ahab

2. Analysis of chapter

Ahab covets Naboth's vineyard. (1-4)
Naboth murdered by Jezebel. (5-16)
Elijah denounces judgments against Ahab. (17-29)

3. Key verse

Verse 2: "And Ahab spake unto Naboth, saying, Give me thy vineyard."

4. Key word / key phrase

Verse 2, "Let me have."

5. Key event / key person / key theme

Naboth's vineyard

6. Key thought

Greed is a killer.

7. Key thing to look out for

Grown-ups as well as children behave like spoilt toddlers.

8. Key Bible cross-reference

Verse 10. See Numbers 35:30; Deuteronomy 17:6.

9. Key "by way of explanation"

Verse 19. Ahab was guilty of committing murder, even though Jezebel had arranged for Naboth to be killed. Numbers 36:7-9 forbad the selling of land one has inherited.

10. Key "Quotable Quote"

"Nothing enslaves us more to the devil, as the desire for more and love for greed."
John Chrysostom

1 Kings chapter 22

1. **Previous chapter**

   Chapter 21: Ahab murders Naboth for his vineyard

2. **Analysis of chapter**

   Jehoshaphat makes a pact with Ahab. (1-14)
   Micaiah predicts the death of Ahab. (15-28)
   Death of Ahab. (29-40)
   Jehoshaphat's good reign over Judah. (41-50)
   Ahaziah's evil reign over Israel. (51-53)

3. **Key verse**

   Verse 37: "So the king died, and was brought to Samaria; and they buried the king in Samaria."

4. **Key word / key phrase**

   Verse 5, "first seek."

5. **Key event / key person / key theme**

   Micaiah prophesies against Ahab

6. **Key thought**

   Even the most wicked ruler will die.

7. **Key thing to look out for**

   The lure of idolatry succeeds in capturing countless hearts.

8. **Key Bible cross-reference**

   Verse 17. See Numbers 27:16,17; Zechariah 13:7.

9. **Key "by way of explanation"**

   Verse 23. The prophets lied because they had chosen to speak from their own evil hearts rather than to follow the truth.

10. **Key "Quotable Quote"**

    "In the time we have it is surely our duty to do all the good we can to all the people we can in all the ways we can."
    William Barclay

2 Kings chapter 1

1. **Following chapter**

   Chapter 2: Elijah hands over to Elisha

2. **Analysis of chapter**

   The rebellion of Moab. Sickness of Ahaziah, king of Israel. (1-8)
   Fire called from heaven by Elijah. Death of Ahaziah. (9-18)

3. **Key verse**

   Verse 8: "And they answered him, He was an hairy man, and girt with a girdle of leather about his loins. And he said, It is Elijah the Tishbite."

4. **Key word / key phrase**

   Verse 3, "the angel of the LORD."

5. **Key event / key person / key theme**

   Failure to consult God

6. **Key thought**

   Elijah followed angelic advice.

7. **Key thing to look out for**

   Elijah was fearless and outspoken in the messages he delivered.

8. **Key Bible cross-reference**

   Verse 8. See Mark 1:6.

9. **Key "by way of explanation"**

   Verse 10. Just as God had answered by fire at Mount Carmel, so here the Lord authenticates his own prophet by answering with fire.

10. **Key "Quotable Quote"**

    "True will power and courage are not on the battlefield, but in every day conquests over our inertia, laziness, boredom."
    Dwight Moody

2 Kings chapter 2

1. Before and after

Previous chapter: Chapter 1: King Ahaziah of Israel
Following chapter: Chapter 3: Rebellion of Moab

2. Analysis of chapter

Elijah divides Jordan. (1-8)
Elijah is taken up into heaven. (9-12)
Elisha is manifested to be Elijah's successor. (13-18)
Elisha heals the waters of Jericho, and those that mocked Elisha are destroyed. (19-25)

3. Key verse

Verse 8: "And Elijah took his mantle, and wrapped it together, and smote the waters, and they were divided hither and thither, so that they two went over on dry ground."

4. Key word / key phrase

Verse 1, "heaven."

5. Key event / key person / key theme

Elijah is taken up to heaven.

6. Key thought

Elijah had served the Lord in many unusual ways and he left earth in an unusual way.

7. Key thing to look out for

God's work does not end just because one person's ministry comes to an end.

8. Key Bible cross-reference

Verse 11. See Genesis 5:24.

9. Key "by way of explanation"

Verse 9. When Elisha asked to "inherit a double portion" from Elijah he was not asking for twice as much as Elijah possessed, but rather that he might inherit Elijah's ministry. A "double portion" was the inheritance a firstborn son received on the death of his father.

10. Key "Quotable Quote"

"We are all in a lifetime of 'ministry.'"
John R.W. Stott

2 Kings chapter 3

1. *Before and after*

Previous chapter: Chapter 2: Elijah hands over to Elisha
Following chapter: Chapter 4: Elisha's miraculous ministry

2. *Analysis of chapter*

Jehoram, king of Israel. (1-5)
War with Moab, and the intercession of Elisha. (6-19)
Water supplied, Moab overcome. (20-27)

3. *Key verse*

Verse 1: "Now Jehoram the son of Ahab began to reign over Israel in Samaria the eighteenth year of Jehoshaphat king of Judah, and reigned twelve years."

4. *Key word / key phrase*

Verse 11, "enquire of the LORD."

5. *Key event / key person / key theme*

God's miraculous provision of water.

6. *Key thought*

The Old Testament prophets were messengers passing on what the Lord had told them.

7. *Key thing to look out for*

An unusual way to win a battle.

8. *Key Bible cross-reference*

Verse 13. See 1 Kings 22:6.

9. *Key "by way of explanation"*

Verse 15. The music was probably to calm everyone down.

10. *Key "Quotable Quote"*

"Prophets are the beating hearts of the Old Testament."
W. Rauschenbusch

2 Kings chapter 4

1. ### Before and after

   Previous chapter: Chapter 3: Rebellion of Moab
   Following chapter: Chapter 5: Healing of Naaman

2. ### Analysis of chapter

   Elisha multiplies the widow's oil. (1-7)
   The Shunammite receives a son. (8-17)
   The Shunammite's son restored to life. (18-37)
   The miracle of healing the stew, and of feeding the sons of the prophets. (38-44)

3. ### Key verse

   Verse 6: "And it came to pass, when the vessels were full, that she said unto her son, Bring me yet a vessel. And he said unto her, There is not a vessel more. And the oil stayed."

4. ### Key word / key phrase

   Verse 14, "What can be done for her?"

5. ### Key event / key person / key theme

   Elisha comes to the rescue of a people in need.

6. ### Key thought

   God's prophets were instantly recognizable.

7. ### Key thing to look out for

   To be able to say, "everything is all right" in the middle of a seeming tragedy displays great faith. See verse 26.

8. ### Key Bible cross-reference

   Verse 1. See Exodus 21:1,2; Leviticus 25:39-41.

9. ### Key "by way of explanation"

   The chapter gives a picture of everyday life at that time.

10. ### Key "Quotable Quote"

    "Do not worry why problems exist in the world. Just respond to people's needs."
    Mother Teresa

2 Kings chapter 5

1. ### Before and after

    Previous chapter: Chapter 4: Elisha's miraculous ministry
    Following chapter: Chapter 6: More of Elisha's miracles

2. ### Analysis of chapter

    Naaman's leprosy. (1-8)
    His cure from leprosy. (9-14)
    Elisha refuses Naaman's gifts. (15-19)
    Gehazi's covetousness and falsehood. (20-27)

3. ### Key verse

    Verse 1: "Now Naaman, captain of the host of the king of Syria, was a great man with his master, and honorable, because by him the LORD had given deliverance unto Syria: he was also a mighty man in valor, but he was a leper."

4. ### Key word / key phrase

    Verse 1, "leprosy."

5. ### Key event / key person / key theme

    The leper Naaman is healed.

6. ### Key thought

    Naaman had to come off his high horse before he could be cured.

7. ### Key thing to look out for

    The role of a young servant girl.

8. ### Key Bible cross-reference

    Verse 3. See verse 9; 2:25; 6:19.

9. ### Key "by way of explanation"

    Verse 14. Naaman's healing can be seen as a message to disobedient Israel who needed to behave like Naaman and trust and obey God if they were to receive God's blessing.

10. ### Key "Quotable Quote"

    "We are all healers who can reach out and offer health, and we are all patients in constant need of help."
    Henri Nouwen

2 Kings chapter 6

1. Before and after

Previous chapter: Chapter 5: Healing of Naaman
Following chapter: Chapter 7: Elisha's prophecies

2. Analysis of chapter

The sons of the prophets enlarge their habitations. Iron made to float. (1-7)
Elisha discloses the counsels of the Syrians. (8-12)
Syrians sent to seize Elisha. (13-23)
Samaria besieged. A famine, and the king sends to kill Elisha. (24-33)

3. Key verse

Verse 1: "And the sons of the prophets said unto Elisha, Behold now, the place where we dwell with thee is too strait for us."

4. Key word / key phrase

Verse 16, "Those who are with us are more than those who are with them."

5. Key event / key person / key theme

Elisha's ministry

6. Key thought

The Lord calls some people to a very varied ministry.

7. Key thing to look out for

Elisha exemplifies the proverb that the Lord's followers should be as shrewd as snakes.

8. Key Bible cross-reference

Verse 16. See 2 Chronicles 32:7,8. 1 John 4:4.

9. Key "by way of explanation"

Verse 6. This miracle shows God's concern for his faithful follower.

10. Key "Quotable Quote"

"Think of it! Multitudes of angels, indescribably mighty, performing the commands of heaven."
Billy Graham

2 Kings chapter 7

1. **Before and after**

   Previous chapter: Chapter 6: More of Elisha's miracles
   Following chapter: Chapter 8: Kings of Syria, Israel, and Judah

2. **Analysis of chapter**

   Elisha prophesies plenty. (1,2)
   The flight of the Syrian army. (3-11)
   Samaria plentifully supplied. (12-20)

3. **Key verse**

   Verse 1: "Then Elisha said, Hear ye the word of the LORD; Thus saith the LORD,
   To morrow about this time shall a measure of fine flour be sold for a shekel,
   and two measures of barley for a shekel, in the gate of Samaria."

4. **Key word / key phrase**

   Verse 5, "not a man was there."

5. **Key event / key person / key theme**

   Elijah's prophecies

6. **Key thought**

   Good news is for sharing.

7. **Key thing to look out for**

   God's prophecies all come true.

8. **Key Bible cross-reference**

   Verse 2. See verse 19; Genesis 8:2; Isaiah 24:18.

9. **Key "by way of explanation"**

   Verse 3. These four lepers were at the "entrance of the city gate" as the law did
   not allow them to live with the healthy people.

10. **Key "Quotable Quote"**

    "God gave the prophecies, not to gratify men's curiosity by enabling them to
    foreknow things, but that after they were fulfilled they might be interpreted
    by the event, and his own providence, not the interpreter's, be thereby
    manifested to the world."
    Isaac Newton

2 Kings chapter 8

1. Before and after

Previous chapter: Chapter 7: Elisha's prophecies
Following chapter: Chapter 9: Jehu is anointed king: Ahab's family is killed

2. Analysis of chapter

A famine in Israel, and the Shunammite receives her land. (1-6)
Elisha consulted by Hazael. Death of Benhadad. (7-15)
Jehoram's wicked reign in Judah. (16-24)
Ahaziah's wicked reign in Judah. (25-29)

3. Key verse

Verse 1: "Then spake Elisha unto the woman, whose son he had restored to life, saying, Arise, and go thou and thine household, and sojourn wheresoever thou canst sojourn: for the LORD hath called for a famine; and it shall also come upon the land seven years."

4. Key word / key phrase

Verse 13, "the LORD has shown me."

5. Key event / key person / key theme

Elisha and King Benhadad

6. Key thought

Power corrupts. Seeking power can completely dominate lives.

7. Key thing to look out for

He was equally at ease with the poor and the powerful.

8. Key Bible cross-reference

Verse 12. See 9:14-16; 10:31; 12:17,18.

9. Key "by way of explanation"

Verse 10. Faced with the tears of the prophet and the dreadful prophecies Hazael shows no sign of repentance.

10. Key "Quotable Quote"

"Two heads are better than one, not because either is infallible, but because they are unlikely to go wrong in the same direction."
C. S. Lewis

2 Kings chapter 9

1. *Before and after*

Previous chapter: Chapter 8: Kings of Syria and Judah
Following chapter: Chapter 10: Baal worshipers killed; death of Jehu

2. *Analysis of chapter*

Elisha sent to anoint Jehu. (1-10)
Jehu and the captains. (11-15)
Joram and Ahaziah killed by Jehu. (16-29)
Jezebel eaten by dogs. (30-37)

3. *Key verse*

Verse 1: "And Elisha the prophet called one of the children of the prophets, and said unto him, Gird up thy loins, and take this box of oil in thine hand, and go to Ramothgilead."

4. *Key word / key phrase*

Verse 2, "Jehu."

5. *Key event / key person / key theme*

Jehu is anointed king.

6. *Key thought*

When Jehu was anointed he was given a specific work to accomplish.

7. *Key thing to look out for*

The role of the prophet was to do what the Lord said, not to do what he felt he would like to do.

8. *Key Bible cross-reference*

Verse 7. See verses 25,26; 1 Kings 21:21-24.

9. *Key "by way of explanation"*

Verse 11. God's prophets often had to suffer in different ways. Here Elisha is referred to as "this madman."

10. *Key "Quotable Quote"*

"In doing what we ought we deserve no praise."
Augustine of Hippo

2 Kings chapter 10

1. *Before and after*

Previous chapter: Chapter 9: Jehu is anointed king: Ahab's family is killed
Following chapter: Chapter 11: Queen Athaliah of Judah

2. *Analysis of chapter*

Ahab's sons and Ahaziah's brethren put to death. (1-14)
Jehu destroys the worshipers of Baal. (15-28)
Jehu follows Jeroboam's sins. (29-36)

3. *Key verse*

Verse 27: "And they brake down the image of Baal, and brake down the house of Baal, and made it a draught house unto this day."

4. *Key word / key phrase*

Verse 18, "Baal."

5. *Key event / key person / key theme*

Baal worshipers killed.

6. *Key thought*

It is easy to be driven by mixed motives.

7. *Key thing to look out for*

To serve the Lord only does not come easily.

8. *Key Bible cross-reference*

Verse 29. See 1 Kings 12:26-32; 13:33,34.

9. *Key "by way of explanation"*

Verses 30,31. Jehu is commended for bringing God's judgment on the house of Ahab. But he went too far and so was condemned in Hosea 1:4 for the "massacre at Jezreel."

10. *Key "Quotable Quote"*

"O Lord, grant that I may do thy will as if it were my will; so that thou mayest do my will as if it were thy will."
Augustine of Hippo

2 Kings chapter 11

1. Before and after

Previous chapter: Chapter 10: Baal worshipers killed; death of Jehu
Following chapter: Chapter 12: King Joash of Judah

2. Analysis of chapter

Athaliah usurps the government of Judah. Jehoash made king. (1-12)
Athaliah put to death. (13-16)
The worship of the Lord restored. (17-21)

3. Key verse

Verse 1: "And when Athaliah the mother of Ahaziah saw that her son was dead, she arose and destroyed all the seed royal."

4. Key word / key phrase

Verse 3, "hidden."

5. Key event / key person / key theme

Queen Athaliah of Judah

6. Key thought

The Lord's covenants were meant to be followed all the time.

7. Key thing to look out for

To ignore God's instructions brings personal and national disaster.

8. Key Bible cross-reference

Verse 17. See Exodus 19:5,6; Deuteronomy 4:20.

9. Key "by way of explanation"

Verse 14. The two pillars outside the temple were called Jakin and Boaz. See 23:3; 1 Kings 7:15-22.

10. Key "Quotable Quote"

"The commands of God are all designed to make us more happy than we can possibly be without them."
Thomas Wilson

2 Kings chapter 12

1. **Before and after**

   Previous chapter: Chapter 11: Queen Athaliah of Judah
   Following chapter: Chapter 13: King Jehoahaz and King Jehoash of Israel

2. **Analysis of chapter**

   Jehoash orders the repair of the temple. (1-16)
   He is killed by his servants. (17-21)

3. **Key verse**

   Verse 2: "And Jehoash did that which was right in the sight of the LORD all his days wherein Jehoiada the priest instructed him."

4. **Key word / key phrase**

   Verse 2, "did what was right."

5. **Key event / key person / key theme**

   King Joash of Judah

6. **Key thought**

   Repairing the temple symbolized making good the spiritual lives of God's people.

7. **Key thing to look out for**

   The Lord's work has to be financed.

8. **Key Bible cross-reference**

   Verse 16. See Leviticus 5:16; 6:5.

9. **Key "by way of explanation"**

   Verse 5. The "treasurers" were the officials who handled the money given in connection with the sacrifices, on behalf of the priests.

10. **Key "Quotable Quote"**

    "Separation from Jesus means sadness. Restoration of fellowship means joy."
    John Piper

2 Kings chapter 13

1. Before and after

Previous chapter: Chapter 12: King Joash of Judah
Following chapter: Chapter 14: King Amaziah of Judah

2. Analysis of chapter

Reign of Jehoahaz. (1-9)
Jehoash, king of Israel. Elisha dying. (10-19)
Elisha's death, and the victories of Jehoash. (20-25)

3. Key verse

Verse 1: "In the three and twentieth year of Joash the son of Ahaziah king of Judah Jehoahaz the son of Jehu began to reign over Israel in Samaria, and reigned seventeen years."

4. Key word / key phrase

Verse 3, "the LORD's anger."

5. Key event / key person / key theme

Jehoahaz king of Israel

6. Key thought

Eradication of idolatry is never easy.

7. Key thing to look out for

It is the devil's ploy to make sin look more attractive than godliness.

8. Key Bible cross-reference

Verse 2. See 1 Kings 12:26-32; 13:33,34.

9. Key "by way of explanation"

Verse 6. The "Asherah pole" was an idol which had been set up by Ahab.

10. Key "Quotable Quote"

"It does not take great men to do great things; it only takes consecrated men."
Phillips Brooks

2 Kings chapter 14

1. **Before and after**

   Previous chapter: Chapter 13: King Jehoahaz and King Jehoash of Israel
   Following chapter: Chapter 15: Azariah of Judah, and five evil kings of Israel

2. **Analysis of chapter**

   Amaziah's good reign. (1-7)
   Amaziah provokes Jehoash king of Israel, and is overcome. (8-14)
   He is killed by conspirators. (15-22)
   Wicked reign of Jeroboam II. (23-29)

3. **Key verse**

   Verse 1: "In the second year of Joash son of Jehoahaz king of Israel reigned Amaziah the son of Joash king of Judah."

4. **Key word / key phrase**

   Verse 26, "the LORD has seen."

5. **Key event / key person / key theme**

   Amaziah King of Judah

6. **Key thought**

   Wholeheartedness in following him is what the Lord asks for.

7. **Key thing to look out for**

   We are not meant to stand in judgment over the lives of these kings but to learn from them.

8. **Key Bible cross-reference**

   Verse 3. See 2 Chronicles 15:14-16.

9. **Key "by way of explanation"**

   Verse 8. In this instance the phrase, "meet me face to face" amounted to a virtual declaration of war.

10. **Key "Quotable Quote"**

    "There, but for the grace of God, goes John Bradford."
    John Bradford, as he saw criminals being taken off to be executed.

2 Kings chapter 15

1. **Before and after**

   Previous chapter: Chapter 14: King Amaziah of Judah
   Following chapter: Chapter 16: King Ahaz of Judah

2. **Analysis of chapter**

   Reign of Azariah, king of Judah. (1-7)
   The latter kings of Israel and invasion of Assyria. (8-31)
   Jotham, king of Judah. (32-38)

3. **Key verse**

   Verse 1: "In the twenty and seventh year of Jeroboam king of Israel began Azariah son of Amaziah king of Judah to reign."

4. **Key word / key phrase**

   Verses 9,18,24,28, "did evil."

5. **Key event / key person / key theme**

   Tiglath Pileser, King of Assyria

6. **Key thought**

   It is easier to please men than to please the Lord.

7. **Key thing to look out for**

   Azariah (Uzziah) was a good king. See the significance of his death for Isaiah (Isaiah 6:1,11).

8. **Key Bible cross-reference**

   Verse 29. See 16:5-9; 2 Chronicles 28:16-21.

9. **Key "by way of explanation"**

   In 734 Tiglath Pileser overran Gilead and Galilee burning and destroying the towns.

10. **Key "Quotable Quote"**

    "A far-reaching reformation of the Church is a prerequisite if it is to commit itself to Jesus' mission of liberating the oppressed."
    Ronald J. Sider

2 Kings chapter 16

1. *Before and after*

    Previous chapter: Chapter 15: Azariah of Judah, and five evil kings of Israel
    Following chapter: Chapter 17: King Hoshea of Israel

2. *Analysis of chapter*

    Ahaz, king of Judah. His wicked reign. (1-9)
    Ahaz copies an idol's altar. (10-16)
    Ahaz robs the temple. (17-20)

3. *Key verse*

    Verse 2: "Twenty years old was Ahaz when he began to reign, and reigned
    sixteen years in Jerusalem, and did not that which was right in the sight of the
    LORD his God, like David his father."

4. *Key word / key phrase*

    Verse 34, "did what was right."

5. *Key event / key person / key theme*

    Verse 37. Danger threatened from the north.

6. *Key thought*

    Morality and belief in God are bound up with each other.

7. *Key thing to look out for*

    Temple improvements

8. *Key Bible cross-reference*

    Verse 3. See Leviticus 18:21.

9. *Key "by way of explanation"*

    Verse 4. The "high places" were originally sites where the pagan Baal was
    worshiped. Later immoral pagan practices took place on these sites.

10. *Key "Quotable Quote"*

    "There is no true and abiding morality that is not founded in religion."
    Henry Ward Beecher

2 Kings chapter 17

1. **Before and after**

   Previous chapter: Chapter 16: King Ahaz of Judah
   Following chapter: Chapter 18: Hezekiah's early reign, and Jerusalem besieged

2. **Analysis of chapter**

   Reign of Hoshea in Israel, and the Israelites carried captives by the Assyrians. (1-6)
   Captivity of the Israelites. (7-23)
   The nations placed in the land of Israel. (24-41)

3. **Key verse**

   Verse 18: "Therefore the LORD was very angry with Israel, and removed them out of his sight: there was none left but the tribe of Judah only."

4. **Key word / key phrase**

   Verse 24, "Samaria."

5. **Key event / key person / key theme**

   The fall of Samaria

6. **Key thought**

   People sin despite being told not to.

7. **Key thing to look out for**

   The writer's summary of the reasons for the fall of Israel.

8. **Key Bible cross-reference**

   Verse 23. See Hosea 10:1-7; Amos 5:27.

9. **Key "by way of explanation"**

   The fall of Samaria took place in the winter of 722/721. The King of Assyria resettled the conquered lands with people of other races. This led to a syncretistic religion. It was the beginning of the Samaritans so hated by later orthodox Jews.

10. **Key "Quotable Quote"**

    "The basic sin is that we usurp God's place at the center of our lives."
    David Watson

2 Kings chapter 18

1. **Before and after**

   Previous chapter: Chapter 17: King Hoshea of Israel
   Following chapter: Chapter 19: Assyria's letter and Hezekiah's faith in God

2. **Analysis of chapter**

   Good reign of Hezekiah in Judah. Idolatry. (1-8)
   Sennacherib invades Judah. (9-16)
   Rabshakeh's blasphemies. (17-37)

3. **Key verse**

   Verse 7: "And the LORD was with him; and he prospered whithersoever he went forth: and he rebelled against the king of Assyria, and served him not."

4. **Key word / key phrase**

   Verse 17, "Jerusalem."

5. **Key event / key person / key theme**

   Sennachrib besieges Jerusalem

6. **Key thought**

   Our extremity is God's opportunity.

7. **Key thing to look out for**

   The extreme desperation of the situation, but the people's refusal to capitulate (verse 36).

8. **Key Bible cross-reference**

   Verse 19. See Psalm 47:2; 48:2; 95:3.

9. **Key "by way of explanation"**

   In Sennacherib's own account of this invasion, he says Hezekiah was trapped "like a bird in a cage."

10. **Key "Quotable Quote"**

    "When you reach rock bottom, that rock is Jesus."
    Author unknown

2 Kings chapter 19

1. **Before and after**

   Previous chapter: Chapter 18: Hezekiah's early reign, and Jerusalem besieged
   Following chapter: Chapter 20: Hezekiah's illness, recovery, and death

2. **Analysis of chapter**

   Messengers sent to Isaiah asking for prayer. Isaiah's reply. (1-7)
   Sennacherib's letter. (8-19)
   His fall is prophesied. (20-34)
   The Assyrian army destroyed. Sennacherib killed. (35-37)

3. **Key verse**

   Verse 1: "And Hezekiah received the letter of the hand of the messengers, and
   read it: and Hezekiah went up into the house of the LORD, and spread it before
   the LORD."

4. **Key word / key phrase**

   Verse 5, "Do not be afraid."

5. **Key event / key person / key theme**

   Isaiah predicts Sennacherib's fall

6. **Key thought**

   The Lord answers prayers that come from the heart and answers in amazing
   ways.

7. **Key thing to look out for**

   Hezekiah's reasons for asking for God's help (verses 15-19).

8. **Key Bible cross-reference**

   Verse 18. See Psalm 115:3-8; 135:15-18.

9. **Key "by way of explanation"**

   Verse 25. Israel's God not only rules his own people but he is the God of
   history for every nation.

10. **Key "Quotable Quote"**

    "By prayer the Christian can open his heart to God, as to a friend, and obtain
    fresh testimony of God's friendship to him."
    John Bunyan

2 Kings chapter 20

1. *Before and after*

   Previous chapter: Chapter 19: Assyria's letter and Hezekiah's faith in God
   Following chapter: Chapter 21: The evil reigns of Manasseh and Amon

2. *Analysis of chapter*

   Hezekiah's sickness. His recovery in answer to prayer. (1-11)
   Hezekiah shows his treasures to the ambassadors from Babylon. His death.
   (12-21)

3. *Key verse*

   Verse 9: "And Isaiah said, This sign shalt thou have of the LORD, that the LORD will do the thing that he hath spoken: shall the shadow go forward ten degrees, or go back ten degrees?"

4. *Key word / key phrase*

   Verses 5,6, "heal . . . deliver."

5. *Key event / key person / key theme*

   Hezekiah's illness

6. *Key thought*

   Miracles are meant to support the faith of God's people.

7. *Key thing to look out for*

   Trusting in God should not make people naïve (verses 12-15).

8. *Key Bible cross-reference*

   Verse 5. See Psalm 139:16 Ephesians s1:11.

9. *Key "by way of explanation"*

   Verse 20. There was no river in Jerusalem. The tunnel, cut through rock to the spring, would ensure a water supply during a siege.

10. *Key "Quotable Quote"*

   "Prayer is not a substitute for work, thinking, watching, suffering, or giving; prayer is a support for all other efforts."
   George Buttrick

2 Kings chapter 21

1. Before and after

Previous chapter: Chapter 20: Hezekiah's illness, recovery, and death
Following chapter: Chapter 22: Josiah repairs the temple and the finding of the book of the law

2. Analysis of chapter

Wicked reign of Manasseh. (1-9)
The prophetic denunciations against Judah. (10-18)
Wicked reign and death of Amon. (19-26)

3. Key verse

Verse 2: "And he did that which was evil in the sight of the LORD, after the abominations of the heathen, whom the LORD cast out before the children of Israel."

4. Key word / key phrase

Verse 1, "Manasseh."

5. Key event / key person / key theme

King Manasseh of Judah

6. Key thought

Some people are evil through and through.

7. Key thing to look out for

Evil needs to be resisted or else it just takes over.

8. Key Bible cross-reference

Verse 2. See 18:3-5; 16:3.

9. Key "by way of explanation"

Verse 13. A "measuring line" and a "plumb-line" were usually used to help with constructing a building. In this instance they are going to be used in the destruction of a building, symbolizing God's judgment.

10. Key "Quotable Quote"

"What greater work is there than training the mind and forming the habits of the young?"
John Chrysostom

2 Kings chapter 22

1. *Before and after*

    Previous chapter: Chapter 21: The evil reigns of Manasseh and Amon
    Following chapter: Chapter 23: Josiah removes pagan worship and celebrates
    the Passover

2. *Analysis of chapter*

    Josiah's good reign, his care for repairing the temple, and the Book of the Law
    found. (1-10)
    Josiah consults Huldah the prophetess. (11-20)

3. *Key verse*

    Verse 1: "Josiah was eight years old when he began to reign, and he reigned
    thirty and one years in Jerusalem."

4. *Key word / key phrase*

    Verse 1, "Josiah."

5. *Key event / key person / key theme*

    The discovery of the Book of the Law

6. *Key thought*

    The Lord never left his people without clear commandments.

7. *Key thing to look out for*

    The Book of the Law gives instructions to nations and individuals.

8. *Key Bible cross-reference*

    Verse 8. See Deuteronomy 31:24,26; 2 Chronicles 34:14.

9. *Key "by way of explanation"*

    Verse 2. Josiah was the last king in David's line who faithfully followed the
    Lord, prior to the Exile.

10. *Key "Quotable Quote"*

    "No man is uneducated who knows the Bible and no one is wise who is
    ignorant of its teachings."
    Samuel Chadwick

2 Kings chapter 23

1. ### Before and after

    Previous chapter: Chapter 22: Josiah repairs the temple and the finding of the
    Book of the Law
    Following chapter: Chapter 24: Nebuchadnezzar captures Jerusalem

2. ### Analysis of chapter

    Josiah reads the law, and renews the covenant. (1-3)
    He destroys idolatry. (4-14)
    The reformation extended to Israel. A Passover kept. (15-24)
    Josiah killed by Pharaoh Neco. (25-30)
    Wicked reigns of Jehoahaz and Jehoiakim. (31-37)

3. ### Key verse

    Verse 2: "And the king went up into the house of the LORD, and all the men of
    Judah and all the inhabitants of Jerusalem with him, and the priests, and the
    prophets, and all the people, both small and great: and he read in their ears all
    the words of the book of the covenant which was found in the house of the
    LORD."

4. ### Key word / key phrase

    Verse 2, "the Book of the Covenant."

5. ### Key event / key person / key theme

    Josiah renews the covenant.

6. ### Key thought

    Some things need to be destroyed if good is to prevail.

7. ### Key thing to look out for

    After evil has been eradicated goodness needs to step in, or else there will be
    a vacuum.

8. ### Key Bible cross-reference

    Verse 3. See Exodus 24:3-8; Deuteronomy 1:34.

9. ### Key "by way of explanation"

    Verse 21. Celebrating the Passover and following the teaching of the Book of
    the Law went hand in hand.

10. ### Key "Quotable Quote"

    "They err who look not to the bright rays of the divine Scriptures, because
    they walk in darkness."
    John Chrysostom

2 Kings chapter 24

1. *Before and after*

Previous chapter: Chapter 23: Josiah removes pagan worship and celebrates the Passover

Following chapter: Chapter 25: The destruction of the temple and exile

2. *Analysis of chapter*

Jehoiakim subdued by Nebuchadnezzar. (1-7)

Jehoiachin captured in Babylon. (8-20)

3. *Key verse*

Verse 1: "In his days Nebuchadnezzar king of Babylon came up, and Jehoiakim became his servant three years: then he turned and rebelled against him."

4. *Key word / key phrase*

Verse 10, "Nebuchadnezzar."

5. *Key event / key person / key theme*

Nebuchadnezzar captures Jerusalem

6. *Key thought*

Even in the face of calamity many refuse to turn to God.

7. *Key thing to look out for*

God punishes evil and sin.

8. *Key Bible cross-reference*

Verse 15. See Jeremiah 22:24-27.

9. *Key "by way of explanation"*

Verse 19. Zedekiah had been given plenty of warnings about the need to repent. See Jeremiah 38:5,19.

10. *Key "Quotable Quote"*

"The Scripture moveth us, in sundry places to acknowledge and confess our manifold sins and wickedness."

Book of Common Prayer

2 Kings chapter 25

1. **Previous chapter**

   Chapter 24: Nebuchadnezzar captures Jerusalem

2. **Analysis of chapter**

   Jerusalem besieged, Zedekiah taken. (1-7)
   The temple burnt, and the people carried into captivity. (8-21)
   The rest of the Jews flee into Egypt, Evil-merodach relieves the captivity of Jehoiachin. (22-30)

3. **Key verse**

   Verse 1: "And it came to pass in the ninth year of his reign, in the tenth month, in the tenth day of the month, that Nebuchadnezzar king of Babylon came, he, and all his host, against Jerusalem, and pitched against it; and they built forts against it round about."

4. **Key word / key phrase**

   Verse 1, "Jerusalem."

5. **Key event / key person / key theme**

   The fall of Jerusalem

6. **Key thought**

   Jerusalem need never have fallen.

7. **Key thing to look out for**

   What can be learned from the fall of Jerusalem?

8. **Key Bible cross-reference**

   Verse 1. See Jeremiah 39:1; 52:4.

9. **Key "by way of explanation"**

   Verse 7. Zedekiah could have prevented God's judgment on Jerusalem if he had only done what Jeremiah told him to do. See Jeremiah 38:14-28. Jerusalem fell in the summer of 586 BC.

10. **Key "Quotable Quote"**

    "God can turn any tragedy into a triumph, if only you will wait and watch."
    Max Lucado

1 Chronicles and
2 Chronicles

1 Chronicles chapter 1

1. **Following chapter**

   Chapter 2: Genealogy from Jacob to David

2. **Analysis of chapter**

   Genealogies, Adam to Abraham. (1-27)
   The descendants of Abraham. (28-54)

3. **Key verse**

   Verse 1: "Adam, Seth, Enosh . . ."

4. **Key word / key phrase**

   Verse 1, "Adam."

5. **Key event / key person / key theme**

   Genealogy from Adam to Abraham

6. **Key thought**

   God has his providential hand over all his people.

7. **Key thing to look out for**

   The orderly arrangement of names has been likened to a garden divided into separate beds.

8. **Key Bible cross-reference**

   Verses 5-23. See Genesis 10:2-29.

9. **Key "by way of explanation"**

   1 and 2 Chronicles were written after the exile to Babylon. In Hebrew Bibles they make up one book and this book is included, not among the historical books, but in the section called the Writings.

10. **Key "Quotable Quote"**

    "The history of the Church ought properly to be called the history of truth." Blaise Pascal

1 Chronicles chapter 2

1. *Before and after*

Previous chapter: Chapter 1: Genealogy from Adam to Abraham, and from Abraham to Jacob

Following chapter: Chapter 3: Genealogy from David to the captivity

2. *Analysis of chapter*

Israel's sons. (1-2)

The line of Judah. (3-55)

3. *Key verse*

Verse 1: "These are the sons of Israel."

4. *Key word / key phrase*

Verse 1, "Israel."

5. *Key event / key person / key theme*

Genealogy from Jacob to David

6. *Key thought*

God is the God of the individual.

7. *Key thing to look out for*

Verse 20. In this list, the Chronicler includes the craftsman Bezalel, who master-minded the building of the tabernacle.

8. *Key Bible cross-reference*

Verses 1,2. See Genesis 29:31–30:24.

9. *Key "by way of explanation"*

In 1 and 2 Chronicles the writer's emphasis is on the priesthood, the temple, and worship.

10. *Key "Quotable Quote"*

"God, so great an artificer in great things, is not less great in small things."
Augustine of Hippo

1 Chronicles chapter 3

1. Before and after

Previous chapter: Chapter 2: Genealogy from Jacob to David
Following chapter: Chapter 4: Genealogy of Judah and Simeon

2. Analysis of chapter

The line of David. (1-24)

3. Key verse

Verse 1: "Now these were the sons of David, which were born unto him in Hebron."

4. Key word / key phrase

Verse 1, "David."

5. Key event / key person / key theme

Genealogy from David to the captivity

6. Key thought

Jesus was happy to be recognized as the son of David.

7. Key thing to look out for

Despite his many faults David was Israel's greatest king.

8. Key Bible cross-reference

Verses 1-9. See 2 Samuel 3:2-5; 5:13-16; 13:1.

9. Key "by way of explanation"

The Chronicler has lifted material from the archives. Slight variations in the lists here and in Kings and Luke 3 probabaly indicate different ways of recording inter-marriages.

10. Key "Quotable Quote"

"Man moves himself, but God leads him."
François Fénelon

1 Chronicles chapter 4

1. **Before and after**

   Previous chapter: Chapter 3: Genealogy from David to the captivity
   Following chapter: Chapter 5: Genealogy of Reuben, Gad, and Manasseh

2. **Analysis of chapter**

   Southern tribal lists. (1-43)

3. **Key verse**

   Verse 1: "The sons of Judah; Pharez, Hezron, and Carmi, and Hur, and Shobal."

4. **Key word / key phrase**

   Verse 1, "Judah."

5. **Key event / key person / key theme**

   Genealogy of Judah and Simeon

6. **Key thought**

   To turn to the Lord in prayer expresses faith and dependence.

7. **Key thing to look out for**

   Verse 10. God loves to answer prayers.

8. **Key Bible cross-reference**

   Verse 13. See Joshua 15:17; Judges 1:13; 3:9-11.

9. **Key "by way of explanation"**

   Verses 9,10. These two verses are an example of the short historical notes which intersperse the list of names in these genealogies.

10. **Key "Quotable Quote"**

    "I have no doubt that the world stands because of the prayers of Christians." Aristides of Athens

1 Chronicles chapter 5

1. Before and after

Previous chapter: Chapter 4: Genealogy of Judah and Simeon
Following chapter: Chapter 6: Genealogy of Levi

2. Analysis of chapter

The line of Reuben. (1-10)
The line of Gad. (11-22)
The half-tribe of Manasseh (23-26)

3. Key verse

Verse 1: "Now the sons of Reuben the firstborn of Israel."

4. Key word / key phrase

Verse 1, "Reuben."

5. Key event / key person / key theme

Genealogy of the tribes who lived across the Jordan.

6. Key thought

Verse 22. God helped his people in their victories.

7. Key thing to look out for

Anything that is good in our lives we should attribute to God.

8. Key Bible cross-reference

Verses 1-26. See Numbers 32:33-42.

9. Key "by way of explanation"

Verse 6. "Tiglath-Pileser" was the Assyrian king who attacked Israel. His personal name was "Pul" and he kept this name as king of Babylon. But as ruler of Assyria he was known as "Tiglath-Pileser."

10. Key "Quotable Quote"

"It is most certain that, where the grace of God reigns, there is also the readiness to obey."
John Calvin

1 Chronicles chapter 6

1. *Before and after*

Previous chapter: Chapter 5: Genealogy of Reuben, Gad, and Manasseh
Following chapter: Chapter 7: Genealogy of Issachar, Benjamin, Naphtali, Manasseh, Ephraim, and Asher

2. *Analysis of chapter*

Descendants of the high priests. (1-15)
Other descendants of Levi. (16-30)
Temple musicians. (31-48)
Descendants of Aaron. (49-53)
Levite territory. (54-80)

3. *Key verse*

Verse 1: "The sons of Levi."

4. *Key word / key phrase*

Verse 1, "Levi."

5. *Key event / key person / key theme*

Genealogy of Levi

6. *Key thought*

The inclusion in the list of temple musicians shows the importance of music in the worship of the Israelites.

7. *Key thing to look out for*

Verse 31. David, himself a singer and musician, established a guild of musicians.

8. *Key Bible cross-reference*

Verses 31-38. See 15:16,27; 25:1-31.

9. *Key "by way of explanation"*

Verse 4-15. These verses give a shortened list of the high priests from the time of Eleazar to the Exile.

10. *Key "Quotable Quote"*

"Pastors have neglected their rightful oversight of worship, including the doctrinal content of the music."
Alliance of Confessing Evangelicals, *The Cambridge Declaration*

1 Chronicles chapter 7

1. **Before and after**

    Previous chapter: Chapter 6: Genealogy of Levi
    Following chapter: Chapter 8: Genealogy of Benjamin

2. **Analysis of chapter**

    Issachar's descendants. (1-5)
    Descendants of Benjamin, Dan, and Naphtali. (6-13)
    Descendants of Manasseh. (14-19)
    Descendants of Ephraim. (20-29).
    Descendants of Asher. (30-40)

3. **Key verse**

    Verse 1: "Now the sons of Issachar were, Tola, and Puah, Jashub, and Shimrom, four."

4. **Key word / key phrase**

    Verse 1, "Issachar."

5. **Key event / key person / key theme**

    Genealogy of Issachar, Benjamin, Naphtali, Manasseh, Ephraim, and Asher

6. **Key thought**

    Every Christian is a member of God's family.

7. **Key thing to look out for**

    Verse 40. How would we wish our descendants to be described?

8. **Key Bible cross-reference**

    Verses 1-5. See Genesis 46:13; Numbers 1:28; 26:23-25.

9. **Key "by way of explanation"**

    Verse 15. The daughters of Zelophehad are linked to the teaching on the inheritance rights of women found in Numbers 26:29-34; 27:1-11.

10. **Key "Quotable Quote"**

    "Every Christian community must realize that not only do the weak need the strong, but also that the strong cannot exist without the weak. The elimination of the weak is the death of the fellowship."
    Dietrich Bonhoeffer

1 Chronicles chapter 8

1. **Before and after**

   Previous chapter: Chapter 7: Genealogy of Issachar, Benjamin, Naphtali, Manasseh, Ephraim, and Asher
   Following chapter: Chapter 9: Genealogy of the remnant

2. **Analysis of chapter**

   Descendants of Benjamin. (1-32)
   Family of King Saul. (33-40)

3. **Key verse**

   Verse 1: "Now Benjamin begat Bela his firstborn, Ashbel the second, and Aharah the third."

4. **Key word / key phrase**

   Verse 1, "Benjamin."

5. **Key event / key person / key theme**

   Genealogy of Benjamin

6. **Key thought**

   Life itself is a gift from God.

7. **Key thing to look out for**

   Families are meant to encourage their members to love the Lord.

8. **Key Bible cross-reference**

   Verse 33. See 1 Samuel 14:49; 31:2.

9. **Key "by way of explanation"**

   Verses 6-27. These verses are among the few verses that are unique to Chronicles.

10. **Key "Quotable Quote"**

   "Behind every saint stands another saint."
   Friedrich von Hugel

1 Chronicles chapter 9

1. Before and after

Previous chapter: Chapter 8: Genealogy of Benjamin
Following chapter: Chapter 10: Death of Saul

2. Analysis of chapter

Returned captives in Jerusalem. (1-9)
Priests and Levites in Jerusalem. (10-16)
Temple guards and other Levites in Jerusalem. (17-34)
Genealogy of King Saul (35-44)

3. Key verse

Verse 1: "So all Israel were reckoned by genealogies; and, behold, they were written in the book of the kings of Israel and Judah, who were carried away to Babylon for their transgression."

4. Key word / key phrase

Verse 22, "positions of trust."

5. Key event / key person / key theme

The work of the Levites

6. Key thought

Christians should excel at being members of a team.

7. Key thing to look out for

Verse 33. Musicians offered praise to God night and day.

8. Key Bible cross-reference

Verses 10-13. See Nehemiah 11:10-14.

9. Key "by way of explanation"

Verses 22-27. A pool of 212 gatekeepers guarded Jerusalem. Seventy-two gatekeepers were on duty each week.

10. Key "Quotable Quote"

"The great cannot exist without the less, nor the less without the great."
Clement of Rome

1 Chronicles chapter 12

(For 1 Chronicles chapter 10, see 1 Samuel 31.)
(For 1 Chronicles chapter 11, see 2 Samuel 5:1-3, 6-10; 23:8-39.)

1. **Before and after**

   Previous chapter: Chapter 11: David becomes king, takes Jerusalem, and his mighty men
   Following chapter: Chapter 13: The failed attempt to take the ark to Jerusalem

2. **Analysis of chapter**

   Those who came to David at Ziklag (where he was still an outlaw). (1-22)
   Those who came to Hebron to proclaim him king. (23-40)

3. **Key verse**

   Verse 1: "Now these are they that came to David to Ziklag, while he yet kept himself close because of Saul the son of Kish: and they were among the mighty men, helpers of the war."

4. **Key word / key phrase**

   Verse 18, "your God will help you."

5. **Key event / key person / key theme**

   David's followers

6. **Key thought**

   So many hundreds of thousands of people were united by their love and loyalty for one man: this ought to be a picture of the Church.

7. **Key thing to look out for**

   The many varied gifts of David's followers.

8. **Key Bible cross-reference**

   Verses 38-40. David's great feast has been taken as a picture of the future Messianic feast. Messianic times are often pictured in terms of a feast. See Matthew 25:1-13; Luke 22:28-30.

9. **Key "by way of explanation"**

   Verses 23-37. Sometimes the Hebrew word for "thousand" stands for a group of men with its own commander. See 13:1.

10. **Key "Quotable Quote"**

    "Imprudent is he whoever arranges only his earthly will and not his heavenly one."
    Basil the Great

1 Chronicles chapter 15

(For 1 Chronicles chapter 13, see 2 Samuel 6:1-12.)
(For 1 Chronicles chapter 14, see 2 Samuel 5:11-25.)

1. **Before and after**

    Previous chapter: Chapter 14: David's prosperous reign
    Following chapter: Chapter 16: Celebrating the ark's arrival in Jerusalem

2. **Analysis of chapter**

    Preparations for the removal of the ark. (1-24)
    The removal of the ark. (25-29)

3. **Key verse**

    Verse 3: "And David gathered all Israel together to Jerusalem, to bring up the ark of the LORD unto his place, which he had prepared for it."

4. **Key word / key phrase**

    Verse 1, "ark."

5. **Key event / key person / key theme**

    The ark is brought to Jerusalem

6. **Key thought**

    Worship is meant to be at the heart of the Christian fellowship.

7. **Key thing to look out for**

    What was the matter with Michal?

8. **Key Bible cross-reference**

    Verses 1-29. See Psalm 132.

9. **Key "by way of explanation"**

    Verse 12. The consecration referred to in this verse means ritual washings and all other activities commanded to avoid ceremonial uncleanness.

10. **Key "Quotable Quote"**

    "Visualize the Lord high and lifted up filling the sanctuary with his presence."
    Richard Foster

1 Chronicles chapter 16

1. ### Before and after

   Previous chapter: Chapter 15: Successfully transporting the ark
   Following chapter: Chapter 17: David is not allowed to build the temple

2. ### Analysis of chapter

   The ark is set down inside the tent with great solemnity. (1-6)
   David's psalm of praise. (7-36)
   Setting in order the worship of God. (37-43)

3. ### Key verse

   Verse 1: "So they brought the ark of God, and set it in the midst of the tent that David had pitched for it: and they offered burnt sacrifices and peace offerings before God."

4. ### Key word / key phrase

   Verse 8, "give thanks."

5. ### Key event / key person / key theme

   David's song of praise

6. ### Key thought

   Praise and thanksgiving should be part of the daily life of God's people.

7. ### Key thing to look out for

   The reasons why God is to be praised.

8. ### Key Bible cross-reference

   Verses 8-36. See Psalm 105:1-15; 96; 106:1,47,48.

9. ### Key "by way of explanation"

   Verse 1-3. David is here linked with the priests as he supervised their sacrifices and blessed the people.

10. ### Key "Quotable Quote"

    "Remember the perfections of that God whom you worship, that he is most holy, pure, and jealous, and therefore to be purely worshipped; and that he is still present with you, and all things are naked and open to him with whom we have to do."
    Richard Baxter

1 Chronicles chapter 22

(For 1 Chronicles chapter 17, see 2 Samuel 7:1-29)
(For 1 Chronicles chapter 18 see 2 Samuel 8:1-18.)
(For 1 Chronicles chapter 19, see 2 Samuel 10.)
(For 1 Chronicles chapter 20, see 2 Samuel 12:29-31; 21:15-22.)
(For 1 Chronicles chapter 21, see 2 Samuel 24.)

1. **Before and after**

   Previous chapter: Chapter 21: David's sinful census
   Following chapter: Chapter 23: The work of the Levites

2. **Analysis of chapter**

   David's preparations for the temple. (1-5)
   David's instructions to Solomon. (6-16)
   The leaders of Israel commanded to assist. (17-19)

3. **Key verse**

   Verse 5: "So David prepared abundantly before his death."

4. **Key word / key phrase**

   Verse 1, "house of the Lord."

5. **Key event / key person / key theme**

   Preparations for building the temple

6. **Key thought**

   Many different skills were needed to build the temple.

7. **Key thing to look out for**

   Verse 19. A crucial instruction.

8. **Key Bible cross-reference**

   Verses 8,9. See 1 Kings 5:3.

9. **Key "by way of explanation"**

   Verses 8,9. David's constant preoccupation with war left him defiled so that
   he was in no state to build the temple.

10. **Key "Quotable Quote"**

    "In a Christian community, everything depends upon whether each
    individual is an indispensable link in a chain. Only when even the smallest
    link is securely interlocked is the chain unbreakable."
    Dietrich Bonhoeffer

1 Chronicles chapter 23

1. Before and after

Previous chapter: Chapter 22: Instructions about building the temple
Following chapter: Chapter 24: Work given to the priests

2. Analysis of chapter

David declares Solomon his successor. (1)
The Levites, their family and work. (2-32)

3. Key verse

Verse 1: "So when David was old and full of days, he made Solomon his son king over Israel."

4. Key word / key phrase

Verse 2, "Levites."

5. Key event / key person / key theme

The work of the Levites

6. Key thought

No job should be too small to do in God's service.

7. Key thing to look out for

The many jobs performed by the Levites.

8. Key Bible cross-reference

Verse 3. See Numbers 4:1-3.

9. Key "by way of explanation"

The Levites were assistants to the priests, and were also in charge of the music (verse 30).

10. Key "Quotable Quote"

"I count that part of my life lost which I spent not in communion with God, or in doing good."
John Donne

1 Chronicles chapter 24

1. **Before and after**

   Previous chapter: Chapter 23: The work of the Levites
   Following chapter: Chapter 25: The temple musicians

2. **Analysis of chapter**

   Work given to the priests. (1-19)
   The rest of the Levites listed. (20-31)

3. **Key verse**

   Verse 1: "Now these are the divisions of the sons of Aaron. The sons of Aaron;
   Nadab, and Abihu, Eleazar, and Ithamar."

4. **Key word / key phrase**

   Verse 1, "sons of Aaron."

5. **Key event / key person / key theme**

   Work given to the priests

6. **Key thought**

   Every Christian can serve the Lord in a unique way.

7. **Key thing to look out for**

   Verse 5. There should be no rivalry or jealousy among the Lord's servants.

8. **Key Bible cross-reference**

   1-19. See 6:3-15; Ezra 2:36-39.

9. **Key "by way of explanation"**

   Verse 4. The priests serving in the temple were divided into twenty-four
   teams or divisions and were chosen by lots.

10. **Key "Quotable Quote"**

    "Blessed is the servant who esteems himself no more highly when he is
    praised and exalted by people than when he is considered worthless, foolish,
    and to be despised; since what a man is before God, that he is and nothing
    more."
    Francis of Assisi

1 Chronicles chapter 25

1. **Before and after**

   Previous chapter: Chapter 24: Work given to the priests
   Following chapter: Chapter 26: The temple guards

2. **Analysis of chapter**

   The temple musicians (all Levites). (1-31)

3. **Key verse**

   Verse 1: "Moreover David and the captains of the host separated to the service of the sons of Asaph, and of Heman, and of Jeduthun, who should prophesy with harps, with psalteries, and with cymbals."

4. **Key word / key phrase**

   Verse 1, "harps, lyres and cymbals."

5. **Key event / key person / key theme**

   The temple musicians

6. **Key thought**

   Music and singing should be an integral part of Christian worship.

7. **Key thing to look out for**

   Here and elsewhere in Chronicles the temple officials had a ministry of prophesying (compare Ehesians 5:18,19).

8. **Key Bible cross-reference**

   Verse 1. See 2 Chronicles 20:14-17; 35:15.

9. **Key "by way of explanation"**

   Verse 1. David's great interest in music would have made him ideal for organizing the singers and musicians in the temple.

10. **Key "Quotable Quote"**

    "The aim and final end of all music should be none other than the glory of God and the refreshment of the soul. If heed is not paid to this, it is not true music but a diabolical bawling and twanging."
    J.S. Bach

1 Chronicles chapter 26

1. **Before and after**

   > Previous chapter: Chapter 25: The temple musicians
   > Following chapter: Chapter 27: Government officials

2. **Analysis of chapter**

   > The temple guards. (1-19)
   > Other temple duties. (20-28)
   > Duties of other Levites (29-32)

3. **Key verse**

   > Verse 1: "Concerning the divisions of the porters: From the Korhites was Meshelemiah the son of Kore, of the sons of Asaph."

4. **Key word / key phrase**

   > Verse 1, "gatekeepers."

5. **Key event / key person / key theme**

   > The temple guards

6. **Key thought**

   > God's word needs guarding in the sense that it should be taught faithfully.

7. **Key thing to look out for**

   > Christian fellowships should guard against being infiltrated by false teachers.

8. **Key Bible cross-reference**

   > Verses 1-19. See 9:17-27; 16:37,38.

9. **Key "by way of explanation"**

   > Verse 29. Work outside Jeruselem. The officers collected tithes for the temple; the judges gave judgment about the application of the law.

10. **Key "Quotable Quote"**

    > "False teachers tear the Bible to pieces, scourge and crucify it, and subject it to all manner of torture until they stretch it sufficiently to apply to their heresy, meaning, and whim."
    > Martin Luther

1 Chronicles chapter 27

1. *Before and after*

Previous chapter: Chapter 26: The temple guards
Following chapter: Chapter 28: David's last words to his officials and to Solomon

2. *Analysis of chapter*

David's military force. (1-15)
Leaders and officers. (16-34)

3. *Key verse*

Verse 1: "Now the children of Israel after their number, to wit, the chief fathers and captains of thousands and hundreds, and their officers that served the king in any matter of the courses, which came in and went out month by month throughout all the months of the year, of every course were twenty and four thousand."

4. *Key word / key phrase*

Verse 1, "commanders of thousands."

5. *Key event / key person / key theme*

Government officials

6. *Key thought*

The desire for unity is meant to be one of the characteristics of Christian workers.

7. *Key thing to look out for*

Verse 24. When does counting numbers arouse God's anger?

8. *Key Bible cross-reference*

Verses 1-15. See 2 Samuel 23:23-37.

9. *Key "by way of explanation"*

Verses 32-34. In these verses David's inner circle of leaders is detailed.

10. *Key "Quotable Quote"*

"It is not our business to succeed, but to do right: when you have done so, the rest lies with God."
C.S. Lewis

1 Chronicles chapter 28

1. Before and after

Previous chapter: Chapter 27: Government officials
Following chapter: Chapter 29: David praises God, and summary of his reign

2. Analysis of chapter

David exhorts the people to fear of the Lord. (1-10)
He gives instructions for the temple. (11-21)

3. Key verse

Verse 8: "Now therefore in the sight of all Israel the congregation of the LORD, and in the audience of our God, keep and seek for all the commandments of the LORD your God: that ye may possess this good land, and leave it for an inheritance for your children after you for ever."

4. Key word / key phrase

Verse 1, "David."

5. Key event / key person / key theme

David's last words to his officials and to Solomon

6. Key thought

God's power should always be the basis for any Christian work.

7. Key thing to look out for

Verses 9,10. David's reasons for urging Solomon to serve God wholeheartedly.

8. Key Bible cross-reference

Verse 19. See Exodus 25:40; 27:8; 31:18.

9. Key "by way of explanation"

Verse 20. The key to David's advice to Solomon comes in this verse with its emphasis on the power and reliability of the Lord.

10. Key "Quotable Quote"

"In God's faithfulness lies eternal security."
Corrie ten Boom

1 Chronicles chapter 29

1. **Previous chapter**

   Chapter 28: David's last words to his officials and to Solomon

2. **Analysis of chapter**

   David induces the leaders and people to offer willingly. (1-9)
   His thanksgiving and prayer. (10-19)
   Solomon enthroned. (20-25)
   David's reign and death. (26-30)

3. **Key verse**

   Verse 6: "Then the chief of the fathers and princes of the tribes of Israel, and the captains of thousands and of hundreds, with the rulers of the king's work, offered willingly."

4. **Key word / key phrase**

   Verse 1, "King David."

5. **Key event / key person / key theme**

   Summary of David's reign

6. **Key thought**

   David nearly always praised God when he prayed.

7. **Key thing to look out for**

   Verse 14. Why were the people so generous?

8. **Key Bible cross-reference**

   Verses 2-9. See Exodus 25:1-8; 35:4-9,20-20.

9. **Key "by way of explanation"**

   Verse 7. A "daric" was a Persian coin, named after King Darius I.

10. **Key "Quotable Quote"**

    "Let us sing how the eternal God, the author of all marvels, first created the heavens for the sons of men as a roof to cover them, and how their almighty Protector gave them the earth to live in."
    Caedmon

2 Chronicles chapter 4

(For 2 Chronicles chapter 1, see 1 Kings 3:4-15; 10:26-29.)
(For 2 Chronicles chapter 2, see 1 Kings 5.)
(For 2 Chronicles chapter 3, see 1 Kings 6.)

1. **Before and after**

   Previous chapter: Chapter 3: Building the temple
   Following chapter: Chapter 5: The ark is taken into the temple

2. **Analysis of chapter**

   Furnishings of the temple. (1-22)

3. **Key verse**

   Verse 2: "Also he made a molten sea of ten cubits from brim to brim, round in compass, and five cubits the height thereof; and a line of thirty cubits did compass it round about."

4. **Key word / key phrase**

   Verse 1, "made."

5. **Key event / key person / key theme**

   Making the furnishings for the temple

6. **Key thought**

   All this craftsmanship was fashioned to bring glory to God.

7. **Key thing to look out for**

   The New Testament speaks of these ceremonies as foreshadowing the cleansing and forgiveness that Christ brought.

8. **Key Bible cross-reference**

   Verse 2. See Exodus 30:18.

9. **Key "by way of explanation"**

   Verse 4. It is likely that the twelve bulls which held up the great Sea represented the twelve tribes of Israel. They had also surrounded the tabernacle with three on each side.

10. **Key "Quotable Quote"**

    "The Old Testament does not occupy itself with how Israel thought of God. Its concern is with how Israel ought to think of God. The fundamental note of the Old Testament is revelation."
    Benjamin B. Warfield

2 Chronicles chapter 5

1. Before and after

> Previous chapter: Chapter 4: The temple's furnishings
> Following chapter: Chapter 6: Solomon's sermon and prayer

2. Analysis of chapter

> The ark placed in the temple. (1-10)
> The temple filled with God's glory. (11-14)

3. Key verse

> Verse 14: "So that the priests could not stand to minister by reason of the cloud: for the glory of the LORD had filled the house of God."

4. Key word / key phrase

> Verse 2, "ark."

5. Key event / key person / key theme

> The ark is brought to the temple

6. Key thought

> The ark symbolized the presence of God.

7. Key thing to look out for

> How did people celebrate one of the greatest events in their history?

8. Key Bible cross-reference

> Verse 2. See 1 Chronicles 15:1–16:6.

9. Key "by way of explanation"

> Verse 10. In addition to the two stone tablets the ark had contained Aaron's staff and a gold jar of manna. Nobody knows what happened to these items.

10. Key "Quotable Quote"

> "Faith is the eye through which the light of God's presence and the vigor of his power stream into the soul."
> Andrew Murray

2 Chronicles chapter 6

1. ## *Before and after*

    Previous chapter: Chapter 5: The ark is taken into the temple
    Following chapter: Chapter 7: The temple's dedication, and the Lord's reply
    to Solomon

2. ## *Analysis of chapter*

    Solomon speaks to the people. (1-11)
    Solomon's prayer. (12-42)

3. ## *Key verse*

    Verse 1: "Then said Solomon, The LORD hath said that he would dwell in the
    thick darkness."

4. ## *Key word / key phrase*

    Verse 1, "Solomon."

5. ## *Key event / key person / key theme*

    Solomon's prayer of dedication

6. ## *Key thought*

    God keeps his promises.

7. ## *Key thing to look out for*

    Recalling our own personal histories with gratitude before God is a healthy
    spiritual exercise.

8. ## *Key Bible cross-reference*

    Verses 8,9. See 1 Chronicles 28:2,3.

9. ## *Key "by way of explanation"*

    Verses 34,35. The Chronicler often states that God gave his people victory in
    answer to prayer.

10. ## *Key "Quotable Quote"*

    "God is my being, my me, my strength, my beatitude, my good, my delight."
    Catherine of Genoa

2 Chronicles chapter 11

(For 2 Chronicles chapter 7, see 1 Kings 8:62-66; 9:1-19.)
(For 2 Chronicles chapter 8, see 1 Kings 9:10-28.)
(For 2 Chronicles chapter 9, see 1 Kings 10:1-29; 11:41-43.)
(For 2 Chronicles chapter 10, see 1 Kings 12:1-24.)

1. ### Before and after

    Previous chapter: Chapter 10: The division of the kingdom
    Following chapter: Chapter 12: Egyptians invade Judah

2. ### Analysis of chapter

    Rehoboam forbidden to fight against Israel. (1-12)
    The priests and Levites find refuge in Judah. (13-23)

3. ### Key verse

    Verse 4: "Thus saith the LORD, Ye shall not go up, nor fight against your brethren: return every man to his house: for this thing is done of me."

4. ### Key word / key phrase

    Verse 1, "Rehoboam."

5. ### Key event / key person / key theme

    Rehoboam fortifies the cities of Judah

6. ### Key thought

    Choosing to follow God's ways is to vote against evil ways.

7. ### Key thing to look out for

    Anything which strengthens goodness should be positively supported.

8. ### Key Bible cross-reference

    Verses 13-17. See 1 Kings 12:26-33.

9. ### Key "by way of explanation"

    Verses 16,17. When the northern tribes rebelled and formed the separate nation of Israel, many people came south to worship in Jerusalem and support Rehoboam.

10. ### Key "Quotable Quote"

    "Man has two great spiritual needs One is for forgiveness. The other is for goodness."
    Billy Graham

2 Chronicles chapter 12

1. *Before and after*

   Previous chapter: Chapter 11: Rehoboam strengthens Jerusalem
   Following chapter: Chapter 13: Abijah of Judah

2. *Analysis of chapter*

   Shishak attacks Jerusalem. (1-12)
   Summary of Rehoboam's reign. (13-16)

3. *Key verse*

   Verse 2: "And it came to pass, that in the fifth year of king Rehoboam Shishak king of Egypt came up against Jerusalem."

4. *Key word / key phrase*

   Verse 2, "Shishak."

5. *Key event / key person / key theme*

   Shishak, king of Egypt, attacks Jerusalem

6. *Key thought*

   Every time we humble ourselves before the Lord we grow spiritually.

7. *Key thing to look out for*

   God's purpose in allowing Judah to become a vassal nation of Egypt (verse 8).

8. *Key Bible cross-reference*

   Verse 1. See 9:30; 10:16; 11:13; 11:3.

9. *Key "by way of explanation"*

   Verse 2. The Chronicler often includes notes which are not found in 1 and 2 Kings. See 11:17; 15:10,19; 16:1,12,13; 17:7: 21:20; 25:15,17,23.

10. *Key "Quotable Quote"*

   "It is only with the heart that one can see rightly; what is essential is invisible to the eye."
   Antoine of St Exupery

2 Chronicles chapter 13

1. *Before and after*

Previous chapter: Chapter 12: Egyptians invade Judah
Following chapter: Chapter 14: Asa's reforms and victory against the Cushites

2. *Analysis of chapter*

Abijah overcomes Jeroboam. (1-22)

3. *Key verse*

Verse 1: "Now in the eighteenth year of king Jeroboam began Abijah to reign over Judah."

4. *Key word / key phrase*

Verse 1, "Abijah."

5. *Key event / key person / key theme*

Abijah goes to war against Jeroboam

6. *Key thought*

In their extremity, Judah cried out to the Lord.

7. *Key thing to look out for*

Verse 10. How the people showed that they had not forsaken God.

8. *Key Bible cross-reference*

Verse 3. See 1 Chronicles 21:5.

9. *Key "by way of explanation"*

Verse 8. This verse shows how David's kingdom stood for the "kingdom of the Lord."

10. *Key "Quotable Quote"*

"There is no point in us traveling abroad to find the kingdom of heaven, or crossing the sea in search of virtue. As the Lord has already told us, God's kingdom is within you."
Antony of Egypt

2 Chronicles chapter 14

1. **Before and after**

   Previous chapter: Chapter 13: Abijah of Judah
   Following chapter: Chapter 15: King Asa's reforms

2. **Analysis of chapter**

   Asa's piety. He strengthens his kingdom. (1-15)

3. **Key verse**

   Verse 2: "And Asa did that which was good and right in the eyes of the LORD his God."

4. **Key word / key phrase**

   Verse 2, "Asa."

5. **Key event / key person / key theme**

   King Asa of Judah defeats the vast Cushite army

6. **Key thought**

   We should never underestimate the power of evil, and its insidious hold on us.

7. **Key thing to look out for**

   What happens when we rely only on God (verses 11,12).

8. **Key Bible cross-reference**

   Verse 5. See 17:6; 20:33.

9. **Key "by way of explanation"**

   Verse 5. Here Asa is said to have "removed the high places." But in 1 Kings 15:14 he is said not to have removed the high places. In the early part of his reign Asa did try to remove them but did not completely succeed, so by the end of his reign the pagan worship still existed.

10. **Key "Quotable Quote"**

    "To be united to Christ by faith is to throw off the thralldom of hostile powers, to enjoy perfect freedom, to gain the mastery over the dominion of evil – because Christ's victory is ours."
    F.F. Bruce

2 Chronicles chapter 15

1. **Before and after**

   Previous chapter: Chapter 14: Asa defeats the Cushites
   Following chapter: Chapter 16: Hanani the prophet, and the end of Asa's reign

2. **Analysis of chapter**

   Asa's reforms. (1-19)

3. **Key verse**

   Verse 1: "And the Spirit of God came upon Azariah the son of Oded."

4. **Key word / key phrase**

   Verse 1, "the Spirit of God."

5. **Key event / key person / key theme**

   King Asa's reforms

6. **Key thought**

   Nobody who seeks God will fail to find him.

7. **Key thing to look out for**

   Whoever decides to forsake God will find himself forsaken by God.

8. **Key Bible cross-reference**

   Verse 12. See Deuteronomy 29:1; 1 Samuel 11:14.

9. **Key "by way of explanation"**

   Verse 3. Priests not only carried out the sacrifices in the temple but also were meant to teach the people.

10. **Key "Quotable Quote"**

    "If you fail to seek God in the small things, you will seek him in vain for the large things."
    Andrew Murray

2 Chronicles chapter 16

1. *Before and after*

   Previous chapter: Chapter 15: King Asa's reforms
   Following chapter: Chapter 17: Jehoshaphat king of Judah

2. *Analysis of chapter*

   Asa seeks help from the Syrians. (1-6)
   The prophet Hanani. (7-10)
   Asa's death. (11-14)

3. *Key verse*

   Verse 2: "Then Asa brought out silver and gold out of the treasures of the house of the LORD and of the king's house, and sent to Benhadad king of Syria."

4. *Key word / key phrase*

   Verse 1, "Asa's."

5. *Key event / key person / key theme*

   King Asa's last years

6. *Key thought*

   Trusting the Lord meant not seeking alliances with foreign powers.

7. *Key thing to look out for*

   The Lord longs for wholeheartedness among his followers.

8. *Key Bible cross-reference*

   Verses 2-9. See 20:35-37; 28:16-21.

9. *Key "by way of explanation"*

   Verse 12. There are a number of examples in the Bible of someone becoming ill as a punishment for sin. See 21:16-20; 26:16-23; Acts 12:23.

10. *Key "Quotable Quote"*

    "Outward uprightness of life is not the chief point of repentance, for God looks into men's hearts."
    John Calvin

2 Chronicles chapter 17

1. *Before and after*

Previous chapter: Chapter 16: Hanani the prophet, and the end of Asa's reign
Following chapter: Chapter 18: Micaiah prophecies against Ahab; Ahab killed

2. *Analysis of chapter*

Jehoshaphat becomes king. (1-9)
Jehoshaphat's greatness. (10-19)

3. *Key verse*

Verse 1: "And Jehoshaphat his son reigned in his stead, and strengthened himself against Israel."

4. *Key word / key phrase*

Verse 4, "sought God."

5. *Key event / key person / key theme*

King Jehoshaphat of Judah

6. *Key thought*

Jehoshaphat's heart was in the right place.

7. *Key thing to look out for*

Right actions stem from being right with the Lord.

8. *Key Bible cross-reference*

17:1–21:3. See 1 Kings 22:1-46.

9. *Key "by way of explanation"*

Verses 7-9. God's Law was not just taught by priests and prophets, but also by officials appointed by the king.

10. *Key "Quotable Quote"*

"Let our hearts and souls burst with love!"
Catherine of Siena

2 Chronicles chapter 19

(For 2 Chronicles chapter 18, see 1 Kings 22.)

1. **Before and after**

    Previous chapter: Chapter 18: Micaiah prophecies against Ahab; Ahab killed

    Following chapter: Chapter 20: Jehoshaphat defeats Moab and Ammon

2. **Analysis of chapter**

    Jehoshaphat is reprimanded. (1-3)

    Jehoshaphat's reforms. (4-11)

3. **Key verse**

    Verse 2: "And Jehu the son of Hanani the seer went out to meet him, and said to king Jehoshaphat, Shouldest thou help the ungodly, and love them that hate the LORD?"

4. **Key word / key phrase**

    Verse 2, "wholeheartedly."

5. **Key event / key person / key theme**

    Micaiah prophecies against Ahab

6. **Key thought**

    A prophet needed courage as well as spiritual insight.

7. **Key thing to look out for**

    How a person reacts to wise advice tells you much about his state of heart.

8. **Key Bible cross-reference**

    Verse 1. See 22:10–23:21.

9. **Key "by way of explanation"**

    Verse 1. In 19:2-3 the prophet condemns the marriage alliance Jehoshaphat made with Ahab.

10. **Key "Quotable Quote"**

    "Watch over your heart."
    Jean Pierre de Caussade

2 Chronicles chapter 20

1. Before and after

Previous chapter: Chapter 19: Jehoshaphat appoints judges
Following chapter: Chapter 21: King Jehoram of Judah

2. Analysis of chapter

The danger and distress of Judah. (1-13)
Jahaziel's prophecy of victory. (14-19)
The thanksgiving of Judah. (20-30)
Jehoshaphat's alliance with Ahaziah. (31-37)

3. Key verse

Verse 3: "And Jehoshaphat feared, and set himself to seek the LORD, and proclaimed a fast throughout all Judah."

4. Key word / key phrase

Verse 15, "the battle . . . is God's."

5. Key event / key person / key theme

Jehoshaphat defeats Moab and Ammon

6. Key thought

How a person is in his or her prayers is how a person is.

7. Key thing to look out for

God's people, equipped with God's Spirit, can face an army.

8. Key Bible cross-reference

Verse 1. See 26:7; 1 Chronicles 4:41.

9. Key "by way of explanation"

Verses 5-12. Jehoshaphat's prayer reveals that his heart is devoted to the Lord.

10. Key "Quotable Quote"

"God made us and God is able to empower us to do whatever he calls us to do."
Warren Wiersbe

2 Chronicles chapter 21

1. Before and after

Previous chapter: Chapter 20: Jehoshaphat defeats Moab and Ammon
Following chapter: Chapter 22: King Ahaziah of Judah

2. Analysis of chapter

The wicked reign of Jehoram. (1-11)
Jehoram's miserable end. (12-20)

3. Key verse

Verse 4: "Now when Jehoram was risen up to the kingdom of his father, he strengthened himself, and slew all his brethren with the sword, and divers also of the princes of Israel."

4. Key word / key phrase

Verse 20, "to no one's regret."

5. Key event / key person / key theme

King Jehoram of Judah

6. Key thought

Not to walk in God's ways always brings down God's judgment.

7. Key thing to look out for

To be a faithful prophet was a tough calling.

8. Key Bible cross-reference

Verse 2. See 11:18-22; 1 Chronicles 25:5.

9. Key "by way of explanation"

Verses 12-15. While 1 Kings and 2 Kings record much information about the prophet Elijah these verses with their reference to a letter from Elijah are the only ones about the prophet in 1 and 2 Chronicles.

10. Key "Quotable Quote"

"It's going to be quite a revealing thing at the last judgment when we see everyone standing naked before God."
Billy Graham

2 Chronicles chapter 24

(For 2 Chronicles chapters 22,23, see 1 Kings 8:25-29; 9:21-29; 11:1-21.)

1. Before and after

Previous chapter: Chapter 23: Rebellion against Athaliah, Jehoiada's reforms
Following chapter: Chapter 25: King Amaziah of Judah

2. Analysis of chapter

Joash, of Judah, and the temple repaired. (1-14)
Joash falls into idolatry. He is killed by his servants. (15-27)

3. Key verse

Verse 4: "And it came to pass after this, that Joash was minded to repair the house of the LORD."

4. Key word / key phrase

Verse 17, "After the death of Jehoiada."

5. Key event / key person / key theme

Joash repairs the temple

6. Key thought

Within one chapter Joash is commended and condemned.

7. Key thing to look out for

Remaining faithful to the Lord throughout one's life challenges all of God's followers.

8. Key Bible cross-reference

Verse 3. See verse 27.

9. Key "by way of explanation"

Verse 19. The destruction of Israel can be traced back to their rejection of the Lord's prophets. See 36:16.

10. Key "Quotable Quote"

"Perseverance in faith, devotion, and virtue is assured by three things: prayer, fasting, and mercy. Prayer knocks at the door, fasting gains entrance, mercy receives. These three things, prayer, fasting, and mercy, are all one and they give life to each other."
Peter Chrysologus

2 Chronicles chapter 25

1. *Before and after*

Previous chapter: Chapter 24: King Josiah of Judah
Following chapter: Chapter 26: King Uzziah of Judah

2. *Analysis of chapter*

Amaziah, king of Judah. (1-13)
Amaziah worships the idols of Edom. (14-16)
Amaziah's rash challenge. (17-28)

3. *Key verse*

Verse 1: "Amaziah was twenty and five years old when he began to reign, and he reigned twenty and nine years in Jerusalem."

4. *Key word / key phrase*

Verse 16, "God had determined."

5. *Key event / key person / key theme*

King Amaziah of Judah

6. *Key thought*

How many people have fallen because they "would not listen," verse 20?

7. *Key thing to look out for*

What turns a seemingly godly person into one who stops following the Lord?

8. *Key Bible cross-reference*

Verses 5-16. See 2 Kings 14:7.

9. *Key "by way of explanation"*

Verses 1-28. Amaziah's life can be studied in two parts: his good years, verses 1-13, and his bad years, verses 14-28.

10. *Key "Quotable Quote"*

"Those who fall away have never been thoroughly imbued with the knowledge of Christ but only had a slight and passing taste of it."
John Calvin

2 Chronicles chapter 26

1. Before and after

Previous chapter: Chapter 25: King Amaziah of Judah
Following chapter: Chapter 27: King Jotham of Judah

2. Analysis of chapter

Uzziah's good reign in Judah. (1-15)
Uzziah's attempt to burn incense. (16-23)

3. Key verse

Verse 16: "But when he was strong, his heart was lifted up to *his* destruction: for he transgressed against the LORD his God, and went into the temple of the LORD to burn incense upon the altar of incense."

4. Key word / key phrase

Verse 16, "pride."

5. Key event / key person / key theme

King Uzziah of Judah

6. Key thought

Leprosy often stands for sin in the Bible.

7. Key thing to look out for

All of God's judgments do not take place in this life.

8. Key Bible cross-reference

Verse 19. See 16:12; 21:12-15.

9. Key "by way of explanation"

Verses 2, 16-21. In 2 Kings 15:5 Uzziah's leprosy is just mentioned. But in 2 Chronicles it is stated that this disease came on Uzziah because of his unfaithfulness to God.

10. Key "Quotable Quote"

"The Christian's battle is first of all with sin."
C.H. Spurgeon

2 Chronicles chapter 27

1. Before and after

Previous chapter: Chapter 26: King Uzziah of Judah
Following chapter: Chapter 28: King Ahaz of Judah

2. Analysis of chapter

Jotham's reign in Judah. (1-9)

3. Key verse

Verse 3: "He built the high gate of the house of the LORD, and on the wall of Ophel he built much."

4. Key word / key phrase

Verse 6, "walked steadfastly."

5. Key event / key person / key theme

King Jotham of Judah

6. Key thought

Walking with God was also used to describe Enoch's relationship with the Lord.

7. Key thing to look out for

To walk with the Lord implies that the person is in step with the Lord in every part of his or her life.

8. Key Bible cross-reference

Verse 7. See 2 Kings 15:37.

9. Key "by way of explanation"

Verses 3-6. Here faithfulness to God results in blessings from God.

10. Key "Quotable Quote"

"Quietness and peace before God are more important than any influence a position may seem to give, for we must stay in step with God to have the power of the Holy Spirit."
Francis A. Schaeffer

2 Chronicles chapter 29

(For 2 Chronicles chapter 28, see 2 Kings 16.)

1. **Before and after**

 Previous chapter: Chapter 28: King Ahaz of Judah
 Following chapter: Chapter 30: Preparations for and two celebrations of the Passover

2. **Analysis of chapter**

 Hezekiah's good reign in Judah. (1-19)
 Hezekiah's sacrifice of atonement. (20-36)

3. **Key verse**

 Verse 1: "Hezekiah began to reign when he was five and twenty years old, and he reigned nine and twenty years in Jerusalem."

4. **Key word / key phrase**

 Verse 5, "consecrate."

5. **Key event / key person / key theme**

 Hezekiah purifies the temple

6. **Key thought**

 To encourage people to be faithful to God is a great privilege and responsibility.

7. **Key thing to look out for**

 Godly people rejoice at the sight of godliness.

8. **Key Bible cross-reference**

 Verse 35. See 7:4-6.

9. **Key "by way of explanation"**

 Verses 7,18,35. Hezekiah has been called a "second Solomon" because of all the arrangements he made for temple worship, as well as because of his wealth and power.

10. **Key "Quotable Quote"**

 "If missions languish, it is because the whole life of godliness is feeble."
 A.T. Pierson

2 Chronicles chapter 30

1. *Before and after*

Previous chapter: Chapter 29: The purification and dedication of the temple
Following chapter: Chapter 31: Hezekiah's religious reforms

2. *Analysis of chapter*

Hezekiah's Passover. (1-12)
The Passover celebrated. (13-20)
The Feast of Unleavened Bread. (21-27)

3. *Key verse*

Verse 1: "And Hezekiah sent to all Israel and Judah, and wrote letters also to Ephraim and Manasseh, that they should come to the house of the LORD at Jerusalem, to keep the Passover unto the LORD God of Israel."

4. *Key word / key phrase*

Verse 20, "heard . . . healed."

5. *Key event / key person / key theme*

Hezekiah celebrates the Passover

6. *Key thought*

Celebrating the Passover reminded God's people that he was their Redeemer.

7. *Key thing to look out for*

The Lord's Supper reminds us that Jesus is our Redeemer.

8. *Key Bible cross-reference*

Verses 18,19. See Mark 7:1-23; John 7:22,23.

9. *Key "by way of explanation"*

Verse 8. The Passover was one of the three annual festivals that had to be celebrated at the temple. See Numbers 28:9–29:39.

10. *Key "Quotable Quote"*

"The reason my sins are forgiven so easily is because the redemption cost God so much."
Oswald Chambers

2 Chronicles chapter 31

1. *Before and after*

Previous chapter: Chapter 30: Preparations for and two celebrations of the Passover

Following chapter: Chapter 32: Assyrians threaten Jerusalem; Hezekiah's wealth, illness, and death

2. *Analysis of chapter*

Hezekiah destroys idolatry. (1-21)

3. *Key verse*

Verse 1: "Now when all this was finished, all Israel that were present went out to the cities of Judah, and brake the images in pieces, and cut down the groves, and threw down the high places and the altars out of all Judah and Benjamin, in Ephraim also and Manasseh, until they had utterly destroyed them all."

4. *Key word / key phrase*

Verse 20, "good and right and faithful."

5. *Key event / key person / key theme*

Hezekiah reforms religious life

6. *Key thought*

Lead by example.

7. *Key thing to look out for*

Praising the Lord and giving thanks to people go hand in hand.

8. *Key Bible cross-reference*

Verse 2. See 8:14.

9. *Key "by way of explanation"*

Verse 3. The example of King Hezekiah giving from "his own possessions" inspired the people to be generous as well.

10. *Key "Quotable Quote"*

"God has given us two hands – one to receive with and the other to give with."
Billy Graham

2 Chronicles chapter 32

1. Before and after

Previous chapter: Chapter 31: Hezekiah's religious reforms
Following chapter: Chapter 33: King Manasseh of Judah

2. Analysis of chapter

The invasion of Sennacherib. His defeat. (1-23)
Hezekiah's sickness. His prosperous reign, and death. (24-33)

3. Key verse

Verse 1: "After these things, and the establishment thereof, Sennacherib king of Assyria came, and entered into Judah, and encamped against the fenced cities, and thought to win them for himself."

4. Key word / key phrase

Verse 8, "with us is the Lord our God."

5. Key event / key person / key theme

Sennacherib threatens Jerusalem

6. Key thought

The time of God's miracles is in God's sovereign hands.

7. Key thing to look out for

Hezekiah was not devoid of pride.

8. Key Bible cross-reference

Verse 18. See 2 Kings 18:26-28; Isaiah 36:11-13.

9. Key "by way of explanation"

Verses 25,26. For all his good qualities Hezekiah's disobedience to the Lord is not skated over.

10. Key "Quotable Quote"

"Pride alienates man from heaven; humility leads to heaven."
Bridget of Sweden

2 Chronicles chapter 33

1. Before and after

Previous chapter: Chapter 32: Assyrians threaten Jerusalem; Hezekiah's wealth, illness, and death

Following chapter: Chapter 34: Josiah's positive religious reforms

2. Analysis of chapter

Manasseh's evil reign. (1-20)

Amon's wicked reign in Judah. (21-25)

3. Key verse

Verse 13: "And prayed unto him: and he was entreated of him, and heard his supplication, and brought him again to Jerusalem into his kingdom. Then Manasseh knew that the LORD he *was* God."

4. Key word / key phrase

Verse 13, "when he prayed."

5. Key event / key person / key theme

King Manasseh of Judah

6. Key thought

Idolatry and sorcery are often linked.

7. Key thing to look out for

Knowing that the Lord is God, verse 13, was the best thing that ever happened to Manasseh.

8. Key Bible cross-reference

Verses 1-20. See 2 Kings 21:1-18.

9. Key "by way of explanation"

Verse 11-17. Defeat is seen as the consequences of Manasseh's evil, while his repentance brings about his restoration.

10. Key "Quotable Quote"

"Oh, the fullness, pleasure, sheer excitement of knowing God on earth! I care not if I never raise my voice again for him, if only I may love him, please him."
Jim Elliot

2 Chronicles chapter 35

(For 2 Chronicles chapter 34, see 2 Kings 22;1-20; 23:1-20.)

1. **Before and after**

   Previous chapter: Chapter 34: Josiah's positive religious reforms
   Following chapter: Chapter 36: Last four kings of Judah; fall of Jerusalem and exile

2. **Analysis of chapter**

   The Passover kept by Josiah. (1-19)
   Josiah killed in battle. (20-27)

3. **Key verse**

   Verse 1: "Moreover Josiah kept a passover unto the LORD in Jerusalem: and they killed the passover [lamb] on the fourteenth day of the first month."

4. **Key word / key phrase**

   Verse 3, "now serve the Lord."

5. **Key event / key person / key theme**

   Josiah celebrates the Passover

6. **Key thought**

   Worshiping the Lord was a great celebration in the Old Testament.

7. **Key thing to look out for**

   The thought of seven days of worship seems alien today.

8. **Key Bible cross-reference**

   Verse 4. See 7:10; 11:17.

9. **Key "by way of explanation"**

   Verse 25. The laments Jeremiah composed for Josiah no longer exist. But the fact that Jeremiah did compose such laments is evidence for Jeremiah's authorship of the book of Lamentations.

10. **Key "Quotable Quote"**

   "Mission is the overflow of our delight in God because mission is the overflow of God's delight in being God."
   John Piper
   (For 2 Chronicles chapter 36, see 2 Kings 23:28–24:20; 25:1-21; Ezra 1:1-3.)

Ezra and Nehemiah

Ezra chapter 1

1. *Following chapter*

Chapter 2: List of exiles who returned

2. *Analysis of chapter*

The proclamation of Cyrus for the rebuilding of the temple. (1-4)
The people provide for their return. (5-11)

3. *Key verse*

Verse 1: "Now in the first year of Cyrus king of Persia, that the word of the LORD by the mouth of Jeremiah might be fulfilled, the LORD stirred up the spirit of Cyrus king of Persia"

4. *Key word / key phrase*

Verse 1, "Cyrus."

5. *Key event / key person / key theme*

Cyrus enables the exiles to return to Jerusalem

6. *Key thought*

God had never forgotten his people during their exile.

7. *Key thing to look out for*

All kinds of unlikely people are used by God to fulfill his will.

8. *Key Bible cross-reference*

Verse 5. See 2:59.

9. *Key "by way of explanation"*

Verse 2. Out of the twenty-two occurrences of the phrase "God of heaven" in the Old Testament, it comes seventeen times in Ezra. Cyrus came to the throne and issued his edict in March 538 BC.

10. *Key "Quotable Quote"*

"The believer is never the victim of the powers of nature or fate. Chance is eliminated."
G.C. Berkouwer

Ezra chapter 2

1. *Before and after*

Previous chapter: Chapter 1: Cyrus allows the exiles to return
Following chapter: Chapter 3: Worship restarted, and the temple foundation laid

2. *Analysis of chapter*

The number of people who returned. (1-35)
The numbers of the priests and Levites. (36-63)
The offerings for the temple. (64-70)

3. *Key verse*

Verse 1: "Now these are the children of the province that went up out of the captivity, of those which had been carried away, whom Nebuchadnezzar the king of Babylon had carried away unto Babylon, and came again unto Jerusalem and Judah, every one unto his city"

4. *Key word / key phrase*

Verse 1, "exiles."

5. *Key event / key person / key theme*

Lists of the exiles who returned

6. *Key thought*

Jeremiah had prophesied that his people would return to Jerusalem after seventy years in exile.

7. *Key thing to look out for*

God always keeps his promises.

8. *Key Bible cross-reference*

Verses 1-70. See Nehemiah 7:6-73.

9. *Key "by way of explanation"*

Verse 2. "Jeshua" means "the Lord saves." It is an Aramaic version of the Hebrew word for "Joshua." In Greek this name is "Jesus."

10. *Key "Quotable Quote"*

"No one is safe by his own strength, but he is safe by the grace and mercy of God."
Cyprian

Ezra chapter 3

1. Before and after

Previous chapter: Chapter 2: List of exiles who returned
Following chapter: Chapter 4: The Jews encounter opposition

2. Analysis of chapter

The altar and festivals. (1-7)
Rebuilding begns. (8-13)

3. Key verse

Verse 10: "And when the builders laid the foundation of the temple of the LORD, they set the priests in their apparel with trumpets, and the Levites the sons of Asaph with cymbals, to praise the LORD, after the ordinance of David king of Israel."

4. Key word / key phrase

Verse 11 "his love to Israel endures."

5. Key event / key person / key theme

The foundations of the temple are laid.

6. Key thought

The rebuilding of the temple is the central feature of Ezra.

7. Key thing to look out for

Verses 11-13. A variety of emotions are expressed as the foundations for rebuilding the temple are laid.

8. Key Bible cross-reference

Verse 7. The Phoenicians supplied timbers and craftsmen, as they had for building the original temple. See 1 Chronicles 14:1.

9. Key "by way of explanation"

Verses 12,13. It was clear that the new temple would lack the magnificence of the first temple, built in the golden era of Solomon.

10. Key "Quotable Quote"

"In the Dark Ages, reform did not arise from the state but from communities of those who remained uncompromising in a compromising age."
Charles Colson

Ezra chapter 4

1. *Before and after*

Previous chapter: Chapter 3: Worship restarted, and the temple foundation laid

Following chapter: Chapter 5: Searching the records

2. *Analysis of chapter*

The adversaries of the temple. (1-5)

The building of the temple is hindered. (6-24)

3. *Key verse*

Verse 3: "But Zerubbabel, and Jeshua, and the rest of the chief of the fathers of Israel, said unto them, Ye have nothing to do with us to build an house unto our God; but we ourselves together will build unto the LORD God of Israel, as king Cyrus the king of Persia hath commanded us."

4. *Key word / key phrase*

Verse 1, "enemies."

5. *Key event / key person / key theme*

Opposition is encountered to rebuilding the temple

6. *Key thought*

Christian activity usually does meet opposition.

7. *Key thing to look out for*

The reason why the Jewish leaders refused to offer of help was because the worship of these enemies (later called Samaritans) was syncretistic.

8. *Key Bible cross-reference*

Verse 15. See 5:17; 6:1; Esther 2:23; 6:1-2.

9. *Key "by way of explanation"*

4:8–6:18 and 7:12-26 are not written in Hebrew, as is nearly all of the Old Testament, but in Aramaic. In the Persian period Aramaic was the international language.

10. *Key "Quotable Quote"*

"They that know anything in this world know that, as the first great opposition of hell, the world, and corrupt nature, is against faith to God by Christ; so the next great opposition made against us, is against our love."
John Owen

Ezra chapter 5

1. Before and after

Previous chapter: Chapter 4: The Jews encounter opposition
Following chapter: Chapter 6: Rebuilding the temple is finished

2. Analysis of chapter

The leaders encourage the building of the temple. (1,2)
Letter against the Jews. (3-17)

3. Key verse

Verse 2: "Then rose up Zerubbabel the son of Shealtiel, and Jeshua the son of Jozadak, and began to build the house of God which is at Jerusalem: and with them were the prophets of God helping them."

4. Key word / key phrase

Verse 2, "rebuild."

5. Key event / key person / key theme

Rebuilding work on the temple continues

6. Key thought

God's prophets knew that the people needed encouragement to rebuild the temple.

7. Key thing to look out for

The prophets did not just shout at the people, they helped them, verses 2.

8. Key Bible cross-reference

Verse 11. See 1 Kings 6:1,38.

9. Key "by way of explanation"

Verse 5. While the inquiry was taking place the Jews were given the benefit of the doubt and their work was not stopped.

10. Key "Quotable Quote"

"To pray when one ought to be working is as much a sin as to work when one ought to be praying."
Dorothy L. Sayers

Ezra chapter 6

1. **Before and after**

   Previous chapter: Chapter 5: Searching the records
   Following chapter: Chapter 7: Ezra arrives in Jerusalem

2. **Analysis of chapter**

   The decree for completing the temple. (1-12)
   The temple is finished. (13-22)

3. **Key verse**

   Verse 1: "Then Darius the king made a decree, and search was made in the house of the rolls, where the treasures were laid up in Babylon."

4. **Key word / key phrase**

   Verse 3, "Cyrus."

5. **Key event / key person / key theme**

   Cyrus' decree is rediscovered

6. **Key thought**

   God sometimes helps his people through the goodwill of those who are not his followers.

7. **Key thing to look out for**

   The rebuilt temple was dedicated to God and joy was the memorable thing about that day, verse 16.

8. **Key Bible cross-reference**

   Verse 3. See 3:12; Haggai 2:3.

9. **Key "by way of explanation"**

   Verse 15. The date for the completion of the rebuilding was March 12th, 516 BC.

10. **Key "Quotable Quote"**

    "Christ is not only a remedy for your weariness and trouble, but he will give you an abundance of the contrary, joy and delight."
    Jonathan Edwards

Ezra chapter 7

1. Before and after

Previous chapter: Chapter 6: Rebuilding the temple is finished
Following chapter: Chapter 8: List of exiles who returned under Ezra

2. Analysis of chapter

Ezra goes up to Jerusalem. (1-10)
The commission to Ezra. (11-26)
Ezra blesses God for his favor. (27,28)

3. Key verse

Verse 10: "For Ezra had prepared his heart to seek the law of the LORD, and to do it, and to teach in Israel statutes and judgments."

4. Key word / key phrase

Verse 28, "the hand of the Lord my God was on me."

5. Key event / key person / key theme

Ezra arrives in Jerusalem

6. Key thought

Verse 10 remains a great example for any pastor or Bible teacher today.

7. Key thing to look out for

Verse 25. The commission given to Ezra.

8. Key Bible cross-reference

Verse 10. See Nehemiah chapter 8.

9. Key "by way of explanation"

Verse 28. For the first time in this book the word "me" is used, indicating that Ezra's memoirs begin at 7:27. They end at 9:15.

10. Key "Quotable Quote"

"No preacher can at one and the same time give the impression that he is clever and that Jesus is great and wonderful."
James Denney

Ezra chapter 8

1. Before and after

Previous chapter: Chapter 7: Ezra arrives in Jerusalem
Following chapter: Chapter 9: Ezra's prayer after learning about inter-
marriage with non-Jews

2. Analysis of chapter

The companions of Ezra. (1-20)
Ezra implores God's blessing. (21-23)
Treasures committed to the priests. (24-30)
Ezra arrives at Jerusalem. (31-36)

3. Key verse

Verse 1: "These are now the chief of their fathers, and this is the genealogy of
them that went up with me from Babylon, in the reign of Artaxerxes the
king."

4. Key word / key phrase

Verse 1, "came up with me."

5. Key event / key person / key theme

Safe arrival in Jerusalem

6. Key thought

Verses 22,23. Ezra was determined to rely only on God for protection as a
public witness to the power of God.

7. Key thing to look out for

In the book of Ezra no blame is attached to those who did not return to
Jerusalem with Ezra, but the excitement of being involved in doing the Lord's
work is obvious.

8. Key Bible cross-reference

Verse 32. See Nehemiah 2:11.

9. Key "by way of explanation"

The 900-mile journey took four months. The people were in great danger
from wild beasts and armed robbers.

10. Key "Quotable Quote"

"It is God who gives our prayer its value and its character, not our interior
dispositions, not our fervor, not our lucidity."
Jacques Ellul

Ezra chapter 9

1. Before and after

Previous chapter: Chapter 8: List of exiles who returned under Ezra
Following chapter: Chapter 10: Ezra's plans to end marriages with non-Jews

2. Analysis of chapter

Ezra mourns for the Jews' behavior. (1-4)
Ezra's confession of sins. (5-15)

3. Key verse

Verse 4: "Then were assembled unto me every one that trembled at the words of the God of Israel, because of the transgression of those that had been carried away; and I sat astonied until the evening sacrifice."

4. Key word / key phrase

Verse 1, "not kept themselves separate."

5. Key event / key person / key theme

Ezra's reaction to news about mixed marriages

6. Key thought

Ezra's response to the crisis was to pray.

7. Key thing to look out for

Ezra was not left unaffected by sin.

8. Key Bible cross-reference

Verse 6. See 8:22.

9. Key "by way of explanation"

Verse 2. Marrying people who did not belong to God was seen as an act of unfaithfulness to God.

10. Key "Quotable Quote"

"Prayer is the central avenue God uses to transform us."
Richard J. Foster

Ezra chapter 10

1. **Previous chapter**

    Chapter 9: Ezra's prayer after learning about inter-marriage with non-Jews

2. **Analysis of chapter**

    Ezra encourages reformation. (1-6)
    He assembles the people. (7-15)
    Reformation effected. (16-44)

3. **Key verse**

    Verse 1: "Now when Ezra had prayed, and when he had confessed, weeping and casting himself down before the house of God, there assembled unto him out of Israel a very great congregation of men and women and children: for the people wept very sore."

4. **Key word / key phrase**

    Verse 1, "confessing."

5. **Key event / key person / key theme**

    The people confess their sins

6. **Key thought**

    Not everyone indulged in mixed marriages, see verse 14.

7. **Key thing to look out for**

    Holiness involves being separate from evil.

8. **Key Bible cross-reference**

    Verse 4. See 1 Chronicles 22:16.

9. **Key "by way of explanation"**

    Verse 1. Ezra threw himself to the ground. Other prophets also acted out their feelings in order to impress their teaching upon the people. See Isaiah 7:3; Jeremiah 13:1-11; Ezekiel 4:1–5:4.

10. **Key "Quotable Quote"**

    "Sometimes truth is lost first in a church, and then holiness and sometimes the decay or hatred of holiness is the cause of the loss of truth. But if either is rejected, the other will not abide."
    John Owen

Nehemiah chapter 1

1. Following chapter

Chapter 2: Nehemiah goes to Jerusalem

2. Analysis of chapter

Nehemiah's distress for the misery of Jerusalem. (1-4)
Nehemiah's prayer. (5-11)

3. Key verse

Verse 4: "And it came to pass, when I heard these words, that I sat down and wept, and mourned certain days, and fasted, and prayed before the God of heaven."

4. Key word / key phrase

Verse 3, "trouble and disgrace."

5. Key event / key person / key theme

Nehemiah's prayer

6. Key thought

Nehemiah combines prayer and action throughout this book.

7. Key thing to look out for

All that can be learned from Nehemiah's prayer about coming to God to pray for success.

8. Key Bible cross-reference

Verse 6. See Psalm 42:3; Jeremiah 9:1.

9. Key "by way of explanation"

Verse 4. Nehemiah shows how profoundly affected he was by the news about Jerusalem. He sat down, wept, mourned, fasted and prayed for three months.

10. Key "Quotable Quote"

"Do what you can and then pray that God will give you the power to do what you cannot."
Augustine of Hippo

Nehemiah chapter 2

1. Before and after

Previous chapter: Chapter 1: Nehemiah learns of Jerusalem's plight
Following chapter: Chapter 3: Nehemiah organizes the work in Jerusalem

2. Analysis of chapter

Nehemiah's request to the king. (1-8)
Nehemiah comes to Jerusalem. (9-18)
The opposition of the adversaries. (19,20)

3. Key verse

Verse 5: "And I said unto the king, If it please the king, and if thy servant have found favor in thy sight, that thou wouldest send me unto Judah, unto the city of my fathers' sepulchers, that I may build it."

4. Key word / key phrase

Verse 2, "so the king asked."

5. Key event / key person / key theme

Artaxerxes sends Nehemiah to Jerusalem

6. Key thought

Nehemiah trusted God in his desire to go to Jerusalem.

7. Key thing to look out for

Nehemiah only shared his God-given task with a few trustworthy people.

8. Key Bible cross-reference

Verse 6. See 5:14.

9. Key "by way of explanation"

Verse 4. Nehemiah was a great one for "arrow" prayers. See 1:4; 4:4,9; 5:19; 6:9,14; 13:14,22;29,31. It is probable that Ezra went to Jerusalem in 458 BC, and Nehemiah went about eighteen years later.

10. Key "Quotable Quote"

"Prayer is not so much an act as it is an attitude – an attitude of dependency, dependency upon God."
Arthur W. Pink

Nehemiah chapter 3

1. **Before and after**

   Previous chapter: Chapter 2: Nehemiah goes to Jerusalem
   Following chapter: Chapter 4: Nehemiah encounters opposition

2. **Analysis of chapter**

   Rebuilding the walls of Jerusalem. (1-16)
   Levites who worked on the wall. (17-21)
   Priests who worked on the wall. (22-26)
   Other builders. (27-32)

3. **Key verse**

   Verse 2: "And next unto him builded the men of Jericho. And next to them builded Zaccur the son of Imri."

4. **Key word / key phrase**

   Verse 1, "rebuilt."

5. **Key event / key person / key theme**

   Rebuilding the walls of Jerusalem

6. **Key thought**

   The faithful work of each team member enabled the repairs to be made.

7. **Key thing to look out for**

   Each group of people doing the rebuilding work had a definite but limited aim.

8. **Key Bible cross-reference**

   Verse 3. See 12:39; 2 Chronicles 33:14; Zephaniah 14:10.

9. **Key "by way of explanation"**

   Verses 1-32. Ten gates are mentioned, as these were the places where people attacking a city concentrated their effort.

10. **Key "Quotable Quote"**

    "The filling with the Spirit happens for the sake of service."
    D. Martyn Lloyd-Jones

Nehemiah chapter 4

1. *Before and after*

   Previous chapter: Chapter 3: Nehemiah organizes the work in Jerusalem
   Following chapter: Chapter 5: The poor are oppressed; Nehemiah's generosity

2. *Analysis of chapter*

   Sanballat and others redicule the builders. (1-6)
   The builders hear of death threats. (7-15)
   Nehemiah's precautions. (16-23)

3. *Key verse*

   Verse 1: "But it came to pass, that when Sanballat heard that we builded the wall, he was wroth, and took great indignation, and mocked the Jews."

4. *Key word / key phrase*

   Verse 14, "remember the LORD."

5. *Key event / key person / key theme*

   Opposition to the rebuilding work

6. *Key thought*

   There are always people who will laugh at work being done for God.

7. *Key thing to look out for*

   Opposition sometimes comes in the form of delaying tactics.

8. *Key Bible cross-reference*

   Verse 14. See Deuteronomy 3:22; 20:3.

9. *Key "by way of explanation"*

   Verse 9 is another example of Nehemiah as a man of prayer and at the same time a man of action.

10. *Key "Quotable Quote"*

    "In our case [as Christians] we are hated for our name."
    Athenagoras

Nehemiah chapter 5

1. *Before and after*

> Previous chapter: Chapter 4: Nehemiah encounters opposition
> Following chapter: Chapter 6: The rebuilding of the walls of Jerusalem is completed

2. *Analysis of chapter*

> The Jews complain of grievances. (1-5)
> Nehemiah redresses the grievances. (6-13)
> Nehemiah's forbearance. (14-19)

3. *Key verse*

> Verse 1: "And there was a great cry of the people and of their wives against their brethren the Jews."

4. *Key word / key phrase*

> Verse 6, "outcry."

5. *Key event / key person / key theme*

> Nehemiah helps the poor

6. *Key thought*

> Before taking action Nehemiah found why some people were so poor and then took to task those who were to blame.

7. *Key thing to look out for*

> Nehemiah acted to remedy the need of the poor.

8. *Key Bible cross-reference*

> Verse 9. See Proverbs 14:31; 1 Peter 2:12-15.

9. *Key "by way of explanation"*

> Verse 6. See Mark 11:15-18; Ephesians 4:26. In the face of dreadful social injustice anger is the appropriate reaction.

10. *Key "Quotable Quote"*

> "Although it is right to campaign for social justice and to expect to improve society further, in order to make it more pleasing to God, we know that we should never perfect it."
> John R.W. Stott

Nehemiah chapter 6

1. Before and after

Previous chapter: Chapter 5: The poor are oppressed; Nehemiah's generosity
Following chapter: Chapter 7: List of those who returned from exile with Zerubbabel

2. Analysis of chapter

Sanballat's plot to hinder Nehemiah. (1-9)
False prophets try to frighten Nehemiah. (10-14)
The wall finished, and treachery of some of the Jews. (15-19)

3. Key verse

Verse 5: "Then sent Sanballat his servant unto me in like manner the fifth time with an open letter in his hand."

4. Key word / key phrase

Verse 15, "the wall was completed."

5. Key event / key person / key theme

More opposition to the rebuilding work

6. Key thought

Fear has caused much of God's work to grind to a halt.

7. Key thing to look out for

When any service for God is completed it is important that glory is only given to God.

8. Key Bible cross-reference

Verse 12. See Deuteronomy 18:20; Isaiah 8:19,20.

9. Key "by way of explanation"

Verse 4. Opposition can be persistent. The only remedy is to be equally persistent.

10. Key "Quotable Quote"

"When your enemies see that you are so determined that neither sickness, fancies, poverty, life, death, nor sins discourage you, but that you will continue to seek the love of Jesus and nothing else, by continuing your prayer and other spiritual works, they will grow enraged and will not spare you the most cruel abuse."
Walter Hilton

Nehemiah chapter 7

1. Before and after

Previous chapter: Chapter 6: The rebuilding of the walls of Jerusalem is completed

Following chapter: Chapter 8: Ezra reads the Law

2. Analysis of chapter

Hananiah and Hanani put in charge of Jerusalem. (1-4)

Register of those who first returned. (5-73)

3. Key verse

Verse 2: "I gave my brother Hanani, and Hananiah the ruler of the palace, charge over Jerusalem: for he was a faithful man, and feared God above many."

4. Key word / key phrase

Verse 5, "my God put it into my heart."

5. Key event / key person / key theme

The exiles who returned to Jerusalem

6. Key thought

God's people in returning to Jerusalem were being given a second chance to be faithful to him there.

7. Key thing to look out for

Nehemiah makes it clear that the initiative for this return came from the Lord, and not from himself, verse 5.

8. Key Bible cross-reference

Verses 6-73. See Ezra 2.

9. Key "by way of explanation"

Verse 3. The gates of Jerusalem were not to be opened at dawn, as would have been normal, in order to guard against any attack taking place while the people were still asleep.

10. Key "Quotable Quote"

"What is sought from Christians is the motivation for selfless service, which once distinguished the Christian heritage."
Klaus Bockmühl

Nehemiah chapter 8

1. *Before and after*

Previous chapter: Chapter 7: List of those who returned from exile with Zerubbabel

Following chapter: Chapter 9: The Jews confess their sins in prayer

2. *Analysis of chapter*

The reading and expounding of the Law. (1-8)
The people called upon to be joyful. (9-12)
The Feast of Tabernacles, and the joy of the people. (13-18)

3. *Key verse*

Verse 8: "And Ezra the priest brought the law before the congregation both of men and women, and all that could hear with understanding, upon the first day of the seventh month."

4. *Key word / key phrase*

Verse 1, "The Book of the Law."

5. *Key event / key person / key theme*

Ezra reads the Law

6. *Key thought*

God's word brings reform and revival.

7. *Key thing to look out for*

Verse 10 says that the source of strength for God's followers is the joy of the Lord.

8. *Key Bible cross-reference*

Verse 3. See Exodus 24:7; Acts 8:30.

9. *Key "by way of explanation"*

Verse 6. The intensity of the feelings of the people is conveyed in the way they repeat the word, "Amen!"

10. *Key "Quotable Quote"*

"We cannot make too much of the word of God."
E.M. Bounds

Nehemiah chapter 9

1. Before and after

Previous chapter: Chapter 8: Ezra reads the Law
Following chapter: Chapter 10: The covenant is renewed

2. Analysis of chapter

A solemn fast. (1-3)
Prayer and confession of sin. (4-38)

3. Key verse

Verse 4: "Then stood up upon the stairs, of the Levites, Jeshua, and Bani, Kadmiel, Shebaniah, Bunni, Sherebiah, Bani, and Chenani, and cried with a loud voice unto the LORD their God."

4. Key word / key phrase

Verse 1, "fasting and wearing sackcloth."

5. Key event / key person / key theme

The Israelites confess their sins

6. Key thought

Nothing is more spiritually therapeutic than confession of sin.

7. Key thing to look out for

God's purpose in giving the Spirit (verse 20).

8. Key Bible cross-reference

Verse 20. See Exodus 31:3.

9. Key "by way of explanation"

Verse 21. The fact that the clothes of the people in the desert did not wear out is given as evidence of God's care for them.

10. Key "Quotable Quote"

"All Word and no Spirit, we dry up; all Spirit and no Word, we blow up; both Word and Spirit, we grow up."
David Watson

Nehemiah chapter 10

1. Before and after

Previous chapter: Chapter 9: The Jews confess their sins in prayer
Following chapter: Chapter 11: The residents of Jerusalem and the people in
the villages

2. Analysis of chapter

The covenant, and those who signed it. (1-29)
A commitment to keep specific parts of the Law recently neglected. (30-39)

3. Key verse

Verse 29: "They clave to their brethren, their nobles, and entered into a curse,
and into an oath, to walk in God's law, which was given by Moses the servant
of God, and to observe and do all the commandments of the LORD our Lord,
and his judgments and his statutes."

4. Key word / key phrase

Verse 1, "sealed."

5. Key event / key person / key theme

The agreement made by the people

6. Key thought

The people promise to live according to God's laws.

7. Key thing to look out for

The link between sin and offerings and atonement is constantly made in the
Old Testament. See verse 33.

8. Key Bible cross-reference

Verse 35. See Exodus 23:19; Ezekiel 44:30.

9. Key "by way of explanation"

Verse 35. Provisions were given to the priests and Levites as they did not have
time to earn a living for themselves.

10. Key "Quotable Quote"

"The greatest good in this life is the union of will between creature and
Creator."
Ignatius of Loyola

Nehemiah chapter 11

1. Before and after

Previous chapter: Chapter 10: The covenant is renewed
Following chapter: Chapter 12: Lists of priests and Levites and other lists of people

2. Analysis of chapter

The people who lived in Jerusalem. (1-24)
People in other cities and towns. (25-36)

3. Key verse

Verse 1: "And the rulers of the people dwelt at Jerusalem: the rest of the people also cast lots, to bring one of ten to dwell in Jerusalem the holy city, and nine parts to dwell in other cities."

4. Key word / key phrase

Verse 1, "Jerusalem."

5. Key event / key person / key theme

The people who lived in Jerusalem

6. Key thought

The resettling of God's people in Jerusalem was one of the high points in the Old Testament. The Lord provided a place for his people to live.

7. Key thing to look out for

Verse 2. God's work is done by some people who are told to do it as well as those who volunteer.

8. Key Bible cross-reference

Verse 1. See Isaiah 48:2; Revelation 11:2.

9. Key "by way of explanation"

Compare 11:1 with 7:4. The city was under-populated.

10. Key "Quotable Quote"

"We ought not to be weary of doing little things for the love of God, who regards not the greatness of the work, but the love with which it is performed."
Brother Lawrence

Nehemiah chapter 12

1. *Before and after*

Previous chapter: Chapter 11: The residents of Jerusalem and the people in the villages

Following chapter: Chapter 13: Nehemiah's reforms

2. *Analysis of chapter*

The priests and Levites who returned. (1-26)

The dedication of the wall. (27-43)

The officers of the temple settled. (44-47)

3. *Key verse*

Verse 27: "And at the dedication of the wall of Jerusalem they sought the Levites out of all their places, to bring them to Jerusalem, to keep the dedication with gladness, both with thanksgivings, and with singing, with cymbals, psalteries, and with harps."

4. *Key word / key phrase*

Verse 27, "dedication."

5. *Key event / key person / key theme*

The dedication of the wall of Jerusalem

6. *Key thought*

God's people have always been given ways in which they are to serve God.

7. *Key thing to look out for*

God gives different talents and different spiritual gifts to his people so we should expect people to be serving God in a great variety of ways.

8. *Key Bible cross-reference*

Verse 43. See 1 Chronicles 29:2.

9. *Key "by way of explanation"*

Verse 30. In times of revival the Levites purified the temple itself as well as everything that was sacred in the temple.

10. *Key "Quotable Quote"*

"God insists that he set up his throne in the heart, and reign in it, without a rival. If we keep him from his right, it will not matter by what competitor."
William Wilberforce

Nehemiah chapter 13

1. *Previous chapter*

Chapter 12: Lists of priests and Levites and other lists of people

2. *Analysis of chapter*

Nehemiah throws out Tobiah's household goods. (1-9)
Nehemiah's reform in the house of God. (10-14)
Sabbath-breaking restrained. (15-22)
Marriage to foreign women denounced. (23-31)

3. *Key verse*

Verse 11: "Then contended I with the rulers, and said, Why is the house of God forsaken?"

4. *Key word / key phrase*

Verse 9, "orders."

5. *Key event / key person / key theme*

Nehemiah's reforms

6. *Key thought*

Following God's laws often proves very hard.

7. *Key thing to look out for*

Nehemiah kept helping God's people to live in ways that pleased the Lord.

8. *Key Bible cross-reference*

Verse 8. See verses 24,25; 5:6,7.

9. *Key "by way of explanation"*

As previously agreed (see 2:5) Nehemiah had returned to Artaxerxes in Babylon. When he later came back to resume his work as governor of Jerusalem he was furious to discover the negligence of the people.

10. *Key "Quotable Quote"*

"Perhaps there cannot be a better way of judging of what manner of spirit we are of, than to see whether the actions of our life are such as we may safely commend them to God in our prayers."
William Law

Esther

Esther chapter 1

1. **Following chapter**

   Chapter 2: Esther becomes the new queen

2. **Analysis of chapter**

   The royal feast of Ahasuerus. (1-9)
   Vashti's refusal to appear, and the king's decree. (10-22)

3. **Key verse**

   Verse 5: ". . . the king made a feast unto all the people that were present in Shushan the palace . . ."

4. **Key word / key phrase**

   Verse 1, "Xerxes."

5. **Key event / key person / key theme**

   Xerxes looks for a new queen

6. **Key thought**

   Drunkenness is often not condemned in ungodly circles.

7. **Key thing to look out for**

   Many other evils go uncensored in godless company.

8. **Key Bible cross-reference**

   Verse 19. See 8:8; Daniel 6:8.

9. **Key "by way of explanation"**

   Verse 3. Esther is full of feasts. There are ten banquets in this book. The story takes place in Persia when Xerxes ruled the Persian Empire (486-465 BC). Susa was his winter residence.

10. **Key "Quotable Quote"**

   "There is practically nothing that men do not prefer to God. "
   François Fénelon

Esther chapter 2

1. *Before and after*

Previous chapter: Chapter 1: Queen Vashti is deposed
Following chapter: Chapter 3: Haman plots to kill the Jews

2. *Analysis of chapter*

Esther chosen as queen. (1-20)
Mordecai discovers a plot against the king. (21-23)

3. *Key verse*

Verse 8: "So it came to pass, when the king's commandment and his decree was heard, and when many maidens were gathered together unto Shushan the palace, to the custody of Hegai, that Esther was brought also unto the king's house, to the custody of Hegai, keeper of the women."

4. *Key word / key phrase*

Verse 22, "plot."

5. *Key event / key person / key theme*

Esther becomes the new queen

6. *Key thought*

Loyalty is a wonderful characteristic.

7. *Key thing to look out for*

The word of "God" does not come in this book, but God's providential hand made the Jewess, Esther, Queen.

8. *Key Bible cross-reference*

Verse 8. See 2 Samuel 11:4.

9. *Key "by way of explanation"*

Verse 10. The fact that nobody knew Esther's background became very important later on, and it is merely mentioned twice, once in this verse and once in verse 20.

10. *Key "Quotable Quote"*

"Circumstances are constantly affecting us and their purpose is to produce our sanctification. Pleasant circumstances and unpleasant circumstances. We should therefore be observant and always watching for lessons, seeking and asking questions."
D. Martyn Lloyd-Jones

Esther chapter 3

1. **Before and after**

    Previous chapter: Chapter 2: Esther becomes the new queen
    Following chapter: Chapter 4: Esther agrees to seek the king's help

2. **Analysis of chapter**

    Haman seeks to destroy the Jews. (1-6)
    He obtains a decree against the Jews. (7-15)

3. **Key verse**

    Verse 6: "Haman sought to destroy all the Jews that were throughout the whole kingdom of Ahasuerus, even the people of Mordecai."

4. **Key word / key phrase**

    Verse 1, "Haman."

5. **Key event / key person / key theme**

    Haman's plot to destroy the Jews

6. **Key thought**

    The Lord had provided for the Jews before Haman tried to exterminate them.

7. **Key thing to look out for**

    Evil is arrogant and callous.

8. **Key Bible cross-reference**

    Verse 8. See 8:11,17; 9:2,12,16,19,20,28.

9. **Key "by way of explanation"**

    Verses 8,9. Although the Jews did have their own laws they had not broken any of the king's laws.

10. **Key "Quotable Quote"**

    "I think we do not attach sufficient importance to the restoration of the Jews."
    C.H. Spurgeon

Esther chapter 4

1. *Before and after*

Previous chapter: Chapter 3: Haman plots to kill the Jews
Following chapter: Chapter 5: Esther goes before the king; Haman plots against Mordecai

2. *Analysis of chapter*

The Jews lament their danger. (1-4)
Esther undertakes to plead for the Jews. (5-17)

3. *Key verse*

Verse 4: "Then was the queen exceedingly grieved; and she sent raiment to clothe Mordecai, and to take away his sackcloth from him: but he received it not."

4. *Key word / key phrase*

Verse 14, "royal position."

5. *Key event / key person / key theme*

Esther risks her life as she agrees to speak up for her people

6. *Key thought*

Sometimes it is not clear how God will use us in the future in his service.

7. *Key thing to look out for*

If Esther had become proud or fearful she would have acted differently.

8. *Key Bible cross-reference*

Verse 14. See Genesis 45:5-7.

9. *Key "by way of explanation"*

Verses 12-16. As God is sovereign he would have acted in some other way had Esther not cooperated with Mordecai's plan.

10. *Key "Quotable Quote"*

"To the Christian, love is the works of love."
Oswald Chambers

Esther chapter 5

1. *Before and after*

   Previous chapter: Chapter 4: Esther agrees to seek the king's help
   Following chapter: Chapter 6: The king honors Mordecai, while Haman sulks

2. *Analysis of chapter*

   Esther's request received. (1-8)
   Haman prepares to hang Mordecai. (9-14)

3. *Key verse*

   Verse 3: "Then said the king unto her, What wilt thou, queen Esther? and what is thy request? it shall be even given thee to the half of the kingdom."

4. *Key word / key phrase*

   Verse 2, "held out to her the gold scepter."

5. *Key event / key person / key theme*

   Esther dares to ask for an audience with the king

6. *Key thought*

   The Lord overruled so that the king granted Esther's wish.

7. *Key thing to look out for*

   The Lord also overruled in the timing of Haman's anger.

8. *Key Bible cross-reference*

   Verses 12,13. See Proverbs 16:18; 29:23.

9. *Key "by way of explanation"*

   Verse 4. Esther does not tell the king at once the nature of her request. This heightens the tension in the whole story.

10. *Key "Quotable Quote"*

    "Life appears to me too short to be spent in nursing animosity or registering wrong."
    Charlotte Brontë

Esther chapter 6

1. Before and after

Previous chapter: Chapter 5: Esther goes before the king; Haman plots against Mordecai

Following chapter: Chapter 7: Haman's fall from grace

2. Analysis of chapter

Providence recommends Mordecai to the king's favor. (1-3)

Haman's counsel honors Mordecai. (4-11)

Haman's friends tell him of his danger. (12-14)

3. Key verse

Verse 1: "On that night could not the king sleep, and he commanded to bring the book of records of the chronicles; and they were read before the king."

4. Key word / key phrase

Verse 3, "honor."

5. Key event / key person / key theme

Mordecai is honored

6. Key thought

The Lord overruled that the king could not sleep that night and so looked through his records.

7. Key thing to look out for

The Lord overruled that on the next day Haman wanted to make his request to the king.

8. Key Bible cross-reference

Verse 1. See Daniel 2:1; 6:18.

9. Key "by way of explanation"

Verse 2. The events the scribe was reading to the king had taken place five years previously. See 3:7 and 2:16.

10. Key "Quotable Quote"

"O love of God, how deep and great.
Far deeper than man's deepest hate."
Corrie ten Boom

Esther chapter 7

1. **Before and after**

     Previous chapter: Chapter 6: The king honors Mordecai, while Haman sulks
     Following chapter: Chapter 8: The king's new decree saves the Jews

2. **Analysis of chapter**

     Esther accuses Haman. (1-6)
     Haman hanged on his own gallows. (7-10)

3. **Key verse**

     Verse 6: "And Esther said, The adversary and enemy is this wicked Haman."

4. **Key word / key phrase**

     Verse 10, "gallows."

5. **Key event / key person / key theme**

     Haman is hanged

6. **Key thought**

     Many men like Haman do receive just rewards for their evil in this life.

7. **Key thing to look out for**

     You do not have to be a follower of God to appreciate justice.

8. **Key Bible cross-reference**

     Verse 4. See 3:9; 4:7.

9. **Key "by way of explanation"**

     Verse 8. It was normal for meals to be eaten reclining on couches. See Amos
     6:4-7; John 13:23.

10. **Key "Quotable Quote"**

     "The day of grace ends with some men before God taketh them out of the
     world."
     John Bunyan

Esther chapter 8

1. Before and after

Previous chapter: Chapter 7: Haman's fall from grace
Following chapter: Chapter 9: The Jews defeat their enemies and institute the
Feast of Purim

2. Analysis of chapter

Mordecai is advanced. (1,2)
Esther pleads for the Jews. (3-14)
Mordecai honored, and the joy of the Jews. (15-17)

3. Key verse

Verse 2: "And the king took off his ring, which he had taken from Haman, and
gave it unto Mordecai."

4. Key word / key phrase

Verse 8, "another decree."

5. Key event / key person / key theme

The king supports the Jews with his second edict

6. Key thought

The king was quick to see how he could save the Jews from their predicament,
which he had unwittingly caused.

7. Key thing to look out for

What could have been an unmitigated tragedy ended in joy and happiness.

8. Key Bible cross-reference

Verse 5. See 4:11; 5:2.

9. Key "by way of explanation"

Verse 8. The king could not revoke his first edict. But he effectively did this by
issuing the second edict.

10. Key "Quotable Quote"

"Christianity is a rescue religion."
John R.W. Stott

Esther chapter 9

1. Before and after

Previous chapter: Chapter 8: The king's new decree saves the Jews
Following chapter: Chapter 10: Mordecai is honored

2. Analysis of chapter

The success of the Jews. (1-19)
The feast of Purim to commemorate this. (20-32)

3. Key verse

Verse 2: "The Jews gathered themselves together in their cities throughout all the provinces of the king Ahasuerus, to lay hand on such as sought their hurt: and no man could withstand them; for the fear of them fell upon all people."

4. Key word / key phrase

Verse 5, "The Jews struck down."

5. Key event / key person / key theme

The Festival of Purim

6. Key thought

The Lord's people should always show their gratitude to the Lord whenever anything good happens to them.

7. Key thing to look out for

The Festival of Purim ensured that the Jews would never forget God's deliverance.

8. Key Bible cross-reference

Verses 2,3. See Genesis 12:3.

9. Key "by way of explanation"

Verses 18,19. To this day Purim is celebrated on different days in different places. In Jerusalem it is celebrated on the 14th, but elsewhere on the 15th.

10. Key "Quotable Quote"

"Worship is the direct acknowledgment to God, of his nature, attributes, ways and claims, whether by the outgoing of the heart in praise and thanksgiving or by deed done in such acknowledgment."
W.E. Vine

Esther chapter 10

1. **Previous chapter**

   The Jews defeat their enemies and institute the Feast of Purim

2. **Analysis of chapter**

   Greatness of Ahasuerus. Mordecai's advancement. (1-3)

3. **Key verse**

   Verse 3: "For Mordecai the Jew was next unto king Ahasuerus, and great among the Jews, and accepted of the multitude of his brethren, seeking the wealth of his people, and speaking peace to all his seed."

4. **Key word / key phrase**

   Verse 3, "pre-eminent."

5. **Key event / key person / key theme**

   Mordecai's greatness

6. **Key thought**

   The Lord raises the humble.

7. **Key thing to look out for**

   Mordecai's good actions are remembered.

8. **Key Bible cross-reference**

   Verse 2. See 1 Chronicles s17:21.

9. **Key "by way of explanation"**

   The word "Purim" came from the Assyrian word *puru*, a small stone, which was used when casting lots.

10. **Key "Quotable Quote"**

    "I read somewhere that this young man, Jesus Christ, went about doing good. But I just go about."
    Toyohiko Kagawa

Job

Job chapter 1

1. *Following chapter*

Chapter 2: Satan's second attack; Job's four friends arrive

2. *Analysis of chapter*

Job's great piety. (1)
His great prosperity. (2-4)
The malice of Satan against him, and the permission he obtained to test him. (6-12)
The surprising troubles that befell him, and the ruin of his estate. (13-17)
The death of his children. (18, 19)
His exemplary patience and piety under these troubles. (20-22)

3. *Key verse*

Verse 21, "And said, Naked came I out of my mother's womb, and naked shall I return thither; the LORD gave, and the LORD hath taken away; blessed be the name of the LORD"

4. *Key word*

Verse 1, "blameless."

5. *Key event / key person / key theme*

Satan's testing of Job's faith in God.

6. *Key thought*

The problem of why innocent people suffer is introduced.

7. *Key thing to look out for*

Job faces up to reality – but does not look for someone or something to blame. He praises God.

8. *Key Bible cross-reference*

Verse 21. See Ecclesiastes 5:15 and 1 Timothy 6:7.

9. *Key "by way of explanation"*

Verse 1, "Job . . . perfect and upright." Job may have been beyond reproach, but this verse does not mean that he was sinless.

10. *Key "Quotable Quote"*

"The greatest poem of ancient and modern times."
Alfred Tennyson (Rhyme is common in English-language poems, but it was rare in Hebrew poetry.)

Job chapter 2

1. *Before and after*

Previous chapter: Chapter 1: Job's circumstances
Following chapter: Chapter 3: Job's first speech

2. *Analysis of chapter*

Satan obtains leave to test Job. (1-6)
Job's sufferings. (7-10)
His friends come to comfort him. (11-13)

3. *Key verse*

Verse 6: "And the LORD said unto Satan, Behold, he is in thine hand; but save his life."

4. *Key word / key phrase*

Verse 1, "Satan."

5. *Key event / key person / key theme*

Job's second test

6. *Key thought*

Satan never rests.

7. *Key thing to look out for*

At this stage Job is still able to answer his wife in a good and positive way.

8. *Key Bible cross-reference*

Verse 3. See 38:2.

9. *Key "by way of explanation"*

Verse 9. Satan attempts to use Job's wife in the same way that he used Eve to tempt Adam.

10. *Key "Quotable Quote"*

"The riddles of God are more satisfying than the solutions of man."
G.K. Chesterton

Job chapter 3

1. *Before and after*

Previous chapter: Chapter 2: Satan's second attack; Job's four friends arrive
Following chapter: Chapter 4: Eliphaz says that the innocent do not suffer

2. *Analysis of chapter*

Job complains that he was born. (1-10)
Job complaining. (11-19)
He complains of his life. (20-26)

3. *Key verse*

Verse 3: "Let the day perish wherein I was born, and the night in which it was
said, There is a man child conceived."

4. *Key word / key phrase*

Verse 3, "may the day of my birth perish."

5. *Key event / key person / key theme*

Job speaks

6. *Key thought*

Job now curses the day he was born.

7. *Key thing to look out for*

Just because godly people commit some serious sin it does not mean that
they will not later repent.

8. *Key Bible cross-reference*

Verses 21,22. Job just wanted to die. See Revelation 9:6.

9. *Key "by way of explanation"*

Verse 8. In the east people used to pronounce curses on people, on days, and
on objects.

10. *Key "Quotable Quote"*

"A believer may pass through much affliction, and yet secure very little
blessing from it all. Abiding in Christ is the secret of securing all that the
Father meant the chastisement to bring us."
Andrew Murray

Job chapters 4 and 5

1. *Before and after*

Previous chapter: Chapter 3: Job's first speech
Following chapter: Chapter 6: Job expresses his deep anguish

2. *Analysis of chapters 4 and 5*

Eliphaz reproves Job. (4:1-6)
And maintains that God's judgments are for the wicked. (4:7-11)
The vision of Eliphaz. (4:12-21)
Eliphaz urges that the sin of sinners is their ruin. (5:1-5)
God is to be taken notice of in affliction. (5:6-16)
The happy end of God's correction. (5:17-27)

3. *Key verse in chapter 4*

Chapter 4, verse 1: "Then Eliphaz the Temanite answered."

4. *Key word / key phrase*

5:17, "Blessed is the man whom God corrects."

5. *Key event / key person / key theme*

Eliphaz replies

6. *Key thought*

It is easy to give unhelpful advice.

7. *Key thing to look out for*

It is wrong to always equate suffering and the Lord's punishment.

8. *Key Bible cross-reference*

4:1. See Genesis 36:11; Amos 1:12; Job 2:11.

9. *Key "by way of explanation"*

4:17-21. Eliphaz tells Job that he should be grateful that God is punishing him.

10. *Key "Quotable Quote"*

"Our affliction is not execution, but a correction."
Thomas Brooks

Job chapters 6 and 7

1. **Before and after**

> Previous chapter: Chapter 5: Eliphaz says that Job is foolish
> Following chapter: Chapter 8: Bildad's first speech

2. **Analysis of chapters**

> Job justifies his complaints. (6:1-7)
> He longs for death. (6:8-13)
> Job reproves his friends as unkind. (6:14-30)
> Job's troubles. (7:1-6)
> Job expostulates with God. (7:7-16)
> He begs release. (7:17-21)

3. **Key verse**

> Chapter 6, verse 2: "Oh that my grief were thoroughly weighed, and my calamity laid in the balances together!"

4. **Key word / key phrase**

> 6:2, "my anguish."

5. **Key event / key person / key theme**

> Job's reply

6. **Key thought**

> To accuse one's "comforters" gets you nowhere, see 6:27.

7. **Key thing to look out for**

> As God knows everything about us it is pointless to justify ourselves before him.

8. **Key Bible cross-reference**

> 6:14,15. See Galatians 6:1.

9. **Key "by way of explanation"**

> Not having entered into the depths of Job's suffering, Eliphaz cannot say anything that will help.

10. **Key "Quotable Quote"**

> "Let us learn like Christians to kiss the rod, and love it."
> John Bunyan

Job chapter 8

1. ### Before and after

   Previous chapter: Chapter 7: Job questions God's continuing trial
   Following chapter: Chapter 9: Job argues his case

2. ### Analysis of chapter

   Bildad reproves Job. (1-7)
   Hypocrites will be destroyed. (8-19)
   Bildad applies God's just dealing to Job. (20-22)

3. ### Key verse

   Verse 1: "Then answered Bildad the Shuhite"

4. ### Key word / key phrase

   Verse 2, "a blustering wind."

5. ### Key event / key person / key theme

   Bildad's advice

6. ### Key thought

   Bildad is a hopeless comforter, calling Job an evildoer, verse 20.

7. ### Key thing to look out for

   Bildad also accuses Job of being a hypocrite, verse 13.

8. ### Key Bible cross-reference

   Verse 9. See 14:2; Psalm 102:11.

9. ### Key "by way of explanation"

   Verse 3. Bildad is rather jumping the gun to ask Job the question, "Does God pervert justice?" when Job has not accused God of that.

10. ### Key "Quotable Quote"

    "Brains can argue, but it takes heart to comfort."
    Samuel Chadwick

Job chapters 9 and 10

1. Before and after

Previous chapter: Chapter 8: Bildad's first speech
Following chapter: Chapter 11: Zophar's first speech

2. Analysis of chapters 9 and 10

Job acknowledges God's justice. (9:1-13)
He is not able to contend with God. (9:14-21)
Men are not to be judged by their outward condition. (9:22-24)
Job complains of troubles. (9:25-35)
Job complains of his hardships. (10:1-7)
He pleads with God as his Maker. (10:8-13)
He complains of God's severity. (10:14-22)

3. Key verse

Chapter 9, verse 13: "If God will not withdraw his anger, the proud helpers do stoop under him."

4. Key word / key phrase

9:1, "righteous before God."

5. Key event / key person / key theme

Job's reply

6. Key thought

When things are difficult it helps to think about God's characteristics.

7. Key thing to look out for

It does not help to question God's existence, especially if we are depressed.

8. Key Bible cross-reference

9:3. Note how Job uses courtroom vocabulary. See also 9:15,32,14,15, 16,19,20,24,32.

9. Key "by way of explanation"

10:8-11 is a poetic description of a baby created by God in the womb. See Psalm 139:13-16.

10. Key "Quotable Quote"

"God does not comfort us to make us comfortable, but to make us comforters."
J.H. Jowett

Job chapter 11

1. Before and after

Previous chapter: Chapter 10: Job questions his oppression
Following chapter: Chapter 12: Job says that only God knows everything

2. Analysis of chapter

Zophar reproves Job. (1-6)
God's perfections and almighty power. (7-12)
Zophar assures Job of blessings if he repents. (13-20)

3. Key verse

Verse 1: "Then answered Zophar the Naamathite."

4. Key word / key phrase

Verse 3, "your idle talk."

5. Key event / key person / key theme

Zophar's speech

6. Key thought

Zophar does not show any compassion toward Job.

7. Key thing to look out for

Zophar accuses Job of being guilty of thoughts and attitudes of which he is
not guilty.

8. Key Bible cross-reference

Verses 8,9. See Ephesians 3:18.

9. Key "by way of explanation"

Verse 4. Job maintained that he was blameless. But Zophar accuses him of
claiming to have reached the heights of sinless perfection.

10. Key "Quotable Quote"

"Comfort yourself with the sovereign Physician of both the soul and the
body."
Brother Lawrence

Job chapters 12, 13, and 14

1. *Before and after*

Previous chapter: Chapter 11: Zophar's first speech
Following chapter: Chapter 15: Eliphaz's second speech

2. *Analysis of chapters 12, 13, and 14*

Job reproves his friends. (12:1-5)
The wicked often prosper.(12:6-11)
Job speaks of the wisdom and power of God. (12:12-25)
Job reproves his friends. (13:1-12)
He professes his confidence in God. (13:13-22)
Job pleads to know his sins. (13:23-28)
Job speaks of man's life. (14:1-6)
Of man's death. (14:7-15)
By sin man is subject to corruption. (14:16-22)

3. *Key verse*

Chapter 12, verse 3: "But I have understanding as well as you; I am not inferior to you."

4. *Key word / key phrase*

12:3, "I am not inferior to you."

5. *Key event / key person / key theme*

Job's reply

6. *Key thought*

Job was helped by the silent sympathy of his friends, 13:5, but not by their advice.

7. *Key thing to look out for*

Job speaks to his three friends, 12:2–13:19, and then to God, 13:14–14:22.

8. *Key Bible cross-reference*

14:2. See Psalm 37:2; Isaiah 40:7,24.

9. *Key "by way of explanation"*

12:20. Job's reaction to the advice of his friends is to reply with biting sarcasm.

10. *Key "Quotable Quote"*

"To comfort a sorrowful conscience is much better than to possess many kingdoms."
Martin Luther

Job chapter 15

1. **Before and after**

   Previous chapter: Chapter 14: Job mourns that man has only one life
   Following chapter: Chapter 16: Job accuses his friends of being miserable comforters

2. **Analysis of chapter**

   Eliphaz reproves Job. (1-16)
   The character of wicked men. (17-35)

3. **Key verse**

   Verse 5: "For thy mouth uttereth thine iniquity, and thou choosest the tongue of the crafty."

4. **Key word / key phrase**

   Verse 3, "useless words."

5. **Key event / key person / key theme**

   Eliphaz's second speech

6. **Key thought**

   Eliphaz again says that the wicked suffer because of their wickedness.

7. **Key thing to look out for**

   Eliphaz does not allow the question, "Why do the innocent suffer?"

8. **Key Bible cross-reference**

   Verse 5. See Matthew 15:11,17-18.

9. **Key "by way of explanation"**

   Verses 7-10. Eliphaz says that Job is guilty of thinking that he can sit alongside members of God's council when he is no wiser than the ordinary person.

10. **Key "Quotable Quote"**

   "In Christ the heart of the Father is revealed, and higher comfort there cannot be than to rest in the Father's heart."
   Andrew Murray

Job chapters 16 and 17

1. Before and after

Previous chapter: Chapter 15: Eliphaz's second speech
Following chapter: Chapter 18: Bildad's second speech

2. Analysis of chapters 16 and 17

Job reproves his friends. (16:1-5)
He represents his case as deplorable. (16:6-16)
Job maintains his innocence. (16:17-22)
Job appeals from man to God. (17:1-9)
His hope is not in life, but in death. (17:10-16)

3. Key verse

Chapter 15, verse 11: "God hath delivered me to the ungodly, and turned me over into the hands of the wicked."

4. Key word / key phrase

16:1, "Job replied."

5. Key event / key person / key theme

Job's reply

6. Key thought

Job calls his three friends, "miserable comforters," 16:1.

7. Key thing to look out for

Job continues to maintain his innocence and to complain about his suffering.

8. Key Bible cross-reference

16:4. See Psalm 22:7; Jeremiah 48:27; Matthew 27:39.

9. Key "by way of explanation"

16:18-21. Job now feels that on earth he will never be vindicated, so his only hope is that he will have a friend in heaven.

10. Key "Quotable Quote"

"Little things console us because little things afflict us."
Blaise Pascal

Job chapter 18

1. **Before and after**

   Previous chapter: Chapter 17: Job feels helpless
   Following chapter: Chapter 19: Job replies to Bildad

2. **Analysis of chapter**

   Bildad reproves Job. (1-4)
   Ruin attends the wicked. (5-10)
   The ruin of the wicked. (11-21)

3. **Key verse**

   Verse 1: "Then answered Bildad the Shuhite."

4. **Key word / key phrase**

   Verse 21, "an evil man."

5. **Key event / key person / key theme**

   Bildad's second speech

6. **Key thought**

   When a person pleads for comfort it is not a good time to start accusing him
   of wrongdoing.

7. **Key thing to look out for**

   Bildad accuses Job of being full of self-pity.

8. **Key Bible cross-reference**

   Verse 21. See Hosea 4:1-2, 6.

9. **Key "by way of explanation"**

   Verses 5-21. Bildad treats Job to another poem about how the wicked suffer.

10. **Key "Quotable Quote"**

    "The hill of comfort is the hill of Calvary; the house of consolation is built
    with the wood of the cross."
    C.H. Spurgeon

Job chapter 19

1. Before and after

Previous chapter: Chapter 18: Bildad's second speech
Following chapter: Chapter 20: Zophar's second speech

2. Analysis of chapter

Job complains of unkindness. (1-7)
God the Author of Job's afflictions. (8-22)
Job's belief in the resurrection. (23-29)

3. Key verse

Verse 6: "Know now that God hath overthrown me, and hath compassed me with his net."

4. Key word / key phrase

Verse 3, "you attack me."

5. Key event / key person / key theme

Job's reply

6. Key thought

Job knows that there is more to existence than just this life.

7. Key thing to look out for

Job is comforted by the thought that one day he will stand in the presence of his Redeemer.

8. Key Bible cross-reference

Verse 3. See Genesis 31:41; 1 Samuel 1:8.

9. Key "by way of explanation"

Verse 25. Despite all his difficulties Job still believes that his Redeemer will vindicate him against all his accusers.

10. Key "Quotable Quote"

"God made the body as well as the soul, and redemption is for the whole man."
Francis A. Schaeffer

Job chapter 20

1. Before and after

Previous chapter: Chapter 19: Job replies to Bildad
Following chapter: Chapter 21: Job replies to Zophar

2. Analysis of chapter

Zophar speaks of the short joy of the wicked. (1-9)
The ruin of the wicked. (10-22)
The portion of the wicked. (23-29)

3. Key verse

Verse 1: "Then answered Zophar the Naamathite."

4. Key word / key phrase

Verse 3, "dishonors me."

5. Key event / key person / key theme

Zophar's second speech

6. Key thought

Zophar points to himself and his own prosperity as proof of his own
righteousness.

7. Key thing to look out for

Do not make unhelpful comparisons when trying to bring comfort.

8. Key Bible cross-reference

Verse 18. See Ecclesiastes 2:18-23.

9. Key "by way of explanation"

Verse 29. Zophar's speech is "remorselessly irrelevant to Job's true situation"
(David Clines).

10. Key "Quotable Quote"

"If we have not quiet in our minds, outward comfort will do no more for us
than a golden slipper on a gouty foot."
John Bunyan

Job chapter 21

1. *Before and after*

   Previous chapter: Chapter 20: Zophar's second speech
   Following chapter: Chapter 22: Eliphaz's third speech

2. *Analysis of chapter*

   Job entreats attention. (1-6)
   The prosperity of the wicked. (7-16)
   The dealings of God's providence. (17-26)
   The judgment of the wicked is in the world to come. (27-34)

3. *Key verse*

   Verse 2: "Hear diligently my speech, and let this be your consolations."

4. *Key word / key phrase*

   Verse 34, "your nonesense."

5. *Key event / key person / key theme*

   Job's reply

6. *Key thought*

   Job points out that it is an observable fact that the wicked do prosper in this
   life.

7. *Key thing to look out for*

   Job expresses his faith in God whom he knows is in control of the world.

8. *Key Bible cross-reference*

   Verse 13. See Psalm 35:20.

9. *Key "by way of explanation"*

   Verse 4. Job complains against God, blaming him for his present suffering.

10. *Key "Quotable Quote"*

   "Sometimes a light surprises
   The Christian while he sings;
   It is the Lord who rises
   With healing in his wings;
   When comforts are declining,
   He grants the soul again;
   A season of clear shining,
   To cheer it after rain."
   William Cowper

Job chapter 22

1. **Before and after**

   Previous chapter: Chapter 21: Job replies to Zophar
   Following chapter: Chapter 23: Job will come out refined like pure gold

2. **Analysis of chapter**

   Eliphaz shows that God does not rebuke piety. (1-4)
   Job accused of wickedness. (5-14)
   The world before the Flood. (15-20)
   Eliphaz exhorts Job to repent. (21-30)

3. **Key verse**

   Verse 2: "Can a man be profitable unto God, as he that is wise may be profitable unto himself?"

4. **Key word / key phrase**

   Verse 21, "submit to God."

5. **Key event / key person / key theme**

   Eliphaz's third speech

6. **Key thought**

   Eliphaz continues to accuse Job of being wicked.

7. **Key thing to look out for**

   Eliphaz thinks that all Job wants is the restoration of his prosperity.

8. **Key Bible cross-reference**

   Verse 9. See 24:3; Isaiah 1:17.

9. **Key "by way of explanation"**

   Chapters 22–26 contain the third round of speeches between Job and his three friends.

10. **Key "Quotable Quote"**

    "God is our true Friend, who always gives us the counsel and comfort we need."
    François Fénelon

Job chapters 23 and 24

1. Before and after

Previous chapter: Chapter 22: Eliphaz's third speech
Following chapter: Chapter 25: Bildad's third speech
2. *Analysis of chapters* 23, *and* 24
Job complains that God has withdrawn. (23:1-7)
He asserts his own integrity. (23:8-12)
Job is terrified. (23:13-17)
Wickedness is often unpunished. (24:1-12)
The wicked shun the light. (24:13-17)
Judgments for the wicked. (24:18-25)

3. Key verse

Chapter 23, verse 2: "Even to day is my complaint bitter: my stroke is heavier than my groaning."

4. Key word / key phrase

23:2, "my complaint is bitter."

5. Key event / key person / key theme

Job's reply

6. Key thought

Job points out how much injustice there is in the world.

7. Key thing to look out for

Job states that evil people rebel against the light, which is found in God's Law.

8. Key Bible cross-reference

24:20. See 21:26; Isaiah 14:11.

9. Key "by way of explanation"

23:8,10. Job agrees that God is testing him, not in order to show up any wickedness in him but to demonstrate that he is pure as gold.

10. Key "Quotable Quote"

"All human comfort is vain and short."
Thomas à Kempis

Job chapter 25

1. Before and after

Previous chapter: Chapter 24: Job says that God seems indifferent to wickedness
Following chapter: Chapter 26: Job replies to Bildad

2. Analysis of chapter

Bildad shows that man cannot be justified before God. (1-6)

3. Key verse

Verse 4: "How then can man be justified with God?"

4. Key word / key phrase

Verse 6, "a maggot."

5. Key event / key person / key theme

Bildad's third speech

6. Key thought

Bildad repeats his previous thoughts. A comforter would do better to be silent than to continually repeat his advice.

7. Key thing to look out for

Bildad emphasizes the depravity of humankind.

8. Key Bible cross-reference

Verses 4-6. See 4:17-19; 15:14-16.

9. Key "by way of explanation"

Verse 3. Bildad states that everything has to submit to God's light.

10. Key "Quotable Quote"

"The broken and the jaded and the twisted are being ministered to by God through the saints who are not overcome by their own panic, who because of their oneness with him are absolutely at rest. Consequently he can work through them."
Oswald Chambers

Job chapter 26

1. Before and after

> Previous chapter: Chapter 25: Bildad's third speech
> Following chapter: Chapter 27: Job boasts of his righteousness

2. Analysis of chapter

> Job reproves Bildad. (1-4)
> Job acknowledges the power of God. (5-14)

3. Key verse

> Verse 3: "How hast thou counseled him that hath no wisdom?"

4. Key word / key phrase

> Verse 3, "without wisdom."

5. Key event / key person / key theme

> Job's reply

6. Key thought

> Job begins with a round of sarcasm.

7. Key thing to look out for

> Verse 4. What spirit moved Bildad?

8. Key Bible cross-reference

> Verse 5. See Proverbs 2:18; Isaiah 14:9; 26:14.

9. Key "by way of explanation"

> Verses 5-14. Job is still able to speak of God's great power.

10. Key "Quotable Quote"

> "You don't have to be alone in your hurt! Comfort is yours. Joy is an option.
> And it's all been made possible by your Savior."
> Joni Eareckson Tada

Job chapter 27

1. *Before and after*

Previous chapter: Chapter 26: Job replies to Bildad
Following chapter: Chapter 28: Job says that men cannot achieve wisdom

2. *Analysis of chapter*

Job protests his sincerity. (1-6)
The hypocrite is without hope. (7-10)
The miserable end of the wicked. (11-23)

3. *Key verse*

Verse 6: "My righteousness I hold fast."

4. *Key word / key phrase*

Verse 11, "I will teach you."

5. *Key event / key person / key theme*

Job's closing discourse

6. *Key thought*

Job continues to state his own innocence.

7. *Key thing to look out for*

Verses 1-6. What does Job hold on to?

8. *Key Bible cross-reference*

Verse 6. See 2:3.

9. *Key "by way of explanation"*

Verse 7. Job asks that his friends may be treated as if they were wicked men!

10. *Key "Quotable Quote"*

"It will greatly comfort you if you can see God's hand in both your losses and your crosses."
C.H. Spurgeon

Job chapter 28

1. **Before and after**

   Previous chapter: Chapter 27: Job boasts of his righteousness
   Following chapter: Chapter 29: Job recalls his happy past

2. **Analysis of chapter**

   Worldly wealth. (1-11)
   Wisdom is of inestimable value. (12-19)
   Wisdom is the gift of God. (20-28)

3. **Key verse**

   Verse 1: "Surely there is a vein for the silver, and a place for gold where they fine it."

4. **Key word / key phrase**

   Verse 28, "wisdom."

5. **Key event / key person / key theme**

   Interlude on wisdom

6. **Key thought**

   Men and women look all over the world for wisdom.

7. **Key thing to look out for**

   Wisdom can only be found in God.

8. **Key Bible cross-reference**

   Verses 25-27. See Proverbs 8:22-31.

9. **Key "by way of explanation"**

   Verses 1-11 give a description of mines in current times. "Wisdom" here means a full understanding of the universe. Although this wisdom is beyond humankind, practical down-to-earth wisdom is within human reach (verse 28).

10. **Key "Quotable Quote"**

    "The beginning of divine wisdom is clemency and gentleness, which arise from greatness of soul and the bearing of infirmities of men."
    Isaac of Nineveh

Job chapter 29

1. *Before and after*

   Previous chapter: Chapter 28: Job says that men cannot achieve wisdom
   Following chapter: Chapter 30: Job outlines his present humiliation

2. *Analysis of chapter*

   Job's former comforts. (1-6)
   The honor paid to Job. His usefulness. (7-17)
   His prospect of prosperity. (18-25)

3. *Key verse*

   Verse 6: "When I washed my steps with butter, and the rock poured me out rivers of oil."

4. *Key word / key phrase*

   Verse 21, "men listened to me."

5. *Key event / key person / key theme*

   Job recalls his previous honor and blessing

6. *Key thought*

   Job speaks about the time when he used to be a repected member of the city council.

7. *Key thing to look out for*

   Verses 12,13. Job reminds his friends that people used to go to him for advice and practical help.

8. *Key Bible cross-reference*

   Verse 14. See Isaiah 59:17; 61:10.

9. *Key "by way of explanation"*

   In chapters 29–31 Job summarizes the position he is in.

10. *Key "Quotable Quote"*

    "Down through the centuries in times of trouble and trial God has brought courage to the hearts of those who love him."
    Billy Graham

Job chapter 30

1. Before and after

Previous chapter: Chapter 29: Job recalls his happy past
Following chapter: Chapter 31: Job maintains that he is innocent

2. Analysis of chapter

Job's honor is turned into contempt. (1-14)
Job is a burden to himself. (15-31)

3. Key verse

Verse 5: "They were driven forth from among men."

4. Key word / key phrase

Verse 1, "mock me."

5. Key event / key person / key theme

Job's present dishonor and suffering

6. Key thought

Job remains very angry with God.

7. Key thing to look out for

The very great contrast between Job's past and present life.

8. Key Bible cross-reference

Verse 11. See 29:20.

9. Key "by way of explanation"

Verse 31. Job says that God has heaped burdens on him which he cannot bear.

10. Key "Quotable Quote"

"Human comfort and divine comfort are of different natures: human comfort
consists in external, visible help, which a man may see, hold, and feel; divine
comfort is only in words and promises, where there is neither seeing, hearing,
nor feeling."
Martin Luther

Job chapter 31

1. *Before and after*

Previous chapter: Chapter 30: Job outlines his present humiliation
Following chapter: Chapter 32: Elihu intervenes in the discussion

2. *Analysis of chapter*

Job declares his uprightness. (1-8)
His integrity. (9-15)
Job is merciful. (16-23)
Job is not guilty of covetousness or idolatry. (24-32)
Job is not guilty of hypocrisy and violence. (33-40)

3. *Key verse*

Verse 5: "If I have walked with vanity, or if my foot hath hasted to deceit."

4. *Key word / key phrase*

Verse 4, "Does he not see my ways?"

5. *Key event / key person / key theme*

Job protests his innocence

6. *Key thought*

Job continues to defend himself as if he is on trial in a courtroom.

7. *Key thing to look out for*

Job states that he is innocent of all the sins he lists.

8. *Key Bible cross-reference*

Verse 16. See 6:2; Proverbs 16:12.

9. *Key "by way of explanation"*

Verses 24-28. Greed and idolatry are both said to be evil in God's sight.

10. *Key "Quotable Quote"*

"The Bible is filled with assurances of God's help and comfort in every kind of trouble which might cause fears to arise in the human heart."
Billy Graham

Job chapters 32 and 33

1. Before and after

Previous chapter: Chapter 31: Job maintains that he is innocent
Following chapter: Chapter 33: Elihu's first proposition

2. Analysis of chapters 32, and 33

Elihu is displeased at the dispute between Job and his friends. (32:1-5)
He reproves them. (32:6-14)
He speaks impartially. (32:15-22)
Elihu offers to reason with Job. (33:1-7)
Elihu blames Job for reflecting upon God. (33:8-13)
God calls men to repentance. (33:14-18)
God sends afflictions for good. (33:19-28)
Elihu entreats Job's attention. (33:29-33)

3. Key verse

Chapter 32, verse 1: "So these three men ceased to answer Job, because he was righteous in his own eyes."

4. Key word / key phrase

32:3, "angry with the three friends."

5. Key event / key person / key theme

Elihu's first speech

6. Key thought

Elihu talks to Job by name, which his other three friends did not.

7. Key thing to look out for

Elihu speaks about redemption being possible through a mediator.

8. Key Bible cross-reference

Verse 6. See Jeremiah 1:6-8; 1 Timothy 4:12.

9. Key "by way of explanation"

32:18. Elihu is indeed "full of words," and his four speeches continue to the end of chapter 37. Verse 1. Job continued to maintain his innocence.

10. Key "Quotable Quote"

"I now possess not merely consolation, but the God of consolation."
Jeanne Guyon

Job chapter 34

1. *Before and after*

Previous chapter: Chapter 33: Elihu's first proposition
Following chapter: Chapter 35: Elihu's third proposition

2. *Analysis of chapter*

Elihu accuses Job of charging God with injustice. (1-9)
God cannot be unjust. (10-15)
God's power and providence. (16-30)
Elihu reproves Job. (31-37)

3. *Key verse*

Verse 9: "For he hath said, It profiteth a man nothing that he should delight himself with God."

4. *Key word / key phrase*

Verse 4, "Let us discern."

5. *Key event / key person / key theme*

Elihu's second proposition

6. *Key thought*

Elihu does not like the way in which Job appeared to make the Lord the author of evil.

7. *Key thing to look out for*

Elihu champions God's glory.

8. *Key Bible cross-reference*

Verse 15. See Ecclesiastes 12:7.

9. *Key "by way of explanation"*

Verses 5,9. Elihu attempts to correct what he deems to be Job's theological errors. 9:14-125; 16:11-17.

10. *Key "Quotable Quote"*

"God does not leave us comfortless, but we have to be in dire need of comfort to know the truth of his promise."
Peter Marshall

Job chapter 35

1. Before and after

Previous chapter: Chapter 34: Elihu's second proposition
Following chapter: Chapter 36: Elihu says that God is disciplining Job

2. Analysis of chapter

Elihu speaks of man's behavior. (1-8)
Why those who cry out under afflictions are not taken notice of. (9-13)
Elihu reproves Job's impatience. (14-26)

3. Key verse

Verse 2: "Thinkest thou this to be right, that thou saidst, My righteousness is more than God's?"

4. Key word / key phrase

Verse 2, "Cleared by God."

5. Key event / key person / key theme

Elihu's third proposition

6. Key thought

Elihu tells Job that he is wrong to accuse God of being silent.

7. Key thing to look out for

Elihu quite misses the point. He seems not to have been listening to what Job has actually been saying.

8. Key Bible cross-reference

Verse 2. See 13:18.

9. Key "by way of explanation"

Verse 9. Elihu includes Job among those who cry out to God but do not believe that he is the God of justice.

10. Key "Quotable Quote"

"Apt words have power to assuage
The tumors of a troubled mind
And are as balm to festered wounds."
John Milton

Job chapters 36 and 37

1. **Before and after**

   Previous chapter: Chapter 35: Elihu's third proposition
   Following chapter: Chapter 38: God reminds Job about the amazing world of nature

2. **Analysis of chapter**

   Elihu desires Job's attention. (36:1-4)
   The methods God uses to deal with people. (36:5-14)
   Elihu counsels Job. (36:15-23)
   The wonders in the works of creation. (36:24-33)
   Elihu observes the power of God. (37:1-13)
   Job required to explain the works of nature. (37:14-20)
   God is great, and is to be feared. (37:21-24)

3. **Key verse**

   36:3: "I will fetch my knowledge from afar, and will ascribe righteousness to my Maker."

4. **Key word / key phrase**

   36:4, "my words are not false."

5. **Key event / key person / key theme**

   Elihu's fourth proposition

6. **Key thought**

   Elihu tells Job to avoid evil and so not come under God's judgment.

7. **Key thing to look out for**

   Elihu points Job to God's magnificent creation.

8. **Key Bible cross-reference**

   36:21. See 1:8; 2:3.

9. **Key "by way of explanation"**

   36:6-9. In contrast to Job's assertions Elihu insists that God rewards the righteous and punishes sinners.

10. **Key "Quotable Quote"**

    "Those who can sit in silence with their fellowman, not knowing what to say but knowing that they should be there, can bring new life in a dying heart."
    Henri J.M. Nouwen

Job chapters 38 and 39

1. Before and after

Previous chapter: Chapter 37: Elihu reminds Job about God's greatness
Following chapter: Chapter 40: God shows Job how feeble he is

2. Analysis of chapters 38, and 39

God calls upon Job to answer. (38:1-3)
God questions Job. (38:4-11)
Light and darkness. (38:12-24)
Other mighty works. (38:25-41)
God asks Job about several animals. (39:1-30)

3. Key verse

38:1: "Then the LORD answered Job out of the whirlwind."

4. Key word / key phrase

38:2, "words without knowledge."

5. Key event / key person / key theme

God reminds Job about the amazing world of nature

6. Key thought

God's creatures point to God's sovereignty.

7. Key thing to look out for

Job is reminded that God cares for the animals.

8. Key Bible cross-reference

38:7. See Psalm 148:2,3.

9. Key "by way of explanation"

God responds, not from a courtroom, but from a storm. Job is challenged to look again at the mystery of the world.

10. Key "Quotable Quote"

"You can look ahead with promise, hope, and joy."
Billy Graham

Job chapter 40

1. *Before and after*

> Previous chapter: Chapter 39: God reminds Job of the animal kingdom
> Following chapter: Chapter 41: God compares Job's power with that of the leviathan

2. *Analysis of chapter*

> Job humbles himself to God. (1-5)
> The Lord reasons with Job to show his righteousness, power, and wisdom. (6-14)
> God's power shown in the behemoth. (15-24)

3. *Key verse*

> Verse 4: "Behold, I am vile; what shall I answer thee?"

4. *Key word / key phrase*

> Verse 3, "I am unworthy."

5. *Key event / key person / key theme*

> Job replies to the Lord

6. *Key thought*

> The Lord demolishes Job's attempts at self-justification.

7. *Key thing to look out for*

> In the opening verses of this chapter God shows Job how feeble he is.

8. *Key Bible cross-reference*

> Verses 11,12. See Isaiah 13:11.

9. *Key "by way of explanation"*

> Verse 15. This "behemoth" is not easy to identify, beyond the fact that it is a very large land animal.

10. *Key "Quotable Quote"*

> "When the house doth sigh and weep,
> And the world is drowned in sleep,
> Yet mine eyes the watch do keep,
> Sweet Spirit comfort me!"
> Robert Herrick

Job chapter 41

1. **Before and after**

    Previous chapter: Chapter 40: God shows Job how feeble he is
    Following chapter: Chapter 42: Job repents and is fully restored

2. **Analysis of chapter**

    Leviathan. (1-34)

3. **Key verse**

    Verse 1: "Canst thou draw out leviathan with an hook?"

4. **Key word / key phrase**

    Verse 11, "everything . . . belongs to me."

5. **Key event / key person / key theme**

    The Lord's second discourse

6. **Key thought**

    No creatures are God's equal.

7. **Key thing to look out for**

    The Lord is not impressed by the proud.

8. **Key Bible cross-reference**

    Verse 11. See Romans 11:35.

9. **Key "by way of explanation"**

    Verse 10. The leviathan is mightier than the behemoth. The Lord is mightier than the leviathan.

10. **Key "Quotable Quote"**

    "My soul cannot be fully comforted or perfectly refreshed, except in God alone, who is the Comforter of the poor in spirit and the Embracer of the humble and low in heart."
    Thomas à Kempis

Job chapter 42

1. Previous chapter

Chapter 41: God compares Job's power with that of the leviathan

2. Analysis of chapter

Job humbly submits unto God. (1-6)
Job intercedes for his friends. (7-9)
His renewed prosperity. (10-17)

3. Key verse

Verse 5: "I have heard of thee by the hearing of the ear: but now mine eye seeth thee."

4. Key word / key phrase

Verse 6, "I . . . repent."

5. Key event / key person / key theme

Job repents

6. Key thought

No final "answer" to the problem of the suffering of the innocent is given.

7. Key thing to look out for

Job is content to rest in God's presence.

8. Key Bible cross-reference

Verse 5. See Isaiah 6:5.

9. Key "by way of explanation"

Verses 7,8. The phrase "my servant Job," repeated four times in these two verses, shows how the Lord viewed Job.

10. Key "Quotable Quote"

"When spiritual comfort is sent to you by God, take it humbly and give thanks meekly for it. But know for certain that it is the great goodness of God that sends it to you, and not because you deserve it."
Thomas à Kempis

Psalms

Psalm 1

1. **Following psalm**

   Psalm 2: The Lord's Anointed

2. **Analysis of psalm**

   The holiness and happiness of a godly man. (1-3)
   The sinfulness and misery of a wicked man, and the reason for both. (4-6)

3. **Key verse**

   Verse 3: "And he shall be like a tree planted by the rivers of water."

4. **Key word / key phrase**

   Verse 1, "blessed."

5. **Key event / key person / key theme**

   The man who is blessed

6. **Key thought**

   There are three steps on the evil path in verse 1.

7. **Key thing to look out for**

   A person blessed by God is like a flourishing tree.

8. **Key Bible cross-reference**

   Verse 3. See Jeremiah 17:8.

9. **Key "by way of explanation"**

   Verse 5. When God judges people nobody will be able to stand in his presence.

10. **Key "Quotable Quote"**

    "The meaning of the psalmist is that it shall be always well with God's devout servants, whose constant endeavor it is to make progress in the study of his law. He teaches us how impossible it is for anyone to apply his mind to meditation upon God's law, who has not first withdrawn and separated himself from the society of the ungodly."
    John Calvin

Psalm 2

1. *Before and after*

   Previous psalm: Psalm 1: Contrasting two ways of life
   Following psalm: Psalm 3: Victory in the face of defeat

2. *Analysis of psalm*

   Warnings against the enemies of Christ's kingdom. (1-6)
   Promise to Christ as the Head of this kingdom. (7-9)
   Counsel to all, to follow its interests. (10-12)

3. *Key verse*

   Verse 11: "Serve the Lord with fear, and rejoice with trembling."

4. *Key word / key phrase*

   Verse 2, "Anointed One."

5. *Key event / key person / key theme*

   The Lord's Anointed

6. *Key thought*

   In the New Testament, where this Psalm is often quoted, the Anointed One is applied to Christ.

7. *Key thing to look out for*

   This Psalm was probably originally written to celebrate the coronation of an heir to David's throne.

8. *Key Bible cross-reference*

   Verses 1,2. See Acts 4:25-28.

9. *Key "by way of explanation"*

   Verse 2. The Hebrew word for "anointed one" is "Messiah." The English word "Christ" comes from the Greek for "anointed one."

10. *Key "Quotable Quote"*

    "For I believe that the whole of human existence, both the dispositions of the soul and the movements of the thoughts, have been measured out and encompassed in those very words of the Psalter. And nothing beyond these is found among men."
    Athanasius the Great

Psalm 3

1. *Before and after*

Previous psalm: Psalm 2: The Lord's Anointed
Following psalm: Psalm 4: Evening prayer for deliverance

2. *Analysis of psalm*

David complains to God about his enemies, and confides in God. (1-3)
He triumphs over his fears, and gives God the glory, and is comforted. (4-8)

3. *Key verse*

Verse 2: "There is no help for him in God."

4. *Key word / key phrase*

Verse 1, "foes."

5. *Key event / key person / key theme*

Victory in the face of defeat

6. *Key thought*

In the face of many threats the psalmist turns to the Lord in prayer.

7. *Key thing to look out for*

All kinds of deliverances belong to the Lord.

8. *Key Bible cross-reference*

Verse 7. See Exodus 12:31.

9. *Key "by way of explanation"*

Verse 5. The psalmist can sleep in peace knowing that he is being protected by
the Lord.

10. *Key "Quotable Quote"*

"For whether there was necessity of repentance or confession, or tribulation
and trial befell us, or someone was persecuted, or, being plotted against, he
was protected . . . or he wants to sing praises and give thanks to the Lord – for
any such eventuality he has instruction in the divine Psalms."
Athanasius the Great

Psalm 4

1. ### Before and after

    Previous psalm: Psalm 3: Victory in the face of defeat
    Following psalm: Psalm 5: Morning prayer for guidance

2. ### Analysis of psalm

    The happiness of godly people. (1-5)
    God's favor is happiness. (6-8)

3. ### Key verse

    Verse 4: "Stand in awe, and sin not."

4. ### Key word / key phrase

    Verse 8, "lie down and sleep."

5. ### Key event / key person / key theme

    Evening prayer for deliverance

6. ### Key thought

    David warns against placing trust in false gods.

7. ### Key thing to look out for

    David warns against anxiety.

8. ### Key Bible cross-reference

    Verse 8. See 3:5,6.

9. ### Key "by way of explanation"

    Verse 1. God is righteous and always acts faithfully toward his people.

10. ### Key "Quotable Quote"

    "Thou hast put gladness in my heart, more than in the time that their corn
    and their wine increased."
    Psalm 4:7

Psalm 5

1. *Before and after*

Previous psalm: Psalm 4: Evening prayer for deliverance
Following psalm: Psalm 6: Prayer for God's mercy

2. *Analysis of psalm*

God will certainly hear prayer: David gives to God the glory, and is comforted. (1-6)
He prayed for himself, that God would guide him, and for all the Lord's people, that God would give them joy, and keep them safe. (7-12)

3. *Key verse*

Verse 2: "Hearken unto the voice of my cry, my King, and my God."

4. *Key word / key phrase*

Verse 3, "in the morning."

5. *Key event / key person / key theme*

Morning prayer for guidance

6. *Key thought*

David warns against trusting what people say.

7. *Key thing to look out for*

David pictures the Lord protecting his people with a shield.

8. *Key Bible cross-reference*

Verse 8. See 23:3.

9. *Key "by way of explanation"*

Verse 10. The curses (or imprecations) in the psalms are cries for justice and the redress of evil.

10. *Key "Quotable Quote"*

"For thou, LORD, wilt bless the righteous; with favor wilt thou compass him as with a shield."
Psalm 5:12

Psalm 6

1. *Before and after*

Previous psalm: Psalm 5: Morning prayer for guidance
Following psalm: Psalm 7: A prayer for justice

2. *Analysis of psalm*

The psalmist deprecates God's wrath, and begs for the return of his favor. (1-7)
He assures himself of an answer of peace. (8-10)

3. *Key verse*

Verse 3: "My soul is also sore vexed."

4. *Key word / key phrase*

Verses 2, "be merciful."

5. *Key event / key person / key theme*

Prayer for God's mercy

6. *Key thought*

The Lord had sent this illness to discipline David.

7. *Key thing to look out for*

David does not attempt to justify himself, but asks for the Lord's mercy.

8. *Key Bible cross-reference*

Verse 4. See Deuteronomy 7:9,12.

9. *Key "by way of explanation"*

This psalm, along with psalms 32; 38; 51; 102; 130; 143, was known as one of the seven penitential psalms in early Christian liturgies.

10. *Key "Quotable Quote"*

"The LORD hath heard my supplication; the LORD will receive my prayer."
Psalm 6:9

Psalm 7

1. Before and after

Previous psalm: Psalm 6: Prayer for God's mercy
Following psalm: Psalm 8: God's glory and humankind's dominion

2. Analysis of psalm

The psalmist prays to God to plead his cause, and judge for him. (1-9)
He expresses confidence in God, and will give him the glory for his deliverance. (10-17)

3. Key verse

Verse 10: "My defense is of God, which saveth the upright in heart."

4. Key word / key phrase

Verse 6, "decree justice."

5. Key event / key person / key theme

A prayer asking for justice

6. Key thought

Because God is just he can be appealed to so that wrongs can be put right.

7. Key thing to look out for

David states that he is innocent and should never have been attacked.

8. Key Bible cross-reference

Verse 2. See 1 Samuel 17:34,35.

9. Key "by way of explanation"

Verse 11. God does not reserve all his judgments for the future but sends some down every day.

10. Key "Quotable Quote"

"And this is a genuine and an undoubted proof of our faith, when, being visited with adversity, we, not withstanding, persevere in cherishing and exercising hope in God. From this, we also learn that the gate of mercy is shut against our prayers if the key of faith do not open it for us."
John Calvin, commenting on verses 1, 2

Psalm 8

1. *Before and after*

Previous psalm: Psalm 7: Wickedness justly rewarded
Following psalm: Psalm 9: Praise for victory over enemies

2. *Analysis of psalm*

God is to be glorified, for making known himself to us. (1,2)
And for making him only a little lower than the angels. (3-9)

3. *Key verse*

Verse 3: "When I consider thy heavens, the work of thy fingers . . ."

4. *Key word / key phrase*

Verse 1, "your glory."

5. *Key event / key person / key theme*

God's glory and humankind's dominion

6. *Key thought*

The greatness of the heavens reflects God's greatness.

7. *Key thing to look out for*

Compare the magnificence of God with the temporary nature of human beings.

8. *Key Bible cross-reference*

Verse 1. See Genesis 1:26-28.

9. *Key "by way of explanation"*

Verses 4-6 are applied to Jesus in Hebrews 2:6-8.

10. *Key "Quotable Quote*

"God is not under the necessity of making war with great power to overcome the faithful, who willingly harken to his voice, and manifest a ready obedience, as soon as he gives the smallest intimation of his will. The providence of God, I confess, shines forth principally for the sake of the faithful, because they only have eyes to behold it. But as they show themselves willing to receive instruction, God teaches them with gentleness; while on the other hand, he arms himself against his enemies, who never submit themselves to him but by constraint."
John Calvin, commentating on verse 2

Psalms 9 and 10

1. Before and after

Previous psalm: Psalm 8: God's glory and humankind's dominion
Following psalm: Psalm 11: God tests the sons of men

2. Analysis of psalms 9, and 10

David praises God for protecting his people. (9:1-10)
And for many reasons to praise him. (9:11-20)
The psalmist complains of the wickedness of the wicked. (10:1-11)
He prays to God to rescue his people. (10:12-18)

3. Key verse

9:11: "Sing praises to the LORD, which dwelleth in Zion."

4. Key word / key phrase

9:3, "enemies."

5. Key event / key person / key theme

Praise for victory over enemies

6. Key thought

In Psalm 9 David says that those who forget God will come to nothing.

7. Key thing to look out for

In Psalm 10 the arrogance of those who oppose God is noted but confidence
in God's righteous reign is also expressed.

8. Key Bible cross-reference

9:5. See Numbers 5:23; 2 Kings 14:27.

9. Key "by way of explanation"

Psalms 10 and 11 were often used together and may even have been one psalm
originally.

10. Key "Quotable Quote"

"I will praise thee, O LORD, with my whole heart; I will show forth all thy
marvelous works."
Psalm 9:1

Psalm 11

1. **Before and after**

   Previous psalm: Psalm 10: Request for God's judgment
   Following psalm: Psalm 12: The pure words of God

2. **Analysis of psalm**

   David's struggle with, and triumph over, a strong temptation to distrust God, and to trust in himself for his own safety, in a time of danger. (1-7)

3. **Key verse**

   Verse 3: "If the foundations be destroyed, what can the righteous do?"

4. **Key word / key phrase**

   Verse 5, "examines the righteous."

5. **Key event / key person / key theme**

   God tests men and women.

6. **Key thought**

   The fearful are reassured that the Lord still reigns on his heavenly throne.

7. **Key thing to look out for**

   David encourages the wavering faith of those around him by expressing his rocklike faith in the Lord.

8. **Key Bible cross-reference**

   Verse 4. This verse is repeated in Habakkuk 2:20.

9. **Key "by way of explanation"**

   Even though the enemies of God's people appear to be overwhelming this psalm expresses complete trust in the Lord's rule.

10. **Key "Quotable Quote"**

    "For the righteous LORD loveth righteousness; his countenance doth behold the upright."
    Psalm 11:7

Psalm 12

1. **Before and after**

   Previous psalm: Psalm 11: God tests the sons of men
   Following psalm: Psalm 13: A prayer asking for God's immediate answer

2. **Analysis of psalm**

   The psalmist begs help from God, because there is no one he dares to trust.
   (1-8)

3. **Key verse**

   Verse 6: "The words of the LORD are pure words."

4. **Key word / key phrase**

   Verse 6, "the words of the Lord."

5. **Key event / key person / key theme**

   The pure words of God

6. **Key thought**

   God's answers the psalmists heartfelt prayer for protection.

7. **Key thing to look out for**

   Despite the way the wicked strut around David expresses his confidence in
   the Lord.

8. **Key Bible cross-reference**

   Verses 1-8. See Micah 7:1-7.

9. **Key "by way of explanation"**

   Verse 6. The words of the Lord are in total contrast to the boastful words of
   the arrogant.

10. **Key "Quotable Quote"**

    "Thou shalt keep them, O LORD, thou shalt preserve them from this
    generation for ever."
    Psalm 12:7

Psalm 13

1. **Before and after**

   Previous psalm: Psalm 12: The pure words of God
   Following psalm: Psalm 14: The characteristics of the godless

2. **Analysis of psalm**

   The psalmist complains that God's presence has been withdrawn for a long time. He earnestly prays for comfort. (1-6)

3. **Key verse**

   Verse 1: "How long wilt thou forget me, O LORD?"

4. **Key word / key phrase**

   Verse 1, "How long, O Lord?"

5. **Key event / key person / key theme**

   A prayer for God's immediate answer

6. **Key thought**

   David calls out pleading to know how long his serious illness will last.

7. **Key thing to look out for**

   David ends this psalm confident of God's salvation.

8. **Key Bible cross-reference**

   Verse 1. See 30:7; 44:24; 88:14.

9. **Key "by way of explanation"**

   Verse 3. This serious illness appears to be life-threatening.

10. **Key "Quotable Quote"**

    "I will sing unto the LORD, because he hath dealt bountifully with me." Psalm 13:6

Psalm 14

1. Before and after

Previous psalm: Psalm 13: A prayer for God's immediate answer
Following psalm: Psalm 15: The characteristics of the godly

2. Analysis of psalm

A description of the depravity of human nature, and the deplorable corruption of a great part of humankind. (1-7)

3. Key verse

Verse 1: "The fool hath said in his heart, There is no God."

4. Key word / key phrase

Verse 4, "evildoers."

5. Key event / key person / key theme

The characteristics of the godless

6. Key thought

Two characteristics of the wicked are that they are violent and they do not trust God.

7. Key thing to look out for

The Lord's people often fall victim to injustice.

8. Key Bible cross-reference

Verses 1-3. See Romans 3:10-12.

9. Key "by way of explanation"

Verse 7. "Jacob" and "Israel" are synonymous. See Genesis 32:28.

10. Key "Quotable Quote"

"Oh that the salvation of Israel were come out of Zion! when the LORD bringeth back the captivity of his people, Jacob shall rejoice, and Israel shall be glad."
Psalm 14:7

Psalm 15

1. Before and after

Previous psalm: Psalm 14: The characteristics of the godless
Following psalm: Psalm 16: A confident prayer about God's goodness

2. Analysis of psalm

The way to heaven, if we want to be happy, is to be holy. We are encouraged to walk in that way. (1-5)

3. Key verse

Verse 1: "LORD, who shall abide in thy tabernacle?"

4. Key word / key phrase

Verse 2, "blameless."

5. Key event / key person / key theme

The characteristics of the godly

6. Key thought

If people live in awe of the Lord they will live their lives according to his will.

7. Key thing to look out for

Godly people should not indulge in common evil practices.

8. Key Bible cross-reference

Verse 1. See 23:6; 27:4-6.

9. Key "by way of explanation"

Verses 2-5. The importance of moral righteousness is stressed here.

10. Key "Quotable Quote"

"He that putteth not out his money to usury, nor taketh reward against the innocent. He that doeth these things shall never be moved."
Psalm 15:5

Psalm 16

1. Before and after

Previous psalm: Psalm 15: The characteristics of the godly
Following psalm: Psalm 17: Hidden under God's wings

2. Analysis of psalm

This psalm begins with expressions of devotion, which may be applied to Christ; but ends with such confidence in a resurrection, which must be applied to Christ, and to him alone. (1-11)

3. Key verse

Verse 6: "The lines are fallen unto me in pleasant places."

4. Key word / key phrase

Verse 2, "You are my Lord."

5. Key event / key person / key theme

A confident prayer about God's goodness

6. Key thought

David has chosen the one good thing.

7. Key thing to look out for

David expresses his joy at being totally secure in the Lord.

8. Key Bible cross-reference

Verse 8. See 73:23; 121:5.

9. Key "by way of explanation"

Verse 5. This "cup" is a cup of blessing for the godly, 23:5; but for the wicked it is a cup of wrath, see Jeremiah 25:15.

10. Key "Quotable Quote"

"Preserve me, O God: for in thee do I put my trust."
Psalm 16:1

Psalm 17

1. **Before and after**

   Previous psalm: Psalm 16: Eternal life for those who trust
   Following psalm: Psalm 18: Thanksgiving for God's deliverance

2. **Analysis of psalm**

   David's integrity. (1-7)
   The character of his enemies. His hope of happiness. (8-15)

3. **Key verse**

   Verse 3: "Thou hast proved mine heart."

4. **Key word / key phrase**

   Verse 8, "the shadow of your wings."

5. **Key event / key person / key theme**

   God's followers are hidden under God's wings

6. **Key thought**

   David's plea for vindication.

7. **Key thing to look out for**

   Note how this psalm is most appropriate for a falsely-accused person to use.

8. **Key Bible cross-reference**

   Verse 8. See Numbers 6:24; Deuteronomy 32:10.

9. **Key "by way of explanation"**

   Verse 8. "Wings" may refer to the cherubim over the ark, 1 Kings 8:6, or, to a mother bird, Matthew 23:37.

10. **Key "Quotable Quote"**

    "Keep me as the apple of the eye, hide me under the shadow of thy wings."
    Psalm 17:8

Psalm 19

(For Psalm 18, see 2 Samuel 22:1-51.)

1. *Before and after*

Previous psalm: Psalm 18: Thanksgiving for God's deliverance
Following psalm: Psalm 20: Trust in God, not in chariots and horses

2. *Analysis of psalm*

The glory of God's works. (1-6)
His holiness and grace as shown in his word. (7-10)
Prayer to benefit from them. (11-14)

3. *Key verse*

Verse 1: "The heavens declare the glory of God."

4. *Key word / key phrase*

Verse 1, "The heavens."

5. *Key event / key person / key theme*

God's glory in creation

6. *Key thought*

The heavenly lights are not divine in themselves but bear witness to the Creator's righteousness.

7. *Key thing to look out for*

The Law sets out the path that leads to life.

8. *Key Bible cross-reference*

Verse 10. See Amos 5:7; 6:12.

9. *Key "by way of explanation"*

Verse 1. The glory of God is seen by looking at the stars, but also in the Law of the Lord.

10. *Key "Quotable Quote"*

"The law of the LORD is perfect, converting the soul: the testimony of the LORD is sure, making wise the simple."
Psalm 19:7

Psalm 20

1. **Before and after**

   Previous psalm: Psalm 19: God's deeds and God's word
   Following psalm: Psalm 21: Triumph of the King

2. **Analysis of psalm**

   This psalm is a prayer for the kings of Israel, but also refers to Christ. (1-9)

3. **Key verse**

   Verse 2: "Send thee help from the sanctuary, and strengthen thee out of Zion."

4. **Key word / key phrase**

   Verse 5, "victorious."

5. **Key event / key person / key theme**

   A prayer asking for victory

6. **Key thought**

   It is crucial that the army trusts in the Lord rather than in chariots and horses.

7. **Key thing to look out for**

   The one thing the army needs is protection and so this is what is prayed for.

8. **Key Bible cross-reference**

   Verses 7,8. See 33:16,17.

9. **Key "by way of explanation"**

   Verse 5. As the king sets out to engage in a battle this prayer is prayed. See 2 Chronicles 20:1-30.

10. **Key "Quotable Quote"**

    "Some trust in chariots, and some in horses: but we will remember the name of the LORD our God."
    Psalm 20:7

Psalm 21

1. *Before and after*

Previous psalm: Psalm 20: Trust in God, not in chariots and horses
Following psalm: Psalm 22: The psalm of the cross

2. *Analysis of psalm*

Thanksgiving for victory. (1-6)
Confidence of further success. (7-13)

3. *Key verse*

Verse 5: "His glory is great in thy salvation."

4. *Key word / key phrase*

Verse 5, "victories."

5. *Key event / key person / key theme*

A prayer of praise after a victory

6. *Key thought*

Unlike earthly blessings, God's blessings are eternal.

7. *Key thing to look out for*

The psalm begins and ends on a note of praise.

8. *Key Bible cross-reference*

Verse 4. See 1 Kings 1:31; Daniel 2:4.

9. *Key "by way of explanation"*

Verse 9. This verse states that the king's victories came about as a result of the Lord's wrath.

10. *Key "Quotable Quote"*

"Be thou exalted, LORD, in thine own strength: so will we sing and praise thy power."
Psalm 21:13

Psalm 22

1. Before and after

Previous psalm: Psalm 21: Triumph of the King
Following psalm: Psalm 23: The psalm of the divine Shepherd

2. Analysis of psalm

Complaints of discouragement. (1-10)
Prayer for deliverance. (11-21)
Praises for mercies and redemption. (22-31)

3. Key verse

Verse 1: "My God, my God, why hast thou forsaken me?"

4. Key word / key phrase

Verse 1, "forsaken me."

5. Key event / key person / key theme

The psalm of the cross

6. Key thought

David cries out because of his godly suffering.

7. Key thing to look out for

Note the links from this psalm to Jesus' death. See Matthew 27:39,43; John 19:34.

8. Key Bible cross-reference

Verse 1. See Matthew 27:46; Mark 15:34.

9. Key "by way of explanation"

Jesus' passion is reflected in the psalm more than any other psalm.

10. Key "Quotable Quote"

"Be not far from me; for trouble is near; for there is none to help."
Psalm 22:11

Psalm 23

1. **Before and after**

   Previous psalm: Psalm 22: The psalm of the cross
   Following psalm: Psalm 24: The psalm of the King of Glory

2. **Analysis of psalm**

   Confidence in God's grace and care. (1-6)

3. **Key verse**

   Verse 1: "The LORD is my shepherd."

4. **Key word / key phrase**

   Verse 1, "my shepherd."

5. **Key event / key person / key theme**

   The Shepherd psalm

6. **Key thought**

   David states that the Lord God is his personal Shepherd.

7. **Key thing to look out for**

   See how many different ways sheep are cared for in this psalm.

8. **Key Bible cross-reference**

   Verse 2. See Isaiah 14:30; 17:2; Jeremiah 33:12.

9. **Key "by way of explanation"**

   Verse 3. "Paths of righteousness." A shepherd leads sheep along safe paths, while the Shepherd-King leads David to eternal security.

10. **Key "Quotable Quote"**

   "The Lord is my shepherd, that's all I want."
   Small child misquoting Psalm 23

Psalm 24

1. **Before and after**

   Previous psalm: Psalm 23: The psalm of the divine Shepherd
   Following psalm: Psalm 25: Acrostic prayer for instruction

2. **Analysis of psalm**

   The kingdom of Christ, and the subjects of that kingdom. (1-6)
   The King of that kingdom. (7-10)

3. **Key verse**

   Verse 3: "Who shall ascend into the hill of the LORD?"

4. **Key word / key phrase**

   Verse 8, "The LORD strong and mighty."

5. **Key event / key person / key theme**

   The psalm of the King of Glory

6. **Key thought**

   This psalm celebrated the Lord entering Zion.

7. **Key thing to look out for**

   Those who are allowed to enter God's city.

8. **Key Bible cross-reference**

   Verse 7. See 3:3; 27:6; 110:7.

9. **Key "by way of explanation"**

   Verse 4. "Clean hands" speak of pure actions, while a "pure heart" focuses on inner motives. The psalmist emphasizes the need for both.

10. **Key "Quotable Quote"**

    "This is the generation of them that seek him, that seek thy face, O Jacob."
    Psalm 24:6

Psalm 25

1. Before and after

Previous psalm: Psalm 24: The psalm of the King of Glory
Following psalm: Psalm 26: A plea to be examined by the Lord

2. Analysis of psalm

Confidence in prayer. (1-7)
Prayer for remission of sins. (8-14)
For help in affliction. (15-22)

3. Key verse

Verse 9: "The meek will he guide in judgment."

4. Key word / key phrase

Verse 4, "teach me your paths."

5. Key event / key person / key theme

A prayer for guidance and protection

6. Key thought

David prays to be delivered from his enemies.

7. Key thing to look out for

David homes in on the blessings of the covenant: God's mercy, grace, and goodness.

8. Key Bible cross-reference

Verse 10. See 103:7; 138:5.

9. Key "by way of explanation"

Verse 4. "Your ways," and "your paths" stand for the covenant and its teaching. See verse 10; Deuteronomy 8:6; Joshua 22:5.

10. Key "Quotable Quote"

"Lead me in thy truth, and teach me: for thou art the God of my salvation; on thee do I wait all the day."
Psalm 25:5

Psalm 26

1. *Before and after*

Previous psalm: Psalm 25: Acrostic prayer for instruction
Following psalm: Psalm 27: Trust in the Lord and do not be afraid

2. *Analysis of psalm*

David, in this psalm, appeals to God pleading his innocence and integrity.
(1-12)

3. *Key verse*

Verse 2: "Examine me, O LORD, and prove me."

4. *Key word / key phrase*

Verses 1,11, "a blameless life."

5. *Key event / key person / key theme*

The prayer of a person longing to be vindicated by the Lord

6. *Key thought*

David refused to settle down with evil people.

7. *Key thing to look out for*

This psalm is shot through with praise and reasons for praising the Lord.

8. *Key Bible cross-reference*

Verse 4. See Proverbs 6:12-14.

9. *Key "by way of explanation"*

"Vindicate," is, in the Hebrew, "judge." The psalm is a call for justice and
deliverance.

10. *Key "Quotable Quote"*

"But as for me, I will walk in mine integrity: redeem me, and be merciful unto
me."
Psalm 26:11

Psalm 27

1. ### Before and after

    Previous psalm: Psalm 26: A plea to be examined by the Lord
    Following psalm: Psalm 28: A prayer for help

2. ### Analysis of psalm

    The psalmist's faith. (1-6)
    His desire for God, and expectation from him. (7-14)

3. ### Key verse

    Verse 8: "Seek ye my face; my heart said unto thee, Thy face, LORD, will I seek."

4. ### Key word / key phrase

    Verse 3, "not fear."

5. ### Key event / key person / key theme

    Trust in the Lord and do not be afraid

6. ### Key thought

    David prays for deliverance from those who seek his life.

7. ### Key thing to look out for

    This psalm gives much insight into the nature of David's faith.

8. ### Key Bible cross-reference

    Verse 4. See 90:17.

9. ### Key "by way of explanation"

    Verse 1, "light." Light often stands for well-being. See 97:11; Job 18:5,6;
    Lamentations 3:2.

10. ### Key "Quotable Quote"

    "One thing have I desired of the LORD, that will I seek after; that I may dwell in
    the house of the LORD all the days of my life, to behold the beauty of the LORD,
    and to inquire in his temple."
    Psalm 27:4

Psalm 28

1. ### Before and after

   Previous psalm: Psalm 27: Trust in the Lord and do not be afraid
   Following psalm: Psalm 29: God's powerful voice

2. ### Analysis of psalm

   A prayer in distress. (1-5)
   Thanksgiving for deliverance. (6-9)

3. ### Key verse

   Verse 1: "Unto thee will I cry, O LORD my rock."

4. ### Key word / key phrase

   Verse 1, "To you I call."

5. ### Key event / key person / key theme

   A prayer for help

6. ### Key thought

   David is in danger of being killed by malicious enemies. So he prays.

7. ### Key thing to look out for

   The psalm includes prayers for all of God's people. David could remember others despite his own pressing trials.

8. ### Key Bible cross-reference

   Verse 2. See 63:4; 134:2.

9. ### Key "by way of explanation"

   Verse 5. The "works of the Lord" encompass a great deal, including, the Exodus, the conquest of the promised land, and David becoming king.

10. ### Key "Quotable Quote"

    "Blessed be the LORD, because he hath heard the voice of my supplications." Psalm 28:6

Psalm 29

1. Before and after

Previous psalm: Psalm 28: Rejoice on account of answered prayer
Following psalm: Psalm 30: Thanksgiving for dramatic deliverance

2. Analysis of psalm

Exhortation to give glory to God. (1-11)

3. Key verse

Verse 4: "The voice of the LORD is powerful."

4. Key word / key phrase

Verse 3, "The voice of the LORD."

5. Key event / key person / key theme

God's powerful voice

6. Key thought

David calls all God's people to worship the Lord.

7. Key thing to look out for

Mighty thunder is likened to the voice of the Lord.

8. Key Bible cross-reference

Verse 5. See Isaiah 2:13.

9. Key "by way of explanation"

Verse 10, "enthroned over the flood." See Genesis 1:2,6-10; 6:17. God is all-powerful, as he showed at creation and during the Flood.

10. Key "Quotable Quote"

"The LORD will give strength unto his people; the LORD will bless his people with peace."
Psalm 29:11

Psalm 30

1. ### Before and after

   Previous psalm: Psalm 29: God's powerful voice
   Following psalm: Psalm 31: Be of good courage

2. ### Analysis of psalm

   Praise to God for deliverance. (1-5)
   Valuable lessons learned. (6-12)

3. ### Key verse

   Verse 2: "O LORD my God, I cried unto thee, and thou hast healed me."

4. ### Key word / key phrase

   Verse 1, "out of the depths."

5. ### Key event / key person / key theme / key theme

   Thanksgiving for dramatic deliverance

6. ### Key thought

   David had been saved, probably from an illness, verse 2, and he gives thanks
   to the Lord for this publicly.

7. ### Key thing to look out for

   David thanks the Lord for all the situations he transforms.

8. ### Key Bible cross-reference

   Verse 1. See 69:2; 130:1; Jonah 2:2.

9. ### Key "by way of explanation"

   Verse 5, "remain for a night." Like a guest who will only stay for one night.

10. ### Key "Quotable Quote"

    "Hear, O LORD, and have mercy upon me: LORD, be thou my helper."
    Psalm 30:10

Psalm 31

1. Before and after

Previous psalm: Psalm 30: Thanksgiving for dramatic deliverance
Following psalm: Psalm 32: The fruit of forgiveness

2. Analysis of psalm

Confidence in God. (1-8)
Prayer in trouble. (9-18)
Praise for God's goodness. (19-24)

3. Key verse

Verse 9: "Have mercy upon me, O LORD, for I am in trouble."

4. Key word / key phrase

Verse 1, "I have taken refuge."

5. Key event / key person / key theme

A prayer expressing trust in the Lord

6. Key thought

David remembers God's wonderful deliverances in the past.

7. Key thing to look out for

David was able to resist his strong enemies because of his constant trust in the Lord.

8. Key Bible cross-reference

Verse 5. See Luke 23:46.

9. Key "by way of explanation"

Verse 5, "commit," literally means to deposit, as in Jeremiah 36:20. So this expression speaks of someone entrusting himself to God's care. See 1 Kings 14:27.

10. Key "Quotable Quote"

"In thee, O LORD, do I put my trust; let me never be ashamed: deliver me in thy righteousness."
Psalm 31:1

Psalm 32

1. Before and after

Previous psalm: Psalm 31: Be of good courage
Following psalm: Psalm 33: God considers all humankind's deeds

2. Analysis of psalm

The happiness of a pardoned sinner. (1,2)
The misery that went before, and the comfort that followed the confession of sins. (3-7)
Sinners instructed, believers encouraged. (8-11)

3. Key verse

Verse 7: "Thou art my hiding place."

4. Key word / key phrase

Verse 1, "transgressions are forgiven."

5. Key event / key person / key theme

The fruit of forgiveness

6. Key thought

David thanks the Lord for the gift of forgiveness and for the joy this brings.

7. Key thing to look out for

Note the repetitions in this psalm and what is repeated (for emphasis.) See verses 1,2,5.

8. Key Bible cross-reference

Verse 9. See Isaiah 1:3.

9. Key "by way of explanation"

Verses 3-5. It appears that David had held on to unacknowledged sin and so had found the Lord's "hand was heavy."

10. Key "Quotable Quote"

"Scripture gives us the warrant to insist that God's normal way of guiding us is rational, not irrational, namely through the very thought processes which he has created in us. Psalm 32 makes this clear. Verse 8 contains a marvelous threefold promise of divine guidance. If we put together the promise and the prohibition, what God is saying to us is this: 'I promise that I will guide you, and show you the way to go. But do not expect me to guide you as you guide horses and mules.'"
John R.W. Stott

Psalm 33

1. ### Before and after

    Previous psalm: Psalm 32: The fruit of forgiveness
    Following psalm: Psalm 34: Seek the Lord

2. ### Analysis of psalm

    God is to be praised. (1-11)
    His people encouraged by his power. (12-22)

3. ### Key verse

    Verse 12: "Blessed is the nation whose God is the LORD."

4. ### Key word / key phrase / key phrase

    Verse 1, "Sing joyfully."

5. ### Key event / key person / key theme

    A song of worship

6. ### Key thought

    This psalm of praise expresses thanks to Israel's God for national deliverance.

7. ### Key thing to look out for

    The psalm starts and ends with three verses which contain a call to praise and a response to praise.

8. ### Key Bible cross-reference

    Verse 4. See 107:20; 147:15,18.

9. ### Key "by way of explanation"

    Verse 3. A "new song" was sung to celebrate God's actions which brought about salvation. See 40:3; Isaiah 42:10; Revelation 14:3.

10. ### Key "Quotable Quote"

    "He loveth righteousness and judgment: the earth is full of the goodness of the LORD."
    Psalm 33:5

Psalm 34

1. **Before and after**

   Previous psalm: Psalm 33: God considers all humankind's deeds
   Following psalm: Psalm 35: Request for God's intervention

2. **Analysis of psalm**

   David praises God, and trusts him. (1-10)
   Exhortations to reverence God. (11-22)

3. **Key verse**

   Verse 3: "O magnify the LORD with me."

4. **Key word / key phrase / key phrase**

   Verse 4, "I sought the LORD."

5. **Key event / key person / key theme**

   Seeking the Lord

6. **Key thought**

   This psalm starts with praise, verse 1-7, and then, verses 8-22, turns to
   instructions for God's followers.

7. **Key thing to look out for**

   The teaching about the fear of the Lord is contained in a number of
   commands, such as: "taste," "fear," "come," and "keep."

8. **Key Bible cross-reference**

   Verse 5. See Isaiah 60:5.

9. **Key "by way of explanation"**

   Verse 7, "angel of the Lord." God's messenger, or heavenly representative, is
   sent to earth to convey and carry out the Lord's will. See 35:5,6.

10. **Key "Quotable Quote"**

    "The angel of the LORD encampeth round about them that fear him, and
    delivereth them."
    Psalm 34:7

Psalm 35

1. Before and after

Previous psalm: Psalm 34: Seek the Lord
Following psalm: Psalm 36: God's loving-kindness

2. Analysis of psalm

David prays for safety. (1-10)
He complains about his enemies. (11-16)
And calls upon God to support him. (17-28)

3. Key verse

Verse 11: "False witnesses did rise up."

4. Key word / key phrase / key phrase

Verse 2, "come to my aid."

5. Key event / key person / key theme

Request for God's intervention

6. Key thought

David appeals to the Lord, his Warrior-King, for help.

7. Key thing to look out for

After a three verse introduction, the psalm has three sections of petitions, verses 4-10; 11-18, and 19-28, each of which concludes with a resolve to praise God.

8. Key Bible cross-reference

Verse 13. See 30:11; Genesis 37:34.

9. Key "by way of explanation"

Verse 15, "stumbled." Here David was brought down, not by immoral actions, but by outside circumstances. See 9:3; 27:2; 37:25; 119:165.

10. Key "Quotable Quote"

"And my tongue shall speak of thy righteousness and of thy praise all the day long."
Psalm 35:28

Psalm 36

1. *Before and after*

   Previous psalm: Psalm 35: Request for God's intervention
   Following psalm: Psalm 37: Rest in the Lord

2. *Analysis of psalm*

   The bad state of the wicked. (1-4)
   The goodness of God. (5-12)

3. *Key verse*

   Verse 6: "Thy righteousness is like the great mountains."

4. *Key word / key phrase / key phrase*

   Verse 1, "sinfulness of the wicked."

5. *Key event / key person / key theme*

   Man's wickedness and God's goodness

6. *Key thought*

   As David reflects on the godlessness of the wicked and the goodness of God, he asks for God's protection.

7. *Key thing to look out for*

   In verses 5-9 David's lists some of the wonderful characteristics of the Lord.

8. *Key Bible cross-reference*

   Verse 3. See 94:8-11; Proverbs 2:9-11.

9. *Key "by way of explanation"*

   Verse 9. "Fountain," that is the source that never dries up.

10. *Key "Quotable Quote"*

    "Let not the foot of pride come against me, and let not the hand of the wicked remove me."
    Psalm 36:11

Psalm 37

1. *Before and after*

   Previous psalm: Psalm 36: God's loving-kindness
   Following psalm: Psalm 38: Sin's heavy burden

2. *Analysis of psalm*

   Evil doers. (1-6)
   Peace, despite the works of evil. (7-20)
   Act justly. (21-33)
   We are at God's disposal. (34-40)

3. *Key verse*

   Verse 7: "Rest in the LORD."

4. *Key word / key phrase / key phrase*

   Verse 4, "Delight yourself in the Lord."

5. *Key event / key person / key theme*

   Rest in the Lord

6. *Key thought*

   This psalm is crammed with teaching about godly wisdom.

7. *Key thing to look out for*

   This teaching is set out in a series of contrasts between the wicked and the righteous.

8. *Key Bible cross-reference*

   Verse 13. See 2:4.

9. *Key "by way of explanation"*

   Verse 10, "A little while." The brevity of time alluded to here underlines the certainty of the event. See 59:9; Job 20:5-11; Haggai 2:6.

10. *Key "Quotable Quote"*

    "But the salvation of the righteous is of the LORD: he is their strength in the time of trouble."
    Psalm 37:39

Psalm 38

1. *Before and after*

   Previous psalm: Psalm 37: Rest in the Lord
   Following psalm: Psalm 39: Recall your lifespan

2. *Analysis of psalm*

   God's displeasure at sin. (1-11)
   The psalmist's sufferings and prayers. (12-22)

3. *Key verse*

   Verse 1: "O Lord, rebuke me not in thy wrath."

4. *Key word / key phrase / key phrase*

   Verse 4, "a burden too heavy to bear."

5. *Key event / key person / key theme*

   Sin's heavy burden

6. *Key thought*

   David pleads, with great urgency, for relief from his severe illness.

7. *Key thing to look out for*

   The psalm divides into five four-verse sections with a two-verse conclusion.

8. *Key Bible cross-reference*

   Verse 18. See 3,4; Psalm 32.

9. *Key "by way of explanation"*

   Verse 16, "when my foot slips." These words refer to some setback David experienced, in this instance, to his health. See 66:9; 94:18; 121:3.

10. *Key "Quotable Quote"*

    "Make haste to help me, O Lord my salvation."
    Psalm 38:22

Psalm 39

1. Before and after

Previous psalm: Psalm 38: Sin's heavy burden
Following psalm: Psalm 40: Delight to do God's will

2. Analysis of psalm

David meditates on human frailty. (1-6)
He asks for pardon and deliverance. (7-13)

3. Key verse

Verse 9: "I was dumb, I opened not my mouth."

4. Key word / key phrase / key phrase

Verse 2, "anguish."

5. Key event / key person / key theme

The confession of a suffering man

6. Key thought

David is in the middle of an acute illness, verses 10,11.

7. Key thing to look out for

David recalls the fragility of human existence on earth and pours out his soul
to the Lord.

8. Key Bible cross-reference

Verse 5. See 90:4; 144:4.

9. Key "by way of explanation"

Verse 6 gives a summary of human life, echoing the book of Ecclesiastes.

10. Key "Quotable Quote"

"And now, Lord, what wait I for? my hope is in thee."
Psalm 39:7

Psalm 40

1. **Before and after**

   Previous psalm: Psalm 39: Recall your lifespan
   Following psalm: Psalm 41: Joy in helping the poor

2. **Analysis of psalm**

   Confidence for deliverance. (1-5)
   Christ's work of redemption. (6-10)
   Prayer for mercy and grace. (11-17)

3. **Key verse**

   Verse 6: "Sacrifice and offering thou didst not desire."

4. **Key word / key phrase**

   Verse 8, "I desire to do your will."

5. **Key event / key person / key theme**

   Delight to do God's will

6. **Key thought**

   This psalm reflects the fact that David's life was filled with praise to the Lord.

7. **Key thing to look out for**

   David spends the first five verses of this psalm reflecting on God's mercies.

8. **Key Bible cross-reference**

   Verse 9. See 68:11; 96:2.

9. **Key "by way of explanation"**

   Verse 12. David is surrounded by unspecified troubles. But he states that they are caused by "my sins."

10. **Key "Quotable Quote"**

    "I waited patiently for the LORD; and he inclined unto me, and heard my cry."
    Psalm 40:1

Psalm 41

1. Before and after

Previous psalm: Psalm 40: Delight to do God's will
Following psalm: Psalm 42: Why are you depressed?

2. Analysis of psalm

God's care for his people. (1-4)
The treachery of David's enemies. (5-13)

3. Key verse

Verse 5: "Mine enemies speak evil of me."

4. Key word / key phrase

Verse 1, "regard for the weak."

5. Key event / key person / key theme

Joy in helping the poor

6. Key thought

David is very ill. He prays.

7. Key thing to look out for

It is possible to be betrayed by even close friends. See John 13:18.

8. Key Bible cross-reference

Verse 1. See 72:2,4,12-14; Proverbs 29:14.

9. Key "by way of explanation"

Verse 13 concludes Book I of the psalms and appropriately ends with a doxology. See 72:18,19; 89:52; 106:48; 150.

10. Key "Quotable Quote"

"Blessed is he that considereth the poor: the LORD will deliver him in time of trouble."
Psalm 41:1

Psalms 42 and 43

1. *Before and after*

Previous psalm: Psalm 41: Joy in helping the poor
Following psalm: Psalm 44: Prayer for God's deliverance

2. *Analysis of psalms 42, 43*

The conflict in the soul of a believer. (42:1-11)
David endeavors to still his spirit, with hope and confidence in God. (43:1-5)

3. *Key verse*

42:3: "My tears have been my meat day and night."

4. *Key word / key phrase*

42:5, "Why are you downcast?"

5. *Key event / key person / key theme*

Why are you depressed?

6. *Key thought*

Taking the two psalms together, Psalms 42 and 43 have four four-verse stanzas each of which concludes with the same thought. See 42:5,11; 43:5.

7. *Key thing to look out for*

The psalmist prays for deliverance and for God's presence.

8. *Key Bible cross-reference*

42:6. See verses 5,11; 43:5.

9. *Key "by way of explanation"*

Psalms 42 and 43 form a single prayer asking for deliverance from an attacking enemy: 42:9; 43:2.

10. *Key "Quotable Quote"*

"Why art thou cast down, O my soul? and why art thou disquieted within me? hope thou in God: for I shall yet praise him, who is the health of my countenance, and my God."
Psalm 42:11

Psalm 44

1. ### Before and after

   Previous psalm: Psalm 43: Hope in God
   Following psalm: Psalm 45: The psalm of the great King

2. ### Analysis of psalm

   A petition for succor and relief. (1-26)

3. ### Key verse

   Verse 6: "For I will not trust in my bow, neither shall my sword save me."

4. ### Key word / key phrase

   Verse 2, "my stronghold."

5. ### Key event / key person / key theme

   A prayer for protection

6. ### Key thought

   Israel has just suffered a major defeat.

7. ### Key thing to look out for

   The whole psalm is a request for God's help.

8. ### Key Bible cross-reference

   Verse 12. See Deuteronomy 32:30; Judges 2:14.

9. ### Key "by way of explanation"

   Verse 19, "you crushed us." The psalmist states that this did not happen because they had disobeyed the Lord. He is pleading Israel's innocence.

10. ### Key "Quotable Quote"

    "In God we boast all the day long, and praise thy name for ever."
    Psalm 44:8

Psalm 45

1. **Before and after**

   Previous psalm: Psalm 44: Prayer for God's deliverance
   Following psalm: Psalm 46: God is our refuge and strength

2. **Analysis of psalm**

   This psalm is a prophecy about the Messiah, the Prince, and points to him as the Bridegroom marrying the Church, and as King. (1-17)

3. **Key verse**

   Verse 1: " . . . my tongue is the pen of a ready writer."

4. **Key word / key phrase**

   Title, "A wedding song."

5. **Key event / key person / key theme**

   A royal wedding song

6. **Key thought**

   This psalm is a great psalm of praise for a king on his wedding day, verse 1.

7. **Key thing to look out for**

   Verses 3-9 are addressed to the king, and verses 10-15 are addressed to the bride.

8. **Key Bible cross-reference**

   Verse 7. See 23:5; Isaiah 61:3.

9. **Key "by way of explanation"**

   Verse 6, "throne." The everlasting nature of this throne is only ultimately fulfilled in Christ, who was rightly known as the Son of David.

10. **Key "Quotable Quote"**

    "I will make thy name to be remembered in all generations: therefore shall the people praise thee for ever and ever."
    Psalm 45:17

Psalm 46

1. *Before and after*

Previous psalm: Psalm 45: The psalm of the great King
Following psalm: Psalm 47: The Lord will subdue all nations

2. *Analysis of psalm*

Confidence in God. (1-5)
An exhortation to see the Lord. (6-11)

3. *Key verse*

Verse 8: "Come, behold the works of the LORD."

4. *Key word / key phrase*

Verse 1, "God is our . . ."

5. *Key event / key person / key theme*

God is with us

6. *Key thought*

This psalm celebrates the security of God's city, Jerusalem.

7. *Key thing to look out for*

Note the numerous reasons why Martin Luther was inspired to write his hymn, "A mighty fortress is our God," which was based on this psalm.

8. *Key Bible cross-reference*

Verse 9. See 76:3; 1 Samuel 2:4.

9. *Key "by way of explanation"*

Verse 10, "Be still." God's great deeds, done on behalf of his people, will bring global recognition. See 22:27; 99:2,3; 102:15.

10. *Key "Quotable Quote"*

"Be still, and know that I am God: I will be exalted among the heathen, I will be exalted in the earth."
Psalm 46:10

Psalm 47

1. *Before and after*

    Previous psalm: Psalm 46: God is our refuge and strength
    Following psalm: Psalm 48: The praise of Mount Zion

2. *Analysis of psalm*

    The people exhorted to praise God. (1-9)

3. *Key verse*

    Verse 1: "O clap your hands, all ye people."

4. *Key word / key phrase*

    Verse 3, "He subdued nations."

5. *Key event / key person / key theme*

    The Lord will subdue all nations

6. *Key thought*

    The psalmist celebrates God's rule over every nation in the world.

7. *Key thing to look out for*

    All the nations are told to praise Israel's God, for he created them.

8. *Key Bible cross-reference*

    Verse 2. See 89:7; 99:3.

9. *Key "by way of explanation"*

    Verses 5,6. The Lord goes to the temple. This is represented by the ark, a symbol of God's throne, going into the temple.

10. *Key "Quotable Quote"*

    "God is gone up with a shout, the LORD with the sound of a trumpet." Psalm 47:5

Psalm 48

1. **Before and after**

   Previous psalm: Psalm 47: The Lord will subdue all nations
   Following psalm: Psalm 49: Riches cannot redeem

2. **Analysis of psalm**

   The glories of the Church of Christ. (1-14)

3. **Key verse**

   Verse 3: "God is known in her palaces for a refuge."

4. **Key word / key phrase**

   Verse 1, "the city of our God."

5. **Key event / key person / key theme**

   Zion is God's city

6. **Key thought**

   This psalm thanks God that his great city gives his people security.

7. **Key thing to look out for**

   The summary of this psalm is found in its central verse, verse 8.

8. **Key Bible cross-reference**

   Verse 2. See 1 Kings 10:1-13.

9. **Key "by way of explanation"**

   Verse 3. The walls of Jerusalem are not Zion's defense. God himself is her defense.

10. **Key "Quotable Quote"**

    "We have thought of thy loving kindness, O God, in the midst of thy temple."
    Psalm 48:9

Psalm 49

1. ## Before and after

   Previous psalm: Psalm 48: The praise of Mount Zion
   Following psalm: Psalm 50: Everyone will be judged by the Lord

2. ## Analysis of psalm

   A call for attention. (1-5)
   Folly of worldliness. (6-14)
   Against fear of death. (15-20)

3. ## Key verse

   Verse 2: "Both low and high, rich and poor, together."

4. ## Key word / key phrase

   Verse 12, "riches."

5. ## Key event / key person / key theme

   Riches cannot redeem

6. ## Key thought

   This psalm is addressed to the rich who trust in their wealth.

7. ## Key thing to look out for

   The psalmist points out how foolish it is to be in the grip of riches and offers wisdom to replace wealth.

8. ## Key Bible cross-reference

   Verse 14. See 96:15; Isaiah 5:14.

9. ## Key "by way of explanation"

   Verse 15, "redeem from the grave." The psalmist looks forward to being in God's presence in heaven. See Luke 16:22.

10. ## Key "Quotable Quote"

    "But God will redeem my soul from the power of the grave: for he shall receive me."
    Psalm 49:15

Psalm 50

1. Before and after

Previous psalm: Psalm 49: Riches cannot redeem
Following psalm: Psalm 51: Confession and forgiveness of sin

2. Analysis of psalm

The glory of God. (1-6)
Sacrifices to be changed for prayers. (7-15)
Sincere obedience required. (16-23)

3. Key verse

Verse 12: "If I were hungry, I would not tell thee."

4. Key word / key phrase

Verse 5, "Gather to me."

5. Key event / key person / key theme

True worship

6. Key thought

This psalm calls God's faithful people to meet before him in worship.

7. Key thing to look out for

The psalm calls God's followers to examine their motives and to root out wickedness.

8. Key Bible cross-reference

Verse 5. See Exodus 24:4-8.

9. Key "by way of explanation"

In Psalm 50 there are seven names or titles for God. Verse 5, "consecrated one," is a reference to Israel, God's covenant people.

10. Key "Quotable Quote"

"The mighty God, even the LORD, hath spoken, and called the earth from the rising of the sun unto the going down thereof."
Psalm 50:1

Psalm 51

1. Before and after

Previous psalm: Psalm 50: Everyone will be judged by the Lord
Following psalm: Psalm 52: The Lord will judge the deceitful

2. Analysis chapter

Pleas for forgiveness. (1-2)
David's understanding of the nature of sin. (3-5).
David's desire for cleansing and renewal. (6-12)
David's resolve to show his gratitude to God. (13-17)
David's prayer for the rebuilding of Jerusalem. (18-19)

3. Key verse

Verse 3: "For I acknowledge my transgressions: and my sin is ever before me."

4. Key word / key phrase

Words expressing heartfelt repentance: "blot out," "wash," and "cleanse," verses 1-2.

5. Key event / key person / key theme

This is explained by the caption at the beginning of the psalm, "To the chief Musician, A Psalm of David, when Nathan the prophet came unto him, after he had gone in to Bathsheba."

6. Key thought

The different ways in which David expresses his sincere repentance.

7. Key thing to look out for

The results that will flow from David's forgiveness by God, healing and restoration.

8. Key biblical cross-reference

2 Samuel chapters 11 – 12 record the events in David's life which caused him to pray this psalm.

9. Key "by way of explanation"

Verse 5, "I was shapen in iniquity; and in sin did my mother conceive me." This is not to suggest that conception or birth are sinful. Rather, "The psalmist confesses his total involvement in human sinfulness, from the very beginning of his existence" A.A. Anderson.

10. Key "Quotable Quote"

"It is generally agreed that this fifty-first psalm is perhaps the classic statement in the Old Testament on the question of repentance [and] is perhaps the classic statement on this whole matter of repentance in the entire Bible."
Martyn Lloyd-Jones

Psalm 52

1. Before and after

Previous psalm: Psalm 51: Confession and forgiveness of sin
Following psalm: Psalm 53: A picture of the godless

2. Analysis of psalm

The enemies of the truth and the Church described, and their destruction. (1-5)
The righteous rejoice. (6-9)

3. Key verse

Verse 6: "The righteous also shall see, and fear, and shall laugh at him."

4. Key word / key phrase

Verse 5, "God will bring you down."

5. Key event / key person / key theme

God's judgment and grace

6. Key thought

Even though David is being attacked he expresses his firm confidence in the Lord.

7. Key thing to look out for

God's enemies will not live forever.

8. Key Bible cross-reference

Verse 8. See 23:6; 27:4.

9. Key "by way of explanation"

Verse 5. The wicked will be brought low. This is expressed by three images in this verse: "bring you down," "snatch you up," and "uproot you."

10. Key "Quotable Quote"

"But I am like a green olive tree in the house of God: I trust in the mercy of God for ever and ever."
Psalm 52:8

Psalm 54

(For Psalm 53, see Psalm 14.)

1. ### Before and after

   Previous psalm: Psalm 53: A picture of the godless
   Following psalm: Psalm 55: Cast your burden on the Lord

2. ### Analysis of psalm

   David complains about the malice of his enemies. (1-3)
   Assurance of the divine favor and protection. (4-7)

3. ### Key verse

   Verse 4: "Behold, God is mine helper."

4. ### Key word / key phrase

   Verse 1, "Save me."

5. ### Key event / key person / key theme

   A prayer for protection from enemies

6. ### Key thought

   As David's life is threatened he turns to the Lord for help.

7. ### Key thing to look out for

   David is not arrogant in his relationship with the Lord, but he is confident that the Lord will answer his cry for help.

8. ### Key Bible cross-reference

   Title, "When the Ziphites . . .," see 1 Samuel 23:19.

9. ### Key "by way of explanation"

   Verse 4. In the psalms the most important verse is often not the first verse, or the last verse, but the central verse. In this case the central verse, verse 4, expresses great confidence in the Lord.

10. ### Key "Quotable Quote"

    "I will freely sacrifice unto thee: I will praise thy name, O LORD; for it is good."
    Psalm 54:6

Psalm 55

1. Before and after

Previous psalm: Psalm 54: The Lord is our Helper
Following psalm: Psalm 56: Fear in the middle of trials

2. Analysis of psalm

Prayer to God to manifest his favor. (1-8)
The great wickedness and treachery of David's enemies. (9-15)
He is sure that God will in due time appear for him. (16-23)

3. Key verse

Verse 2: "Attend unto me, and hear me."

4. Key word / key phrase

Verse 22, "Cast your cares."

5. Key event / key person / key theme

Cast your burden on the Lord

6. Key thought

David is under great pressure as he is the object of a conspiracy against him
in Jerusalem.

7. Key thing to look out for

In his longing to escape from his trouble David says that he will cast his
worries on the Lord.

8. Key Bible cross-reference

Verse 22. See 1 Peter 5:7.

9. Key "by way of explanation"

Verse 18, "ransom." The Lord is said to "ransom," "rescue," and "redeem" his
people. See Isaiah 50:2; Jeremiah 31:11.

10. Key "Quotable Quote"

"Cast thy burden upon the LORD, and he shall sustain thee: he shall never
suffer the righteous to be moved."
Psalm 55:22

Psalm 56

1. Before and after

Previous psalm: Psalm 55: Cast your burden on the Lord
Following psalm: Psalm 57: Prayer in the middle of trouble

2. Analysis of psalm

David seeks mercy from God, in the middle of the malice of his enemies. (1-7) He rests his faith on God's promises, and declares his obligation to praise him for mercies. (8-13)

3. Key verse

Verse 8: "Thou tellest my wanderings: put thou my tears into thy bottle."

4. Key word / key phrase

Verse 3, "I will trust in you."

5. Key event / key person / key theme

Trust in God, despite outward circumstances

6. Key thought

The title to this psalm supplies its background: "When the Philistines had seized him [David] in Gath."

7. Key thing to look out for

Because David trusts in God he says he will not be afraid of the most frightening situation.

8. Key Bible cross-reference

Verse 12. See 66:14.

9. Key "by way of explanation"

Verse 4, "word." The Lord had often promised to go to the help of his people if they called on him. See 50:15; 130:5.

10. Key "Quotable Quote"

"In God will I praise his word: in the LORD will I praise his word."
Psalm 56:10

Psalm 57

1. *Before and after*

   Previous psalm: Psalm 56: Fear in the middle of trials
   Following psalm: Psalm 58: Wicked judges will be judged

2. *Analysis of psalm*

   David begins with prayer and complaint. (1-6)
   He concludes with joy and praise. (7-11)

3. *Key verse*

   Verse 8: "Awake up, my glory; awake, psaltery and harp."

4. *Key word / key phrase*

   Verse 2, "I cry out to God."

5. *Key event / key person / key theme*

   A prayer for help in trouble

6. *Key thought*

   David spends a night in acute danger and so pleads for deliverance.

7. *Key thing to look out for*

   This psalm has a simple structure of two groups of verses, 1-5 and 6-11, both
   asking for God's help. Both of these sets of verses end with an identical
   refrain. See verses 5,11.

8. *Key Bible cross-reference*

   Verse 5. See Exodus 14:4; Isaiah 59:19.

9. *Key "by way of explanation"*

   Verse 7. This verse explains why David was no longer in the grip of fear.

10. *Key "Quotable Quote"*

    "For thy mercy is great unto the heavens, and thy truth unto the clouds."
    Psalm 57:10

Psalm 58

1. **Before and after**

   Previous psalm: Psalm 57: Prayer in the middle of trouble
   Following psalm: Psalm 59: Prayer for deliverance from violent people

2. **Analysis of psalm**

   Wicked judges described and reproved. (1-5)
   A prayer that they may fall, and their ruin predicted. (6-11)

3. **Key verse**

   Verse 6: "Break their teeth, O God, in their mouth."

4. **Key word / key phrase**

   Verse 2, "injustice."

5. **Key event / key person / key theme**

   Wicked judges will be punished

6. **Key thought**

   As God is the supreme Judge, David appeals to him to judge the human judges.

7. **Key thing to look out for**

   The first and last verses state that God will judge unjust judges.

8. **Key Bible cross-reference**

   Verse 4. See 140:3; Matthew 23:33.

9. **Key "by way of explanation"**

   Verses 6-8. The language used here looks rather vicious at first sight. The psalmist was making use of the curses which were commonly used at that time in the ancient Near East.

10. **Key "Quotable Quote"**

   "So that a man shall say, Verily there is a reward for the righteous: verily he is a God that judgeth in the earth."
   Psalm 58:11

Psalm 59

1. **Before and after**

   Previous psalm: Psalm 58: Wicked judges will be judged
   Following psalm: Psalm 60: Prayer for the deliverance of the nation

2. **Analysis of psalm**

   David prays for deliverance from his enemies. (1-7)
   He foresees their destruction. (8-17)

3. **Key verse**

   Verse 8: "But thou, O LORD, shalt laugh at them."

4. **Key word / key phrase**

   Verse 1, "Deliver me."

5. **Key event / key person / key theme**

   Prayer for deliverance from violent people

6. **Key thought**

   David is being spied on by Saul's men, and so David turns to the Lord for help.

7. **Key thing to look out for**

   David often suffered verbal attacks. See verses 3-5.

8. **Key Bible cross-reference**

   Verse 11. See 78:11; 106:13.

9. **Key "by way of explanation"**

   Verse 2. The people who maliciously attack the psalmist are often labeled "evildoers" or "bloodthirsty men."

10. **Key "Quotable Quote"**

    "Unto thee, O my strength, will I sing: for God is my defense, and the God of my mercy."
    Psalm 59:17

Psalm 60

1. **Before and after**

   Previous psalm: Psalm 59: Prayer for deliverance from violent people
   Following psalm: Psalm 61: A prayer when overwhelmed

2. **Analysis of psalm**

   David prays for the deliverance of Israel from their enemies. (1-5)
   He asks God to carry on and complete their victories. (6-12)

3. **Key verse**

   Verse 6: "God hath spoken in his holiness."

4. **Key word / key phrase**

   Verse 5, "save us."

5. **Key event / key person / key theme**

   A heavy defeat from their enemies, probably Edom (verse 9)

6. **Key thought**

   God's people now seek the Lord's deliverance.

7. **Key thing to look out for**

   Israel is comforted as they recognize the Lord as their Warrior-King.

8. **Key Bible cross-reference**

   Title. See 2 Samuel 8:13; 1 Chronicles 18:12.

9. **Key "by way of explanation"**

   Verse 7. The land that the Israelites conquered and settled in belonged to the
   Lord and so was under his rule.

10. **Key "Quotable Quote"**

   "Give us help from trouble: for vain is the help of man."
   Psalm 60:11

Psalm 61

1. **Before and after**

    Previous psalm: Psalm 60: Prayer for the deliverance of the nation
    Following psalm: Psalm 62: Wait for God

2. **Analysis of psalm**

    As David seeks God he remembers past deliverance. (1-4)
    He vows to serve God. (5-8)

3. **Key verse**

    Verse 4: "I will abide in thy tabernacle for ever."

4. **Key word / key phrase**

    Verse 4, "the shelter of your wings."

5. **Key event / key person / key theme**

    A prayer when overwhelmed

6. **Key thought**

    This psalm asks for God to be present among his people.

7. **Key thing to look out for**

    The psalmist knows that he can appeal to the Lord for help, as the Lord has never failed him.

8. **Key Bible cross-reference**

    Verse 5. See 16:6; 37:18.

9. **Key "by way of explanation"**

    Verse 2. The psalmist likens security in the Lord to being on a rock.

10. **Key "Quotable Quote"**

    "So will I sing praise unto thy name for ever, that I may daily perform my vows."
    Psalm 61:8

Psalm 62

1. **Before and after**

   Previous psalm: Psalm 61: A prayer when overwhelmed
   Following psalm: Psalm 63: Thirst for God

2. **Analysis of psalm**

   David's confidence in God. (1-7)
   No trust is to be put in worldly things. (8-12)

3. **Key verse**

   Verse 5: "My soul, wait thou only upon God."

4. **Key word / key phrase**

   Verse 5, "find rest."

5. **Key event / key person / key theme**

   Wait for God

6. **Key thought**

   David's trust in God is expressed most wonderfully in this psalm.

7. **Key thing to look out for**

   David wrote this psalm from a position of weakness and some think it may
   have been written in his old age.

8. **Key Bible cross-reference**

   Verse 12. See Jeremiah 17:10; Revelation 2:23.

9. **Key "by way of explanation"**

   Verse 3. The "leaning wall" and "tottering fence" are expressions of David's
   fragile state.

10. **Key "Quotable Quote"**

   "Trust in him at all times; ye people, pour out your heart before him: God is a
   refuge for us."
   Psalm 62:8

Psalm 63

1. Before and after

Previous psalm: Psalm 62: Wait for God
Following psalm: Psalm 64: A prayer for God's protection

2. Analysis of psalm

David's desire for God. (1,2)
His satisfaction in God. (3-6)
His dependence upon God, and assurance of safety. (7-11)

3. Key verse

Verse 3: "Because thy loving kindness is better than life, my lips shall praise thee."

4. Key word / key phrase

Verse 1, "earnestly I seek you."

5. Key event / key person / key theme

The psalmist's thirst for God

6. Key thought

The psalm starts with longing but ends with joy.

7. Key thing to look out for

The intensity of David's longing for God is seen in his earnestly seeking God, and in his seeking God night and day.

8. Key Bible cross-reference

Title. See 1 Samuel 13:14.

9. Key "by way of explanation"

Verse 1 mentions thirst, and verse 5 mentions hunger as ways of expressing David's longing for God.

10. Key "Quotable Quote"

"Thus will I bless thee while I live: I will lift up my hands in thy name."
Psalm 63:4

Psalm 64

1. ### Before and after

   Previous psalm: Psalm 63: Thirst for God
   Following psalm: Psalm 65: God's care of nature

2. ### Analysis of psalm

   Prayer for deliverance. (1-6)
   The destruction of the wicked, and encouragement for the righteous. (7-10)

3. ### Key verse

   Verse 2: "Hide me from the secret counsel of the wicked."

4. ### Key word / key phrase

   Verse 1, "protect my life."

5. ### Key event / key person / key theme

   A prayer for God's protection

6. ### Key thought

   The main weapon the enemy uses against David in this psalm, as in some others, is his tongue.

7. ### Key thing to look out for

   David's enemies are full of contempt for him.

8. ### Key Bible cross-reference

   Verse 3. See 59:7.

9. ### Key "by way of explanation"

   Verses 9,10 contrast God's judgments on men and his blessings on them.

10. ### Key "Quotable Quote"

    "The righteous shall be glad in the LORD, and shall trust in him; and all the upright in heart shall glory."
    Psalm 64:10

Psalm 65

1. *Before and after*

   Previous psalm: Psalm 64: A prayer for God's protection
   Following psalm: Psalm 66: Remember what God has done

2. *Analysis of psalm*

   God is to be praised in the kingdom of grace. (1-5)
   In the kingdom of providence. (6-13)

3. *Key verse*

   Verse 11: "Thou crownest the year with thy goodness."

4. *Key word / key phrase*

   Verse 5, "you answer us."

5. *Key event / key person / key theme*

   A hymn in praise of God's goodness

6. *Key thought*

   International events are not beyond the Lord's control.

7. *Key thing to look out for*

   The beauty and fruitfulness of nature comes from the Lord.

8. *Key Bible cross-reference*

   Verse 5. See 66:3; Isaiah 64:3.

9. *Key "by way of explanation"*

   Verse 8. One day everyone will acknowledge God and his salvation.

10. *Key "Quotable Quote"*

    "The pastures are clothed with flocks; the valleys also are covered over with corn; they shout for joy, they also sing."
    Psalm 65:13

Psalm 66

1. *Before and after*

> Previous psalm: Psalm 65: God's provision through nature
> Following psalm: Psalm 67: God will rule the earth

2. *Analysis of psalm*

> Praise for God's sovereign power in the creation. (1-7)
> For his favor to his Church. (8-12)
> And the psalmist's praise for his experience of God's goodness. (13-20)

3. *Key verse*

> Verse 8: "O bless our God, ye people, and make the voice of his praise to be heard."

4. *Key word / key phrase*

> Verse 5, "his works."

5. *Key event / key person / key theme*

> Remember what God has done

6. *Key thought*

> All deliverances by God demonstrate his power.

7. *Key thing to look out for*

> Remembering what God has done leads naturally to praising the Lord.

8. *Key Bible cross-reference*

> Verse 6. See Exodus 14:21; Joshua 3:14-17.

9. *Key "by way of explanation"*

> This psalm dovetails in well with the events in 2 Kings 19 where Judah is miraculously delivered from the Assyrians.

10. *Key "Quotable Quote"*

> "Come and hear, all ye that fear God, and I will declare what he hath done for my soul."
> Psalm 66:16

Psalm 67

1. **Before and after**

   Previous psalm: Psalm 66: Remember what God has done
   Following psalm: Psalm 68: God is the Father of the fatherless

2. **Analysis of psalm**

   A prayer for the enlargement of Christ's kingdom. (1-7)

3. **Key verse**

   Verse 1: "God be merciful unto us, and bless us."

4. **Key word / key phrase**

   Verse 4, "guide the nations."

5. **Key event / key person / key theme**

   God will rule the earth

6. **Key thought**

   Nobody is the same after being blessed by the Lord.

7. **Key thing to look out for**

   The fruits of the earth and sea are provided by the Lord.

8. **Key Bible cross-reference**

   Verse 1. See Numbers 6:24-26.

9. **Key "by way of explanation"**

   Verse 2. This prayer asks that the whole world may know God's goodness.

10. **Key "Quotable Quote"**

    "Let the people praise thee, O God; let all the people praise thee."
    Psalm 67:3

Psalm 68

1. Before and after

Previous psalm: Psalm 67: God will rule the earth
Following psalm: Psalm 69: Prayer for God to come close

2. Analysis of psalm

A prayer: The greatness and goodness of God. (1-6)
The wonderful works God performed for his people. (7-14)
The presence of God in his Church. (15-21)
The victories of Christ. (22-28)
The growth of the Church. (29-31)
The glory and grace of God. (32-35)

3. Key verse

Verse 8: "The earth shook, the heavens also dropped at the presence of God."

4. Key word / key phrase

Verse 5, "a father."

5. Key event / key person / key theme

God is the Father of the fatherless.

6. Key thought

God's people are meant to be distinct, righteous, and holy.

7. Key thing to look out for

The Lord promises to bear our burdens, whatever they may be.

8. Key Bible cross-reference

Verse 18. See Ephesians 4:8.

9. Key "by way of explanation"

Verse 6. Ruth is a perfect example of the truth of this verse. See Ruth 4:14-17.

10. Key "Quotable Quote"

"Ascribe ye strength unto God: his excellency is over Israel, and his strength is in the clouds."
Psalm 68:34

Psalm 69

1. *Before and after*

Previous psalm: Psalm 68: God is the Father of the fatherless
Following psalm: Psalm 70: Prayer for the poor and needy

2. *Analysis of psalm*

David complains of great distress. (1-12)
And begs for succor. (13-21)
He declares the judgments of God. (22-29)
He concludes with joy and praise. (30-36)

3. *Key verse*

Verse 1: "Save me, O God; for the waters are come in unto my soul."

4. *Key word / key phrase*

Verse 18, "rescue me."

5. *Key event / key person / key theme*

A cry for help

6. *Key thought*

After Psalm 22 this psalm is the most quoted psalm in the New Testament because of its foreshadowings of Christ's suffering.

7. *Key thing to look out for*

Observe the different reasons given for praising the Lord.

8. *Key Bible cross-reference*

Verse 4. See 35:19; John 15:25

9. *Key "by way of explanation"*

Verse 9. David's devotion to the temple burnt in him like a fire. But this was even more the case with Jesus, John 2:17.

10. *Key "Quotable Quote"*

"Draw nigh unto my soul, and redeem it: deliver me because of mine enemies."
Psalm 69:18

Psalm 71

(For Psalm 70, see Psalm 40:13-17.)

1. ### Before and after

   Previous psalm: Psalm 70: Prayer for the poor and needy
   Following psalm: Psalm 72: The Messiah's rule

2. ### Analysis of psalm

   Prayers that God would deliver and save. (1-13)
   Believing praises. (14-24)

3. ### Key verse

   Verse 3: "Be thou my strong habitation."

4. ### Key word / key phrase

   Verse 6, "from my birth."

5. ### Key event / key person / key theme

   Prayer for the poor and needy

6. ### Key thought

   As the psalmist feels that his strength is fading he turns to the Lord in prayer for help.

7. ### Key thing to look out for

   Even though he is confronted by so many troubles the psalmist says that he still relies on the Lord.

8. ### Key Bible cross-reference

   Verse 5. See 22:9.

9. ### Key "by way of explanation"

   Verses 16,17. The Lord's "mighty acts" which he performed for his people reveal his righteousness and so are also called "righteous acts" in verse 24.

10. ### Key "Quotable Quote"

    "Let my mouth be filled with thy praise and with thy honor all the day." Psalm 71:8

Psalm 72

1. *Before and after*

> Previous psalm: Psalm 71: Prayer for the elderly
> Following psalm: Psalm 73: The perspective of eternity

2. *Analysis of psalm*

> David begins with a prayer for Solomon. (1)
> He moves on to a prophecy of the glories of his reign, and of Christ's kingdom. (2-17)
> Praise to God. (18-20)

3. *Key verse*

> Verse 7: "In his days shall the righteous flourish."

4. *Key word / key phrase*

> Verse 8, "rule from sea to sea."

5. *Key event / key person / key theme*

> The Messiah's rule

6. *Key thought*

> Justice and righteousness are the characteristics of the king described in this psalm.

7. *Key thing to look out for*

> The early Christian Church applied this psalm to Jesus as Messiah.

8. *Key Bible cross-reference*

> Verse 8. See Zechariah 9:10.

9. *Key "by way of explanation"*

> Verses 18,19. As at the end of Book I, these verses are in the form of a doxology and conclude Book II of the five books of the psalms.

10. *Key "Quotable Quote"*

> "He shall spare the poor and needy, and shall save the souls of the needy."
> Psalm 72:13

Psalm 73

1. **Before and after**

   Previous psalm: Psalm 72: The Messiah's rule
   Following psalm: Psalm 74: A prayer asking God to remember his covenant

2. **Analysis of psalm**

   The psalmist's temptation. (1-14)
   How he gained a victory over it. (15-20)
   How he benefited by it. (21-28)

3. **Key verse**

   Verse 1: "Truly God is good to Israel."

4. **Key word / key phrase**

   Verse 24, "into glory."

5. **Key event / key person / key theme**

   The perspective of eternity

6. **Key thought**

   The destinies of the godly and wicked are compared.

7. **Key thing to look out for**

   The righteous can become too absorbed in worrying about the wickedness of
   the wicked.

8. **Key Bible cross-reference**

   Verse 14. See Proverbs :12; 23:13,14.

9. **Key "by way of explanation"**

   Verse 24. The psalmist expresses his sure hope that the Lord will be with him
   after this life.

10. **Key "Quotable Quote"**

    "Thou shalt guide me with thy counsel, and afterward receive me to glory."
    Psalm 73:24

Psalm 74

1. ### Before and after
   Previous psalm: Psalm 73: The perspective of eternity
   Following psalm: Psalm 75: God is the Judge

2. ### Analysis of psalm
   The desolations of the sanctuary. (1-11)
   Pleas for encouraging faith. (12-17)
   Petitions for deliverance. (18-23)

3. ### Key verse
   Verse 13: "Thou didst divide the sea by thy strength."

4. ### Key word / key phrase
   Verse 2, "remember."

5. ### Key event / key person / key theme
   A prayer asking God to remember his covenant

6. ### Key thought
   God is the all-powerful King.

7. ### Key thing to look out for
   The second verse and penultimate verse of this psalm include the key word "remember."

8. ### Key Bible cross-reference
   Verse 14. See Job 41:1; Isaiah 27:1.

9. ### Key "by way of explanation"
   Verse 2. The Lord purchased or acquired, or created, or chose, the people of Israel to be his people and always cared for them, as was seen during the Exodus.

10. ### Key "Quotable Quote"
    "The day is thine, the night also is thine: thou hast prepared the light and the sun."
    Psalm 74:16

Psalm 75

1. *Before and after*

   Previous psalm: Psalm 74: A prayer asking God to remember his covenant
   Following psalm: Psalm 76: God's wonderful power

2. *Analysis of psalm*

   The psalmist declares his resolution to execute judgment. (1-5)
   He rebukes the wicked, and concludes with resolutions to praise God. (6-10)

3. *Key verse*

   Verse 7: "But God is the judge."

4. *Key word / key phrase*

   Verse 2, "judge uprightly."

5. *Key event / key person / key theme*

   God is the Judge.

6. *Key thought*

   This psalm states that the Lord will judge the wicked and the arrogant.

7. *Key thing to look out for*

   The psalm starts with thanksgiving and ends with praise.

8. *Key Bible cross-reference*

   Verse 8. See Proverbs 2,5; Isaiah 65:11.

9. *Key "by way of explanation"*

   Verse 4, "Do not lift up your horns." A "horn" often stood for strength in the
   Bible and to "lift up one's horn" meant to attack or defy someone.

10. *Key "Quotable Quote"*

    "Unto thee, O God, do we give thanks, unto thee do we give thanks: for that
    thy name is near thy wondrous works declare."
    Psalm 75:1

Psalm 76

1. *Before and after*

Previous psalm: Psalm 75: God is the Judge
Following psalm: Psalm 77: When overwhelmed, recall God's greatness

2. *Analysis of psalm*

The psalmist speaks of God's power. (1-6)
All have to fear and to trust in him. (7-12)

3. *Key verse*

Verse 8: "Thou didst cause judgment to be heard from heaven."

4. *Key word / key phrase*

Verse 3, "broke."

5. *Key event / key person / key theme*

God's wonderful power

6. *Key thought*

The Lord revealed himself through his saving actions among the people of Israel.

7. *Key thing to look out for*

God's people are urged to acknowledge all that the Lord has done for them.

8. *Key Bible cross-reference*

Verse 6. See Job 26:11; Nahum 1:4.

9. *Key "by way of explanation"*

A great victory has just been won at Jerusalem. This psalm may have originally celebrated the capture of Jerusalem by David.

10. *Key "Quotable Quote"*

"In Judah is God known: his name is great in Israel."
Psalm 76:1

Psalm 77

1. Before and after

Previous psalm: Psalm 76: God's wonderful power
Following psalm: Psalm 78: God continues to guide, despite unbelief

2. Analysis of psalm

The psalmist's troubles and temptation. (1-10)
He encourages himself by remembering God's help of his people. (11-20)

3. Key verse

Verse 2: "In the day of my trouble I sought the Lord."

4. Key word / key phrase

Verse 2, "distress."

5. Key event / key person / key theme

An overwhelmed person

6. Key thought

This psalm is designed to bring comfort in times of distress.

7. Key thing to look out for

Verse 15 points Christians to the death and resurrection of Christ. See Matthew 28:2; Ephesians 1:18-23.

8. Key Bible cross-reference

Verse 13. See Exodus 15:11.

9. Key "by way of explanation"

Verses 1-9. God's people have never found it easy to cope with times when the Lord seems to be doing nothing and they have to wait for him to act.

10. Key "Quotable Quote"

"I will meditate also of all thy work, and talk of thy doings."
Psalm 77:12

Psalm 78

1. ### Before and after

   Previous psalm: Psalm 77: When overwhelmed, recall God's greatness
   Following psalm: Psalm 79: Jerusalem's defilement will be avenged

2. ### Analysis of psalm

   Attention called for. (1-8)
   The history of Israel. (9-39)
   Their settlement in Canaan. (40-55)
   The mercies of God to Israel contrasted with their ingratitude. (56-72)

3. ### Key verse

   Verse 1: "Give ear, O my people, to my law."

4. ### Key word / key phrase

   Verse 2, "parables."

5. ### Key event / key person / key theme

   God continues to guide, despite unbelief.

6. ### Key thought

   The psalmist remembers how often Israel has rebelled against the Lord.

7. ### Key thing to look out for

   God's followers have been chosen by the Lord to follow him, just as he chose
   the tribe of Judah.

8. ### Key Bible cross-reference

   Verse 2. See Matthew 13:35.

9. ### Key "by way of explanation"

   Verse 2, "parables." The Lord taught his people in a wide variety of ways,
   including riddles, proverbs, and parables.

10. ### Key "Quotable Quote"

    "He brought streams also out of the rock, and caused waters to run down like
    rivers."
    Psalm 78:16

Psalm 79

1. *Before and after*

Previous psalm: Psalm 78: God continues to guide, despite unbelief
Following psalm: Psalm 80: Israel pleads for God's mercy

2. *Analysis of psalm*

The deplorable condition of the people of God. (1-5)
A prayer for help. (6-13)

3. *Key verse*

Verse 5: "How long, LORD? wilt thou be angry for ever?"

4. *Key word / key phrase*

Verse 1, "defiled."

5. *Key event / key person / key theme*

Jerusalem's defilement will be avenged.

6. *Key thought*

God's people ask for the Lord's judgment to fall on their enemies. Some of the evil acts of these people are listed in this psalm.

7. *Key thing to look out for*

The psalmist asks for the Lord's forgiveness on Israel's sins and for his help.

8. *Key Bible cross-reference*

Verse 1. See 2 Kings 25:8-10; 2 Chronicles 36:17-19.

9. *Key "by way of explanation"*

Verse 3. See 2 Kings 21:16.

10. *Key "Quotable Quote"*

"Help us, O God of our salvation, for the glory of thy name: and deliver us, and purge away our sins, for thy name's sake."
Psalm 79:9

Psalm 80

1. *Before and after*

    Previous psalm: Psalm 79: Jerusalem's defilement will be avenged
    Following psalm: Psalm 81: God's longing for Israel's obedience

2. *Analysis of psalm*

    The psalmist complains of the miseries endured by God's people. (1-7)
    Their former prosperity and present desolation. (8-16)
    A prayer for mercy. (17-19)

3. *Key verse*

    Verse 1: "Give ear, O Shepherd of Israel."

4. *Key word / key phrase*

    Verse 3, "restore us."

5. *Key event / key person / key theme*

    Israel pleads for God to restore them.

6. *Key thought*

    The vine/vineyard metaphor is used to bring comfort to the Lord's people.

7. *Key thing to look out for*

    Israel has been attacked and defeated by a foreign power. Now she turns to the
    Lord and asks for his restoration.

8. *Key Bible cross-reference*

    Verse 1. See Exodus 25:22.

9. *Key "by way of explanation"*

    Verses 3,7,19. These verses each have a similar refrain in them. But their appeal
    increases in urgency each time: "Lord God," "O God Almighty;" and "O Lord
    God Almighty."

10. *Key "Quotable Quote"*

    "Turn us again, O God of hosts, and cause thy face to shine; and we shall be
    saved."
    Psalm 80:7

Psalm 81

1. ***Before and after***

    Previous psalm: Psalm 80: Israel pleads for God's mercy
    Following psalm: Psalm 82: Israel's judges rebuked

2. ***Analysis of psalm***

    God is praised for what he has done for his people. (1-7)
    Their obligations to him. (8-16)

3. ***Key verse***

    Verse 8: "Hear, O my people, and I will testify unto thee."

4. ***Key word / key phrase***

    Verse 8, "if you would but listen to me."

5. ***Key event / key person / key theme***

    God's longing for Israel's obedience

6. ***Key thought***

    The psalm states that the Lord who has always heard and delivered his people
    seeks their allegiance.

7. ***Key thing to look out for***

    God's people are told off for not listening to the Lord.

8. ***Key Bible cross-reference***

    Verse 7. See Numbers 20:1-13.

9. ***Key "by way of explanation"***

    Verse 3, the "new moon" marks the first day of the month. The "first" is
    probably the Feast of Tabernacles, a great seven day long autumn festival,
    beginning on the 15th of the month, when the moon is full.

10. ***Key "Quotable Quote"***

    "Sing aloud unto God our strength: make a joyful noise unto the God of
    Jacob"
    Psalm 81:1

Psalm 82

1. ### Before and after

   Previous psalm: Psalm 81: God's longing for Israel's obedience
   Following psalm: Psalm 83: Plea for God to destroy Israel's enemies

2. ### Analysis of psalm

   An exhortation to judges. (1-5)
   The doom of evil rulers. (6-8)

3. ### Key verse

   Verse 1: "God standeth in the congregation of the mighty."

4. ### Key word / key phrase

   Verse 2, "show partiality."

5. ### Key event / key person / key theme

   Israel's judges rebuked

6. ### Key thought

   Many of Israel's judges were unjust. This psalm says that the Lord will call
   them to account.

7. ### Key thing to look out for

   The desperate needs of the poor and weak are highlighted in this psalm.

8. ### Key Bible cross-reference

   Verse 6. See John 10:34.

9. ### Key "by way of explanation"

   Verse 1, "great assembly." This pictures a Hall of Justice where the Lord
   presides as the supreme Judge. See 1 Kings 7:7; 22:19.

10. ### Key "Quotable Quote"

    "Deliver the poor and needy: rid them out of the hand of the wicked."
    Psalm 82:4

Psalm 83

1. **Before and after**

   Previous psalm: Psalm 82: Israel's judges rebuked
   Following psalm: Psalm 84: The joy of living with God

2. **Analysis of psalm**

   The purposes of the enemies of Israel. (1-8)
   Earnest prayer for their defeat. (9-18)

3. **Key verse**

   Verse 13: "O my God, make them like a wheel; as the stubble before the wind."

4. **Key word / key phrase**

   Verse 2, "enemies."

5. **Key event / key person / key theme**

   Plea for God to destroy Israel's enemies

6. **Key thought**

   As the whole world seem to be against Israel, God's people ask the Lord to crush their enemies.

7. **Key thing to look out for**

   The psalm ends with the prayer that even Israel's enemies would turn to the Lord.

8. **Key Bible cross-reference**

   Verse 11. See Judges 7:25; 8:12.

9. **Key "by way of explanation"**

   Verse 1, "do not keep silent." This was another way of asking the Lord to act on behalf of his people.

10. **Key "Quotable Quote"**

    "Keep not thou silence, O God: hold not thy peace, and be not still, O God."
    Psalm 83:1

Psalm 84

1. Before and after

Previous psalm: Psalm 83: Plea for God to destroy Israel's enemies
Following psalm: Psalm 85: A prayer for revival

2. Analysis of psalm

The pilgrim's longing to be in the temple. (1-3)
The happy pilgrim. (4-7)
A prayer for God's blessing. (8-12)

3. Key verse

Verse 1: "How amiable are thy tabernacles, O LORD of hosts!"

4. Key word / key phrase

Verse 4, "Blessed."

5. Key event / key person / key theme

The joy of living with God

6. Key thought

The psalmist longs to enter the Lord's temple so he can rest in the Lord's presence.

7. Key thing to look out for

The psalmist seeks refreshment from the Lord as he travels along on his tough pilgrimage.

8. Key Bible cross-reference

Verse 7. See Isaiah 40:31.

9. Key "by way of explanation"

Verse 5, "those whose strength is in you." The Lord gives his strength to those who acknowledge him as their deliverer.

10. Key "Quotable Quote"

"Blessed are they that dwell in thy house: they will be still praising thee."
Psalm 84:4

Psalm 85

1. Before and after

Previous psalm: Psalm 84: The joy of living with God
Following psalm: Psalm 86: Teach my your way, O Lord

2. Analysis of psalm

Prayers for the continuance of former mercies. (1-7)
Trust in God's goodness. (8-13)

3. Key verse

Verse 4: "Turn us, O God of our salvation, and cause thine anger toward us to cease."

4. Key word / key phrase

Verse 6, "revive."

5. Key event / key person / key theme

A prayer for revival

6. Key thought

God's people, in their distress, express their great desire to be renewed by the Lord.

7. Key thing to look out for

The psalmist recalls how the Lord has refreshed and restored his people in past times.

8. Key Bible cross-reference

Verse 9. See Numbers 14:22; Ezekiel 39:21.

9. Key "by way of explanation"

Verse 10. God's mercy and grace towards his people is expressed in four wonderful personifications: "Love and faithfulness . . . righteousness and peace."

10. Key "Quotable Quote"

"Show us thy mercy, O Lord, and grant us thy salvation."
Psalm 85:7

Psalm 86

1. Before and after

Previous psalm: Psalm 85: A prayer for revival
Following psalm: Psalm 87: Glorious Zion, city of God

2. Analysis of psalm

The psalmist pleads his earnestness, and the mercy of God, as reasons why his prayer should be heard. (1-7)
He renews his requests for help. (8-17)

3. Key verse

Verse 3: "Be merciful unto me, O Lord: for I cry unto thee daily."

4. Key word / key phrase

Verse 11, "walk in your truth."

5. Key event / key person / key theme

Teach my your way, O Lord

6. Key thought

The psalmist feels battered. He looks to the Lord for mercy and protection.

7. Key thing to look out for

The psalmist knows that the Lord pours down his love on those to turn to him in prayer.

8. Key Bible cross-reference

Verse 9. See Revelation 15:4.

9. Key "by way of explanation"

Verse 11 "teach me." The psalmist recognizes that he must follow the Lord's ways and that it is not enough that his enemies should stop attacking him.

10. Key "Quotable Quote"

"In the day of my trouble I will call upon thee: for thou wilt answer me."
Psalm 86:7

Psalm 87

1. **Before and after**

   Previous psalm: Psalm 86: Teach my your way, O Lord
   Following psalm: Psalm 88: Crying from the depths of affliction

2. **Analysis of psalm**

   The glory of Mount Zion, the site of Jerusalem. (1-3)
   It is filled with the divine blessing. (4-7)

3. **Key verse**

   Verse 3: "Glorious things are spoken of thee, O city of God."

4. **Key word / key phrase**

   Verse 2, "Zion."

5. **Key event / key person / key theme**

   God's city is glorious

6. **Key thought**

   This is the only psalm to picture other nations coming in to Jerusalem to be citizens alongside Israel in God's presence (verse 4).

7. **Key thing to look out for**

   Music and song in praise of God are to be heard in the Lord's city.

8. **Key Bible cross-reference**

   Verse 1. See Isaiah 14:32.

9. **Key "by way of explanation"**

   Verse 7, "All my fountains." Everything that refreshes the soul is found in Zion, God's city.

10. **Key "Quotable Quote"**

    "Glorious things are spoken of thee, O city of God."
    Psalm 87:3

Psalm 88

1. ***Before and after***

   Previous psalm: Psalm 87: Glorious Zion, city of God
   Following psalm: Psalm 89: Claiming God's promises in affliction

2. ***Analysis of psalm***

   The psalmist pours out his soul to God in lamentation. (1-9)
   He wrestles by faith, in his prayer to God for comfort. (10-18)

3. ***Key verse***

   Verse 3: "For my soul is full of troubles."

4. ***Key word / key phrase***

   Verse 1, "I cry out."

5. ***Key event / key person / key theme***

   Crying from the depths of affliction

6. ***Key thought***

   The psalmist says he is on the edge of death. He prays to the Lord about his situation.

7. ***Key thing to look out for***

   From the depths of his troubles the psalmist says that he knows salvation is with the Lord.

8. ***Key Bible cross-reference***

   Verse 10. See Isaiah 14:9.

9. ***Key "by way of explanation"***

   This is "the saddest psalm in the whole Psalter" (Kirkpatrick, quoted by L. Allen). Yet in the darkness the psalmist continues to pray.

10. ***Key "Quotable Quote"***

    "Let my prayer come before thee: incline thine ear unto my cry."
    Psalm 88:2

Psalm 89

1. Before and after

Previous psalm: Psalm 88: Crying from the depths of affliction
Following psalm: Psalm 90: Teach us to number our days

2. Analysis of psalm

God's mercy and truth, and his covenant. (1-4)
The glory and perfection of God. (5-14)
The happiness of those in communion with him. (15-18)
God's covenant with David, as a type of Christ. (19-37)
A calamitous state lamented. Prayer for redress. (38-52)

3. Key verse

Verse 5: "And the heavens shall praise thy wonders, O LORD."

4. Key word / key phrase

Verse 2. "Your love stands."

5. Key event / key person / key theme

Claiming God's promises in affliction

6. Key thought

The psalmist mourns over the fall of David's dynasty, verses 38-45, and feels totally rejected.

7. Key thing to look out for

The psalmist does, however, also express his trust in the Lord's righteousness and faithfulness.

8. Key Bible cross-reference

Title. See 1 Samuel 13:14.

9. Key "by way of explanation"

Verse 10, "Rahab" refers to a mythical monster, supposed to live in the deepest waters, and can be compared with leviathan, 104:26.

10. Key "Quotable Quote"

"I will sing of the mercies of the LORD for ever: with my mouth will I make known thy faithfulness to all generations."
Psalm 89:1

Psalm 90

1. *Before and after*

    Previous psalm: Psalm 89: Claiming God's promises in affliction
    Following psalm: Psalm 91: Living under the shadow of the Almighty

2. *Analysis of psalm*

    The eternity of God, the frailty of humans. (1-6)
    Submission to divine chastisements. (7-11)
    Prayer for mercy and grace. (12-17)

3. *Key verse*

    Verse 1: "Lord, thou hast been our dwelling place in all generations."

4. *Key word / key phrase*

    Verse 12, "Teach us to number our days."

5. *Key event / key person / key theme*

    Numbering our days

6. *Key thought*

    The Lord's everlasting nature is compared with transitory human life.

7. *Key thing to look out for*

    This psalm expresses man's state of hopelessness before the Lord, but does not forget the Lord's unfailing love.

8. *Key Bible cross-reference*

    Verse 4. See 2 Peter 3:8.

9. *Key "by way of explanation"*

    Verse 14 "morning." After the dark "night" of God's wrath, the psalmist is confident that God's love will come in the morning.

10. *Key "Quotable Quote"*

    "For a thousand years in thy sight are but as yesterday when it is past, and as a watch in the night."
    Psalm 90:4

Psalm 91

1. *Before and after*

   Previous psalm: Psalm 90: Teach us to number our days
   Following psalm: Psalm 92: It is good to praise the Lord

2. *Analysis of psalm*

   The safety of those who have God for their refuge. (1-8)
   Their favor with him. (9-16)

3. *Key verse*

   Verse 11: "For he shall give his angels charge over thee, to keep thee in all thy ways."

4. *Key word / key phrase*

   Verse 1, "shelter."

5. *Key event / key person / key theme*

   Living under the shadow of the Almighty

6. *Key thought*

   This psalm was composed out of a heart that was brimming over with the experience of God's presence.

7. *Key thing to look out for*

   The psalm states that the godly will be protected from four threats, verses 5,6, and from four beasts, verse 13.

8. *Key Bible cross-reference*

   Verse 11. See Matthew 4:6; Luke 4:10.

9. *Key "by way of explanation"*

   Verse 1, "shelter." It is in the temple that God's followers find the Lord's security and protection.

10. *Key "Quotable Quote"*

    "He that dwelleth in the secret place of the most High shall abide under the shadow of the Almighty."
    Psalm 91:1

Psalm 92

1. **Before and after**

   Previous psalm: Psalm 91: Living under the shadow of the Almighty
   Following psalm: Psalm 93: God's majesty

2. **Analysis of psalm**

   Praise is the business of the Sabbath. (1-6)
   The wicked shall perish, but God's people shall be exalted. (7-15)

3. **Key verse**

   Verse 6: "A brutish man knoweth not; neither doth a fool understand this."

4. **Key word / key phrase**

   Verse 4, "I sing for joy."

5. **Key event / key person / key theme**

   It is good to praise the Lord

6. **Key thought**

   The psalmist looks to God, reflecting on how high he is exalted, and concludes that his enemies will be defeated.

7. **Key thing to look out for**

   Those who live in God's presence may rest secure.

8. **Key Bible cross-reference**

   Verse 13. See 2 Kings 21:5; 23:11,12.

9. **Key "by way of explanation"**

   Verse 6. "Fools" have a completely godless outlook on life.

10. **Key "Quotable Quote"**

    "It is a good thing to give thanks unto the LORD, and to sing praises unto thy name, O most High."
    Psalm 92:1

Psalm 93

1. *Before and after*

   Previous psalm: Psalm 92: It is good to praise the Lord
   Following psalm: Psalm 94: Revenge belongs only to God

2. *Analysis of psalm*

   The majesty, power, and holiness of Christ's kingdom. (1-5)

3. *Key verse*

   Verse 3: "The floods have lifted up, O LORD."

4. *Key word / key phrase*

   Verse 1, "majesty."

5. *Key event / key person / key theme*

   The Lord reigns

6. *Key thought*

   This psalm, in common with psalms 47, 94-100, praises the Lord for his global reign.

7. *Key thing to look out for*

   The psalmist longs for the prayer, "thy kingdom come" to be realized.

8. *Key Bible cross-reference*

   Verse 3. See Job 38:8-11.

9. *Key "by way of explanation"*

   Verse 5, "statutes." These refer to the Lord's laws which do not change and which need to be followed if people are to live in harmony with God and each other.

10. *Key "Quotable Quote"*

    "Thy testimonies are very sure: holiness becometh thine house, O LORD, for ever."
    Psalm 93:5

Psalm 94

1. *Before and after*

Previous psalm: Psalm 93: God's majesty
Following psalm: Psalm 95: A call to worship the Lord

2. *Analysis of psalm*

The danger and folly of persecutors. (1-11)
Comfort and peace to the persecuted. (12-23)

3. *Key verse*

Verse 6: "They slay the widow and the stranger, and murder the fatherless."

4. *Key word / key phrase*

Verse 1, "God who avenges."

5. *Key event / key person / key theme*

Revenge belongs only to God

6. *Key thought*

In the face of blatant injustice and oppression of the poor the psalmist cries
out to the Judge of the world.

7. *Key thing to look out for*

The psalmist takes comfort in the thought that God knows all about the evil
that is being perpetrated in the world.

8. *Key Bible cross-reference*

Verse 11. See 1 Corinthians 3:20.

9. *Key "by way of explanation"*

Verse 17, "silence of death." If it had not been for the Lord's help the wicked
would never have been exposed and the psalmist would lie in silence in his
grave.

10. *Key "Quotable Quote"*

"The LORD knoweth the thoughts of man, that they are vanity."
Psalm 94:11

Psalm 95

1. **Before and after**

   Previous psalm: Psalm 94: Revenge belongs only to God
   Following psalm: Psalm 96: Make known God's glory

2. **Analysis of psalm**

   An exhortation to praise God. (1-7)
   A warning not to tempt him. (7-11)

3. **Key verse**

   Verse 2: "Let us come before his presence with thanksgiving."

4. **Key word / key phrase**

   Verse 1, "Let us sing . . . to the Lord."

5. **Key event / key person / key theme**

   A call to worship the Lord

6. **Key thought**

   The psalmist gives reasons for praising the Lord: he is superior to any other supposed god, and the whole world belongs to him.

7. **Key thing to look out for**

   Every godly person is called to worship.

8. **Key Bible cross-reference**

   Verses 8,9. See Exodus 17:1-7; Numbers 20:2-13.

9. **Key "by way of explanation"**

   Verses 4,5. God rules everywhere, including all the extremes and corners of the universe, the "depths . . . mountain peaks . . . sea . . . dry land."

10. **Key "Quotable Quote"**

    "O come, let us worship and bow down: let us kneel before the LORD our maker."
    Psalm 95:6

Psalm 97

(For Psalm 96, see 1 Chronicles 16:23-33.)

1. **Before and after**

   Previous psalm: Psalm 96: Make known God's glory
   Following psalm: Psalm 98: Sing a new song to the Lord

2. **Analysis of psalm**

   The Lord reigns in power that cannot be resisted. (1-7)
   His care of his people, and his provision for them. (8-12)

3. **Key verse**

   Verse 11: "Light is sown for the righteous, and gladness for the upright in heart."

4. **Key word / key phrase**

   Verse 1, "The Lord reigns."

5. **Key event / key person / key theme**

   The Lord is the supreme ruler

6. **Key thought**

   The psalmist is filled with joy because God reigns over the universe.

7. **Key thing to look out for**

   Those who worship idols will be disgraced.

8. **Key Bible cross-reference**

   Verse 8. See Isaiah 26:9.

9. **Key "by way of explanation"**

   Verse 6, "proclaim his righteousness." By looking into the night sky people can praise God, for they know that all nature testifies to the Creator.

10. **Key "Quotable Quote"**

    "Rejoice in the LORD, ye righteous; and give thanks at the remembrance of his holiness."
    Psalm 97:12

Psalm 98

1. *Before and after*

Previous psalm: Psalm 97: Rejoice! The Lord rules
Following psalm: Psalm 99: Exult in the Lord our God

2. *Analysis of psalm*

The glory of the Redeemer. (1-3)
The joy of the Redeemer. (4-9)

3. *Key verse*

Verse 4: "Make a joyful noise unto the LORD."

4. *Key word / key phrase*

Verse 1, "a new song."

5. *Key event / key person / key theme*

Israel's God is a glorious King

6. *Key thought*

All of God's characteristics, including his rule and his righteousness, are worthy of celebration

7. *Key thing to look out for*

The reasons why God is to be praised.

8. *Key Bible cross-reference*

Verse 2. See Isaiah 52:10.

9. *Key "by way of explanation"*

Verse 2. "Salvation" and "righteousness" are often linked in the psalms, as the Lord's actions which bring about his salvation also demonstrate his righteousness.

10. *Key "Quotable Quote"*

"Let the floods clap their hands: let the hills be joyful together."
Psalm 98:8

Psalm 99

1. **Before and after**

   Previous psalm: Psalm 98: Sing a new song to the Lord
   Following psalm: Psalm 100: Serve the Lord with gladness

2. **Analysis of psalm**

   God rules the world. (1-3)
   God rules over Israel. (4-5)
   This holy God is also a merciful God. (6-9)

3. **Key verse**

   Verse 9: "Exalt the LORD our God, and worship at his holy hill."

4. **Key word / key phrase**

   Verses 3,5,9. "he is holy."

5. **Key event / key person / key theme**

   Holiness

6. **Key thought**

   The psalmist depicts the Lord as the awesome and holy King to whom all
   nations should bow.

7. **Key thing to look out for**

   In the middle of worshiping the Lord, the psalmist recalls that he is a forgiving
   God.

8. **Key Bible cross-reference**

   Verse 7. See Exodus 33:9.

9. **Key "by way of explanation"**

   In verse 6, "Moses . . . Aaron . . . Samuel" are selected as they represented the
   Lord to the Israelites in their moments of special difficulty.

10. **Key "Quotable Quote"**

    "The LORD reigneth; let the people tremble: he sitteth between the cherubims;
    let the earth be moved."
    Psalm 99:1

Psalm 100

1. Before and after

Previous psalm: Psalm 99: Exult in the Lord our God
Following psalm: Psalm 101: Commitment to a holy life

2. Analysis of psalm

An exhortation to praise God, and rejoice in him. (1-5)

3. Key verse

Verse 1: "Make a joyful noise unto the LORD, all ye lands."

4. Key word / key phrase

Verse 1, "joy."

5. Key event / key person / key theme

Serve the Lord with gladness

6. Key thought

The title to this psalm states that it was used as a prayer of thanksgiving.

7. Key thing to look out for

Reasons for worshiping the Lord with gladness

8. Key Bible cross-reference

Verse 5. See Ezra 3:11; Jeremiah 33:11.

9. Key "by way of explanation"

Verse 1, "all the earth." Even though only God's people have a special relationship with the Lord, everyone on earth is summoned to worship God.

10. Key "Quotable Quote"

"For the LORD is good; his mercy is everlasting; and his truth endureth to all generations."
Psalm 100:5

Psalm 101

1. ### Before and after

   Previous psalm: Psalm 100: Serve the Lord with gladness
   Following psalm: Psalm 102: The prayer of an overwhelmed believer

2. ### Analysis of psalm

   David's vow and profession of godliness. (1-8)

3. ### Key verse

   Verse 2: "I will behave myself wisely in a perfect way."

4. ### Key word / key phrase

   Verse 2, "a blameless heart."

5. ### Key event / key person / key theme

   Commitment to a holy life

6. ### Key thought

   This psalm is cast in the form of a pledge in which the king promises to rule with justice.

7. ### Key thing to look out for

   The psalmist determines not to serve the Lord intermittently, but "every morning," verse 8.

8. ### Key Bible cross-reference

   Verse 2. See 1 Kings 3:7-9.

9. ### Key "by way of explanation"

   Verse 8. "Every morning," that is, in the daily courts of justice presided over by the king.

10. ### Key "Quotable Quote"

    "I will sing of mercy and judgment: unto thee, O Lord, will I sing."
    Psalm 101:1

Psalm 102

1. *Before and after*

   Previous psalm: Psalm 101: Commitment to a holy life
   Following psalm: Psalm 103: Bless the Lord, all you people!

2. *Analysis of psalm*

   A sorrowful complaint of great afflictions. (1-11)
   Future hope. (12-22)
   The unchangeableness of God. (23-28)

3. *Key verse*

   Verse 7: "I watch, and am as a sparrow alone upon the house top."

4. *Key word / key phrase*

   Verse 1, "my cry for help."

5. *Key event / key person / key theme*

   The prayer of an overwhelmed believer

6. *Key thought*

   This psalmist is in great distress. But it is second nature to him to turn to the Lord in prayer.

7. *Key thing to look out for*

   From the depths of his own situation the psalmist raises his eyes to see the Lord sitting on his throne and ruling the world.

8. *Key Bible cross-reference*

   Verses 25-27. See Hebrews 1:10-12.

9. *Key "by way of explanation"*

   Verse 14, "dear to your servants." God's people love Jerusalem. How much more does the Lord love his own city, and thus his people who worship him in it.

10. *Key "Quotable Quote"*

    "Hear my prayer, O LORD, and let my cry come unto thee."
    Psalm 102:1

Psalm 103

1. *Before and after*

Previous psalm: Psalm 102: The prayer of an overwhelmed believer
Following psalm: Psalm 104: A psalm remembering God's creation

2. *Analysis of psalm*

An exhortation to bless God for his mercy. (1-5)
And to the Church and to all men. (6-14)
For the constancy of his mercy. (15-18)
For the government of the world. (19-22)

3. *Key verse*

Verse 15: "As for man, his days are as grass."

4. *Key word / key phrase*

Verse 1, "Praise."

5. *Key event / key person / key theme*

Bless the Lord

6. *Key thought*

Among many other things, the psalmist thanks the Lord for the personal blessings he has received.

7. *Key thing to look out for*

The psalmists many reasons for praising the Lord.

8. *Key Bible cross-reference*

Verse 8. See James 5:11.

9. *Key "by way of explanation"*

Verses 1,2,22, "O my soul." This was a normal way to speak to oneself. See 116:7.

10. *Key "Quotable Quote"*

"Bless the LORD, O my soul: and all that is within me, bless his holy name." Psalm 103:1

Psalm 104

1. *Before and after*

Previous psalm: Psalm 103: Bless the Lord, all you people!
Following psalm: Psalm 105: Remember, God keeps his promises

2. *Analysis of psalm*

God's majesty in the heavens, and the creation of the sea, and the dry land. (1-9)
His provision for all creatures. (10-18)
The regular course of day and night, and God's sovereign power over all the creatures. (19-30)
A resolution to continue praising God. (31-35)

3. *Key verse*

Verse 2: "Who coverest thyself with light as with a garment."

4. *Key word / key phrase*

Verse 5, "sets the earth."

5. *Key event / key person / key theme*

God's creation

6. *Key thought*

The Lord God is the Creator and the psalmist therefore worships him.

7. *Key thing to look out for*

Many of the psalms follow a particular pattern. This one has stanzas grouped in the following sets of verses: three, five, nine, five, three.

8. *Key Bible cross-reference*

Verse 4. See Hebrews 1:7.

9. *Key "by way of explanation"*

Verses 1-4 picture the forces of nature being used in God's service. His robe is "light" in verse 2, and his "chariot" is the "clouds" in verse 3.

10. *Key "Quotable Quote"*

"The glory of the LORD shall endure for ever: the LORD shall rejoice in his works."
Psalm 104:31

Psalm 105

1. **Before and after**

   Previous psalm: Psalm 104: A psalm remembering God's creation
   Following psalm: Psalm 106: We have sinned

2. **Analysis of psalm**

   A solemn call to praise and serve the Lord. (1-7)
   His gracious dealings with Israel. (8-23)
   Their deliverance from Egypt, and their settlement in Canaan. (24-45)

3. **Key verse**

   Verse 5: "Remember his marvelous works that he hath done."

4. **Key word / key phrase**

   Verse 8, "he remembers."

5. **Key event / key person / key theme**

   Remember, God keeps his promises

6. **Key thought**

   The countless ways in which God acted on behalf of his people.

7. **Key thing to look out for**

   The plagues show that the Lord rules over the hearts of even evil men.

8. **Key Bible cross-reference**

   Verse 16. See Genesis 41:53-57.

9. **Key "by way of explanation"**

   Verse 5. "Remember." The Lord has remembered his people, and his people
   are duty bound to remember him.

10. **Key "Quotable Quote"**

    "He is the LORD our God: his judgments are in all the earth."
    Psalm 105:7

Psalm 106

1. Before and after

Previous psalm: Psalm 105: Remember, God keeps his promises
Following psalm: Psalm 107: God satisfies the longing soul

2. Analysis of psalm

The happiness of God's people. (1-5)
Israel's sins. (6-12)
Their provocations. (13-33)
Their rebellions in Canaan. (34-46)
Prayer for more complete deliverance. (47,48)

3. Key verse

Verse 7: "Our fathers understood not thy wonders in Egypt."

4. Key word / key phrase

Verse 6, "We have sinned."

5. Key event / key person / key theme

Confessing sin to God

6. Key thought

The psalmist recalls Israel's unfaithfulness, but nevertheless asks for the Lord's salvation.

7. Key thing to look out for

The psalmist counts on God's faithfulness, despite the unfaithfulness of his people.

8. Key Bible cross-reference

Verse 1. See 136:1; Jeremiah 33:11.

9. Key "by way of explanation"

Verse 31, "This was credited to him as righteousness." This phrase reminds us of Abram's faith in the Lord, Genesis 15:6. But in this verse it is applied to Phinehas' intervention as a result of which the plague was checked.

10. Key "Quotable Quote"

"Then believed they his words; they sang his praise."
Psalm 106:12

Psalm 107

1. Before and after

Previous psalm: Psalm 106: We have sinned

Following psalm: Psalm 109: A song of those who have been slandered

2. Analysis of psalm

God's providential care of the children of men in times of distress, in banishment, and dispersion. (1-9)

In captivity. (10-16)

In sickness. (17-22)

Danger at sea. 23-32)

God's power to be seen by his own people. (33-43)

3. Key verse

Verse 9: "For he satisfieth the longing soul, and filleth the hungry soul with goodness."

4. Key word / key phrase

Verse 9, "satisfies."

5. Key event / key person / key theme

God satisfies the longing soul

6. Key thought

The psalmist vocalizes his great need of the Lord and looks to him for deliverance.

7. Key thing to look out for

The psalmist does not skate over the times when the Lord disciplined his followers so that they would be more faithful to him.

8. Key Bible cross-reference

Verse 1. See 100:5; 106:1.

9. Key "by way of explanation"

Verse 10. "Darkness" and "gloom" portray the great distress God's people are going through. They are likened to prisoners who live with little hope.

10. Key "Quotable Quote"

"He maketh the storm a calm, so that the waves thereof are still."

Psalm 107:29

Psalm 109

(For Psalm 108: 1-5, see Psalm 57:7-11; Psalm 108: 6-13, see Psalm 60:5-12.)

1. Before and after

Previous psalm: Psalm 108: A prayer for help against enemies
Following psalm: Psalm 110: The coming of the Priest-King-Judge

2. Analysis of psalm

David complains about his enemies. (1-5)
He prophesies their destruction. (6-20)
Prayers and praises. (21-31)

3. Key verse

Verse 1: "Hold not thy peace, O God of my praise."

4. Key word / key phrase

Verse 4, "they accuse."

5. Key event / key person / key theme

A positive response to slander

6. Key thought

The psalmist is falsely accused. He asks for the Lord to vindicate him.

7. Key thing to look out for

The psalmist gives voice to the great afflictions he is enduring.

8. Key Bible cross-reference

Verse 8. See Acts 1:20.

9. Key "by way of explanation"

Verse 4. To be "a man of prayer" is to be a person who totally leans on God for help in life.

10. Key "Quotable Quote"

"I will greatly praise the LORD with my mouth; yea, I will praise him among the multitude."
Psalm 109:30

Psalm 110

1. Before and after

Previous psalm: Psalm 109: A song of those who have been slandered
Following psalm: Psalm 111: Praise for God's tender care

2. Analysis of psalm

Christ's kingdom. (1-7)

3. Key verse

Verse 2: "The LORD shall send the rod of thy strength out of Zion."

4. Key word / key phrase

Verse 4, "Melchizedek."

5. Key event / key person / key theme

The coming of the Priest-King-Judge

6. Key thought

This psalm was interpreted by Jesus and by New Testament writers as a reference to the coming Messiah.

7. Key thing to look out for

The psalmist portrays the Priest-King of this psalm as one who has great power to rule over the nations.

8. Key Bible cross-reference

Verse 4. See Hebrews 5:6; 6:20.

9. Key "by way of explanation"

Melchizedeh was a priest-king who had ruled over Jerusalem (Genesis 14: 18-20). David later conquered Jerusalem, so acquired the rights and position of Jebusite kingship, and was therefore, in title, a priest.

10. Key "Quotable Quote"

"The LORD hath sworn, and will not repent, Thou art a priest for ever after the order of Melchizedek."
Psalm 110:4

Psalm 111

1. **Before and after**

   Previous psalm: Psalm 110: The coming of the Priest-King-Judge
   Following psalm: Psalm 112: The blessings of those who fear God

2. **Analysis of psalm**

   The Lord is to be praised for his works. (1-10)

3. **Key verse**

   Verse 2: "The works of the LORD are great."

4. **Key word / key phrase**

   Verse 5, "He provides food."

5. **Key event / key person / key theme**

   Praise for God's tender care

6. **Key thought**

   This psalm starts with a note of praise and ends on the theme of wisdom.

7. **Key thing to look out for**

   God's great deeds performed for his people take center stage in this psalm.

8. **Key Bible cross-reference**

   Verse 10. See Job 28:28; Proverbs 1:7.

9. **Key "by way of explanation"**

   Verse 10. This statement about the fear of the Lord being the beginning of
   wisdom is the foundation of the Old Testament's teaching about wisdom.

10. **Key "Quotable Quote"**

    "They stand fast for ever and ever, and are done in truth and uprightness."
    Psalm 111:8

Psalm 112

1. Before and after

Previous psalm: Psalm 111: Praise for God's tender care
Following psalm: Psalm 113: God's wonderful grace

2. Analysis of psalm

The blessedness of the righteous. (1-10)

3. Key verse

Verse 7: "He shall not be afraid of evil tidings."

4. Key word / key phrase

Verse 1, "blessed."

5. Key event / key person / key theme

The blessings of those who fear God

6. Key thought

Even bad news need not crush the godly.

7. Key thing to look out for

A heart that is fixed on God need fear nothing and nobody.

8. Key Bible cross-reference

Verse 9. See 2 Corinthians 9:9.

9. Key "by way of explanation"

Verse 4, "darkness" often stands for troubles and serious problems in the Bible.

10. Key "Quotable Quote"

"Praise ye the LORD. Blessed is the man that feareth the LORD, that delighteth greatly in his commandments."
Psalm 112:1

Psalm 113

1. Before and after

Previous psalm: Psalm 112: The blessings of those who fear God
Following psalm: Psalm 114: Praise God for the Exodus

2. Analysis of psalm

An exhortation to praise God. (1-9)

3. Key verse

Verse 5: "Who is like unto the LORD our God, who dwelleth on high,"

4. Key word / key phrase

Verse 7, "raises the poor."

5. Key event / key person / key theme

God's wonderful grace

6. Key thought

The psalmist points out how merciful the Lord is, especially to those most in need.

7. Key thing to look out for

The Lord provides for people who have little or no hope.

8. Key Bible cross-reference

Verses 7,8. See 1 Samuel 2:8.

9. Key "by way of explanation"

This psalm, along with 114–118, was known as the "Egyptian Hallel." These psalms were used at the major Jewish festivals. At the Passover, Psalms 113–114 were said before the meal, and Psalms 115–118 after the meal.

10. Key "Quotable Quote"

"He maketh the barren woman to keep house, and to be a joyful mother of children. Praise ye the LORD."
Psalm 113:9

Psalm 114

1. *Before and after*

Previous psalm: Psalm 113: God's wonderful grace
Following psalm: Psalm 115: To God alone be the glory

2. *Analysis of psalm*

An exhortation to fear God. (1-8)

3. *Key verse*

Verse 3: "The sea saw it, and fled: Jordan was driven back."

4. *Key word / key phrase*

Verse 1, "Egypt."

5. *Key event / key person / key theme*

Praise God for the Exodus

6. *Key thought*

This psalm was written in order to remind the Israelites to give thanks to the Lord for the Exodus.

7. *Key thing to look out for*

The Exodus was the most important miracle in the history of God's people.

8. *Key Bible cross-reference*

Verse 3. See Exodus 14:21; Joshua 3:16.

9. *Key "by way of explanation"*

Verse 2. "Judah" and "Israel," the northern and southern countries respectively, are here thought of as one people: God's people.

10. *Key "Quotable Quote"*

"Judah was his sanctuary, and Israel his dominion."
Psalm 114:2

Psalm 115

1. **Before and after**

   Previous psalm: Psalm 114: Praise God for the Exodus
   Following psalm: Psalm 116: Remember all that God has done

2. **Analysis of psalm**

   Glory to be ascribed to God. (1-8)
   By trusting in him and praising him. (9-18)

3. **Key verse**

   Verse 1: "Not unto us, O LORD, not unto us, but unto thy name give glory."

4. **Key word / key phrase**

   Verse 1, "glory."

5. **Key event / key person / key theme**

   To God alone be the glory

6. **Key thought**

   Whenever the psalmist remembers the Lord's faithfulness he breaks into praise.

7. **Key thing to look out for**

   The idea that idols possess power is quite false. No glory should ever be given to them.

8. **Key Bible cross-reference**

   Verses 4-8. See 135:15-18; Revelation 9:20.

9. **Key "by way of explanation"**

   Verse 1, "Not to us . . . not to us." Israel is quite sure that they do not deserve any credit for their own existence and that everything is due to God's grace. Therefore, to him alone glory must be given.

10. **Key "Quotable Quote"**

    "O Israel, trust thou in the LORD: he is their help and their shield."
    Psalm 115:9

Psalm 116

1. **Before and after**

   Previous psalm: Psalm 115: To God alone be the glory
   Following chapter: Psalm 117: The praise of God's people

2. **Analysis of psalm**

   The psalmist declares his love to the Lord. (1-9)
   His desire to be thankful. (10-19)

3. **Key verse**

   Verse 5: "Gracious is the LORD, and righteous; yea, our God is merciful."

4. **Key word / key phrase**

   Verse 17, "thank-offering."

5. **Key event / key person / key theme**

   Remember all that God has done

6. **Key thought**

   Verses 2,13,17. The psalmist will always call on the Lord in prayer.

7. **Key thing to look out for**

   The psalmist rejoices because he knows that the Lord listens to him and saves him.

8. **Key Bible cross-reference**

   Verse 10. See 2 Corinthians 4:13.

9. **Key "by way of explanation"**

   Verse 15, "precious." None of God's followers die, without the Lord knowing about this and being concerned about it.

10. **Key "Quotable Quote"**

    "I will take the cup of salvation, and call upon the name of the LORD."
    Psalm 116:13

Psalm 117

1. *Before and after*

Previous psalm: Psalm 116: Remember all that God has done
Following psalm: Psalm 118: It is better to trust God than any human being

2. *Analysis of psalm*

All people called upon to praise God. (1-2)

3. *Key verse*

Verse 1: "O praise the LORD, all ye nations: praise him, all ye people."

4. *Key word / key phrase*

Verse 1, "praise."

5. *Key event / key person / key theme*

The praise of God's people

6. *Key thought*

The shortest psalm, and shortest chapter in the Bible, is like an extended Hallelujah.

7. *Key thing to look out for*

This psalm explains that the reason for praising the Lord lies in his lov" and faithfulness.

8. *Key Bible cross-reference*

Verse 1. See Amos 9:11,12; Micah 5:7-9.

9. *Key "by way of explanation"*

Verse 1 shows that it was always the Lord's intention that non-Jews should be saved. This verse is quoted to this effect in Romans 15:11.

10. *Key "Quotable Quote"*

"For his merciful kindness is great toward us: and the truth of the LORD endureth for ever. Praise ye the LORD."
Psalm 117:2

Psalm 118

1. ### Before and after
   Previous psalm: Psalm 117: The praise of God's people
   Following psalm: Psalm 119: An acrostic psalm in praise of the Scriptures

2. ### Analysis of psalm
   It is good to trust in the Lord. (1-18)
   The coming of Christ in his kingdom. (19-29)

3. ### Key verse
   Verse 8: "It is better to trust in the LORD than to put confidence in man."

4. ### Key word / key phrase
   Verse 8, "refuge."

5. ### Key event / key person / key theme
   It is better to trust God than any human being

6. ### Key thought
   The psalmist starts with praising the Lord and then moves on to remembering how oppressed he has been.

7. ### Key thing to look out for
   The psalmist's many reasons for thanking the Lord.

8. ### Key Bible cross-reference
   Verse 6. See Hebrews 13:6.

9. ### Key "by way of explanation"
   Verse 18, "chastened me." The Old Testament teaches that the Lord disciplines his people for their good. Here the psalmist acknowledges that his afflictions were the Lord's severe affliction of him.

10. ### Key "Quotable Quote"
    "O give thanks unto the LORD; for he is good: because his mercy endureth for ever."
    Psalm 118:1

Psalm 119

1. Before and after

Previous psalm: Psalm 118: It is better to trust God than any human
Following psalm: Psalm 120: A cry from the depths of distress

2. Analysis of psalm

The psalm consists of twenty-two stanzas, each having eight verses. Each stanza starts with the following letter of the Hebrew Bible. This psalm is an elaborate acrostic. It has twenty-two eight-line stanzas, corresponding to the twenty-two letters of the Hebrew alphabet. Then in each stanzas, every line starts with the letter at the beginning of its stanza.

3. Key verse

Verse 105: "Thy word is a lamp unto my feet, and a light unto my path."

4. Key word / key phrase

Verse 2, "statutes."

5. Key event / key person / key theme

An acrostic psalm in praise of the Scriptures

6. Key thought

The general scope and design of this psalm is to magnify the divine law, and make it honorable.

7. Key thing to look out for

The centrality of the word of God.

8. Key Bible cross-reference

Verse 3. See Genesis 17:1.

9. Key "by way of explanation"

The psalmist uses eight synonyms for God's law, each with a slight variation of meaning. In some stanzas he includes all eight synonyms, and he never has fewer than six.

10. Key "Quotable Quote"

"The law is no do-it-yourself manual which God has handed over to man. It is the written part of a life-long teach-in. With it comes the assurance of his living presence."
Leslie C. Allen

Psalm 120

1. Before and after

Previous psalm: Psalm 119: An acrostic psalm in praise of the Scriptures

Following psalm: Psalm 121: God is our Protector

2. Analysis of psalm

The psalmist prays to God to deliver him from false and malicious tongues. (1-4)

He complains about wicked neighbors. (5-7)

3. Key verse

Verse 1: "In my distress I cried unto the LORD, and he heard me."

4. Key word / key phrase

Verse 1, "in my distress."

5. Key event / key person / key theme

A cry from the depths of distress

6. Key thought

The psalmist has been falsely accused and he asks the Lord to deliver him from his accusers.

7. Key thing to look out for

Verse 4, "sharp arrows." The tongue is said to be a weapon used against the psalmist as he had to cope with endless insults.

8. Key Bible cross-reference

Verse 3. See 1 Samuel 3:17.

9. Key "by way of explanation"

Psalm 120 begins a group of fifteen psalms each called "a song of ascents." The word probably refers to a pilgrimage up to the temple in Jerusalem and the psalm would have been sung by pilgrims traveling to the temple. They were not all, however, written as pilgrim songs. Some, like Psalm 120, had a different original purpose.

10. Key "Quotable Quote"

"Deliver my soul, O LORD, from lying lips, and from a deceitful tongue." Psalm 120:2

Psalm 121

1. *Before and after*

Previous psalm: Psalm 120: A cry from the depths of distress
Following psalm: Psalm 122: Pray for the peace of Jerusalem

2. *Analysis of psalm*

The safety of the godly. (1-8)

3. *Key verse*

Verse 1: "I will lift up mine eyes unto the hills, from whence cometh my help."

4. *Key word / key phrase*

Verse 1, "my help."

5. *Key event / key person / key theme*

God is our Protector

6. *Key thought*

The psalmist answers his own opening rhetorical question by expressing his trust in the Lord.

7. *Key thing to look out for*

The psalmist expresses his certainty of the Lord's protection.

8. *Key Bible cross-reference*

Verse 3. See 1 Kings 18:27.

9. *Key "by way of explanation"*

Verse 1, "hills." Jerusalem is surrounded by hills, and is itself set on a hill.

10. *Key "Quotable Quote"*

"Behold, he that keepeth Israel shall neither slumber nor sleep."
Psalm 121:4

Psalm 122

1. ### Before and after

   Previous psalm: Psalm 121: God is our Protector
   Following psalm: Psalm 123: A plea for God's mercy

2. ### Analysis of psalm

   Esteem for Jerusalem. (1-5)
   Concern for its welfare. (6-9)

3. ### Key verse

   Verse 2: "Our feet shall stand within thy gates, O Jerusalem."

4. ### Key word / key phrase

   Verse 6, "the peace of Jerusalem."

5. ### Key event / key person / key theme

   Pray for the peace of Jerusalem

6. ### Key thought

   The pilgrim's joy as he enters Jerusalem.

7. ### Key thing to look out for

   For God's people Jerusalem was the most significant city in all the world.

8. ### Key Bible cross-reference

   Verse 1. See 2 Samuel 7:5.

9. ### Key "by way of explanation"

   Verse 6, "peace." When the psalmist prayed for the peace of Jerusalem, in addition to peace as the absence of war, he would have been praying for the spiritual prosperity of the city.

10. ### Key "Quotable Quote"

    "Pray for the peace of Jerusalem: they shall prosper that love thee."
    Psalm 122:6

Psalm 123

1. Before and after

Previous psalm: Psalm 122: Pray for the peace of Jerusalem
Following psalm: Psalm 124: God is on our side

2. Analysis of psalm

Trust in God, in spite of ridicule and contempt from the oppressor. (1-4)

3. Key verse

Verse 1: "Unto thee lift I up mine eyes, O thou that dwellest in the heavens."

4. Key word / key phrase

Verse 3, "Have mercy on us."

5. Key event / key person / key theme

A plea for God's mercy

6. Key thought

The Lord's throne is both in Jerusalem and in heaven.

7. Key thing to look out for

Kyrie eleison, long-prayed by the Church.

8. Key Bible cross-reference

Verse 1. See 122:5; 132:14.

9. Key "by way of explanation"

Verse 2, "slaves" and "a maid" stand for a powerful image of God's servants who look to their Master in everything.

10. Key "Quotable Quote"

"Behold, as the eyes of servants look unto the hand of their masters, and as the eyes of a maiden unto the hand of her mistress; so our eyes wait upon the LORD our God, until that he have mercy upon us."
Psalm 123:2

Psalm 124

1. ## *Before and after*

   Previous psalm: Psalm 123: A plea for God's mercy
   Following psalm: Psalm 125: Trust in the Lord

2. ## *Analysis of psalm*

   The deliverance of the Church. (1-5)
   Thankfulness for the deliverance. (6-8)

3. ## *Key verse*

   Verse 5: "Then the proud waters had gone over our soul."

4. ## *Key word / key phrase*

   Verse 2, "on our side."

5. ## *Key event / key person / key theme*

   God is on our side

6. ## *Key thought*

   Had it not been for the Lord, Israel would have ceased to exist.

7. ## *Key thing to look out for*

   The psalmist feels that the Lord's people only escaped by the skin of their
   teeth.

8. ## *Key Bible cross-reference*

   Verse 2. See 123:4.

9. ## *Key "by way of explanation"*

   Verses 4,5. The psalmist feels overwhelmed by his attackers, as if they were a
   "flood," a "torrent" and "raging waters".

10. ## *Key "Quotable Quote"*

   "Our help is in the name of the LORD, who made heaven and earth."
   Psalm 124:8

Psalm 125

1. Before and after

Previous psalm: Psalm 124: God is on our side
Following psalm: Psalm 126: Sow in tears, reap in joy

2. Analysis of psalm

The security of the righteous. (1-3)
Prayer for them, and the ruin of the wicked. (4,5)

3. Key verse

Verse 1: "They that trust in the LORD shall be as mount Zion."

4. Key word / key phrase

Verse 1, "trust."

5. Key event / key person / key theme

Trust in the Lord

6. Key thought

There is a constant battle between the godly and the ungodly.

7. Key thing to look out for

The Lord's people are described in a variety of ways throughout this psalm.

8. Key Bible cross-reference

Verse 5. See Numbers 6:24-26.

9. Key "by way of explanation"

Verse 2, "surrounds his people." Just as Jerusalem is immovable as she is set in a mountainous area so the Lord will make his people immoveable.

10. Key "Quotable Quote"

"As the mountains are round about Jerusalem, so the LORD is round about his people from henceforth even for ever."
Psalm 125:2

Psalm 126

1. *Before and after*

Previous psalm: Psalm 125: Trust in the Lord
Following psalm: Psalm 127: Children are God's gift

2. *Analysis of psalm*

Those returned out of captivity are to be thankful. (1-3)
Those still in captivity are encouraged. (4-6)

3. *Key verse*

Verse 5: "They that sow in tears shall reap in joy."

4. *Key word / key phrase*

Verse 6, "Goes out weeping."

5. *Key event / key person / key theme*

Sow in tears, reap in joy

6. *Key thought*

Out of sorry God brings great joy.

7. *Key thing to look out for*

The good that comes out of suffering.

8. *Key Bible cross-reference*

Verses 5,6. See 20:5.

9. *Key "by way of explanation"*

Verse 1, "brought back." This psalm exactly fits the circumstances of God's
people returning to Jerusalem after their exile.

10. *Key "Quotable Quote"*

"The LORD hath done great things for us; whereof we are glad."
Psalm 126:3

Psalm 127

1. ## Before and after

    Previous psalm: Psalm 126: Sow in tears, reap in joy
    Following psalm: Psalm 128: May God's blessing rest on the God-fearing

2. ## Analysis of psalm

    The value of the divine blessing. (1-5)

3. ## Key verse

    Verse 3: "Lo, children are an heritage of the LORD."

4. ## Key word / key phrase

    Verse 3, "children."

5. ## Key event / key person / key theme

    Children are God's gift

6. ## Key thought

    Children are to be greatly valued.

7. ## Key thing to look out for

    Children should be considered as a sign of God's love.

8. ## Key Bible cross-reference

    Verse 2. See Matthew 6:25-34; 1 Peter 5:7.

9. ## Key "by way of explanation"

    Verse 2, "grants sleep." The psalmist teaches that a good harvest is not to be
    seen as just the result of hard work, but the result of God's blessing.

10. ## Key "Quotable Quote"

    "Among the Psalmist's music deep,
    Now tell me if that any is,
    For gift of grace, surpassing this:
    'He giveth his beloved – sleep.'"
    Elizabeth Barrett Browning

Psalm 128

1. *Before and after*

> Previous psalm: Psalm 127: Children are God's gift
> Following psalm: Psalm 129: A cry of the persecuted

2. *Analysis of psalm*

> The blessings of those who fear God. (1-6)

3. *Key verse*

> Verse 6: "Yea, thou shalt see thy children's children, and peace upon Israel."

4. *Key word / key phrase*

> Verse 2, "blessings and prosperity."

5. *Key event / key person / key theme*

> May God's blessing rest on the God-fearing

6. *Key thought*

> Verses 1,4. The secret of blessing.

7. *Key thing to look out for*

> God's blessing is meant to flow from one generation to the next generation.

8. *Key Bible cross-reference*

> Verse 6. See 125:5.

9. *Key "by way of explanation"*

> Verse 3, "vine." A vine was taken to be a symbol of fruitfulness in the Old
> Testament. See Genesis 49:22.

10. *Key "Quotable Quote"*

> "Blessed is every one that feareth the LORD; that walketh in his ways."
> Psalm 128:1

Psalm 129

1. **Before and after**

   Previous psalm: Psalm 128: May God's blessing rest on the God-fearing
   Following psalm: Psalm 130: My soul waits for the Lord

2. **Analysis of psalm**

   Thankfulness for former deliverances. (1-4)
   A believing prospect of the destruction of the enemies of Zion. (5-8)

3. **Key verse**

   Verse 5: "Let them all be confounded and turned back that hate Zion."

4. **Key word / key phrase**

   Verse 2, "greatly oppressed."

5. **Key event / key person / key theme**

   A cry of the persecuted

6. **Key thought**

   The psalmist was all too familiar with persecution. See verse 3.

7. **Key thing to look out for**

   Those who opposed God's people would be opposed by God.

8. **Key Bible cross-reference**

   Verse 8. See Ruth 2:4.

9. **Key "by way of explanation"**

   Verse 6, "like grass on the roof." This refers to one -tory houses with flat roofs
   on which grass might just manage to grow, but as it has no depth of soil to
   sustain it quickly withers.

10. **Key "Quotable Quote"**

    "Many a time have they afflicted me from my youth: yet they have not
    prevailed against me."
    Psalm 129:2

Psalm 130

1. *Before and after*

Previous psalm: Psalm 129: A cry of the persecuted
Following psalm: Psalm 131: A childlike faith

2. *Analysis of psalm*

The psalmist's hope in prayer. (1-4)
His patience in hope. (5-8)

3. *Key verse*

Verse 1: "Out of the depths have I cried unto thee, O Lord."

4. *Key word / key phrase*

Verse 5, "wait."

5. *Key event / key person / key theme*

My soul waits for the Lord

6. *Key thought*

The psalmist gives a personal testimony to his trust in the Lord.

7. *Key thing to look out for*

The psalmist tells Israel to put their hope for complete redemption in the Lord.

8. *Key Bible cross-reference*

Verse 8. See Matthew 1:21; Titus 2:14.

9. *Key "by way of explanation"*

Verse 4, "feared." Appropriate synonyms for the word "feared" in this context would be "served," or "worshiped" or "trusted."

10. *Key "Quotable Quote"*

"I wait for the Lord, my soul doth wait, and in his word do I hope."
Psalm 130:5

Psalm 131

1. ## Before and after

   Previous psalm: Psalm 130: My soul waits for the Lord
   Following psalm: Psalm 132: Trust in the God of David

2. ## Analysis of psalm

   The psalmist's humility. Believers encouraged to trust in God. (1-3)

3. ## Key verse

   Verse 3: "Let Israel hope in the LORD from henceforth and for ever."

4. ## Key word / key phrase

   Verse 2, "Like a weaned child."

5. ## Key event / key person / key theme

   A childlike faith

6. ## Key thought

   The psalmist knew that the one thing the Lord could not abide was a proud
   heart.

7. ## Key thing to look out for

   Israel is encouraged to keep on placing its hope in the Lord, rather than just
   doing so now and again.

8. ## Key Bible cross-reference

   Verse 1. See 2 Samuel 6:21,22.

9. ## Key "by way of explanation"

   Verse 2, "a weaned child" could be a child as old as four or five years old. For
   in those days children were not weaned as babies, but as toddlers of a few
   years old.

10. ## Key "Quotable Quote"

    "Surely I have behaved and quieted myself, as a child that is weaned of his
    mother: my soul is even as a weaned child."
    Psalm 131:2

Psalm 132

1. *Before and after*

    Previous psalm: Psalm 131: A childlike faith
    Following psalm: Psalm 133: The beauty unity among God's people

2. *Analysis of psalm*

    David's care for the ark. (1-10)
    The promises of God. (11-18)

3. *Key verse*

    Verse 1: "LORD, remember David, and all his afflictions."

4. *Key word / key phrase*

    Verse 1, "David."

5. *Key event / key person / key theme*

    Trust in the God of David

6. *Key thought*

    The psalmist asks the Lord to treat him mercifully, just as he did David.

7. *Key thing to look out for*

    The psalmist is constantly expressing his desire to worship the Lord.

8. *Key Bible cross-reference*

    Verse 17. See 1 Kings 11:36.

9. *Key "by way of explanation"*

    Verse 12, "statutes." These refer back to the laws which the Lord gave Moses on Mount Sinai.

10. *Key "Quotable Quote"*

    "I find that the psalms are like a mirror, in which one can see oneself and the movements of one's own heart."
    Athanasius

Psalm 133

1. **Before and after**

    Previous psalm: Psalm 132: Trust in the God of David
    Following psalm: Psalm 134: Praise the Lord in the evening

2. **Analysis of psalm**

    The excellency of brotherly love. (1-3)

3. **Key verse**

    Verse 1: "Behold, how good and how pleasant it is for brethren to dwell together in unity!"

4. **Key word / key phrase**

    Verse 1, "live together."

5. **Key event / key person / key theme**

    Unity

6. **Key thought**

    God blesses his people when they are united.

7. **Key thing to look out for**

    What is conveyed by the two similies?

8. **Key Bible cross-reference**

    Verse 2. See 89:20; Zechariah 4:14.

9. **Key "by way of explanation"**

    Verse 3, "dew." "Dew" symbolizes the Lord's blessing on his people.

10. **Key "Quotable Quote"**

    "I'll make David sing like a Christian."
    Isaac Watts

Psalm 134

1. **Before and after**

   Previous psalm: Psalm 133: The beauty of unity among God's people
   Following psalm: Psalm 135: God has done great things

2. **Analysis of psalm**

   An exhortation to bless the Lord. (1-3)

3. **Key verse**

   Verse 2: "Lift up your hands in the sanctuary, and bless the LORD."

4. **Key word / key phrase**

   Verse 1, "Praise the Lord."

5. **Key event / key person / key theme**

   A call to praise the Lord

6. **Key thought**

   There are no exceptions made among God's people about worshiping the Lord.

7. **Key thing to look out for**

   The psalms are full of short blessings, like the one in verse three of this psalm.

8. **Key Bible cross-reference**

   Verse 3. See 124:8; 135:6.

9. **Key "by way of explanation"**

   Verse 1, "night." Services were held in the night during the Feast of Tabernacles.

10. **Key "Quotable Quote"**

    "The psalms were written as songs and should be read in the spirit of lyric poetry rather than as doctrinal treatises or sermons."
    C.S. Lewis

Psalm 135

1. *Before and after*

   Previous psalm: Psalm 134: Praise the Lord in the evening
   Following psalm: Psalm 136: God's mercy endures forever

2. *Analysis of psalm*

   God to be praised for his mercy. (1-4)
   For his power and judgments. (5-14)
   The vanity of idols. (15-21)

3. *Key verse*

   Verse 8: "Who smote the firstborn of Egypt, both of man and beast."

4. *Key word / key phrase*

   Verse 13, "your renown."

5. *Key event / key person / key theme*

   God has done great things

6. *Key thought*

   The psalmist gives very important reasons for worshiping the Lord.

7. *Key thing to look out for*

   Three good reasons to worship the Lord are because the Lord rules over the
   world of nature, and over the nations, and because he is Israel's Redeemer.

8. *Key Bible cross-reference*

   Verses 15-18. See Psalm 115:4-8; Revelation 9:20.

9. *Key "by way of explanation"*

   Verses 15-18. The powerlessness of the false gods is constantly being exposed
   by the writers of the Old Testament.

10. *Key "Quotable Quote"*

    "The psalms are the anatomy of all the parts of the soul."
    John Calvin

Psalm 136

1. Before and after

Previous psalm: Psalm 135: God has done great things
Following psalm: Psalm 137: Tears in exile

2. Analysis of psalm

God to be praised as the Creator of the world. (1-9)
As Israel's God and Savior. (10-22)
For his blessings to all. (23-26)

3. Key verse

Verse 1: "O give thanks unto the LORD; for he is good."

4. Key word / key phrase

Verse 1, "endures."

5. Key event / key person / key theme

God's mercy endures forever

6. Key thought

The psalmist praises the Lord for the critical moments in Israel's history.

7. Key thing to look out for

This psalm shows how the Lord is Creator, Deliverer, Conqueror and Provider.

8. Key Bible cross-reference

Verse 20. See Numbers 21:31-35.

9. Key "by way of explanation"

This psalm is written so worshipers could join in with an easily memorized refrain.

10. Key "Quotable Quote"

"No part of the Old Testament is more frequently quoted or referred to in the New as the psalms."
Matthew Henry

Psalm 137

1. **Before and after**

   Previous psalm: Psalm 136: God's mercy endures forever
   Following psalm: Psalm 138: God answered my prayer

2. **Analysis of psalm**

   The Jews bewail their captivity. (1-4)
   Their affection for Jerusalem. (5-9)

3. **Key verse**

   Verse 4: "How shall we sing the LORD's song in a strange land?"

4. **Key word / key phrase**

   Verse 1, "wept."

5. **Key event / key person / key theme**

   Tears in exile

6. **Key thought**

   This psalm reflects the sad times of God's people in exile, where they were cut of from their city and their temple, and so, some thought, from their God.

7. **Key thing to look out for**

   The Israelites were in no mood to play their harps and sing happy songs.

8. **Key Bible cross-reference**

   Verse 8. See Revelation 18:6.

9. **Key "by way of explanation"**

   Verse 1. The "rivers" here refer to the River Tigris and the River Euphrates, and their many tributaries.

10. **Key "Quotable Quote"**

    "The most valuable thing the Psalms do for me is to express that same delight in God which made David dance."
    C.S. Lewis

Psalm 138

1. **Before and after**

   Previous psalm: Psalm 137: Tears in exile
   Following psalm: Psalm 139: Search me, O God

2. **Analysis of psalm**

   The psalmist praises God for answering prayer. (1-5)
   The Lord's dealing with the humble and the proud. (6-8)

3. **Key verse**

   Verse 7: "Though I walk in the midst of trouble, thou wilt revive me."

4. **Key word / key phrase**

   Verse 3, "answered."

5. **Key event / key person / key theme**

   God answered my prayer

6. **Key thought**

   Answered prayer is a great spur to keep on praying.

7. **Key thing to look out for**

   It is clear from this psalm why the Lord looks on some people with favor and
   looks on other people with disdain.

8. **Key Bible cross-reference**

   Verse 7. See 124:3; 145:8.

9. **Key "by way of explanation"**

   Verse 2, "your word." This especially refers to the promises of the Lord that, as
   his followers discovered, were always kept.

10. **Key "Quotable Quote"**

    "In the day when I cried thou answeredst me, and strengthenedst me with
    strength in my soul."
    Psalm 138:3

Psalm 139

1. Before and after

Previous psalm: Psalm 138: God answered my prayer
Following psalm: Psalm 140: Protect me from violent people

2. Analysis of psalm

God knows all things. (1-6)
He is everywhere. (7-16)
The psalmist's hatred of sin, and desire to be led by God. (17-24)

3. Key verse

Verse 7: "Whither shall I go from thy spirit? or whither shall I flee from thy presence?"

4. Key word / key phrase

Verse 1, "searched."

5. Key event / key person / key theme

Search me, O God

6. Key thought

The psalmist shows his loyalty to the Lord. He is even prepared to be examined by the Lord.

7. Key thing to look out for

There is nowhere that a godly person can go to hide from the Lord's Spirit.

8. Key Bible cross-reference

Verse 8. See 63:9; 143:7.

9. Key "by way of explanation"

Verse 6, "too wonderful." The Lord's knowledge is "too wonderful" in the sense that humans are not able to fully appreciate and understand it.

10. Key "Quotable Quote"

"Psalms: a 'Little Bible' since it contains, set out in the briefest and most beautiful form, all that is to be found in the whole Bible."
Martin Luther

Psalm 140

1. **Before and after**

   Previous psalm: Psalm 139: Search me, O God
   Following psalm: Psalm 141: Set a guard, O Lord, over my mouth

2. **Analysis of psalm**

   David encourages himself in God. (1-7)
   He prays for, and prophesies the destruction of, his persecutors. (8-13)

3. **Key verse**

   Verse 1: "Deliver me, O LORD, from the evil man."

4. **Key word / key phrase**

   Verse 1, "men of violence."

5. **Key event / key person / key theme**

   Protect me from violent people

6. **Key thought**

   Evil men with cruel plots surrounded the psalmist. He pleads for the Lord to
   rescue him.

7. **Key thing to look out for**

   The poor and the needy are never far from the Lord's care.

8. **Key Bible cross-reference**

   Verse 3. See Romans 13:3.

9. **Key "by way of explanation"**

   Verse 13, "will love before you." This promise, given to the righteous, stands in
   stark contrast to the destiny of the wicked.

10. **Key "Quotable Quote"**

    "Surely the righteous shall give thanks unto thy name: the upright shall dwell
    in thy presence."
    Psalm 140:13

Psalm 141

1. Before and after

Previous psalm: Psalm 140: Protect me from violent people
Following psalm: Psalm 142: A prayer for help

2. Analysis of psalm

David prays for God's acceptance and assistance. (1-4)
That God would appear for his rescue. (5-10)

3. Key verse

Verse 3: "Set a watch, O Lord, before my mouth; keep the door of my lips."

4. Key word / key phrase

Verse 3, "my lips."

5. Key event / key person / key theme

Deliverance from evil – within the self, and from outside.

6. Key thought

The psalmist prays that he will never join the ranks of the wicked.

7. Key thing to look out for

The psalmist makes striking contrasts between the wicked and the righteous.

8. Key Bible cross-reference

Verse 2. See Revelation 5:8.

9. Key "by way of explanation"

Verse 4, "their delicacies." The tables of the wealthy were strewn with ill-
gotten gains from the poor and oppressed. The psalmist asks to be delivered
from even desiring such things.

10. Key "Quotable Quote"

"But mine eyes are unto thee, O God the Lord: in thee is my trust; leave not
my soul destitute."
Psalm 141:8

Psalm 142

1. ## Before and after

    Previous psalm: Psalm 141: Set a guard, O Lord, over my mouth
    Following psalm: Psalm 143: Teach me to do your will

2. ## Analysis of psalm

    David's comfort in prayer. (1-7)

3. ## Key verse

    Verse 7: "Bring my soul out of prison."

4. ## Key word / key phrase

    Verse 5, "my portion."

5. ## Key event / key person / key theme

    A prayer for help

6. ## Key thought

    In the grip of powerful enemies, the psalmist appeals for the Lord to rescue him with his greater power.

7. ## Key thing to look out for

    When the psalmist was in real need he made a point of bringing that before the Lord in prayer.

8. ## Key Bible cross-reference

    Title. See 1 Samuel 22:1; 24:3.

9. ## Key "by way of explanation"

    Verse 7, "prison." The word "prison" is often used in a metaphorical way to indicate being caught up and fettered by some kind of suffering.

10. ## Key "Quotable Quote"

    "I cried unto the LORD with my voice; with my voice unto the LORD did I make my supplication."
    Psalm 142:1

Psalm 143

1. **Before and after**

     Previous psalm: Psalm 142: A prayer for help
     Following psalm: Psalm 144: What is man?

2. **Analysis of psalm**

     An appeal for help based on Gold's covenant love. (1-6)
     He prays for comfort, guidance, and deliverance. (7-12)

3. **Key verse**

     Verse 1: "Hear my prayer, O LORD, give ear to my supplications."

4. **Key word / key phrase**

     Verse 1, "my cry."

5. **Key event / key person / key theme**

     The psalmist calls on God's grace in his desperate situation.

6. **Key thought**

     Weakness is not a sin. Rather it is something to pray about.

7. **Key thing to look out for**

     The psalmist is desperate and asks for immediate help.

8. **Key Bible cross-reference**

     Verse 2. See Romans 3:20; Galatians 2:16.

9. **Key "by way of explanation"**

     Verse 6, "spread out my hands." This was one of the ways in which people
     prayed. See 44:20; Exodus 9:29.

10. **Key "Quotable Quote"**

     "And enter not into judgment with thy servant: for in thy sight shall no man
     living be justified."
     Psalm 143:2

Psalm 144

1. **Before and after**

    Previous psalm: Psalm 143: Teach me to do your will
    Following psalm: Psalm 145: Speak of God's great deeds

2. **Analysis of psalm**

    David acknowledges the great goodness of God, and prays for help. (1-8)
    He prays for the prosperity of his kingdom. (9-15)

3. **Key verse**

    Verse 4: "Man is like to vanity: his days are as a shadow that passeth away."

4. **Key word / key phrase**

    Verse 4, "What is man?"

5. **Key event / key person / key theme**

    Victory comes from God

6. **Key thought**

    In the face of foreign aggression, the psalmist calls on the Lord.

7. **Key thing to look out for**

    The Israelites believed that the Lord gave them victory on the battlefield and
    in all other kinds of conflict.

8. **Key Bible cross-reference**

    Verse 3. See Job 7:17,18.

9. **Key "by way of explanation"**

    Verse 12, "daughters . . . like pillars carved." On the Acropolis in Athens, as in
    other temples, it was not very unusual to find columns carved in the shape of
    women.

10. **Key "Quotable Quote"**

    "I will sing a new song unto thee, O God: upon a psaltery and an instrument
    of ten strings will I sing praises unto thee."
    Psalm 144:9

Psalm 145

1. ### Before and after

   Previous psalm: Psalm 144: What is man?
   Following psalm: Psalm 146: Do not place your trust in princes

2. ### Analysis of psalm

   David extols the power, goodness, and mercy of the Lord. (1-9)
   The glory of God's kingdom, and his care of those that love him. (10-21)

3. ### Key verse

   Verse 10: "All thy works shall praise thee, O Lord; and thy saints shall bless
   thee."

4. ### Key word / key phrase

   Verse 4, "mighty acts."

5. ### Key event / key person / key theme

   God's kingship

6. ### Key thought

   Praise

7. ### Key thing to look out for

   God's followers are meant to speak up about God's goodness and greatness.

8. ### Key Bible cross-reference

   Verse 11. See 144:7; Proverbs 6:3.

9. ### Key "by way of explanation"

   Verse 4, "your works." In the psalms the Lord's "works" or "deeds," usually
   refer to creation, the Exodus, and the conquest of the promised land.

10. ### Key "Quotable Quote"

    "I will extol thee, my God, O king; and I will bless thy name for ever and ever."
    Psalm 145:1

Psalm 146

1. Before and after

Previous psalm: Psalm 145: Speak of God's great deeds
Following psalm: Psalm 147: God heals the broken-hearted

2. Analysis of psalm

Why we should not trust in men. (1-4)
Why we should trust in God. (5-10)

3. Key verse

Verse 5: "Happy is he that hath the God of Jacob for his help."

4. Key word / key phrase

Verse 3, "mortal men."

5. Key event / key person / key theme

Do not place your trust in princes.

6. Key thought

Psalm 146 is the first of five psalms of praise which close the whole book of Psalms.

7. Key thing to look out for

The Lord acts out of love.

8. Key Bible cross-reference

Verse 6. See Acts 4:24; 14:15.

9. Key "by way of explanation"

Verse 6, "Maker of heaven and earth." By referring to the Lord as "Maker of heaven and earth" the psalmist is calling attention to the mighty power and infinite goodness of the Lord God Almighty.

10. Key "Quotable Quote"

"The LORD shall reign for ever, even thy God, O Zion, unto all generations. Praise ye the LORD."
Psalm 146:10

Psalm 147

1. **Before and after**

   Previous psalm: Psalm 146: Do not place your trust in princes
   Following psalm: Psalm 148: All creation praises the Lord

2. **Analysis of psalm**

   The people of God are exhorted to praise him for his mercies and care. (1-11)
   For the salvation and prosperity that he gives. (12-20)

3. **Key verse**

   Verse 9: "He giveth to the beast his food, and to the young ravens which cry."

4. **Key word / key phrase**

   Verse 3, "binds up their wounds."

5. **Key event / key person / key theme**

   God heals the broken-hearted.

6. **Key thought**

   The Lord is Lord of all of creation, but he also had a unique relationship with
   his people, the Israelites.

7. **Key thing to look out for**

   Peace and prosperity come from the hand of the Lord.

8. **Key Bible cross-reference**

   Verse 5. See 136:5; Proverbs 1:2.

9. **Key "by way of explanation"**

   Verse 3, "broken-hearted." There could be no greater example of the "broken-
   hearted" than the Lord's people in exile from their beloved Jerusalem.

10. **Key "Quotable Quote"**

    "Great is our Lord, and of great power: his understanding is infinite."
    Psalm 147:5

Psalm 148

1. *Before and after*

   Previous psalm: Psalm 147: God heals the broken-hearted
   Following psalm: Psalm 149: The Lord takes pleasure in his people

2. *Analysis of psalm*

   Praise from the heavens. (1-6)
   Praise from the earth.. (7-14)

3. *Key verse*

   Verse 2: "Praise ye him, all his angels: praise ye him, all his hosts."

4. *Key word / key phrase*

   Verse 2, "all his heavenly hosts."

5. *Key event / key person / key theme*

   All creation praises the Lord.

6. *Key thought*

   The whole of the created order is to sing the Lord's praises.

7. *Key thing to look out for*

   God's people are to join in the praises of creation and worship the Lord alone.

8. *Key Bible cross-reference*

   Verse 7. See 104:26; Isaiah 27:1.

9. *Key "by way of explanation"*

   Verse 14, "horn," refers here to the victorious king.

10. *Key "Quotable Quote"*

    "Let them praise the name of the LORD: for his name alone is excellent; his glory is above the earth and heaven."
    Psalm 148:13

Psalm 149

1. Before and after

Previous psalm: Psalm 148: All creation praises the Lord
Following psalm: Psalm 150: Praise the Lord

2. Analysis of psalm

Joy to all the people of God. (1-5)
Terror to their enemies. (6-9)

3. Key verse

Verse 3: "Let them praise his name in the dance."

4. Key word / key phrase

Verse 4, "crowns."

5. Key event / key person / key theme

The Lord takes pleasure in his people.

6. Key thought

Dancing and music are to accompany the praises of the godly.

7. Key thing to look out for

The Israelites praised the Lord for being their Maker and for being their Redeemer.

8. Key Bible cross-reference

Verse 1. See 144:9; Proverbs 19:4.

9. Key "by way of explanation"

Verse 7, "vengeance." Christians are armed for the spiritual battle with the sword of the Spirit, Ephesians 6:12,17.

10. Key "Quotable Quote"

"Praise ye the LORD. Sing unto the LORD a new song, and his praise in the congregation of saints."
Psalm 149:1

Psalm 150

1. **Previous psalm**

   Psalm 149: The Lord takes pleasure in his people

2. **Analysis of psalm**

   A psalm of praise. (1-6)

3. **Key verse**

   Verse 6: "Let every thing that hath breath praise the LORD. Praise ye the LORD."

4. **Key word / key phrase**

   Verse 1, "praise God."

5. **Key event / key person / key theme**

   Praise the Lord

6. **Key thought**

   This grand musical hallelujah is a fitting conclusion to Book V of the psalms.

7. **Key thing to look out for**

   Everyone is to praise the Lord.

8. **Key Bible cross-reference**

   Verse 2. See 138:2; Daniel 3:26.

9. **Key "by way of explanation"**

   Verse 4, "flute." The Lord is to be praised with the eight instruments of the full orchestra.

10. **Key "Quotable Quote"**

    "Praise ye the LORD. Praise God in his sanctuary: praise him in the firmament of his power."
    Psalm 150:1

Proverbs

Proverbs 1

1. **Following chapter**

   Chapter 2: Seek wisdom

2. **Analysis of chapter**

   The use of the proverbs. (1-6)
   Exhortations to fear God and obey parents. (7-9)
   To avoid sinners. (10-19)
   The address of Wisdom to sinners. (20-33)

3. **Key verse**

   Verse 1: "The proverbs of Solomon the son of David, king of Israel."

4. **Key word / key phrase**

   Verse 3: "acquiring."

5. **Key event / key person / key theme**

   The value of proverbs

6. **Key thought**

   Solomon was renowned for his wisdom.

7. **Key thing to look out for**

   The importance of gaining wisdom is introduced.

8. **Key Bible cross-reference**

   Verse 1. See 1 Kings 4:32.

9. **Key "by way of explanation"**

   Verse 6, "riddles." This word can mean "allegories" as well as "riddles." See Ezekiel 17:2.

10. **Key "Quotable Quote"**

    "The fear of the LORD is the beginning of knowledge: but fools despise wisdom and instruction."
    Proverbs 1:7

Proverbs 2

1. Before and after

Previous chapter: Chapter 1: The purpose of proverbs
Following chapter: Chapter 3: The benefits of wisdom

2. Analysis of chapter

Promises to those who seek wisdom. (1-9)
The advantages of wisdom. (10-22)

3. Key verse

Verse 1: "My son, if thou wilt receive my words, and hide my commandments with thee."

4. Key word / key phrase

Verse 2, "applying your heart to understanding."

5. Key event / key person / key theme

Seek wisdom

6. Key thought

The many benefits of wisdom.

7. Key thing to look out for

The danger of leaving the straight and narrow.

8. Key Bible cross-reference

Verse 7. See Psalm 147:1

9. Key "by way of explanation"

Verse 13, "dark ways." Jesus warned that ungodly people naturally prefer darkness to light.

10. Key "Quotable Quote"

"For the LORD giveth wisdom: out of his mouth cometh knowledge and understanding."
Proverbs 2:6

Proverbs 3

1. Before and after

Previous chapter: Chapter 2: Seek wisdom
Following chapter: Chapter 4: Avoid the wicked and guard your heart

2. Analysis chapter

Exhortations to obedience and faith. (1-6)
To piety, and to improve afflictions. (7-12)
To gain wisdom. (13-20)
Guidance of Wisdom. (21-26)
The wicked and the upright. (27-35)

3. Key verse

Verse 5: "Trust in the LORD with thine heart; and lean not unto thine own understanding."

4. Key word / key phrase

God's wisdom. Note each occurrence or reference to the word, or a linked idea (verses 13,14,15,16,17,18,19,20,21,35).

5. Key event / key person / key theme

The benefits of wisdom

6. Key thought

The benefits to be derived from divine wisdom are incalculable.

7. Key thing to look out for

The practical outworking of wisdom in everyday life.

8. Key biblical cross-reference

God's wisdom revealed in Jesus Christ, 1 Corinthians 1:19-31.

9. Key "by way of explanation"

Verse 18. Wisdom is described as "a tree of life." This is the source of life and may be linked with the tree in the Garden of Eden, Genesis 2:9.

10. Key "Quotable Quote"

"The great folly of man in trials is leaning to or on his own understanding and counsels. What is the result of this? Whenever in our trials we consult our own understanding, listen to our own reason, even though they appear to be good, the principle of living by faith is stifled, and we will in this way be let down by our own counsels."
John Owen, commenting on verse 5.

Proverbs 4

1. **Before and after**

    Previous chapter: Chapter 3: The benefits of wisdom
    Following chapter: Chapter 5: Adultery is out, faithfulness is in

2. **Analysis of chapter**

    Exhortation to the study of wisdom. (1-13)
    Warnings against bad company. Exhortation to faith and holiness. (14-27)

3. **Key verse**

    Verse 14: "Enter not into the path of the wicked, and go not in the way of evil men."

4. **Key word / key phrase**

    Verse 19, "the road of the wicked."

5. **Key event / key person / key theme**

    The righteous and the wicked

6. **Key thought**

    Wisdom is the supreme way of life.

7. **Key thing to look out for**

    The choice between following wisdom or following evil is always before us.

8. **Key Bible cross-reference**

    Verse 26. See Hebrews 12:13.

9. **Key "by way of explanation"**

    Verse 19, "deep darkness." Evil leads on to more and more evil. It eventually leads to destruction.

10. **Key "Quotable Quote"**

    "Keep thy heart with all diligence; for out of it are the issues of life."
    Proverbs 4:23

Proverbs 5

1. ### Before and after

   Previous chapter: Chapter 4: Avoid the wicked and guard your heart
   Following chapter: Chapter 6: Do not be lazy

2. ### Analysis of chapter

   Exhortations to wisdom. The evils of adultery. (1-14)
   Remedies against adultery, and the miserable end of the wicked. (15-23)

3. ### Key verse

   Verse 15: "Drink waters out of thine own cistern, and running waters out of
   thine own well."

4. ### Key word / key phrase

   Verse 3, "the lips of an adulteress."

5. ### Key event / key person / key theme

   Adultery is out, faithfulness is in

6. ### Key thought

   The book of Proverbs is full of warnings against adultery.

7. ### Key thing to look out for

   Self-discipline is essential.

8. ### Key Bible cross-reference

   Verse 4. See Psalm 106:33.

9. ### Key "by way of explanation"

   Verse 19, "doe . . . deer," are descriptions of a wife, focusing on her beauty.

10. ### Key "Quotable Quote"

    "He shall die without instruction; and in the greatness of his folly he shall go
    astray."
    Proverbs 5:23

Proverbs 6

1. ### Before and after

   Previous chapter: Chapter 5: Adultery is out, faithfulness is in
   Following chapter: Chapter 7: Do not commit adultery

2. ### Analysis of chapter

   Warnings against rash lending. (1-5)
   A rebuke to slothfulness. (6-11)
   Seven things God hates. (12-19)
   Exhortations to walk according to God's commandments. (20-35)

3. ### Key verse

   Verse 6: "Go to the ant, thou sluggard; consider her ways, and be wise."

4. ### Key word / key phrase

   Verse 6, "sluggard."

5. ### Key event / key person / key theme

   Do not be lazy.

6. ### Key thought

   How to avoid being foolish.

7. ### Key thing to look out for

   More warnings against adultery.

8. ### Key Bible cross-reference

   Verses 10,11. See 24:33,34.

9. ### Key "by way of explanation"

   Verse 12, "corrupt mouth." The pernicious words of a gossip are spread by a "corrupt mouth."

10. ### Key "Quotable Quote"

    "A naughty person, a wicked man, walketh with a froward mouth."
    Proverbs 6:12

Proverbs 7

1. *Before and after*

Previous chapter: Chapter 6: Do not be lazy
Following chapter: Chapter 8: In praise of wisdom

2. *Analysis of chapter*

Invitations to learn wisdom. (1-5)
The ways of seducers, with warnings against them. (6-27)

3. *Key verse*

Verse 4: "Say unto wisdom, Thou art my sister."

4. *Key word / key phrase*

Verse 10, "dressed like a prostitute."

5. *Key event / key person / key theme*

Do not commit adultery.

6. *Key thought*

Adultery ends in death.

7. *Key thing to look out for*

Being wise can prevent adultery.

8. *Key Bible cross-reference*

Verse 22. See Isaiah 14:21.

9. *Key "by way of explanation"*

Verse 16, "colored lines from Egypt" were linked with the wealthy as Egyptian linen fetched the top price. See Ezekiel 7:7.

10. *Key "Quotable Quote"*

"My son, keep my words, and lay up my commandments with thee."
Proverbs 7:1

Proverbs 8

1. *Before and after*

Previous chapter: Chapter 7: Do not commit adultery
Following chapter: Chapter 9: Wisdom and folly are contrasted

2. *Analysis of chapter*

Christ, as Wisdom, calls to the sons of men. (1-11)
The nature and riches of Wisdom. (12-21)
Christ one with the Father, in the creation of the world, and rejoicing in his work for the salvation of humankind. (22-31)
Exhortations to hear Christ's word. (32-36)

3. *Key verse*

Verse 12: "I wisdom dwell with prudence, and find out knowledge of witty inventions."

4. *Key word / key phrase*

Verse 1, "Does not wisdom call out?"

5. *Key event / key person / key theme*

In praise of wisdom

6. *Key thought*

Wisdom is personified. She longs to be followed.

7. *Key thing to look out for*

What wisdom is said to hate, the Lord hates; and what wisdom gives, the Lord gives.

8. *Key Bible cross-reference*

Verse 22. See Revelation 3:14.

9. *Key "by way of explanation"*

Verse 15, "By me kings reign." At the start of his reign as king, Solomon, in his dream, asked for the wisdom he needed to help him rule.

10. *Key "Quotable Quote"*

"Hear instruction, and be wise, and refuse it not."
Proverbs 8:33

Proverbs 9

1. *Before and after*

   Previous chapter: Chapter 8: In praise of wisdom
   Following chapter: Chapter 10: The godly and the wicked are contrasted

2. *Analysis of chapter*

   The invitations of Wisdom. (1-12)
   The invitations of Folly. (13-18)

3. *Key verse*

   Verse 1: "Wisdom hath builded her house, she hath hewn out her seven pillars."

4. *Key word / key phrase*

   Verse 1, "seven pillars."

5. *Key event / key person / key theme*

   Wisdom and Folly are contrasted

6. *Key thought*

   The choice between listening to Wisdom and Folly.

7. *Key thing to look out for*

   The fear of the Lord and wisdom are said to be one.

8. *Key Bible cross-reference*

   Verse 10. See Job 28:28.

9. *Key "by way of explanation"*

   Verse 17, "Stolen water." Anything that is stolen may be pleasurable at the time but it is certain to bring disaster in its wake.

10. *Key "Quotable Quote"*

    "Give instruction to a wise man, and he will be yet wiser: teach a just man, and he will increase in learning."
    Proverbs 9:9

Proverbs 10

1. **Before and after**

   Previous chapter: Chapter 9: Foolish women
   Following chapter: Chapter 11: The godly and the wicked are contrasted

2. **Analysis of chapter**

   Proverbs of Solomon. (1-32)

3. **Key verse**

   Verse 1: "A wise son maketh a glad father: but a foolish son is the heaviness of his mother."

4. **Key word / key phrase**

   Verse 1, "A wise son . . . a foolish son."

5. **Key event / key person / key theme**

   The godly and the wicked are contrasted

6. **Key thought**

   Following the paths of wisdom brings happiness and prosperity.

7. **Key thing to look out for**

   "Through the whole of the Proverbs, we are to look for somewhat beyond the first sense the passage may imply, and this we shall find to be Christ. He is the Wisdom so often spoken of in this book." Matthew Henry

8. **Key Bible cross-reference**

   Verse 12. See 1 Peter 4:8.

9. **Key "by way of explanation"**

   Verse 5, "sleeps during harvest." Condemnation of the person who does not work when he should.

10. **Key "Quotable Quote"**

    "The blessing of the LORD, it maketh rich, and he addeth no sorrow with it." Proverbs 10:22

Proverbs 11

1. *Before and after*

Previous chapter: Chapter 10: The godly and the wicked are contrasted
Following chapter: Chapter 12: The godly and the wicked are contrasted

2. *Analysis of chapter*

Proverbs of Solomon. (1-31)

3. *Key verse*

Verse 1: "A false balance is abomination to the LORD: but a just weight is his delight."

4. *Key word / key phrase*

Verse 2, "pride . . . humility."

5. *Key event / key person / key theme*

The godly and the wicked are contrasted

6. *Key thought*

There is wisdom here for the individual as well as for nations.

7. *Key thing to look out for*

Do not give your heart to the love of money.

8. *Key Bible cross-reference*

Verse 31. See 1 Peter 4:18

9. *Key "by way of explanation"*

Verse 5, "a straight way" enables a traveler to reach his destination.

10. *Key "Quotable Quote"*

"As righteousness tendeth to life: so he that pursueth evil pursueth it to his own death."
Proverbs 11:19

Proverbs 12

1. **Before and after**

   Previous chapter: Chapter 11: The godly and the wicked are contrasted
   Following chapter: Chapter 13: The godly and the wicked are contrasted

2. **Analysis of chapter**

   Proverbs of Solomon. (1-28)

3. **Key verse**

   Verse 4: "A virtuous woman is a crown to her husband."

4. **Key word / key phrase**

   Verse 2, "good man . . . crafty man."

5. **Key event / key person / key theme**

   The godly and the wicked are contrasted

6. **Key thought**

   Observe the contrasts in most of the verses.

7. **Key thing to look out for**

   The way to cope with an insult is given here.

8. **Key Bible cross-reference**

   Verse 18. See Ecclesiastes 3:3.

9. **Key "by way of explanation"**

   Verse 4. A wife is a husband's "crown" when she honors him.

10. **Key "Quotable Quote"**

    "The lip of truth shall be established for ever: but a lying tongue is but for a moment."
    Proverbs 12:19

Proverbs 13

1. **Before and after**

   Previous chapter: Chapter 12: The godly and the wicked are contrasted
   Following chapter: Chapter 14: The godly and the wicked are contrasted

2. **Analysis of chapter**

   Proverbs of Solomon. (1-25)

3. **Key verse**

   Verse 5: "A righteous man hateth lying: but a wicked man is loathsome, and cometh to shame."

4. **Key word / key phrase**

   Verse 3, "guards his lips . . . speaks rashly."

5. **Key event / key person / key theme**

   The godly and the wicked are contrasted

6. **Key thought**

   Wisdom is linked to what many in today's society would call "old-fashioned" virtues.

7. **Key thing to look out for**

   The value of accepting advice, heeding wisdom, and seeking instruction is commended.

8. **Key Bible cross-reference**

   Verse 9. See Ecclesiastes 2:13.

9. **Key "by way of explanation"**

   Verse 17, "bring healing." It is possible to pour oil on troubled waters or to inflame a situation.

10. **Key "Quotable Quote"**

    "Hope deferred maketh the heart sick: but when the desire cometh, it is a tree of life."
    Proverbs 13:12

Proverbs 14

1. **Before and after**

   Previous chapter: Chapter 13: The godly and the wicked are contrasted
   Following chapter: Chapter 15: The godly and the wicked are contrasted

2. **Analysis of chapter**

   Proverbs of Solomon. (1-35)

3. **Key verse**

   Verse 5: "A faithful witness will not lie: but a false witness will utter lies."

4. **Key word / key phrase**

   Verse 5, "truthful witness . . . false witness."

5. **Key event / key person / key theme**

   The godly and the wicked are contrasted

6. **Key thought**

   The good things which are commended are to be sought after.

7. **Key thing to look out for**

   The proverbs assume that there is plenty of scope for improvement in our lives.

8. **Key Bible cross-reference**

   Verse 12. See Proverbs 16:25.

9. **Key "by way of explanation"**

   Verse 31, "shows contempt for their Maker." The Lord made both the rich and the poor. Both are created in his image. So, for the rich to mistreat the poor is to show contempt for their "Maker."

10. **Key "Quotable Quote"**

   "The house of the wicked shall be overthrown: but the tabernacle of the upright shall flourish."
   Proverbs 14:11

Proverbs 15

1. ### Before and after

    Previous chapter: Chapter 14: The godly and the wicked are contrasted
    Following chapter: Chapter 16: Encouraging godly lives

2. ### Analysis of chapter

    Proverbs of Solomon. (1-33)

3. ### Key verse

    Verse 1: "A soft answer turneth away wrath: but grievous words stir up anger."

4. ### Key word / key phrase

    Verse 32, "ignores discipline . . . heeds correction."

5. ### Key event / key person / key theme

    The godly and the wicked are contrasted

6. ### Key thought

    Once again the fear of the Lord tops the list.

7. ### Key thing to look out for

    It is possible for a very proud person to read this list of evil traits and to think that none of them apply to him or her.

8. ### Key Bible cross-reference

    Verse 27. See Psalm 26:10.

9. ### Key "by way of explanation"

    Verse 11, "Death" and "Destruction" are where there is no praise given to God and where the dead abide. See Ecclesiastes 9:10; Psalm 88:10.

10. ### Key "Quotable Quote"

    "The eyes of the LORD are in every place, beholding the evil and the good."
    Proverbs 15:3

Proverbs 16

1. *Before and after*

Previous chapter: Chapter 15: The godly and the wicked are contrasted
Following chapter: Chapter 17: Encouraging godly lives

2. *Analysis of chapter*

Proverbs of Solomon. (1-33)

3. *Key verse*

Verse 8: "Better is a little with righteousness than great revenues without right."

4. *Key word / key phrase*

Verse 3, "Commit to the Lord."

5. *Key event / key person / key theme*

Encouraging godly living

6. *Key thought*

The proverbs are often not linked to each other, but taken together, they give a vast amount of wisdom.

7. *Key thing to look out for*

Ways to avoid evil.

8. *Key Bible cross-reference*

Verse 25. See 14:12.

9. *Key "by way of explanation"*

Verse 15, "his favor is like a rain cloud in spring." For the barley crop to produce a good harvest in the summer, spring rain was essential. It was a sign that the expected good things would indeed follow.

10. *Key "Quotable Quote"*

"How much better is it to get wisdom than gold! and to get understanding rather to be chosen than silver!"
Proverbs 16:16

Proverbs 17

1. **Before and after**

   Previous chapter: Chapter 16: Encouraging godly lives
   Following chapter: Chapter 18: Encouraging godly lives

2. **Analysis of chapter**

   Proverbs of Solomon. (1-28)

3. **Key verse**

   Verse 10: "A reproof entereth more into a wise man than an hundred stripes into a fool."

4. **Key word / key phrase**

   Verse 24, "a discerning man."

5. **Key event / key person / key theme**

   Encouraging godly lives

6. **Key thought**

   In Proverbs, many of the good qualities, like discernment, seem to be at a premium.

7. **Key thing to look out for**

   The proverbs hit out at wrongdoing wherever it is to be found.

8. **Key Bible cross-reference**

   Verse 21. See Ecclesiastes 7:3.

9. **Key "by way of explanation"**

   Verse 3, "the crucible for silver and the furnace for gold." Both metals were refined in a fire and came out purified of impurities. In the same way, the Lord disciplines us to refine our characters.

10. **Key "Quotable Quote"**

    "A friend loveth at all times, and a brother is born for adversity."
    Proverbs 17:17

Proverbs 18

1. Before and after

Previous chapter: Chapter 17: Encouraging godly lives
Following chapter: Chapter 19: Encouraging godly lives

2. Analysis of chapter

Proverbs of Solomon. (1-24)

3. Key verse

Verse 9: "He also that is slothful in his work is brother to him that is a great waster."

4. Key word / key phrase

Verse 10, "The name of the Lord."

5. Key event / key person / key theme

Encouraging godly lives

6. Key thought

Many of the things we take for granted should become things we take care to thank the Lord for.

7. Key thing to look out for

The proverbs give warning about taking care over how we speak, since words can kill or give life.

8. Key Bible cross-reference

Verse 24. See Psalm 119:89.

9. Key "by way of explanation"

Verse 10, "the name" of a person stood for his personality and character.

10. Key "Quotable Quote"

"A man that hath friends must show himself friendly: and there is a friend that sticketh closer than a brother."
Proverbs 18:24

Proverbs 19

1. *Before and after*

Previous chapter: Chapter 18: Encouraging godly lives
Following chapter: Chapter 20: Encouraging godly lives

2. *Analysis of chapter*

Proverbs of Solomon. (1-29)

3. *Key verse*

Verse 4: "Wealth maketh many friends; but the poor is separated from his neighbor."

4. *Key word / key phrase*

Verse 8, "He who gets wisdom."

5. *Key event / key person / key theme*

Encouraging godly lives

6. *Key thought*

These proverbs teach that evil will be punished.

7. *Key thing to look out for*

The poor should be looked after.

8. *Key Bible cross-reference*

Verse 26. See Job 24:21.

9. *Key "by way of explanation"*

Verse 26, "robs his father and drives out his mother." There was no state aid in those days. The children were expected to look after their ill or elderly parents.

10. *Key "Quotable Quote"*

"Slothfulness casteth into a deep sleep; and an idle soul shall suffer hunger." Proverbs 19:15

Proverbs 20

1. **Before and after**

   Previous chapter: Chapter 19: Encouraging godly lives
   Following chapter: Chapter 21: Encouraging godly lives

2. **Analysis of chapter**

   Proverbs of Solomon. (1-30)

3. **Key verse**

   Verse 15: "There is gold, and a multitude of rubies: but the lips of knowledge
   are a precious jewel."

4. **Key word / key phrase**

   Verse 3, "avoid strife."

5. **Key event / key person / key theme**

   Encouraging godly lives

6. **Key thought**

   In the early chapters of Proverbs blame for adultery is often attached to the
   woman. Verse 6 of this chapter appears to find it impossible to find a faithful
   man.

7. **Key thing to look out for**

   Many of the proverbs are directly linked to the Lord and his wishes and
   actions.

8. **Key Bible cross-reference**

   Verse 27. See Acts 23:1.

9. **Key "by way of explanation"**

   Verse 9, "without sin." No one in this life can reach sinless perfection. But
   after our sin is confessed to God and forgiven it may be said that we are
   "without sin" and so "pure" and "clean."

10. **Key "Quotable Quote"**

    "Wine is a mocker, strong drink is raging: and whosoever is deceived thereby
    is not wise."
    Proverbs 20:1

Proverbs 21

1. **Before and after**

   Previous chapter: Chapter 20: Encouraging godly lives
   Following chapter: Chapter 22: Encouraging godly lives

2. **Analysis of chapter**

   Proverbs of Solomon. (1-31)

3. **Key verse**

   Verse 21: "To do justice and judgment is more acceptable to the LORD than sacrifice."

4. **Key word / key phrase**

   Verse 4, "Haughty eyes."

5. **Key event / key person / key theme**

   Encouraging godly lives

6. **Key thought**

   The proud, the lazy, and the loud-mouthed come off worst in this chapter.

7. **Key thing to look out for**

   Wisdom and victory are attributed to the Lord.

8. **Key Bible cross-reference**

   Verse 20. See Lamentations 4:5.

9. **Key "by way of explanation"**

   Verse 26, "give without sparing." Generosity should be a characteristic of the righteous. The righteous may also prosper and so find that they are in a better position to help the poor.

10. **Key "Quotable Quote"**

    "Every way of a man is right in his own eyes: but the LORD pondereth the hearts."
    Proverbs 21:2

Proverbs 22

1. *Before and after*

Previous chapter: Chapter 21: Encouraging godly lives
Following chapter: Chapter 23: Proverbs concerning a variety of situations

2. *Analysis of chapter*

Proverbs of Solomon. (1-16)
Sayings of the wise. (17-29)

3. *Key verse*

Verse 4: "By humility and the fear of the LORD are riches, and honor, and life."

4. *Key word / key phrase*

Verse 17, "the sayings of the wise."

5. *Key event / key person / key theme*

Encouraging godly lives

6. *Key thought*

The heart is often under scrutiny in these proverbs.

7. *Key thing to look out for*

A recurrent theme is the need to choose friends wisely.

8. *Key Bible cross-reference*

Verse 28. See Psalm 99:4.

9. *Key "by way of explanation"*

Verse 13, "the sluggard." When a lazy person does not want to work he is full of excuses and plausible reasons for not lifting a finger.

10. *Key "Quotable Quote"*

"Train up a child in the way he should go: and when he is old, he will not depart from it."
Proverbs 22:6

Proverbs 23

1. **Before and after**

   Previous chapter: Chapter 22: Encouraging godly lives
   Following chapter: Chapter 24: Proverbs concerning a variety of situations

2. **Analysis of chapter**

   Sayings of the wise. (1-35)

3. **Key verse**

   Verse 10: "Remove not the old landmark; and enter not into the fields of the fatherless."

4. **Key word / key phrase**

   Verse 5, "riches."

5. **Key event / key person / key theme**

   Evils bring short-lived pleasures.

6. **Key thought**

   Envy and fear of the Lord are contrasted in the same verse.

7. **Key thing to look out for**

   Warnings to drunkards and gluttons, and a vivid description of what it is like to be drunk.

8. **Key Bible cross-reference**

   Verse 2. See Isaiah 56:11.

9. **Key "by way of explanation"**

   Verse 4, "Do not wear yourself out to get rich." This warning is phrased in this way because amassing wealth can ruin a person emotionally, physically, and spiritually.

10. **Key "Quotable Quote"**

    "Labor not to be rich: cease from thine own wisdom."
    Proverbs 23:4

Proverbs 24

1. *Before and after*

Previous chapter: Chapter 23: Proverbs concerning a variety of situations
Following chapter: Chapter 25: Relationships with kings, neighbors, enemies, and yourself

2. *Analysis of chapter*

Sayings of the wise. (1-22)
More wise sayings. (23-34)

3. *Key verse*

Verse 10: "If thou faint in the day of adversity, thy strength is small."

4. *Key word / key phrase*

Verse 3, "By wisdom a house is built."

5. *Key event / key person / key theme*

What to do in the face of different types of wrongdoing.

6. *Key thought*

A godly person should not be envious of evil people, even if they appear to prosper in their evil ways for a time.

7. *Key thing to look out for*

A wise person never seeks or exacts revenge.

8. *Key Bible cross-reference*

Verse 14. See Lamentations 1:20.

9. *Key "by way of explanation"*

Verse 12, "weighs the heart." The Lord knows everyone's inner motives and can read our minds and thoughts.

10. *Key "Quotable Quote"*

"Be not thou envious against evil men, neither desire to be with them."
Proverbs 24:1

Proverbs 25

1. Before and after

Previous chapter: Chapter 24: Proverbs concerning a variety of situations
Following chapter: Chapter 26: Relationships with fools, the lazy, and gossips

2. Analysis of chapter

More of Solomon's proverbs. (1-28)

3. Key verse

Verse 11: "A word fitly spoken is like apples of gold in pictures of silver."

4. Key word / key phrase

Verse 17, "your neighbor's house."

5. Key event / key person / key theme

Proverbs concerning a variety of situations

6. Key thought

Many proverbs in this chapter are little cameos which are meant to be visualized so that they stay in our memories and we learn from them.

7. Key thing to look out for

A number of proverbs teach that enough is as good as a feast.

8. Key Bible cross-reference

Verses 6,7. See Luke 14:8-10.

9. Key "by way of explanation"

Verse 14. "Like clouds . . . without rain." In Jude's letter, verse 12, this idea is applied to men who should have been pastors of the flock but are just out to satisfy their own whims.

10. Key "Quotable Quote"

"He that hath no rule over his own spirit is like a city that is broken down, and without walls."
Proverbs 25:28

Proverbs 26

1. ## *Before and after*

    Previous chapter: Chapter 25: Relationships with kings, neighbors, enemies, and yourself
    Following chapter: Chapter 27: Proverbs concerning various activities

2. ## *Analysis of chapter*

    More of Solomon's proverbs. (1-28)

3. ## *Key verse*

    Verse 3: "A whip for the horse, a bridle for the ass, and a rod for the fool's back."

4. ## *Key word / key phrase*

    Verse 13, "The sluggard says."

5. ## *Key event / key person / key theme*

    Relationships with fools, the lazy, and gossips

6. ## *Key thought*

    Gossips and lazy people are warned against in this chapter.

7. ## *Key thing to look out for*

    There are more negative qualities to avoid in this chapter than good ones to emulate.

8. ## *Key Bible cross-reference*

    Verse 9. See Ecclesiastes 12:11.

9. ## *Key "by way of explanation"*

    Verse 8, "like tying a stone in a sling." If a stone is tied in a sling it will not fly through the air. In the same way, although a fool may have a position of honor, he is unable to act honorably.

10. ## *Key "Quotable Quote"*

    "As the door turneth upon his hinges, so doth the slothful upon his bed."
    Proverbs 26:14

Proverbs 27

1. **Before and after**

   Previous chapter: Chapter 26: Relationships with fools, the lazy, and gossips
   Following chapter: Chapter 28: Proverbs concerning various activities

2. **Analysis of chapter**

   More of Solomon's proverbs. (1-27)

3. **Key verse**

   Verse 2: "Let another man praise thee, and not thine own mouth; a stranger, and not thine own lips."

4. **Key word / key phrase**

   Verse 1, "tomorrow."

5. **Key event / key person / key theme**

   Proverbs concerning various activities

6. **Key thought**

   There are helpful and unhelpful ways to help a friend.

7. **Key thing to look out for**

   Being prudent is commended.

8. **Key Bible cross-reference**

   Verse 1. See James 4:13-16.

9. **Key "by way of explanation"**

   Verse 24, "crown is not secure." Even a king should not think that he is secure in his position.

10. **Key "Quotable Quote"**

    "Open rebuke is better than secret love."
    Proverbs 27:5

Proverbs 28

1. **Before and after**

   Previous chapter: Chapter 27: Proverbs concerning various activities
   Following chapter: Chapter 29: Proverbs concerning various activities

2. **Analysis of chapter**

   More of Solomon's proverbs. (1-28)

3. **Key verse**

   Verse 11: "The rich man is wise in his own conceit; but the poor that hath understanding searcheth him out."

4. **Key word / key phrase**

   Verse 6, "a poor man . . . a rich man."

5. **Key event / key person / key theme**

   Just and unjust rulers

6. **Key thought**

   Trusting in the Lord is highlighted.

7. **Key thing to look out for**

   Good and evil men are compared.

8. **Key Bible cross-reference**

   Verse 9. See Ecclesiastes 8:5.

9. **Key "by way of explanation"**

   Verse 3, "driving rain." Different types of rain stand for different things. In Psalm 72:6,7 gentle rain is linked to the righteous, here driving rain probably refers to the power of the Assyrian army.

10. **Key "Quotable Quote"**

    "Evil men understand not judgment: but they that seek the LORD understand all things."
    Proverbs 28:5

Proverbs 29

1. *Before and after*

    Previous chapter: Chapter 28: Proverbs concerning various activities
    Following chapter: Chapter 30: The proverbs of Agur

2. *Analysis of chapter*

    More of Solomon's proverbs. (1-27)

3. *Key verse*

    Verse 5: "A man that flattereth his neighbor spreadeth a net for his feet."

4. *Key word / key phrase*

    Verse 4, "justice."

5. *Key event / key person / key theme*

    Destruction comes to the wicked.

6. *Key thought*

    Pride and anger are exposed for what they are.

7. *Key thing to look out for*

    Unpopular things like justice and discipline are recommended.

8. *Key Bible cross-reference*

    Verse 11. See Ecclesiastes 7:5.

9. *Key "by way of explanation"*

    Verse 18, "people cast off restraint." This probably refers to the Israelites
    making and worshiping the golden calf in Exodus 32:25.

10. *Key "Quotable Quote"*

    "Where there is no vision, the people perish: but he that keepeth the law,
    happy is he."
    Proverbs 29:18

Proverbs 30

1. **Before and after**

   Previous chapter: Chapter 29: Proverbs concerning various activities
   Following chapter: Chapter 31: The wise woman

2. **Analysis of chapter**

   Sayings of Agur. (1-6)
   More proverbs. (7-33)

3. **Key verse**

   Verse 1: "The words of Agur the son of Jakeh.".

4. **Key word / key phrase**

   Verse 8, "daily bread."

5. **Key event / key person / key theme**

   The proverbs of Agur

6. **Key thought**

   Size is not everything.

7. **Key thing to look out for**

   The value of God's word is highlighted.

8. **Key Bible cross-reference**

   Verse 1. See Psalm 132:11.

9. **Key "by way of explanation"**

   Verse 14, "teeth . . . jaws." Wicked people are compared to wild animals who tear into their prey with their teeth and jaws.

10. **Key "Quotable Quote"**

    "Every word of God is pure: he is a shield unto them that put their trust in him."
    Proverbs 30:5

Proverbs 31

1. **Previous chapter**

    Chapter 30: The proverbs of Agur

2. **Analysis of chapter**

    An exhortation to king Lemuel to take heed of sin, and to carry out his duties. (1-9)

    The description of a virtuous woman. (10-31)

3. **Key verse**

    Verse 1: "The words of king Lemuel."

4. **Key word / key phrase**

    Verse 10, "a wife."

5. **Key event / key person / key theme**

    The wise woman

6. **Key thought**

    All the activities of the good wife stem from her noble character.

7. **Key thing to look out for**

    The secret of her success is given in verse 30.

8. **Key Bible cross-reference**

    Verse 2. See Song of Songs 1:16.

9. **Key "by way of explanation"**

    Verse 25, "laugh at the days to come." This exemplary wife is not burdened by care and worry and does not fear the future. This song of praise is an acrostic.

10. **Key "Quotable Quote"**

    "Who can find a virtuous woman? for her price is far above rubies."
    Proverbs 31:10

Ecclesiastes

Ecclesiastes chapter 1

1. *Following chapter*

   Chapter 2: Proof from experience that "All is vanity"

2. *Analysis of chapter*

   Without God, all human actions are meaningless and empty. (1-3)
   Man's toil and lack of satisfaction. (4-8)
   There is nothing new. (9-11)
   The pointlessness in pursuing knowledge. (12-18)

3. *Key verse*

   Verse 1: "The words of the Preacher, the son of David, king in Jerusalem."

4. *Key word / key phrase*

   Verse 2, "meaningless."

5. *Key event / key person / key theme*

   Everything seems meaningless

6. *Key thought*

   Life without God is seen to have no meaning.

7. *Key thing to look out for*

   Human wisdom has its limits.

8. *Key Bible cross-reference*

   Verse 16. See 1 Kings 4:29-31.

9. *Key "by way of explanation"*

   Verse 3, "under the sun." This expression, which comes twenty-nine times in
   Ecclesiastes, refers to this earthly world and our life in it.

10. *Key "Quotable Quote"*

    "I believe that nothing that happens to me is meaningless, and that it is good
    for us all that it should be so, even if it runs counter to our own wishes."
    Dietrich Bonhoeffer

Ecclesiastes chapter 2

1. **Before and after**

   Previous chapter: Chapter 1: Illustrations of vanity
   Following chapter: Chapter 3: God's plans cannot be changed

2. **Analysis of chapter**

   The vanity of mirth, sensual pleasure, riches, and pomp. (1-11)
   Human wisdom is insufficient. (12-17)
   This world to be used according to the will of God. (18-26)

3. **Key verse**

   Verse 2: "I said of laughter, It is mad: and of mirth, What doeth it?"

4. **Key word / key phrase**

   Verse 20, "toilsome labor."

5. **Key event / key person / key theme**

   Proof from experience that "All is vanity"

6. **Key thought**

   Pleasures are meaningless.

7. **Key thing to look out for**

   Daily work has no meaning.

8. **Key Bible cross-reference**

   Verses 4-8. See 1 Kings 10:23-27.

9. **Key "by way of explanation"**

   Verse 17, "meaningless." This is a key word in this book, appearing thirty-five times, and refers to any life lived without God.

10. **Key "Quotable Quote"**

    "The meaning of earthly existence lies, not as we have grown used to thinking, in prospering, but in the development of the soul."
    A. I. Solzhenitsyn

Ecclesiastes chapter 3

1. ## Before and after

   Previous chapter: Chapter 2: Proof of "All is vanity" from experience
   Following chapter: Chapter 4: Inequalities of life

2. ## Analysis of chapter

   The changes of human affairs. (1-10)
   The divine counsels are unchangeable. (11-15)
   The vanity of worldly power. (16-22)

3. ## Key verse

   Verse 1: "To every thing there is a season, and a time to every purpose under
   the heaven."

4. ## Key word / key phrase

   Verse 1, "a season for every activity."

5. ## Key event / key person / key theme

   God's plans cannot be changed

6. ## Key thought

   Everything has been given its time.

7. ## Key thing to look out for

   As we are creatures of eternity nothing in time is found to be satisfying.

8. ## Key Bible cross-reference

   Verse 20. See Genesis 3:19.

9. ## Key "by way of explanation"

   Verse 1, "everything," refers to all activities which are engaged in without
   reference to God.

10. ## Key "Quotable Quote"

    "More men fail through lack of purpose than through lack of talent."
    Billy Sunday

Ecclesiastes chapter 4

1. **Before and after**

   Previous chapter: Chapter 3: God's plans cannot be changed
   Following chapter: Chapter 5: Insufficiencies of wealth

2. **Analysis of chapter**

   Miseries from oppression. (1-3)
   Troubles from envy. (4-6)
   The folly of covetousness. (7,8)
   The advantages of mutual help. (9-12)
   The changes of royalty. (13-16)

3. **Key verse**

   Verse 7: "Then I returned, and I saw vanity under the sun."

4. **Key word / key phrase**

   Verse 1, "tears of the oppressed."

5. **Key event / key person / key theme**

   Inequalities of life

6. **Key thought**

   Look at all the oppression in the world.

7. **Key thing to look out for**

   Even advancement is meaningless.

8. **Key Bible cross-reference**

   Verse 2. See Jeremiah 20:14-18.

9. **Key "by way of explanation"**

   Verse 4, "a chasing after wind," is a key phrase in this book, coming nine times
   in the first half. It is a description of any futile activity.

10. **Key "Quotable Quote"**

    "The whole meaning of the soul is to express the spirit."
    Oswald Chambers

Ecclesiastes chapter 5

1. Before and after

Previous chapter: Chapter 4: Inequalities of life
Following chapter: Chapter 6: Vanity of life is inescapable

2. Analysis of chapter

What makes devotion vain. (1-3)
Vows, and oppression. (4-8)
The vanity of riches. (9-7)
The right use of riches. (18-20)

3. Key verse

Verse 5: "Better is it that thou shouldest not vow, than that thou shouldest vow and not pay."

4. Key word / key phrase

Verse 10, "Whoever loves money."

5. Key event / key person / key theme

Insufficiencies of wealth

6. Key thought

Stand in reverence of God.

7. Key thing to look out for

Even gaining wealth is meaningless.

8. Key Bible cross-reference

Verse 4. See Psalm 66:13,14.

9. Key "by way of explanation"

Verse 4, "fools." "Fools" in the Bible do not usually refer to stupid or uneducated people, but rather to those who refuse to learn.

10. Key "Quotable Quote"

"Meaninglessness doesn't come from being weary of pain but from being weary of pleasure."
Ravi Zacharias

Ecclesiastes chapter 6

1. Before and after

Previous chapter: Chapter 5: Insufficiencies of wealth
Following chapter: Chapter 7: Wisdom and folly contrasted

2. Analysis of chapter

The vanity of riches, long life and flourishing families. (1-6)
The little advantage any one has in outward things. (7-12)

3. Key verse

Verse 7: "All the labor of man is for his mouth, and yet the appetite is not filled."

4. Key word / key phrase

Verse 3, "he cannot enjoy."

5. Key event / key person / key theme

The emptiness of life is inescapable.

6. Key thought

Nothing seems to bring fulfillment.

7. Key thing to look out for

Even a good man's life seems meaningless.

8. Key Bible cross-reference

Verse 12. See 1 Chronicles 29:15.

9. Key "by way of explanation"

Verse 3, "does not receive a proper burial." Anyone who was not honored in their death or lamented over, see Jeremiah 22:18,19, would not have received "a proper burial."

10. Key "Quotable Quote"

"Atheism turns out to be too simple. If the whole universe has no meaning, we should never have found out that it has no meaning: just as, if there were no light in the universe and therefore no creatures with eyes, we should never know it was dark."
C.S. Lewis

Ecclesiastes chapter 7

1. *Before and after*

Previous chapter: Chapter 6: Vanity of life is inescapable
Following chapter: Chapter 8: Inability to understand all of God's actions

2. *Analysis of chapter*

The benefit of a good name; of death above life; of sorrow over vain mirth. (1-6)
Oppression, anger, and discontentment. (7-10)
Advantages of wisdom. (11-22)
Experience of the evil of sin. (23-29)

3. *Key verse*

Verse 7: "Surely oppression maketh a wise man mad; and a gift destroyeth the heart."

4. *Key word / key phrase*

Verse 7, "turns a wise man into a fool."

5. *Key event / key person / key theme*

Wisdom and folly contrasted

6. *Key thought*

Some wise proverbs to ponder.

7. *Key thing to look out for*

Further thoughts about the meaninglessness of life.

8. *Key Bible cross-reference*

Verse 9. See James 1:19.

9. *Key "by way of explanation"*

Verse 15, "righteous man perishing." Just because someone is righteous that does not mean to say that he or she will not meet an early death.

10. *Key "Quotable Quote"*

"The truly wise are those whose souls are in Christ."
Ambrose

Ecclesiastes chapter 8

1. *Before and after*

Previous chapter: Chapter 7: Wisdom and folly contrasted; the power of wisdom

Following chapter: Chapter 9: Judgment, enjoyment of life, and the value of wisdom

2. *Analysis of chapter*

Commendations of wisdom. (1-5)
To prepare for sudden evils and death. (6-8)
It will be well with the righteous, but not with the wicked. (9-13)
Mysteries of providence. (14-17)

3. *Key verse*

Verse 11: "Because sentence against an evil work is not executed speedily, therefore the heart of the sons of men is fully set in them to do evil."

4. *Key word / key phrase*

Verse 1, "explanation."

5. *Key event / key person / key theme*

Inability to understand all of God's actions

6. *Key thought*

The wicked and the righteous are contrasted.

7. *Key thing to look out for*

The key to the meaning in life is found in reverence for God.

8. *Key Bible cross-reference*

Verses 8,9. See 2 Corinthians 5:1-10.

9. *Key "by way of explanation"*

Verse 17, "no one can comprehend." God has not revealed everything we would like to know, only what he thinks we need to know. See Deuteronomy 29:29.

10. *Key "Quotable Quote"*

"We are ensnared by the wisdom of the serpent; we are set free by the foolishness of God."
Augustine of Hippo

Ecclesiastes chapter 9

1. *Before and after*

Previous chapter: Chapter 8: Inability to understand all of God's actions
Following chapter: Chapter 10: Wisdom's characteristics

2. *Analysis of chapter*

Good and bad men fare alike as to this world. (1-3)
All men must die. (4-10)
Disappointments are experienced by everyone. (11,12)
Benefits of wisdom. (13-18)

3. *Key verse*

Verse 9: "For to him that is joined to all the living there is hope: for a living dog is better than a dead lion."

4. *Key word / key phrase*

Verse 2, "a common destiny."

5. *Key event / key person / key theme*

Judgment, enjoyment of life, and the value of wisdom

6. *Key thought*

Wisdom is superior to folly.

7. *Key thing to look out for*

War and sin bring devastating consequences.

8. *Key Bible cross-reference*

Verse 10. See Colossians 3:23.

9. *Key "by way of explanation"*

Verse 12, "hour." In the Bible an "hour" often refers to the moment of a disaster or the time of a crisis.

10. *Key "Quotable Quote"*

"Our wisdom, in so far as it ought to be deemed true and solid wisdom, consists almost entirely of two parts: the knowledge of God and of ourselves."
John Calvin

Ecclesiastes chapter 10

1. *Before and after*

Previous chapter: Chapter 9: Judgment, enjoyment of life, and the value of wisdom

Following chapter: Chapter 11: Wisdom and business; wisdom and youth

2. *Analysis of chapter*

To preserve a character for wisdom. (1-3)

Subjects and rulers. (4-10)

Foolish talk. (11-15)

Duties of rulers and subjects. (16-20)

3. *Key verse*

Verse 6: "Folly is set in great dignity, and the rich sit in low place."

4. *Key word / key phrase*

Verse 12, "Words from a wise man's mouth."

5. *Key event / key person / key theme*

Wisdom's characteristics

6. *Key thought*

Wisdom and foolishness are compared.

7. *Key thing to look out for*

The lazy will achieve little.

8. *Key Bible cross-reference*

Verse 8. See Proverbs 26:27.

9. *Key "by way of explanation"*

Verse 12, "words." "Words" are a frequent theme in all biblical wisdom literature.

10. *Key "Quotable Quote"*

"Wisdom and goodness are twin-born, one heart
Must hold both sisters, never seen apart."
William Cowper

Ecclesiastes chapter 11

1. Before and after

Previous chapter: Chapter 10: Wisdom's characteristics
Following chapter: Chapter 12: Remember God in your youth

2. Analysis of chapter

Exhortation to liberality. (1-6)
An admonition to prepare for death, and to young people to be religious. (7-10)

3. Key verse

Verse 1: "Cast thy bread upon the waters: for thou shalt find it after many days"

4. Key word / key phrase

Verse 4, "Whoever watches the wind."

5. Key event / key person / key theme

Wisdom and business; wisdom and youth

6. Key thought

The steps of a wise person.

7. Key thing to look out for

Advice to young people.

8. Key Bible cross-reference

Verse 1. See Proverbs 11:24.

9. Key "by way of explanation"

Verse 2, "Give portions of seven," is an instruction to be generous.

10. Key "Quotable Quote"

"Not until we have become humble and teachable, standing in awe of God's holiness and sovereignty . . . acknowledging our own littleness, distrusting our own thoughts, and willing to have our minds turned upside down, can divine wisdom become ours."
J.I. Packer

Ecclesiastes chapter 12

1. ### Previous chapter

    Chapter 11: Wisdom and business; wisdom and youth

2. ### Analysis of chapter

    A description of the infirmities of age. (1-7)
    All is vanity: also a warning of the judgment to come. (8-14)

3. ### Key verse

    Verse 1: "Remember now thy Creator in the days of thy youth."

4. ### Key word / key phrase

    Verse 1, "The days of your youth."

5. ### Key event / key person / key theme

    Remember God in your youth

6. ### Key thought

    Remember God before decrepitude sets in. Contrast with this the Christian's
    hope as the body grows frail (2 Corinthians 4:16-18).

7. ### Key thing to look out for

    Verses 2-4. A poetic and powerful description of old age

8. ### Key Bible cross-reference

    Verse 14. See Romans 2:16.

9. ### Key "by way of explanation"

    Verse 13, "Fear God." The basis of all wisdom is a heart full of love and
    reverence for God.

10. ### Key "Quotable Quote"

    "I believe that God has made me and all creatures; that he has given and still
    preserves to me my body and soul, eyes, ears, and all my members, my reason
    and all my senses; also clothing and shoes, meat and drink, house and home,
    wife and child, land, cattle and all my goods."
    Martin Luther

Song of Songs

Song of Songs chapter 1

1. **Following chapter**

   Chapter 2: Second song

2. **Analysis of chapter**

   The title. (1)
   The Church confesses her wrong ways. (2-6)
   The Church asks Christ to lead her to the resting-place of his people. (7,8)
   Christ's commendation of the Church, her esteem for him. (9-17)

3. **Key verse**

   Verse 1: "The song of songs, which is Solomon's."

4. **Key word / key phrase**

   Verse 4, "Take me away with you."

5. **Key event / key person / key theme**

   The first song

6. **Key thought**

   The characters are introduced.

7. **Key thing to look out for**

   The lover uses flattering language.

8. **Key Bible cross-reference**

   Verse 12. See John 12:3.

9. **Key "by way of explanation"**

   Verse 1, the phrase "Song of Songs," means the greatest of songs ever
   composed. The Song of Solomon has often been viewed as an allegory of
   Christ and the Church.

10. **Key "Quotable Quote"**

    "The historical books I may compare to the outer courts of the temple; the
    gospels, the epistles and the psalms bring us into the holy place, or the court
    of the priests; but the Song of Songs is the most holy place – the holy of
    holies, before which the veil still hangs to many an untaught believer."
    C.H. Spurgeon

Song of Songs chapter 2

1. *Before and after*

   Previous chapter: Chapter 1: First song
   Following chapter: Chapter 3: Third song

2. *Analysis of chapter*

   The mutual love of Christ and his Church. (1-7)
   The hope and calling of the Church. (8-13)
   Christ's care of the Church, her faith and hope. (14-17)

3. *Key verse*

   Verse 1: "I am the rose of Sharon, and the lily of the valleys."

4. *Key word / key phrase*

   Verse 8, "Listen! My lover!"

5. *Key event / key person / key theme*

   The second song

6. *Key thought*

   The beloved expresses his love.

7. *Key thing to look out for*

   The beloved longs to be in the company of the lover.

8. *Key Bible cross-reference*

   Verse 9. See Isaiah 35:6.

9. *Key "by way of explanation"*

   Verse 9, "gazelle." The beauty of a gazelle was renowned.

10. *Key "Quotable Quote"*

   "Most men need patience to die, but a saint who understands what death
   admits him to should rather need patience to live. I think he should often look
   out and listen on a deathbed for his Lord's coming; and when he receives the
   news of his approaching change he should say, 'The voice of my beloved!
   behold, he cometh leaping over the mountains, skipping upon the hills' 2:8."
   John Flavel

Song of Songs chapter 3

1. ## Before and after

   Previous chapter: Chapter 2: Second song
   Following chapter: Chapter 4: The groom praises the bride

2. ## Analysis of chapter

   The trials of the Church by the withdrawing of Christ. (1-5)
   The excellences of the Church, and the care of Christ for her. (6-11)

3. ## Key verse

   Verse 3: "The watchmen that go about the city found me."

4. ## Key word / key phrase

   Verse 6, "coming up from the desert."

5. ## Key event / key person / key theme

   The third song

6. ## Key thought

   The woman expresses her love.

7. ## Key thing to look out for

   Night and day the beloved's mind is filled with thoughts of her lover.

8. ## Key Bible cross-reference

   Verse 8. See Psalm 91:5.

9. ## Key "by way of explanation"

   Verse 3, "watchmen." These guards were posted at the gates of a city and kept a look-out for any enemies, especially at night.

10. ## Key "Quotable Quote"

    "The Song comes to us in this world of sin, where lust and passion are on every hand, where fierce temptation assails us, and try to turn us aside from the God-given standard of marriage."
    E.J. Young

Song of Songs chapter 4

1. ## Before and after

   Previous chapter: Chapter 3: Third song
   Following chapter: Chapter 5: Fourth song

2. ## Analysis of chapter

   Christ sets out the graces of the Church. (1-7)
   Christ's love to the Church. (8-15)
   The Church desires further influences of divine grace. (16)

3. ## Key verse

   Verse 1: "Behold, thou art fair, my love; behold, thou art fair; thou hast doves' eyes within thy locks: thy hair is as a flock of goats, that appear from mount Gilead."

4. ## Key word / key phrase

   Verse 9, "you have stolen my heart."

5. ## Key event / key person / key theme

   The groom praises the bride

6. ## Key thought

   The groom is totally attentive to his bride.

7. ## Key thing to look out for

   The bride is happy to accept the love of the groom.

8. ## Key Bible cross-reference

   Verse 11. See Proverbs 5:3.

9. ## Key "by way of explanation"

   Verse 14, "saffron." This flower has beautiful purple flowers and was also used as a spice.

10. ## Key "Quotable Quote"

    "The Song reminds us, in particularly beautiful fashion, how pure and noble true love is."
    E.J. Young

Song of Songs chapter 5

1. Before and after

Previous chapter: Chapter 4: Third song
Following chapter: Chapter 6: Fifth song

2. Analysis of chapter

Christ's answer. (1)
The disappointments of the Church from her own folly. (2-8)
The excellences of Christ. (9-16)

3. Key verse

Verse 8: "I charge you, O daughters of Jerusalem, if ye find my beloved, that ye tell him, that I am sick of love."

4. Key word / key phrase

Verse 2, "my heart was awake."

5. Key event / key person / key theme

The fourth song

6. Key thought

The bride praises the groom.

7. Key thing to look out for

The bride is not abandoned by her friends.

8. Key Bible cross-reference

Verse 10. See 1 Samuel 16:12.

9. Key "by way of explanation"

Verse 15, "choice as its cedars." The cedars of Lebanon were known for their size, beauty and strength. The temple was constructed from them.

10. Key "Quotable Quote"

"The imagery of The Song is not eidetic; by this is meant it does not, like much modern writing, draw the picture in such realistic detail that the reader imagines himself a participant."
R.W. Orr

Song of Songs chapter 6

1. Before and after

Previous chapter: Chapter 5: Fourth song
Following chapter: Chapter 7: Fifth song

2. Analysis of chapter

Inquiry where Christ must be sought. (1)
Where Christ may be found. (2,3)
Christ's commendations of the Church. (4-10)
The work of grace in the believer. (11-13)

3. Key verse

Verse 3: "I am my beloved's, and my beloved is mine: he feedeth among the lilies."

4. Key word / key phrase

Verse 4, "You are beautiful."

5. Key event / key person / key theme

The fifth song, part one

6. Key thought

The groom praises the bride.

7. Key thing to look out for

True love is selfless.

8. Key Bible cross-reference

Verse 9. See Genesis 22:2.

9. Key "by way of explanation"

Verse 4, "as troops with banners." Soldiers were greatly inspired to march under the banner of their king and country.

10. Key "Quotable Quote"

"The Song is impressionistic: the symbolic imagery cools the imagination."
E.W. Orr

Song of Songs chapter 7

1. *Before and after*

> Previous chapter: Chapter 6: Fifth song
> Following chapter: Chapter 8: Sixth song

2. *Analysis of chapter*

> The graces of the Church. (1-9)
> The delight of the Church in Christ. (10-13)

3. *Key verse*

> Verse 10: "I am my beloved's, and his desire is toward me."

4. *Key word / key phrase*

> Verse 6, "how beautiful you are."

5. *Key event / key person / key theme*

> The fifth song, part two

6. *Key thought*

> The groom praises the bride again.

7. *Key thing to look out for*

> The bride responds to her groom's praises.

8. *Key Bible cross-reference*

> Verse 10. See Genesis 3:16.

9. *Key "by way of explanation"*

> Verse 5, "royal tapestry," refers to cloth used by royalty which was usually purple in color.

10. *Key "Quotable Quote"*

> "The community of the Bride and Groom is far above mere sexuality."
> E.W. Orr

Song of Songs chapter 8

1. *Previous chapter*

   Chapter 7: Fifth song

2. *Analysis of chapter*

   Desire for communion with Christ. (1-4)
   The vehemence of this desire. (5-7)
   The Church pleads for others. (8-12)
   And prays for Christ's coming. (13,14)

3. *Key verse*

   Verse 14: "Make haste, my beloved, and be thou like to a roe or to a young hart upon the mountains of spices."

4. *Key word / key phrase*

   Verse 6, "my love is as strong as death."

5. *Key event / key person / key theme*

   The sixth song

6. *Key thought*

   The power and value of love is expressed.

7. *Key thing to look out for*

   True love draws a man and a woman together.

8. *Key Bible cross-reference*

   Verse 10. See Ezekiel 16:7,8.

9. *Key "by way of explanation"*

   Verse 6, "seal." Seals were closely guarded and were highly prized as they bore the owner's name on them.

10. *Key "Quotable Quote"*

    "The Song is charged with psychical energy of nuclear fusion released when two hearts, distanced by the Creator when he made them male and female, approach each other for union in a life-long bond."
    E.W. Orr

Isaiah

Isaiah chapter 1

1. **Following chapter**

   Chapter 2: The day of judgment

2. **Analysis of chapter**

   The corruptions prevailing among the Jews. (1-9)
   Severe censures. (10-15)
   Exhortations to repentance. (16-20)
   The state of Judah is lamented; with gracious promises of the gospel times.
   (21-31)

3. **Key verse**

   Verse 1: "The vision of Isaiah the son of Amoz, which he saw concerning
   Judah and Jerusalem in the days of Uzziah, Jotham, Ahaz, and Hezekiah,
   kings of Judah."

4. **Key word / key phrase**

   Verse 4, "sinful nation."

5. **Key event / key person / key theme**

   God reprimands his people

6. **Key thought**

   Judah is accused for breaking the covenant.

7. **Key thing to look out for**

   God's judgment is certain.

8. **Key Bible cross-reference**

   Verse 9. See Genesis 19:24.

9. **Key "by way of explanation"**

   Verse 6, "oil," was used to bind up wounds, see Luke 10:34. Verse 1, Isaiah's
   prophecies were made during the tumultuous reigns of Judah's last kings.
   Isaiah was a contemporary of Amos, Hosea, and Micah.

10. **Key "Quotable Quote"**

    "God's mill grinds slow, but sure."
    George Herbert

Isaiah chapter 2

1. **Before and after**

   Previous chapter: Chapter 1: Judah's sickness
   Following chapter: Chapter 3: Society's breakdown

2. **Analysis of chapter**

   The conversion of the Gentiles. Description of the sinfulness of Israel. (1-9)
   The awful punishment of unbelievers. (10-22)

3. **Key verse**

   Verse 2: "Enter into the rock, and hide thee in the dust, for fear of the LORD,
   and for the glory of his majesty."

4. **Key word / key phrase**

   Verse 12, "a day in store."

5. **Key event / key person / key theme**

   The day of judgment

6. **Key thought**

   God's people will come to Jerusalem.

7. **Key thing to look out for**

   "That day" will be a day of judgment.

8. **Key Bible cross-reference**

   Verse 4. See Joel 3:10.

9. **Key "by way of explanation"**

   Verse 11, "in that day." This phrase comes seven times in chapters two, three,
   and four, and refers to God's judgment, or, the Day of the Lord.

10. **Key "Quotable Quote"**

    "The judgment of all men and women is ultimately going to be in terms of
    their relationship to the Lord Jesus Christ."
    D. Martyn Lloyd-Jones

Isaiah chapter 3

1. Before and after

Previous chapter: Chapter 2: The day of judgment
Following chapter: Chapter 4: The Day of the Lord: the branch

2. Analysis of chapter

The calamities about to come on the land. (1-9)
The wickedness of the people. (10-15)
The distress of the proud, wealthy women of Zion. (16-26)

3. Key verse

Verse 1: "For, behold, the Lord, the LORD of hosts, doth take away from Jerusalem and from Judah the stay and the staff, the whole stay of bread, and the whole stay of water."

4. Key word / key phrase

Verse 12, "your guides lead you astray."

5. Key event / key person / key theme

Society's breakdown

6. Key thought

Jerusalem will be punished because of her sin.

7. Key thing to look out for

The women of Jerusalem will be cut down in their pride.

8. Key Bible cross-reference

Verse 2. See 2 Chronicles 33:6.

9. Key "by way of explanation"

Verse 14, "vineyard." The vineyard is a picture of Israel, see Isaiah 5:1.

10. Key "Quotable Quote"

"The passions expelled by grace return to an arrogant soul."
Peter of Damascus

Isaiah chapter 4

1. ### Before and after

    Previous chapter: Chapter 3: Society's breakdown
    Following chapter: Chapter 5: The Song of the Vineyard

2. ### Analysis of chapter

    The havoc caused by war. (1)
    The times of the Messiah. (2-6)

3. ### Key verse

    Verse 2: "In that day shall the branch of the LORD be beautiful and glorious, and the fruit of the earth shall be excellent and comely for them that are escaped of Israel."

4. ### Key word / key phrase

    Verse 2, "the Branch of the Lord."

5. ### Key event / key person / key theme

    The Day of the Lord: the branch

6. ### Key thought

    The Branch of the Lord speaks of God's redemption.

7. ### Key thing to look out for

    The Lord God shelters and shields his people.

8. ### Key Bible cross-reference

    Verse 5. See Exodus 13:21.

9. ### Key "by way of explanation"

    Verse 3, "holy." This means separate in the sense of being totally and exclusively devoted to God.

10. ### Key "Quotable Quote"

    "Christ is our Redeemer, Savior, peace, atonement and satisfaction, and has made amends or satisfaction toward God for all the sin which they that repent, consenting to the law and believing the promises, do, have done, or shall do."
    William Tyndale

Isaiah chapter 5

1. **Before and after**

    Previous chapter: Chapter 4: The Day of the Lord: the branch
    Following chapter: Chapter 6: Isaiah's vision and calling

2. **Analysis of chapter**

    The state and behavior of the Jewish nation. (1-7)
    The coming judgments. (8-23)
    Those who will carry out these judgments. (24-30)

3. **Key verse**

    Verse 1: "Now will I sing to my well beloved a song of my beloved touching his vineyard."

4. **Key word / key phrase**

    Verse 1, "vineyard."

5. **Key event / key person / key theme**

    The Song of the Vineyard

6. **Key thought**

    The Lord could have done nothing more for his people.

7. **Key thing to look out for**

    Rejecting the Lord's love brings the Lord's judgment.

8. **Key Bible cross-reference**

    Verses 1,2. See Luke 20:9.

9. **Key "by way of explanation"**

    Verse 10. The tiny crops from this ten-acre site indicate how God punished his people.

10. **Key "Quotable Quote"**

    "Never before on this earth has there been such a huge number of people who freely and easily, without any shame, without any pangs of conscience 'call evil good, and good evil; that put darkness for light, and light for darkness; that put bitter for sweet, and sweet for bitter!' (Isaiah 5:20)."
    Archbishop Averky of Syracuse

Isaiah chapter 6

1. *Before and after*

Previous chapter: Chapter 5: The Song of the Vineyard
Following chapter: Chapter 7: The sign of Immanuel

2. *Analysis of chapter*

The vision which Isaiah saw in the temple. (1-8)
The Lord declares the blindness to come upon the Jewish nation, and the destruction which would follow. (9-13)

3. *Key verse*

Verse 3: "And one cried unto another, and said, Holy, holy, holy, is the LORD of hosts: the whole earth is full of his glory."

4. *Key word / key phrase*

Verse 8, "Whom shall I send?"

5. *Key event / key person / key theme*

Isaiah's vision and calling

6. *Key thought*

Every Christian is called to serve the Lord in some way.

7. *Key thing to look out for*

Isaiah needed to have his sin dealt with before he could serve the Lord.

8. *Key Bible cross-reference*

Verse 3. See Revelation 4:8.

9. *Key "by way of explanation"*

Verse 7, "touched my mouth." This was a purging of the prophet's sin. But it also indicated that Isaiah would speak for the Lord. See Jeremiah 1:9. Uzziah died in 740 BC.

10. *Key "Quotable Quote"*

"The Lord called me by the way of simplicity and humility."
Francis of Assisi

Isaiah chapter 7

1. Before and after

Previous chapter: Chapter 6: Isaiah's vision and calling
Following chapter: Chapter 8: Comfort and warning

2. Analysis of chapter

Ahaz threatened by Israel and Syria; and is assured their attack would be in vain. (1-9)
God gives a sure sign by the promise of the long-expected Messiah. (10-16)
The folly and sin of seeking relief from Assyria are reproved. (17-25)

3. Key verse

Verse 14: "Therefore the Lord himself shall give you a sign; Behold, a virgin shall conceive, and bear a son, and shall call his name Immanuel."

4. Key word / key phrase

Verse 14, "a sign."

5. Key event / key person / key theme

The sign of Immanuel

6. Key thought

Many prophecies were fulfilled in more than one way.

7. Key thing to look out for

Matthew refers to verse 14 as he applies the name "Immanuel" to Jesus. See Matthew 1:23.

8. Key Bible cross-reference

Verse 1. See 2 kings 16:5.

9. Key "by way of explanation"

Verse 20, "Shave . . . heads . . . beards." To have one's beard shaved off was considered a great insult. See 2 Samuel 10:4,5.

10. Key "Quotable Quote"

"Immanuel, God with us in our nature, in our sorrow, in our lifework, in our punishment, in our grave, and now with us, or rather we with him, in resurrection, ascension, triumph, and Second Advent splendor."
C.H. Spurgeon

Isaiah chapter 8

1. Before and after

> Previous chapter: Chapter 7: The sign of Immanuel
> Following chapter: Chapter 9: The sign of the Prince of Peace

2. Analysis of chapter

> Exhortations and warnings. (1-8)
> Comfort for those who fear God. (9-16)
> Afflictions to idolaters. (17-22)

3. Key verse

> Verse 10: "Take counsel together, and it shall come to nought; speak the word, and it shall not stand: for God is with us."

4. Key word / key phrase

> Verse 11, "warning me."

5. Key event / key person / key theme

> Comfort and warning

6. Key thought

> Assyria is to become the Lord's instrument.

7. Key thing to look out for

> Isaiah trusted in the Lord even though he seemed to be hidden from him.

8. Key Bible cross-reference

> Verse 17. See Hebrews 2:13.

9. Key "by way of explanation"

> Verse 12, "conspiracy." When the prophet Isaiah told God's people not to form an alliance with Assyria, as a way of defending themselves against an attack from Israel, it amounted to treason in their eyes.

10. Key "Quotable Quote"

> "To wait upon God is the perfection of activity."
> Oswald Chambers

Isaiah chapter 9

1. Before and after

Previous chapter: Chapter 8: Comfort and warning
Following chapter: Chapter 10: A remnant will survive

2. Analysis of chapter

The Son that should be born, and his kingdom. (1-7)
The judgments to come upon Israel, and on the enemies of the kingdom of Christ. (8-21)

3. Key verse

Verse 6: "For unto us a child is born, unto us a son is given: and the government shall be upon his shoulder: and his name shall be called Wonderful, Counselor, The mighty God, The everlasting Father, The Prince of Peace."

4. Key word / key phrase

Verse 6, "Prince of Peace."

5. Key event / key person / key theme

The sign of the Prince of Peace

6. Key thought

See how the titles in verse 6 relate to Jesus.

7. Key thing to look out for

The Lord will not put up with ungodliness.

8. Key Bible cross-reference

Verse 7. See Luke 1:32,33.

9. Key "by way of explanation"

Verse 6, "Mighty God." In the Old Testament the Lord was sometimes pictured as a strong warrior fighting for his people.

10. Key "Quotable Quote"

"There is no peace without the Prince of Peace."
Augustine of Hippo

Isaiah chapter 10

1. **Before and after**

    Previous chapter: Chapter 9: The sign of the Prince of Peace
    Following chapter: Chapter 11: God's future king

2. **Analysis of chapter**

    Woes against proud oppressors. (1-4)
    The Assyrians are but an instrument in the hand of God for the punishment of his people. (5-19)
    The deliverance from the aggressor. (20-34)

3. **Key verse**

    Verse 5: "O Assyrian, the rod of mine anger, and the staff in their hand is mine indignation."

4. **Key word / key phrase**

    Verse 20, "the remnant of Israel."

5. **Key event / key person / key theme**

    A remnant will survive

6. **Key thought**

    Today, the Christian Church is viewed as God's remnant.

7. **Key thing to look out for**

    Assyria was but a tool (verse 15), and would be punished for its pride.

8. **Key Bible cross-reference**

    Verses 5-34. See Isaiah 14:24-27; Nahum 1:1–3:19; Zephaniah 2:13-15.

9. **Key "by way of explanation"**

    When Isaiah gave this poem, Israel (the northern kingdom) had fallen to Assyria, and now Jerusalem itself was threatened (27-32).

10. **Key "Quotable Quote"**

    "What is impossible to God? Not that which is difficult to his power, but that which is contrary to his nature."
    Ambrose

Isaiah chapter 11

1. **Before and after**

    Previous chapter: Chapter 10: A remnant will survive
    Following chapter: Chapter 12: A song of salvation

2. **Analysis of chapter**

    The peaceful character of Christ's kingdom and subjects. (1-9)
    The conversion of the Gentiles and Jews. (10-16)

3. **Key verse**

    Verse 2: "And the spirit of the LORD shall rest upon him, the spirit of wisdom
    and understanding, the spirit of counsel and might, the spirit of knowledge
    and of the fear of the LORD."

4. **Key word / key phrase**

    Verse 1, "the stump of Jesse."

5. **Key event / key person / key theme**

    God's future king

6. **Key thought**

    Verses from this chapter are read at Christmas time as they speak of the
    coming of the Messiah.

7. **Key thing to look out for**

    Note what is said about the stump and the Root of Jesse in verses 1 and 10.

8. **Key Bible cross-reference**

    Verse 9. See Romans 9:27.

9. **Key "by way of explanation"**

    Verse 2, "the Spirit." One of the genuine signs of the coming of the Messiah
    would be that the Spirit would rest on him.

10. **Key "Quotable Quote"**

    "The great King, immortal, invisible, the divine person called the Holy Ghost,
    it is he that quickens the soul."
    C.H. Spurgeon

Isaiah chapter 12

1. **Before and after**

   Previous chapter: Chapter 11: God's future king
   Following chapter: Chapter 13: Prophecies against Babylon

2. **Analysis of chapter**

   This is a hymn of praise appropriate for the times of the Messiah. (1-6)

3. **Key verse**

   Verse 5: "Sing unto the LORD; for he hath done excellent things: this is known in all the earth."

4. **Key word / key phrase**

   Verse 6, "sing for joy."

5. **Key event / key person / key theme**

   A song of salvation

6. **Key thought**

   Songs of praise should always be sung to the Savior.

7. **Key thing to look out for**

   Worship should lead to evangelism. See verse 4.

8. **Key Bible cross-reference**

   Verse 2. See Exodus 15:2.

9. **Key "by way of explanation"**

   Verse 3, "wells." Wells of salvation refer to the Lord himself who saves his people as they draw live-giving water from him.

10. **Key "Quotable Quote"**

    "There is no more urgent and critical question in life than that of your personal relationship with God and your eternal salvation."
    Billy Graham

Isaiah chapter 13

1. Before and after

Previous chapter: Chapter 12: A song of salvation
Following chapter: Chapter 14: Prophecies against Assyria and Philistia

2. Analysis of chapter

The armies of God's wrath. (1-5)
The conquest of Babylon. (6-18)
Its final desolation. (19-22)

3. Key verse

Verse 6: "Howl ye; for the day of the LORD is at hand; it shall come as a destruction from the Almighty."

4. Key word / key phrase

Verse 1, "concerning Babylon."

5. Key event / key person / key theme

Prophecies against Babylon

6. Key thought

No matter how powerful great nations appear, God controls their destiny. The beautiful and powerful city of Babylon fell into ruins in the time of Christ, and has never been rebuilt.

7. Key thing to look out for

Note how God is pictured as a warrior summoning his troops for battle.

8. Key Bible cross-reference

Verse 21. See Isaiah 34:14.

9. Key "by way of explanation"

Verse 10, "not show their light." On the Lord's judgment day darkness fills the land. See Joel 2:10,31. Chapters 13–27 speak of God's purposes for the nations of the world.

10. Key "Quotable Quote"

"God hath appointed a day, wherein he will judge the world by Jesus Christ, when everyone shall receive according to his deed; the wicked shall go into everlasting punishment; the righteous, into everlasting life."
James Boyce

Isaiah chapter 14

1. **Before and after**

   Previous chapter: Chapter 13: Prophecies against Babylon
   Following chapter: Chapter 15: Prophecies against Moab

2. **Analysis of chapter**

   The destruction of Babylon, and the death of its proud monarch. (1-23)
   Assurance of the destruction of Assyria. (24-27)
   The destruction of the Philistines. (28-32)

3. **Key verse**

   Verse 4: "That thou shalt take up this proverb against the king of Babylon, and
   say, How hath the oppressor ceased! the golden city ceased!"

4. **Key word / key phrase**

   Verse 24, "as I planned, so it will be."

5. **Key event / key person / key theme**

   An end of oppression

6. **Key thought**

   The Lord is full of compassion.

7. **Key thing to look out for**

   The world's greatest superpower is puny when compared with the Lord.

8. **Key Bible cross-reference**

   Verse 12. See Revelation 8:10.

9. **Key "by way of explanation"**

   Verse 8, "pine trees . . . cedars." Isaiah was fond of personifying something
   from nature.

10. **Key "Quotable Quote"**

    "A prophet is one who knows his times and what God is trying to say to the
    people of his times."
    A.W. Tozer

Isaiah chapter 15

1. Before and after

Previous chapter: Chapter 14: Prophecies against Assyria and Philistia
Following chapter: Chapter 16: Moab's hopeless situation

2. Analysis of chapter

The divine judgments about to come upon the Moabites. (1-9)

3. Key verse

Verse 1: "The burden of Moab."

4. Key word / key phrase

Verse 1, "concerning Moab."

5. Key event / key person / key theme

Moab, Israel's constant enemy, will be judged by God.

6. Key thought

Verse 5. Isaiah feels sympathy for Moab.

7. Key thing to look out for

God's judgment falls on those who reject him.

8. Key Bible cross-reference

Verse 2. See 2 Chronicles 32:12.

9. Key "by way of explanation"

Verse 2, "high places," were pagan shrines.

10. Key "Quotable Quote"

"It is one thing to fall victim to the flood or to fall prey to cancer; it is another thing to fall into the hands of the living God."
R.C. Sproul

Isaiah chapter 16

1. *Before and after*

   Previous chapter: Chapter 15: Prophecies against Moab
   Following chapter: Chapter 17: Prophecies against Damascus and Israel

2. *Analysis of chapter*

   Moab is exhorted to obedience. (1-5)
   The pride and the judgments of Moab. (6-14)

3. *Key verse*

   Verse 6: "We have heard of the pride of Moab; he is very proud: even of his
   haughtiness, and his pride, and his wrath: but his lies shall not be so."

4. *Key word / key phrase*

   Verse 6, "Moab's pride."

5. *Key event / key person / key theme*

   Moab's hopeless situation

6. *Key thought*

   Moab's pride is her downfall.

7. *Key thing to look out for*

   Note in how many different ways Isaiah focuses on Moab's pride in this
   chapter.

8. *Key Bible cross-reference*

   Verse 6. See Jeremiah 48:29.

9. *Key "by way of explanation"*

   Verse 10, "treads out wine." After grapes had been picked they were trodden
   on in the winepress, and the juice ran out into a trough.

10. *Key "Quotable Quote"*

    "Pride is spiritual cancer; it eats the very possibility of love or contentment, or
    even common sense."
    C.S. Lewis

Isaiah chapter 17

1. **Before and after**

   Previous chapter: Chapter 16: Prophecies against Moab
   Following chapter: Chapter 18: Prophecies against Egypt

2. **Analysis of chapter**

   A prophecy against Damascus.. (1-3)
   A prophecy against Israel. (4-14)

3. **Key verse**

   Verse 1: "The burden of Damascus. Behold, Damascus is taken away from being a city, and it shall be a ruinous heap."

4. **Key word / key phrase**

   Verse 9, "desolation."

5. **Key event / key person / key theme**

   The invasion of Judah by the armies of Damascus and Israel in 734 BC.

6. **Key thought**

   God's enemies will eventually be defeated.

7. **Key thing to look out for**

   Forgetting the Lord and all he had done was Israel's besetting sin.

8. **Key Bible cross-reference**

   Verses 1-3. See Zechariah 9:1.

9. **Key "by way of explanation"**

   Verse 1, "Damascus," the capital of Aram (Syria) had been Israel's great enemy since the time of David.

10. **Key "Quotable Quote"**

    "I remember two things: that I am a great sinner and that Christ is a great Savior."
    John Newton

Isaiah chapter 18

1. **Before and after**

   Previous chapter: Chapter 17: Prophecies against Damascus and Israel
   Following chapter: Chapter 19: Prophecies against Egypt

2. **Analysis of chapter**

   Prophecy againt Egypt (here called Cush).. (1-7)

3. **Key verse**

   Verse 1: "Woe to the land shadowing with wings, which is beyond the rivers of Ethiopia [Cush]."

4. **Key word / key phrase**

   Verse 5, "cut down."

5. **Key event / key person / key theme**

   The king of Egypt had sent envoys to Hezekiah in an attempt to get Hezekiah to join in a coalition against Assyria.

6. **Key thought**

   All who are against God's people are called "people of the world" and are under God's judgment.

7. **Key thing to look out for**

   The graphic pictures in the Bible of God's judgment should move us.

8. **Key Bible cross-reference**

   Verses 18:1-7. See Zephaniah 2:12.

9. **Key "by way of explanation"**

   Verse 1, "Cush," is the name of a country to the south of Egypt. This country, the ancient Ethiopia, was close to our modern Ethiopia. The prophecy is a description of Egypt, which is addressed as "Cush" because in 715 BC a Cushite dynasty had come to power in Egypt.

10. **Key "Quotable Quote"**

    "Truly, when the day of judgment comes, we shall not be examined as to what we have read, but what we have done, not how well we have spoken but how we have lived."
    Thomas à Kempis

Isaiah chapter 19

1. **Before and after**

    Previous chapter: Chapter 18: Prophecies against Egypt
    Following chapter: Chapter 20: Prophecies against Egypt

2. **Analysis of chapter**

    Judgments upon Egypt. (1-17)
    Its deliverance, and the conversion of the people. (18-25)

3. **Key verse**

    Verse 1: "The burden of Egypt. Behold, the LORD rideth upon a swift cloud, and shall come into Egypt."

4. **Key word / key phrase**

    Verse 1, "concerning Egypt."

5. **Key event / key person / key theme**

    Prophecies against Egypt

6. **Key thought**

    The repetition of the words "in that day" emphasizes the certainty of God's impending judgment.

7. **Key thing to look out for**

    The hope offered in verse 25.

8. **Key Bible cross-reference**

    1-25. See Jeremiah 46:2-26.

9. **Key "by way of explanation"**

    Verse 15, "head or tail, palm branch or reed." These words refer to Egyptian leaders. See 9:14,15 where they refer to Israel's leaders.

10. **Key "Quotable Quote"**

    "The death of Jesus means the verdict which God will pronounce over us on the day of judgment has been brought into the present. We therefore do not need to fear the judgment day."
    Anthony Hoekema

Isaiah chapter 20

1. **Before and after**

    Previous chapter: Chapter 19: Prophecies against Egypt
    Following chapter: Chapter 21: Prophecies against Babylon, Edom, and
    Arabia

2. **Analysis of chapter**

    The invasion and conquest of Egypt and its rulers. (1-6)

3. **Key verse**

    Verse 4: "So shall the king of Assyria lead away the Egyptians prisoners, and
    the Ethiopians captives, young and old, naked and barefoot, even with their
    buttocks uncovered, to the shame of Egypt."

4. **Key word / key phrase**

    Verse 2, "stripped and barefoot."

5. **Key event / key person / key theme**

    For three years before the fall of Ashdod (in 712/11 BC) Isaiah had walked
    around Jerusalem stripped and barefoot as a warning to the people of coming
    disaster.

6. **Key thought**

    It is fatal to rely on human aid.

7. **Key thing to look out for**

    The Lord's people are not to ally themselves with the people of this world.

8. **Key Bible cross-reference**

    Verse 3. See 47:3.

9. **Key "by way of explanation"**

    Verse 5, "boasted in Egypt." Judah's king, Hezekiah, was advised to make a
    pact with Egypt, but Isaiah warned him against this. See 30:1-2; 31:1.

10. **Key "Quotable Quote"**

    "Separation from evil is the necessary first principle of communion with the
    Lord."
    J.N. Darby

Isaiah chapter 21

1. *Before and after*

Previous chapter: Chapter 20: Prophecies against Egypt
Following chapter: Chapter 22: Prophecies against Jerusalem

2. *Analysis of chapter*

The taking of Babylon. (1-10)
The Edomites. (11,12)
The Arabs. (13-17)

3. *Key verse*

Verse 11: "The burden of Dumah. He calleth to me out of Seir, Watchman, what of the night? Watchman, what of the night?"

4. *Key word / key phrase*

Verse 9, "Babylon has fallen."

5. *Key event / key person / key theme*

Prophecies against Babylon, Edom, and Arabia

6. *Key thought*

No country or evil group of people are strong enough to withstand the Lord's power.

7. *Key thing to look out for*

When the Bible says that God has "spoken," as in verse 17, it means that the action is as good as done.

8. *Key Bible cross-reference*

Verse 10. See Proverbs 25:25.

9. *Key "by way of explanation"*

Verse 9, "its gods lie shattered." When a country was defeated its gods, too, were disgraced.

10. *Key "Quotable Quote"*

"Evil is that which God does not will."
Emil Brunner

Isaiah chapter 22

1. Before and after

Previous chapter: Chapter 21: Prophecies against Babylon, Edom, and Arabia
Following chapter: Chapter 23: Prophecies against Tyre

2. Analysis of chapter

Jerusalem under siege. (1-11)
Godless revelry condemned. (12-14)
The displacing of the steward Shebna, and the promotion of Eliakim, applied
to the Messiah. (15-25)

3. Key verse

Verse 22: "And the key of the house of David will I lay upon his shoulder; so
he shall open, and none shall shut; and he shall shut, and none shall open."

4. Key word / key phrase

Verse 9, "the city of David."

5. Key event / key person / key theme

Jerusalem under servere threat

6. Key thought

When God lifted the danger the people let go of God.

7. Key thing to look out for

God's people, if they are sinful, will not escape God's judgment.

8. Key Bible cross-reference

Verse 13. See 1 Corinthians 15:32.

9. Key "by way of explanation"

Verses 1-14 probably refer to Sennacherib's siege in 701 BC, and the behavior of
the citizens when the siege was miraculously ended.

10. Key "Quotable Quote"

"If God doesn't bring judgment on America soon, he will have to apologize
to Sodom and Gomorrah."
Ruth Graham

Isaiah chapter 23

1. **Before and after**

   Previous chapter: Chapter 22: Prophecies against Jerusalem
   Following chapter: Chapter 24: Warning about coming judgment

2. **Analysis of chapter**

   The overthrow of Tyre. (1-14)
   It is established again. (15-18)

3. **Key verse**

   Verse 1: "The burden of Tyre. Howl, ye ships of Tarshish; for it is laid waste, so that there is no house, no entering in: from the land of Chittim it is revealed to them."

4. **Key word / key phrase**

   Verse 1, "Tyre is destroyed."

5. **Key event / key person / key theme**

   Prophecies against Tyre

6. **Key thought**

   God is the God of the nations and in charge of their rise and fall.

7. **Key thing to look out for**

   The timing of events in history is in the Lord's hands.

8. **Key Bible cross-reference**

   Verses 1-18. See Luke 10:13,14.

9. **Key "by way of explanation"**

   Verse 15, "seventy years." This was also the length of the exile in Babylon, Jeremiah 25:11; 29:10.

10. **Key "Quotable Quote"**

    "The judgments of God are like thunderclaps. Punishment to one, terror to all."
    John Boys

Isaiah chapter 24

1. *Before and after*

Previous chapter: Chapter 23: Prophecies against Tyre
Following chapter: Chapter 25: Praise for kingdom blessings

2. *Analysis of chapter*

The desolation of the land. (1-12)
A few will be preserved. (13-15)
God's kingdom advanced by his judgments. (16-23)

3. *Key verse*

Verse 5: "The earth also is defiled under the inhabitants thereof; because they have transgressed the laws, changed the ordinance, broken the everlasting covenant."

4. *Key word / key phrase*

Verse 3, "completely laid waste."

5. *Key event / key person / key theme*

Warning about coming judgment

6. *Key thought*

The images in the Bible about God's judgment all combine to tell us to take it seriously.

7. *Key thing to look out for*

Some of the reasons for God's judgments are clearly set out in this chapter.

8. *Key Bible cross-reference*

Verse 16. See Jeremiah 9:2.

9. *Key "by way of explanation"*

Verse 2. When God's judgment comes all sections of society will be judged.

10. *Key "Quotable Quote"*

"Learn from examples in history lest thou be made an example."
John Boys

Isaiah chapter 25

1. Before and after

Previous chapter: Chapter 24: Warning about coming judgment
Following chapter: Chapter 26: Israel's song of salvation

2. Analysis of chapter

A song of praise. (1-5)
A declaration of the gospel blessings. (6-8)
The destruction of the enemies of God's people. (9-12)

3. Key verse

Verse 6: "And in this mountain shall the LORD of hosts make unto all people a feast of fat things, a feast of wines on the lees, of fat things full of marrow, of wines on the lees well refined."

4. Key word / key phrase

Verse 1, "I will exult you."

5. Key event / key person / key theme

Praise for kingdom blessings

6. Key thought

A terrifying chapter about God's judgment is followed by an exhilarating chapter in praise of God.

7. Key thing to look out for

Notice how often it is stated that people are brought down because of their pride.

8. Key Bible cross-reference

Verse 8. See Revelation 7:17; 21:4.

9. Key "by way of explanation"

Verse 8, "swallow up death." Paul quotes part of this verse in 1 Corinthians 15:4. Death has now itself been swallowed up, thanks to Jesus' resurrection.

10. Key "Quotable Quote"

"The Immortal put on mortality in order to die for us, and by his death to slay the death of us all."
Augustine of Hippo

Isaiah chapter 26

1. **Before and after**

   Previous chapter: Chapter 25: Praise for kingdom blessings
   Following chapter: Chapter 27: Future restoration

2. **Analysis of chapter**

   The divine mercies encourage confidence in God. (1-4)
   His judgments. (5-11)
   His people exhorted to wait on him. (12-19)
   Deliverance promised. (20,21)

3. **Key verse**

   Verse 4: "Trust ye in the LORD for ever: for in the LORD JEHOVAH is everlasting strength."

4. **Key word / key phrase**

   Verse 1, "this song will be sung."

5. **Key event / key person / key theme**

   Israel's song of salvation

6. **Key thought**

   Only the Lord can establish peace.

7. **Key thing to look out for**

   The many reasons for praising the Lord

8. **Key Bible cross-reference**

   Verse 11. See Hebrews 10:27.

9. **Key "by way of explanation"**

   Verse 19, "your dead will live." This was a reference to the restoration of Israel. For Christians it reminds us about the resurrection of the body.

10. **Key "Quotable Quote"**

    "If a man does not say in his heart, 'In the world there is only myself and God,' he will not gain peace."
    Abba Alonius

Isaiah chapter 27

1. **Before and after**

   Previous chapter: Chapter 26: Israel's song of salvation
   Following chapter: Chapter 28: Israel and Judah are warned

2. **Analysis of chapter**

   God's care for his people. (1-5)
   Judgment followed by redemption. (6-13)

3. **Key verse**

   Verse 2: "In that day sing ye unto her, A vineyard of red wine."

4. **Key word / key phrase**

   Verse 2, "a fruitful vineyard."

5. **Key event / key person / key theme**

   Probably the destruction of the northern kingdom of Israel

6. **Key thought**

   God's tender care of his vineyard

7. **Key thing to look out for**

   Fruitfulness can only be achieved by abiding in the true Vine (John 15:1-16).

8. **Key Bible cross-reference**

   Verse 1. See Job 41:1.

9. **Key "by way of explanation"**

   Verse 13, "trumpet will sound." Trumpets were used to call soldiers to fight
   and often refer to God's judgment.

10. **Key "Quotable Quote"**

   "We get no deeper into Christ than we allow him to get into us."
   J.H. Jowett

Isaiah chapter 28

1. Before and after

Previous chapter: Chapter 27: Future restoration
Following chapter: Chapter 29: Jerusalem is warned

2. Analysis of chapter

The desolations of Samaria, capital of the northern kingdom. (1-13)
Rebuke to the northern kingdom. (14-15)
Christ is pointed out as the sure Foundation for all believers. (16-22)
God's dealings with his people. (23-29)

3. Key verse

Verse 1: "Woe to the crown of pride, to the drunkards of Ephraim, whose glorious beauty is a fading flower, which are on the head of the fat valleys of them that are overcome with wine!"

4. Key word / key phrase

Verse 1, "the pride of Ephraim."

5. Key event / key person / key theme

The folly of refusing to take God seriously

6. Key thought

A cornerstone for Zion is promised.

7. Key thing to look out for

Concluding verses containing God's wisdom.

8. Key Bible cross-reference

Verse 16. See 1 Peter 2:6.

9. Key "by way of explanation"

Verse 7, "wine . . . beer." The prophets were too drunk to receive God's messages.

10. Key "Quotable Quote"

"Anything which increases the authority of the body over the mind is an evil thing."
Susannah Wesley, letter to her son John

Isaiah chapter 29

1. Before and after

Previous chapter: Chapter 28: Israel and Judah are warned
Following chapter: Chapter 30: The obstinate are warned

2. Analysis of chapter

Judgments on Jerusalem and on its enemies. (1-8)
The senselessness and hypocrisy of the prophets. (9-12)
God will bring about his plans. (13-24)

3. Key verse

Verse 9: "Stay yourselves, and wonder; cry ye out, and cry: they are drunken, but not with wine; they stagger, but not with strong drink."

4. Key word / key phrase

Verse 1, "the city where David settled."

5. Key event / key person / key theme

Jerusalem is warned

6. Key thought

The siege of Jerusalem is prophesied.

7. Key thing to look out for

The Lord hates hypocrisy and exposes it.

8. Key Bible cross-reference

Verse 10. See Romans 11:8.

9. Key "by way of explanation"

Verse 13. Jesus quotes from this verse to highlight the hypocrisy of the Pharisees.

10. Key "Quotable Quote"

"The knowledge of God, and the remembrance of his all-seeing presence, are the most powerful means against hypocrisy."
Richard Baxter

Isaiah chapter 30

1. **Before and after**

   Previous chapter: Chapter 29: Jerusalem is warned
   Following chapter: Chapter 31: Warning against an Egyptian alliance

2. **Analysis of chapter**

   The Jews reproved for seeking help from Egypt. (1-7)
   Judgments as a result of their contempt of God's word. (8-18)
   God's mercies to his people. (19-26)
   The ruin of the Assyrian army, and of all God's enemies. (27-33)

3. **Key verse**

   Verse 8: "Now go, write it before them in a table, and note it in a book, that it
   may be for the time to come for ever and ever."

4. **Key word / key phrase**

   Verse 1, "obstinate children."

5. **Key event / key person / key theme**

   The obstinate are warned

6. **Key thought**

   God's mercies are highlighted, even though his followers disobey him.

7. **Key thing to look out for**

   To reject the Lord, verse 15, is to miss out on his wonderful blessings.

8. **Key Bible cross-reference**

   Verse 6. See Revelation 12:3.

9. **Key "by way of explanation"**

   Verse 20, "bread of adversity . . . water of affliction." This refers to the bread
   and water diet of prison. The oracles in this chapter relate to the time when
   Hezekiah rebelled against Assyria.

10. **Key "Quotable Quote"**

    "Man calls it an accident, God calls it abomination.
    Man calls it a defect, God calls it a disease.
    Man calls it an error, God calls it an enmity.
    Man calls it a liberty, God calls it lawlessness.
    Man calls it a trifle, God calls it a tragedy.
    Man calls it a mistake, God calls it a madness.
    Man calls it a weakness, God calls it willfulness."
    Author unknown

Isaiah chapter 31

1. **Before and after**

   Previous chapter: Chapter 30: The obstinate are warned
   Following chapter: Chapter 32: The King is coming

2. **Analysis of chapter**

   The sin and folly of seeking help from Egypt. (1-5)
   God's care for Jerusalem. (6-9)

3. **Key verse**

   Verse 1: "Woe to them that go down to Egypt for help; and stay on horses, and trust in chariots, because they are many; and in horsemen, because they are very strong; but they look not unto the Holy One of Israel, neither seek the LORD!"

4. **Key word / key phrase**

   Verse 1, "those who go down to Egypt."

5. **Key event / key person / key theme**

   Warning against an Egyptian alliance

6. **Key thought**

   The folly of seeking help from the wrong people.

7. **Key thing to look out for**

   God's great care for Jerusalem is like a protective shield.

8. **Key Bible cross-reference**

   Verse 2. See Proverbs 22:23.

9. **Key "by way of explanation"**

   Verse 9, "fire . . . furnace." God's judgment will be like fire when it falls on people.
   Nineveh was destroyed by Babylon in 612 BC.

10. **Key "Quotable Quote"**

    "Let us not underestimate how hard it is to be compassionate."
    Henri Nouwen

Isaiah chapter 32

1. **Before and after**

   Previous chapter: Chapter 31: Warning against an Egyptian alliance
   Following chapter: Chapter 33: A hymn of thanksgiving

2. **Analysis of chapter**

   Times of peace and happiness. (1-8)
   An interval of trouble, yet comfort and blessings in the end. (9-20)

3. **Key verse**

   Verse 4: "The heart also of the rash shall understand knowledge, and the tongue of the stammerers shall be ready to speak plainly."

4. **Key word / key phrase**

   Verse 1, "A king will reign."

5. **Key event / key person / key theme**

   The King is coming

6. **Key thought**

   Complacency is severely rebuked.

7. **Key thing to look out for**

   Verses 17-20, the fruit of righteousness

8. **Key Bible cross-reference**

   Verse 11. See Jeremiah 17:8.

9. **Key "by way of explanation"**

   Verses 5-8. These verses are similar to the wisdom literature of the Bible where comparisons between the wise and the foolish are constantly made. See Proverbs 9:13-18.

10. **Key "Quotable Quote"**

   "Complacency is a deadly foe of all spiritual growth."
   A.W. Tozer

Isaiah chapter 33

1. ## Before and after

   Previous chapter: Chapter 32: The King is coming
   Following chapter: Chapter 34: A warning to the nations

2. ## Analysis of chapter

   God's judgments against the enemies of his people. (1-14)
   The happiness of his people. (15-24)

3. ## Key verse

   Verse 2: "O LORD, be gracious unto us; we have waited for thee: be thou their arm every morning, our salvation also in the time of trouble."

4. ## Key word / key phrase

   Verse 5, "the Lord is exalted."

5. ## Key event / key person / key theme

   A hymn of thanksgiving

6. ## Key thought

   The promise for a wonderful future is given.

7. ## Key thing to look out for

   No matter what circumstances we face, the Lord can be our strength each morning.

8. ## Key Bible cross-reference

   Verse 18. See Matthew 5:46.

9. ## Key "by way of explanation"

   Verse 23, "rigging." The picture here is of Jerusalem as a warship.

10. ## Key "Quotable Quote"

    "To be in Christ is the source of the Christian's life; to be like Christ is the sum of his excellence; to be with Christ is the fullness of his joy."
    Charles Hodge

Isaiah chapter 34

1. Before and after

Previous chapter: Chapter 33: A hymn of thanksgiving
Following chapter: Chapter 35: The promise of restoration and transformation

2. Analysis of chapter

God's vengeance against the enemies of his people. (1-8)
Their desolation. (9-17)

3. Key verse

Verse 9: "And the streams thereof shall be turned into pitch, and the dust thereof into brimstone, and the land thereof shall become burning pitch."

4. Key word / key phrase

Verse 1, "pay attention, you peoples!"

5. Key event / key person / key theme

A warning to the nations: Edom, Israel's long-time enemy, represents all his enemies.

6. Key thought

God's enemies will never ultimately escape from God's punishment.

7. Key thing to look out for

Contemplating God's judgment is a terrifying spectacle.

8. Key Bible cross-reference

Verse 4. See Mark 13:25.

9. Key "by way of explanation"

Verse 11, "desert owl." These are the birds you would expect to find in deserted cities and among ruins.

10. Key "Quotable Quote"

"No man is condemned for anything he has done: he is condemned for continuing to do wrong. He is condemned for not coming out of the darkness, for not coming to the light."
George MacDonald

Isaiah chapter 35

1. **Before and after**

   Previous chapter: Chapter 34: A warning to the nations
   Following chapter: Chapter 40: Comfort because of Israel's deliverance

2. **Analysis of chapter**

   The ultimate joy and peace of the people of God. (1-4)
   The privileges of his people. (5-10)

3. **Key verse**

   Verse 5: "Then the eyes of the blind shall be opened, and the ears of the deaf shall be unstopped."

4. **Key word / key phrase**

   Verse 2, "burst into bloom."

5. **Key event / key person / key theme**

   The promise of restoration and transformation

6. **Key thought**

   Any blossoming flower can remind us that God is victorious.

7. **Key thing to look out for**

   The joy a Christian experiences is for now and for eternity.

8. **Key Bible cross-reference**

   Verse 3. See Hebrews 12:12.

9. **Key "by way of explanation"**

   Verse 9, "ferocious beast." Prowling wild animals, such as lions, made all travel dangerous.

10. **Key "Quotable Quote"**

    "A joyless life is not a Christian life, for joy is one constant in the recipe for Christian living."
    William Barclay

Isaiah chapter 40

(Isaiah chapters 36, 37, 38, 39 are almost identical with 2 Kings 18:13-20:19.)

1. **Before and after**

   Previous chapter: Chapter 35: The promise of restoration and transformation
   Following chapter: Chapter 41: Comfort because of God's greatness

2. **Analysis of chapter**

   The preaching of the gospel, and good news of the coming of Christ. (1-11)
   The almighty power of God. (12-17)
   The folly of idolatry. (18-31)

3. **Key verse**

   Verse 1: "Comfort ye, comfort ye my people, saith your God."

4. **Key word / key phrase**

   Verse 2, "speak tenderly."

5. **Key event / key person / key theme**

   Comfort because of Israel's deliverance

6. **Key thought**

   This chapter contains some of the most glorious words of hope found in the Bible.

7. **Key thing to look out for**

   Israel's God cannot be compared with any other so-called "gods."

8. **Key Bible cross-reference**

   Verse 3. See Matthew 3:3.

9. **Key "by way of explanation"**

   Verse 3, "voice." Each "voice" mentioned, verses 3,6,9, brings a message of comfort.

10. **Key "Quotable Quote"**

    "If you wish to leave much wealth to your children, leave them in God's care."
    John Chrysostom

Isaiah chapter 41

1. *Before and after*

Previous chapter: Chapter 40: Comfort because of Israel's deliverance
Following chapter: Chapter 42: Comfort because of God's Servant

2. *Analysis of chapter*

God's care of his people. (1-9)
They are encouraged not to fear. (10-20)
The vanity and folly of idolatry. (21-29)

3. *Key verse*

Verse 1: "Keep silence before me, O islands; and let the people renew their strength: let them come near; then let them speak: let us come near together to judgment."

4. *Key word / key phrase*

Verse 4, "with the first of them and with the last."

5. *Key event / key person / key theme*

God's supremacy

6. *Key thought*

God is in control of world events.

7. *Key thing to look out for*

It is God himself who promises to help his followers.

8. *Key Bible cross-reference*

Verse 8. See 2 Chronicles 20:7.

9. *Key "by way of explanation"*

Verse 14, "worm." This describes the desperate and despised state of the exiles in Babylon.

10. *Key "Quotable Quote"*

"God is always present, always available."
Jacques Ellul

Isaiah chapter 42

1. *Before and after*

Previous chapter: Chapter 41: Comfort because of God's greatness
Following chapter: Chapter 43: God is Israel's Redeemer

2. *Analysis of chapter*

The character and coming of Christ. (1-4)
The blessings of his kingdom. (5-12)
The prevalence of true religion. (13-17)
Unbelief and blindness reproved. (18-25)

3. *Key verse*

Verse 1: "Behold my servant, whom I uphold; mine elect, in whom my soul delighteth; I have put my spirit upon him: he shall bring forth judgment to the Gentiles."

4. *Key word / key phrase*

Verse 1, "my servant."

5. *Key event / key person / key theme*

Comfort because of God's Servant

6. *Key thought*

God's promises provide help in a multitude of different ways.

7. *Key thing to look out for*

Singing God's praises revitalizes us spiritually.

8. *Key Bible cross-reference*

Verse 1. See Matthew 3:17.

9. *Key "by way of explanation"*

Verse 14, "for a long time." The seventy-year long exile seemed to be a time when God's people were cut off from him, being away from their city and temple.

10. *Key "Quotable Quote"*

"When your heart is full of Christ, you want to sing."
C.H. Spurgeon

Isaiah chapter 43

1. **Before and after**

   Previous chapter: Chapter 42: Comfort because of God's Servant
   Following chapter: Chapter 44: The absurdity of idolatry

2. **Analysis of chapter**

   God's unchangeable love for his people. (1-7)
   Apostates and idolaters addressed. (8-13)
   The deliverance from Babylon, and the conversion of the Gentiles. (14-21)
   Admonition to repent of sin. (22-28)

3. **Key verse**

   Verse 1: "But now thus saith the LORD that created thee, O Jacob, and he that
   formed thee, O Israel, Fear not: for I have redeemed thee, I have called thee by
   thy name; thou art mine."

4. **Key word / key phrase**

   Verse 1, "I have redeemed you."

5. **Key event / key person / key theme**

   The promise of release

6. **Key thought**

   Israel never forget the way God had rescued them from Egypt.

7. **Key thing to look out for**

   The force of the argument is: If God so acted in the past, will you not trust him
   for the present?

8. **Key Bible cross-reference**

   Verse 28. See Nehemiah 13:18.

9. **Key "by way of explanation"**

   Verse 2, "pass through the waters." God's people knew that it was only God's
   power and presence that had enabled them to cross over the water out of
   Egypt.

10. **Key "Quotable Quote"**

    "Jesus saves: indeed, but that means not only saving your soul out of the
    shipwreck of this world! His saving grace redeems us here and now. He is able
    to redeem us, really and truly, not just 'spiritually' in a narrow sense."
    H.R. Rookmaaker

Isaiah chapter 44

1. *Before and after*

    Previous chapter: Chapter 43: God is Israel's Redeemer
    Following chapter: Chapter 45: Comfort through God using Cyrus

2. *Analysis of chapter*

    Here are promises of the influences of the Holy Spirit. (1-8)
    An exposure of the folly of idolatry. (9-20)
    Also the deliverance of God's people. (21-28)

3. *Key verse*

    Verse 6: "Thus saith the LORD the King of Israel, and his redeemer the LORD of hosts; I am the first, and I am the last; and beside me there is no God."

4. *Key word / key phrase*

    Verse 9, "All who make idols."

5. *Key event / key person / key theme*

    The absurdity of idolatry

6. *Key thought*

    Jacob was a cheat. But God chose to bless him. From sheer grace every Christian is called by God.

7. *Key thing to look out for*

    Our God is both the Creator of the world and our personal Savior.

8. *Key Bible cross-reference*

    Verse 6. See Revelation 22:13.

9. *Key "by way of explanation"*

    Verse 2, "formed you in the womb," shows how much the Lord cared for us, even before we were born.

10. *Key "Quotable Quote"*

    "We are a long time in learning that all our strength and salvation is in God."
    David Brainerd

Isaiah chapter 45

1. *Before and after*

Previous chapter: Chapter 44: The absurdity of idolatry
Following chapter: Chapter 46: Destruction of Babylon's idols

2. *Analysis of chapter*

An oracle addressed to Cyrus, God's anointed. (1-7)
God calls for obedience to his almighty power. (8-10)
The settlement of his people. (11-19)
The conversion of the Gentiles. (20-25)

3. *Key verse*

Verse 1: "Thus saith the LORD to his anointed, to Cyrus, whose right hand I
have holden, to subdue nations before him."

4. *Key word / key phrase*

Verse 1, "Cyrus."

5. *Key event / key person / key theme*

Cyrus, a pagan emperor, was used to bring about God's plans.

6. *Key thought*

The all-powerful God will fulfill his purposes in his way.

7. *Key thing to look out for*

The Lord God is our Creator God as well as the Lord of history.

8. *Key Bible cross-reference*

Verse 9. See Romans 9:20.

9. *Key "by way of explanation"*

Cyrus, the founder of the Persian Empire, captured Babylon in October 539
BC. In the first year of his reign he issued a decree permitting the exiles to
return to Jerusalem. He authorized the rebuilding of the temple.

10. *Key "Quotable Quote"*

"God has no need of his creatures, but everything created has need of him."
Meister Eckhart

Isaiah chapter 46

1. **Before and after**

    Previous chapter: Chapter 45: Comfort through God using Cyrus
    Following chapter: Chapter 47: Destruction of Babylon

2. **Analysis of chapter**

    The idols could not save themselves, but God saves his people. (1-4)
    The folly of worshiping idols. (5-13)

3. **Key verse**

    Verse 5: "To whom will ye liken me, and make me equal, and compare me,
    that we may be like?"

4. **Key word / key phrase**

    Verse 1, "Bel . . . Nebo."

5. **Key event / key person / key theme**

    Destruction of Babylon's idols

6. **Key thought**

    God's message to an idol-infested society is: "I alone am God."

7. **Key thing to look out for**

    The other side of the coin of salvation and forgiveness is judgment and God's
    wrath.

8. **Key Bible cross-reference**

    Verse 12. See Proverbs 29:1.

9. **Key "by way of explanation"**

    Verse 11, "bird of prey." Cyrus, like a bird of prey, was characterized by power
    and swift action.

10. **Key "Quotable Quote"**

    "Love can forbear, and Love can forgive but Love can never be reconciled to
    an unlovely object."
    Thomas Traherne

Isaiah chapter 47

1. **Before and after**

   Previous chapter: Chapter 46: Destruction of Babylon's idols
   Following chapter: Chapter 48: Israel is stubborn

2. **Analysis of chapter**

   God's judgments on Babylon. (1-6)
   Carelessness and confidence shall not prevent the evil. (7-15)

3. **Key verse**

   Verse 4: "As for our redeemer, the LORD of hosts is his name, the Holy One of
   Israel."

4. **Key word / key phrase**

   Verse 1, "Sit in the dust."

5. **Key event / key person / key theme**

   Destruction of Babylon

6. **Key thought**

   God may stay his hand, but when his judgment does come it is decisive.

7. **Key thing to look out for**

   The way of darkness and sorcery is certain to lead to death.

8. **Key Bible cross-reference**

   Verses 8,9. See Revelation 18:7,8.

9. **Key "by way of explanation"**

   Verse 7, "I will continue forever." Many cruel dictators have echoed such
   words, including Nebuchadnezzar, Daniel 4:30.

10. **Key "Quotable Quote"**

    "Arrogance has its own built-in misery. The arrogant person may offend
    others, but he hurts himself more."
    Billy Graham

Isaiah chapter 48

1. **Before and after**

   Previous chapter: Chapter 47: Destruction of Babylon
   Following chapter: Chapter 49: The Messiah's mission

2. **Analysis of chapter**

   The Jews reproved for their idolatry. (1-8)
   Yet their deliverance is promised. (9-15)
   Solemn warnings of judgment on those who persisted in evil. (16-22)

3. **Key verse**

   Verse 9: "For my name's sake will I defer mine anger, and for my praise will I
   refrain for thee, that I cut thee not off."

4. **Key word / key phrase**

   Verse 4, "stubborn."

5. **Key event / key person / key theme**

   Israel is stubborn

6. **Key thought**

   God's love can melt the hardest of hearts.

7. **Key thing to look out for**

   God's teaching, verse 17, will only be accepted when it is realized that it is all
   for our own good.

8. **Key Bible cross-reference**

   Verse 12. See Revelation 1:17.

9. **Key "by way of explanation"**

   Verse 13, "spread out the heavens" – one of Isaiah's ways of referring to God as
   the Creator. Isaiah was constantly returning to this theme.

10. **Key "Quotable Quote"**

    "To see a World in a grain of sand,
    And a Heaven in a wild flower,
    Hold Infinity in the palm of your hand,
    And Eternity in an hour."
    William Blake

Isaiah chapter 49

1. **Before and after**

    Previous chapter: Chapter 48: Israel is stubborn
    Following chapter: Chapter 50: The Messiah's obedience

2. **Analysis of chapter**

    The unbelief and rejection of the people. (1-6)
    Gracious promise to the Gentiles. (7-12)
    God's love for his chosen people. (13-17)
    Their increase. (18-23)
    And deliverance. (24-26)

3. **Key verse**

    Verse 1: "Listen, O isles, unto me; and hearken, ye people, from far; The LORD hath called me from the womb."

4. **Key word / key phrase**

    Verse 6, "to restore."

5. **Key event / key person / key theme**

    The Messiah's mission

6. **Key thought**

    Isaiah remained conscious of his pre-natal election.

7. **Key thing to look out for**

    Nothing and no one is beyond the Lord's restoration.

8. **Key Bible cross-reference**

    Verse 1. See Jeremiah 1:5.

9. **Key "by way of explanation"**

    Verse 2l, "polished arrow." Arrows depict God's judgment. See Deuteronomy 32:23,42. A "polished" arrow ensures sure and swift flight.

10. **Key "Quotable Quote"**

    "He who undertakes anything without a divine call seeks his own glory."
    D'Aubigne

Isaiah chapter 50

1. *Before and after*

   Previous chapter: Chapter 49: The Messiah's mission
   Following chapter: Chapter 51: The Messiah's encouragement to Israel

2. *Analysis of chapter*

   A temporary separation. (1-3)
   The sufferings and exaltation of the Messiah. (4-9)
   Consolation to the believer, and warning to the unbeliever. (10,11)

3. *Key verse*

   Verse 4: "The Lord GOD hath given me the tongue of the learned, that I should know how to speak a word in season to him that is weary: he wakeneth morning by morning, he wakeneth mine ear to hear as the learned."

4. *Key word / key phrase*

   Verse 10, "obeys."

5. *Key event / key person / key theme*

   The Messiah's obedience

6. *Key thought*

   Verse 10 gives a picture of abiding in the Lord.

7. *Key thing to look out for*

   Obedience was one of the key characteristics of God's Servant.

8. *Key Bible cross-reference*

   Verse 6. See Mark 14:65.

9. *Key "by way of explanation"*

   Verse 5, "opened my ears." This symbolizes a person who obeys God because he follows what God has enabled him to hear.

10. *Key "Quotable Quote"*

    "Remember to eat your bread, or your heart will wither away. Fill your soul with richness and strength."
    Bernard of Clairvaux

Isaiah chapter 51

1. Before and after

Previous chapter: Chapter 50: The Messiah's obedience
Following chapter: Chapter 52: The Messiah's atonement

2. Analysis of chapter

Exhortations to trust the Messiah. (1-3)
The power of God, and the weakness of man. (4-8)
Christ defends his people. (9-16)
Their afflictions and deliverances. (17-23)

3. Key verse

Verse 1: "Hearken to me, ye that follow after righteousness, ye that seek the LORD: look unto the rock whence ye are hewn, and to the hole of the pit whence ye are digged."

4. Key word / key phrase

Verse 3, "comfort Zion."

5. Key event / key person / key theme

The Messiah's encouragement to Israel

6. Key thought

All suffering will one day end.

7. Key thing to look out for

The salvation the Lord offers is everlasting salvation.

8. Key Bible cross-reference

Verse 17. See Revelation 14:10; 16:19.

9. Key "by way of explanation"

Verse 1, "rock." "Rock" usually refers to the Lord, especially in the psalms, but here it refers to Abraham, through whose faithfulness God's people were established.

10. Key "Quotable Quote"

"The Bible declares that the salvation of sinful men is a matter of grace."
Loraine Boettner

Isaiah chapter 52

1. **Before and after**

Previous chapter: Chapter 51: The Messiah's encouragement to Israel
Following chapter: Chapter 53: The Messiah's atonement

2. **Analysis of chapter**

The welcome news of Christ's kingdom. (1-12)
The humiliation of the Messiah. (13-15)

3. **Key verse**

Verse 7: "How beautiful upon the mountains are the feet of him that bringeth good tidings, that publisheth peace; that bringeth good tidings of good, that publisheth salvation; that saith unto Zion, Thy God reigneth!"

4. **Key word / key phrase**

Verse 10, "the salvation of our God."

5. **Key event / key person / key theme**

The Messiah's atonement

6. **Key thought**

God's rescue plan includes physical as well as spiritual blessings.

7. **Key thing to look out for**

God's people would have been surprised to learn that God's special Servant whould be a suffering Servant.

8. **Key Bible cross-reference**

Verse 5. See Romans 2:24.

9. **Key "by way of explanation"**

Verse 7, "the feet of those who bring good news." God's messengers, preachers, teachers, evangelists are not praised for having beautiful feet, but because of the wonderful message they carry.

10. **Key "Quotable Quote"**

"If Mark's is the Gospel of Christ the suffering Servant, and Luke's the Gospel of Christ the universal Savior, Matthew's is the Gospel of Christ the ruling King."
John R.W. Stott

Isaiah chapter 53

1. *Before and after*

   Previous chapter: Chapter 52: The Messiah's atonement
   Following chapter: Chapter 54: The Messiah's promise of Israel's restoration

2. *Analysis of chapter*

   The person. (1-3)
   Sufferings. (4-9)
   Humiliation, and exaltation of Christ, are described in detail; with the blessings to humankind from his death. (10-12)

3. *Key verse*

   Verse 6: "All we like sheep have gone astray; we have turned every one to his own way; and the LORD hath laid on him the iniquity of us all."

4. *Key word / key phrase*

   Verse 6, "laid on him."

5. *Key event / key person / key theme*

   The Messiah's atonement

6. *Key thought*

   Verse 6 is one of the clearest pictures of atonement in the Bible.

7. *Key thing to look out for*

   No other chapter in Isaiah speaks so much about Jesus' crucifixion as this one.

8. *Key Bible cross-reference*

   Verse 1. See John 12:38.

9. *Key "by way of explanation"*

   Verse 6, "laid on him the iniquity." This pictures the priest laying his hands on the scapegoat, as God's people thought of their sins being taken away.

10. *Key "Quotable Quote"*

   "We are also told in Isaiah 53 that Christ's death is to be vicarious."
   D. Martyn Lloyd-Jones

Isaiah chapter 54

1. **Before and after**

   Previous chapter: Chapter 53: The Messiah's atonement
   Following chapter: Chapter 55: The Messiah's global invitation

2. **Analysis of chapter**

   Jerusalem's future prosperity. (1-17)

3. **Key verse**

   Verse 4: "Fear not; for thou shalt not be ashamed: neither be thou confounded; for thou shalt not be put to shame: for thou shalt forget the shame of thy youth, and shalt not remember the reproach of thy widowhood any more."

4. **Key word / key phrase**

   Verse 2, "enlarge the place of your tent."

5. **Key event / key person / key theme**

   The Messiah's promise of Israel's restoration

6. **Key thought**

   God's love stretches out in front of us and will never end.

7. **Key thing to look out for**

   Jerusalem is promised a wonderful future, as are God's followers.

8. **Key Bible cross-reference**

   Verse 1. See Genesis 4:27.

9. **Key "by way of explanation"**

   Verses 11,12. Jerusalem is pictured in a highly figurative and wonderful way, just as the new Jerusalem is in Revelation 21:10,18-21.

10. **Key "Quotable Quote"**

    "Christ is the desire of nations, the joy of angels, the delight of the Father. What solace then must that soul be filled with that hath the possession of him to all eternity!"
    John Bunyan

Isaiah chapter 55

1. Before and after

Previous chapter: Chapter 54: The Messiah's promise of Israel's restoration
Following chapter: Chapter 56: The basis of worship

2. Analysis of chapter

An invitation to receive freely the blessings of the Savior. (1-5)
Gracious offers of pardon and peace. (6-13)

3. Key verse

Verse 1: "Ho, every one that thirsteth, come ye to the waters, and he that hath no money; come ye, buy, and eat; yea, come, buy wine and milk without money and without price."

4. Key word / key phrase

Verse 1, "all."

5. Key event / key person / key theme

The Messiah's global invitation

6. Key thought

Salvation is all of grace. But this should not stop people seeking God.

7. Key thing to look out for

The Bible is full of descriptions of the joy of salvation, not just of warnings about God's judgment.

8. Key Bible cross-reference

Verse 1. See Revelation 21:6.

9. Key "by way of explanation"

Verse 2, "richest of fare." God's blessings are often likened to a feast in the Bible. See Jeremiah 31:14.

10. Key "Quotable Quote"

"If the pleasures of love can attract a man to a woman, if hunger and loneliness can make a man travel miles in search of food and shelter, how much more will the desire for truth and holiness make a man seek God."
Augustine of Hippo

Isaiah chapter 56

1. **Before and after**

    Previous chapter: Chapter 55: The Messiah's global invitation
    Following chapter: Chapter 57: The Messiah rebukes the wicked

2. **Analysis of chapter**

    A charge to keep the divine precepts. (1,2)
    Blessings promised. (3-8)
    Reproof to the careless watchmen, the teachers and rulers of the Jews. (9-12)

3. **Key verse**

    Verse 9: "All ye beasts of the field, come to devour, yea, all ye beasts in the forest."

4. **Key word / key phrase**

    Verse 6, "worship him."

5. **Key event / key person / key theme**

    The basis of worship

6. **Key thought**

    God's promise of salvation includes those everyone else would exclude.

7. **Key thing to look out for**

    Despite all God did his people were unfaithful to him.

8. **Key Bible cross-reference**

    Verse 7. See Luke 19:46.

9. **Key "by way of explanation"**

    Verse 4, "eunuchs" were considered to be ceremonially unclean. Yet the Lord promises to give them "an everlasting name."

10. **Key "Quotable Quote"**

    "Seek not to explore the heights of the divine majesty, but to find salvation in the saving deeds of God our Savior."
    William of St Thierry

Isaiah chapter 57

1. Before and after

Previous chapter: Chapter 56: The basis of worship
Following chapter: Chapter 58: The blessings of true worship

2. Analysis of chapter

The blessed death of the righteous. (1,2)
The abominable idolatries of the Jewish nation. (3-12)
Promises to the humble and contrite. (13-21)

3. Key verse

Verse 2: "He shall enter into peace: they shall rest in their beds, each one walking in his uprightness."

4. Key word / key phrase

Verse 4, "a brood of rebels."

5. Key event / key person / key theme

The Messiah rebukes the wicked

6. Key thought

God's judgments are meant to be pondered in our hearts.

7. Key thing to look out for

God's many promises of help include healing.

8. Key Bible cross-reference

Verse 19. See Ephesians 2:17.

9. Key "by way of explanation"

Verse 9, "Molech," was the chief Ammonite "god."

10. Key "Quotable Quote"

"I have prayed hundreds, if not thousands, of times for the Lord to heal me – and he finally healed me of the need to be healed."
Tim Hansel

Isaiah chapter 58

1. *Before and after*

Previous chapter: Chapter 57: The Messiah rebukes the wicked
Following chapter: Chapter 59: Israel's sins

2. *Analysis of chapter*

Hypocrisy reproved. (1,2)
A counterfeit and a true fast, with promises to real godliness. (3-12)
The keeping of the Sabbath. (13,14)

3. *Key verse*

Verse 8: "Then shall thy light break forth as the morning, and thine health shall spring forth speedily: and thy righteousness shall go before thee; the glory of the LORD shall be thy reward."

4. *Key word / key phrase*

Verse 7, "share your food."

5. *Key event / key person / key theme*

The blessings of true worship

6. *Key thought*

If ever Christians need a chapter in the Bible to turn to about social action this is it.

7. *Key thing to look out for*

Doing God's will always results in joy.

8. *Key Bible cross-reference*

Verse 7. See Matthew 25:25.

9. *Key "by way of explanation"*

Verse 7, "provide . . . shelter" – helping the less well off is a sign of behaving in a righteous way.

10. *Key "Quotable Quote"*

"The loving service which God sends his people into the world to render includes both evangelism and social action, for each is in itself an authentic expression of love, and neither needs the other to justify it."
John R.W. Stott

Isaiah chapter 59

1. *Before and after*

Previous chapter: Chapter 58: The blessings of true worship
Following chapter: Chapter 60: A vision of the new Jerusalem

2. *Analysis of chapter*

Reproofs of sin and wickedness. (1-8)
Confession of sin, and lamentation for the consequences. (9-15)
Promises of deliverance. (16-21)

3. *Key verse*

Verse 1: "Behold, the LORD's hand is not shortened, that it cannot save; neither his ear heavy, that it cannot hear."

4. *Key word / key phrase*

Verse 2, "your iniquities."

5. *Key event / key person / key theme*

Israel's sins

6. *Key thought*

The seriousness of sin is explained in this chapter.

7. *Key thing to look out for*

The only way to deal with sin is to confess it to God.

8. *Key Bible cross-reference*

Verse 17. See 1 Thessalonians 5:8.

9. *Key "by way of explanation"*

Verse 17, "righteousness as his breastplate." We can only be righteous because of God's righteousness.

10. *Key "Quotable Quote"*

"The most important ingredient of righteousness is to render to God the service and homage due to him. He is shamefully cheated whenever we do not submit to his authority."
John Calvin

Isaiah chapter 60

1. **Before and after**

   Previous chapter: Chapter 59: Israel's sins
   Following chapter: Chapter 61: The year of the Lord's favor

2. **Analysis of chapter**

   The glories of the Church of God, when the fullness of the Gentiles will come in. (1-8)
   The Jews will be converted and gathered from their dispersions. (9-14)
   The kingdoms of this world will become the kingdom of our Lord, and of his Christ. (15-22)

3. **Key verse**

   Verse 1: "Arise, shine; for thy light is come, and the glory of the LORD is risen upon thee."

4. **Key word / key phrase**

   Verse 14, "Zion of the Holy One of Israel."

5. **Key event / key person / key theme**

   A vision of the new Jerusalem

6. **Key thought**

   Today nearly all nations ignore God. One day all nations will worship God.

7. **Key thing to look out for**

   How wonderful to live in a town walled by salvation and guarded with gates of praise.

8. **Key Bible cross-reference**

   Verse 11. See Revelation 21:25,26.

9. **Key "by way of explanation"**

   Verse 13, "glory of Lebanon." This refers to the magnificent cedar trees of Lebanon from which the temple was built.

10. **Key "Quotable Quote"**

   "The whole work of salvation was finished and the whole debit paid, so there is nothing for me to do but to fall down on my knees and accept the Savior."
   Hudson Taylor

Isaiah chapter 61

1. *Before and after*

   Previous chapter: Chapter 60: A vision of the new Jerusalem
   Following chapter: Chapter 62: Jerusalem's future

2. *Analysis of chapter*

   The Messiah, his character and office. (1-3)
   His promises of future blessedness. (4-9)
   Praise to God for these mercies. (10,11)

3. *Key verse*

   Verse 1: "The Spirit of the Lord GOD is upon me; because the LORD hath anointed me to preach good tidings unto the meek; he hath sent me to bind up the brokenhearted, to proclaim liberty to the captives, and the opening of the prison to them that are bound."

4. *Key word / key phrase*

   Verse 2, "proclaim the year of the Lord's favor."

5. *Key event / key person / key theme*

   The year of the Lord's favor

6. *Key thought*

   Without the Spirit of the Lord there is never any spiritual life.

7. *Key thing to look out for*

   Note how these verses apply to Jesus. See Luke 4:16-21.

8. *Key Bible cross-reference*

   Verse 1. See Matthew 11:5.

9. *Key "by way of explanation"*

   Verse 3, "oil of gladness." In times of joy people were anointed with olive oil. The imagery is based on the year of Jubilee (Leviticus 25).

10. *Key "Quotable Quote"*

   "We who have Christ's eternal life need to throw away our own lives."
   George Verwer

Isaiah chapter 62

1. **Before and after**

    Previous chapter: Chapter 61: The year of the Lord's favor
    Following chapter: Chapter 63: Salvation and judgment

2. **Analysis of chapter**

    God's care of his people. (1-5)
    The people urged to a life of prayer. (6-9)
    Every hindrance will be removed from the way of salvation. (10-12)

3. **Key verse**

    Verse 6: "I have set watchmen upon thy walls, O Jerusalem, which shall never hold their peace day nor night."

4. **Key word / key phrase**

    Verse 4, "your land will be married."

5. **Key event / key person / key theme**

    Jerusalem's future

6. **Key thought**

    God's workers need to model themselves on these faithful watchmen.

7. **Key thing to look out for**

    Note how verse 11 is quoted in Matthew 21:5 to such good effect.

8. **Key Bible cross-reference**

    Verse 11. See Revelation 22:12.

9. **Key "by way of explanation"**

    Verse 11, "daughters of Jerusalem," is a personification of Jerusalem and for all its inhabitants.

10. **Key "Quotable Quote"**

    "I think the first essential mark of the difference between true and false assurance is to be found in the fact that the true brings about humility. There is nothing in the world that works such satanic, profound, God-defiant pride as false assurance; nothing works such utter humility, or brings to such utter self-emptiness, as the child-like spirit of true assurance."
    A.A. Hodge

Isaiah chapter 63

1. *Before and after*

Previous chapter: Chapter 62: Jerusalem's future
Following chapter: Chapter 64: A prayer for deliverance

2. *Analysis of chapter*

Christ's victory over his enemies. (1-6)
His mercy toward his people. (7-14)
Prayer for God's deliverance. (15-19)

3. *Key verse*

Verse 4: "For the day of vengeance is in mine heart, and the year of my redeemed is come."

4. *Key word / key phrase*

Verse 3, "in my wrath."

5. *Key event / key person / key theme*

Salvation and judgment

6. *Key thought*

The time of redemption and the day of vengeance are spoken of in the same verse, verse 4.

7. *Key thing to look out for*

A key part of the prophet's message was to speak about "the kindness of the Lord," verse 7.

8. *Key Bible cross-reference*

Verses 1-6. See Amos 1:11,12.

9. *Key "by way of explanation"*

Verse 7, "kindness," includes all the ways in which God has been faithful to his covenant promises to his people.

10. *Key "Quotable Quote"*

"To me, God and compassion are one and the same. Compassion is the joy of sharing. It's doing small things for the love of each other – just a smile, or carrying a bucket of water, or showing some simple kindness. These are the small things that make up compassion."
Mother Teresa of Calcutta

Isaiah chapter 64

1. *Before and after*

Previous chapter: Chapter 63: Salvation and judgment
Following chapter: Chapter 65: The Lord's answer to the remnant

2. *Analysis of chapter*

Prayer for God's power to be revealed. (1-5)
A confession of sin. (6-12)

3. *Key verse*

Verse 1: "Oh that thou wouldest rend the heavens, that thou wouldest come
down, that the mountains might flow down at thy presence,"

4. *Key word / key phrase*

Verse 4, "acts on behalf of those who wait for him."

5. *Key event / key person / key theme*

A prayer for deliverance

6. *Key thought*

Godly people would never dream that they could ever outgrow the need to
confess their sin to God.

7. *Key thing to look out for*

The "awesome things," (verse 3) that must be remembered.

8. *Key Bible cross-reference*

Verse 4. See 1 Corinthians 2:9.

9. *Key "by way of explanation"*

Verse 7, "No one calls on your name." Just the opposite of this needs to be
true, especially in times of trouble.

10. *Key "Quotable Quote"*

"We need prayer as much as we need water. All of us need times of quiet
before God."
Johann Heinrich Arnold

Isaiah chapter 65

1. *Before and after*

Previous chapter: Chapter 64: A prayer for deliverance
Following chapter: Chapter 66: A new heaven and a new earth

2. *Analysis of chapter*

God castigates those who have refused to listen. (1-7)
The Lord will preserve a remnant. (8-10)
Judgments on the wicked. (11-16)
The future happy and flourishing state of God's faithful people. (17-25)

3. *Key verse*

Verse 1: "I am sought of them that asked not for me; I am found of them that sought me not."

4. *Key word / key phrase*

Verse 9, "my chosen people."

5. *Key event / key person / key theme*

The Lord's answer to the remnant

6. *Key thought*

From verse 17 this chapter reads like the book of Revelation, see Revelation 21:4.

7. *Key thing to look out for*

We cannot think of heaven too often.

8. *Key Bible cross-reference*

Verse 1. See Romans 10:20.

9. *Key "by way of explanation"*

Verse 7, "burned sacrifices on the mountains" refers to the high places were sacrifices were offered to Baal.

10. *Key "Quotable Quote"*

"I saw the heavens opened, and God sitting on his great white throne."
G.F. Handel, explaining how he was inspired during his writing of the Hallelujah chorus.

Isaiah chapter 66

1. **Previous chapter**

    Chapter 65: The Lord's answer to the remnant

2. **Analysis of chapter**

    God looks at the heart, and vengeance is threatened for guilt. (1-4)
    Jew and Gentile will be gathered to the Redeemer. (5-14)
    Every enemy will be destroyed, and the final ruin of the ungodly will be seen. (15-24)

3. **Key verse**

    Verse 1: "Thus saith the LORD, The heaven is my throne, and the earth is my footstool: where is the house that ye build unto me? and where is the place of my rest?"

4. **Key word / key phrase**

    Verse 1, "heaven is my throne."

5. **Key event / key person / key theme**

    A new heaven and a new earth

6. **Key thought**

    Jerusalem's future (and the future of all Christians) is secure and will be glorious.

7. **Key thing to look out for**

    Verses 12 and 13 picture the loving nature of the Lord God Almighty.

8. **Key Bible cross-reference**

    Verse 1. See Matthew 5:34,35.

9. **Key "by way of explanation"**

    Verse 15, "fire," is often linked with God's judgment. See 1:31; 30:27.

10. **Key "Quotable Quote"**

    "Never can father or mother embrace their child, nor any person embrace another with so much love as God Almighty embraces."
    Angela of Foligno

Jeremiah and Lamentations

Jeremiah chapter 1

1. *Following chapter*

   Chapter 2: Judah's deliberate sins

2. *Analysis of chapter*

   Jeremiah's call to the prophetic office. (1-10)
   A vision of an almond tree and a boiling pot, divine protection is promised.
   (11-19)

3. *Key verse*

   Verse 1: "The words of Jeremiah the son of Hilkiah, of the priests that were in
   Anathoth in the land of Benjamin."

4. *Key word / key phrase*

   Verse 4, "The word of the Lord came to me."

5. *Key event / key person / key theme*

   Jeremiah's call

6. *Key thought*

   Jeremiah was called before he was born.

7. *Key thing to look out for*

   Jeremiah endured a tough prophetic ministry but is told at the start of it not
   to be afraid.

8. *Key Bible cross-reference*

   Verse 3. See 2 Chronicles 36:5-8; 11:21.

9. *Key "by way of explanation"*

   Jeremiah preached from about 620–580 BC. He lived in tumultuous times,
   witnessing the rise of Babylonian power and the fall of Jerusalem.

10. *Key "Quotable Quote"*

   "Learn the lesson that, if you are to do the work of a prophet what you need
   is not a scepter but a hoe."
   Bernard of Clairvaux

Jeremiah chapter 2

1. Before and after

Previous chapter: Chapter 1: Jeremiah's call
Following chapter: Chapter 3: Judah ignores Israel's example

2. Analysis of chapter

God expostulates with his people. (1-8)
Their revolt beyond precedent. (9-13)
Guilt the cause of sufferings. (14-19)
The sins of Judah. (20-28)
Their false confidence. (29-37)

3. Key verse

Verse 9: "Wherefore I will yet plead with you, saith the LORD, and with your children's children will I plead."

4. Key word / key phrase

Verse 8, "worthless idols."

5. Key event / key person / key theme

Judah's deliberate sins

6. Key thought

When repentance is necessary it is essential to confess the relevant sin to God.

7. Key thing to look out for

Unfaithfulness always ends in punishment.

8. Key Bible cross-reference

Verse 3. See Deuteronomy 7:6.

9. Key "by way of explanation"

Verse 24, "wild donkey." The Israelites are likened to the stubborn and untamed nature of such an animal.

10. Key "Quotable Quote"

"Some men, not content with Christ alone, are borne hither and thither from one hope to another; even if they concern themselves chiefly with him, they nevertheless stray from the right way in turning some part of their thinking in another direction."
John Calvin

Jeremiah chapter 3

1. Before and after

Previous chapter: Chapter 2: Judah's deliberate sins
Following chapter: Chapter 4: Judah's destruction from the north

2. Analysis of chapter

Exhortations to repentance. (1-5)
Judah more guilty than Israel. (6-11)
But pardon is promised. (12-20)
The children of Israel express their sorrow and repentance. (21-25)

3. Key verse

Verse 6: "The LORD said also unto me in the days of Josiah the king, Hast thou seen that which backsliding Israel hath done?"

4. Key word / key phrase

Verse 12, "faithless Israel."

5. Key event / key person / key theme

It is not too late to repent.

6. Key thought

In the prophet's message to Israel to repent, the Lord is likened to a loving and faithful husband.

7. Key thing to look out for

No matter how faithless a person has been, the Lord welcomes back the repentant sinner with open arms.

8. Key Bible cross-reference

Verse 6. See 2 Kings 22:1–23:30

9. Key "by way of explanation"

"Israel" refers to the northern kingdom of Israel, now destroyed by the Assyrians and her people taken captive. Many were resettled in Assyria's northern province (verse 12).

10. Key "Quotable Quote"

"I will love you, O Lord, and thank you, and confess to your name, because you have forgiven me my evil and nefarious deeds."
Augustine of Hippo

Jeremiah chapter 4

1. **Before and after**

   Previous chapter: Chapter 3: Judah ignores Israel's example
   Following chapter: Chapter 5: Judah's sins

2. **Analysis of chapter**

   Exhortations and promises. (1-2)
   Judah exhorted to repentance. (3-4)
   Judgments denounced. (5-18)
   The approaching ruin of Judah. (19-31)

3. **Key verse**

   Verse 3: "For thus saith the LORD to the men of Judah and Jerusalem, Break up your fallow ground, and sow not among thorns."

4. **Key word / key phrase**

   Verse 7, "a lion has come."

5. **Key event / key person / key theme**

   Judah's destruction from the north

6. **Key thought**

   Jeremiah expresses his sorrow for his people's sins.

7. **Key thing to look out for**

   People who turn from the Lord do not become stupid, but skilled in evil.

8. **Key Bible cross-reference**

   Verse 3. See Hosea 10:12.

9. **Key "by way of explanation"**

   Verse 11, "scorching wind." This dry desert wind, called the *sirocco* wind, brought dust and sand and so caused great aggravation.

10. **Key "Quotable Quote"**

    "Repentance is a grace, and must have its daily operation, as well as other graces."
    Thomas Brooks

Jeremiah chapter 5

1. **Before and after**

   Previous chapter: Chapter 4: Judah's destruction from the north
   Following chapter: Chapter 6: Jerusalem will be destroyed

2. **Analysis of chapter**

   The people's profession of religion was hypocritical. (1-9)
   The destroyer is summoned. (10-18)
   Their apostasy and idolatry. (19-31)

3. **Key verse**

   Verse 1: "Run ye to and fro through the streets of Jerusalem, and see now, and know, and seek in the broad places thereof, if ye can find a man, if there be any that executeth judgment, that seeketh the truth; and I will pardon it."

4. **Key word / key phrase**

   Verse 7, "forsaken me."

5. **Key event / key person / key theme**

   Judah's sins

6. **Key thought**

   The sins of God's people are recorded in some detail so that future generations of God's followers will learn from their unfaithfulness.

7. **Key thing to look out for**

   Our reaction to the sin of other people gives us a good guide to the state of our own spiritual life.

8. **Key Bible cross-reference**

   Verse 21. See Ezekiel 12:2.

9. **Key "by way of explanation"**

   Verse 6, "backslidings." This word indicates that their sin was no passing whim, but a constant apostasy.

10. **Key "Quotable Quote"**

    "For to sin, indeed is human: but to persevere in sin is not human but altogether satanic."
    John Chrysostom

Jeremiah chapter 6

1. **Before and after**

    Previous chapter: Chapter 5: Judah's sins
    Following chapter: Chapter 7: The externals of religion

2. **Analysis of chapter**

    No safety in Jerusaelem. (1-8)
    The justice of God's judgment. (9-17)
    All methods used to change the people of Judah have been unsuccessful. (18-30)

3. **Key verse**

    Verse 3: "The shepherds with their flocks shall come unto her; they shall pitch their tents against her round about; they shall feed every one in his place."

4. **Key word / key phrase**

    Verse 1, "Flee from Jerusalem.!"

5. **Key event / key person / key theme**

    Jerusalem will be destroyed

6. **Key thought**

    The Lord never punishes his people without giving them ample warning and opportunity to repent.

7. **Key thing to look out for**

    It often appears that no amount of reasoning can stop some people from choosing to reject the Lord.

8. **Key Bible cross-reference**

    Verse 14. See Ezekiel 13:10.

9. **Key "by way of explanation"**

    Verse "peace . . . when there is no peace." This was the cry of a number of unfaithful prophets. "Shepherds," that is, "rulers."

10. **Key "Quotable Quote"**

    "As heat is opposed to cold, and light to darkness, so grace is opposed to sin."
    Thomas Benton Brooks

Jeremiah chapter 7

1. **Before and after**

   Previous chapter: Chapter 6: Jerusalem will be destroyed
   Following chapter: Chapter 8: Judgment on Judah is imminent

2. **Analysis of chapter**

   Confidence in the temple is vain. (1-16)
   The provocation by persisting in idolatry. (17-20)
   God justifies his dealings with them. (21-28)
   And threatens vengeance. (29-34)

3. **Key verse**

   Verse 4: "Trust ye not in lying words, saying, The temple of the LORD, The
   temple of the LORD, The temple of the LORD, are these."

4. **Key word / key phrase**

   Verse 3, "Reform your ways."

5. **Key event / key person / key theme**

   The externals of religion

6. **Key thought**

   God's anger should not make us think negatively about God, but about
   human sin.

7. **Key thing to look out for**

   The result of following "the ancient paths" (verse 16).

8. **Key Bible cross-reference**

   Verse 11. See Matthew 21:13.

9. **Key "by way of explanation"**

   God had saved Jerusalem in the days of Hezekiah. People believed that the
   temple was God's dwelling-place, a holy place, and he would never let it be
   destroyed. Therefore, they were safe.

10. **Key "Quotable Quote"**

    "I am convinced that the first step toward attaining a higher standard of
    holiness is to realize more fully the amazing sinfulness of sin."
    J.C. Ryle

Jeremiah chapter 8

1. *Before and after*

   Previous chapter: Chapter 7: The externals of religion
   Following chapter: Chapter 9: Description of Judah's judgment

2. *Analysis of chapter*

   The bones of the dead exposed. (1-3)
   The stupidity of the people, compared with the instinct of the brute creation. (4-13)
   A prophetic description of the devastation that will be caused by the invasion, and a lamentation. (14-22)

3. *Key verse*

   Verse 5: "Why then is this people of Jerusalem slidden back by a perpetual backsliding?"

4. *Key word / key phrase*

   Verse 12, "when they are punished."

5. *Key event / key person / key theme*

   Judgment on Judah is imminent

6. *Key thought*

   If idolatry is not removed voluntarily God will remove it himself.

7. *Key thing to look out for*

   In Jeremiah's lament the heart of a true pastor is revealed.

8. *Key Bible cross-reference*

   Verse 11. See Ezekiel 13:10.

9. *Key "by way of explanation"*

   Verse 8, "lying pen." This phrase stands for the misuse of God's Law.

10. *Key "Quotable Quote"*

    "We must feel toward our people as a father toward his children."
    Richard Baxter

Jeremiah chapter 9

1. **Before and after**

   Previous chapter: Chapter 8: Judgment on Judah is imminent
   Following chapter: Chapter 10: The Lord is sovereign

2. **Analysis of chapter**

   A prophecy of the destruction of Jerusalem. (1-11)
   The captives will suffer in a foreign land. (12-22)
   God's loving-kindness. He threatens the enemies of his people. (23-26)

3. **Key verse**

   Verse 8: "Their tongue is as an arrow shot out; it speaketh deceit: one speaketh peaceably to his neighbor with his mouth, but in heart he layeth his wait."

4. **Key word / key phrase**

   Verse 11, "a heap of ruins."

5. **Key event / key person / key theme**

   Description of Judah's coming judgment

6. **Key thought**

   Israel's great sin was her idolatry, and this chapter spells out why it was so evil in the Lord's sight.

7. **Key thing to look out for**

   Even in the middle of these warnings the kindness of the Lord is mentioned.

8. **Key Bible cross-reference**

   Verse 24. See 1 Corinthians 1:31.

9. **Key "by way of explanation"**

   Verse 22, "reaper." Death is often personified as the grim reaper. This verse is the background to such an idea.

10. **Key "Quotable Quote"**

    "Measure not God's love and favor by your own feelings."
    Richard Sibbes

Jeremiah chapter 10

1. ## Before and after

   Previous chapter: Chapter 9: Description of Judah's judgment
   Following chapter: Chapter 11: Judah and the broken covenant

2. ## Analysis of chapter

   The absurdity of idolatry. (1-16)
   Coming destruction. (17-25)

3. ## Key verse

   Verse 10: "But the LORD is the true God, he is the living God, and an everlasting king: at his wrath the earth shall tremble, and the nations shall not be able to abide his indignation."

4. ## Key word / key phrase

   Verse 12, "God made the earth."

5. ## Key event / key person / key theme

   The Lord is sovereign

6. ## Key thought

   The prophets often praised the Lord as they contemplated his power in creation and nature.

7. ## Key thing to look out for

   Verse 23 is a good verse for anyone seeking guidance.

8. ## Key Bible cross-reference

   Verse 7. See Revelation 15:4.

9. ## Key "by way of explanation"

   Verse 18, "hurl out." When David used his sling a stone was "hurled" out with great force. This is what will happen to the people of Jerusalem.

10. ## Key "Quotable Quote"

    "Self-sacrifice is what the Bible means by love."
    John R.W. Stott

Jeremiah chapter 11

1. **Before and after**

   Previous chapter: Chapter 10: The Lord is sovereign
   Following chapter: Chapter 12: Jeremiah's complaint, and God's reply

2. **Analysis of chapter**

   The disobedient Jews reproved for breaking their covenant with God. (1-10)
   Their utter ruin. (11-17)
   Plots against Jeremiah. (18-23)

3. **Key verse**

   Verse 9: "And the LORD said unto me, A conspiracy is found among the men
   of Judah, and among the inhabitants of Jerusalem."

4. **Key word / key phrase**

   Verse 3, "the man who does not obey."

5. **Key event / key person / key theme**

   Judah and the broken covenant

6. **Key thought**

   Disobeying God brings devastating consequences.

7. **Key thing to look out for**

   It is never safe to be God's representative, as Jeremiah discovered.

8. **Key Bible cross-reference**

   Verse 12. Deuteronomy 32:28.

9. **Key "by way of explanation"**

   Verse 10, "refused." The sin here was deliberate and willful. Verse 21, Anathoth
   was Jeremiah's home-town.

10. **Key "Quotable Quote"**

    "We sin two kinds of sin. We sin one kind of sin as though we trip off the curb,
    and it overtakes us by surprise. We sin a second kind of sin when we
    deliberately set ourselves up to fall."
    Francis A. Schaeffer

Jeremiah chapter 12

1. *Before and after*

Previous chapter: Chapter 11: Judah and the broken covenant
Following chapter: Chapter 13: Enacted warnings

2. *Analysis of chapter*

Jeremiah complains about the prosperity of the wicked. (1-6)
The heavy judgments to come upon the nation. (7-13)
Divine mercy to them, and even to the nations around. (14-17)

3. *Key verse*

Verse 7: "I have forsaken mine house, I have left mine heritage; I have given the dearly beloved of my soul into the hand of her enemies."

4. *Key word / key phrase*

Verse 1, "a case before you."

5. *Key event / key person / key theme*

Jeremiah's complaint, and God's reply

6. *Key thought*

Many of the prophets questioned the Lord, as Jeremiah does here.

7. *Key thing to look out for*

"God's answer is to brace Jeremiah for yet fiercer, and often subtler, opposition from his family" (D.J. Wiseman).

8. *Key Bible cross-reference*

Verse 1. See Ezra 9:15

9. *Key "by way of explanation"*

Verse 5: if Jeremiah cannot cope with opposition in his own town, how will he manage in Jerusalem? There were lions and other wild animals in the dense jungle-like vegetation of the Jordan valley.

10. *Key "Quotable Quote"*

"Though our Savior's passion is over, his compassion is not."
William Penn

Jeremiah chapter 13

1. **Before and after**

   Previous chapter: Chapter 12: Jeremiah's complaint, and God's reply
   Following chapter: Chapter 14: Judah's drought is described

2. **Analysis of chapter**

   The glory of the Jews was to be marred. (1-11)
   All ranks would suffer misery. An earnest exhortation to repentance. (12-17)
   An awful message to Jerusalem and its king. (18-27)

3. **Key verse**

   Verse 12: "Every bottle shall be filled with wine: and they shall say unto thee,
   Do we not certainly know that every bottle shall be filled with wine?"

4. **Key word / key phrase**

   Verse 2, "I brought a belt."

5. **Key event / key person / key theme**

   The close relationship of God and his people (the belt) is now ruined.

6. **Key thought**

   God's truth can be conveyed in a host of different ways.

7. **Key thing to look out for**

   The danger of pride and trusting in the self.

8. **Key Bible cross-reference**

   Verse 22. See Kings 9:9.

9. **Key "by way of explanation"**

   Verse 6, "Many days later," probably stands for the seventy-year long exile in
   Babylon.

10. **Key "Quotable Quote"**

    "Illustrations are just servants."
    D. Martyn Lloyd-Jones

Jeremiah chapter 14

1. Before and after

Previous chapter: Chapter 13: Enacted warnings
Following chapter: Chapter 15: Jeremiah complains again to the Lord

2. Analysis of chapter

A drought on the land of Judah. (1-7)
A confession of sin in the name of the people. (8-9)
The divine purpose to punish is declared. (10-16)
The people ask for help. (17-22)

3. Key verse

Verse 1: "The word of the LORD that came to Jeremiah concerning the dearth."

4. Key word / key phrase

Verse 3, "no water."

5. Key event / key person / key theme

Judah's drought is described

6. Key thought

Even when God's judgments were crystal clear some people would not repent.

7. Key thing to look out for

The best prophets, like Nehemiah, identified with the sin of God's people and confessed such sin as if it were their own.

8. Key Bible cross-reference

Verse 11. See Exodus 32:10.

9. Key "by way of explanation"

Verse 17, "virgin daughter," was a name by which Jerusalem was known.

10. Key "Quotable Quote"

"I thank God that now when I preach I shall be able to say instead of 'dear brethren,' 'my fellow lepers.'"
Joseph de Veuster

Jeremiah chapter 15

1. **Before and after**

   Previous chapter: Chapter 14: Judah's drought is described
   Following chapter: Chapter 16: When God departs

2. **Analysis of chapter**

   The destruction of the wicked described. (1-9)
   The prophet complains, and is reproved. (10-14)
   He asks for pardon, and is promised protection. (15-21)

3. **Key verse**

   Verse 10: "Woe is me, my mother, that thou hast borne me a man of strife and
   a man of contention to the whole earth!"

4. **Key word / key phrase**

   Verse 10, "everyone curses me."

5. **Key event / key person / key theme**

   God's promise of protection for Jeremiah.

6. **Key thought**

   It is never right to blame the Lord when things go wrong.

7. **Key thing to look out for**

   Without being irreverent, it is right to tell the Lord how one is feeling.

8. **Key Bible cross-reference**

   Verse 2. See Revelation 13:10.

9. **Key "by way of explanation"**

   Verse 1. In the days of Moses and Samuel the people had listened and
   repented. But not any longer. Only exile will bring them to their senses.

10. **Key "Quotable Quote"**

    "Honesty and transparency make you vulnerable. Be honest and transparent
    anyway."
    Mother Teresa of Calcutta

Jeremiah chapter 16

1. *Before and after*

   Previous chapter: Chapter 15: Jeremiah complains again to the Lord
   Following chapter: Chapter 17: The results of sin

2. *Analysis of chapter*

   Jeremiah's life is to be a sign. (1-9)
   The justice of God in these judgments. (10-13)
   Future restoration of the Jews, and the conversion of the Gentiles. (14-21)

3. *Key verse*

   Verse 16: "Behold, I will send for many fishers, saith the LORD, and they shall fish them; and after will I send for many hunters, and they shall hunt them from every mountain, and from every hill, and out of the holes of the rocks."

4. *Key word / key phrase*

   Verse 10, "a great disaster."

5. *Key event / key person / key theme*

   When God departs

6. *Key thought*

   Within this single chapter disaster and restoration are spoken of.

7. *Key thing to look out for*

   Power and might do not belong to political leaders but to the Lord.

8. *Key Bible cross-reference*

   Verse 9. See Revelation 18:23.

9. *Key "by way of explanation"*

   Verse 19, "refuge." The Lord is often pictured in ways that portray his power and strength, especially in the psalms.

10. *Key "Quotable Quote"*

   "There is no greater joy than the peace and assurance of knowing that, whatever the future may hold, you are secure in the loving arms of the Savior."
   Billy Graham

Jeremiah chapter 17

1. Before and after

Previous chapter: Chapter 16: When God departs
Following chapter: Chapter 18: Learning from the potter

2. Analysis of chapter

The fatal consequences of the idolatry of the Jews. (1-4)
The happiness of the people who trust in God; the end of those who do not. (5-11)
The malice of the prophet's enemies. (12-18)
The observance of the Sabbath. (19-27)

3. Key verse

Verse 1: "The sin of Judah is written with a pen of iron."

4. Key word / key phrase

Verse 6, "parched places."

5. Key event / key person / key theme

The results of sin

6. Key thought

We know how true it is that environmental mismanagement ruins the earth. This principle is just as true in the spiritual realm.

7. Key thing to look out for

Health, wholeness, and salvation are all linked with each other.

8. Key Bible cross-reference

Verse 8. See Psalm 1:3.

9. Key "by way of explanation"

Verse 20, "kings of Judah," refers to all the kings of David's dynasty.

10. Key "Quotable Quote"

"The Bible deals with heaven and hell, good and bad, God and the devil, right and wrong, salvation and damnation; we like to deal with things in-between."
Oswald Chambers

Jeremiah 18

1. *Before and after*

Previous chapter: Chapter 17: The results of sin
Following chapter: Chapter 19: The sign of the broken flask

2. *Analysis of chapter*

God's power over his creatures is represented by the potter. (1-10)
The Jews exhorted to repent, and judgments predicted. (11-17)
The prophet appeals to God. (18-23)

3. *Key verse*

Verse 6: "O house of Israel, cannot I do with you as this potter?"

4. *Key word*

Verse 8, "Repents."

5. *Key event / key person / key theme*

Jeremiah receives a message from God as a result of his visit to a potter's workshop.

6. *Key thought*

"God is always using everyday objects and the experiences of life to show us truths about himself. Because God is both Creator and Savior it is natural that he should use the created world to develop our spiritual lives." Stephen Travis

7. *Key thing to look out for*

The "if . . . then" sequence in verses 7-10. If the warning of disaster results in turning back to God then God will avert the disaster. But if God's promise of blessing is met with disobedience, then the blessing will end in disaster. Note that the word "if" comes four times in these verses.

8. *Key biblical cross-reference*

With verse 15, see Isaiah 17:10-11: both give the results of forgetting God.

9. *Key "by way of explanation"*

Verse 3, "Working at the wheel." In Hebrew this is "the two stone-wheels." The lower wheel, which was turned by the potter's feet, made the upper wheel spin round. The potter's hands were thus free to work the clay on the upper wheel.

10. *Key "Quotable Quote"*

"Like the New Testament parables, not every part must be pressed for its symbolism for neither nations nor men are lifeless lumps of clay. . . . It is God who molds, breaking down, rebuilds. This power is not exercised arbitrarily and the possibility of renewal by God is conditional on a change of heart." D.J. Wiseman

Jeremiah chapter 19

1. *Before and after*

Previous chapter: Chapter 18: Learning from the potter
Following chapter: Chapter 20: Jeremiah put in the stocks

2. *Analysis of chapter*

By the type of breaking an earthen vessel, Jeremiah is to predict the destruction of Judah. (1-15)

3. *Key verse*

Verse 15: "Behold, I will bring upon this city and upon all her towns all the evil that I have pronounced against it, because they have hardened their necks, that they might not hear my words."

4. *Key word / key phrase*

Verse 10, "break the jar."

5. *Key event / key person / key theme*

The sign of the broken flask

6. *Key thought*

One of the worst condemnations found in the Bible is that people do not listen to God's words.

7. *Key thing to look out for*

Even when Jeremiah knew that the people would not repent he carried out the Lord's commands faithfully.

8. *Key Bible cross-reference*

Verse 5. See Leviticus 18:21.

9. *Key "by way of explanation"*

Verse 13, "to all the starry hosts." The sun, moon, and stars were worshiped by some of the people of Judah.

10. *Key "Quotable Quote"*

"A strong and faithful pulpit is no mean safeguard of a nation's life."
John Hall

Jeremiah chapter 20

1. Before and after

Previous chapter: Chapter 19: The sign of the broken flask
Following chapter: Chapter 21: Jerusalem's defeat is predicted

2. Analysis of chapter

The doom of Pashur, who ill-treated the prophet. (1-6)
Jeremiah complains about being persecuted. (7-13)
He regrets ever being born. (14-18)

3. Key verse

Verse 1: "Now Pashur the son of Immer the priest, who was also chief governor in the house of the LORD, heard that Jeremiah prophesied these things."

4. Key word / key phrase

Verse 2, "put in the stocks."

5. Key event / key person / key theme

Jeremiah put in the stocks

6. Key thought

Most of the leading early disciples of Jesus were martyred or persecuted.

7. Key thing to look out for

The great, fearless, Jeremiah knew what it was like to wish he was dead.

8. Key Bible cross-reference

Verses 14-18. See Job 3:1-19.

9. Key "by way of explanation"

Verse 16, "towns the Lord overthrew." The fate of Sodom and Gomorrah was well known in Jeremiah's day.

10. Key "Quotable Quote"

"If we only spent more of our time in looking at him we should soon forget ourselves."
D. Martyn Lloyd-Jones

Jeremiah chapter 21

1. **Before and after**

   Previous chapter: Chapter 20: Jeremiah put in the stocks
   Following chapter: Chapter 22: Kings condemned

2. **Analysis of chapter**

   The only way of deliverance is to surrender to the Babylonians. (1-10)
   The wickedness of the king and his household. (11-14)

3. **Key verse**

   Verse 4: "Thus saith the LORD God of Israel; Behold, I will turn back the
   weapons of war that are in your hands, wherewith ye fight against the king of
   Babylon, and against the Chaldeans, which besiege you without the walls, and
   I will assemble them into the midst of this city."

4. **Key word / key phrase**

   Verse 4, "I am about to turn against you."

5. **Key event / key person / key theme**

   Jerusalem's defeat is predicted

6. **Key thought**

   The choice given in verse 8 is true for each of us every day.

7. **Key thing to look out for**

   Note why the Lord says he is "against" Jerusalem, verse 13.

8. **Key Bible cross-reference**

   Verse 2. See 2 Kings 25:1-11.

9. **Key "by way of explanation"**

   Verse 13, "valley." Jerusalem is set on a high mound, surrounded by valleys.

10. **Key "Quotable Quote"**

    "Every Christian must refer always and everywhere to the Scriptures for all
    his choices, becoming like a child before it, seeking in it the most effective
    remedy against all his various weaknesses, and not daring to take a step
    without being illuminated by the divine rays of those words."
    Pope John Paul II

Jeremiah chapter 22

1. *Before and after*

Previous chapter: Chapter 21: Jerusalem's defeat is predicted
Following chapter: Chapter 23: The Righteous Branch

2. *Analysis of chapter*

Justice is recommended, and destruction threatened in case of disobedience. (1-9)
The captivity of Jehoiakim, and the end of Jeconiah. (10-19)
The doom of the royal family. (20-30)

3. *Key verse*

Verse 3: "Execute ye judgment and righteousness, and deliver the spoiled out of the hand of the oppressor: and do no wrong, do no violence to the stranger, the fatherless, nor the widow, neither shed innocent blood in this place."

4. *Key word / key phrase*

Verse 13, "woe to him who builds his palace by unrighteousness."

5. *Key event / key person / key theme*

Kings condemned

6. *Key thought*

The highest power in the land is subject to God's judgment.

7. *Key thing to look out for*

The same old sins are repeated again and again.

8. *Key Bible cross-reference*

Verse 5. See Matthew 23:38.

9. *Key "by way of explanation"*

Verse 9, "forsaken the covenant," that is, by breaking the first and second commandment of the Ten Commandments, they have broken the binding agreement they made with God.

10. *Key "Quotable Quote"*

"What destroys faith is that disobedience that hardens into unbelief."
Os Guinness

Jeremiah chapter 23

1. Before and after

Previous chapter: Chapter 22: Kings condemned
Following chapter: Chapter 24: Two baskets of figs

2. Analysis of chapter

The restoration of the Jews to their own land. (1-8)
The wickedness of the priests and prophets of Judah, and the people exhorted
not to listen to false promises. (9-22)
False prophets are warned. (23-32)
Those who scoff at genuine prophecy. (33-40)

3. Key verse

Verse 6: "In his days Judah shall be saved, and Israel shall dwell safely: and this
is his name whereby he shall be called, THE LORD OUR RIGHTEOUSNESS."

4. Key word / key phrase

Verse 5, "a righteous Branch."

5. Key event / key person / key theme

The Righteous Branch

6. Key thought

Faithless shepherds of God's flock are no novelty.

7. Key thing to look out for

It is possible to lie in God's name as well as to prophecy faithfully in God's
name.

8. Key Bible cross-reference

Verse 14. See Genesis 18:20.

9. Key "by way of explanation"

Verse 6, "Judah . . . Israel." All of God's people will be united and restored.

10. Key "Quotable Quote"

"Christ is with those of humble mind, not with those who exalt themselves
over his flock."
Clement of Rome

Jeremiah chapter 24

1. *Before and after*

Previous chapter: Chapter 23: The Righteous Branch
Following chapter: Chapter 25: The seventy-year captivity

2. *Analysis of chapter*

Good figs (that is the Jews in captivity), and the rotten figs (those left behind).
(1-10)

3. *Key verse*

Verse 1: "The LORD showed me, and, behold, two baskets of figs were set
before the temple of the LORD . . ."

4. *Key word / key phrase*

Verse 6, "I will build them up."

5. *Key event / key person / key theme*

Two baskets of figs

6. *Key thought*

Note the characteristics of those symbolized by the bad figs.

7. *Key thing to look out for*

Note the characteristics of those symbolized by the good figs.

8. *Key Bible cross-reference*

Verse 1. See 2 Kings 24:12-16.

9. *Key "by way of explanation"*

Verse 2, "that ripen early." The figs which ripen in June were noted for being
especially succulent. When Jerusalem was captured in March 597 the leaders
of the people, and the craftsmen were deported.

10. *Key "Quotable Quote"*

"Give us a pure heart
That we may see thee,
A humble heart
That we may hear thee,
A heart of love
That we may serve thee,
A heart of faith
That we may live thee."
Dag Hammarskjöld

Jeremiah chapter 25

1. Before and after

Previous chapter: Chapter 24: Two baskets of figs
Following chapter: Chapter 26: Jeremiah on trial

2. Analysis of chapter

The Jews rebuked for not obeying calls to repentance. (1-7)
Their captivity during seventy years is specifically foretold. (8-14)
Destruction on the nations shown by the cup of wrath. (15-29)
The judgments again declared. (30-38)

3. Key verse

Verse 1: "The word that came to Jeremiah concerning all the people of Judah in the fourth year of Jehoiakim the son of Josiah king of Judah, that was the first year of Nebuchadrezzar king of Babylon."

4. Key word / key phrase

Verse 11, "seventy years."

5. Key event / key person / key theme

The seventy-year captivity

6. Key thought

God's judgment will fall on everyone.

7. Key thing to look out for

God's mercy is for those who turn to him.

8. Key Bible cross-reference

Verse 1. See Daniel 1:1-2.

9. Key "by way of explanation"

Verse 15, "the wine of my wrath." "Wine" often represents God's wrath and righteous anger.

10. Key "Quotable Quote"

"A day will come when those who are not born again will wish that they had never been born at all."
J.C. Ryle

Jeremiah chapter 26

1. Before and after

Previous chapter: Chapter 25: The seventy-year captivity
Following chapter: Chapter 27: Jeremiah wears an ox yoke

2. Analysis of chapter

The destruction of the temple and city foretold. (1-6)
Jeremiah's life is threatened. (7-15)
He is defended by the elders. (16-24)

3. Key verse

Verse 8: "Now it came to pass, when Jeremiah had made an end of speaking all that the LORD had commanded him to speak unto all the people, that the priests and the prophets and all the people took him, saying, Thou shalt surely die."

4. Key word / key phrase

Verse 8, "the priests, the prophets and the people seized him."

5. Key event / key person / key theme

Jeremiah on trial

6. Key thought

Jeremiah's innocence was clear to all impartial observers.

7. Key thing to look out for

Jesus was also accused of speaking against the temple.

8. Key Bible cross-reference

Verse 18. See Micah 3:12.

9. Key "by way of explanation"

Verse 10, the "officials of Judah" were responsible for dealing with disputes, within the temple area.

10. Key "Quotable Quote"

"If the biographer gives me credit for being a plodder, he will describe me justly. Anything beyond this will be too much. I can plod. I can persevere in any definite pursuit. To this I owe everything."
William Carey

Jeremiah chapter 27

1. Before and after

Previous chapter: Chapter 26: Jeremiah on trial
Following chapter: Chapter 28: Jeremiah's conflict with the prophet Hananiah

2. Analysis of chapter

The neighboring nations to be subdued. (1-11)
Zedekiah is warned to give in. (12-18)
The temple treasures to be carried to Babylon, but later would be restored. (19-22)

3. Key verse

Verse 1: "In the beginning of the reign of Jehoiakim the son of Josiah king of Judah came this word unto Jeremiah from the LORD."

4. Key word / key phrase

Verse 2, "make a yoke."

5. Key event / key person / key theme

Jeremiah wears an ox yoke

6. Key thought

Like Ezekiel Jeremiah acted out what the Lord would do in the future.

7. Key thing to look out for

Many of the of the chapters in the Bible which focus on God's punishment also contain a message of hope, as this one does. See verse 22.

8. Key Bible cross-reference

Verse 1. See 2 Chronicles 36:11-13.

9. Key "by way of explanation"

Jeremiah's messages are not given in chronological order. Chapters 27-29 describe events in about 593 BC.

10. Key "Quotable Quote"

"Lord, make us instruments of thy peace.
Where there is hatred, let us sow love.
Where there is injury, pardon.
Where there is discord, union.
Where there is doubt, faith.
Where there is despair, hope.
Where there is darkness, light ..."
Francis of Assisi

Jeremiah chapter 28

1. **Before and after**

   Previous chapter: Chapter 27: Jeremiah wears an ox yoke
   Following chapter: Chapter 29: Jeremiah's letter to the Jews in Babylonia

2. **Analysis of chapter**

   A false prophet opposes Jeremiah. (1-9)
   The false prophet warned of his approaching death. (10-17)

3. **Key verse**

   Verse 1: "And it came to pass the same year, in the beginning of the reign of Zedekiah king of Judah, in the fourth year, and in the fifth month, that Hananiah the son of Azur the prophet, which was of Gibeon, spake unto me in the house of the LORD."

4. **Key word / key phrase**

   Verse 1, "the prophet Hananiah."

5. **Key event / key person / key theme**

   Jeremiah's conflict with the prophet Hananiah

6. **Key thought**

   Many of the worst enemies facing Christians are found within the ranks of the Church.

7. **Key thing to look out for**

   The last verse of this chapter reads like God's epitaph on Hananiah.

8. **Key Bible cross-reference**

   Verse 1. See 2 Kings 24:18-20.

9. **Key "by way of explanation"**

   Hananiah "thought too much of Israel's privelege and too little of Israel's responsibility." (quoted by D.J. Wiseman)

10. **Key "Quotable Quote"**

    "Satan labors with all his strength by false teachers, which are his messengers and ambassadors, to deceive, delude and forever destroy the precious souls of men."
    Thomas Brooks

Jeremiah chapter 29

1. *Before and after*

Previous chapter: Chapter 28: Jeremiah's conflict with the prophet Hananiah
Following chapter: Chapter 30: Restoration of the land

2. *Analysis of chapter*

Two letters to the captives in Babylon; in the first, they are recommended to be patient and composed. (1-19)
In the second, judgments are denounced against the false prophets who deceived them. (20-32)

3. *Key verse*

Verse 5: "Build ye houses, and dwell in them; and plant gardens, and eat the fruit of them."

4. *Key word / key phrase*

Verse 1, "the letter."

5. *Key event / key person / key theme*

Jeremiah's letter to the Jews in Babylonia

6. *Key thought*

The priority of prayer is apparent in this letter.

7. *Key thing to look out for*

God has plans for our lives.

8. *Key Bible cross-reference*

Verse 13. See Deuteronomy 4:29.

9. *Key "by way of explanation"*

Verse 15, "prophets . . . in Babylon." There were false prophets everywhere, even in Babylon. Jeremiah is writing from Jerusalem to the religious and civil leaders who had been taken to Babylon with Jehoiachin (2 Kings 24:17-20).

10. *Key "Quotable Quote"*

"Inconsistent professors injure the gospel more than the sneering critic or the infidel."
C.H. Spurgeon

Jeremiah chapter 30

1. *Before and after*

Previous chapter: Chapter 29: Jeremiah's letter to the Jews in Babylonia
Following chapter: Chapter 31: Israel will return home

2. *Analysis of chapter*

Troubles which will occur before the restoration of Israel. (1-11)
Encouragement to trust divine promises. (12-17)
The blessings under Christ, and the wrath on the wicked. (18-24)

3. *Key verse*

Verse 10: "Therefore fear thou not, O my servant Jacob, saith the LORD; neither be dismayed, O Israel: for, lo, I will save thee from afar, and thy seed from the land of their captivity; and Jacob shall return, and shall be in rest, and be quiet, and none shall make him afraid."

4. *Key word / key phrase*

Verse 3, "back from captivity."

5. *Key event / key person / key theme*

Restoration of the land

6. *Key thought*

Salvation of every kind is attributed to the Lord.

7. *Key thing to look out for*

Salvation includes discipline.

8. *Key Bible cross-reference*

Verses 10-11. See 46:27,28.

9. *Key "by way of explanation"*

Verse 8, "tear off their bonds." The chains which bind God's people to foreign domination will be broken.

10. *Key "Quotable Quote"*

"Discipline is the secret of godliness. You must learn to discipline yourself for the purpose of godliness."
Jay E. Adams

Jeremiah chapter 31

1. Before and after

Previous chapter: Chapter 30: Restoration of the land
Following chapter: Chapter 32: Rebuilding Jerusalem

2. Analysis of chapter

The restoration of Israel. (1-14)
Promises of guidance and happiness; Rachel lamenting. (15-17)
Ephraim [Israel] laments his errors. (18-20)
The promised Savior. (21-26)
The new covenant. (27-34)
Peace and prosperity in the time of the gospel. (35-40)

3. Key verse

Verse 31: "Behold, the days come, saith the LORD, that I will make a new covenant with the house of Israel, and with the house of Judah."

4. Key word / key phrase

Verse 31, "a new covenant."

5. Key event / key person / key theme

Restoration of both Israel and Judah

6. Key thought

This is the first mention of the new covenant.

7. Key thing to look out for

The characteristic of the new covenant is that it will be an internal one to be kept in one's heart.

8. Key Bible cross-reference

Verse 15. See Matthew 2:18.

9. Key "by way of explanation"

Verse 15, at Ramah the exiles were chained up before being deported (40:1).

10. Key "Quotable Quote"

"A covenant cannot be terminated. It can only be violated."
Ross T. Bender

Jeremiah chapter 32

1. Before and after

Previous chapter: Chapter 31: Israel will return home
Following chapter: Chapter 33: Reconfirming the covenant

2. Analysis of chapter

Jeremiah buys a field. (1-15)
The prophet's prayer. (16-25)
God declares that he will give up his people, but promises to restore them. (26-44)

3. Key verse

Verse 6: "And Jeremiah said, The word of the LORD came unto me, saying, Behold, Hanameel the son of Shallum thine uncle shall come unto thee, saying, Buy thee my field that is in Anathoth: for the right of redemption is thine to buy it."

4. Key word / key phrase

Verse 43, "fields will be bought in this land."

5. Key event / key person / key theme

Jeremiah buys a field: future restoration

6. Key thought

To buy a field at such a time was a great act of faith and symbol of hope.

7. Key thing to look out for

Nothing is too hard for the Lord.

8. Key Bible cross-reference

Verse 28. See 2 Kings 25:1-11.

9. Key "by way of explanation"

Verse 12, "Baruch," is mentioned here for the first time. He later became very important in preserving Jeremiah's words. Jeremiah bought the field in 588/7 when Jerusalem had been under siege for a year.

10. Key "Quotable Quote"

"In the midst of worldly employments, there should be some thoughts of sin, death, judgment, and eternity, with at least a word or two of ejaculatory prayer to God."
Samuel Rutherford

Jeremiah chapter 33

1. *Before and after*

Previous chapter: Chapter 32: Rebuilding Jerusalem
Following chapter: Chapter 34: Prophecies in Zedekiah's reign

2. *Analysis of chapter*

The restoration of the Jews. (1-13)
The Messiah promised; happiness of his times. (14-26)

3. *Key verse*

Verse 3: "Call unto me, and I will answer thee, and show thee great and mighty things, which thou knowest not."

4. *Key word / key phrase*

Verse 2, "who made the earth."

5. *Key event / key person / key theme*

Reconfirming the covenant

6. *Key thought*

These wonderful promises were made to Jeremiah while he was still under arrest.

7. *Key thing to look out for*

"The Lord Our Righteousness," verse 16, summarizes the whole point of Jesus' death on the cross.

8. *Key Bible cross-reference*

Verse 11. See Psalm 100:5.

9. *Key "by way of explanation"*

Verse 8, "forgive all their sins." The covenant was founded on the confession of sin and the forgiveness of sin.

10. *Key "Quotable Quote"*

"The greatest of physicians has come to us and forgiven all our sins."
Augustine of Hippo

Jeremiah chapter 34

1. Before and after

Previous chapter: Chapter 33: Reconfirming the covenant
Following chapter: Chapter 35: Message to the Recabites

2. Analysis of chapter

Zedekiah's death at Babylon foretold. (1-7)
The Jews reproved for compelling their poor brethren, forced by debt to become slaves, to remain in slavery.. (8-22)

3. Key verse

Verse 4: "Yet hear the word of the LORD, O Zedekiah king of Judah; Thus saith the LORD of thee, Thou shalt not die by the sword."

4. Key word / key phrase

Verse 17, "not obeyed me."

5. Key event / key person / key theme

A covenant commitment overthrown (verses 10,11

6. Key thought

Under the covenant, slaves were set free every seven years. By going back on their promise to keep this covenant commitment, the people had dishonored God.

7. Key thing to look out for

God's judgment on sin is inevitable as night follows day.

8. Key Bible cross-reference

Verse 14. See Exodus 21:2.

9. Key "by way of explanation"

Verse 1, "all the empires and peoples." Nebuchadnezzar's empire was vast. The attack by the Babylonians came in 589 after Zedekiah had rebelled. Though the siege was temporarily lifted (21) Jerusalem was eventually captured.

10. Key "Quotable Quote"

"There is your brother, naked and crying! And you stand confused over choice of floor covering."
Ambrose

Jeremiah chapter 35

1. **Before and after**

   Previous chapter: Chapter 34: Prophecies in Zedekiah's reign
   Following chapter: Chapter 36: Scroll burning

2. **Analysis of chapter**

   The obedience of the Recabites. (1-11)
   The Jews' disobedience to the Lord. (12-19)

3. **Key verse**

   Verse 3: "Then I took Jaazaniah the son of Jeremiah, the son of Habaziniah, and his brethren, and all his sons, and the whole house of the Rechabites."

4. **Key word / key phrase**

   Verse 2, "the Recabite family."

5. **Key event / key person / key theme**

   Message to the Recabites

6. **Key thought**

   The Recabites are held up as an example of loyalty in the middle of adversity.

7. **Key thing to look out for**

   Verse 13 asks the pertinent question, "Will you not learn a lesson . . .?"

8. **Key Bible cross-reference**

   Verse 1. See 2 Chronicles 36:5-7.

9. **Key "by way of explanation"**

   The Recabites were a nomad clan who were true worshipers of God, and lived in the desert in protest against the evils of society. They had come into Jerusalem for protection from raiding enemy armies. The events of chapters 35-36 follow chapter 26 (609-598 BC).

10. **Key "Quotable Quote"**

    "When Christians stand up for righteousness and justice, they evidence the power of the living God."
    Charles Colson

Jeremiah chapter 36

1. *Before and after*

Previous chapter: Chapter 35: Message to the Recabites
Following chapter: Chapter 37: Jeremiah imprisoned

2. *Analysis of chapter*

Baruch is to write down the prophecies of Jeremiah. (1-8)
The leaders advise them to hide themselves. (9-19)
The king having heard some of Jeremiah's words, burns the scroll. (20-32)

3. *Key verse*

Verse 2: "Take thee a roll of a book, and write therein all the words that I have spoken unto thee against Israel, and against Judah, and against all the nations, from the day I spake unto thee, from the days of Josiah, even unto this day."

4. *Key word / key phrase*

Verse 27, "the king burned the scroll."

5. *Key event / key person / key theme*

The kings refused to listen to Jeremiah's prophecies.

6. *Key thought*

Endless attempts to snuff out God's word have been made by destroying Bibles.

7. *Key thing to look out for*

Note how Jeremiah reacted, verse 32, to this scroll burning.

8. *Key Bible cross-reference*

Verse 1. See 2 Chronicles 36:5-7.

9. *Key "by way of explanation"*

Verse 6, "a day of fasting." God's people fasted in times of crisis.

10. *Key "Quotable Quote"*

"Do not let only your mouth fast, but also the eye and the ear and the feet and the hands and all the members of our bodies.
Let the hands fast, by being free of avarice.
Let the feet fast, by ceasing to run after sin.
Let the eyes fast, by disciplining them not to glare at that which is sinful.
Let the ear fast, by not listening to evil talk and gossip.
Let the mouth fast from foul words and unjust criticism."
John Chrysostom

Jeremiah chapter 37

1. **Before and after**

   Previous chapter: Chapter 36: Scroll burning
   Following chapter: Chapter 38: Jeremiah dumped in a cistern

2. **Analysis of chapter**

   The Babylonian army will return. (1-10)
   Jeremiah is imprisoned. (11-21)

3. **Key verse**

   Verse 5: "Then Pharaoh's army was come forth out of Egypt: and when the Chaldeans that besieged Jerusalem heard tidings of them, they departed from Jerusalem."

4. **Key word / key phrase**

   Verse 16, "in a dungeon"

5. **Key event / key person / key theme**

   Jeremiah imprisoned

6. **Key thought**

   Some of God's servants undergo severe times of persecution in their lives.

7. **Key thing to look out for**

   Jeremiah was imprisoned for being faithful to the Lord.

8. **Key Bible cross-reference**

   Verse 1. See 2 Chronicles 36:10.

9. **Key "by way of explanation"**

   Verse 21, "courtyard of the guard." Jeremiah's imprisonment was made much more bearable. At the end of the Acts Paul had a not dissimilar experience when he was under house-arrest for two years.

10. **Key "Quotable Quote"**

    "Those persecutions, which we must suffer for the testimony of the Gospel, are remnants of the sufferings of Christ."
    John Calvin

Jeremiah chapter 38

1. Before and after

Previous chapter: Chapter 37: Jeremiah imprisoned
Following chapter: Chapter 39: Ebed-Melech rewarded; Jerusalem captured

2. Analysis of chapter

Jeremiah is thrown into a cistern, from where he is rescued by an Ethiopian. (1-13)
He advises the king to surrender to the Chaldeans. (14-28)

3. Key verse

Verse 6: "Then took they Jeremiah, and cast him into the dungeon of Malchiah the son of Hammelech, that was in the court of the prison: and they let down Jeremiah with cords."

4. Key word / key phrase

Verse 6, "into the cistern."

5. Key event / key person / key theme

Jeremiah dumped in a cistern

6. Key thought

Without someone to rescue him God's prophet would have died in the cistern.

7. Key thing to look out for

The faithful action of a few godly people can do an enormous amount of good.

8. Key Bible cross-reference

Verse 28. See Ezekiel 33:21.

9. Key "by way of explanation"

Verse 12, "put these old rags . . . under your arms." Ebed-Melech took practical and kind action as he rescued Jeremiah.

10. Key "Quotable Quote"

"It is impossible to comfort men's hearts with the love of God when their feet are perishing with cold."
William Booth

Jeremiah chapter 39

1. *Before and after*

Previous chapter: Chapter 38: Jeremiah dumped in a cistern
Following chapter: Chapter 40: Jeremiah freed

2. *Analysis of chapter*

The taking of Jerusalem. (1-10)
Jeremiah used well. (11-14)
Promises of safety to Ebed-melech. (15-18)

3. *Key verse*

Verse 1: "In the ninth year of Zedekiah king of Judah, in the tenth month, came Nebuchadrezzar king of Babylon and all his army against Jerusalem, and they besieged it."

4. *Key word / key phrase*

Verse 1, "Jerusalem was taken."

5. *Key event / key person / key theme*

Ebed-Melech rewarded; Jerusalem captured

6. *Key thought*

All of God's prophecies will be fulfilled.

7. *Key thing to look out for*

Whether in this life or in the next life God's faithful servants are rewarded.

8. *Key Bible cross-reference*

Verse 7. See Numbers 16:14.

9. *Key "by way of explanation"*

Verse 16, "Go and tell." It is clear that Jeremiah had contact with the outside world, even though he was confined to prison.

10. *Key "Quotable Quote"*

"In this life, all things go in pairs: practice and spiritual knowledge, free will and grace, fear and hope, struggle and reward."
Peter of Damascus

Jeremiah chapter 40

1. **Before and after**

   Previous chapter: Chapter 39: Ebed-Melech rewarded; Jerusalem captured
   Following chapter: Chapter 41: Murder and massacre

2. **Analysis of chapter**

   Jeremiah is directed to go to Gedaliah. (1-6)
   A conspiracy against Gedaliah. (7-16)

3. **Key verse**

   Verse 2: "And the captain of the guard took Jeremiah, and said unto him, The LORD thy God hath pronounced this evil upon this place."

4. **Key word / key phrase**

   Verse 1, "He had found Jeremiah bound in chains."

5. **Key event / key person / key theme**

   Jeremiah freed

6. **Key thought**

   Jeremiah knows that the future lay with the exiles in Babylon, yet he decided to stay with the poorest in the land (verse 7).

7. **Key thing to look out for**

   Jeremiah could have had comfortable old age if he had gone to Babylon (verse 4).

8. **Key Bible cross-reference**

   Verses 7-9. See 2 Kings 25:22-24.

9. **Key "by way of explanation"**

   Verses 13-16, the warning was justified (41:1-3). Gedaliah failed to recognize wise counsel. Gedaliah was based at Mizpah.

10. **Key "Quotable Quote"**

    "Our professed love of freedom is increasingly shown to be a sophistry that replaces wisdom and righteousness with self-gratification."
    Carl Henry

Jeremiah chapter 41

1. Before and after

Previous chapter: Chapter 40: Jeremiah freed
Following chapter: Chapter 42: "Don't flee to Egypt"

2. Analysis of chapter

Ishmael murders Gedaliah at Mizpah. (1-3)
Ishael murders a group of pilgrims and flees with the people of Mizpah as his prisoners. (11-18)

3. Key verse

Verse 4: "And it came to pass the second day after he had slain Gedaliah, and no man knew it,"

4. Key word / key phrase

Verse 2, "struck down Gedaliah."

5. Key event / key person / key theme

Murder and massacre

6. Key thought

The escalation of evil.

7. Key thing to look out for

Verse 5, there were still godly people in Israel.

8. Key Bible cross-reference

Verses 1-3. See 2 Kings 25:25.

9. Key "by way of explanation"

Verse 7, "cistern." Cisterns were used to dump people in whether they were dead or alive. To murder someone while you were eating together was a gross violation of the laws of hospitality. The other murders were probably to silence witnesses.

10. Key "Quotable Quote"

"We cannot love good if we do not hate evil."
Jerome

Jeremiah chapter 42

1. **Before and after**

   Previous chapter: Chapter 41: Murder and massacre
   Following chapter: Chapter 43: Jeremiah taken to Egypt

2. **Analysis of chapter**

   Johanan wants Jeremiah to seek God's counsel. (1-6)
   God promises them safety in in Judea, but destruction in Egypt. (7-22)

3. **Key verse**

   Verse 3: "That the LORD thy God may show us the way wherein we may walk, and the thing that we may do."

4. **Key word / key phrase**

   Verse 19, "Do not go to Egypt."

5. **Key event / key person / key theme**

   "Don't flee to Egypt."

6. **Key thought**

   Verse 11, God was with the people, and he was greater than the kings of Babylon, so they must not run away.

7. **Key thing to look out for**

   Jeremiah could see that their minds were already made up: a sign of arrogance

8. **Key Bible cross-reference**

   Verse 12. See Exodus 3:21.

9. **Key "by way of explanation"**

   Verse 6, "we will obey the Lord our God." 43:2 shows how shallow this assertion proved to be.

10. **Key "Quotable Quote"**

    "I need Thy presence every passing hour:
    What but Thy grace can foil the tempter's power?"
    Henry Francis Lyte

Jeremiah chapter 43

1. Before and after

Previous chapter: Chapter 42: "Don't flee to Egypt"
Following chapter: Chapter 44: The Lord's message to the Jews in Egypt

2. Analysis of chapter

The leaders carry the people to Egypt. (1-7)
Jeremiah predicts the conquest of Egypt. (8-13)

3. Key verse

Verse 7: "So they came into the land of Egypt: for they obeyed not the voice of
the LORD: thus came they even to Tahpanhes."

4. Key word / key phrase

Verse 7, "they entered Egypt."

5. Key event / key person / key theme

Jeremiah taken to Egypt

6. Key thought

Verse 8, even in Egypt Jeremiah continued to warn the people. He did not give
up.

7. Key thing to look out for

Safety only lies with following the Lord.

8. Key Bible cross-reference

Verses 5-7. See 2 Kings 25:26.

9. Key "by way of explanation"

Verse 10, "my servant Nebuchadnezzar." God can use even pagan leaders to
carry out his will.

10. Key "Quotable Quote"

"One of the outstanding glories of the Gospel is its promise of eternal security
to all who truly believe it."
A.W. Pink

Jeremiah chapter 44

1. Before and after

Previous chapter: Chapter 43: Jeremiah taken to Egypt
Following chapter: Chapter 45: A message for Baruch

2. Analysis of chapter

The Jews in Egypt persist in idolatry. (1-14)
They refuse to reform. (15-19)
Jeremiah then pronounces destruction on them. (20-30)

3. Key verse

Verse 10: "They are not humbled even unto this day, neither have they feared, nor walked in my law, nor in my statutes, that I set before you and before your fathers."

4. Key word / key phrase

Verse 11, "to bring disaster."

5. Key event / key person / key theme

The Lord's message to the Jews in Egypt

6. Key thought

Human sinfulness again brings down divine wrath.

7. Key thing to look out for

The consequences of idolatry are incalculable.

8. Key Bible cross-reference

Verse 9. See Judges 2:19.

9. Key "by way of explanation"

Verse 17, "Queen of Heaven," refers to Ishtar, one of the main goddesses among the Babylonian pantheon. Jeremiah's last message to the Jews is dated about 585 BC.

10. Key "Quotable Quote"

"A man is first startled by sin; then it becomes pleasing, then easy, then delightful, then frequent, then habitual, then confirmed."
Jeremy Taylor

Jeremiah chapter 45

1. *Before and after*

Previous chapter: Chapter 44: The Lord's message to the Jews in Egypt
Following chapter: Chapter 46: Prophecies against Egypt

2. *Analysis of chapter*

An encouragement sent to Baruch. (1-5)

3. *Key verse*

Verse 1: "The word that Jeremiah the prophet spake unto Baruch the son of Neriah, when he had written these words in a book at the mouth of Jeremiah,"

4. *Key word / key phrase*

Verse 1, "Baruch."

5. *Key event / key person / key theme*

A message for Baruch, Jeremiah's faithful secretary.

6. *Key thought*

Verse 5, "great things." Selfish ambition has no place in the life of the godly person.

7. *Key thing to look out for*

All of God's followers need human encouragement.

8. *Key Bible cross-reference*

Verse 1. See 2 Kings 24:1,2.

9. *Key "by way of explanation"*

This message was written in 605/4 BC (out of chronological order). Baruch's brother held an important office (51:59), and they came from an aristocratic family.

10. *Key "Quotable Quote"*

"What brings joy to the heart is not so much the friend's gift as the friend's love."
Aelred of Rievaulx

Jeremiah chapter 46

1. *Before and after*

Previous chapter: Chapter 45: A message for Baruch
Following chapter: Chapter 47: Prophecies against Philistia

2. *Analysis of chapter*

The defeat of the Egyptians. (1-12)
Their overthrow after the siege of Tyre. (13-26)
A promise of comfort to the Jews. (27,28)

3. *Key verse*

Verse 2: "Against Egypt, against the army of Pharaohnecho king of Egypt,"

4. *Key word / key phrase*

Verse 2, "Concerning Egypt."

5. *Key event / key person / key theme*

Prophecies against Egypt

6. *Key thought*

The battle belongs to the Lord.

7. *Key thing to look out for*

Kingdoms rise and fall but God's kingdom is everlasting.

8. *Key Bible cross-reference*

Verse 13. See Jeremiah 43:10-13.

9. *Key "by way of explanation"*

Verse 2, "defeated at Carchemish." This reference to Carchemish alludes to one of the most famous battles in the ancient world when Egypt was defeated by the Babylonians. It took place in 605 BC

10. *Key "Quotable Quote"*

"Beware of resting in the word of the kingdom, without the spirit and power of the kingdom of that gospel."
John Bunyan

Jeremiah chapter 47

1. *Before and after*

Previous chapter: Chapter 46: Prophecies against Egypt
Following chapter: Chapter 48: Prophecies against Moab

2. *Analysis of chapter*

The calamities of the Philistines. (1-7)

3. *Key verse*

Verse 1: "The word of the LORD that came to Jeremiah the prophet against the Philistines, before that Pharaoh smote Gaza."

4. *Key word / key phrase*

Verse 1, "Concerning the Philistines."

5. *Key event / key person / key theme*

Prophecies against Philistia

6. *Key thought*

No country can truly prosper if it defies the living God.

7. *Key thing to look out for*

The Philistines were doomed because they loved to attack and crush God's people.

8. *Key Bible cross-reference*

Verses 1-47. See Amos 2:1-3; Zephaniah 2:8-11.

9. *Key "by way of explanation"*

Verse 3, "hands hang limp." This condition was brought about by fear and terror. Verse 5, "Cut yourself," was a mark of mourning.

10. *Key "Quotable Quote"*

"If we desire to live in honor and to be esteemed by our neighbors, then we shall never be solidly rooted in God our Lord, and it will be impossible for us to remain undisturbed when insults come our way."
Ignatius of Loyola

Jeremiah chapter 48

1. Before and after

Previous chapter: Chapter 47: Prophecies against Philistia
Following chapter: Chapter 49: Prophecies against Ammon, Edom, Damascus, Kedar, and Hazor

2. Analysis of chapter

Prophecies against Moab for pride and security. (1-13)
For trust in people and contempt of God. (14-47)

3. Key verse

Verse 13: "And Moab shall be ashamed of Chemosh, as the house of Israel was ashamed of Bethel their confidence."

4. Key word / key phrase

Verse 1, "Concerning Moab."

5. Key event / key person / key theme

Prophecies against Moab

6. Key thought

Judgment falls on Chemosh and on all who worship him.

7. Key thing to look out for

The people who despised Israel so much become despicable themselves.

8. Key Bible cross-reference

Verse 7. See Psalm 49:6.

9. Key "by way of explanation"

Verse 7, "Chemosh," was worshiped by the Moabites as their national god.

10. Key "Quotable Quote"

"Christians must seek their delights in a higher sphere than the insipid frivolities of the world!"
C.H. Spurgeon

Jeremiah chapter 49

1. Before and after

Previous chapter: Chapter 48: Prophecies against Moab
Following chapter: Chapter 50: Babylon's defeat and desolation

2. Analysis of chapter

Prophecies about the Ammonites. (1-6)
The Edomites. (7-22)
The Syrians. (23-27)
The Kedarenes. (28-33)
The Elamites. (34-39)

3. Key verse

Verse 1: "Concerning the Ammonites,"

4. Key word / key phrase

Verses 1,7 "The Lord Almighty says."

5. Key event / key person / key theme

Prophecies against Ammon, Edom, Damascus, Kedar, and Hazor

6. Key thought

It is true that the world seems to be in the grip of the evil one.

7. Key thing to look out for

The deeper truth is that the world is in the loving embrace of its Creator and
Sustainer, who is also the God of history.

8. Key Bible cross-reference

Verse 18. See Genesis 19:24,25.

9. Key "by way of explanation"

Verse 1, "Molech." He was the leading god among the Ammonites.

10. Key "Quotable Quote"

"The almighty and everywhere present power of God; whereby, as it were by
his hand, he upholds and governs heaven, earth, and all creatures; so that
herbs and grass, rain and drought, fruitful and barren years, meat and drink,
health and sickness, riches and poverty, yea, and all things come, not by
chance, but by his fatherly hand."
Heidelberg Catechism

Jeremiah chapter 50

1. **Before and after**

   Previous chapter: Chapter 49: Prophecies against Ammon, Edom, Damascus, Kedar, and Hazor
   Following chapter: Chapter 51: Babylon's destiny

2. **Analysis of chapter**

   The ruin of Babylon. (1-3,8-16,21-32,35-46)
   The redemption of God's people. (4-7,17-20,33,34)

3. **Key verse**

   Verse 1: "The word that the LORD spake against Babylon and against the land of the Chaldeans [Babylonians] by Jeremiah the prophet."

4. **Key word / key phrase**

   Verse 1, "concerning Babylon."

5. **Key event / key person / key theme**

   Babylon's defeat and desolation

6. **Key thought**

   Babylon, Israel's major enemy, will be punished by God.

7. **Key thing to look out for**

   The greatest enemies of God's followers should not make godly people quake with fear.

8. **Key Bible cross-reference**

   Verse 8. See Revelation 18:6.

9. **Key "by way of explanation"**

   Babylon was the dominant power from 627 to 539 BC when the empire fell to Cyrus (verse 3).

10. **Key "Quotable Quote"**

    "It is men, not God, who have produced racks, whips, prisons, slavery, guns, bayonets, and bombs; it is by human avarice or human stupidity, not by the churlishness of nature, that we have poverty and overwork."
    C.S. Lewis

Jeremiah chapter 51

1. *Before and after*

Previous chapter: Chapter 50: Babylon's defeat and desolation
Following chapter: Chapter 52: Jerusalem captured, the exile, and signs of
hope

2. *Analysis of chapter*

Babylon's doom; God's controversy with her; encouragements from this for
the Israel of God. (1-58)
This is confirmed. (59-64)

3. *Key verse*

Verse 6: "Flee out of the midst of Babylon, and deliver every man his soul: be
not cut off in her iniquity; for this is the time of the LORD's vengeance; he will
render unto her a recompense."

4. *Key word / key phrase*

Verse 1, "against Babylon."

5. *Key event / key person / key theme*

Babylon's destiny

6. *Key thought*

Wrongs will be put right.

7. *Key thing to look out for*

If we believed that God was totally in control of our world how our worldview
would change.

8. *Key Bible cross-reference*

Verse 13. See Revelation 17:1.

9. *Key "by way of explanation"*

Verse 9, "reaches to the skies." This is clearly a form of poetic speech.
However, the truth it conveys remains true and the vivid expression only
reinforces the point.

10. *Key "Quotable Quote"*

"The teaching of the New Testament is that the whole time the world has been
'lying in the wicked one'."
D. Martyn Lloyd-Jones

Jeremiah chapter 52

1. *Previous chapter*

Chapter 51: Babylon's destiny

2. *Analysis of chapter*

The fate of Zedekiah. (1-11)
The destruction of Jerusalem. (12-23)
The captivities. (24-30)
The advancement of Jehoiachin. (31-34)

3. *Key verse*

Verse 11: "Then he put out the eyes of Zedekiah; and the king of Babylon bound him in chains, and carried him to Babylon, and put him in prison till the day of his death."

4. *Key word / key phrase*

Verse 7, "the city wall was broken through."

5. *Key event / key person / key theme*

Jerusalem captured, the exile, and signs of hope

6. *Key thought*

Verse 27 is one of the saddest verses in the Old Testament.

7. *Key thing to look out for*

Jehoiachin's release means that the book of Jeremiah ends on a note of hope with the first step in the restoration being recorded.

8. *Key Bible cross-reference*

Verse 4. See Ezekiel 24:2.

9. *Key "by way of explanation"*

The last chapter of the book of Jeremiah is an additional historical appendix to the book.

10. *Key "Quotable Quote"*

"Hope has two beautiful daughters Their names are anger and courage; anger at the way things are, and courage to see that they do not remain the way they are."
Augustine of Hippo

Lamentations chapter 1

1. *Following chapter*

Chapter 2: God's anger

2. *Analysis of chapter*

The miserable state of Jerusalem, the just results of its sins. (1-11)
Jerusalem represented as a captive, lamenting, and seeking the mercy of God.
(12-22)

3. *Key verse*

Verse 1: "How doth the city sit solitary, that was full of people! how is she
become as a widow."

4. *Key word / key phrase*

Verse 2, "bitterly she weeps."

5. *Key event / key person / key theme*

Jerusalem's desolation

6. *Key thought*

Mourning is necessary if there is ever to be any recovery.

7. *Key thing to look out for*

For the Israelites their city in ruins was tantamount to their God being
defeated.

8. *Key Bible cross-reference*

Verse 1. See Leviticus 26:43.

9. *Key "by way of explanation"*

Verse 1. The opening phrase of the book, "how deserted lies the city", sets the
sad and almost desperate atmosphere which pervades every chapter.

10. *Key "Quotable Quote"*

"Especially judge not the sons and daughters of sorrow."
C.H. Spurgeon

Lamentations chapter 2

1. *Before and after*

   Previous chapter: Chapter 1: Jerusalem's destruction
   Following chapter: Chapter 3: A prayer for mercy

2. *Analysis of chapter*

   Lamentation for the misery of Jerusalem. (1-22)

3. *Key verse*

   Verse 5: "The Lord was as an enemy: he hath swallowed up Israel, he hath swallowed up all her palaces: he hath destroyed his strong holds, and hath increased in the daughter of Judah mourning and lamentation."

4. *Key word / key phrase*

   Verse 2, "in his wrath."

5. *Key event / key person / key theme*

   God's anger

6. *Key thought*

   God's people will not escape God's judgment if they are not faithful.

7. *Key thing to look out for*

   Jerusalem itself was punished dreadfully.

8. *Key Bible cross-reference*

   Verse 1. See Jeremiah 12:7.

9. *Key "by way of explanation"*

   Verse 9, "prophets no longer find visions." One of the signs of God withdrawing from his people was the lack of visions and prophetic messages.

10. *Key "Quotable Quote"*

    "We are healed of grief only when we express it to the full."
    Charles R. Swindoll

Lamentations chapter 3

1. **Before and after**

   Previous chapter: Chapter 2: God's anger
   Following chapter: Chapter 4: Jerusalem, after its fall

2. **Analysis of chapter**

   The faithful lament their calamities, and hope in God's mercies. (1-66)

3. **Key verse**

   Verse 22: "It is of the LORD's mercies that we are not consumed, because his compassions fail not."

4. **Key word / key phrase**

   Verse 23, "great is your faithfulness."

5. **Key event / key person / key theme**

   A prayer for mercy

6. **Key thought**

   To express faith in God when all around speaks of the opposite is faith indeed.

7. **Key thing to look out for**

   Even in the middle of the greatest tragedy God's love should be remembered.

8. **Key Bible cross-reference**

   Verse 26. See Isaiah 7:4.

9. **Key "by way of explanation"**

   Verse 22, "great love." This includes all the promises God made to his people in his covenants.

10. **Key "Quotable Quote"**

    "Truly, it is in darkness that one finds the light, so when we are in sorrow, then this light is nearest to all of us."
    Meister Eckhart

Lamentations chapter 4

1. *Before and after*

Previous chapter: Chapter 3: A prayer for mercy
Following chapter: Chapter 5: A prayer for restoration

2. *Analysis of chapter*

The deplorable state of the nation is contrasted with its ancient prosperity.
(1-22)

3. *Key verse*

Verse 13: "It is of the LORD'S mercies that we are not consumed, because his compassions fail not."

4. *Key word / key phrase*

Verse 18, "men stalked us at every step."

5. *Key event / key person / key theme*

Jerusalem, after its fall

6. *Key thought*

The destruction of Jerusalem is open for all to view.

7. *Key thing to look out for*

Verse 14 indicates that the sins of Israel's spiritual leaders brought down God's judgment on God's city.

8. *Key Bible cross-reference*

Verse 6. See Genesis 19:24.

9. *Key "by way of explanation"*

Verse 15, "unclean." The whole of the devastated city of Jerusalem is likened to an unclean leper.

10. *Key "Quotable Quote"*

"And no one ever told me about the laziness of grief. Not only writing but even reading a letter is too much. Even shaving. What does it matter now whether my cheek is rough or smooth?"
C.S. Lewis

Lamentations chapter 5

1. **Previous chapter**

   Chapter 4: Jerusalem besieged

2. **Analysis of chapter**

   The Jewish nation asking for divine favor. (1-22)

3. **Key verse**

   Verse 19: "Thou, O LORD, remainest for ever; thy throne from generation to generation."

4. **Key word / key phrase**

   Verse 1, "Remember, O Lord."

5. **Key event / key person / key theme**

   A prayer for restoration

6. **Key thought**

   A prayer of deep repentance is the only appropriate action on certain occasions.

7. **Key thing to look out for**

   Not only is there hope for the individual (chapter 3) but hope for the community, because God still reigns (verses 19-22).

8. **Key Bible cross-reference**

   Verse 20. See Psalm 13:1.

9. **Key "by way of explanation"**

   Verse 16, "crown." The "crown" refers to the regal nature of God's city and now that it has fallen shows how the city's glory has been lost.

10. **Key "Quotable Quote"**

    "There is a command to rejoice evermore, but nowhere is it written, mourn continually."
    Richard Sibbes

Ezekiel

Ezekiel chapter 1

1. **Following chapter**

   Chapter 2: Ezekiel is sent to Israel

2. **Analysis of chapter**

   Ezekiel's vision of God, and of the angelic host. (1-14)
   Divine providence. (15-25)
   A revelation of the Son of man on his heavenly throne. (26-28)

3. **Key verse**

   Verse 1: "Now it came to pass in the thirtieth year, in the fourth month, in the fifth day of the month, as I was among the captives by the river of Chebar, that the heavens were opened, and I saw visions of God."

4. **Key word / key phrase**

   Verse 28, "the likeness of the glory of the Lord."

5. **Key event / key person / key theme**

   Ezekiel sees the glory of God

6. **Key thought**

   God's glory is beyond human description.

7. **Key thing to look out for**

   From this vision observe what is said about God's nature.

8. **Key Bible cross-reference**

   Verse 1. See Revelation 19:11.

9. **Key "by way of explanation"**

   Ezekiel was one of the Jews deported to Babylon in 597 BC. Here, at Tel Abib (3:15), God calls him to be a prophet.

10. **Key "Quotable Quote"**

    "Power in the Christian life depends upon our connection with the source of power."
    L. Nelson Bell

Ezekiel chapter 2

1. Before and after

Previous chapter: Chapter 1: Ezekiel sees the glory of God
Following chapter: Chapter 3:Ezekiel is instructed about his ministry

2. Analysis of chapter

The prophet is told what he is to do. (1-5)
And encouraged to be resolute, faithful, and devoted. (6-10)

3. Key verse

Verse 6: "And thou, son of man, be not afraid of them, neither be afraid of their words, though briers and thorns be with thee, and thou dost dwell among scorpions."

4. Key word / key phrase

Verse 3, "I am sending you to the Israelites."

5. Key event / key person / key theme

Ezekiel is commissioned to give God's message to the exiles in Babylonia.

6. Key thought

The prophets accepted God's call, even when it meant they would have to suffer.

7. Key thing to look out for

Ezekiel is warned of danger but told not to fear.

8. Key Bible cross-reference

Verses 9,10. See Revelation 5:1.

9. Key "by way of explanation"

Verse 1, "Son of man," that is, "human being." The phrase emphasizes Ezekiel's humanity and his weakness when compared with God.

10. Key "Quotable Quote"

"We are not made of iron, we are not like rocks, we are mortal men full of fragility."
John Calvin

Ezekiel chapter 3

1. Before and after

Previous chapter: Chapter 2: Ezekiel is sent to Israel
Following chapter: Chapter 4: Three symbolic actions

2. Analysis of chapter

The preparation of the prophet for his work. (1-11)
His office, as a watchman. (12-21)
The restraining and restoring of his speech. (22-27)

3. Key verse

Verse 5: "For thou art not sent to a people of a strange speech and of an hard language, but to the house of Israel."

4. Key word / key phrase

Verse 1, "eat this scroll."

5. Key event / key person / key theme

Ezekiel is instructed about his ministry.

6. Key thought

Opposition should not be an excuse to stop us witnessing.

7. Key thing to look out for

The different arguments that are put up against following God.

8. Key Bible cross-reference

Verses 1-3. See Revelation 10:9,10.

9. Key "by way of explanation"

Verse 15, "seven days." This was the usual time for mourning and indicates Ezekiel's frame of mind.

10. Key "Quotable Quote"

"Oh, that there were more crying persons, when there are so many crying sins."
Ralph Venning

Ezekiel chapter 4

1. **Before and after**

    Previous chapter: Chapter 3:Ezekiel is instructed about his ministry
    Following chapter: Chapter 5: A fourth symbolic action, and symbolic
    actions explained

2. **Analysis of chapter**

    Ezekiel draws a plan of the siege of Jerusalem. (1-3)
    The prophet lies on the ground for 430 days by the miniature Jerusalem. (4-8)
    Starvation-rations, ceremonially polluted. (9-17)

3. **Key verse**

    Verse 2: "And lay siege against it, and build a fort against it, and cast a mount
    against it; set the camp also against it, and set battering rams against it round
    about."

4. **Key word / key phrase**

    Verse 1, "Draw the city of Jerusalem."

5. **Key event / key person / key theme**

    A symbolic acting-out of the siege of Jerusalem

6. **Key thought**

    Actions speak louder than words.

7. **Key thing to look out for**

    Verse 4, Ezekiel's complete identification with the sinful people: he *symbolized*
    the sin; cf. Christ who removed sin (Isaiah 53:11).

8. **Key Bible cross-reference**

    Verse 16. See Psalm 105:16.

9. **Key "by way of explanation"**

    Verse 3, "a sign to the house of Israel," is that they should not place their hope
    in Jerusalem's survival. Ezekiel's rations were 8oz of poor quality bread and
    two pints of water.

10. **Key "Quotable Quote"**

    "The Christian hope is hope in the power of God."
    William Barclay

Ezekiel chapter 5

1. *Before and after*

Previous chapter: Chapter 4: Three symbolic actions
Following chapter: Chapter 6: Destruction because of idolatry

2. *Analysis of chapter*

A type of hair, showing the judgments about to come upon the Jews. (1-4)
These awful judgments are declared. (5-17)

3. *Key verse*

Verse 1: "And thou, son of man, take thee a sharp knife, take thee a barber's razor, and cause it to pass upon thine head and upon thy beard: then take thee balances to weigh, and divide the hair."

4. *Key word / key phrase*

Verse 1, "Shave your head and beard."

5. *Key event / key person / key theme*

A fourth symbolic action, and symbolic actions explained

6. *Key thought*

Verses 12-17, the destruction will be terrible

7. *Key thing to look out for*

These images were not man-made, but given by the Lord.

8. *Key Bible cross-reference*

Verse 10. See Lamentations 4:10.

9. *Key "by way of explanation"*

Verse 13, the two phrases "they will know" and "I the LORD have spoken," are two themes in Ezekiel.

10. *Key "Quotable Quote"*

"Sin is the most expensive thing in the universe, pardoned or unforgiven: pardoned, its cost falls on the atoning sacrifice; unforgiven, it must forever lie upon the impenitent soul."
Charles G. Finney

Ezekiel chapter 6

1. *Before and after*

Previous chapter: Chapter 5: A fourth symbolic action, and symbolic actions explained

Following chapter: Chapter 7: The day of destruction described

2. *Analysis of chapter*

The divine judgments for idolatry. (1-7)

A remnant shall be saved. (8-10)

The calamities are to be lamented. (11-14)

3. *Key verse*

Verse 11: "Smite with thine hand, and stamp with thy foot, and say, Alas for all the evil abominations of the house of Israel!"

4. *Key word / key phrase*

Verse 6, "high places demolished."

5. *Key event / key person / key theme*

Destruction upon all the land because of idolatry

6. *Key thought*

What form does idolatry take today?

7. *Key thing to look out for*

The Lord will not put up with certain things.

8. *Key Bible cross-reference*

Verse 5. See Leviticus 19:16.

9. *Key "by way of explanation"*

Verse 13, "under every spreading tree." Such trees marked the sites of pagan worship.

10. *Key "Quotable Quote"*

"The very heart and root of sin is an independent spirit. We erect the idol self, and not only wish others to worship, but worship it ourselves."

Richard Cecil

Ezekiel chapter 7

1. *Before and after*

Previous chapter: Chapter 6: Destruction because of idolatry
Following chapter: Chapter 8: Four abominations

2. *Analysis of chapter*

The imminent desolation of the land. (1-15)
The distress of the few who should escape. (16-22)
The captivity. (23-27)

3. *Key verse*

Verse 23: "Make a chain: for the land is full of bloody crimes, and the city is full of violence."

4. *Key word / key phrase*

Verse 2, "the end has come."

5. *Key event / key person / key theme*

The day of destruction described

6. *Key thought*

How can the wrong use of money be a stumbling block today?

7. *Key thing to look out for*

The catalogue of wrongdoing: spelled out for emphasis

8. *Key Bible cross-reference*

Verse 14. See Job 39:24.

9. *Key "by way of explanation"*

Verse 22, "my treasured place," refers to the temple, and possibly to the holy of holies in particular. Verse 26, the ultimate horror.

10. *Key "Quotable Quote"*

"To live without hope is to cease to live."
Fyodor Dostoevsky

Ezekiel chapter 8

1. Before and after

Previous chapter: Chapter 7: The day of destruction described
Following chapter: Chapter 9: Vision of killing in Jerusalem

2. Analysis of chapter

The Spirit transports Ezekiel to Jerusalem. (1-4)
The detestable worship: first Canaanite. (5-6)
Second, Egyptian. (7-13)
Third, Sumerian. (14,15)
Fourth, sun-worship by the priests themselves. 16-18)

3. Key verse

Verse 3: ". . . the spirit lifted me up between the earth and the heaven, and brought me in the visions of God to Jerusalem, to the door of the inner gate that looketh toward the north; where was the seat of the image of jealousy, which provoketh to jealousy."

4. Key word / key phrase

Verses 6,10,14,17, "detestable."

5. Key event / key person / key theme

The glory of the Lord has been driven out of the holy of holies (verse 4), and will soon leave the temple (verse 6).

6. Key thought

Idolatry is thriving even in God's temple.

7. Key thing to look out for

What steps can we take to ensure that we avoid the worship of false gods?

8. Key Bible cross-reference

Verse 4. See 1:28.

9. Key "by way of explanation"

Verse 3, "took me by the hair of my head." Later, Ezekiel realized that he was describing an ecstatic experience. Verse 1, "the elders of Judah," community life has been re-established.

10. Key "Quotable Quote"

"The dearest idol I have known,
Whate'er that idol be.
Help me to tear it from the throne,
And worship only thee."
William Cowper

Ezekiel chapter 9

1. **Before and after**

   Previous chapter: Chapter 8: Four abominations
   Following chapter: Chapter 10: God's glory leaves the temple

2. **Analysis of chapter**

   A vision denoting the destruction of the inhabitants of Jerusalem, and the departure of the symbol of the divine presence. (1-11)

3. **Key verse**

   Verse 3: "And the glory of the God of Israel was gone up from the cherub."

4. **Key word / key phrase**

   Verse 5, "kill."

5. **Key event / key person / key theme**

   Vision of killing in Jerusalem

6. **Key thought**

   The severity of the punishment shows the seriousness of the sin.

7. **Key thing to look out for**

   How does the Lord answer the prophet's question?

8. **Key Bible cross-reference**

   Verse 4. See Revelation 7:3; 9:4; 14:1.

9. **Key "by way of explanation"**

   Verse 4, "put a mark." This "mark" was the last letter of the Hebrew alphabet, "taw". It was some kind of protective mark.

10. **Key "Quotable Quote"**

    "In all our actions, when we come in or go out, when we dress, when we wash, at our meals, before retiring to sleep, we make on our foreheads the sign of the cross. These practices are not committed by a formal law of Scripture, but tradition teaches them, custom confirms them, faith observes them."
    Tertullian

Ezekiel chapter 10

1. Before and after

Previous chapter: Chapter 9: Vision of killing in Jerusalem
Following chapter: Chapter 11: The promise of restoration

2. Analysis of chapter

A vision of the burning of the city. (1-7)
The divine glory departing from the temple. (8-22)

3. Key verse

Verse 8: "And there appeared in the cherubims the form of a man's hand under their wings."

4. Key word / key phrase

Verse 18, "the glory of the Lord departed."

5. Key event / key person / key theme

God's glory leaves the temple

6. Key thought

Can God's presence leave a Christian fellowship?

7. Key thing to look out for

What was the point of the burning coals?

8. Key Bible cross-reference

Verse 12. See Revelation 4:8.

9. Key "by way of explanation"

Verse 4, "The cloud filled." Just as God's glory filled the temple when it was first dedicated.

10. Key "Quotable Quote"

"The great end of God's work which is variously expressed in Scripture, is indeed but one; and this one end is most properly and comprehensively called, 'the glory of God.'"
Jonathan Edwards

Ezekiel chapter 11

1. Before and after

Previous chapter: Chapter 10: God's glory leaves the temple
Following chapter: Chapter 12: Pictures of the exile

2. Analysis of chapter

Divine judgments against the wicked at Jerusalem. (1-13)
Divine favor toward those in captivity. (14-21)
The divine presence forsakes the city. (22-25)

3. Key verse

Verse 6: "Ye have multiplied your slain in this city, and ye have filled the streets thereof with the slain."

4. Key word / key phrase

Verse 17, "I will gather you from the nations."

5. Key event / key person / key theme

The promise of restoration

6. Key thought

Do present-day events in Israel have any bearing on what God promised in the Bible about the land of Israel being given back to the Israelites?

7. Key thing to look out for

Why were the leaders in Jerusalem wrong to think that they were safe?

8. Key Bible cross-reference

Verses 19,20. See 36:26-28.

9. Key "by way of explanation"

Verse 16, "I have been a sanctuary for them." The Lord could live among his people in exile.

10. Key "Quotable Quote"

"Love divine, all loves excelling,
Joy of heaven, to earth come down,
Fix in us thy humble dwelling,
And thy faithful mercies crown."
Charles Wesley

Ezekiel chapter 12

1. *Before and after*

Previous chapter: Chapter 11: The promise of restoration
Following chapter: Chapter 13: False prophets are condemned

2. *Analysis of chapter*

The approaching captivity. (1-16)
An emblem of the consternation of the Jews. (17-20)
Answers to the objections of scoffers. (21-28)

3. *Key verse*

Verse 5: "Dig thou through the wall in their sight, and carry out thereby."

4. *Key word / key phrase*

Verse 3, "pack your belongings."

5. *Key event / key person / key theme*

Pictures of the exile

6. *Key thought*

Note how people reacted to these warning?

7. *Key thing to look out for*

Is there any lesson here to apply to people's attitudes to Jesus' second coming?

8. *Key Bible cross-reference*

Verse 2. See Isaiah 6:9-10.

9. *Key "by way of explanation"*

Verse 13, "my net . . . my snare," refers to the Lord taking his people into exile.

10. *Key "Quotable Quote"*

"I will be a pastor to none that will not be under discipline: That were to be half pastor, and indulge men in an unruliness and contempt of the ordinance of Christ."
Richard Baxter

Ezekiel chapter 13

1. **Before and after**

   Previous chapter: Chapter 12: Pictures of the Exile
   Following chapter: Chapter 14: Idolatry is condemned

2. **Analysis of chapter**

   Heavy judgments against lying prophets. (1-9)
   The insufficiency of their work. (10-16)
   Woes against false prophetesses. (17-23)

3. **Key verse**

   Verse 4: "O Israel, thy prophets are like the foxes in the deserts."

4. **Key word / key phrase**

   Verse 1, "prophecy against the prophets."

5. **Key event / key person / key theme**

   False prophets are condemned

6. **Key thought**

   What results did these false prophets produce?

7. **Key thing to look out for**

   In what terms are the false prophets described?

8. **Key Bible cross-reference**

   Verse 10. See Jeremiah 6:14.

9. **Key "by way of explanation"**

   Verse 2, "prophesy against the prophets of Israel." False teachers may be accredited by fellow false teachers and hold positions of authority among God's people.

10. **Key "Quotable Quote"**

    "By entertaining of strange persons, men sometimes entertain angels unawares: but by entertaining of strange doctrines, many have entertained devils unawares."
    John Flavel

Ezekiel chapter 14

1. Before and after

Previous chapter: Chapter 13: False prophets are condemned
Following chapter: Chapter 15: The parable of the vine

2. Analysis of chapter

Idolatry among the exiles: warnings against hypocrites. (1-11)
God's purpose to punish Jerusaelm, but a few are be saved. (12-23)

3. Key verse

Verse 6: "Repent, and turn yourselves from your idols; and turn away your faces from all your abominations."

4. Key word / key phrase

Verse 9, "I will . . . destroy him from among my people."

5. Key event / key person / key theme

Judgment from God

6. Key thought

God punishes sin.

7. Key thing to look out for

What is the point in offering guidance to those who do not sincerely want it?

8. Key Bible cross-reference

Verse 21. See Revelation 6:8.

9. Key "by way of explanation"

Verse 8, "I will set my face against that man." Idolatry was such a serious sin that it resulted in this terrible divine punishment.

10. Key "Quotable Quote"

"If we do not preach about sin and God's judgment on it, we cannot present Christ as Savior from sin and the wrath of God."
J.I. Packer

Ezekiel chapter 15

1. **Before and after**

   Previous chapter: Chapter 14: Idolatry is condemned
   Following chapter: Chapter 16: Parable of Israel's marriage

2. **Analysis of chapter**

   Jerusalem like an unfruitful vine.(1-8)

3. **Key verse**

   Verse 8: "And I will make the land desolate, because they have committed a trespass, saith the Lord GOD."

4. **Key word / key phrase**

   Verse 2, "the wood of a vine."

5. **Key event / key person / key theme**

   Parable of the good-for-nothing vine

6. **Key thought**

   How did this vine apply to Israel?

7. **Key thing to look out for**

   How does John 15 apply to us today?

8. **Key Bible cross-reference**

   Verse 3. See Isaiah 22:23.

9. **Key "by way of explanation"**

   Verse 7, "although they have come out of the fire." Jerusalem escaped destruction in 597 BC, but there would be no escape next time.

10. **Key "Quotable Quote"**

    "Sin, in short, is that vast moral disease which affects the whole human race and justly deserves God's wrath and damnation."
    J.C. Ryle

Ezekiel chapter 16

1. **Before and after**

   Previous chapter: Chapter 15: The parable of the vine
   Following chapter: Chapter 17: Parable of the two eagles

2. **Analysis of chapter**

   A parable showing the state of the Jewish nation, its prosperity, idolatries, and punishment. (1-63)

3. **Key verse**

   Verse 12: "And I put a jewel on thy forehead, and earrings in thine ears, and a beautiful crown upon thine head."

4. **Key word / key phrase**

   Verse 4, "on the day you were born."

5. **Key event / key person / key theme**

   God's covenat with Israel pictured as a marriage

6. **Key thought**

   By worshiping idols, Israel betrayed the marriage, turning herself into a prostitute.

7. **Key thing to look out for**

   How can we show our gratitude to the Lord who has loved and forgiven us?

8. **Key Bible cross-reference**

   Verse 22. See Psalm 25:7.

9. **Key "by way of explanation"**

   Verse 44, "Like mother, like daughter." The present inhabitants of Jerusalem are like the pagan Canaanites who originally lived there. An adulteress was publically shamed and stoned to death.

10. **Key "Quotable Quote"**

    "Sin is cosmic treason. Sin is treason against a perfectly pure Sovereign."
    R.C. Sproul

Ezekiel chapter 17

1. Before and after

Previous chapter: Chapter 16: Parable of Israel's marriage
Following chapter: Chapter 18: Personal judgment on personal sin

2. Analysis of chapter

An allegory relating to the Jewish nation. (1-10)
An added explanation. (11-21)
A direct promise of the Messiah. (22-24)

3. Key verse

Verse 5: "He took also of the seed of the land, and planted it in a fruitful field; he placed it by great waters, and set it as a willow tree."

4. Key word / key phrase

Verse 3, "a great eagle."

5. Key event / key person / key theme

Zedekiah's attempt to rebel against Babylon

6. Key thought

God's will can never be thwarted by human action.

7. Key thing to look out for

With verses 13-16 compare 2 Chronicles 36:13. What sin is attacked?

8. Key Bible cross-reference

Verses 12-15. See 2 Kings 24:15-20.

9. Key "by way of explanation"

The last eagle is the king of Babylon; Lebanon is Jerusalem; the topmost branch is Jehoiachin, taken to Babylon; the "seed" is Zedekiah, a vassal king in a lowly position (a low vine). The second eagle is Egypt. The cedar (verse 22) refers to the house of David.

10. Key "Quotable Quote"

"Where there is no mission, there is no Church, and where there is neither Church nor mission, there is no faith."
Emil Brunner

Ezekiel chapter 18

1. *Before and after*

Previous chapter: Chapter 17: Parable of the two eagles
Following chapter: Chapter 19: Lament for Israel's princes

2. *Analysis of chapter*

The soul who sins will die. (1-20)
The divine providence is vindicated. (21-29)
A gracious invitation to repent. (30-32)

3. *Key verse*

Verse 2: "What mean ye, that ye use this proverb concerning the land of Israel, saying, The fathers have eaten sour grapes, and the children's teeth are set on edge?"

4. *Key word / key phrase*

Verse 4. "The soul who sins is the one who will die."

5. *Key event / key person / key theme*

Personal responsibility

6. *Key thought*

How does verse 4 answer the question of verse 2?

7. *Key thing to look out for*

Verse 32. "I take no pleasure in the death of anyone." Because this is God's nature he extends his hand of mercy out to all.

8. *Key Bible cross-reference*

Verse 20. See Deuteronomy 24:16.

9. *Key "by way of explanation"*

Ezekiel was here correcting a tendency among the exiles to evade responsibility and to say they were suffering because of the mistakes of previous kings (see 2 Kings 21:10-15). This was only partially true.

10. *Key "Quotable Quote"*

"God's mercy is infinite. Everything about it is infinite. It proceeds from infinite Being, flows through the medium of an infinite sacrifice, surmounts obstacles that are infinite, and addresses itself to those that are infinitely unworthy and ill-deserving."
Gardiner Spring

Ezekiel chapter 19

1. Before and after

Previous chapter: Chapter 18: Personal judgment on personal sin
Following chapter: Chapter 20: Looking back on Israel's past rebellion

2. Analysis of chapter

A parable lamenting the ruin of Jehoahaz and Jehoiakim. (1-9)
Another describing the desolation of the people. (10-14)

3. Key verse

Verse 6: "And he went up and down among the lions, he became a young lion, and learned to catch the prey, and devoured men."

4. Key word / key phrase

Verse 1, "Take up a lament."

5. Key event / key person / key theme

Lament for three of the kings of Judah

6. Key thought

What did these kings of Judah do wrong?

7. Key thing to look out for

How can unfruitfulness in God's service be avoided?

8. Key Bible cross-reference

Verse 2. See Numbers 23:24.

9. Key "by way of explanation"

Verse 12, "the east wind made it shrivel." This is a reference to Nebuchadnezzar and his powerful empire. Verse 2, the mother was the tribe of Judah, whose emblem was a lion. Verse 10, here Judah is a vine.

10. Key "Quotable Quote"

"A man who imagines to arrive at grace by doing all that he is able to do, adds sin to sin, and is doubly guilty."
Martin Luther

Ezekiel chapter 20

1. *Before and after*

Previous chapter: Chapter 19: Lament for Israel's princes
Following chapter: Chapter 21: Jerusalem's great sins

2. *Analysis of chapter*

The elders of Israel are reminded of the idolatry in Egypt. (1-9)
In the desert. (10-26)
In Canaan. (27-32)
God promises to pardon and restore them. (33-44)
Prophecy against Jerusalem. (45-49)

3. *Key verse*

Verse 8: "But they rebelled against me, and would not hearken unto me: they did not every man cast away the abominations of their eyes, neither did they forsake the idols of Egypt."

4. *Key word / key phrase*

Verse 4, "detestable practices."

5. *Key event / key person / key theme*

Looking back on Israel's past rebellion

6. *Key thought*

Verses 42-44, note how the Lord says he wants his people to respond to him.

7. *Key thing to look out for*

Why does God not just wipe everybody out from the face of the earth?

8. *Key Bible cross-reference*

Verse 15. See Numbers 14:26-35.

9. *Key "by way of explanation"*

Verse 33, "outstretched arm," is a deliberate reference back to God's spectacular deliverance at the Red Sea.

10. *Key "Quotable Quote"*

"No other blessing of the common grace of God is as great as the universal and sincere offer of salvation, nor is any other more obviously a fruit of the atonement."
R.B. Kuiper

Ezekiel chapter 21

1. *Before and after*

Previous chapter: Chapter 20: Looking back on Israel's past rebellion
Following chapter: Chapter 22: God's judgment on Jerusalem

2. *Analysis of chapter*

The ruin of Judah under the emblem of a sharp sword. (1-17)
The approach of the king of Babylon described. (18-27)
The destruction of the Ammonites. (28-32)

3. *Key verse*

Verse 2: "Son of man, set thy face toward Jerusalem, and drop thy word toward the holy places, and prophesy against the land of Israel."

4. *Key word / key phrase*

Verse 3, "I will draw my sword."

5. *Key event / key person / key theme*

Jerusalem's great sins

6. *Key thought*

God judged his people by means of a pagan king. Is there any lesson to draw from this?

7. *Key thing to look out for*

When human leaders fail where should we look for leadership?

8. *Key Bible cross-reference*

Verses 28-32. See Amos 1:13-15.

9. *Key "by way of explanation"*

Verse 28, "about their insults," refers to their malicious delight in the fall of Jerusalem.

10. *Key "Quotable Quote"*

"To ignore evil is to become an accomplice to it."
Martin Luther King, Jr.

Ezekiel chapter 22

1. Before and after

Previous chapter: Chapter 21: Jerusalem's great sins
Following chapter: Chapter 23: Parable of two adulterous sisters

2. Analysis of chapter

The sins of Jerusalem. (1-16)
Israel is condemned as dross. (17-22)
As the corruption is general, so shall be the punishment. (23-31)

3. Key verse

Verse 3: "The city sheddeth blood in the midst of it, that her time may come, and maketh idols against herself to defile herself."

4. Key word / key phrase

Verse 3, "brings on herself doom."

5. Key event / key person / key theme

God's judgment on Jerusalem

6. Key thought

Verses 17-22, elsewhere in the scriptures the imagery of a furnace is used of purification, here it means destruction.

7. Key thing to look out for

What are the social and religious sins that are highlighted?

8. Key Bible cross-reference

Verse 12. See Exodus 22:25; 23:8.

9. Key "by way of explanation"

Verse 24, "a land that has no rain." Rain was thought of as a blessing coming down from the Lord.

10. Key "Quotable Quote"

"Grace comes into the soul, as the morning sun into the world; first a dawning, then a light; and at last the sun in his full and excellent brightness."
Thomas Adams

Ezekiel chapter 23

1. Before and after

Previous chapter: Chapter 22: God's judgment on Jerusalem
Following chapter: Chapter 24: Jerusalem is besieged

2. Analysis of chapter

A history of the apostasy of God's people from him. (1-49)

3. Key verse

Verse 2: "Son of man, there were two women, the daughters of one mother."

4. Key word / key phrase

Verse 3, "prostitutes in Egypt."

5. Key event / key person / key theme

Parable of two adulterous sisters

6. Key thought

Jerusalem followed the wicked ways of Samaria.

7. Key thing to look out for

How can Christians today heed the warning this chapter gives?

8. Key Bible cross-reference

Verse 2. See Jeremiah 3:7.

9. Key "by way of explanation"

Verse 25, "They will cut off your noses." Jerusalem will suffer punishment similar to that handed out to some adulterers.

10. Key "Quotable Quote"

"No life ever grows great until it is focused, dedicated, disciplined."
Harry Emerson Fosdick

Ezekiel chapter 24

1. Before and after

Previous chapter: Chapter 23: Parable of two adulterous sisters
Following chapter: Chapter 25: Judgment against Ammon, Moab, Edom, and Philistia

2. Analysis of chapter

The fate of Jerusalem. (1-14)
The extent of the sufferings of the Jews. (15-27)

3. Key verse

Verse 3: "Set on a pot, set it on, and also pour water into it."

4. Key word / key phrase

Verse 2, "the king of Babylon has laid siege to Jerusalem."

5. Key event / key person / key theme

Jerusalem is besieged

6. Key thought

Note God's estimate of the people of Jerusalem.

7. Key thing to look out for

Is there anything positive to be gleaned from the death of Ezekiel's wife?

8. Key Bible cross-reference

Verse 13. See Isaiah 22:14.

9. Key "by way of explanation"

Verse 6, "empty it piece by piece," refers to the people being deported from Jerusalem.

10. Key "Quotable Quote"

"God does not discipline us to subdue us, but to condition us for a life of usefulness and blessedness."
Billy Graham

Ezekiel chapter 25

1. *Before and after*

Previous chapter: Chapter 24: Jerusalem is besieged
Following chapter: Chapter 26: Destruction of Tyre

2. *Analysis of chapter*

Judgments against the Ammonites. (1-7)
Against the Moabites, Edomites, and Philistines. (8-17)

3. *Key verse*

Verse 2: "Son of man, set thy face against the Ammonites, and prophesy against them."

4. *Key word / key phrase*

Verse 2, "set your face against the Ammonites."

5. *Key event / key person / key theme*

Judgment against Ammon, Moab, Edom, and Philistia

6. *Key thought*

Note the different ways unbelievers act toward God's people when the latter are brought down.

7. *Key thing to look out for*

What are we to think when injustice is not put right?

8. *Key Bible cross-reference*

Verses 12-14. See Malachi 1:2-5.

9. *Key "by way of explanation"*

Verse 16, "I will cut off the Kerethites." The Kerethites were a synonym for the Philistines.

10. *Key "Quotable Quote"*

"God's wounds cure, sin's kisses kill."
William Gurnall

Ezekiel chapter 26

1. Before and after

Previous chapter: Chapter 25: Judgment against Ammon, Moab, Edom, and Philistia

Following chapter: Chapter 27: Lament over Tyre

2. Analysis of chapter

A prophecy against Tyre.(1-21)

3. Key verse

Verse 4: "And they shall destroy the walls of Tyrus, and break down her towers: I will also scrape her dust from her, and make her like the top of a rock."

4. Key word / key phrase

Verse 4, "they will destroy the walls of Tyre."

5. Key event / key person / key theme

Destruction of Tyre, a city on an island, was the capital of Phoenicia (Lebanon)

6. Key thought

Note the reason for Tyre's downfall. See verse 2.

7. Key thing to look out for

In view of what happened in this chapter to mighty Tyre how should we view today's mighty nations?

8. Key Bible cross-reference

Verse 13. See Revelation 18:22.

9. Key "by way of explanation"

Verse 2, "the gate to the nations is broken." Once Jerusalem fell the customs barrier between Tyre and the countries in the south was removed.

10. Key "Quotable Quote"

"God is none other than the Savior of our wretchedness. So we can only know God well by knowing our iniquities."

Blaise Pascal

Ezekiel chapter 27

1. Before and after

Previous chapter: Chapter 26: Destruction of Tyre
Following chapter: Chapter 28: The fall of the ruler of Tyre

2. Analysis of chapter

The merchandise of Tyre. (1-25)
Its fall and ruin. (26-36)

3. Key verse

Verse 7: "Fine linen with broidered work from Egypt was that which thou spreadest forth to be thy sail; blue and purple from the isles of Elishah was that which covered thee."

4. Key word / key phrase

Verse 2, "take up a lament concerning Tyre."

5. Key event / key person / key theme

Lament over Tyre

6. Key thought

Where did Tyre go wrong?

7. Key thing to look out for

Today, how do nations make shipwreck of their countries?

8. Key Bible cross-reference

Verses 25-36. See Revelation 18:11-19.

9. Key "by way of explanation"

Tyre is pictured as a great trading ship, which sinks on the high seas. Ezekiel has a thorough grasp of trade and commerce.

10. Key "Quotable Quote"

"The corruption [of original sin] is constantly called sin by Paul while the things which spring from it such as adultery, fornication, theft, hatred, murder and revelings, he calls sins. Sins are the fruit of sin."
John Calvin

Ezekiel chapter 28

1. Before and after

Previous chapter: Chapter 27: Lament over Tyre
Following chapter: Chapter 29: Prophecies against Egypt

2. Analysis of chapter

Two oracles against the ruler of Tyre. (1-19)
The fall of Sidon. (20-23)
The restoration of Israel. (24-26)

3. Key verse

Verse 3: "Behold, thou art wiser than Daniel; there is no secret that they can hide from thee."

4. Key word / key phrase

Verse 2, "say to the ruler of Tyre."

5. Key event / key person / key theme

The fall of the ruler of Tyre

6. Key thought

The downfall of the King of Tyre was caused by pride.

7. Key thing to look out for

From the prophecy against Sidon, verses 20-26, what do we learn about the purpose of God's judgments, especially in relation to his own followers?

8. Key Bible cross-reference

Verses 20-26. See Matthew 11:21,22.

9. Key "by way of explanation"

Verse 18, "desecrated your sanctuaries." They did this by the temple treasury money which had been gained unjustly. In verse 11 Ezekiel draws on a Phoenician version of the Eden story in which the first man is splendidly adorned.

10. Key "Quotable Quote"

"You will notice that you far oftener meet a man laboring under a sense of sin than one laboring under a sense of mercies."
Andrew Bonar

Ezekiel chapter 29

1. Before and after

Previous chapter: Chapter 28: The fall of the ruler of Tyre
Following chapter: Chapter 30: Egypt will be destroyed

2. Analysis of chapter

The desolation of Egypt. (1-16)
Also a promise of mercy to Israel. (17-21)

3. Key verse

Verse 3: "Behold, I am against thee, Pharaoh king of Egypt."

4. Key word / key phrase

Verse 2, "set your face against Pharaoh king of Egypt."

5. Key event / key person / key theme

Prophecies against Egypt

6. Key thought

Pharaoh's downfall is caused by arrogance.

7. Key thing to look out for

What does this chapter teach about God's treatment of ungodly nations?

8. Key Bible cross-reference

Verse 6. See Isaiah 36:6.

9. Key "by way of explanation"

Verse 18, "every shoulder made raw," as a result of carrying heavy loads of
military equipment. Verse 1, the date is January 7th, 587 BC.

10. Key "Quotable Quote"

"Today we need prophetic preachers; not preachers of prophesy merely, but
preachers with a gift of prophecy. The word of wisdom is missing."
A.W. Tozer

Ezekiel chapter 30

1. *Before and after*

Previous chapter: Chapter 29: Prophecies against Egypt
Following chapter: Chapter 31: Egypt will fall like a cedar

2. *Analysis of chapter*

A prophecy against Egypt. (1-19)
Another prophecy against Egypt. (20-26)

3. *Key verse*

Verse 6: "They also that uphold Egypt shall fall."

4. *Key word / key phrase*

Verse 4, "a sword will come against Egypt."

5. *Key event / key person / key theme*

Egypt will be destroyed

6. *Key thought*

Why will a nation never ultimately prosper that trusts in the power of its own rulers?

7. *Key thing to look out for*

How does verse 6 apply to many nations today?

8. *Key Bible cross-reference*

Verse 8. See Jeremiah 49:27.

9. *Key "by way of explanation"*

Verse 11, "dry up the streams of the Nile." This refers to the Nile delta. If this dried up life in Egypt would at once be threatened.

10. *Key "Quotable Quote"*

"Where sin rules and sin reigns sin ruins."
Author unknown

Ezekiel chapter 31

1. **Before and after**

   Previous chapter: Chapter 30: Egypt will be destroyed
   Following chapter: Chapter 32: Further prophecies against Egypt

2. **Analysis of chapter**

   The glory of Assyria. (1-9)
   Its fall. (10-18)

3. **Key verse**

   Verse 7: "Thus was he fair in his greatness, in the length of his branches: for his root was by great waters."

4. **Key word / key phrase**

   Verse 2, "say to Pharaoh king of Egypt."

5. **Key event / key person / key theme**

   Egypt will fall like a cedar

6. **Key thought**

   What had happened to Assyria would also happen to Egypt.

7. **Key thing to look out for**

   What effect should the destruction of the tree have on other nations?

8. **Key Bible cross-reference**

   Verse 8. See Genesis 2:9.

9. **Key "by way of explanation"**

   Verse 9, "the garden of God," is a reference to the Garden of Eden in which the opening chapters of Genesis are set.

10. **Key "Quotable Quote"**

    "Our attitude towards sin is more self-centered than God-centered. We are more concerned about our own 'victory' over sin than we are about the fact that our sin grieves the heart of God."
    Jerry Bridges

Ezekiel chapter 32

1. *Before and after*

     Previous chapter: Chapter 31: Egypt will fall like a cedar
     Following chapter: Chapter 33: Ezekiel the watchman

2. *Analysis of chapter*

     The fall of Egypt. (1-16)
     A dirge: Egypt in the land of the dead. (17-32)

3. *Key verse*

     Verse 2: "Son of man, take up a lamentation for Pharaoh king of Egypt."

4. *Key word / key phrase*

     Verse 2, "concerning Pharaoh king of Egypt."

5. *Key event / key person / key theme*

     Egypt, caught up in God's fishing net, is thrown up on the land

6. *Key thought*

     God's agent in the destruction of Egypt is Babylon (verse 11).

7. *Key thing to look out for*

     Note how often the personal pronoun "I" is used in this chapter, with reference to the Lord, and how this emphasizes his power in the world.

8. *Key Bible cross-reference*

     Verse 7. See Isaiah 13:10.

9. *Key "by way of explanation"*

     Verse 7, "I will cover the heavens." This kind of darkness indicated that great political chaos was about to come.

10. *Key "Quotable Quote"*

     "There is only one thing to be feared, and that is sin."
     John Chrysostom

Ezekiel chapter 33

1. *Before and after*

Previous chapter: Chapter 32: Further prophecies against Egypt
Following chapter: Chapter 34: Message to the shepherds

2. *Analysis of chapter*

Ezekiel's commission to be a watchman. (1-20)
The desolation of the land. (21-29)
Judgments on the mockers of the prophets. (30-33)

3. *Key verse*

Verse 6: "But if the watchman see the sword come, and blow not the trumpet, and the people be not warned; if the sword come, and take any person from among them, he is taken away in his iniquity; but his blood will I require at the watchman's hand."

4. *Key word / key phrase*

Verse 2, "their watchman."

5. *Key event / key person / key theme*

Ezekiel the watchman

6. *Key thought*

In what sense are Christians pastor to be watchmen today?

7. *Key thing to look out for*

In what ways are all Christians to be watchmen?

8. *Key Bible cross-reference*

Verse 21. See 2 Kings 25:3-10.

9. *Key "by way of explanation"*

Verse 2, "When I bring the sword against a land." The prophets often state that a country is plunged into war as a form of divine punishment.

10. *Key "Quotable Quote"*

"Sin pays – but it pays in remorse, regret, and failure."
Billy Graham

Ezekiel chapter 34

1. ### Before and after

   Previous chapter: Chapter 33: Ezekiel the watchman
   Following chapter: Chapter 35: Judgment on Edom

2. ### Analysis of chapter

   The rulers reproved. (1-6)
   The people are to be restored to their own land. (7-16)
   The kingdom of Christ. (17-31)

3. ### Key verse

   Verse 10: "Behold, I am against the shepherds."

4. ### Key word / key phrase

   Verse 2, "prophecy against the shepherds of Israel."

5. ### Key event / key person / key theme

   Message to the shepherds

6. ### Key thought

   What did the bad shepherds do wrong?

7. ### Key thing to look out for

   In what ways is Jesus, the Good Shepherd, different from these false shepherds?

8. ### Key Bible cross-reference

   Verse 5. See Numbers 27:17.

9. ### Key "by way of explanation"

   Verse 6, "I will search for the lost." This is exactly what the Jesus said the Son of Man would do. See Luke 19:10.

10. ### Key "Quotable Quote"

   "Do you wish to see God's love? Look at the cross. Do you wish to see God's wrath? Look at the cross."
   D.A. Carson

Ezekiel chapter 35

1. Before and after

Previous chapter: Chapter 34: Message to the shepherds
Following chapter: Chapter 36: A new heart and a new spirit

2. Analysis of chapter

A prophecy against Edom. (1-15)

3. Key verse

Verse 2: "Son of man, set thy face against mount Seir, and prophesy against it."

4. Key word / key phrase

Verse 2, "set your face against Mount Seir."

5. Key event / key person / key theme

Judgment on Edom

6. Key thought

For what sins is Edom condemned?

7. Key thing to look out for

Note how the punishment Edom will receive matches her sins.

8. Key Bible cross-reference

Verse 13. See Daniel 7:8.

9. Key "by way of explanation"

Verse 3, "the Lord was there." The Edomites had no business to take over the land for it belonged to the Lord.

10. Key "Quotable Quote"

"The pervasive sinfulness of man becomes evident when contrasted with the radiant holiness of God."
Richard J. Foster

Ezekiel chapter 36

1. *Before and after*

Previous chapter: Chapter 35: Judgment on Edom
Following chapter: Chapter 37: New life for dry bones

2. *Analysis of chapter*

The land shall be delivered from heathen oppressors. (1-15)
The people are reminded of former sins, and promised deliverance. (16-24)
Also holiness, and gospel blessings. (25-38)

3. *Key verse*

Verse 11: "And I will multiply upon you man and beast; and they shall increase and bring fruit: and I will settle you after your old estates, and will do better unto you than at your beginnings: and ye shall know that I am the LORD."

4. *Key word / key phrase*

Verse 26, "I will give you a new heart."

5. *Key event / key person / key theme*

A new heart and a new spirit

6. *Key thought*

God promises a radical cleansing and a new nature, a teachable heart ("heart of flesh") and knowledge of God by his Spirit.

7. *Key thing to look out for*

What spiritual blessings that Christians enjoy today are mirrored in these verses?

8. *Key Bible cross-reference*

Verses 26-28. See 11:19,20.

9. *Key "by way of explanation"*

Verse 26, "new spirit." Once people have this new heart and new spirit, which is nothing other than God's Spirit they will be enabled to keep God's covenant.

10. *Key "Quotable Quote"*

"Spirit-filled souls are ablaze for God. They love with a love that glows. They believe with a faith that kindles. They serve with a devotion that consumes. They hate sin with a fierceness that burns. They rejoice with a joy that radiates. Love is perfected in the fire of God."
Samuel Chadwick

Ezekiel chapter 37

1. Before and after

Previous chapter: Chapter 36: A new heart and a new spirit
Following chapter: Chapter 38: Prophecy against Gog

2. Analysis of chapter

God restores dried bones to life. (1-14)
The whole house of Israel is represented as enjoying the blessings of Christ's kingdom. (15-28)

3. Key verse

Verse 1: "The hand of the LORD was upon me, and carried me out in the spirit of the LORD, and set me down in the midst of the valley which was full of bones."

4. Key word / key phrase

Verse 2, "bones that were very dry."

5. Key event / key person / key theme

New life for dry bones

6. Key thought

There is no life at all in the bones: "the most unpromising congregation that any preacher ever addressed" (F.F. Bruce).

7. Key thing to look out for

What conclusions are we to draw from the dry bones coming to life?

8. Key Bible cross-reference

Verse 27. See 2 Corinthians 6:16.

9. Key "by way of explanation"

Verse 10, "breath entered them." This is reminiscent of God the Creator breathing life into the nostrils of the first man. The Hebrew word, *ruah*, means "breath," "wind," and "spirit."

10. Key "Quotable Quote"

"The Spirit of God is given to the true saints to dwell in them, as his proper lasting abode; and to influence their hearts, as a principle of new nature or as a divine supernatural spring of life and action."
Jonathan Edwards

Ezekiel chapter 38

1. *Before and after*

   Previous chapter: Chapter 37: New life for dry bones
   Following chapter: Chapter 39: God's plans for Israel

2. *Analysis of chapter*

   The army and malice of Gog. (1-13)
   God's judgments. (14-23)

3. *Key verse*

   Verse 2: "Son of man, set thy face against Gog, the land of Magog."

4. *Key word / key phrase*

   Verse 2, "set your face against Gog."

5. *Key event / key person / key theme*

   An attack from the north by a mighty coalition of aggresors.

6. *Key thought*

   Verse 4, God is in control

7. *Key thing to look out for*

   How will God make himself known to the nations?

8. *Key Bible cross-reference*

   Verse 2. See Revelation 20:8.

9. *Key "by way of explanation"*

   Verse 16, "when I show myself holy through you." Israel's God used even these
   ungodly people to demonstrate his own holiness.

10. *Key "Quotable Quote"*

    "The first and most important thing we know about God is that we know
    nothing about him except what he himself makes known."
    Emil Brunner

Ezekiel chapter 39

1. **Before and after**

   Previous chapter: Chapter 38: Prophecy against Gog
   Following chapter: Chapter 40: The new temple

2. **Analysis of chapter**

   The destruction of Gog. (1-10)
   Its extent. (11-22)
   Israel again favored. (23-29)

3. **Key verse**

   Verse 1: "Thus saith the Lord GOD; Behold, I am against thee, O Gog, the chief prince of Meshech and Tubal."

4. **Key word / key phrase**

   Verse 25, "I will now bring Jacob back from captivity."

5. **Key event / key person / key theme**

   God's plans for Israel

6. **Key thought**

   How are God's compassion and holiness linked in verse 25?

7. **Key thing to look out for**

   How can one benefit from a time during which God "hides" himself from us?

8. **Key Bible cross-reference**

   Verses 17-20. See Revelation 19:17,18.

9. **Key "by way of explanation"**

   Verse 7, "the Holy One in Israel." This is a slight variation of the more familiar title given to God, "the Holy One of Israel."

10. **Key "Quotable Quote"**

    "What men stand most in need of is the knowledge of God."
    François Fénelon

Ezekiel chapter 40

1. Before and after

Previous chapter: Chapter 39: God's plans for Israel
Following chapter: Chapter 41: The holy place, holy of holies, and interior furniture

2. Analysis of chapter

Ezekiel is taken to Jerusalem. (1-4)
The east gate to the outer court. (5-16)
The outer court. (17-19)
The north gate and the south gate. (20-27).
Gates to the inner court. (28-37)
Buildings near the north gate. (38-46)
The inner courtyard and the temple building. (47-49)

3. Key verse

Verse 2: "In the visions of God brought he me into the land of Israel, and set me upon a very high mountain, by which was as the frame of a city on the south."

4. Key word / key phrase

Verse 5, "the temple area."

5. Key event / key person / key theme

The new temple

6. Key thought

"A purified people implies a purified land . . . the new temple, the holiest place of all – because the divine glory which had abandoned the first temple returns (44:4)" (F.F. Bruce).

7. Key thing to look out for

In verse 4 what responsibilities are placed on Ezekiel?

8. Key Bible cross-reference

Verse 2. See Revelation 21:10.

9. Key "by way of explanation"

Verse 3, "a man whose appearance was like bronze." This is a description of a celestial being, as in Daniel 10:6 in which the "man" had "arms and legs like the gleam of burnished bronze."

10. Key "Quotable Quote"

"We love the Invisible and know what is beyond understanding."
Richard J. Foster

Ezekiel chapter 41

1. *Before and after*

   Previous chapter: Chapter 40: The new temple
   Following chapter: Chapter 42: The priests' rooms and overall dimensions of the temple

2. *Analysis of chapter*

   The temple. (1-26)

3. *Key verse*

   Verse 1: "Afterward he brought me to the temple."

4. *Key word / key phrase*

   Verse 1, "to the outer sanctuary."

5. *Key event / key person / key theme*

   The holy place, holy of holies, and interior furniture

6. *Key thought*

   What privileges do Christians have today which Ezekiel did not have?

7. *Key thing to look out for*

   Compare verses 3,4 with Hebrews 9:6-9,24; 10:19-22.

8. *Key Bible cross-reference*

   Verse 18. See 1 Kings 6:18.

9. *Key "by way of explanation"*

   Verse 3, "he went into the inner sanctuary." This corresponds to the holy of holies of Solomon's temple into which only the high priest was allowed to enter once a year.

10. *Key "Quotable Quote"*

    "Nothing is so easily obtained as the possession and enjoyment of God. He is more present to us than we are to ourselves. He is more desirous of giving himself to us than we are to possess him; we only need to know how to seek him, and the way is easier and more natural to us than breathing."
    Jeanne Guyon

Ezekiel chapter 42

1. *Before and after*

Previous chapter: Chapter 41: The holy place, holy of holies, and interior furniture

Following chapter: Chapter 43: God's glory returns to the temple

2. *Analysis of chapter*

Two buildings near the temple. (1-14)

Measurements of the temple area. (15-20)

3. *Key verse*

Verse 1: "Then he brought me forth into the utter court, the way toward the north: and he brought me into the chamber that was over against the separate place, and which was before the building toward the north."

4. *Key word / key phrase*

Verse 1, "the outer court."

5. *Key event / key person / key theme*

The priests' rooms and overall dimensions of the temple

6. *Key thought*

In what ways is God's holiness underlined in this chapter?

7. *Key thing to look out for*

How should this effect our walk with the Holy One of Israel?

8. *Key Bible cross-reference*

Verse 13. See Leviticus 6:29.

9. *Key "by way of explanation"*

Verse 14, "these are holy." The priests were told to remove the clothes they wore while they ministered, as they were not to mix with people in the outer court in such sanctified garments.

10. *Key "Quotable Quote"*

"I want to be open to God, not to what human beings say about God."
Madeleine L'Engle

Ezekiel chapter 43

1. Before and after

> Previous chapter: Chapter 42: The priests' rooms and overall dimensions of the temple
>
> Following chapter: Chapter 44: Laws for the priesthood

2. Analysis of chapter

> The Lord returns to the temple. (1-12)
> The altar. (13-17)
> Consecration of the altar. (18-27)

3. Key verse

> Verse 2: "And, behold, the glory of the God of Israel came from the way of the east: and his voice was like a noise of many waters: and the earth shined with his glory."

4. Key word / key phrase

> Verse 5, "the glory of the Lord filled the temple."

5. Key event / key person / key theme

> God's glory returns to the temple

6. Key thought

> How should God's glory be visible in a Christian today?

7. Key thing to look out for

> In what ways should Christian fellowships display God's glory?

8. Key Bible cross-reference

> Verse 2. See 10:3,4,18,19; 11:22,23.

9. Key "by way of explanation"

> Verse 2, "the glory of God," now returns and fills the new temple as it did in the tabernacle and first temple.

10. Key "Quotable Quote"

> "The person who loves God values knowledge of God more than anything created by God, and pursues such knowledge ardently and ceaselessly."
> Maximus the Confessor

Ezekiel chapter 44

1. Before and after

Previous chapter: Chapter 43: God's glory returns to the temple
Following chapter: Chapter 45: Rules for the prince; and the festivals

2. Analysis of chapter

Use of east gate. (1-3)
Admission into the temple. (4-9)
Excluded Levites. (10-14)
Priests. (15-31)

3. Key verse

Verse 9: "Thus saith the Lord GOD; No stranger, uncircumcised in heart, nor uncircumcised in flesh, shall enter into my sanctuary, of any stranger that is among the children of Israel."

4. Key word / key phrase

Verse 5, "regulations regarding the temple."

5. Key event / key person / key theme

Laws for the priesthood

6. Key thought

What place should rules and regulations have in a Christian's life today?

7. Key thing to look out for

What can we learn from the judgments of God that fell on faithful and unfaithful service in this chapter?

8. Key Bible cross-reference

Verse 21. See Leviticus 10:9.

9. Key "by way of explanation"

Verse 9, "uncircumcised in heart and flesh." More important than literal uncircumcision is impiety in the heart. Verse 3, the "prince" is not a messianic figure but a lay ruler/administrator.

10. Key "Quotable Quote"

"What were we made for? To know God.
What aim should we have in life? To know God.
What is the eternal life that Jesus gives? To know God.
What is the best thing in life? To know God.
What in humans gives God most pleasure? Knowledge of himself."
J.I. Packer

Ezekiel chapter 45

1. Before and after

Previous chapter: Chapter 44: Laws for the priesthood
Following chapter: Chapter 46: Additional princely duties

2. Analysis of chapter

Division of the land. (1-12)
Offerings and holy days. (13-25)

3. Key verse

Verse 1: "Moreover, when ye shall divide by lot the land for inheritance, ye shall offer an oblation unto the LORD."

4. Key word / key phrase

Verse 1, "When you allot the land."

5. Key event / key person / key theme

Rules for the prince (the secular ruler); and the festivals

6. Key thought

Where in this chapter can one deduce that God's holiness should affect our morality?

7. Key thing to look out for

What does this chapter tell us about God's attitude to injustice and oppression?

8. Key Bible cross-reference

Verse 10. See Leviticus 19:36.

9. Key "by way of explanation"

Verse 7, "the prince." The people had to give their offering to the prince as part of his work was to provide the public with their necessary sacrifices. Verses 1-8, an area of land, about 8 miles from north to south was to be set apart. This was where the Levites and priests would live. The temple enclosure was in the center of the land allocated to the priests.

10. Key "Quotable Quote"

"The right doctrines mentally assented to are not an end in themselves, but should only be the vestibule to a personal and loving communion with God." Francis A. Schaeffer

Ezekiel chapter 46

1. *Before and after*

Previous chapter: Chapter 45: Rules for the prince; and the festivals
Following chapter: Chapter 47: The river flowing from the temple

2. *Analysis of chapter*

The prince and the festivals. (1-12)
Daily offering. (13-15)
The prince and the land. (16-18)
Temple kitchens. (19-24)

3. *Key verse*

Verse 3: "Likewise the people of the land shall worship at the door of this gate before the LORD in the Sabbaths and in the new moons."

4. *Key word / key phrase*

Verse 1, "the gate of the inner court."

5. *Key event / key person / key theme*

Additional princely duties

6. *Key thought*

How can we ensure that we worship God "in spirit and in truth" at every Christian worship service?

7. *Key thing to look out for*

Does the style of worship service matter to God?

8. *Key Bible cross-reference*

Verse 17. See Leviticus 25:10.

9. *Key "by way of explanation"*

Verse 16, "his descendants." In Ezekiel's vision some kind of hereditary rulership is in view.

10. *Key "Quotable Quote"*

"When we encounter God, the totality of our creatureliness breaks upon us and shatters the myth that we have believed about ourselves, the myth that we are demi-gods, junior-grade deities who will try to live forever."
R.C. Sproul

Ezekiel chapter 47

1. **Before and after**

   Previous chapter: Chapter 46: Additional princely duties
   Following chapter: Chapter 48: Division of the land among the tribes

2. **Analysis of chapter**

   River flowing from the temple. (1-12)
   Boundaries of the land. (13-23)

3. **Key verse**

   Verse 1: "Afterward he brought me again unto the door of the house; and, behold, waters issued out from under the threshold of the house eastward: for the forefront of the house stood toward the east, and the waters came down from under from the right side of the house, at the south side of the altar."

4. **Key word / key phrase**

   Verse 1, "I saw water coming out."

5. **Key event / key person / key theme**

   The river flowing from the temple – a prophecy of the outpoured Spirit of God

6. **Key thought**

   What does this chapter teach about the principles that should guide us about reforming our society or our Church?

7. **Key thing to look out for**

   How are the living waters of spiritual life from the Lord Jesus Christ to be increased in the life of individual Christians?

8. **Key Bible cross-reference**

   Verse 1. See John 7:38.

9. **Key "by way of explanation"**

   Verse 1, "I saw water." In Ezekiel's vision a river rises in the temple and flows down the Kidron Valley to the Dead Sea. Joel and Zechariah also prophecy that living water will flow from Jerusalem.

10. **Key "Quotable Quote"**

    "The true knowledge of God will result, not in our being puffed up with conceit at how knowledgeable we are, but in our falling on our faces before God in sheer wonder."
    John R.W. Stott

Ezekiel chapter 48

1. **Previous chapter**

   Chapter 47: The river flowing from the temple

2. **Analysis of chapter**

   Division of the land. (1-29)
   Gates of Jerusalem. (30-35)

3. **Key verse**

   Verse 11: "It shall be for the priests that are sanctified of the sons of Zadok; which have kept my charge, which went not astray when the children of Israel went astray, as the Levites went astray."

4. **Key word / key phrase**

   Verse 1, "These are the tribes, listed by name."

5. **Key event / key person / key theme**

   Division of the land among the tribes

6. **Key thought**

   Verse 35. What does God's name for the city tell us about God himself?

7. **Key thing to look out for**

   What abiding lessons are there to draw from the whole book of Ezekiel?

8. **Key Bible cross-reference**

   Verses 30-34. See Revelation 21:12,13.

9. **Key "by way of explanation"**

   Verse 35, "the name of the city." The city is called, "The Lord is there." This is the most important reason for calling the city the "holy" city.

10. **Key "Quotable Quote"**

    "If you keep watch over your hearts, and listen for the voice of God and learn of him, in one short hour you can learn more from him than you could learn from man in a thousand years."
    Johann Tauler

Daniel

Daniel chapter 1

1. **Following chapter**

   Chapter 2: Nebuchadnezzar's dream of the great image

2. **Analysis of chapter**

   The captivity of Daniel and his companions. (1-7)
   Their refusal to eat the king's meat. (8-16)
   Their improvement in wisdom. (17-21)

3. **Key verse**

   Verse 1: "In the third year of the reign of Jehoiakim king of Judah came Nebuchadnezzar king of Babylon unto Jerusalem, and besieged it."

4. **Key word / key phrase**

   Verse 6, "Daniel."

5. **Key event / key person / key theme**

   The personal history of Daniel

6. **Key thought**

   Daniel could have thought that he would have no life at all as an exile.

7. **Key thing to look out for**

   The great understanding Daniel had was a gift from God.

8. **Key Bible cross-reference**

   Verse 1. See 2 Kings 24:1.

9. **Key "by way of explanation"**

   Verse 5, "assigned them a daily amount." Babylon had a highly organized bureaucracy and the same rations to foreigners were given in many different parts of their empire. The date is probably late 605 BC.

10. **Key "Quotable Quote"**

    "Go, labor on; spend and be spent –
    Thy joy to do the Father's will;
    It is the way the Master went;
    Should not the servant tread it still?"
    Horatius Bonar

Daniel chapter 2

1. **Before and after**

>   Previous chapter: Chapter 1: The personal history of Daniel
>   Following chapter: Chapter 3: Nebuchadnezzar's image of gold

2. **Analysis of chapter**

>   Nebuchadnezzar's dream. (1-13)
>   It is revealed to Daniel. (14-23)
>   He obtains admission to the king. (24-30)
>   The dream and the interpretation. (31-45)
>   Honors to Daniel and his friends. (46-49)

3. **Key verse**

>   Verse 1: "And in the second year of the reign of Nebuchadnezzar Nebuchadnezzar dreamed dreams, wherewith his spirit was troubled, and his sleep brake from him."

4. **Key word / key phrase**

>   Verse 28, "There is a God in heaven who reveals mysteries."

5. **Key event / key person / key theme**

>   Nebuchadnezzar's dream of the great image

6. **Key thought**

>   God's timing is perfect.

7. **Key thing to look out for**

>   Daniel's promotion was very similar to Joseph's.

8. **Key Bible cross-reference**

>   Verse 2. See Genesis 41:8.

9. **Key "by way of explanation"**

>   Verse 19, "God of heaven." This description of God, to which "and earth" was sometimes added, focuses on his universal and transcendent reign.

10. **Key "Quotable Quote"**

>   "God in nature is God above us; God in providence is God beyond us; God in law is God against us: but God in Christ is God with us, for us, and in us."
>   Author unknown

Daniel chapter 3

1. Before and after

Previous chapter: Chapter 2: Nebuchadnezzar's dream of the great image
Following chapter: Chapter 4: Nebuchadnezzar's vision of a great tree

2. Analysis of chapter

Nebuchadnezzar's golden image. (1-7)
Shadrach and his companions refuse to worship it. (8-18)
They are thrown into a furnace, but are miraculously preserved. (19-27)
Nebuchadnezzar gives glory to Jehovah. (28-30)

3. Key verse

Verse 7: "Therefore at that time, when all the people heard the sound of the
cornet, flute, harp, sackbut, psaltery, and all kinds of music, all the people, the
nations, and the languages, fell down and worshipped the golden image that
Nebuchadnezzar the king had set up."

4. Key word / key phrase

Verse 1, "Nebuchadnezzar made an image of gold."

5. Key event / key person / key theme

God deliverance of his loyal servants

6. Key thought

Promotion of self is a sin none can claim to be free of.

7. Key thing to look out for

God protected these three faithful men, but some of God's followers become
martyrs.

8. Key Bible cross-reference

Verse 9: See Nehemiah 2:3.

9. Key "by way of explanation"

Verse 12, "pay no attention to you." This is meant to show how good the king
was and how disloyal these three were being to him.

10. Key "Quotable Quote"

"It is unnatural for Christianity to be popular."
Billy Graham

Daniel chapter 4

1. Before and after

Previous chapter: Chapter 3: Nebuchadnezzar's image of gold
Following chapter: Chapter 5: Belshazzar and handwriting on the wall

2. Analysis of chapter

Nebuchadnezzar acknowledges the power of Yahweh. (1-18)
Daniel interprets his dream. (19-27)
Its fulfillment. (28-37)

3. Key verse

Verse 8: "But at the last Daniel came in before me, whose name was Belteshazzar, according to the name of my god, and in whom is the spirit of the holy gods."

4. Key word / key phrase

Verse 10, "a tree in the middle of the land."

5. Key event / key person / key theme

Nebuchadnezzar's vision of a great tree

6. Key thought

Pride comes before a fall.

7. Key thing to look out for

God's mercy is seen in the restoration of Nebuchadnezzar.

8. Key Bible cross-reference

Verse 14. See Job 24:20.

9. Key "by way of explanation"

Verse 26, "Heaven rules." This means that God rules, (cf. Luke 15:18). This is the first time this expression is used in the Bible.

10. Key "Quotable Quote"

"Jesus shall reign where e'er the sun
Doth his successive journeys run;
His kingdom stretch from shore to shore
Till moons shall wax and wane no more."
Isaac Watts

Daniel chapter 5

1. ### Before and after

   Previous chapter: Chapter 4: Nebuchadnezzar's vision of a great tree
   Following chapter: Chapter 6: Darius' foolish decree

2. ### Analysis of chapter

   Belshazzar's impious feast; the handwriting on the wall. (1-9)
   Daniel is sent for to interpret it. (10-17)
   Daniel warns the king of his destruction. (18-31)

3. ### Key verse

   Verse 30: "In that night was Belshazzar the king of the Chaldeans slain."

4. ### Key word / key phrase

   Verse 5, "fingers of a human hand appeared."

5. ### Key event / key person / key theme

   Belshazzar and handwriting on the wall

6. ### Key thought

   God's judgment can strike at any time.

7. ### Key thing to look out for

   God does not view people in the way that the world does.

8. ### Key Bible cross-reference

   Verse 11. See Genesis 41:38.

9. ### Key "by way of explanation"

   Verse 8, "could not read the writing." Although the words were written in ordinary Aramaic nobody could make head or tail of them. They could read them but not understand them.

10. ### Key "Quotable Quote"

   "God's actual divine essence and his will, administration and works – are absolutely beyond all human thought, human understanding or wisdom; in short, they are and ever will be incomprehensible, inscrutable, and altogether hidden to human reason."
   Martin Luther

Daniel chapter 6

1. Before and after

Previous chapter: Chapter 5: Belshazzar and handwriting on the wall
Following chapter: Chapter 7: Daniel's vision of four beasts

2. Analysis of chapter

The malice of Daniel's enemies. (1-5)
His constancy in prayer. (6-10)
He is thrown into the lion's den. (11-17)
His miraculous preservation. (18-24)
The decree of Darius. (25-28)

3. Key verse

Verse 10: "Now when Daniel knew that the writing was signed, he went into his house; and his windows being open in his chamber toward Jerusalem, he kneeled upon his knees three times a day, and prayed, and gave thanks before his God, as he did aforetime."

4. Key word / key phrase

Verse 7, "issue an edict."

5. Key event / key person / key theme

Darius' foolish decree

6. Key thought

Accepting flattery is a sign of a warped character. The centrality of prayer in Daniel's life.

7. Key thing to look out for

Even if Daniel had not been unharmed his faith in God would have remained.

8. Key Bible cross-reference

Verse 15. See Esther 8:8.

9. Key "by way of explanation"

Verse 16, "the lions' den." Lions were kept in this way so kings could chase them when they were released.

10. Key "Quotable Quote"

"Let gratitude for the past inspire us with trust for the future."
François Fénelon

Daniel chapter 7

1. Before and after

Previous chapter: Chapter 6: Darius' foolish decree
Following chapter: Chapter 8: Daniel's vision of a ram and a goat

2. Analysis of chapter

Daniel's vision of the four beasts. (1-8)
And of Christ's kingdom. (9-14)
The interpretation. (15-28)

3. Key verse

Verse 4: "The first was like a lion, and had eagle's wings."

4. Key word / key phrase

Verse 1, "a dream, and visions."

5. Key event / key person / key theme

Daniel's vision of four beasts

6. Key thought

Commentators are not agreed on the identification of the beasts but what is clear is that the future is in God's control, and all evil powers are subservient to him (verse 21).

7. Key thing to look out for

The description of God's kingdom

8. Key Bible cross-reference

Verses 4-6. See Revelation 13:2.

9. Key "by way of explanation"

Verse 18, "the saints" is a phrase rarely found in the Bible. See its equivalent in 8:25; Psalm 16:3; 24:10. It means "the holy ones." The date is about 553 BC, after the death of Nebuchadnezzar but before the supremacy of Persia.

10. Key "Quotable Quote"

"To attain holiness we must follow the example that Christ gave us, not only in his gentleness, humility, and patience during life, but also in his death."
Basil the Great

Daniel chapter 8

1. **Before and after**

Previous chapter: Chapter 7: Daniel's vision of four beasts
Following chapter: Chapter 9: Daniel's vision of seventy weeks

2. **Analysis of chapter**

Daniel's vision of the ram and the he-goat. (1-14)
Its interpretation. (15-27)

3. **Key verse**

Verse 3: "Then I lifted up mine eyes, and saw, and, behold, there stood before the river a ram which had two horns: and the two horns were high; but one was higher than the other, and the higher came up last."

4. **Key word / key phrase**

Verse 3, "a ram with two horns."

5. **Key event / key person / key theme**

Daniel's vision of a ram and a goat – representing Cyrus (Persia), and then Alexander the Great (Greece).

6. **Key thought**

Verse 19, "the time of wrath," that is, God's anger against Israel.

7. **Key thing to look out for**

Verse 17, "the time of the end." These words indicate that the events in chapter 8, point beyond themselves to future events, of which they are shadows.

8. **Key Bible cross-reference**

Verse 16. See Luke 1:19,26.

9. **Key "by way of explanation"**

Verse 11. "Daily sacrifice." This refers to the sacrifice prescribed in Exodus 29:38-42 which had to take place every morning and evening. The little lion (9-14 and 23-25) is Antiochus Epiphanes, against whom the Jews rose up. He stopped the daily temple offerings (verse 11). "Rebels" (verse 23) were Jews who forsook God's Law.

10. **Key "Quotable Quote"**

"Many souls, to whom visions have never come, are incomparably more advanced in the way of perfection than others to whom many have been given."
John of the Cross

Daniel chapter 9

1. Before and after

Previous chapter: Chapter 8: Daniel's vision of a ram and a goat
Following chapter: Chapter 10: The appearance of the messenger

2. Analysis of chapter

Daniel considers the time of the captivity. (1-3)
His confession of sin, and prayer for national restoration. (4-19)
The revelation about the coming of the Messiah. (20-27)

3. Key verse

Verse 5: "We have sinned, and have committed iniquity, and have done wickedly, and have rebelled, even by departing from thy precepts and from thy judgment."

4. Key word / key phrase

Verse 24, "seventy 'sevens'."

5. Key event / key person / key theme

Daniel's vision of seventy weeks

6. Key thought

Daniel prays to the Lord, the covenant God (verse 4) – and therefore, with the Sinai covenant in mind, immediately confesses sin.

7. Key thing to look out for

Daniel's attitude toward God throughout his prayer.

8. Key Bible cross-reference

Verse 2. See Jeremiah 25:11.

9. Key "by way of explanation"

Verse 13, "We have not sought the favor of the Lord." The only solution to their sufferings would be found in repentance. Many conflicting attempts have been made to add up the numbers. They may, however, be symbolic. What is certain is that wickedness will end and the Anointed One will bring in everlasting righteousness.

10. Key "Quotable Quote"

"True repentance is to cease from sin."
Ambrose

Daniel chapter 10

1. *Before and after*

Previous chapter: Chapter 9: Daniel's vision of seventy weeks
Following chapter: Chapter 11: A vision of kings

2. *Analysis of chapter*

Daniel's vision near the river Tigris. (1-9)
He is to expect a discovery of future events. (10-21)

3. *Key verse*

Verse 1: "In the third year of Cyrus king of Persia a thing was revealed unto Daniel, whose name was called Belteshazzar; and the thing was true, but the time appointed was long: and he understood the thing, and had understanding of the vision."

4. *Key word / key phrase*

Verse 5, "a man dressed in linen."

5. *Key event / key person / key theme*

The messenger (since he says he was sent, verse 11, and needed help (verse 13) may be an angel – perhaps Gabriel.

6. *Key thought*

All the heavenly powers involved in the great conflict of good against evil

7. *Key thing to look out for*

What does verse 15 tell us about Daniel's character?

8. *Key Bible cross-reference*

Verses 5,6. See Revelation 1:13-15.

9. *Key "by way of explanation"*

The date is 536. A party of Jews, headed by Zerubbabel has returned to Jerusalem, but Daniel has not gone with them. Verse 1, "a revelation was given." Many different words are used of the divine revelation Daniel received. This one is unique.

10. *Key "Quotable Quote"*

"The Christian does not begin with what the human intellect has discovered. The Christian begins with what God has revealed."
William Barclay

Daniel chapter 11

1. **Before and after**

   Previous chapter: Chapter 10: The appearance of the messenger
   Following chapter: Chapter 12: The end time

2. **Analysis of chapter**

   The kingdoms of Egypt and Syria. (1-20)
   The evil king of Syria. (21-45)

3. **Key verse**

   Verse 5: "And the king of the south shall be strong, and one of his princes; and
   he shall be strong above him, and have dominion; his dominion shall be a
   great dominion."

4. **Key word / key phrase**

   Verse 2, "three more kings."

5. **Key event / key person / key theme**

   A vision of kings

6. **Key thought**

   What is the lesson from verse 32?

7. **Key thing to look out for**

   Verse 36 remains a warning to all rulers.

8. **Key Bible cross-reference**

   Verse 36. See 2 Thessalonians 2:3,4.

9. **Key "by way of explanation"**

   Verse 22, "a prince of the covenant," refers either to Ptolemy V or the high
   priest Onias III. The identity of some of the people described in Daniel is not
   certain.

10. **Key "Quotable Quote"**

    "What is offered to man's apprehension in any specific revelation is not truth
    concerning God but the living God himself."
    William Temple

Daniel chapter 12

1. **Previous chapter**

    Chapter 11: A vision of kings

2. **Analysis of chapter**

    The end times. (1-13)

3. **Key verse**

    Verse 4: "But thou, O Daniel, shut up the words, and seal the book, even to the time of the end: many shall run to and fro, and knowledge shall be increased."

4. **Key word / key phrase**

    Verse 12, "a time of distress."

5. **Key event / key person / key theme**

    The end time

6. **Key thought**

    Daniel remained faithful to God throughout his long life.

7. **Key thing to look out for**

    What comfort can be drawn from the concluding verses of this book?

8. **Key Bible cross-reference**

    Verse 11. See Mark 13:14.

9. **Key "by way of explanation"**

    Verse 2, "everlasting life." This is a phrase that is well-known to Christians because of Jesus' teaching. This is the first occurrence of it in the Bible.

10. **Key "Quotable Quote"**

    "Our hope for everlasting life permits no evasion of death's hard reality."
    Amy Plantinga Pauw

The Minor Prophets

Hosea

Joel

Amos

Obadiah

Jonah

Micah

Nahum

Habakkuk

Zephaniah

Haggai

Zechariah

Malachi

Hosea chapter 1

1. *Following chapter*

   Chapter 2: Israel's unfaithfulness, God's faithfulness

2. *Analysis of chapter*

   The shameful idolatry of the ten tribes. (1-7)
   The calling of the Gentiles, and the uniting Israel and Judah under the Messiah. (8-11)

3. *Key verse*

   Verse 1: "The word of the LORD that came unto Hosea, the son of Beery, in the days of Uzziah, Jotham, Ahaz, and Hezekiah, kings of Judah, and in the days of Jeroboam the son of Joash, king of Israel."

4. *Key word / key phrase*

   Verse 2, "Take to yourself an adulterous wife."

5. *Key event / key person / key theme*

   Hosea's marriage

6. *Key thought*

   Verse 2, "for the land is guilty of the vilest adultery." The purpose of Hosea's book is to expose Israel's unfaithfulness to the Lord and to affirm God's forgiving love. Hosea' own domestic tragedy is a parable of this situation.

7. *Key thing to look out for*

   The Lord was constantly telling his people to be faithful to him.

8. *Key Bible cross-reference*

   Verse 10. See Romans 9:26.

9. *Key "by way of explanation"*

   Hosea married Gomer, who proved to be unfaithful, and left him for another man. He later found her for sale as a slave. In deep love he bought her and eventually took her back as his wif.

10. *Key "Quotable Quote"*

    "The lukewarmness of our prayers is the source of all our other infidelities." François Fénelon

Hosea chapter 2

1. **Before and after**

   Previous chapter: Chapter 1: Hosea's marriage
   Following chapter: Chapter 3: Hosea buys his wife back

2. **Analysis of chapter**

   The idolatry of the people. (1-5)
   God's judgments against them. (6-13)
   His promises of reconciliation. (14-23)

3. **Key verse**

   Verse 8: "For she did not know that I gave her corn, and wine, and oil, and multiplied her silver and gold, which they prepared for Baal."

4. **Key word / key phrase**

   Verse 17, "I will remove the names of the Baals from her lips."

5. **Key event / key person / key theme**

   Israel's unfaithfulness, God's faithfulness

6. **Key thought**

   Note the ways in which Israel's unfaithfulness is detailed.

7. **Key thing to look out for**

   How does God say he will act in this situation?

8. **Key Bible cross-reference**

   Verse 15. See Joshua 7:24-26.

9. **Key "by way of explanation"**

   Hosea lived and preached in the northern kingdom during its final years. He probably died before the fall of Samaria. Hosea's ministry overlapped with the ministries of Amos, Micah and Isaiah.

10. **Key "Quotable Quote"**

    "Incomprehensible and immutable is the love of God."
    Augustine of Hippo

Hosea chapter 3

1. **Before and after**

   Previous chapter: Chapter 2: Israel's unfaithfulness, God's faithfulness
   Following chapter: Chapter 4: Israel's sins

2. **Analysis of chapter**

   Hosea reconciled with his wife. (1-5)

3. **Key verse**

   Verse 2: "So I bought her to me for fifteen pieces of silver, and for an homer of barley, and an half homer of barley."

4. **Key word / key phrase**

   Verse 1, "Show your love to your wife again."

5. **Key event / key person / key theme**

   Hosea buys his wife back

6. **Key thought**

   God's very great love, shown in his willingness to receive Israel back

7. **Key thing to look out for**

   How does God "buy us back?"

8. **Key Bible cross-reference**

   Verse 5. See Isaiah 9:13.

9. **Key "by way of explanation"**

   Verse 5, "return." This is the key word in the whole book. "Return" or "go back" are repeatedly stated in this book. See 2:7; 5:4; 6:1; 7:10; 11:5; 12:6; 14:1-2.

10. **Key "Quotable Quote"**

    "God created man because God loves and wanted an object to love. He created man so that he could return his love."
    Billy Graham

Hosea chapter 4

1. **Before and after**

   Previous chapter: Chapter 3: Hosea buys his wife back
   Following chapter: Chapter 5: Eventual restoration of Israel

2. **Analysis of chapter**

   God's judgments against the sins of the people, (1-5)
   and of the priests. (6-11)
   Idolatry is reproved, and Judah is admonished. (12-19)

3. **Key verse**

   Verse 6: "My people are destroyed for lack of knowledge."

4. **Key word / key phrase**

   Verse 1, "the Lord has a charge to bring against you."

5. **Key event / key person / key theme**

   Israel's sins

6. **Key thought**

   There is never any point in trying to hide our sins from God.

7. **Key thing to look out for**

   No matter how many and how bad our sins, they must be owned up to.

8. **Key Bible cross-reference**

   Verse 16. See Exodus 32:9.

9. **Key "by way of explanation"**

   Verse 1, "charge." Hosea was the Lord's spokesman and he had charges to bring against his people since they had broken God's covenant.

10. **Key "Quotable Quote"**

    "Knowledge without repentance will be but a torch to light men to hell."
    Thomas Watson

Hosea chapter 5

1. **Before and after**

   Previous chapter: Chapter 4: Israel's sins
   Following chapter: Chapter 6: The covenant is deliberately broken

2. **Analysis of chapter**

   The divine judgments against Israel. (1-7)
   Approaching desolations threatened. (8-15)

3. **Key verse**

   Verse 5: "And the pride of Israel doth testify to his face: therefore shall Israel and Ephraim fall in their iniquity; Judah also shall fall with them."

4. **Key word / key phrase**

   Verse 15, "they will seek my face."

5. **Key event / key person / key theme**

   Eventual restoration of Israel

6. **Key thought**

   Why did Israel find it so difficult to admit her guilt? See verse 15.

7. **Key thing to look out for**

   There is never a time when we should not seek the Lord.

8. **Key Bible cross-reference**

   Verse 12. See Job 13:28.

9. **Key "by way of explanation"**

   Verse 6, "seek the Lord." This was to be done in different ways, including through prayer and through offering sacrifices. See 3:5; Amos 5:4,5.

10. **Key "Quotable Quote"**

    "Sitting still will lose you heaven, as well as if you run from it."
    Richard Baxter

Hosea chapter 6

1. *Before and after*

Previous chapter: Chapter 5: Eventual restoration of Israel
Following chapter: Chapter 7: Deliberate refusal to return to the Lord

2. *Analysis of chapter*

A superficial repentance. (1-3)
Israel's instability and breaking of the covenant. (4-11)

3. *Key verse*

Verse 2: "After two days will he revive us: in the third day he will raise us up, and we shall live in his sight."

4. *Key word / key phrase*

Verse 6, "mercy."

5. *Key event / key person / key theme*

God sees through a shallow casual repentance (see verses 1-4 and 7:14).

6. *Key thought*

Why can there be no progress if we refuse to repent?

7. *Key thing to look out for*

What is verse 6 saying?

8. *Key Bible cross-reference*

Verse 6. See Matthew 9:13.

9. *Key "by way of explanation"*

Verse 6, "mercy" translates the Hebrew word *hesed*, often used to describe God's covenant love for his people. Here it can refer to being loyal to the Lord or acting in the right way toward people. Here it probably includes both of these meanings.

10. *Key "Quotable Quote"*

"There's a wideness in God's mercy,
Like the wideness of the sea;
There's a kindness in his justice,
Which is more than liberty."
F.W. Faber

Hosea chapter 7

1. *Before and after*

Previous chapter: Chapter 6: The covenant is deliberately broken
Following chapter: Chapter 8: Deliberate idolatry

2. *Analysis of chapter*

The many sins of Israel. (1-7)
Their senselessness and hypocrisy. (8-16)

3. *Key verse*

Verse 8: "Ephraim [Israel], he hath mixed himself among the people; Ephraim is a cake not turned."

4. *Key word / key phrase*

Verse 1, "whenever I would heal Israel."

5. *Key event / key person / key theme*

Deliberate refusal to return to the Lord

6. *Key thought*

How can such people be helped?

7. *Key thing to look out for*

The causes of Israel's many sins and difficulties

8. *Key Bible cross-reference*

Verse 2. See Jeremiah 14:10.

9. *Key "by way of explanation"*

Verse 2, "I remember." Nothing is hidden from the Lord, and the Lord never forgets anything.

10. *Key "Quotable Quote"*

"I am constrained to express my adoration of the Author of my existence for his forgiving mercy revealed to the world through Jesus Christ, through whom I hope for never ending happiness in a future state."
Robert Treat Paine, Signer of the Declaration

Hosea chapter 8

1. Before and after

Previous chapter: Chapter 7: Deliberate refusal to return to the Lord
Following chapter: Chapter 9: God will reject Israel

2. Analysis of chapter

Destruction threatened for the impiety of Israel. (1-4)
For their idolatry. (5-10)
Further warnings for the same sins. (11-14)

3. Key verse

Verse 3: "Israel hath cast off the thing that is good: the enemy shall pursue him."

4. Key word / key phrase

Verse 6, "this calf."

5. Key event / key person / key theme

The state of the nation: deliberate idolatry and unfortunate foreign alliances

6. Key thought

The cause of their troubles: "Israel has forgotten" verse 14

7. Key thing to look out for

What instances of God's love are nevertheless found in this chapter?

8. Key Bible cross-reference

Verse 1. See Numbers 10:2.

9. Key "by way of explanation"

Verse 5, "calf-idol." Golden calves had been set up in Bethel and Dan by Jeroboam I. See 1 Kings 12:28-33.

10. Key "Quotable Quote"

"Repentance means that everything must be changed."
Johann Heinrich Arnold

Hosea chapter 9

1. Before and after

Previous chapter: Chapter 8: Deliberate idolatry
Following chapter: Chapter 10: God's judgment on Israel

2. Analysis of chapter

The distress to come upon Israel. (1-6)
The approach of the day of trouble. (7-10)
Judgments on Israel. (11-17)

3. Key verse

Verse 7: "The days of visitation are come, the days of recompense are come; Israel shall know it: the prophet is a fool, the spiritual man is mad, for the multitude of thine iniquity, and the great hatred."

4. Key word / key phrase

Verse 17, "My God will reject them."

5. Key event / key person / key theme

Israel's disobedience

6. Key thought

Reflect on God's grace to you throughout your life.

7. Key thing to look out for

God only drives Israel away from him to bring her to her senses.

8. Key Bible cross-reference

Verse 7. See Luke 21:22.

9. Key "by way of explanation"

Verse 10, "grapes . . . fruit on the fig-tree." Grapes in the desert and the early figs, refreshing fruit, stand for God's delight in Israel's acceptance of the covenant.

10. Key "Quotable Quote"

"No powers can separate us from God's love in Christ. Unmasked, revealed in their true nature, they have lost their mighty grip on men. The cross has disarmed them."
Hendrik Berkhof

Hosea chapter 10

1. *Before and after*

Previous chapter: Chapter 9: God will reject Israel
Following chapter: Chapter 11: God's love for Israel

2. *Analysis of chapter*

The idolatry of Israel. (1-8)
They are exhorted to repent. (9-15)

3. *Key verse*

Verse 1: "Israel is an empty vine, he bringeth forth fruit unto himself: according to the multitude of his fruit he hath increased the altars; according to the goodness of his land they have made goodly images."

4. *Key word / key phrase*

Verse 15, "the king of Israel will be completely destroyed."

5. *Key event / key person / key theme*

God's judgment on Israel

6. *Key thought*

Israel's prosperity (verse 1), led her to depend on her own strength (verse 13) and that proved fatal.

7. *Key thing to look out for*

Why is sin so appealing?

8. *Key Bible cross-reference*

Verse 8. See Luke 23:30.

9. *Key "by way of explanation"*

Verse 11, "yoke" is a reference to the law. Steadily doing what is right, showing love and seeking God, will lead to the outpouring of God's blessings.

10. *Key "Quotable Quote"*

"All of God's people are ordinary people who have been made extraordinary by the purpose he has given them."
Oswald Chambers

Hosea chapter 11

1. Before and after

Previous chapter: Chapter 10: God's judgment on Israel
Following chapter: Chapter 12: Israel and Judah are condemned

2. Analysis of chapter

God's tender love for Israel; their ingratitude. (1-7)
The divine mercy yet in store. (8-12)

3. Key verse

Verse 3: "I taught Ephraim also to go, taking them by their arms; but they knew not that I healed them."

4. Key word / key phrase

Verse 1, "I loved him."

5. Key event / key person / key theme

God's love for Israel

6. Key thought

God never stops loving his people.

7. Key thing to look out for

Life with God is the best life. See verse 11.

8. Key Bible cross-reference

Verse 1. See Exodus 4:22.

9. Key "by way of explanation"

Verse 3, "walk." Here the picture depicts a father gently teaching his child to walk – a beautiful picture of God's love for his people.

10. Key "Quotable Quote"

"The atonement was not the cause but the effect of God's love."
A.W. Pink

Hosea chapter 12

1. *Before and after*

Previous chapter: Chapter 11: God's love for Israel
Following chapter: Chapter 13: Only God's love can save Israel

2. *Analysis of chapter*

Jacob's deceit. (1-6)
Out of Egypt. (7-14)

3. *Key verse*

Verse 6: "Therefore turn thou to thy God: keep mercy and judgment, and wait on thy God continually."

4. *Key word / key phrase*

Verse 2, "a change to bring."

5. *Key event / key person / key theme*

A look back to the past

6. *Key thought*

Like father (Jacob) like son (Israel, cheating at business, cheating on God)

7. *Key thing to look out for*

The waywardness of God's people is meant to be a lesson for us.

8. *Key Bible cross-reference*

Verse 3. See Genesis 25:26.

9. *Key "by way of explanation"*

Verse 8, "I am very rich." One of the downsides of riches is that they tend to make people complacent and self-sufficient.

10. *Key "Quotable Quote"*

"No friend of gold ever became a friend of Christ or a friend of people."
John Chrysostom

Hosea chapter 13

1. Before and after

Previous chapter: Chapter 12: Israel and Judah are condemned
Following chapter: Chapter 14: God's promise to restore Israel

2. Analysis of chapter

The abuse of God's favor leads to punishment. (1-8)
A promise of God's mercy. (9-16)

3. Key verse

Verse 14: "I will ransom them from the power of the grave; I will redeem them from death."

4. Key word / key phrase

Verse 4, "no Savior except me."

5. Key event / key person / key theme

Only God's love can save Israel

6. Key thought

God insists on being the only God in Israel's life.

7. Key thing to look out for

Note the sinfulness of sin, in verse 2, for example.

8. Key Bible cross-reference

Verse 14. See 1 Corinthians 15:55.

9. Key "by way of explanation"

Verse 14, "I will ransom." This promise states that the Lord will redeem people from death and is echoed in 1 Corinthians 15.

10. Key "Quotable Quote"

"He that hath one foot in heaven need not fear to put the other into the grave."
John Flavel

Hosea chapter 14

1. *Previous chapter*

   Chapter 13: Only God's love can save Israel

2. *Analysis of chapter*

   An exhortation to repent. (1-3)
   Blessings promised, showing the great benefits of the gospel. (4-8)
   The just and the wicked. (9)

3. *Key verse*

   Verse 4: "I will heal their backsliding, I will love them freely: for mine anger is turned away from him."

4. *Key word / key phrase*

   Verse 1, "Return."

5. *Key event / key person / key theme*

   God's promise to restore Israel

6. *Key thought*

   God always extends his forgiving arms to his repentant people.

7. *Key thing to look out for*

   Note how everything that is good in us comes from God, see verse 8.

8. *Key Bible cross-reference*

   Verse 1. See Isaiah 19:22.

9. *Key "by way of explanation"*

   Verse 2, "take words." Sacrifices would not be sufficient. The words that had to be taken needed to be words of repentance.

10. *Key "Quotable Quote"*

    "Repentance is in every view so desirable, so necessary, so suited to honor God, that I seek that above all. The tender heart, the broken and contrite spirit, are to me far above all the joys that I could ever hope for in this vale of tears."
    Charles Simeon

Joel chapter 1

1. *Following chapter*

Chapter 2: The Day of the Lord will bring destruction

2. *Analysis of chapter*

A plague of locusts. (1-7)
All sorts of people are called to lament it. (8-13)
They are to look to God. (14-20)

3. *Key verse*

Verse 12: "The vine is dried up, and the fig tree languisheth; the pomegranate tree, the palm tree also, and the apple tree, even all the trees of the field, are withered: because joy is withered away from the sons of men."

4. *Key word / key phrase*

Verse 4, "the locust swarm."

5. *Key event / key person / key theme*

The devastating plague of locusts

6. *Key thought*

A good question to ask of any disaster is: "What can I learn from God in this situation?"

7. *Key thing to look out for*

In God's sight we always need to repent.

8. *Key Bible cross-reference*

Verse 28-32. See Acts 2:17-21.
6. See Revelation 9:8.

9. *Key "by way of explanation"*

Verse 11, "all the trees of the field." The extent of the damage caused by locusts went beyond the corn and vines to the trees, which included apple trees, fig-trees, and pomegranates. There are no historical details in the book, so the date of Joel is uncertain.

10. *Key "Quotable Quote"*

"If God exists, and if He judges good and evil, then we must realize that those who trample on his great gifts will one day know his judgment. The scriptures bear solemn witness to this. Our nation is not immune."
Francis A. Schaeffer

Joel chapter 2

1. Before and after

Previous chapter: Chapter 1: The devastating plague of locusts
Following chapter: Chapter 3: Judgment on the nations

2. Analysis of chapter

God's judgments. (1-14)
Exhortations to fasting and prayer; blessings promised. (15-27)
A promise of the Holy Spirit, and of future mercies. (28-32)

3. Key verse

Verse 1: "Blow ye the trumpet in Zion, and sound an alarm in my holy mountain: let all the inhabitants of the land tremble: for the day of the LORD cometh, for it is nigh at hand."

4. Key word / key phrase

Verse 1, "the day of the Lord is coming."

5. Key event / key person / key theme

The Day of the Lord will bring destruction

6. Key thought

How do you link up the Day of the Lord with the second coming of Jesus?

7. Key thing to look out for

Note how verse 13 goes to the heart of the matter.

8. Key Bible cross-reference

Verses 2:28-32. See Acts 2:17-21.

9. Key "by way of explanation"

Verse 12, "even now." God's judgment had already started. But "even now" it was not too late to escape it if the people repented.

10. Key "Quotable Quote"

"All true repentance has its root in faith."
Horatius Bonar

Joel chapter 3

1. **Previous chapter**

   Chapter 2: The Day of the Lord will bring destruction

2. **Analysis of chapter**

   God's judgments in the latter days. (1-8)
   The extent of these judgments. (9-17)
   The blessings the messianic age. (18-21)

3. **Key verse**

   Verse 10: "Beat your plowshares into swords, and your pruninghooks into spears: let the weak say, I am strong."

4. **Key word / key phrase**

   Verse 4, "what have you against me?"

5. **Key event / key person / key theme**

   Judgment on the nations

6. **Key thought**

   Godless nations will be judged by God because of their treatment of God's people

7. **Key thing to look out for**

   What spiritual blessings are alluded to in verses 17-21?

8. **Key Bible cross-reference**

   Verses 4-8. See Luke 10:13,14.

9. **Key "by way of explanation"**

   Verse 18, "valley of acacias," suggests a dry and hot ravine, similar to those that go down to the Dead Sea. "The water flowing from the temple of God will be sufficient for even the most remote and waterless ravine" (Paul E. Leonard). See Ezekiel 47:1-12.

10. **Key "Quotable Quote"**

    "The Law by which God rules us, is as dear to him as the Gospel by which he saves us."
    William Secker

Amos chapter 1

1. *Following chapter*

   Chapter 2: Moab, Judah, and Israel condemned

2. *Analysis of chapter*

   Introduction. (1-2)
   Judgments against Israel's neighbors. (3-15)

3. *Key verse*

   Verse 1: "The words of Amos, who was among the herdmen of Tekoa, which he saw concerning Israel in the days of Uzziah king of Judah, and in the days of Jeroboam the son of Joash king of Israel, two years before the earthquake."

4. *Key word / key phrase*

   Verse 3, "three sins of Damascus."

5. *Key event / key person / key theme*

   The sins of Damascus, Philistia, Phoenicia, Edom, and Ammon

6. *Key thought*

   Be sure your sin will find you out.

7. *Key thing to look out for*

   All humans beings are responsible people with consciences.

8. *Key Bible cross-reference*

   Verse 1. See 2 Kings 15:1-7.

9. *Key "by way of explanation"*

   Amos, who lived near Bethlehem in Judah, was sent by God to preach at Bethel in Israel, probably about 760-750, during a time of temporary prosperity for both kingdoms. He was not a priest, like Jeremiah and Ezekiel, but a shepherd. He also tended sycamore-fig trees (1:1; 7:14).

10. *Key "Quotable Quote"*

    "Alas! that prisons should have been peopled, and thousands immolated on the pyre, for the sake of opinions; and that nothing but death could atone for the horrible crime of individual judgment, instead of allowing each to stand or fall to their own Master."
    John Foxe

Amos chapter 2

1. ### Before and after

   Previous chapter: Chapter 1:The sins of Damascus, Philistia, Phoenicia, Edom, and Ammon
   Following chapter: Chapter 3: God's judgment

2. ### Analysis of chapter

   Judgments against Moab and Judah. (1-8)
   The ingratitude and ruin of Israel. (9-16)

3. ### Key verse

   Verse 4: "Thus saith the LORD."

4. ### Key word / key phrase

   Verse 6, "For three sins of Israel."

5. ### Key event / key person / key theme

   The climax: sins of Israel

6. ### Key thought

   It is easy to sit in judgment on others and to ignore our own sins. Israel will have been shocked when Amos suddenly turned to the sins of Israel.

7. ### Key thing to look out for

   God's people very often rebel against the Lord God.

8. ### Key Bible cross-reference

   Verse 9. See Deuteronomy 3:8-11.

9. ### Key "by way of explanation"

   Verse 8, "garments taken in pledge." This describes the usual way in which a loan was secured. If you wanted to borrow money you would leave your cloak as surety for your debt. Verse 3, "For three . . . even four" a literary device that emphasizes the sin named.

10. ### Key "Quotable Quote"

    "Original sin is the only rational solution of the undeniable fact of the deep, universal and early manifested sinfulness of men in all ages, of every class, and in every part of the world."
    Charles Hodge

Amos chapter 3

1. *Before and after*

    Previous chapter: Chapter 2: Moab, Judah, and Israel condemned
    Following chapter: Chapter 4: The willfulness of Israel

2. *Analysis of chapter*

    Judgments against Israel. (1-8)
    Judgments against other nations. (9-15)

3. *Key verse*

    Verse 10: "For they know not to do right, saith the LORD, who store up violence and robbery in their palaces."

4. *Key word / key phrase*

    Verse 14, "I punish Israel."

5. *Key event / key person / key theme*

    God's judgment

6. *Key thought*

    That fact that God chose his people to follow him in the first place, verse 2, is mentioned here because that alone should have brought Israel back to her senses.

7. *Key thing to look out for*

    Verse 7 shows how God plans everything and that his plans were often conveyed through his prophets.

8. *Key Bible cross-reference*

    Verse 14. See 2 Kings 23:15.

9. *Key "by way of explanation"*

    Verse 15, "houses adorned with ivory." This indicates great wealth obtained at the expense of the poor. Craftsmen were used to inlay the ivory.

10. *Key "Quotable Quote"*

    "None are true saints except those who have the true character of compassion and concern to relieve the poor, indignant, and afflicted."
    Jonathan Edwards

Amos chapter 4

1. ### Before and after

   Previous chapter: Chapter 3: God's judgment
   Following chapter: Chapter 5: Judgment on Israel is deserved

2. ### Analysis of chapter

   Israel is reproved. (1-5)
   Their impenitence shown. (6-13)

3. ### Key verse

   Verse 4: "Come to Bethel, and transgress."

4. ### Key word / key phrase

   Verse 1, "women who oppress the poor."

5. ### Key event / key person / key theme

   The willfulness of Israel's sins

6. ### Key thought

   The Bible often uses very unflattering language, verse 1, to startle people into paying attention.

7. ### Key thing to look out for

   Natural justice dictates that the poor should not be trodden under foot. Of all people, God's followers should not have allowed this to happen.

8. ### Key Bible cross-reference

   Verse 11. See Genesis 19:24.

9. ### Key "by way of explanation"

   Verse 6, "yet you have not returned to me." This refrain comes at the close of the description of the five natural disasters, verses 6,8,9,10,11, and parallels Pharaoh's response to the plagues.

10. ### Key "Quotable Quote"

    "It is human to err; it is devilish to remain willfully in error."
    Augustine of Hippo

Amos chapter 5

1. *Before and after*

Previous chapter 4: The willfulness of Israel
Following chapter 6: Israel's end is near

2. *Analysis chapter*

Israel is called to seek the Lord. (1-6)
Earnest exhortations to repent. (7-17)
Warnings about idolatry. (18-27)

3. *Key verse*

Verse 24: "But let judgment run down as waters, and righteousness as a mighty stream."

4. *Key word / key phrase*

"Hate," verses 10, 15, 21. It is always instructive to see what God and God's prophets "hate."

5. *Key event / key person / key theme*

Judgment on Israel is deserved

6. *Key thought*

God's assessment of Israel's worship is that it is: "your religious feasts, your assemblies, and your songs," verses 21-23.

7. *Key thing to look out for*

The prophetic call for social justice is repeated in the New Testament.

8. *Key biblical cross-reference*

Verse 15. See Isaiah 1:17; Romans 12:9.

9. *Key "by way of explanation"*

Verse 2 "Fallen is Virgin Israel." The word "Virgin" emphasizes Israel's premature death. Amos says, in effect, "How sad that a whole life of potential love and fruitfulness was cut short."

10. *Key "Quotable Quote"*

"Concern for the rights and welfare of all [God's] people flows, like a mighty river, from his own heart. Whoever would truly serve him must go with that flow."
D.A. Hubbard, on verse 24

Amos chapter 6

1. **Before and after**

   Previous chapter: Chapter 5: Israel's judgment is deserved
   Following chapter: Chapter 7: Visions of doom: locusts, fire, and plumb line

2. **Analysis of chapter**

   The danger of luxury and false security. (1-7)
   Punishment of sins. (8-14)

3. **Key verse**

   Verse 1: "Woe to them that are at ease in Zion."

4. **Key word / key phrase**

   Verse 14, "I will stir up a nation against you."

5. **Key event / key person / key theme**

   Israel's end is near

6. **Key thought**

   Why is luxurious living and feasting picked on as being so sinful?

7. **Key thing to look out for**

   Complacency, verse 1, heads the list of sins. Why is it so dangerous?

8. **Key Bible cross-reference**

   Verse 10. See 1 Samuel 31:12.

9. **Key "by way of explanation"**

   Verse 8, "the Sovereign Lord has sworn." This phrase is used three times in this book. See also 4:2; 8:7. It introduces the Lord's impending judgment.

10. **Key "Quotable Quote"**

    "Jesus Christ is no longer on trial before men – men are now on trial before him!"
    A.W. Tozer

Amos chapter 7

1. ### Before and after

    Previous chapter: Chapter 6: Israel's end is near
    Following chapter: Chapter 8: Vision of the summer fruit

2. ### Analysis of chapter

    Visions of judgments to come upon Israel. (1-9)
    Amaziah threatens Amos. (10-17)

3. ### Key verse

    Verse 7: "Thus he showed me: and, behold, the Lord stood upon a wall made by a plumb line, with a plumb line in his hand."

4. ### Key word / key phrase

    Verse 4, "judgment by fire."

5. ### Key event / key person / key theme

    Visions of doom: locusts, fire, and plumb line

6. ### Key thought

    When we are brought to the end of ourselves, verses 2, what should we do?

7. ### Key thing to look out for

    Only people with discernment can detect a false prophet.

8. ### Key Bible cross-reference

    Verse 13. See Joshua 7:2.

9. ### Key "by way of explanation"

    Verse 6, "the LORD relented." This does not imply that the Lord gave up, regretted or stopped his actions through remorse. Rather it shows that the Lord God himself was personally involved with his people.

10. ### Key "Quotable Quote"

    "You can't drink your way out of loneliness. Drugs won't take you out of it. God says to you that there is an answer to loneliness. It lies in a personal relationship with the Lord Jesus Christ."
    Billy Graham

Amos chapter 8

1. **Before and after**

   Previous chapter: Chapter 7: Visions of doom: locusts, fire, and plumb line
   Following chapter: Chapter 9: God's destruction, but hope for the future

2. **Analysis of chapter**

   The impending ruin of Israel. (1-3)
   Oppression reproved. (4-10)
   A famine of the word of God. (11-14)

3. **Key verse**

   Verse 4: "Hear this, O ye that swallow up the needy, even to make the poor of the land to fail."

4. **Key word / key phrase**

   Verse 1, "a basket of ripe fruit."

5. **Key event / key person / key theme**

   Vision of the summer fruit

6. **Key thought**

   Social injustice is abhorrent in God's sight.

7. **Key thing to look out for**

   God can send spiritual famines as a judgment.

8. **Key Bible cross-reference**

   Verse 9. See Job 5:14.

9. **Key "by way of explanation"**

   Verse 7, "the Pride of Jacob." God's people were very proud of the fact that the Lord God was with them, always went with them, and that he was their God.

10. **Key "Quotable Quote"**

    "When God measures man, he puts the tape around the heart, not the head." Author unknown

Amos chapter 9

1. **Previous chapter**

   Chapter 8: Vision of the summer fruit

2. **Analysis of chapter**

   The ruin of Israel. (1-10)
   The restoration of the Jews and the gospel blessing. (11-15)

3. **Key verse**

   Verse 8: "Behold, the eyes of the Lord GOD are upon the sinful kingdom, and I will destroy it from off the face of the earth; saving that I will not utterly destroy the house of Jacob, saith the LORD."

4. **Key word / key phrase**

   Verse 1, "none will escape."

5. **Key event / key person / key theme**

   God's destruction, but hope for the future

6. **Key thought**

   Some things have to be torn down before a building can progress.

7. **Key thing to look out for**

   From verse 11 we observe the Lord's loving heart in his promise of restoration.

8. **Key Bible cross-reference**

   Verses 11,12. See Acts 15:16-18.

9. **Key "by way of explanation"**

   Verse 6, "his lofty place." The comparison here is between puny man whose buildings are threatened by the slightest earthquake and God who can build up into the heavens.

10. **Key "Quotable Quote"**

    "At the end of life, we shall be judged by love."
    St John of the Cross

Obadiah

1. **The judgment of Edom**

2. **Analysis of chapter**

   Destruction to come on Edom. Their offences against Jacob. (1-16)
   The restoration of the Jews, and their flourishing state in the latter times.
   (17-21)

3. **Key verse**

   Verse 10: "For thy violence against thy brother Jacob shame shall cover thee,
   and thou shalt be cut off for ever."

4. **Key word / key phrase**

   Verse 1, "about Edom."

5. **Key event / key person / key theme**

   The callous behavior of Edom

6. **Key thought**

   Some people seem to spend all their lives being openly hostile to God.

7. **Key thing to look out for**

   Verse 12 is a warning to all people, not just the Edomites.

8. **Key Bible cross-reference**

   Verses 1-14. See Isaiah 34:5-17; 63:1-6.

9. **Key "by way of explanation"**

   Verse 10, "your brother Jacob." What made Edom's sins all the worse is that
   her evil actions were committed against Jacob, her brother nation. The date of
   this book is uncertain but verses 11-14 seem to indicate the recent destruction
   of Jerusalem by Babylon in which Edom joined in.

10. **Key "Quotable Quote"**

    "Jesus will judge us not only for what we did, but also for what we could have
    done and didn't."
    George Otis

Jonah chapter 1

1. **Following chapter**

   Chapter 2: Jonah prays from inside the great fish

2. **Analysis of chapter**

   Jonah, sent to Nineveh, flees to Tarshish. (1-3)
   He is caught in a storm at sea. (4-7)
   His conversation with the sailors. (8-12)
   He is thrown into the sea, and miraculously preserved. (13-17)

3. **Key verse**

   Verse 1: "Now the word of the LORD came unto Jonah the son of Amittai."

4. **Key word / key phrase**

   Verse 3, "Jonah ran away."

5. **Key event / key person / key theme**

   Jonah is thrown overboard

6. **Key thought**

   It is possible to run away from God's wishes, but not to evade them forever.

7. **Key thing to look out for**

   God's plan B is always better than our own disobedience.

8. **Key Bible cross-reference**

   Verse 17. See Matthew 12:40.

9. **Key "by way of explanation"**

   Joppa (and Tarsish) are in the opposite direction to Nineveh. A probable date for the book of Jonah is after the ministries of Amos and Hosea, and before the fall of Israel and Samaria to Assyria in 722-721 BC.

10. **Key "Quotable Quote"**

    "It will not do to say that you have no special call to go to China. With these facts before you and with the command of the Lord Jesus to go and preach the gospel to every creature, you need rather to ascertain whether you have a special call to stay at home."
    James Hudson Taylor

Jonah chapter 2

1. *Before and after*

   Previous chapter: Chapter 1: Jonah is thrown overboard
   Following chapter: Chapter 3: Jonah goes to Nineveh

2. *Analysis of chapter*

   The prayer of Jonah. (1-9)
   He is delivered from the fish. (10)

3. *Key verse*

   Verse 10: "And the LORD spake unto the fish, and it vomited out Jonah upon the dry land."

4. *Key word / key phrase*

   Verse 1, "From inside the fish Jonah prayed."

5. *Key event / key person / key theme*

   Jonah prays from inside the great fish

6. *Key thought*

   In desperate trouble, Jonah turned to the Lord in sincere prayer.

7. *Key thing to look out for*

   Verse 2, "I called . . . he answered." This is thus Jonah's second prayer: a prayer of thanksgiving for answered prayer.

8. *Key Bible cross-reference*

   Verse 3. See Psalm 88:6.

9. *Key "by way of explanation"*

   Verse 3, "all your waves and breakers swept over me." The four Hebrew words which make up this sentence are also found in Psalm 42:7. Either Jonah was quoting the psalmist or the psalmist was quoting Jonah.

10. *Key "Quotable Quote"*

   "I am convinced that the really great issues before us will be settled on our knees."
   D.A. Carson

Jonah chapter 3

1. *Before and after*

Previous chapter: Chapter 2: Jonah prays from inside the great fish
Following chapter: Chapter 4: The people of Nineveh repent

2. *Analysis of chapter*

Jonah sent again to Nineveh, preaches there. (1-4)
Nineveh is spared as the inhabitants repent. (5-10)

3. *Key verse*

Verse 5: "So the people of Nineveh believed God, and proclaimed a fast, and put on sackcloth, from the greatest of them even to the least of them."

4. *Key word / key phrase*

Verse 2, "the great city of Nineveh."

5. *Key event / key person / key theme*

Jonah goes to Nineveh

6. *Key thought*

Witnessing should not be governed by the reaction that is expected.

7. *Key thing to look out for*

God always has compassion on people who repent.

8. *Key Bible cross-reference*

Verses 3,4. See Matthew 12:41.

9. *Key "by way of explanation"*

Verse 10. "God had compassion," but previously had threatened his judgment on Nineveh. When people repent the Bible is never worried about saying that God shows mercy, and in this sense "changed his mind."

10. *Key "Quotable Quote"*

"Prayer is the midwife of mercy, that helps to bring it forth."
Matthew Henry

Jonah chapter 4

1. **Previous chapter**

   Chapter 3: Jonah goes to Nineveh

2. **Analysis of chapter**

   Jonah sulks because of God's mercy to Nineveh, and is reproved. (1-4)
   He is taught by the withering of a gourd that he did wrong. (5-11)

3. **Key verse**

   Verse 1: "But it displeased Jonah exceedingly, and he was very angry..

4. **Key word / key phrase**

   Verse 11, "should I not be concerned?"

5. **Key event / key person / key theme**

   God's pity for the people of Nineveh

6. **Key thought**

   Some of the Lord's most faithful followers have also made Jonah's request:
   "take away my life," verse 3.

7. **Key thing to look out for**

   God's provision takes many forms, some of them most unexpected.

8. **Key Bible cross-reference**

   Verse 2. See Exodus 34:6.

9. **Key "by way of explanation"**

   Verse 8, "a scorching east wind." This wind, known as the *sirocco*, was a
   particularly dry and hot wind which blew off the desert. It would have
   certainly increased Jonah's discomfort.

10. **Key "Quotable Quote"**

    "Repentance must not be mistaken for remorse. It does not consist in feeling
    terribly sorry that things went wrong in the past; it is an active, positive
    attitude which consists in moving in the right direction."
    Metropolitan Anthony of Sourozh

Micah chapter 1

1. Following chapter

Chapter 2: People who exploit the poor will be punished

2. Analysis of chapter

The wrath of God against Israel. (1-7)
Also against Jerusalem and other cities, and the precautions they take in vain.
(8-16)

3. Key verse

Verse 1: "The word of the LORD that came to Micah the Morasthite in the days
of Jotham, Ahaz, and Hezekiah, kings of Judah, which he saw concerning
Samaria and Jerusalem."

4. Key word / key phrase

Verse 1, "vision."

5. Key event / key person / key theme

Samaria will be destroyed; the enemy approaches Jerusalem

6. Key thought

Idolatry is again mentioned. It kept on leading people away from God.

7. Key thing to look out for

Repentance and mourning is the order of the day.

8. Key Bible cross-reference

Verse 1. See 2 Kings 15:32–16:20.

9. Key "by way of explanation"

Verse 13 "Lachish," a border town and one of Judah's largest towns. It received
its chariots and horses from Egypt. Micah was a contemporary of Isaiah and
Hosea. He preached t the northern kingdom.

10. Key "Quotable Quote"

"All sin is against God, and for that reason he who truly grieves for his own
sin will grieve for other men's too."
Ralph Venning

Micah chapter 2

1. Before and after

Previous chapter: Chapter 1: Samaria will be destroyed; the enemy approaches Jerusalem

Following chapter: Chapter 3: The leaders are judged

2. Analysis of chapter

The sins and desolations of Israel. (1-5)

Their evil practices. (6-11)

A promise of restoration. (12,13)

3. Key verse

Verse 6: "Prophesy ye not, say they to them that prophesy: they shall not prophesy to them, that they shall not take shame."

4. Key word / key phrase

Verse 2, "defraud a man of his home."

5. Key event / key person / key theme

The corruption and greed of the rich

6. Key thought

Note the timelessness of Micah's message. These conditions still prevail in the world today.

7. Key thing to look out for

The message of false prophets and false teachers often sounds very plausible.

8. Key Bible cross-reference

Verse 1. See Isaiah 29:20.

9. Key "by way of explanation"

Verse 2, "They covet fields and seize them." They not only buy up land which came on the open market but they stole fields that belonged to poor families who could not stop them.

10. Key "Quotable Quote"

"Any religion that professes to be concerned with the souls of men and is not concerned with the slums that damn them, the economic conditions that strangle them, and the social conditions that cripple them, is a dry-as-dust religion."

Martin Luther King, Jr.

Micah chapter 3

1. *Before and after*

Previous chapter: Chapter 2: People who exploit the poor will be punished
Following chapter: Chapter 4: The Lord's future reign, and the return from exile

2. *Analysis of chapter*

The cruelty of the princes. The false prophets. (1-8)
Their false security. (9-12)

3. *Key verse*

Verse 8: "But truly I am full of power by the spirit of the LORD, and of judgment, and of might, to declare unto Jacob his transgression, and to Israel his sin."

4. *Key word / key phrase*

Verse 3, "Listen, you leaders of Jacob."

5. *Key event / key person / key theme*

The leaders are judged.

6. *Key thought*

Verse 8, a description of a genuine spiritual leader

7. *Key thing to look out for*

Verse 4. Jesus also warned that some people may cry out to the Lord and be turned away (Matthew 7:21).

8. *Key Bible cross-reference*

Verse 12. See Jeremiah 26:18.

9. *Key "by way of explanation"*

Verse 3, "who eat my people's flesh." These leaders live in such an evil way that they are no better than cannibals. This is not meant to be taken literally but as a description of their dreadful behavior.

10. *Key "Quotable Quote"*

"True greatness, true leadership, is achieved not by reducing men to one's service but in giving oneself in selfless service to them."
Oswald Sanders

Micah chapter 4

1. Before and after

Previous chapter: Chapter 3: The leaders are judged
Following chapter: Chapter 5: The promise about the coming King

2. Analysis of chapter

The peace of the kingdom of Christ. (1-8)
The judgments to come on Jerusalem, but the final triumph of God's people.
(9-13)

3. Key verse

Verse 5: "For all people will walk every one in the name of his god, and we will
walk in the name of the LORD our God for ever and ever."

4. Key word / key phrase

Verse 6, "I will assemble the exiles."

5. Key event / key person / key theme

The Lord's future reign, and the return from exile

6. Key thought

God always has a positive plan, no matter how desperate the situation.

7. Key thing to look out for

God always wants to bless his people.

8. Key Bible cross-reference

Verse 3. See Joel 3:10.

9. Key "by way of explanation"

Verses 1,2, "let us go up to the mountain of the Lord. . . . He will teach us."
Jerusalem would become the pre-eminent place where people would be
taught about God's revelation.

10. Key "Quotable Quote"

"I was more convinced than ever that preaching like an Apostle, without
joining together those that are awakened and training them up in the ways of
God, is only begetting children for the murderer."
John Wesley

Micah chapter 5

1. Before and after

Previous chapter: Chapter 4: The Lord's future reign, and the return from exile

Following chapter: Chapter 6: The Lord pleads for repentance

2. Analysis of chapter

The birth of Christ and conversion of the Gentiles. (1-6)

Deliverance of the remnant and destruction of idolatry. (7-15)

3. Key verse

Verse 2: "But thou, Bethlehem Ephratah, though thou be little among the thousands of Judah, yet out of thee shall he come forth unto me that is to be ruler in Israel; whose goings forth have been from of old, from everlasting."

4. Key word / key phrase

Verse 5, "he will be their peace."

5. Key event / key person / key theme

The promise about the coming King

6. Key thought

Bethlehem was only a small town, but important because it was chosen by God.

7. Key thing to look out for

Deliverance and destruction are both attributed to God's power.

8. Key Bible cross-reference

Verse 2. See Matthew 2:6.

9. Key "by way of explanation"

Verse 3, "abandoned until . . . she . . . gives birth." Israel will be handed over to her enemies, but only temporarily. When the Messiah is born; God's family will be reunited.

10. Key "Quotable Quote"

"Bethlehem and Golgotha, the Manger and the Cross, the birth and the death, must always be seen together, if the real Christmas is to survive."
J. Sidlow Baxter

Micah chapter 6

1. Before and after

Previous chapter: Chapter 5: The promise about the coming King
Following chapter: Chapter 7: The promise of final salvation

2. Analysis of chapter

God's controversy with Israel. (1-5)
The duties God requires. (6-8)
The wickedness of Israel. (9-16)

3. Key verse

Verse 8: "He hath showed thee, O man, what is good; and what doth the LORD require of thee, but to do justly, and to love mercy, and to walk humbly with thy God?"

4. Key word / key phrase

Verse 8, "what does the Lord require of you?"

5. Key event / key person / key theme

The Lord pleads for repentance

6. Key thought

Verse 8 sums up how all God's followers should live.

7. Key thing to look out for

Being unfaithful to God is a most fearful prospect.

8. Key Bible cross-reference

Verse 4. See Exodus 4:10-16.

9. Key "by way of explanation"

Verse 5, "Balaam," had been asked to curse Balak's enemies but he blessed them three times.

10. Key "Quotable Quote"

"You will never make yourself feel that you are a sinner, because there is a mechanism in you as a result of sin which will always be defending you against every accusation. We are all on very good terms with ourselves, and we can always put up a good case for ourselves even if we try to make ourselves feel that we are sinners; we will never do it. There is only one way to know that we are sinners, and that is to have some dim, glimmering conception of God."
D. Martyn Lloyd-Jones

Micah chapter 7

1. **Previous chapter**

   Chapter 6: The Lord pleads for repentance

2. **Analysis of chapter**

   The general prevalence of wickedness. (1-7)
   Reliance on God, and triumph over enemies. (8-13)
   Promises and encouragements for Israel. (14-20)

3. **Key verse**

   Verse 7: "Therefore I will look unto the LORD; I will wait for the God of my salvation: my God will hear me."

4. **Key word / key phrase**

   Verse 18, "who pardons sin."

5. **Key event / key person / key theme**

   The promise of final salvation

6. **Key thought**

   Micah thanked God for his past mercies.

7. **Key thing to look out for**

   Micah's prayer shows how much he appreciated all that God had done.

8. **Key Bible cross-reference**

   Verse 6. See Luke 12:53.

9. **Key "by way of explanation"**

   Verse 8, "Though I have fallen." This is Micah looking forward to the future even though he writes as if the event, the destruction of Jerusalem in 586 BC, had already taken place.

10. **Key "Quotable Quote"**

    "If any one would tell you the shortest, surest way to all happiness and all perfection, he must tell you to make it a rule to yourself to thank and praise God for everything that happens to you."
    William Law

Nahum chapter 1

1. **Following chapter**

   Chapter 2: Nineveh's destruction described

2. **Analysis of chapter**

   The justice and power of the Lord. (1-8)
   The overthrow of the Assyrians. (9-15)

3. **Key verse**

   Verse 2: "God is jealous, and the LORD revengeth; the LORD revengeth, and is furious; the LORD will take vengeance on his adversaries, and he reserveth wrath for his enemies."

4. **Key word / key phrase**

   Verse 2, "The Lord is jealous."

5. **Key event / key person / key theme**

   A portrait of God

6. **Key thought**

   If we did not sin we would not have to be confronted with God's righteous reaction to it.

7. **Key thing to look out for**

   Verse 7 deserves to be meditated upon.

8. **Key Bible cross-reference**

   Verse 15. See Isaiah 52:7.

9. **Key "by way of explanation"**

   Verse 13, "I will break their yoke." Judah was ruled by Assyria. But this is a promise that in the future the Assyrian yoke around Judah's neck will be broken and Judah will be free. Nineveh fell to Babylon in 612 BC. Thebes, described as already conquered (3:10) was taken in 663. Therefore, it is probable that Nahum gave his prophecy between these two dates.

10. **Key "Quotable Quote"**

    "It is only the doctrine of the wrath of God, of his irreconcilable hostility to all evil, which makes human life tolerable in such a world as ours."
    Stephen Neill

Nahum chapter 2

1. *Before and after*

Previous chapter: Chapter 1: A portrait of God
Following chapter: Chapter 3: Nineveh's destruction is deserved

2. *Analysis of chapter*

Nineveh's destruction foretold. (1-10)
The real reason, their sinning against God, and his appearing against them. (11-13)

3. *Key verse*

Verse 6: "The gates of the rivers shall be opened, and the palace shall be dissolved."

4. *Key word / key phrase*

Verse 1, "An attacker advances against you, Nineveh."

5. *Key event / key person / key theme*

Nineveh's destruction described

6. *Key thought*

God's enemies are no match for God's power.

7. *Key thing to look out for*

Spiritual renewal is a gift from God.

8. *Key Bible cross-reference*

Verse 1. See Jeremiah 51:20.

9. *Key "by way of explanation"*

Verse 13, "I will burn up." The prophecy states that Nineveh's fall will not simply be due to weapons of war but because the Lord God himself has stepped in.

10. *Key "Quotable Quote"*

"I believe, that, being fallen in Adam, my first father, I am by nature a child of wrath, under the condemnation of God and corrupted in body and soul, prone to evil and liable to eternal death."
Benjamin B. Warfield

Nahum chapter 3

1. **Previous chapter**

   Chapter 2: Nineveh's destruction described

2. **Analysis of chapter**

   The sins and judgments of Nineveh. (1-7)
   Its utter destruction. (8-19)

3. **Key verse**

   Verse 1: "Woe to the bloody city! it is all full of lies and robbery; the prey departeth not."

4. **Key word / key phrase**

   Verse 5, "I am against you."

5. **Key event / key person / key theme**

   Nineveh's destruction is deserved

6. **Key thought**

   God makes no mistakes in his judgments.

7. **Key thing to look out for**

   Evil will not win.

8. **Key Bible cross-reference**

   Verse 1. See Ezekiel 22:2.

9. **Key "by way of explanation"**

   Verse 19, "your injury is fatal." Nineveh will be so overrun that she could not be rebuilt. A few centuries after this prophecy, all that was left of Nineveh was under wind-blown sand.

10. **Key "Quotable Quote"**

    "No sin, but the sin of final impenitence, can prove a man reprobate."
    John Bunyan

Habakkuk chapter 1

1. **Following chapter**

   Chapter 2: God's hatred of injustice

2. **Analysis of chapter**

   Habakkuk's first problem: why does God allow injustice? (1-4)
   God's reply: punishment will come at the hand of the Babylonians. (5-11)
   Habakkuk's response: How can a holy God possibly use Babylon? (12–2:1)

3. **Key verse**

   Verse 1: "The burden which Habakkuk the prophet did see."

4. **Key word / key phrase**

   Verse 2, "How long, O Lord, must I call for help?"

5. **Key event / key person / key theme**

   God's apparent inaction in the face of wrongdoing
   What

6. **Key thought**

   Whatever the problem or difficulty the way through is to keep on telling God
   exactly and truthfully how we feel.

7. **Key thing to look out for**

   Why did Habakkuk feel that God was not listening to him? See verse 2.

8. **Key Bible cross-reference**

   Verse 5. See Acts 13:41.

9. **Key "by way of explanation"**

   Habakkuk was a contemporary of Jeremiah. He lived and preached in Judah.
   His book takes the form of a dialogue between God and his prophet.

10. **Key "Quotable Quote"**

    "Though Satan instills his poison, and fans the flames of our corrupt desires
    within us, we are yet not carried by any external force to the commission of
    sin, but our own flesh entices us, and we willingly yield to its allurements."
    John Calvin

Habakkuk chapter 2

1. Before and after

Previous chapter: Chapter 1: Habakkuk's complaints
Following chapter: Chapter 3: Habakkuk's prayer

2. Analysis of chapter

God's second answer, judgment will come on the Babylonians. (2-20)

3. Key verse

Verse 4: "Behold, his soul which is lifted up is not upright in him: but the just shall live by his faith."

4. Key word / key phrase

Verse 9, "unjust gain."

5. Key event / key person / key theme

God's hatred of injustice

6. Key thought

Verse 4, "Faith," that is faithfulness. In contrast to the works of the wicked, the righteous exercise trust in their great God.

7. Key thing to look out for

Note the importance of silent worship, verse 20.

8. Key Bible cross-reference

Verses 3,4. See Hebrews 10:37,38. See also Romans 1:17; Galatians 3:11.

9. Key "by way of explanation"

Verse 9, "nest on high." The Babylonians thought that their military power was as mighty as the swooping eagle who built her nest where no one could reach.

10. Key "Quotable Quote"

"God's spiritual 'law of gravity' humbles the high and exalts the low."
Anne Graham Lotz

Habakkuk chapter 3

1. **Previous chapter**

   Chapter 2: God's hatred of injustice

2. **Analysis of chapter**

   The prophet beseeches God for his people. (1,2)
   He calls to mind previous deliverances. (3-15)
   His firm trust in God's mercy. (16-19)

3. **Key verse**

   Verse 4: "And his brightness was as the light; he had horns coming out of his hand: and there was the hiding of his power."

4. **Key word / key phrase**

   Verse 2, "I stand in awe of your deeds."

5. **Key event / key person / key theme**

   Habakkuk's prayer

6. **Key thought**

   The world around us reflects the glory of God.

7. **Key thing to look out for**

   After all his complaints Habakkuk ends up by praising God for his power and righteous judgments, and affirming his trust in God, come what may.

8. **Key Bible cross-reference**

   Verse 19. See 2 Samuel 22:34.

9. **Key "by way of explanation"**

   Verse 5, "plague went before him." God often used plagues and pestilence as a form of punishment on those who rejected him.

10. **Key "Quotable Quote"**

    "When my attitudes and actions become marked by pride, it's usually been much too long since I've repented and experienced the key discipline of mourning."
    Gary Thomas

Zephaniah chapter 1

1. *Following chapter*

    Chapter 2: Oracles against the nations

2. *Analysis of chapter*

    Warnings against sinners. (1-6)
    More warnings. (7-13)
    Fear of the approaching judgments. (14-18)

3. *Key verse*

    Verse 1: "The word of the LORD which came unto Zephaniah the son of Cushi,
    the son of Gedaliah, the son of Amariah, the son of Hizkiah, in the days of
    Josiah the son of Amon, king of Judah."

4. *Key word / key phrase*

    Verse 4, "I will stretch out my hand against Judah."

5. *Key event / key person / key theme*

    Judah is judged

6. *Key thought*

    Beware of complacency, see verse 12.

7. *Key thing to look out for*

    God visits, either to judge or to bless.

8. *Key Bible cross-reference*

    Verse 1. See 2 Kings 22:1–23:30.

9. *Key "by way of explanation"*

    Zephaniah was a contemporary of Jeremiah, Nahum, and Habbakuk. He
    lived in Jerusalem and his prophecy was probably given early in Josiah's reign,
    before Josiah's reforms.

10. *Key "Quotable Quote"*

    "If a man is called to be a street sweeper, he should sweep streets even as
    Michelangelo painted, or Beethoven played music, or Shakespeare wrote
    poetry."
    Martin Luther King, Jr.

Zephaniah chapter 2

1. *Before and after*

Previous chapter: Chapter 1: Judah is judged
Following chapter: Chapter 3: Salvation on the Day of the Lord

2. *Analysis of chapter*

An exhortation to repent. (1-3)
Judgments on other nations. (4-15)

3. *Key verse*

Verse 3: "Seek ye the LORD, all ye meek of the earth, which have wrought his judgment; seek righteousness, seek meekness: it may be ye shall be hid in the day of the LORD'S anger."

4. *Key word / key phrase*

Verse 8, "the insults of Moab."

5. *Key event / key person / key theme*

Oracles against the nations

6. *Key thought*

If people will not listen to God he will eliminate them.

7. *Key thing to look out for*

God always tells people how they should serve him, see verse 3.

8. *Key Bible cross-reference*

Verses 4-7. See Isaiah 14:29-31.

9. *Key "by way of explanation"*

Verse 9, "like Sodom . . . Gomorrah." The destruction of the cities of Sodom and Gomorrah was also remembered as an instance of the way God dealt with evil people.

10. *Key "Quotable Quote"*

"Before God can deliver us we must undeceive ourselves."
Augustine of Hippo

Zephaniah chapter 3

1. **Previous chapter**

   Chapter 2: Oracles against the nations

2. **Analysis of chapter**

   Further reproofs for sin. (1-7)
   Encouragement to look for mercy. (8-13)
   Promises of future favor and prosperity. (14-20)

3. **Key verse**

   Verse 6: "I have cut off the nations: their towers are desolate; I made their streets waste, that none passeth by: their cities are destroyed, so that there is no man, that there is none inhabitant."

4. **Key word / key phrase**

   Verse 14, "Sing, O Daughter of Zion."

5. **Key event / key person / key theme**

   Salvation on the Day of the Lord

6. **Key thought**

   Blessed are the meek. See verse 12.

7. **Key thing to look out for**

   God promises to restore his people.

8. **Key Bible cross-reference**

   Verse 13. See Revelation 14:5.

9. **Key "by way of explanation"**

   Verse 14, "Sing . . . with all your heart." In Hebrew thinking the "heart" was the center of a person, especially his intellect. Unlike the unthinking worshipers of Baal, God's followers were to use their minds as they worshiped.

10. **Key "Quotable Quote"**

   "God hears no more than the heart speaks; and if the heart be dumb, God will certainly be deaf."
   Thomas Brooks

Haggai chapter 1

1. **Following chapter**

   Chapter 2: Looking to the future

2. **Analysis of chapter**

   Haggai's first message: he reproves the Jews for neglecting the temple. (1-11)
   He promises them God's assistance. (12-15)

3. **Key verse**

   Verse 1: "In the second year of Darius the king, in the sixth month, in the first
   day of the month, came the word of the LORD by Haggai the prophet unto
   Zerubbabel the son of Shealtiel, governor of Judah, and to Joshua the son of
   Josedech, the high priest."

4. **Key word / key phrase**

   Verse 8, "build the house."

5. **Key event / key person / key theme**

   A call to build the house of the Lord

6. **Key thought**

   What personal activities do we substitute for getting on with the Lord's work?

7. **Key thing to look out for**

   God's presence is promised to all who serve him.

8. **Key Bible cross-reference**

   Verse 1. See Ezra 4:24–5:2.

9. **Key "by way of explanation"**

   Haggai's four messages were given over a four-month period in 520 BC,
   seventeen years after the first group of exiles, led by Zerubbabel, had returned
   to Jerusalem, and started rebuilding the temple. After two years, in the face of
   severe opposition the work had stopped but when Darius the Great became
   Emperor in 522, he encouraged the rebuilding and gave generous financial
   support. Ezra 4:5; 4:24–5:2; 6:14 give this historical background.

10. **Key "Quotable Quote"**

    "The false and the genuine prophet will be known by their ways. If a prophet
    teaches the truth but does not practice what he teaches, he is a false prophet."
    Didache

Haggai chapter 2

1. *Previous chapter*

    Chapter 2: A call to build the house of the Lord

2. *Analysis of chapter*

    Second message: an encouragement to work. (1-5)
    Greater glory promised for the second temple than for the first. (6-9)
    Third message: sins hindered the work. (10-19)
    Fourth message: promise to Zerubbabel. (20-23)

3. *Key verse*

    Verse 9: "The glory of this latter house shall be greater than of the former, saith the LORD of hosts: and in this place will I give peace, saith the LORD of hosts."

4. *Key word / key phrase*

    Verse 23, "On that day."

5. *Key event / key person / key theme*

    The kingdom of Christ foretold (20-23)

6. *Key thought*

    God's Spirit is meant to be always with God's people.

7. *Key thing to look out for*

    God's glory is meant to be the abiding concern of God's people.

8. *Key Bible cross-reference*

    Verse 6. See Hebrews 12:26.

9. *Key "by way of explanation"*

    Verse 8, "The silver is mine and the gold is mine." All the silver and gold used in the construction of the temple belonged to the Lord.

10. *Key "Quotable Quote"*

    "Numerous passages of Scripture assert that the manifestation of the glory of God is the great end of creation, that he has himself chiefly in view in all his works and dispensations, and that it is a purpose in which he requires that all his intelligent creatures should acquiesce, and seek and promote it as their first and paramount duty."
    Robert Haldane

Zechariah chapter 1

1. **Following chapter**

   Chapter 2: The man with the measuring line

2. **Analysis of chapter**

   An exhortation to repent. (1-6)
   First vision: horseman among the myrtle trees. (7-17)
   Second vision: the four horns and four craftsmen. (18-21)

3. **Key verse**

   Verse 1: "In the eighth month, in the second year of Darius, came the word of the LORD unto Zechariah, the son of Berechiah, the son of Iddo the prophet."

4. **Key word / key phrase**

   Verse 8, "During the night I had a vision."

5. **Key event / key person / key theme**

   The ministry of angels, who act as interpreters (first vision); the defeat of Judah's enemies (second vision)

6. **Key thought**

   Note the results of repentance. See verse 6.

7. **Key thing to look out for**

   The prophet is happy to show his total dependence on the Lord.

8. **Key Bible cross-reference**

   Verse 8. See Revelation 6:2-8.

9. **Key "by way of explanation"**

   Verse 8, "red, brown and white horses." Horses were also seen in John's vision, see Revelation 6:1-8. Horses symbolized power and dominance. Zechariah was a priest and a contemporary of Haggai (Ezra 5:1). He continued his ministry after Haggai, perhaps because he was younger (2:4). He was born in Babylonia, and returned with the first group of exiles led by Zerubbabel.

10. **Key "Quotable Quote"**

    "Repentance ranges from regretting obvious sins like murder, adultery, abuse, swearing, and stealing to the realization that not loving (loving your brother as yourself) is a murder, and that an evil look is adultery and the love of praise is stealing God's glory."
    John Chrysostom

Zechariah chapter 2

1. ***Before and after***

    Previous chapter: Chapter 1: Two visions: the man on the red horse; the four horns

    Following chapter: Chapter 3: Joshua the priest is accused and acquitted

2. ***Analysis of chapter***

    Third vision: man with a measuring line.
    The prosperity of Jerusalem. (1-5)
    The Jews called to return to their own land. (6-9)
    A promise of God's presence. (10-13)

3. ***Key verse***

    Verse 6: "Ho, ho, come forth, and flee from the land of the north."

4. ***Key word / key phrase***

    Verse 10, "Shout and be glad, O Daughter of Zion."

5. ***Key event / key person / key theme***

    Full restoration for people, temple, and city

6. ***Key thought***

    There is nothing that God does not know about us.

7. ***Key thing to look out for***

    Verse 13 commends stillness in God's presence.

8. ***Key Bible cross-reference***

    Verse 5. See Isaiah 26:1.

9. ***Key "by way of explanation"***

    Verse 12, "the holy land." This is the only place where this phrase comes in the Bible. But also see Psalm 2:6; 15:1; 99:9. This land was the national home for God's people and given over to God.

10. ***Key "Quotable Quote"***

    "Jewish infidelity shall be overthrown. The Jews in all their dispersions shall cast away their old infidelity, and shall have their hearts wonderfully changed, and abhor themselves for their past unbelief and obstinacy."
    Jonathan Edwards

Zechariah chapter 3

1. **Before and after**

   Previous chapter: Chapter 2: The man with the measuring line
   Following chapter: Chapter 4: The golden lampstand and the olive trees

2. **Analysis of chapter**

   Fourth vision: clean clothes for the high priest
   Restoration. (1-5)
   A promise about the Messiah. (6-10)

3. **Key verse**

   Verse 7: "I will give thee places to walk among these that stand by."

4. **Key word / key phrase**

   Verse 1, "to accuse him."

5. **Key event / key person / key theme**

   Joshua the priest is accused and acquitted

6. **Key thought**

   Verse 4 should fill us with wonder and gratitude.

7. **Key thing to look out for**

   God requires us to serve him in certain specific ways.

8. **Key Bible cross-reference**

   Verse 2. See Jude 9.

9. **Key "by way of explanation"**

   Verse 3, "filthy clothes." Joshua's clothes were like those someone wore who
   had escaped from a fire. The clothes symbolized the sins of the people and so
   needed to be exchanged for "rich garments."

10. **Key "Quotable Quote"**

    "Purity is 'that which is undiluted by other substances.' Now, join that to the
    place Jesus pointed at, to the heart of a man: that's where God seeks undiluted
    commitment."
    Jack Hayford

Zechariah chapter 4

1. Before and after

Previous chapter: Chapter 3: Joshua the priest is accused and acquitted
Following chapter: Chapter 5: The flying scroll, and the woman in the basket

2. Analysis of chapter

Fifth vision: gold lampstand, with two olive trees. (1-7)
Further encouragement. (8-10)
An explanation about the olive trees. (11-14)

3. Key verse

Verse 2: "And said unto me, What seest thou? And I said, I have looked, and behold a candlestick all of gold."

4. Key word / key phrase

Verse 2, "a solid gold lampstand."

5. Key event / key person / key theme

The temple would not be built through shear labor, or by human power and ability, but by the Spirit.

6. Key thought

There is no light without oil. There is not spiritual light without God's Spirit.

7. Key thing to look out for

The only way to serve the Lord successfully is summarized in verse 6.

8. Key Bible cross-reference

Verse 3. See Revelation 11:4.

9. Key "by way of explanation"

Verse 2, the bowl will have contained oil for the lamps; seven symbolizes perfection of light. The two olive trees are the two lines of leadership, the priestly line and the royal line. The lampstand represents the testimony of the people of God. The oil is God's power and God's anointing.

10. Key "Quotable Quote"

"All of us who have received one and the same Spirit, that is, the Holy Spirit, are in a sense blended together with one another and with God."
Cyril of Alexandria

Zechariah chapter 5

1. **Before and after**

   Previous chapter: Chapter 4: The golden lampstand and the olive trees
   Following chapter: Chapter 6: The vision of the four chariots

2. **Analysis of chapter**

   Sixth vision: the flying scroll. (1-4)
   Seventh vision: a woman in a basket. (5-11)

3. **Key verse**

   Verse 1: "Then I turned, and lifted up mine eyes, and looked, and behold a flying roll."

4. **Key word / key phrase**

   Verse 1, "a flying scroll."

5. **Key event / key person / key theme**

   Three evils which need to be dealt with: theft, false witness, unrighteousness

6. **Key thought**

   God is constantly giving us warnings to heed.

7. **Key thing to look out for**

   When we clearly see what we must do we still need to rely on God for his help.

8. **Key Bible cross-reference**

   Verse 11. See Genesis 10:10.

9. **Key "by way of explanation"**

   Verse 1, "a flying scroll." This could be read by everyone and depicts the renewed interest in the law in the days after the Exile.

10. **Key "Quotable Quote"**

   "God's truth judges created things out of love, and Satan's truth judges them out of envy and hatred."
   Dietrich Bonhoeffer

Zechariah chapter 6

1. *Before and after*

Previous chapter: Chapter 5: The flying scroll, and the woman in the basket
Following chapter: Chapter 7: A call to repentance

2. *Analysis of chapter*

Eighth vision: the four chariots. (1-8)
Joshua, the high priest, crowned as a type of Christ. (9-15)

3. *Key verse*

Verse 1: "And I turned, and lifted up mine eyes, and looked, and, behold, there came four chariots out from between two mountains; and the mountains were mountains of brass."

4. *Key word / key phrase*

Verse 1, "four chariots."

5. *Key event / key person / key theme*

The angelic spirits are the symbols and agents of God's judgment

6. *Key thought*

God's presence among his people is symbolized by the temple.

7. *Key thing to look out for*

God longs to rule in our hearts.

8. *Key Bible cross-reference*

Verse 5. See Revelation 7:1.

9. *Key "by way of explanation"*

Verse 11, "crown." This special crowning of the high priest looks forward to the time when all prophecy will be consummated in the rule of the messianic Priest-King.

10. *Key "Quotable Quote"*

"That book [Bible], sir, is the rock on which our republic rests."
Andrew Jackson

Zechariah chapter 7

1. *Before and after*

Previous chapter: Chapter 6: The vision of the four chariots
Following chapter: Chapter 8: Jerusalem's wonderful future

2. *Analysis of chapter*

The captives' inquiry about fasting. (1-7)
Sin is the reason for their captivity. (8-14)

3. *Key verse*

Verse 9: "Execute true judgment, and show mercy and compassions every man to his brother."

4. *Key word / key phrase*

Verse 13, "When I called."

5. *Key event / key person / key theme*

A call to repentance

6. *Key thought*

Verse 13 is a picture of the basis of all sin.

7. *Key thing to look out for*

Over and over again the prophets emphasize the need for social justice. See verses 9,10.

8. *Key Bible cross-reference*

Verse 1. See Ezra 5:1.

9. *Key "by way of explanation"*

Verse 9, "justice." This is proper ordering of every society. See 8:16; Isaiah 42:1,4; Micah 6:8.

10. *Key "Quotable Quote"*

"The Christian's goal is not power but justice. We are to seek to make the institutions of power just, without being corrupted by the process necessary to do this."
Charles Colson

Zechariah chapter 8

1. *Before and after*

Previous chapter: Chapter 7: A call to repentance
Following chapter: Chapter 9: Judgment on the surrounding nations, and the Messiah-King

2. *Analysis of chapter*

The restoration of Jerusalem. (1-8)
The people encouraged by promises of God's favor, and exhorted to holiness. (9-17)
The Jews in the latter days. (18-23)

3. *Key verse*

Verse 8: "And I will bring them, and they shall dwell in the midst of Jerusalem: and they shall be my people, and I will be their God, in truth and in righteousness."

4. *Key word / key phrase*

Verse 3, "I will . . . dwell in Jerusalem."

5. *Key event / key person / key theme*

Jerusalem's wonderful future

6. *Key thought*

The greatest blessing we can receive from the Lord is his presence.

7. *Key thing to look out for*

This chapter has ten promises, each beginning, "The LORD Almighty says."

8. *Key Bible cross-reference*

Verse 16. See Ephesians 4:25.

9. *Key "by way of explanation"*

Verse 2, "jealous." The Hebrew word indicates very strong feelings. An alternative translation might be, "with great zeal."

10. *Key "Quotable Quote"*

"The main hinge on which faith turns is this: we must not imagine that the Lord's promises are true objectively but not in our experience. We must make them ours by embracing them in our hearts."
John Calvin

Zechariah chapter 9

1. Before and after

Previous chapter: Chapter 8: Jerusalem's wonderful future
Following chapter: Chapter 10: The Lord promises deliverance

2. Analysis of chapter

God's defense of his people. (1-8)
Christ's coming and his kingdom. (9-11)
Promises to God's people. (12-17)

3. Key verse

Verse 9: "Rejoice greatly, O daughter of Zion; shout, O daughter of Jerusalem: behold, thy King cometh unto thee: he is just, and having salvation; lowly, and riding upon an ass, and upon a colt the foal of an ass."

4. Key word / key phrase

Verse 5, "Gaza will lose her king."

5. Key event / key person / key theme

Judgment on the surrounding nations, and the Messiah-King

6. Key thought

It is not up to us to take revenge on people, God will punish them in due course.

7. Key thing to look out for

God is majestic. God is humble. See verse 9.

8. Key Bible cross-reference

Verse 10. See Psalm 72:8.

9. Key "by way of explanation"

Verse 9, "gentle and riding on a donkey." This verse is quoted in the New Testament, Matthew 21:5; John 12:15, to refer to the Messiah entering his city, that is, to Jesus entering Jerusalem on Palm Sunday. Chapters 9 to 14 consist of a series of prophecies about the end times.

10. Key "Quotable Quote"

"Our personal afflictions involve the living God; the only way in which Satan can persecute or afflict God is through attacking the people of God. The only way we can have personal victory in the midst of these flying arrows raining down on us is to call upon the Lord for help. It is his strength, supplied to us in our weakness, that makes victory after victory possible."
Edith Schaeffer

Zechariah chapter 10

1. Before and after

Previous chapter: Chapter 9: Judgment on the surrounding nations, and the Messiah-King

Following chapter: Chapter 11: The good shepherd and the bad shepherds

2. Analysis of chapter

Blessings to be sought from the Lord. (1-5)

God will restore his people. (6-12)

3. Key verse

Verse 6: "And I will strengthen the house of Judah, and I will save the house of Joseph, and I will bring them again to place them; for I have mercy upon them: and they shall be as though I had not cast them off: for I am the LORD their God, and will hear them."

4. Key word / key phrase

Verse 6, "I will strengthen the house of Judah."

5. Key event / key person / key theme

The Lord promises deliverance

6. Key thought

Jesus echoed verse 2 in Mark 6:34 where also showed his compassion for people needing spiritual care.

7. Key thing to look out for

Only God can redeem people. See verse 8.

8. Key Bible cross-reference

Verse 1. See Leviticus 26:4.

9. Key "by way of explanation"

Verse 8, "redeem." This Hebrew word refers to rescuing people from slavery or leading them out of captivity. See Isaiah 35:10; 1 Peter 1:18,19.

10. Key "Quotable Quote"

"When a man undergoes treatment from a doctor, he does not need to know the way in which the drug works on his body in order to be cured. There is a sense in which Christianity is like that. At the heart of Christianity there is a mystery, but it is not the mystery of intellectual appreciation; it the mystery of redemption."

William Barclay

Zechariah chapter 11

1. **Before and after**

   Previous chapter: Chapter 10: The Lord promises deliverance
   Following chapter: Chapter 12: Jerusalem is saved, and the way of salvation

2. **Analysis of chapter**

   Destruction to come on the Jews. (1-3)
   The Lord's dealing with the Jews. (4-14)
   The emblem and curse of a foolish shepherd. (15-17)

3. **Key verse**

   Verse 10: "And I took my staff, even Beauty, and cut it asunder, that I might break my covenant which I had made with all the people."

4. **Key word / key phrase**

   Verse 4, "Pasture the flock."

5. **Key event / key person / key theme**

   The good shepherd and the bad shepherds

6. **Key thought**

   We are all pastors to the people with whom we live and work.

7. **Key thing to look out for**

   Which shepherd do we resemble?

8. **Key Bible cross-reference**

   Verse 12. See Matthew 26:15.

9. **Key "by way of explanation"**

   Verse 9, "eat one another's flesh." The siege of Jerusalem in AD 70 was so severe that the historian Josephus claims that cannibalism took place.

10. **Key "Quotable Quote"**

    "It takes some of us a lifetime to learn that Christ, our Good Shepherd, knows exactly what he is doing with us. He understands us perfectly."
    Phillip Keller

Zechariah chapter 12

1. **Before and after**

   Previous chapter: Chapter 11: The good shepherd and the bad shepherds
   Following chapter: Chapter 13: Impurity abolished, and the remnant refined

2. **Analysis of chapter**

   Punishment of the enemies of Judah. (1-8)
   Repentance and sorrow of the Jews. (9-14)

3. **Key verse**

   Verse 3: "And in that day will I make Jerusalem a burdensome stone for all
   people: all that burden themselves with it shall be cut in pieces, though all the
   people of the earth be gathered together against it."

4. **Key word / key phrase**

   Verse 2, "I am going to make Jerusalem a cup."

5. **Key event / key person / key theme**

   Jerusalem is saved, and the way of salvation

6. **Key thought**

   Verse 8 is a good verse for when we feel feeble.

7. **Key thing to look out for**

   Verse 10 speaks of God pouring out his Spirit of grace. How can we receive
   this today?

8. **Key Bible cross-reference**

   Verse 10. See John 19:37.

9. **Key "by way of explanation"**

   Verse 4, "panic . . . madness . . . blind." In Deuteronomy 28:28 these are said to
   be the afflictions God will bring down on his people. Now they will rest on
   Israel's enemies. "Cup," that is Jerusalem will be the agent of God's judgment
   (drinking strong wine is often a metaphor for the experience of God's
   judgment, e.g. Isaiah 51:17).

10. **Key "Quotable Quote"**

    "The true way to mourn the dead is to take care of the living who belong to
    them."
    Edmund Burke

Zechariah chapter 13

1. *Before and after*

     Previous chapter: Chapter 12: Jerusalem is saved, and the way of salvation
     Following chapter: Chapter 14: The Messiah's reign

2. *Analysis of chapter*

     The fountain for the remission of sins, and the conviction of the false
     prophets. (1-6)
     The death of Christ, and the saving of a remnant of the people. (7-9)

3. *Key verse*

     Verse 1: "In that day there shall be a fountain opened to the house of David
     and to the inhabitants of Jerusalem for sin and for uncleanness."

4. *Key word / key phrase*

     Verse 1, "cleanse them from sin and impurity."

5. *Key event / key person / key theme*

     Impurity abolished, and the remnant refined

6. *Key thought*

     If God disciplines us it is to make us more godly.

7. *Key thing to look out for*

     Nobody can any longer strike and scatter the Good Shepherd's flock.

8. *Key Bible cross-reference*

     Verse 7. See Mark 14:27.

9. *Key "by way of explanation"*

     Verse 7, "my shepherd." This refers to the Good Shepherd, see 11:4-14, and
     contrasts with the faithless shepherds, see 11:15-17.

10. *Key "Quotable Quote"*

     "Our speech, our thoughts, our actions, our reactions, our relationships, our
     goals, our values – all are transformed if only we live in the self-conscious
     enjoyment of the love of Christ."
     D.A. Carson

Zechariah chapter 14

1. **Previous chapter**

   Chapter 13: Impurity abolished, and the remnant refined

2. **Analysis of chapter**

   The sufferings of Jerusalem. (1-7)
   Encouraging prospects, and the destruction of her enemies. (8-15)
   The holiness of the latter days. (16-21)

3. **Key verse**

   Verse 3: "Then shall the LORD go forth, and fight against those nations, as when he fought in the day of battle."

4. **Key word / key phrase**

   Verse 10, "Jerusalem will be raised up and remain in its place."

5. **Key event / key person / key theme**

   The Messiah's reign

6. **Key thought**

   Every day should be a holy day.

7. **Key thing to look out for**

   Everything we do should be done to the glory of our holy God.

8. **Key Bible cross-reference**

   Verse 8. See John 7:38.

9. **Key "by way of explanation"**

   Verse 20, "HOLY TO THE LORD." This inscription was engraved on a gold plate and worn on the turban of the high priest, see Exodus 28:36-38.

10. **Key "Quotable Quote"**

    "Sever me from myself
       that I may be grateful to you;
    may I perish to myself
       that I may be safe in you;
    may I die to myself
       that I may live in you;
    may I wither to myself
       that I may blossom in you;
    may I be emptied of myself
       that I may abound in you;
    may I be nothing to myself
       that I may be all in you."
    Desiderius Erasmus

Malachi chapter 1

1. *Following chapter*

Chapter 2: Israel's faithlessness in worship and marriage

2. *Analysis of chapter*

The ingratitude of Israel. (1-5)
They are careless about God's institutions. (6-14)

3. *Key verse*

Verse 1: "The burden of the word of the LORD to Israel by Malachi."

4. *Key word / key phrase*

Verse 2, "I have loved you."

5. *Key event / key person / key theme*

God loves Israel, but indicts the priests

6. *Key thought*

So often, God's leaders seem to be unfaithful to God.

7. *Key thing to look out for*

The existence of God's people is founded on God's love.

8. *Key Bible cross-reference*

Verses 2-3. See Romans 9:13.

9. *Key "by way of explanation"*

Verse 3, "Esau I have hated." This does not mean that God literally "hated" Esau. Rather it contrasts God's great love for Jacob, in comparison with which it might be said that he hated Esau. Malachi was probably a contemporary of Nehemiah. The book may have been written about 433 BC when Nehemiah returned to Persia, after the city walls has been rebuilt.

10. *Key "Quotable Quote"*

"The love which brought the Son of God's love from heaven to earth, from earth to the cross, from the cross to the grave, from the grave to glory – that love which was weary, hungry, tempted, scorned, scourged, buffeted, spat upon, crucified, pierced – which fasted, prayed, taught, healed, wept, sweated, bled, died, that love will eternally embrace you."
Richard Baxter

Malachi chapter 2

1. Before and after

Previous chapter: Chapter 1: God loves Israel, but indicts the priests
Following chapter: Chapter 3: Robbing God, tithing and God's blessing

2. Analysis of chapter

The priests reproved for neglecting the covenant. (1-9)
The people reproved for their evil practices. (10-17)

3. Key verse

Verse 6: "The law of truth was in his mouth, and iniquity was not found in his lips: he walked with me in peace and equity, and did turn many away from iniquity."

4. Key word / key phrase

Verse 1, "this abomination is for you, O priests."

5. Key event / key person / key theme

Israel's (that is, all the Jews who had returned from exile) faithlessness in worship and marriage

6. Key thought

Not listening to God seems to be the first step we take in falling away from God.

7. Key thing to look out for

There can be no excuse for deliberately breaking God's laws.

8. Key Bible cross-reference

Verse 4. See Numbers 3:11-13.

9. Key "by way of explanation"

Verse 5, "a covenant of life and peace." This is the only occurrence of this phrase in the Bible. To enter into a covenant relationship with God is the beginning of spiritual life and this leads to peace and health and salvation.

10. Key "Quotable Quote"

"When everything we receive from him is received and prized as a pledge of his covenant love, then his bounties, instead of being set up as rivals and idols to draw our heart from him, awaken us to fresh exercises of gratitude and furnish us with fresh motives of cheerful obedience every hour."
John Newton

Malachi chapter 3

1. *Before and after*

Previous chapter: Chapter 2: Israel's faithlessness in worship and marriage
Following chapter: Chapter 4: The Day of the Lord, and the coming of Elijah

2. *Analysis of chapter*

The coming of God's messenger. (1-5)
The Jews reproved for their corruptions. (6-12)
God's care of his people. The distinction between the righteous and the wicked. (13-18)

3. *Key verse*

Verse 1: "Behold, I will send my messenger, and he shall prepare the way before me: and the Lord, whom ye seek, shall suddenly come to his temple, even the messenger of the covenant, whom ye delight in: behold, he shall come, saith the LORD of hosts."

4. *Key word / key phrase*

Verse 8, "Will a man rob God?"

5. *Key event / key person / key theme*

Robbing God, tithing and God's blessing

6. *Key thought*

Everything belongs to God. We own nothing. At best, we are tenants.

7. *Key thing to look out for*

Trusting our finances to the Lord seems to be about the last thing we ever do.

8. *Key Bible cross-reference*

Verse 1. See Matthew 11:10.

9. *Key "by way of explanation"*

Verses 1-5, the messenger is a future prophet who will make the people ready for the Day of the Lord. This prophecy was fulfilled when John the Baptist started preaching (see also 4:5-6).

10. *Key "Quotable Quote"*

"May I be patient! It is so difficult to make real what one believes, and to make these trials, as they are intended, real blessings."
John Henry Newman

Malachi chapter 4

1. **Previous chapter**

   Chapter 3: Robbing God, tithing and God's blessing

2. **Analysis of chapter**

   The judgments on the wicked, and the happiness of the righteous. (1-3)
   Regard for the Law. John the Baptist promised as the Messiah's forerunner. (4-6)

3. **Key verse**

   Verse 5: "Behold, I will send you Elijah the prophet before the coming of the great and dreadful day of the LORD."

4. **Key word / key phrase**

   Verse 5, "I will send you the prophet Elijah."

5. **Key event / key person / key theme**

   The Day of the Lord, and the coming of Elijah

6. **Key thought**

   Any visitation from the Lord is characterized by joy.

7. **Key thing to look out for**

   We seek no new message, but just follow the old one of repentance.

8. **Key Bible cross-reference**

   Verse 5. See Matthew 11:14; 17:10-13.

9. **Key "by way of explanation"**

   Verse 5, "Elijah." Malachi concludes his prophecy by looking forward to a future prophet who will have a ministry similar to the prophet Elijah and call people back to God in repentance.

10. **Key "Quotable Quote"**

    "He shows himself worthy, in that he confesses himself unworthy."
    Augustine of Hippo

THE NEW TESTAMENT

Matthew

Matthew chapter 1

1. **Following chapter**

   Chapter 2: Jesus' infancy

2. **Analysis of chapter**

   The genealogy of Jesus. (1-17)
   An angel appears to Joseph. (18-25)

3. **Key verse**

   Verse 1: "A record of the genealogy of Jesus Christ the son of David, the son of Abraham."

4. **Key word / key phrase**

   Verse 1, "the genealogy of Jesus Christ."

5. **Key event / key person / key theme**

   Jesus' family tree

6. **Key thought**

   God planned our salvation a long time ago.

7. **Key thing to look out for**

   Jesus' birth was natural and supernatural.

8. **Key Bible cross-reference**

   Verse 23. See Isaiah 7:14.

9. **Key "by way of explanation"**

   Verse 18, "pledged to be married." Betrothal was much more binding than our modern engagements and if broken required a legal divorce settlement.

10. **Key "Quotable Quote"**

    "Immanuel, God with us in our nature, in our sorrow, in our lifework, in our punishment, in our grave, and now with us, or rather we with him, in resurrection, ascension, triumph, and second Advent splendor."
    C.H. Spurgeon

Matthew chapter 2

1. Before and after

Previous chapter: 1: Jesus' family tree and birth
Following chapter: 3: John the Baptist and the baptism of Jesus

2. Analysis of chapter

The wise men's search for Christ. (1-8)
The wise men worship Jesus. (9-12)
Jesus taken to Egypt. (13-15)
Herod's massacre of the infants of Bethlehem. (16-18)
Death of Herod, Jesus taken to Nazareth. (19-23)

3. Key verse

Verse 3: "When King Herod heard this he was disturbed, and all Jerusalem with him."

4. Key word / key phrase

Verse 1: "Jesus was born."

5. Key event / key person / key theme

Jesus' infancy

6. Key thought

King Herod epitomizes the evil people who have always been seeking to destroy Christianity.

7. Key thing to look out for

The number of times Matthew refers to the fulfillment of prophesy.

8. Key Bible cross-reference

Verse 6. See Micah 5:2.

9. Key "by way of explanation"

Verse 11, "house." By the time the Magi visited Jesus, Mary and Joseph had managed for find better accommodation.

10. Key "Quotable Quote"

"The Word was made man in order that we might be made divine."
Athanasius

Matthew chapter 3

1. *Before and after*

Previous chapter: Chapter 2: Jesus' infancy
Following chapter: Chapter 4: The temptation of Jesus

2. *Analysis of chapter*

John the Baptist, his preaching, lifestyle, and baptism. (1-6)
John reproves the Pharisees and Sadducees. (7-12)
The baptism of Jesus. (13-17)

3. *Key verse*

Verse 11: "I baptize you with water for repentance. But after me will come one who is more powerful than I, whose sandals I am not fit to carry. He will baptize you with the Holy Spirit and with fire."

4. *Key word / key phrase*

Verse 1, "John the Baptist."

5. *Key event / key person / key theme*

John the Baptist and the baptism of Jesus

6. *Key thought*

John the Baptist shows courage as he challenges people to repent.

7. *Key thing to look out for*

John the Baptist shows humility in the way he relates to Jesus.

8. *Key Bible cross-reference*

Verse 3. See Isaiah 40:3.

9. *Key "by way of explanation"*

Verse 3. This verse quotes Isaiah 40:3. Matthew, Mark, and Luke all apply this verse to John the Baptist.

10. *Key "Quotable Quote"*

"The beginning of repentance proceeds from fear of God."
Boniface

Matthew chapter 4

1. *Before and after*

Previous chapter: 3: John the Baptist and the baptism of Jesus
Following chapter: 5: The Beatitudes, salt and light, and the Law

2. *Analysis of chapter*

The temptation of Christ. (1-11)
The start of Christ's ministry in Galilee. (12-17)
Call of Simon and others. (18-22)
Jesus teaches and performs miracles. (23-25)

3. *Key verse*

Verse 8: "Again, the devil took him to a very high mountain and showed him
all the kingdoms of the world and their splendor."

4. *Key word / key phrase*

Verse 17, "Repent, for the kingdom of heaven is near."

5. *Key event / key person / key theme*

The temptation of Jesus

6. *Key thought*

If Jesus was tempted we should hardly be surprised that we are.

7. *Key thing to look out for*

Jesus resisted temptation by quoting from the Old Testament.

8. *Key Bible cross-reference*

Verse 7. See Deuteronomy 6:16.

9. *Key "by way of explanation"*

Verse 3, "If you are the Son of God." The devil is not saying that Jesus was not
the Son of God, but rather, was trying to make him use his powers in a selfish
way.

10. *Key "Quotable Quote"*

"The devil tempts that he may ruin; God tests that he may crown."
St Ambrose

Matthew chapter 5

1. Before and after

Previous chapter: Chapter 4: The temptation of Jesus
Following chapter: Chapter 6: Jesus rejects pharisaical practices

2. Analysis of chapter

Christ's Sermon on the Mount. (1,2)
Who are blessed. (3-12)
Exhortations and warnings. (13-16)
Christ came to confirm the Law. (17-20)
The sixth commandment. (21-26)
The seventh commandment. (27-32)
The third commandment. (33-37)
The law of retaliation. (38-42)
The law of love explained. (43-48)

3. Key verse

Verse 5: "Blessed are the meek, for they will inherit the earth."

4. Key word / key phrase

Verse 2, "He began to teach."

5. Key event / key person / key theme

The Beatitudes

6. Key thought

The Sermon on the Mount describes the way of life of those who belong to Christ's kingdom.

7. Key thing to look out for

Ways in which Jesus brought out the true meaning (fulfilled) of the law.

8. Key Bible cross-reference

Verse 8. See Psalm 24:3,4.

9. Key "by way of explanation"

Verse 22, "Raca." This word involves speaking to someone as if you think that person is contemptible.

10. Key "Quotable Quote"

"Good morning, theologians! You wake and sing. But I, old fool, know less than you and worry over everything, instead of simply trusting in the heavenly Father's care."
Martin Luther, talking to birds

Matthew chapter 6

1. *Before and after*

Previous chapter: Chapter 5: The Beatitudes, salt and light, and the Law
Following chapter: Chapter 7: Jesus encourages true religion

2. *Analysis of chapter*

Against hypocrisy in giving money. (1-4)
Against hypocrisy in prayer. (5-8)
How to pray. (9-15)
About fasting. (16-18)
The evil of being worldly-minded. (19-24)
Trust in God commended. (25-34)

3. *Key verse*

Verse 8: "Do not be like them, for your Father knows what you need before you ask him."

4. *Key word / key phrase*

Verse 16, "hypocrites."

5. *Key event / key person / key theme*

Right motives

6. *Key thought*

A right way and a wrong way to give.

7. *Key thing to look out for*

There is no better model prayer than the Lord's Prayer.

8. *Key Bible cross-reference*

Verse 29. See 1 Kings 10:4-7.

9. *Key "by way of explanation"*

Verse 48, "be perfect." This side of heaven no one will reach perfection. But Jesus said we should still aim for perfection.

10. *Key "Quotable Quote"*

"If you say, 'It is enough. I have reached perfection,' all is lost, since it is the function of perfection to make one know one's imperfections."
Augustine of Hippo

Matthew chapter 7

1. Before and after

Previous chapter: Chapter 6: Jesus rejects pharisaical practices
Following chapter: Chapter 8: Healing miracles and the demands of discipleship

2. Analysis of chapter

Christ reproves rash judgment. (1-6)
Encouragements to prayer. (7-11)
The broad and narrow way. (12-14)
Against false prophets. (15-20)
To be doers of the word, not hearers only. (21-29)

3. Key verse

Verse 12: "So in everything, do to others what you would have them do to you, for this sums up the Law and the Prophets."

4. Key word / key phrase

Verse 15, "false prophets."

5. Key event / key person / key theme

The road that leads to life.

6. Key thought

There is no room in the Christian life for judging other people.

7. Key thing to look out for

While it is true that God searches us out this should never stop us seeking God with all our hearts.

8. Key Bible cross-reference

Verse 23. See Psalm 6:8.

9. Key "by way of explanation"

Verse 12. This verse is known as "the Golden Rule." While a negative version of it is found in Judaism, Hinduism, Buddhism and Confucianism, only Jesus said it in this positive way.

10. Key "Quotable Quote"

"We cannot be truly Christian people so long as we flaunt the central teachings of Jesus: brotherly love and the Golden Rule."
Martin Luther King, Jr.

Matthew chapter 8

1. *Before and after*

Previous chapter: Chapter 7: Jesus encourages true religion
Following chapter: Chapter 9: More miracles

2. *Analysis of chapter*

Crowds follow Christ. (1)
He heals a leper. (2-4)
A centurion's servant healed. (5-13)
Peter's wife's mother healed. (14-17)
The scribe's zealous proposal. (18-22)
Christ in a storm. (23-27)
He heals two possessed with devils. (28-34)

3. *Key verse*

Verse 1: "When he came down from the mountainside, large crowds followed him."

4. *Key word / key phrase*

Verse 3, "he was cured."

5. *Key event / key person / key theme*

Healing miracles

6. *Key thought*

Jesus demonstrated his love for people and he healed them.

7. *Key thing to look out for*

Jesus showed his power over many kinds of evil.

8. *Key Bible cross-reference*

Verse 17. See Isaiah 53:4.

9. *Key "by way of explanation"*

Verse 22, "let the dead bury their dead." Jews thought it most important that children should look after the funeral arrangements of their parents. Jesus says there is a higher loyalty than family loyalty.

10. *Key "Quotable Quote"*

"Christ does not want to win numbers but dedicated hearts."
Johann Heinrich Arnold

Matthew chapter 9

1. Before and after

Previous chapter: Chapter 8: Healing miracles and demands of discipleship
Following chapter: Chapter 10: The mission of the Twelve

2. Analysis of chapter

Jesus returns to Capernaum, and heals a paralytic. (1-8)
Matthew called. (9)
Matthew's feast. (10-13)
Objections of John's disciples. (14-17)
Christ raises the daughter of Jairus. He heals a woman with bleeding. (18-26)
He heals two blind men. (27-31)
Christ expels a dumb spirit. (32-34)
He sends out the apostles. (35-38)

3. Key verse

Verse 9: "Matthew got up and followed him."

4. Key word / key phrase

Verse 9, "Follow me."

5. Key event / key person / key theme

What God desires

6. Key thought

Matthew shows his delight in following Jesus but throwing a party.

7. Key thing to look out for

Verses 36-38, Jesus' response to the crowds.

8. Key Bible cross-reference

Verse 13. See Hosea 6:6.

9. Key "by way of explanation"

Verse 23, "flute players," were used in bereavement rituals. People were also
hired to lament and cry out, forming a "noisy crowd."

10. Key "Quotable Quote"

"A Pharisee is a righteous man whose righteousness is nourished by the blood
of sinners."
Thomas Merton

Matthew chapter 10

1. *Before and after*

Previous chapter: Chapter 9: More miracles
Following chapter: Chapter 11: Jesus' answer about John the Baptist

2. *Analysis of chapter*

The apostles called. (1-4)
The apostles instructed and sent out. (5-15)
Directions to the apostles. (16-42)

3. *Key verse*

Verse 1: "He called his twelve disciples to him and gave them authority to drive out evil spirits and to heal every disease and sickness."

4. *Key word / key phrase*

Verse 10, "He called his twelve."

5. *Key event / key person / key theme*

Fearless into danger and difficulty

6. *Key thought*

"If the love of ourselves hinders us from following Christ, we must resist it courageously." John Calvin

7. *Key thing to look out for*

Jesus chose disciples for mission.

8. *Key Bible cross-reference*

Verse 15. See Genesis 19:24-28.

9. *Key "by way of explanation"*

Verse 38, "take his cross." This is the first time Matthew mentions the cross, a Roman instrument for torture and execution. When Jesus spoke of it he was challenging people to follow him unreservedly.

10. *Key "Quotable Quote"*

"Those who are excessively desirous of an earthly life, take pains to guard themselves with unfounded confidence, as if they were looking well to themselves, but their life, though defended by such powerful safeguards, will pass away; for they will bring to them everlasting ruin. On the other hand, when believers surrender themselves to die, their soul, which appears to vanish in a moment, passes into a better life."
John Calvin, commentating on Matthew 10:37

Matthew chapter 11

1. **Before and after**

   Previous chapter: Chapter 10: The mission of the Twelve
   Following chapter: Chapter 12: The opposition of the Pharisees

2. **Analysis of chapter**

   Christ's preaching. (1)
   Christ's answer to John's disciples. (2-6)
   Christ's testimony to John the Baptist. (7-15)
   The perverseness of the Jews. (16-24)
   The gospel revealed to the simple. The heavy-laden invited. (25-30)

3. **Key verse**

   Verse 11: "I tell you the truth: Among those born of women there has not risen anyone greater than John the Baptist; yet he who is least in the kingdom of heaven is greater than he."

4. **Key word / key phrase**

   Verse 4, "report to John what you hear and see."

5. **Key event / key person / key theme**

   Jesus fulfilled the Old Testament prophecies about the Messiah.

6. **Key thought**

   Why did people comment about John the Baptist in the way that is recorded in verse 18?

7. **Key thing to look out for**

   The kind of rest Jesus offered his followers was much greater than absence from work.

8. **Key Bible cross-reference**

   Verse 5. See Isaiah 35:5,6.

9. **Key "by way of explanation"**

   Verse 12, "forceful men laid hold of it." This does not mean that you have to be violent to become a Christian but that this may require great effort and concentrated attention.

10. **Key "Quotable Quote"**

    "Our Lord's words are not, 'Do this, or don't do that,' but – 'Come to me.'"
    Oswald Chambers

Matthew chapter 12

1. Before and after

Previous chapter: Chapter 11: Jesus' answer about John the Baptist
Following chapter: Chapter 13: The parables of the kingdom

2. Analysis of chapter

Jesus defends his disciples for picking corn on the Sabbath day. (1-8)
Jesus heals a man with a withered hand on the Sabbath. (9-13)
The malice of the Pharisees. (14-21)
Jesus heals a demoniac. (22-30)
Blasphemy of the Pharisees. (31,32)
Evil words come from an evil heart. (33-37)
The scribes and Pharisees told off for seeking a sign. (38-45)
The disciples of Christ are his closest relations. (46-50)

3. Key verse

Verse 12: "How much more valuable is a man than a sheep! Therefore it is lawful to do good on the Sabbath."

4. Key word / key phrase

Verse 2, "When the Pharisees."

5. Key event / key person / key theme

The opposition of the Pharisees

6. Key thought

Clear teaching is given here about the perplexing topic of "blasphemy against the Spirit."

7. Key thing to look out for

The importance of the mission of Jonah is underlined by Jesus himself.

8. Key Bible cross-reference

Verses 18-21. See Isaiah 42:1-4.

9. Key "by way of explanation"

Verse 31, "blasphemy against the Spirit" will not be forgiven because such a person is attributing Jesus' miracles to Satan. Such a person has written off the work of God's Spirit, yet the Spirit which is the only way to find salvation.

10. Key "Quotable Quote"

"The disciple who is in the condition of abiding in Jesus is in the will of God, and his apparent free choices are God's foreordained decrees. Mysterious? Logically absurd? But a glorious truth to a saint."
Oswald Chambers

Matthew chapter 13

1. *Before and after*

Previous chapter: Chapter 12: The opposition of the Pharisees
Following chapter: Chapter 14: Execution of John the Baptist

2. *Analysis of chapter*

The parable of the sower. (1-23)
The parable of the weeds. (24-30; 36-43)
The parables of the mustard seed and the leaven. (31-35)
The parables of the hidden treasure, the pearl of great price, the net thrown into the sea, and the owner of a house. (44-52)
Jesus is again rejected at Nazareth. (53-58)

3. *Key verse*

Verse 3: "A farmer went out to sow his seed."

4. *Key word / key phrase*

Verse 3, "in parables."

5. *Key event / key person / key theme*

The parables of the kingdom

6. *Key thought*

The amazing increase produced by each fruitful seed is sometimes missed here.

7. *Key thing to look out for*

What are the weeds?

8. *Key Bible cross-reference*

Verse 35. See Psalm 78:2.

9. *Key "by way of explanation"*

Verse 33. Teaching about "the kingdom of heaven," God's present rule and God's forthcoming rule, is the main plank of Jesus' teaching. Matthew mentions it over fifty times.

10. *Key "Quotable Quote"*

"Each of us ought to endeavor to tear the thorns out of his heart, if we do not choose that the word of God should be choked; for there is not one of us whose heart is not filled with a vast quantity, and, I may say, a thick forest, of thorns. And, indeed, we perceive how few there are that reach maturity; for there is scarcely one individual out of ten that labors, I do not say to root out, but even to cut down the thorns."
John Calvin

Matthew chapter 14

1. **Before and after**

   Previous chapter: Chapter 13: The parables of the kingdom
   Following chapter: Chapter 15: Rejection by scribes and Pharisees

2. **Analysis of chapter**

   Death of John the Baptist. (1-12)
   Five thousand people miraculously fed. (13-21)
   Jesus walks on the water. (22-33)
   Jesus heals the sick. (34-36)

3. **Key verse**

   Verse 14: "When Jesus landed and saw a large crowd, he had compassion on them and healed their sick."

4. **Key word / key phrase**

   Verse 10, "John beheaded."

5. **Key event / key person / key theme**

   Execution of John the Baptist

6. **Key thought**

   John's outspoken faithfulness caused him to lose his head.

7. **Key thing to look out for**

   Jesus shows that he is the bread of life in a most unforgettable way.

8. **Key Bible cross-reference**

   Verse 4. See Leviticus 18:16.

9. **Key "by way of explanation"**

   Verse 6. The Gospels do not tell us the name of the dancing "daughter of Herodias." But Josephus (*Ant.* XVIII. v. 4) records that she was called Salome.

10. **Key "Quotable Quote"**

    "Why, they ask, do not those miracles, which you preach as of past events, happen nowadays? I might reply that they were necessary before the world believed, to bring the world to believe; but whoever is still looking for prodigies to make him believe is himself a great prodigy for refusing to believe where the world believes."
    Augustine of Hippo

Matthew chapter 15

1. Before and after

Previous chapter: Chapter 14: Execution of John the Baptist
Following chapter: Chapter 16: Warnings about religious leaders, and Peter's confession

2. Analysis of chapter

Jesus speaks about human traditions. (1-9)
He warns about things which really defile. (10-20)
He heals the daughter of a Canaanite woman. (21-28)
Jesus heals the sick, and miraculously feeds four thousand. (29-39)

3. Key verse

Verse 2: "Why do your disciples break the tradition of the elders? They don't wash their hands before they eat!"

4. Key word / key phrase

Verse 1, "Pharisees and teachers of the law."

5. Key event / key person / key theme

Rejection by scribes and Pharisees

6. Key thought

In some of the recorded conversations people had with Jesus, Jesus appears to be almost harsh. But all he did was to draw out people's faith in him.

7. Key thing to look out for

It is all too easy to honor God with our lips in a Sunday worship service and to dishonor him a little later.

8. Key Bible cross-reference

Verse 4. See Exodus 20:12.

9. Key "by way of explanation"

Verse 26, "their dogs." Jesus is referring to a pet dog here. Even though Jesus is saying the gospel was for the Jews first of all, the woman would not be put off, and persists and reveals the depth of her faith in Jesus.

10. Key "Quotable Quote"

"Some people think that having reasons for faith is an insult to God. But verification itself depends on the unchanging authority and stability of the Word of God. We are not insulting God but bringing glory to him by taking his Word as the stable, authoritative truth it is."
Os Guinness

Matthew chapter 16

1. *Before and after*

Previous chapter: Chapter 15: Rejection by scribes and Pharisees
Following chapter: Chapter 17: Jesus' transfiguration and teaching the Twelve

2. *Analysis of chapter*

The Pharisees and Sadducees ask a sign. (1-4)
Jesus warns against the teaching of the Pharisees. (5-12)
Peter's testimony that Jesus is the Christ. (13-20)
Christ predicts his sufferings, and rebukes Peter. (21-23)
The necessity of self-denial. (24-28)

3. *Key verse*

Verse 1: "The Pharisees and Sadducees came to Jesus and tested him by asking him to show them a sign from heaven."

4. *Key word / key phrase*

Verse 16, "You are the Christ."

5. *Key event / key person / key theme*

Peter's confession

6. *Key thought*

A miracle in itself is by no means guaranteed to elicit faith.

7. *Key thing to look out for*

Peter had divine insight to see who Jesus really was.

8. *Key Bible cross-reference*

Verse 27. See Psalm 62:12.

9. *Key "by way of explanation"*

Verse 19 "bind . . . loose." What is conferred on Peter here is not the authority to determine who is guilty and who is innocent, but just the responsibility to announce this.

10. *Key "Quotable Quote"*

"He is no fool who gives what he cannot keep to gain what he cannot lose." Jim Elliot, the young American missionary killed by Auca Indians in Ecuador in 1956, reflecting on Jesus' words in verses 24-26.

Matthew chapter 17

1. Before and after

Previous chapter: Chapter 16: Warnings about religious leaders, and Peter's confession
Following chapter: Chapter 18: The Church's lifestyle

2. Analysis of chapter

The transfiguration of Christ. (1-13)
Jesus expels a dumb and deaf spirit. (14-21)
He again predicts his sufferings. (22,23)
He performs a miracle to pay the temple tax. (24-27)

3. Key verse

Verses 20,21: "Because you have so little faith. I tell you the truth, if you have faith as small as a mustard seed, you can say to this mountain, 'Move from here to there' and it will move. Nothing will be impossible for you."

4. Key word / key phrase

Verse 2, "he was transfigured."

5. Key event / key person / key theme

Jesus' transfiguration

6. Key thought

For a brief moment part of the glory is made visible to the human eye.

7. Key thing to look out for

Peter shows his obedience and faith in Jesus in verses 24-27.

8. Key Bible cross-reference

Verse 16. See Deuteronomy 19:15.

9. Key "by way of explanation"

Verse 24. The "two-drachma tax" was the annual temple tax. Every male over the age of twenty had to pay it.

10. Key "Quotable Quote"

"As Moses and Elijah stood with Jesus on the Mount of Transfiguration, the Law, with its requirement and its sacrifices, and prophecy, with its forward-looking gaze, stood there in their representatives and bore witness that their converging lines meet in Jesus. Their presence and their speech were the acknowledgment that this was he whom they had seen from afar."
Alexander MacLaren

Matthew chapter 18

1. Before and after

Previous chapter: Chapter 17: Jesus' transfiguration and teaching the Twelve
Following chapter: Chapter 19: Divorce, children, and a rich young man

2. Analysis of chapter

The importance of humility. (1-6)
Warning about causing people to sin. (7-9)
The parable of the lost sheep. (10-14)
The brother who sins against you. (15-20)
Forgiving your brother, and the parable of the unmerciful servant. (21-35)

3. Key verse

Verse 4: "Therefore, whoever humbles himself like this child is the greatest in the kingdom of heaven."

4. Key word / key phrase

Verse 1, "Who is the greatest?"

5. Key event / key person / key theme

The Church's lifestyle

6. Key thought

The greatest in the kingdom is in stark contrast to greatness in the world.

7. Key thing to look out for

Jesus' great love is illustrated wonderfully in the short parable in verses 12-14.

8. Key Bible cross-reference

Verse 4. See Genesis 1:27; 5:2.

9. Key "by way of explanation"

Verse 9, "fire of hell." In 5:22,29,30 this is called Gehenna, after the "Valley of Hinnom" which was a rubbish dump outside Jerusalem. It was always on fire.

10. Key "Quotable Quote"

"God forgives talents; we cannot forgive pence. God forgives a hundred thousand; we cannot forgive a hundred (Matthew 18). We look that God should forgive us, and we will not forgive others."
Thomas Manton

Matthew chapter 19

1. Before and after

Previous chapter: Chapter 18: The Church's lifestyle
Following chapter: Chapter 20: Parable of the workers in the vineyard, and Jesus in Judea

2. Analysis of chapter

Jesus enters Judea. (1,2)
The Pharisees' question about divorce. (3-12)
Young children brought to Jesus. (13-15)
The rich young man's question. (16-22)
The reward for Christ's followers. (23-30)

3. Key verse

Verse 3: "Is it lawful for a man to divorce his wife for any and every reason?"

4. Key word / key phrase

Verse 22, "he had great wealth."

5. Key event / key person / key theme

A rich young man

6. Key thought

Jesus reveals much about his attitude to children in verses 13-15.

7. Key thing to look out for

This man was in the grip of his riches.

8. Key Bible cross-reference

Verse 18. See Exodus 20:13-16.

9. Key "by way of explanation"

Verse 16, "what good thing must I do?" The rich man thought that he could enter heaven by doing some great deed. Jesus pointed out that he needed to give his most treasured possessions to God and that the rich man was not prepared to do.

10. Key "Quotable Quote"

"It is the one exception that gives prominence to the illegitimacy of every other reason. Preoccupation with the one exception should never be permitted to obscure the force of the negation of all others."
John Murray, commentating on Matthew 5:32 and 19:9

Matthew chapter 20

1. *Before and after*

Previous chapter: Chapter 19: Divorce, children, and a rich young man
Following chapter: Chapter 21: Jesus enters Jerusalem and his public ministry there

2. *Analysis of chapter*

The parable of the workers in the vineyard. (1-16)
Jesus again predicts his sufferings. (17-19)
The ambition of James and John. (20-28)
Jesus heals two blind men near Jericho. (29-34)

3. *Key verse*

Verse 28: "just as the Son of Man did not come to be served, but to serve, and to give his life as a ransom for many."

4. *Key word / key phrase*

Verse 16, "the first will be last."

5. *Key event / key person / key theme*

Parable of the workers in the vineyard

6. *Key thought*

To claim that Jesus was taken unawares and crucified flies in the face of the most cursory reading of the Gospels.

7. *Key thing to look out for*

Verses 21 and 32. A question that Jesus still asks.

8. *Key Bible cross-reference*

Verse 8. See Leviticus 19:13.

9. *Key "by way of explanation"*

Verse 22, "drink the cup." This meant to experience something and in this instance refers to Jesus' suffering. See Jeremiah 25:15; Ezekiel 23:32.

10. *Key "Quotable Quote"*

"We must first make up our minds about Christ before coming to conclusions about the miracles attributed to him."
F.F. Bruce

Matthew chapter 21

1. Before and after

Previous chapter: Chapter 20: Parable of the workers in the vineyard, and Jesus in Judea

Following chapter: Chapter 22: Parables and questions

2. Analysis of chapter

Christ enters Jerusalem. (1-11)

He drives out those who profaned the temple. (12-17)

The barren fig tree cursed. (18-22)

Jesus' teaching in the temple. (23-27)

The parable of the two sons. (28-32)

The parable of the wicked landowner. (33-46)

3. Key verse

Verse 8: "A very large crowd spread their cloaks on the road, while others cut branches from the trees and spread them on the road."

4. Key word / key phrase

Verse 22, "If you believe."

5. Key event / key person / key theme

Jesus enters Jerusalem

6. Key thought

One minute a crowd welcome Jesus, later in the week they call for his blood.

7. Key thing to look out for

The chief priests knew where Jesus' authority came from, but they just did not care to bow before God.

8. Key Bible cross-reference

Verse 5. See Zechariah 9:9.

9. Key "by way of explanation"

Verse 33, "watchtower." The watchtower was for shelter and for a lookout post for any enemies.

10. Key "Quotable Quote"

"Jesus promised his disciples three things – that they would be completely fearless, absurdly happy and in constant trouble."

G.K. Chesterton

Matthew chapter 22

1. **Before and after**

   Previous chapter: Chapter 21: Jesus enters Jerusalem and his public ministry there

   Following chapter: Chapter 23: Jesus denounces the Pharisees and teachers of the law, and weeps over Jerusalem

2. **Analysis of chapter**

   The parable of the marriage feast. (1-14)
   The Pharisees question Jesus about paying taxes to Caesar. (15-22)
   The Sadducees and the resurrection. (23-33)
   The greatest commandment. (34-40)
   Jesus questions the Pharisees. (41-46)

3. **Key verse**

   Verse 37: "'Love the Lord your God with all your heart and with all your soul and with all your mind.'"

4. **Key word / key phrase**

   Verse 22, "in parables."

5. **Key event / key person / key theme**

   Parables and questions

6. **Key thought**

   Verse 35 was a much-debated question among the rabbis. Until Jesus came, no one had ever put the two separate commandments together to from one whole.

7. **Key thing to look out for**

   In the Old Testament, "Love your neighbor" meant your fellow-Jew. Jesus gave it a new meaning: "Love your fellow human being."

8. **Key Bible cross-reference**

   Verse 24. See Deuteronomy 25:5.

9. **Key "by way of explanation"**

   Verse 11, "not wearing wedding clothes." Some of the people at the banquet had been hauled in from the streets. They would have had to avail themselves of a wedding garment from the host. If they were not wearing one it shows that they had deliberately refused to put one on.

10. **Key "Quotable Quote"**

    "Only our refusal to trust him . . . can hinder his purposes in our lives."
    Joni Eareckson Tada

Matthew chapter 23

1. Before and after

Previous chapter: Chapter 22: Parables and questions
Following chapter: Chapter 24: Jesus teaches about the end of the age

2. Analysis of chapter

Jesus reproves the scribes and Pharisees. (1-12)
Evil actions of the Pharisees. (13-33)
The guilt of Jerusalem. (34-39)

3. Key verse

Verse 12: "For whoever exalts himself will be humbled, and whoever humbles himself will be exalted."

4. Key word / key phrase

Verse 13, "Woe to you."

5. Key event / key person / key theme

Jesus denounces the Pharisees

6. Key thought

Jesus called some Pharisees, "you snakes," verse 33, to help them face the reality of their vile selves.

7. Key thing to look out for

Serious times call for serious talking.

8. Key Bible cross-reference

Verse 29. See Isaiah 13:10.

9. Key "by way of explanation"

Verse 35, "Abel to . . . Zechariah." This was Jesus' summary of the people who had been martyred in the Old Testament. Zechariah is "Zechariah son of Jehoiada" who comes in 2 Chronicles 24:20-22. According to the Hebrew arrangement of the book of the Old Testament, 2 Chronicles came last.

10. Key "Quotable Quote"

"Jesus offered us, not an excursion, but an execution."
Billy Graham

Matthew chapter 24

1. *Before and after*

Previous chapter: Chapter 23: Jesus denounces the Pharisees and teachers of the law, and weeps over Jerusalem

Following chapter: Chapter 25: Jesus predicts judgment at his coming

2. *Analysis of chapter*

Christ predicts the destruction of the temple. (1-3)

The troubles before the destruction of Jerusalem. (4-28)

Christ predicts other signs. The end of the world. (29-41)

Exhortations to be watchful. (42-51)

3. *Key verse*

Verse 4: "Watch out that no one deceives you."

4. *Key word / key phrase*

Verse 3, "the end of the age."

5. *Key event / key person / key theme*

Jesus teaches about the end of the age

6. *Key thought*

When someone says he knows when the world will end we know he must be wrong.

7. *Key thing to look out for*

The end of the world is certain and Jesus warns people to be alert and ready for it.

8. *Key Bible cross-reference*

Verse 29. See Isaiah 13:10; 34:4.

9. *Key "by way of explanation"*

Verse 28, "vultures." When Jesus does come again it will be clear for all to see, as obvious as vultures circling over some dead body.

10. *Key "Quotable Quote"*

"He who loves the coming of the Lord is not he who affirms it is far off, nor is it he who says it is near. It is he who, whether it be far or near, awaits it with sincere faith, steadfast hope, and fervent love."

Augustine of Hippo

Matthew chapter 25

1. Before and after

Previous chapter: Chapter 24: Jesus teaches about the end of the age
Following chapter: Chapter 26: The Last Supper and Jesus on trial

2. Analysis of chapter

The parable of the ten virgins. (1-13)
The parable of the talents. (14-30)
The judgment. (31-46)

3. Key verse

Verse 14: "Again, it will be like a man going on a journey, who called his servants and entrusted his property to them."

4. Key word / key phrase

Verse 30, "into the darkness."

5. Key event / key person / key theme

Jesus predicts judgment at his coming

6. Key thought

Talents are to be used, not hidden away.

7. Key thing to look out for

God's day of judgment will certainly come.

8. Key Bible cross-reference

Verse 46. See Daniel 12:2.

9. Key "by way of explanation"

Verses 34-40. The "rewards" given to the faithful are not given because they "merit" them. Everyone is saved by grace, but everyone should also serve Jesus and his kingdom, "seeking for no reward."

10. Key "Quotable Quote"

"The kingdom of heaven" is the great theme of Matthew's Gospel.
John R.W. Stott

Matthew chapter 26

1. Before and after

Previous chapter: Chapter 25: Jesus predicts judgment at his coming
Following chapter: Chapter 27: Jesus before Pilate, and his death and burial

2. Analysis of chapter

The rulers plot against Christ. (1-5)
Christ anointed at Bethany. (6-13)
Judas agrees to betray Christ. (14-16)
The Passover. (17-25)
Christ institutes his holy supper. (26-30)
He warns his disciples. (31-35)
His agony in the garden. (36-46)
He is betrayed. (47-56)
Christ before Caiaphas. (57-68)
Peter denies him. (69-75)

3. Key verse

Verse 4: ". . . they plotted to arrest Jesus in some sly way and kill him."

4. Key word / key phrase

Verse 17, "to eat the Passover."

5. Key event / key person / key theme

The Last Supper

6. Key thought

God's covenant with the Jews was a refrain that runs throughout the Old Testament. That covenant was based on God's Law. Jesus here inaugurates a new covenant. By his death people enter into a covenant of grace and love.

7. Key thing to look out for

Jesus' command in verse 41.

8. Key Bible cross-reference

Verse 2. See Exodus 12:1-27.

9. Key "by way of explanation"

Verse 63, "I charge you under oath." This meant that Jesus was legally bound to answer the question.

10. Key "Quotable Quote"

"He said to Judas when he betrayed him: 'Friend, wherefore art thou come?' Just as if he had said: 'Thou hatest me, and art mine enemy, yet I love thee, and am thy friend.'"
Theologia Germanica

Matthew chapter 27

1. Before and after

Previous chapter: Chapter 26: The Last Supper and Jesus on trial
Following chapter: Chapter 28: The resurrection of Jesus

2. Analysis of chapter

Christ handed over to Pilate, and the despair of Judas. (1-10)
Christ before Pilate. (11-25)
Barabbas freed, Christ mocked. (26-30)
Christ led to be crucified. (31-34)
He is crucified. (35-44)
The death of Christ. (45-50)
Events at the crucifixion. (51-56)
The burial of Christ. (57-61)
The sepulcher secured. (62-66)

3. Key verse

Verse 45: "From the sixth hour until the ninth hour darkness came over all the land."

4. Key word / key phrase

Verse 35, "when they had crucified him."

5. Key event / key person / key theme

Jesus is crucified

6. Key thought

Verse 46. See 2 Corinthians 5:21: "God made him who had no sin to be sin for us." The major characteristic of sin is that it separates the sinners from God.

7. Key thing to look out for

Note the first thing Matthew records after Jesus' death, verse 51.

8. Key Bible cross-reference

Verses 9,10. See Zechariah 11:12,13.

9. Key "by way of explanation"

Verse 51, "curtain." This separated the Holy Place from the innermost Most Holy Place in the temple. Now it was torn in half and the way to God was open. Verse 46: the words are in Aramaic, one of the languages spoken in Palestine.

10. Key "Quotable Quote"

"No other death has aroused one hundredth part of the interest, or been remembered with one hundredth part of the intensity and concern."
Malcolm Muggeridge

Matthew chapter 28

1. *Previous chapter*

Chapter 27: Jesus before Pilate, and his death and burial

2. *Analysis of chapter*

Christ's resurrection. (1-8)
He appears to the women. (9,10)
The guards' report. (11-15)
Christ's commission to his disciples. (16-20)

3. *Key verse*

Verse 20: "And surely I am with you always, to the very end of the age."

4. *Key word / key phrase*

Verse 6, "he has risen."

5. *Key event / key person / key theme*

Jesus' resurrection

6. *Key thought*

The resurrection is the proof of Jesus' deity (Romans 1:4) and the guarantee of our resurrection and salvation.

7. *Key thing to look out for*

Note Jesus' last recorded words, verses 18-20.

8. *Key Bible cross-reference*

Verse 19. See Acts 1:8.

9. *Key "by way of explanation"*

Verse 20, "with you." Matthew, in his opening chapter, announced that God was "with us," 1:23, now he writes that Jesus will be "with you" forever.

10. *Key "Quotable Quote"*

"Of all the things in the world that can set the heart burning, there is none like the presence of Jesus."
C.H. Spurgeon

Mark

Mark chapter 1

1. **Following chapter**

   Chapter 2: Jesus heals a paralyzed man, calls Levi, and answers questions

2. **Analysis of chapter**

   John the Baptist is introduced. (1-8)
   The baptism and temptation of Christ. (9-13)
   Christ preaches and calls disciples. (14-22)
   He expels an unclean spirit. (23-28)
   He heals many ill people. (29-39)
   He heals a leper. (40-45)

3. **Key verse**

   Verse 1: "The beginning of the gospel about Jesus Christ, the Son of God."

4. **Key word / key phrase**

   Verse 32, "the people brought to Jesus all the sick."

5. **Key event / key person / key theme**

   The gospel of Jesus in action

6. **Key thought**

   The reality of Satan

7. **Key thing to look out for**

   The basis for Jesus' healing ministry is found in verse 41.

8. **Key Bible cross-reference**

   Verse 2. See Malachi 3:1.

9. **Key "by way of explanation"**

   Verse 41, "touched the man." According to Mosaic law you became ceremonially unclean if you touched a leper. By his actions Jesus showed his great care for this man.

10. **Key "Quotable Quote"**

    "Humility consists, not in condemning our conscience, but in recognizing God's grace and compassion."
    St. Mark the Ascetic

Mark chapter 2

1. *Before and after*

Previous chapter: Chapter 1: Jesus' baptism, temptation, and first followers
Following chapter: Chapter 3: Jesus appoints the Twelve

2. *Analysis of chapter*

Christ heals a paralytic. (1-12)
Levi's call, and the dinner given to Jesus. (13-17)
Why Christ's disciples did not fast. (18-22)
He justifies his disciples for picking corn on the Sabbath. (23-28)

3. *Key verse*

Verse 8: "Immediately Jesus knew in his spirit that this was what they were thinking in their hearts."

4. *Key word / key phrase*

Verse 9, "Get up."

5. *Key event / key person / key theme*

Jesus heals

6. *Key thought*

Jesus knows everything. We can hide nothing about our motives or anything else from him, verse 8.

7. *Key thing to look out for*

Jesus' purpose in coming.

8. *Key Bible cross-reference*

Verse 23. See Deuteronomy 23:25.

9. *Key "by way of explanation"*

Verse 17, "I have not come to call the righteous." The person who thinks he does not need God will not go to God for help.

10. *Key "Quotable Quote"*

"Unless you humble yourself before God in the dust, and confess before him your iniquities and sins, the gate of heaven, which is open only for sinners, saved by grace, must be shut against you forever."
D.L. Moody

Mark chapter 3

1. Before and after

Previous chapter: Chapter 2: Jesus heals a paralyzed man, calls Levi, and answers questions

Following chapter: Chapter 4: Four parables and the calming of the lake

2. Analysis of chapter

Christ heals a man with a shriveled hand. (1-5)
Crowds follow Christ. (6-12)
The apostles called. (13-21)
The blasphemy of the scribes. (22-30)
Christ's relatives. (31-35)

3. Key verse

Verse 7: "Jesus withdrew with his disciples to the lake, and a large crowd from Galilee followed."

4. Key word / key phrase

Verse 14, "He appointed twelve."

5. Key event / key person / key theme

Jesus appoints the Twelve

6. Key thought

The spirit world was all too aware of who Jesus was and of his great power.

7. Key thing to look out for

The Jesus family is united by spiritual factors, not by ordinary family ties.

8. Key Bible cross-reference

Verse 21. See Acts 26:24.

9. Key "by way of explanation"

Verse 14, "appointed twelve." The word "disciple" means "pupil" or "student." Moses, Gamaliel, and John the Baptist all had disciples. Those who followed Jesus as a result of the ministry of the Twelve were also called disciples, Matthew 28:19; Acts 11:26.

10. Key "Quotable Quote"

"Now do I begin to be a disciple of my Master, Christ."
Ignatius of Antioch, traveling cheerfully to the place where he was to be thrown to the lions.

Mark chapter 4

1. **Before and after**

   Previous chapter: Chapter 3: Jesus appoints the Twelve
   Following chapter: Chapter 5: Four miracles

2. **Analysis of chapter**

   The parable of the sower. (1-20)
   Other parables. (21-34)
   Christ stills a storm. (35-41)

3. **Key verse**

   Verse 11: "The secret of the kingdom of God has been given to you."

4. **Key word / key phrase**

   Verse 3, "A farmer went out to sow."

5. **Key event / key person / key theme**

   Four parables

6. **Key thought**

   What conclusions should be drawn from these parables?

7. **Key thing to look out for**

   Jesus' power extended over the natural order.

8. **Key Bible cross-reference**

   Verse 12. See Isaiah 6:9,10.

9. **Key "by way of explanation"**

   Verses 26-29. This parable is only recorded by Mark. It stresses the great and
   mysterious power of the seed. The gospel has unique spiritual power.

10. **Key "Quotable Quote"**

    "We must meditate on what we read in the Gospels. This even the most
    unlearned person can do, and will do, if he has a will to do it."
    John Henry Newman

Mark chapter 8

(For Mark chapter 5:1-20, see Luke 8:26-39; for Mark 5:22-43, see Luke8:41-56.
For Mark chapter 6:1-6, see Matthew 13:54-58; for Mark 6:7-11, see Matthew 10:1,9-14;
for Mark 6:14-29, see Matthew 14:1-12; for Mark 6:32-44, see John 6:5-13.
For Mark chapter 7:1-23, see Matthew 15:1-20; for Mark 7:24-30, see Matthew 15:21-28;
for Mark 7:31-37, see Matthew 15:29-31.)

1. **Before and after**

   Previous chapter: Chapter 7: Inner purity and two healing miracles
   Following chapter: Chapter 9: Transfiguration, demon-possession, and prediction of death

2. **Analysis of chapter**

   Four thousand people miraculously fed. (1-10)
   Christ warns against the Pharisees and Herodians. (11-21)
   A blind man healed. (22-26)
   Peter's testimony to Christ. (27-33)
   Christ must be followed. (34-38)

3. **Key verse**

   Verse 6: "He told the crowd to sit down on the ground. When he had taken the seven loaves and given thanks, he broke them and gave them to his disciples to set before the people, and they did so."

4. **Key word / key phrase**

   Verse 34, "take up his cross."

5. **Key event / key person / key theme**

   Four thousand are fed

6. **Key thought**

   What is Jesus warning his hearers against in verses 14-21?

7. **Key thing to look out for**

   As soon as Peter says who Jesus is, Jesus speaks of his death. Peter shows how little he understands, so that Jesus even has to call him "Satan."

8. **Key Bible cross-reference**

   Verse 18. See Jeremiah 5:21.

9. **Key "by way of explanation"**

   Verse 15, "Yeast" often stands for corruption and evil.

10. **Key "Quotable Quote"**

    "To take up the cross means that you take your stand for the Lord Jesus no matter what it costs."
    Billy Graham

Mark chapter 9

1. Before and after

Previous chapter: Chapter 8: Jesus feeds four thousand, and Peter's confession

Following chapter: Chapter 10: Jesus teaches his disciples and heals Bartimaeus

2. Analysis of chapter

The transfiguration. (1-13)
An evil spirit expelled. (14-29)
The apostles reproved. (30-40)
Pain to be preferred to sin. (41-50)

3. Key verse

Verse 3: "His clothes became dazzling white, whiter than anyone in the world could bleach them."

4. Key word / key phrase

Verse 2, "he was transfigured."

5. Key event / key person / key theme

Jesus' transfiguration

6. Key thought

The vital importance of prayer is stressed by Jesus, verse 29.

7. Key thing to look out for

God's command.

8. Key Bible cross-reference

Verses 2-7. See 2 Peter 1:17,18.

9. Key "by way of explanation"

Verse 7, "a voice came from the cloud." Clouds stood for God's presence and his ability to protect people and to guide them.

10. Key "Quotable Quote"

"The key to missions is not work, but prayer. Too often work is used as a substitute for, or a by-pass to, fervent prayer."
Oswald Chambers

Mark chapter 11

(For Mark chapter 10:1-12, see Matthew 19:1-9; for Mark 10:13-16, see Matthew 19:13-15; 10:17-31, see Matthew 19:16-30, for Mark 10:32-52, see Matthew 20:17-34)

1. Before and after

Previous chapter: Chapter 10: Jesus teaches his disciples and heals Bartimaeus
Following chapter: Chapter 12: Opposition from the leaders in Jerusalem

2. Analysis of chapter

Christ's triumphant entry into Jerusalem. (1-11)
The barren fig tree cursed, and the temple cleansed. (12-18)
Prayer in faith. (19-26)
The priests and elders questioned about John the Baptist. (27-33)

3. Key verse

Verse 8: "Many people spread their cloaks on the road, while others spread branches they had cut in the fields."

4. Key word / key phrase

Verse 22, "Have faith in God."

5. Key event / key person / key theme

Jesus enters Jerusalem

6. Key thought

The Gospel writers were deeply conscious of the way Jesus fulfilled Old Testament prophecy.

7. Key thing to look out for

Jesus' cursing of the fig tree was an enacted parable (c.f. Ezekiel's symbolic actions). What was he condemning?

8. Key Bible cross-reference

Verse 9. See Psalm 118:25,26.

9. Key "by way of explanation"

Verse 17, "a house of prayer for all nations." Non-Jews could take comfort in the fact that Isaiah had given this name to the temple (Isaiah 56:7). But the Jews allowed the Court of the Gentiles to be taken over by a noisy market.

10. Key "Quotable Quote"

"What is needed desperately today is prophetic insight. Scholars can interpret the past; it takes prophets to interpret the present."
A.W. Tozer

Mark chapter 13

(For Mark chapter 12:1-27, see Luke 20:9-38; 12:28-37, see Matthew 22:34-46; 12:38-40, see Luke 20:45-47; 12:41-44, see Luke 21:1-4.
For Mark chapter 13, see Matthew 24:1-51)

1. **Before and after**

   Previous chapter: Chapter 12: Opposition from the leaders in Jerusalem
   Following chapter: Chapter 14: The Last Supper and Gethsemane

2. **Analysis of chapter**

   The destruction of the temple predicted. (1-4)
   Christ's prophetic declaration. (5-13)
   Christ's prophesy. (14-23)
   More prophetic declarations. (24-27)
   Watchfulness urged. (28-37)

3. **Key verse**

   Verse 9: "You must be on your guard. You will be handed over to the local councils and flogged in the synagogues."

4. **Key word / key phrase**

   Verse 4, "what will be the sign?"

5. **Key event / key person / key theme**

   Jesus teaches about the future

6. **Key thought**

   Jesus mentioned specific signs which would usher in the end of the age.

7. **Key thing to look out for**

   The last word in this chapter gives the Christian response to the teaching it contains.

8. **Key Bible cross-reference**

   Verse 24. See Joel 2:10,31.

9. **Key "by way of explanation"**

   Verse 32. "No one knows" the timing of Jesus' return. If we did it might hinder our life of faith.

10. **Key "Quotable Quote"**

    "I hope that when Christ comes He will find me either praying or preaching."
    Augustine of Hippo

Mark chapter 14

1. Before and after

Previous chapter: Chapter 13: Jesus teaches about the future
Following chapter: Chapter 15: Pilate, and Jesus' crucifixion and burial

2. Analysis of chapter

Christ anointed at Bethany. (1-11)
The Passover, Jesus declares that Judas will betray him. (12-21)
The Lord's Supper instituted. (22-31)
Christ's agony in the garden. (32-42)
He is betrayed and arrested. (43-52)
Christ before the high priest. (53-65)
Peter denies Christ. (66-72)

3. Key verse

Verse 3: "While he was in Bethany, reclining at the table in the home of a man known as Simon the Leper, a woman came with an alabaster jar of very expensive perfume, made of pure nard. She broke the jar and poured the perfume on his head."

4. Key word / key phrase

Verse 34, "Keep watch."

5. Key event / key person / key theme

Gethsemane

6. Key thought

Jesus had a betrayer among his disciples.

7. Key thing to look out for

Peter did not heed Jesus' warning.

8. Key Bible cross-reference

Verse 18. See Psalm 41:9.

9. Key "by way of explanation"

Verse 51, "young man." This unidentified person may have been the author of this Gospel, John Mark.

10. Key "Quotable Quote"

"The saddest road to hell is that which runs under the pulpit, past the Bible and through the midst of warnings and invitations."
J.C. Ryle

Mark chapter 15

1. *Before and after*

Previous chapter: Chapter 14: The Last Supper and Gethsemane
Following chapter: Chapter 16: Jesus' resurrection

2. *Analysis of chapter*

Christ before Pilate. (1-14)
Christ led out to be crucified. (15-21)
The crucifixion. (22-32)
The death of Christ. (33-41)
His body buried. (42-47)

3. *Key verse*

Verse 3: "The chief priests accused him of many things."

4. *Key word / key phrase*

Verse 39, "saw how he died."

5. *Key event / key person / key theme*

Jesus' death and burial

6. *Key thought*

Few people come out well in the trials and death of Jesus.

7. *Key thing to look out for*

Jesus' physical pain is certainly not the central focus in the description of his death. What is?

8. *Key Bible cross-reference*

Verse 21. See Romans 16:13.

9. *Key "by way of explanation"*

Verse 37, "with a loud cry." Most crucified people endured agony which led to exhaustion and then unconsciousness before death. Jesus' great cry indicates that he did not die an ordinary death.

10. *Key "Quotable Quote"*

"Those who belong to Christ have 'crucified' their flesh or sinful nature. It is an astonishing metaphor. For crucifixion was a horrible, brutal form of execution. Yet it illustrates graphically what our attitude to our fallen nature is to be. We are not to coddle or cuddle it, not to pamper or spoil it, not to give it any encouragement or even toleration."
John R.W. Stott

Mark chapter 16

1. Previous chapter

Chapter 15: Pilate, and Jesus' crucifixion and burial

2. Analysis of chapter

Christ's resurrection made known to the women. (1-8)
Christ appears to Mary Magdalene and other disciples. (9-13)
His commission to the apostles. (14-18)
Christ's ascension. (19,20)

3. Key verse

Verse 8: "Trembling and bewildered, the women went out and fled from the tomb. They said nothing to anyone, because they were afraid."

4. Key word / key phrase

Verse 6, "He has risen!"

5. Key event / key person / key theme

Jesus' resurrection

6. Key thought

Verse 6. How could Jesus' resurrection cause anyone to be alarmed?

7. Key thing to look out for

Verse 14. Lack of faith was rebuked by Jesus.

8. Key Bible cross-reference

Verse 15. See Acts 1:8.

9. Key "by way of explanation"

Verse 3, "who will roll the stone away?" The stone rolled in front of a tomb fell into a hollow. It could not possibly have been rolled back by a group of women.

10. Key "Quotable Quote"

"Worship...is the most appropriate response that can be made to resurrection."
Eugene H. Peterson

Luke

Luke chapter 1

1. Following chapter

Chapter 2: The birth of Jesus and events during his childhood

2. Analysis of chapter

The preface. (1-4)
Zechariah and Elizabeth. (5-25)
Christ's birth announced. (26-38)
Mary visits Elizabeth. (39-56)
The birth of John the Baptist. (57-66)
The Song of Zechariah. (67-80)

3. Key verse

Verse 3: "Therefore, since I myself have carefully investigated everything from the beginning, it seemed good also to me to write an orderly account for you, most excellent Theophilus."

4. Key word / key phrase

Verse 31, "you will be with child."

5. Key event / key person / key theme

Jesus' birth is foretold

6. Key thought

Luke gives his reasons for writing his "orderly account" verses 1-4.

7. Key thing to look out for

Note the links between two expectant mothers.

8. Key Bible cross-reference

Verse 37. See Genesis 18:14.

9. Key "by way of explanation"

Verse 25, "taken away my disgrace." In Jewish society in those days childlessness was thought to be a sign of God's disfavor.

10. Key "Quotable Quote"

"Earth grows into heaven, as we come to live and breathe in the atmosphere of the incarnation. Jesus makes heaven wherever he is."
F.W. Faber

Luke chapter 2

1. Before and after

Previous chapter: Chapter 1: Events before Jesus' birth and birth of John the Baptist

Following chapter: Chapter 3: John the Baptist's ministry and Jesus' baptism

2. Analysis of chapter

The birth of Christ. (1-7)
It is made known to the shepherds. (8-20)
Christ presented in the temple. (21-24)
Simeon prophesies about Jesus. (25-35)
Anna prophesies about him. (36-40)
Christ with the teachers in the temple. (41-52)

3. Key verse

Verse 7: ". . . she gave birth to her firstborn, a son. She wrapped him in cloths and placed him in a manger, because there was no room for them in the inn."

4. Key word / key phrase

Verse 7, "she gave birth to her firstborn."

5. Key event / key person / key theme

Jesus' birth and childhood

6. Key thought

Shepherd's work made it impossible for him to keep all the demands of the ceremonial law. He was therefore despised by religious people. Yet shepherds were God's first witness of the birth of the baby.

7. Key thing to look out for

See how the different people who met Jesus react to him.

8. Key Bible cross-reference

Verse 32. See Isaiah 42:6.

9. Key "by way of explanation"

Verse 14, "Glory to God in the highest." From the Latin translation of these words in the *Vulgate* translation of the Bible this angelic prayer is now known as the *Gloria in Excelsis Deo.*"

10. Key "Quotable Quote"

"Thirty years of our Lord's life are hidden in the words, 'He was subject unto them.'"
Jacques Benigne Bossuet

Luke chapter 3

1. *Before and after*

Previous chapter: Chapter 2: The birth of Jesus and events during his childhood

Following chapter: Chapter 4: Jesus' temptation, rejection at Nazareth, and early miracles

2. *Analysis of chapter*

John the Baptist's ministry. (1-14)
John the Baptist testifies about Christ. (15-20)
The baptism of Christ. (21,22)
The genealogy of Christ. (23-38)

3. *Key verse*

Verses 3,4: "He went into all the country around the Jordan, preaching a baptism of repentance for the forgiveness of sins. As is written in the book of the words of Isaiah the prophet."

4. *Key word / key phrase*

Verse 3, "preaching a baptism of repentance."

5. *Key event / key person / key theme*

John the Baptist's ministry

6. *Key thought*

In his baptism Jesus was saying yes to John's work as forerunner and identifying with all those who were coming to be baptized by John.

7. *Key thing to look out for*

Verses 10-14: what does repentance involve?

8. *Key Bible cross-reference*

Verse 22. See Genesis 22:2.

9. *Key "by way of explanation"*

Verse 4, "prepare the way." Just as roads and highways were repaired good before a king set out on a journey, so John the Baptist was sent ahead of Jesus to prepare people's hearts for his coming and his message. It was a slave's job to take off a man's sandals.

10. *Key "Quotable Quote"*

"God gets down on his knees among us; gets on our level and shares himself with us. He does not reside afar off and send diplomatic messages."
Eugene H. Peterson

Luke chapter 4

1. *Before and after*

Previous chapter: Chapter 3: John the Baptist's ministry and Jesus' baptism
Following chapter: Chapter 5: Miracles of Jesus and the calling of Levi

2. *Analysis of chapter*

The temptation of Christ. (1-13)
Christ in the synagogue of Nazareth. (14-30)
He expels an unclean spirit and heals the sick. (31-44)

3. *Key verse*

Verse 1: "Jesus, full of the Holy Spirit, returned from the Jordan and was led by the Spirit in the desert."

4. *Key word / key phrase*

Verse 2, "he was tempted by the devil."

5. *Key event / key person / key theme*

Jesus' temptation

6. *Key thought*

"The question facing Jesus was, 'What does it mean to live as the obedient Son of God?'" (Stephen Travis)

7. *Key thing to look out for*

Jesus came to minister to people. Luke records the opening scenes of Jesus' compassionate work here.

8. *Key Bible cross-reference*

Verse 12. See Deuteronomy 6:16.

9. *Key "by way of explanation"*

Verse 23, "this proverb." The Greek word used here for "proverb" is *parabole*. It is taken from a verb which means to set things side by side next to each other so that they may be compared with each other. This word is used in the New Testament for both a short descriptive story, and for a proverb.

10. *Key "Quotable Quote"*

"Let him who would indeed be a Christian learn from the lives of eminent Christians the best ways to overcome temptation and to grow in every aspect of holiness."
William Wilberforce

Luke chapter 5

1. Before and after

Previous chapter: Chapter 4: Jesus' temptation, rejection at Nazareth, and early miracles

Following chapter: Chapter 6: Jesus chooses the Twelve and teaches them

2. Analysis of chapter

The miraculous catch of fish. Peter, James, and John called. (1-11)

A leper healed. (12-16)

A paralytic cured. (17-26)

Levi called. Christ's answer to the Pharisees. (27-39)

3. Key verse

Verse 5: "Master, we've worked hard all night and haven't caught anything. But because you say so, I will let down the nets."

4. Key word / key phrase

Verse 17, "to heal the sick."

5. Key event / key person / key theme

Miracles

6. Key thought

The startling newness of the Christian life.

7. Key thing to look out for

Jesus was constantly being questioned by people who had no sympathy with him.

8. Key Bible cross-reference

Verse 14. See Leviticus 14:1-32.

9. Key "by way of explanation"

Verse 17, "Pharisees." The name "Pharisee" refers to a religious party and means "Separated One." In order, as they thought, to please God, Pharisees sought to keep every minute requirement of the Law – not only the law of Moses, but the extensive elaborations of it. The "scribes" were men whose full-time job it was to interpret, teach and apply the Law. Most scribes came from the party of the Pharisees. Scribes and Pharisees were held in great respect by ordinary people.

10. Key "Quotable Quote"

"God is in the hypocrite's mouth, but the world is in his heart."
William Gurnall

Luke chapter 6

1. Before and after

Previous chapter: Chapter 5: Miracles of Jesus and the calling of Levi
Following chapter: Chapter 7: Two miracles, John the Baptist, and in the home of a Pharisee

2. Analysis of chapter

The disciples pick corn on the Sabbath. (1-5)
Works of mercy allowed on the Sabbath day. (6-11)
The apostles chosen. (12-19)
Blessings and woes declared. (20-26)
Christ teaches about mercy. (27-36)
And justice and sincerity. (37-49)

3. Key verse

Verse 7: "The Pharisees and the teachers of the law were looking for a reason to accuse Jesus, so they watched him closely to see if he would heal on the Sabbath."

4. Key word / key phrase

Verse 13, "chose twelve."

5. Key event / key person / key theme

Jesus chooses the Twelve

6. Key thought

"Love your enemies" must have always seemed to be an impossible command to carry out.

7. Key thing to look out for

The more we appreciate God's mercy the more merciful we should be.

8. Key Bible cross-reference

Verse 4. See Leviticus 24:9.

9. Key "by way of explanation"

Verse 37, "do not judge." Jesus forbade his followers from indulging in hypocritical judging of other people. This is not the same as exercising discernment between right and wrong, which Jesus did encourage.

10. Key "Quotable Quote"

"If we had no faults ourselves, we should not take so much delight in noticing those of others."
François duc de La Rochefoucauld

Luke chapter 7

1. *Before and after*

Previous chapter: Chapter 6: Jesus chooses the Twelve and teaches them
Following chapter: Chapter 8: The parable of the sower and three miracles

2. *Analysis of chapter*

The centurion's servant healed. (1-10)
The widow's son raised. (11-18)
John the Baptist's question about Jesus. (19-35)
Christ anointed in the house of the Pharisee and the parable of the two debtors. (36-50)

3. *Key verse*

Verse 12: "As he approached the town gate, a dead person was being carried out – the only son of his mother, and she was a widow."

4. *Key word / key phrase*

Verse 50, "your faith has saved you."

5. *Key event / key person / key theme*

Jesus brings back to life the son of the widow of Nain

6. *Key thought*

This chapter is full of people with remarkable faith.

7. *Key thing to look out for*

Note how the four people demonstrated their faith in Jesus.

8. *Key Bible cross-reference*

Verse 22. See Isaiah 61:1.

9. *Key "by way of explanation"*

Verse 14, "coffin." When Jesus spoke to the dead man he told him to sit up. This indicates that he was carried in an open coffin which was common Jewish practice.

10. *Key "Quotable Quote"*

"She sat and wept, and with her untressed hair
She wiped the feet she was blest to touch;
And he wiped off the soiling despair
From her sweet soul – because she loved so much."
Dante Gabriel Rossetti

Luke chapter 8

1. *Before and after*

Previous chapter: Chapter 7: Two miracles, John the Baptist, and in the home of a Pharisee

Following chapter: Chapter 9: Feeding of the five thousand, Jesus' transfiguration, and Peter's confession

2. *Analysis of chapter*

The ministry of Christ. (1-3)
The parable of the sower. (4-21)
Christ calms the storm and heals a demon-possessed man. (22-40)
The daughter of Jairus restored to life. (41-56)

3. *Key verse*

Verse 21: "My mother and brothers are those who hear God's word and put it into practice."

4. *Key word / key phrase*

Verse 25, "Who is this?"

5. *Key event / key person / key theme*

Parable of the sower

6. *Key thought*

Note the different things that prevent spiritual growth according to the parable of the sower.

7. *Key thing to look out for*

Verse 18 places a heavy responsibility on the shoulders of those who have been blessed with special talents and opportunities.

8. *Key Bible cross-reference*

Verse 10. See Isaiah 6:9,10.

9. *Key "by way of explanation"*

Verse 18, "consider carefully how you listen." This was especially important for these first disciples since what they heard they taught to others. See also Luke 19:26.

10. *Key "Quotable Quote"*

"Whatever you have received more than others in health, talents, abilities, success, a pleasant childhood, or in harmonious conditions of home life, all this you must not take to yourself as a matter of course. In gratitude for your good fortune, render some sacrifice of your own life for another life."
Albert Schweitzer

Luke chapter 9

1. Before and after

Previous chapter: Chapter 8: The parable of the sower and three miracles
Following chapter: Chapter 10: The mission of the seventy-two disciples and
the parable of the good Samaritan

2. Analysis chapter

The apostles sent out. (1-9)
The multitude miraculously fed. (10-17)
Peter's testimony to Christ. Self-denial commanded. (18-27)
The transfiguration. (28-36)
An evil spirit expelled. (37-42)
Christ checks the ambition of his disciples. (43-50)
He reproves their mistaken zeal. (51-56)
Everything to be given up for Christ. (57-62)

3. Key verse

Verse 23: "If anyone would come after me, he must deny himself and take up
his cross daily and follow me."

4. Key word / key phrase

Verse 29, "as bright as a flash of lightning."

5. Key event / key person / key theme

Jesus' transfiguration

6. Key thought

Here is the truth about being a disciple of Jesus.

7. Key thing to look out for

The frequent references made to Jesus' impending death. When Jesus set out
"resolutely" (verse 51) for Jerusalem, he had the cross in view.

8. Key biblical cross-reference

Verses 3-5. See Acts 13:51.

9. Key "by way of explanation"

Verse 30: "departure." When Jesus was transfigured Moses and Elijah spoke of
his "departure." In Greek, the word is "exodus." Jesus' death is linked to God's
rescue of his people from Egypt.

10. Key "Quotable Quote"

Verse 22: "The Son of Man must suffer." "The 'must' is not of resignation to
fate but of self-giving to God's plan of salvation."
J.C. Ryle

Luke chapter 10

1. Before and after

Previous chapter: Chapter 9: Feeding of the five thousand, Jesus' transfiguration, and Peter's confession

Following chapter: Chapter 11: The Lord's Prayer and further teaching

2. Analysis of chapter

Seventy-two disciples sent out. (1-16)
The joy of Christ's disciples. (17-24)
The good Samaritan. (25-37)
Jesus at the home of Martha and Mary. (38-42)

3. Key verse

Verse 1: "After this the Lord appointed seventy-two others and sent them two by two ahead of him to every town and place where he was about to go."

4. Key word / key phrase

Verse 37, "Go and do likewise."

5. Key event / key person / key theme

The good Samaritan

6. Key thought

As the harvest is still plentiful what should happen?

7. Key thing to look out for

Note, verse 21, what made Jesus full of joy.

8. Key Bible cross-reference

Verse 7. See 1 Corinthians 9:14.

9. Key "by way of explanation"

Verse 27, "Love . . . God . . . Love your neighbor." When Jesus said this he was linking together Deuteronomy 6:5 and Leviticus 19:18. Jesus demanded nothing short of total devotion to God and dedication to helping people. Verse 1: some early manuscripts have seventy-two, and others have seventy here.

10. Key "Quotable Quote"

"Attitudes displayed in the parable of the good Samaritan
1. The Robbers: What's yours is mine if I can get it.
2. The Priest: What's mine is mine if I can keep it.
3. The Innkeeper: What's mine is yours if you can pay for it.
4. The Samaritan: What's mine is yours if you need it."
Tear Fund

Luke chapter 11

1. Before and after

Previous chapter: Chapter 10: The mission of the seventy-two disciples and
the parable of the good Samaritan
Following chapter: Chapter 12: Jesus teaches a large crowd

2. Analysis of chapter

The disciples taught to pray. (1-4)
Christ encourages believing prayer. (5-13)
Christ expels a devil, and the blasphemy of the Pharisees. (14-26)
True happiness. (27,28)
Christ reproves the Jews. (29-36)
He reproves the Pharisees. (37-54)

3. Key verse

Verse 1: "Lord, teach us to pray, just as John taught his disciples."

4. Key word / key phrase

Verse 2, "when you pray."

5. Key event / key person / key theme

The Lord's Prayer

6. Key thought

"Your kingdom come." The word "kingdom" does not refer to a place but to a
"situation in which God is King." "Wherever God is in control, his sovereignty
accepted and his will obeyed, there is God's kingship." (R.T. France)

7. Key thing to look out for

How to avoid three terrible states: the empty soul (verse 25), the soul full of
darkness (verse 34), the soul full of greed and wickedness (verse 39).

8. Key Bible cross-reference

Verse 42. See Leviticus 27:30.

9. Key "by way of explanation"

Verse 46, "load people down." Experts in the Law knew ways round the Law
but made existing laws sit even more heavily on the shoulders of ordinary
people by adding to them and by not helping anyone to keep them.

10. Key "Quotable Quote"

"True religion disposes persons to be much alone in solitary places for holy
meditation and prayer."
Jonathan Edwards

Luke chapter 12

1. Before and after

Previous chapter: Chapter 11: The Lord's Prayer and further teaching
Following chapter: Chapter 13: A healing, three kingdom parables, and weeping over Jerusalem

2. Analysis of chapter

Christ reproves the interpreters of the Law. (1-12)
A caution against greed. The parable of the rich man. (13-21)
Worldly care reproved. (22-40)
Watchfulness commanded. (41-53)
A warning to be reconciled to God. (54-59)

3. Key verse

Verse 13: "Teacher, tell my brother to divide the inheritance with me."

4. Key word / key phrase

Verse 1, "a crowd of many thousands."

5. Key event / key person / key theme

Jesus teaches a large crowd

6. Key thought

Called to be watchful and fearless.

7. Key thing to look out for

What can be learned from the warnings in this chapter?

8. Key Bible cross-reference

Verse 53. See Micah 7:6.

9. Key "by way of explanation"

Verse 29, "worry." This word in the Greek describes a storm-tossed ship which is literally raised between heaven and earth. Worry achieves nothing. Jesus points out that it is irrational to worry.

10. Key "Quotable Quote"

"There is no Christian solution of the problems presented by self-will; but there is a Christian cure and if that is effective, the problem is abolished. So when a man wanted Jesus to divide an inheritance, that is to arbitrate between two self-centered claims, he refused. He did not settle the dispute; but he did tell them how to avoid continuing the dispute. 'Take heed and keep yourselves from covetousness.'"
William Temple

Luke chapter 13

1. Before and after

Previous chapter: Chapter 12: Jesus teaches a large crowd
Following chapter: Chapter 14: Jesus teaches the Pharisees, and teaches about discipleship

2. Analysis of chapter

Christ exhorts people to repent, using the example of the Galileans and others. (1-5)
Parable of the barren fig tree. (6-9)
A crippled woman healed. (10-17)
The parables of the mustard seed, and yeast. (18-22)
Command to enter through the narrow gate. (23-30)
Christ's reproof to Herod, and to the people of Jerusalem. (31-35)

3. Key verse

Verse 14: "There are six days for work. So come and be healed on those days, not on the Sabbath."

4. Key word / key phrase

Verse 34, "O Jerusalem, Jerusalem."

5. Key event / key person / key theme

Jesus weeps over Jerusalem

6. Key thought

Jesus never minced his words.

7. Key thing to look out for

Note the fate of those who refuse to repent.

8. Key Bible cross-reference

Verse 27. See Psalm 6:8.

9. Key "by way of explanation"

Verse 15, "untie his ox." Leading Jews had many clever ways of circumventing the law. They could justify assisting their own ox on the Sabbath, but this did not stop them from accusing Jesus of breaking the Sabbath for working on it, and healing someone.

10. Key "Quotable Quote"

"Superstition, idolatry, and hypocrisy have ample wages, but truth goes a begging."
Martin Luther

Luke chapter 14

1. **Before and after**

    Previous chapter: Chapter 13: A healing, three kingdom parables, and weeping over Jerusalem
    Following chapter: Chapter 15: The lost sheep, lost coin, and lost son

2. **Analysis of chapter**

    Christ heals a man on the Sabbath. (1-6)
    He teaches humility. (7-14)
    Parable of the great supper. (15-24)
    The necessity for consideration and self-denial. (25-35)

3. **Key verse**

    Verse 7: "When he noticed how the guests picked the places of honor at the table, he told them this parable."

4. **Key word / key phrase**

    Verse 1, "a prominent Pharisee."

5. **Key event / key person / key theme**

    Jesus teaches the Pharisees

6. **Key thought**

    Jesus insists on humility.

7. **Key thing to look out for**

    Jesus never underestimated the cost involved in following him.

8. **Key Bible cross-reference**

    Verse 35. See Jeremiah 22:5.

9. **Key "by way of explanation"**

    Verse 26, "hate his father." Jesus is clearly exaggerating to make a point here. As he had told people to love their neighbors he would not now tell them to hate their fathers. The expression sets out absolute priorities. Loyalty to Jesus always comes first.

10. **Key "Quotable Quote"**

    "Luke 14:33 shows what is meant by the calculation of expenses, with which Christ enjoins his followers to begin: it is to lead them to consider that they must forsake all. In vain do persons who are delighted with an easy, indolent life, and with exemption from the cross, undertake a profession of Christianity."
    John Calvin

Luke chapter 15

1. *Before and after*

Previous chapter: Chapter 14: Jesus teaches the Pharisees, and teaches about discipleship
Following chapter: Chapter 16: Jesus teaches about money

2. *Analysis of chapter*

Parables of the lost sheep, and the piece of silver. (1-10)
The prodigal son, his wickedness and distress. (11-16)
His repentance and pardon. (17-24)
The elder brother is offended. (25-32)

3. *Key verse*

Verse 11: "There was a man who had two sons."

4. *Key word / key phrase*

Verses 4,9,32, "lost."

5. *Key event / key person / key theme*

Three "lost" parables

6. *Key thought*

Jesus welcomes sinners (verse 2).

7. *Key thing to look out for*

Where did the elder son go wrong?

8. *Key Bible cross-reference*

Verse 20. See Genesis 45:14,15.

9. *Key "by way of explanation"*

Verse 15, "to feed pigs." That was the last thing a Jew would dream of doing, as pigs were regarded as "unclean" animals.

10. *Key "Quotable Quote"*

"His father saw him – there were eyes of mercy;
he ran to meet him – there were legs of mercy;
he put his arms round his neck – there were arms of mercy;
he kissed him – there were kisses of mercy;
he said to him – there were words of mercy;
Bring here the best robe – there were deeds of mercy;
Wonders of mercy – all mercy!
Oh, what a God of mercy he is!"
Matthew Henry

Luke chapter 16

1. *Before and after*

Previous chapter: Chapter 15: The lost sheep, lost coin, and lost son
Following chapter: Chapter 17: 10 lepers cured, and teaching on the Second
Coming

2. *Analysis of chapter*

The parable of the unjust steward. (1-12)
Christ reproves the hypocrisy of the covetous Pharisees. (13-18)
The rich man and Lazarus. (19-31)

3. *Key verse*

Verse 8: "For the people of this world are more shrewd in dealing with their
own kind than are the people of the light."

4. *Key word / key phrase*

Verse 1, "there was a rich man."

5. *Key event / key person / key theme*

Jesus teaches about money

6. *Key thought*

Note the point commended in the parable about the manager.

7. *Key thing to look out for*

Where did the rich man go wrong in the parable of the rich man and Lazarus?

8. *Key Bible cross-reference*

Verse 18. See 1 Corinthians 7:10,11.

9. *Key "by way of explanation"*

Verse 9, "use worldly wealth." There are many warnings about the dangers of
riches in the Bible. But this verse teaches that wealth can be thought of as
talent which should be fully employed in God's service.

10. *Key "Quotable Quote"*

"The fulfillment of the Lord's mercy does not depend upon believers' works,
but . . . in those who are directed to the good by his Spirit he recognizes the
only genuine insignia of his children."
John Calvin

Luke chapter 17

1. Before and after

Previous chapter: Chapter 16: Jesus teaches about money
Following chapter: Chapter 18: Jesus and prayer, children, sacrifice, and his own death and resurrection

2. Analysis of chapter

Sin, faith, duty. (1-10)
Ten lepers cleansed. (11-19)
Christ's kingdom. (20-37)

3. Key verse

Verse 6: "If you have faith as small as a mustard seed, you can say to this mulberry tree, 'Be uprooted and planted in the sea,' and it will obey you."

4. Key word / key phrase

Verse 12, "ten men who had leprosy."

5. Key event / key person / key theme

Gratitude

6. Key thought

What does ingratitude indicate?

7. Key thing to look out for

The point about faith is not its size but in whom it is placed.

8. Key Bible cross-reference

Verse 27. See Genesis 7:6-24.

9. Key "by way of explanation"

Verse 2, "millstone." The point about the very heavy stones used for grinding is that it conjures up a terrible picture of punishment: death by drowning.

10. Key "Quotable Quote"

"The first element in faith is what we can only call receptivity. Faith is the response of trust of a man's total personality to the love of God as shown to us in the life and death of Jesus Christ."
William Barclay

Luke chapter 18

1. Before and after

Previous chapter: Chapter 17: Ten lepers cured, and teaching on the Second Coming

Following chapter: Chapter 19: Zacchaeus, entering Jerusalem, and cleansing the temple

2. Analysis of chapter

The parable of the persistent widow. (1-8)
The Pharisee and the tax-collector. (9-14)
Children brought to Christ. (15-17)
The ruler hindered by his riches. (18-30)
Christ talks of his death. (31-34)
A blind man restored to sight. (35-43)

3. Key verse

Verse 27: "What is impossible with men is possible with God."

4. Key word / key phrase

Verse 16, "Jesus called the children to him."

5. Key event / key person / key theme

Jesus and prayer

6. Key thought

The only way to enter the kingdom of heaven is as a little child.

7. Key thing to look out for

What do the stories and conversations in this chapter have to say about prayer?

8. Key Bible cross-reference

Verse 32. See Genesis 19:26.

9. Key "by way of explanation"

Verse 31, "everything that is written by the prophets." The death of the Messiah is prophesied in a number of places in the Old Testament, such as Psalm 22, Isaiah 53, and Zechariah 13:7.

10. Key "Quotable Quote"

"What the Church needs today is not more or better machinery, not new organizations, or more novel methods; but men whom the Holy Spirit can use – men of prayer, men mighty in prayer."
E.M. Bounds

Luke chapter 19

1. *Before and after*

Previous chapter: Chapter 18: Jesus and prayer, children, sacrifice, and his own death and resurrection

Following chapter: Chapter 20: Jesus' public teaching in Jerusalem

2. *Analysis of chapter*

The conversion of Zacchaeus. (1-10)
The parable of the nobleman and his servants. (11-27)
Christ enters Jerusalem. (28-40)
Christ weeps over Jerusalem. (41-48)

3. *Key verse*

Verse 2: "A man was there by the name of Zacchaeus; he was a chief tax collector and was wealthy"

4. *Key word / key phrase*

Verse 10, "to seek and to save what was lost."

5. *Key event / key person / key theme*

Entering Jerusalem

6. *Key thought*

In the parable about the ten minas Jesus praises faithfulness.

7. *Key thing to look out for*

The many different responses to Jesus

8. *Key Bible cross-reference*

Verse 38. See Psalm 118:26.

9. *Key "by way of explanation"*

Verse 30, "colt." Jesus entered Jerusalem in the most humble way imaginable. He was also doing so in a most public way. He was the son of David entering his city as King.

10. *Key "Quotable Quote"*

"Humility is the secret of blessing, our salvation, true heavenly-mindedness, the primacy in the Church, the only ladder to honor in God's kingdom, the most essential element of discipleship."
Andrew Murray

Luke chapter 21

(Luke chapter 20:1-8, see Matthew 21:23-27; 20:9-19, see Matthew 21:33-46; 20-47, see Matthew 22:15–23:7.)

1. Before and after

Previous chapter: Chapter 20: Jesus' public teaching in Jerusalem
Following chapter: Chapter 22: The Last Supper, Gethsemane, and Peter's denial

2. Analysis of chapter

Christ commends a poor widow. (1-4)
His prophecy. (5-28)
Christ commands watchfulness. (29-38)

3. Key verse

Verse 2: "He also saw a poor widow put in two very small copper coins."

4. Key word / key phrase

Verse 8, "Watch out that you are not deceived."

5. Key event / key person / key theme

Jesus teaches about the future

6. Key thought

At every point of our lives Jesus responds to our motives.

7. Key thing to look out for

What do dissipation, drunkenness and anxiety have in common?

8. Key Bible cross-reference

Verse 25. See Ezekiel 32:7.

9. Key "by way of explanation"

Verse 1, "the temple treasury" consisted of thirteen boxes in the court of women into which people put their gifts for the temple.

10. Key "Quotable Quote"

"A sacrifice without a heart, without salt, without fire, of what value is it?"
John Owen

Luke chapter 22

1. Before and after

Previous chapter: Chapter 21: Jesus teaches about the future
Following chapter: Chapter 23: Jesus' trials, crucifixion, and burial

2. Analysis of chapter

The treachery of Judas. (1-6)
The Passover. (7-18)
The Lord's Supper instituted. (19,20)
Christ admonishes the disciples. (21-38)
Christ's agony in the garden. (39-46)
Christ betrayed. (47-53)
The fall of Peter. (54-62)
Christ declares himself to be the Son of God. (63-71)

3. Key verse

Verse 8: "Go and make preparations for us to eat the Passover."

4. Key word / key phrase

Verse 54, "Peter followed at a distance."

5. Key event / key person / key theme

The last supper; Jesus arrested

6. Key thought

Nobody forced Judas to betray Jesus.

7. Key thing to look out for

Even at the last supper the disciples were quarrelling about who was the most important.

8. Key Bible cross-reference

Verse 20. See Jeremiah 31:31-34.

9. Key "by way of explanation"

Verse 44, "drops of blood," could have been a mingling of sweat and blood, known as haematidrosis, or just a description of perspiration. Either way, these words highlight Jesus' anguish. There was an interrogation in the middle of the night followed by a formal trial at daybreak before a full session of the Sanhedrin.

10. Key "Quotable Quote"

"The death of Jesus was not the death of a martyr, it was the revelation of the eternal heart of God."
Oswald Chambers

Luke chapter 23

1. Before and after

Previous chapter: Chapter 22: The Last Supper, Gethsemane, and Peter's denial

Following chapter: Chapter 24: Jesus' resurrection and ascension

2. Analysis of chapter

Christ before Pilate. (1-5)

Christ before Herod. (6-12)

Barabbas preferred to Christ. (13-25)

Christ speaks about the destruction of Jerusalem. (26-31)

The crucifixion, and the repentant criminal. (32-43)

The death of Christ. (44-49)

The burial of Christ. (50-56)

3. Key verse

Verse 7: "When he learned that Jesus was under Herod's jurisdiction, he sent him to Herod, who was also in Jerusalem at that time."

4. Key word / key phrase

Verse 33, "they crucified him."

5. Key event / key person / key theme

The death of Jesus

6. Key thought

Even there in the mess and horror and torture of the cross, we see Jesus' deep compassion for others and communion with the Father (verse 46).

7. Key thing to look out for

The differing responses of the people: at the foot of the cross, including those who ignored Jesus. Where do we place ourselves?

8. Key Bible cross-reference

Verse 30. See Hosea 10:8.

9. Key "by way of explanation"

Under Roman law the Sanhedrin did not have authority to pass a death sentence on Jesus. He therefore had to be taken to Pilate. Verse 38, "written notice." Above the head of the dying criminal a notice was placed on which was written his crime. Pilate's notice would have greatly annoyed the Jews.

10. Key "Quotable Quote"

"It costs God nothing, so far as we know, to create nice things: but to convert rebellious wills cost him crucifixion."

C.S. Lewis

Luke chapter 24

1. Previous chapter

Chapter 23: Jesus' trials, crucifixion, and burial

2. Analysis of chapter

The resurrection of Christ. (1-12)
He appears to two disciples on the way to Emmaus. (13-27)
And makes himself known to them. (28-35)
Christ appears to the other disciples. (36-49)
His ascension. (50-53)

3. Key verse

Verse 6: "He is not here; he has risen!"

4. Key word / key phrase

Verse 15, "Jesus himself . . . walked along with them."

5. Key event / key person / key theme

Jesus' resurrection appearances

6. Key thought

Verse 45 indicates that our minds need to be opened when reading the Bible.

7. Key thing to look out for

"There is no worse screen to block out the Spirit than confidence in our own intelligence."
John Calvin commenting on Luke 24:45

8. Key Bible cross-reference

Verse 49. See Acts 1:4.

9. Key "by way of explanation"

Verse 9, "to the Eleven and to all the others." After Judas had committed suicide Jesus' twelve disciples were reduced in number to eleven, and this verse indicates that they were known as the "Eleven." However, even after Judas' death, they were still called the "Twelve" sometimes. John 20:24.

10. Key "Quotable Quote"

"True discrimination between right and wrong does not then depend on the acuteness of our intelligence, but on the wisdom of the Spirit."
John Calvin commenting on Luke 24:16

John

John chapter 1

1. Following chapter

Chapter 2: Water into wine and cleansing the temple

2. Analysis of chapter

The divinity of Christ. (1-5)
His divine and human nature. (6-14)
John the Baptist's testimony to Christ. (15-18)
John's public testimony about Christ. (19-28)
Other testimonies of John about Christ. (29-36)
Andrew and Simon Peter follow Jesus. (37-42)
Philip and Nathanael are called to follow Jesus. (43-51)

3. Key verse

Verse 1: "In the beginning was the Word, and the Word was with God, and the Word was God."

4. Key word / key phrase

Verse 17, "grace and truth came through Jesus Christ."

5. Key event / key person / key theme

The Word becomes flesh

6. Key thought

Note how John opens his Gospel is a totally different way from the other three Gospels.

7. Key thing to look out for

How does someone become a child of God?

8. Key Bible cross-reference

Verse 51. See Genesis 28:12.

9. Key "by way of explanation"

Verse 29, "Lamb of God." This verse and verse 36 are the only places where this expression is found in the Bible. But under the Old Testament law, lambs were sacrificed regularly for the sins of the people. See Isaiah 53:7; Jeremiah 11:19.

10. Key "Quotable Quote"

"The four Gospels all had the same purpose: to point out Christ. The first three Gospels show his body, so to speak, but John shows his soul. For this reason I usually say that this Gospel is a key to understanding the rest; for whoever understands the power of Christ strikingly pictured here will then profit by reading what the others tell about the Redeemer who appeared."
John Calvin

John chapter 2

1. *Before and after*

   Previous chapter: Chapter 1: Special introduction, John the Baptist, and first disciples
   Following chapter: Chapter 3: Jesus and Nicodemus

2. *Analysis of chapter*

   The miracle at Cana. (1-11)
   Christ throw the traders out of the temple. (12-22)
   Many believe in Christ. (23-25)

3. *Key verse*

   Verse 11: "This, the first of his miraculous signs, Jesus performed at Cana in Galilee. He thus revealed his glory, and his disciples put their faith in him."

4. *Key word / key phrase*

   Verse 1, "a wedding . . . at Cana."

5. *Key event / key person / key theme*

   The wedding at Cana

6. *Key thought*

   John always refers to Jesus' miracles as "signs," verse 11. In this way he highlights the fact that the purpose of the miracles was to point to the identity of Jesus and stimulate faith.

7. *Key thing to look out for*

   The fine wine was a symbol of the new covenant inaugurated by Jesus. What was the effect of this first sign?

8. *Key Bible cross-reference*

   Verse 17. See Psalm 69:9.

9. *Key "by way of explanation"*

   Verse 1, "a wedding." Celebrations after a wedding often went on for up to a week. To run out of wine would have been more than a slight embarrassment. It would have been thought of as a major sign of inhospitality.

10. *Key "Quotable Quote"*

    "I prefer you to make mistakes in kindness than work miracles in unkindness."
    Mother Teresa of Calcutta

John chapter 3

1. Before and after

Previous chapter: Chapter 2: Water into wine and cleansing the temple
Following chapter: Chapter 4: Jesus and the woman of Samaria

2. Analysis of chapter

Christ's conversation with Nicodemus. (1-21)
John the Baptist's testimony about Christ. (22-36)

3. Key verse

Verse 16: "For God so loved the world that he gave his one and only Son, that whoever believes in him shall not perish but have eternal life."

4. Key word / key phrase

Verse 1, "a member of the Jewish ruling council."

5. Key event / key person / key theme

Jesus and Nicodemus

6. Key thought

Note the context of the most famous verse in the Bible, verse 16.

7. Key thing to look out for

Jesus insists on the necessity of the new birth.

8. Key Bible cross-reference

Verse 14. See Numbers 21:9.

9. Key "by way of explanation"

Verse 2, "at night." Nicodemus came to Jesus at night. Maybe he wanted to speak with Jesus when others would not see him, or maybe he wanted an unhurried time with Jesus, which the bustle of Jesus' day would have prevented.

10. Key "Quotable Quote"

"The Church is largely wasting her time in talking politics, and in imagining that, if you give people the Christian ethic and urge them to practice it, the problems of the world will be solved. It cannot be done: regeneration is essential."
D. Martyn Lloyd-Jones

John chapter 4

1. Before and after

Previous chapter: Chapter 3: Jesus and Nicodemus
Following chapter: Chapter 5: Opposition at the feast in Jerusalem

2. Analysis of chapter

Christ goes to Galilee. (1-3)
His conversation with the Samaritan woman. (4-26)
The effects of Christ's conversation with the woman of Samaria. (27-42)
Christ heals the nobleman's son. (43-54)

3. Key verse

Verse 42: "We no longer believe just because of what you said; now we have heard for ourselves, and we know that this man really is the Savior of the world."

4. Key word / key phrase

Verse 14, "a spring of water welling up to eternal life."

5. Key event / key person / key theme

Jesus and the woman of Samaria

6. Key thought

This woman witnessed immediately and many Samaritans believed in Jesus.

7. Key thing to look out for

Note how Jesus turns the conversation to spiritual matters.

8. Key Bible cross-reference

Verse 9. See Ezra 4:1-5.

9. Key "by way of explanation"

Verse 42, "the Savior of the world." Only John, in 1 John 4:14 and here in this verse, uses this expression. It points to Jesus as the Savior, and to his global significance. John gives only seven "signs" (miracles) in his Gospel. The healing of the nobleman's son is the second.

10. Key "Quotable Quote"

"He who in his preaching neglects to lead men to a fuller knowledge of God and to the way of eternal salvation may be called an idle declaimer, but not a preacher of the Gospel."
Pope Benedict XV

John chapter 5

1. Before and after

Previous chapter: Chapter 4: Jesus and the woman of Samaria
Following chapter: Chapter 6: Jesus is the bread of life

2. Analysis of chapter

The healing at the pool of Bethesda. (1-9)
The Jews' displeasure. (10-16)
Christ reproves the Jews. (17-23)
Christ's teaching. (24-47)

3. Key verse

Verse 14: "See, you are well again. Stop sinning or something worse may happen to you."

4. Key word / key phrase

Verse 16, "the Jews persecuted him."

5. Key event / key person / key theme

Jesus faces opposition

6. Key thought

Verse 24 must rank as one of the clearest verses about eternal life to be found in the Gospels.

7. Key thing to look out for

What Jesus looked for in people was the love of God in their hearts, verse 42.

8. Key Bible cross-reference

Verse 29. See Daniel 12:2.

9. Key "by way of explanation"

Verse 30, "By myself I can do nothing." Jesus often explained that without his heavenly Father he was unable to achieve anything.

10. Key "Quotable Quote"

"It is a destructive addition to add anything to Christ."
Richard Sibbes

John chapter 6

1. ### Before and after

   Previous chapter: Chapter 5: Opposition at the feast in Jerusalem
   Following chapter: Chapter 7: Jesus is the water of life

2. ### Analysis of chapter

   Five thousand miraculously fed. (1-14)
   Jesus walks on the sea. (15-21)
   He teaches about spiritual food. (22-27)
   His teaching to the crowds. (28-65)
   Many disciples turned back from following Christ. (66-71)

3. ### Key verse

   Verse 15: "Jesus, knowing that they intended to come and make him king by force, withdrew again to a mountain by himself."

4. ### Key word / key phrase

   Verse 35, "I am the bread of life."

5. ### Key event / key person / key theme

   Jesus is the bread of life

6. ### Key thought

   Jesus' actions, verses 1-15, always shed light on who he is, verse 35.

7. ### Key thing to look out for

   Grumbling has no place among those who seek God, verse 43.

8. ### Key Bible cross-reference

   Verse 45. See Isaiah 54:13.

9. ### Key "by way of explanation"

   Verse 35, "I am." Jesus' use of this phrase was deliberate. This is the first of seven times that it is recorded by John. The words are emphatic in the Greek and echo Exodus 3:14.

10. ### Key "Quotable Quote"

    "I don't preach a social gospel; I preach the Gospel, period. The gospel of our Lord Jesus Christ is concerned for the whole person. When people were hungry, Jesus didn't say, 'Now is that political or social?' He said, 'I feed you.' Because the good news to a hungry person is bread."
    Desmond Tutu

John chapter 7

1. Before and after

Previous chapter: Chapter 6: Jesus is the bread of life
Following chapter: Chapter 8: The woman caught in adultery, and Jesus the Light of the world

2. Analysis of chapter

Christ goes to the Feast of Tabernacles. (1-13)
His teaching at the Feast. (14-39)
The people argue about Christ. (40-53)

3. Key verse

Verse 16: "My teaching is not my own. It comes from him who sent me."

4. Key word / key phrase

Verse 37, "come to me and drink."

5. Key event / key person / key theme

Jesus is the water of life

6. Key thought

Wherever Jesus went he caused a division among his hearers.

7. Key thing to look out for

The religious leaders were Jesus' fiercest enemies.

8. Key Bible cross-reference

Verse 2. See Leviticus 23:34.

9. Key "by way of explanation"

Verse 39, "glorified," refers to Jesus' death, resurrection, and ascension. The Feast of Tabernacles was the Harvest Festival, and the time when the Jews remembered God's care for them in the wilderness.

10. Key "Quotable Quote"

"Spirituality really means 'Holy Spirit at work.'"
Leon Joseph Suenens

John chapter 8

1. Before and after

Previous chapter: Chapter 7: Jesus is the water of life
Following chapter: Chapter 9: Jesus heals a blind man

2. Analysis of chapter

The Pharisees and the adulteress. (1-11)
Christ's teaching with the Pharisees. (12-59)

3. Key verse

Verse 12: "I am the light of the world. Whoever follows me will never walk in darkness, but will have the light of life."

4. Key word / key phrase

Verse 12, "I am the light of the world."

5. Key event / key person / key theme

Jesus the Light of the world

6. Key thought

Jesus is the one who takes away our darkness.

7. Key thing to look out for

Considering how genuinely humble Jesus was, is it not remarkable that he was so outspoken about who he was?

8. Key Bible cross-reference

Verse 5. See Leviticus 20:10.

9. Key "by way of explanation"

Verse 12, "I am." This is the second of Jesus' "I ams." See also John 6:35; 9:5; 10:7,9;10:11,14; 11:25; 14:6; 15:1,5.

10. Key "Quotable Quote"

"We live in a world full of people struggling to be, or at least to appear strong, in order not to be weak; and we follow a gospel which says that when I am weak, then I am strong. And this gospel is the only thing that brings healing."
N.T. Wright

John chapter 9

1. Before and after

Previous chapter: Chapter 8: The woman caught in adultery, and Jesus the light of the world

Following chapter: Chapter 10: Jesus is the good shepherd

2. Analysis of chapter

Christ heals a man born blind. (1-7)
The account given by the blind man. (8-12)
The Pharisees question the man who had been blind. (13-17)
They ask about him. (18-23)
They throw him out. (24-34)
Christ's words to the man that had been blind. (35-38)
He reproves the Pharisees. (39-41)

3. Key verse

Verse 2: "Rabbi, who sinned, this man or his parents, that he was born blind?"

4. Key word / key phrase

Verse 7, "came home seeing."

5. Key event / key person / key theme

Jesus heals a blind man.

6. Key thought

Note the links between physical and spiritual sight in this chapter.

7. Key thing to look out for

Verse 38 puts belief in Jesus and worship of Jesus side by side.

8. Key Bible cross-reference

Verse 31. See Genesis 18:23-32.

9. Key "by way of explanation"

Verse 18, "the Jews" were among Jesus' most strident opponents. Instead of seeing Jesus' actions as miraculous they tried to undermine his every step and every statement.

10. Key "Quotable Quote"

"There is no strength in unbelief."
George MacDonald

John chapter 10

1. *Before and after*

Previous chapter: Chapter 9: Jesus heals a blind man
Following chapter: Chapter 11: Jesus brings Lazarus back to life

2. *Analysis of chapter*

The parable of the good shepherd. (1-5)
Christ the Door. (6-9)
Christ the good shepherd. (10-18)
The Jews' opinion about Jesus. (19-21)
His teaching at the Feast of Dedication. (22-30)
The Jews attempt to stone Jesus. (31-38)
He leaves Jerusalem. (39-42)

3. *Key verse*

Verse 11: "I am the good shepherd. The good shepherd lays down his life for the sheep."

4. *Key word / key phrase*

Verse 11, "I am the good shepherd."

5. *Key event / key person / key theme*

Jesus is the Good Shepherd

6. *Key thought*

Verse 15, "I lay down my life." This is the gospel of Jesus in a nutshell. It shows that his death was voluntary and purposeful and for others.

7. *Key thing to look out for*

This chapter indicates how often Jesus' opponents longed to get their hands on him.

8. *Key Bible cross-reference*

Verse 33. See Leviticus 24:16.

9. *Key "by way of explanation"*

In the Old Testament God was called the Shepherd. "The gate" or "door." The sheepfolds on the hillsides that shepherds build in the summer did not have doors. The shepherd himself would lie across the opening.

10. *Key "Quotable Quote"*

"To Christ all the types and shadows point! Of Christ all the prophecies give witness! While all the glory of the Scriptures, from Genesis to Revelation, culminates at the cross of Christ."
Octavius Winslow

John chapter 11

1. Before and after

Previous chapter: Chapter 10: Jesus is the good shepherd
Following chapter: Chapter 12: Jesus enters Jerusalem and teaches

2. Analysis of chapter

Lazarus' illness. (1-6)
Christ returns to Judea. (7-10)
The death of Lazarus. (11-16)
Christ arrives at Bethany. (17-32)
He raises Lazarus. (33-46)
The Pharisees call a meeting about Jesus. (47-53)
The Jews look for him. (54-57)

3. Key verse

Verse 25: "I am the resurrection and the life. He who believes in me will live, even though he dies."

4. Key word / key phrase

Verse 43, "Lazarus, come out!"

5. Key event / key person / key theme

Jesus brings Lazarus back to life

6. Key thought

Note the link between the "I am" of Jesus, verse 25, and Jesus bringing Lazarus back to life.

7. Key thing to look out for

The purpose of the raising of Lazarus. Note also John 20:31.

8. Key Bible cross-reference

Verse 24. See Daniel 12:2.

9. Key "by way of explanation"

Verse 35, "Jesus wept." This is the shortest verse in the Bible. It refers to shedding tears rather than loud wailing.

10. Key "Quotable Quote"

"Jesus Christ's claim of divinity is the most serious claim anyone ever made. Everything about Christianity hinges on his incarnation, crucifixion, and resurrection. That's what Christmas, Good Friday, and Easter are all about."
Luis Palau

John chapter 12

1. Before and after

Previous chapter: Chapter 11: Jesus brings Lazarus back to life
Following chapter: Chapter 13: Jesus washes his disciples' feet

2. Analysis of chapter

Christ anointed by Mary. (1-11)
He enters Jerusalem. (12-19)
Greeks ask to see Jesus. (20-26)
A voice from heaven bears testimony to Christ. (27-33)
His teaching the people. (34-36)
Unbelief of the Jews. (37-43)
Christ speaks to them. (44-50)

3. Key verse

Verse 32: "But I, when I am lifted up from the earth, will draw all men to myself."

4. Key word / key phrase

Verse 23, "the hour has come."

5. Key event / key person / key theme

Jesus teaches about his death

6. Key thought

Bringing Lazarus back to life did have an effect on some people, verses 17,18.

7. Key thing to look out for

Sheer jealousy seems to have held sway in the hearts of the Pharisees, verse 19.

8. Key Bible cross-reference

Verse 15. See Zechariah 9:9.

9. Key "by way of explanation"

Verse 12, "great crowd." This large number of people would have been in Jerusalem at this time for the Passover Feast. It was one of the three annual festivals that Jewish men had to attend.

10. Key "Quotable Quote"

"No more energy must be wasted in the wrangling and jealousy that can only lead to death."
Clement of Rome

John chapter 13

1. Before and after

Previous chapter: Chapter 12: Jesus enters Jerusalem and teaches
Following chapter: Chapter 14: Jesus teaches about the promised Holy Spirit

2. Analysis of chapter

Christ washes the disciples' feet. (1-17)
The treachery of Judas foretold. (18-30)
Christ commands the disciples to love one another. (31-38)

3. Key verse

Verse 5: "After that, he poured water into a basin and began to wash his disciples' feet, drying them with the towel that was wrapped around him."

4. Key word / key phrase

Verse 14, "you also should wash one another's feet."

5. Key event / key person / key theme

Jesus washes his disciples' feet

6. Key thought

Verse 34, "A new command." It may be asked in what sense this command, which was really an old one, see Leviticus 19:18, could be called a "new" one. It was new in the sense that it showed the quality of the love followers of Jesus should have, as a result of Jesus' love for them.

7. Key thing to look out for

Note that Jesus is in control of all the events of the last few days of his life.

8. Key Bible cross-reference

Verse 18. See Psalm 41:9.

9. Key "by way of explanation"

At a meal a host would frequently offer a special tit-bit to one of the diners. It was a token of special friendship.

10. Key "Quotable Quote"

"Jesus said love one another. He didn't say love the whole world."
Mother Teresa of Calcutta

John chapter 14

1. **Before and after**

   Previous chapter: Chapter 13: Jesus washes his disciples' feet
   Following chapter: Chapter 15: Jesus is the true vine

2. **Analysis of chapter**

   Christ comforts his disciples. (1-4)
   Seeing the Father. (5-11)
   The purpose of faith. (12-14)
   The Holy Spirit (15-31)

3. **Key verse**

   Verse 3: "And if I go and prepare a place for you, I will come back and take you to be with me that you also may be where I am."

4. **Key word / key phrase**

   Verse 26, "the Counselor, the Holy Spirit."

5. **Key event / key person / key theme**

   Jesus teaches about the promised Holy Spirit

6. **Key thought**

   Verse 1. Trusting in Jesus is the same as trusting in the Father.

7. **Key thing to look out for**

   What did Jesus promise about the Holy Spirit?

8. **Key Bible cross-reference**

   Verse 1. See Psalm 4:5.

9. **Key "by way of explanation"**

   Verse 17, "the Spirit of truth." Everything about the Holy Spirit is linked to and characterized by truth. The Holy Spirit leads people to the truth about God and to God himself, who is the truth.

10. **Key "Quotable Quote"**

    "Christianity is not a system of philosophy, nor a ritual, nor a code of laws; it is the impartation of a divine vitality. Without the way there is no going, without the truth there is no knowing, without life there is no living."
    Merrill Tenney

John chapter 15

1. Before and after

Previous chapter: Chapter 14: Jesus teaches about the promised Holy Spirit
Following chapter: Chapter 16: Jesus gives the Holy Spirit and predicts his own death and resurrection

2. Analysis of chapter

Christ the true vine. (1-8)
His love for his disciples. (9-17)
Persecution predicted. (18-25)
The Comforter promised. (26,27)

3. Key verse

Verse 5: "I am the vine; you are the branches. If a man remains in me and I in him, he will bear much fruit; apart from me you can do nothing."

4. Key word / key phrase

Verse 3, "Remain in me."

5. Key event / key person / key theme

Jesus is the true vine

6. Key thought

If we wish to know what "abiding" means, there is no better chapter in the Bible than this.

7. Key thing to look out for

Verse 9 explains, as no other Bible verse does, how much we are loved, and by whom we are loved.

8. Key Bible cross-reference

Verse 25. See Psalm 35:19.

9. Key "by way of explanation"

Verse 15, "servants . . . friends." To be a servant of Jesus is a great enough privilege. To be his friend blows the mind. But that is what is stated here.

10. Key "Quotable Quote"

"The true, the genuine worship is when man, through his spirit, attains to friendship and intimacy with God."
William Barclay

John chapter 16

1. *Before and after*

Previous chapter: Chapter 15: Jesus is the true vine
Following chapter: Chapter 17: Jesus prays to his Father

2. *Analysis of chapter*

Persecution predicted. (1-6)
The promise of the Holy Spirit, and his ministry. (7-15)
Christ's departure and return. (16-22)
Encouragement to pray. (23-27)
Christ and the Father. (28-33)

3. *Key verse*

Verse 16: "In a little while you will see me no more, and then after a little while you will see me."

4. *Key word / key phrase*

Verse 28, "I am leaving the world."

5. *Key event / key person / key theme*

Jesus predicts his own death and resurrection

6. *Key thought*

Jesus explains the work of the Holy Spirit in salvation.

7. *Key thing to look out for*

Verse 33. Jesus offers peace in a turbulent world. Rather, Jesus offers himself. This brings peace.

8. *Key Bible cross-reference*

Verse 2. See Revelation 6:9.

9. *Key "by way of explanation"*

Verse 23, "you will no longer ask me anything." This does not mean that the disciples should cease to ask for things in prayer. Rather they will not have any need for information. After the Resurrection and Pentecost they will understand what has hitherto baffled them.

10. *Key "Quotable Quote"*

"Oh, if thou knewest what peace to thyself thy holy life should bring . . . and what joy to others, me thinketh thou wouldst be more zealous for spiritual profit."
Thomas à Kempis

John chapter 17

1. **Before and after**

   Previous chapter: Chapter 16: Jesus gives the Holy Spirit and predicts his own death and resurrection
   Following chapter: Chapter 18: Jesus' arrest and trials

2. **Analysis of chapter**

   Christ's prayer for himself. (1-5)
   His prayer for his disciples. (6-20)
   His prayer for all believers. (21-26)

3. **Key verse**

   Verse 4: "I have brought you glory on earth by completing the work you gave me to do."

4. **Key word / key phrase**

   Verse 21, "that all of them may be one."

5. **Key event / key person / key theme**

   Jesus prays to his Father

6. **Key thought**

   Verse 4 explains what bringing glory to God involves.

7. **Key thing to look out for**

   Jesus never outgrew his need for prayer.

8. **Key Bible cross-reference**

   Verse 12. See Psalm 41:9.

9. **Key "by way of explanation"**

   Verse 12, "I protected them." In his own prayer Jesus shows that he has power to keep his followers safe. In that sense people have said that Christians are under God's special protection.

10. **Key "Quotable Quote"**

    "We stand at better advantage to find truth, and keep it also, when devoutly praying for it, than fiercely wrangling and contending about it."
    William Gurnall

John chapter 18

1. **Before and after**

   Previous chapter: Chapter 17: Jesus prays to his Father
   Following chapter: Chapter 19: Jesus' death and burial

2. **Analysis of chapter**

   Christ arrested in the garden. (1-12)
   Christ before Annas and Caiaphas. (13-27)
   Christ before Pilate. (28-40)

3. **Key verse**

   Verse 3: "So Judas came to the grove, guiding a detachment of soldiers and some officials from the chief priests and Pharisees."

4. **Key word / key phrase**

   Verse 12, "arrested Jesus."

5. **Key event / key person / key theme**

   Jesus' arrest

6. **Key thought**

   Jesus only went to the cross because he was following his Father's will.

7. **Key thing to look out for**

   Peter, the rock, reveals his feet of clay.

8. **Key Bible cross-reference**

   Verse 1. See 2 Samuel 15:23.

9. **Key "by way of explanation"**

   Verse 17, "the girl at the door." It is remarkable that all four Gospels pick up this detail that the first person to suggest to Peter that he knew Jesus was a slave girl. Such a person would have been totally despised in society in those days.

10. **Key "Quotable Quote"**

    "When we are right with God, he gives us our desires and aspirations. Our Lord had only one desire, and that was to do the will of his Father, and to have this desire is characteristic of a disciple."
    Oswald Chambers

John chapter 19

1. Before and after

Previous chapter: Chapter 18: Jesus' arrest and trials
Following chapter: Chapter 20: Jesus' resurrection and first resurrection appearances

2. Analysis of chapter

Christ condemned and crucified. (1-18)
Christ on the cross. (19-30)
His side pierced. (31-37)
The burial of Jesus. (38-42)

3. Key verse

Verse 7: "We have a law, and according to that law he must die, because he claimed to be the Son of God."

4. Key word / key phrase

Verse 30, "It is finished."

5. Key event / key person / key theme

Jesus' death

6. Key thought

"Our Lord's death on the cross is the supreme manifestation of the love of God."
D. Martyn Lloyd-Jones

7. Key thing to look out for

Even on the cross Jesus shows his care for others.

8. Key Bible cross-reference

Verse 24. See Psalm 22:18.

9. Key "by way of explanation"

Verse 20, "this sign." The wording on the sign was in three languages so everyone who passed by would be able to read it. It was in one of the Jewish languages, Aramaic, in the official language of the Romans, Latin, and the everyday language used throughout the Empire, Greek.

10. Key "Quotable Quote"

"There is only one answer to the question as to why Christ had to die – the holiness of God!"
D. Martyn Lloyd-Jones

John chapter 20

1. Before and after

Previous chapter: Chapter 19: Jesus' death and burial
Following chapter: Chapter 21: Further resurrection appearances of Jesus

2. Analysis of chapter

The sepulcher is found to be empty. (1-10)
Christ appears to Mary. (11-18)
He appears to the disciples. (19-25)
The unbelief of Thomas. (26-29)
Conclusion. (30,31)

3. Key verse

Verse 2: "They have taken the Lord out of the tomb, and we don't know where they have put him!"

4. Key word / key phrase

Verse 8, "he saw and believed."

5. Key event / key person / key theme

Jesus' resurrection

6. Key thought

Without the resurrection appearances the disciples would have understood little.

7. Key thing to look out for

What encouragement is there from the experience of Thomas?

8. Key Bible cross-reference

Verse 22. See Galatians 3:2.

9. Key "by way of explanation"

Verse 22, "Receive the Holy Spirit." This foreshadowed what would take place on the Day of Pentecost. A disciple might receive God's commission but would never be able to carry it out without the Spirit's help.

10. Key "Quotable Quote"

"Christ's call is to save the lost, not the stiff-necked; He came not to call scoffers but sinners to repentance; not to build and furnish comfortable chapels, churches, and cathedrals at home in which to rock Christian professors to sleep by means of clever essays, stereotyped prayers, and artistic musical performances, but to capture men from the devil's clutches and the very jaws of Hell. This can be accomplished only by a red-hot devotion, in the power of the Holy Spirit, to the Lord Jesus Christ."
C.T. Studd

John chapter 21

1. Previous chapter

Chapter 20: Jesus' resurrection and first resurrection appearances

2. Analysis of chapter

Christ appears to his disciples. (1-14)
His teaching with Peter. (15-19)
Christ's declaration about John. (20-24)
The conclusion. (25)

3. Key verse

Verse 25: "Jesus did many other things as well. If every one of them were written down, I suppose that even the whole world would not have room for the books that would be written."

4. Key word / key phrase

Verse 15, "Feed my lambs."

5. Key event / key person / key theme

Resurrection appearances of Jesus.

6. Key thought

From Peter we learn that failure need never be the end of the story.

7. Key thing to look out for

John 21:19, "Follow me." (Cf the same words in Mark 1:17). What do these words now mean to Peter?

8. Key Bible cross-reference

Verse 16. See Ezekiel 34:2.

9. Key "by way of explanation"

Verse 19, "the kind of death." This verse indicates that Peter would be killed against his will. According to tradition Peter was martyred, upside-down, on a cross.

10. Key "Quotable Quote"

"Fear had denied Christ three times. Three times love confessed him. A threefold negation, the desertion of truth; a threefold confession, the witness of love."
John Calvin

Acts

Acts chapter 1

1. **Following chapter**

   Chapter 2: The coming of the Holy Spirit and Peter's sermon

2. **Analysis of chapter**

   Proofs of Christ's resurrection. (1-5)
   Christ's ascension. (6-11)
   The apostles unite in prayer. (12-14)
   Matthias chosen in the place of Judas. (15-26)

3. **Key verse**

   Verse 3: "After his suffering, he showed himself to these men and gave many convincing proofs that he was alive. He appeared to them over a period of forty days and spoke about the kingdom of God."

4. **Key word / key phrase**

   Verse 9, "he was taken up."

5. **Key event / key person / key theme**

   The ascension of Jesus

6. **Key thought**

   The beginning of the chapter makes a helpful link between the life of the early Church and the Gospels.

7. **Key thing to look out for**

   Verse 8 states that "witnessing" was to be the job of Jesus' followers.

8. **Key Bible cross-reference**

   Verse 20. See Psalm 69:25.

9. **Key "by way of explanation"**

   Verse 3. "In Acts 1, Luke tells us that Jesus showed himself alive by many infallible proofs (en pollois tekmeriois), an expression indicating the strongest type of legal evidence." Bernard Ramm

10. **Key "Quotable Quote"**

    "When Jesus ascended, he changed his presence for his omnipresence."
    F.P. Wood

Acts chapter 2

1. *Before and after*

Previous chapter: Chapter 1: The ascension of Jesus, and waiting for the Spirit
Following chapter: Chapter 3: Peter heals and preaches

2. *Analysis of chapter*

The arrival of the Holy Spirit on the Day of Pentecost. (1-4)
The apostles speak in different languages. (5-13)
Peter's sermon to the Jews. (14-36)
Three thousand people converted. (37-41)
The fellowship of the believers. (42-47)

3. *Key verse*

Verse 3: "They saw what seemed to be tongues of fire that separated and came to rest on each of them."

4. *Key word / key phrase*

Verse 4, "filled with the Holy Spirit."

5. *Key event / key person / key theme*

The coming of the Holy Spirit

6. *Key thought*

No wonder Pentecost has been called the birthday of the Christian Church.

7. *Key thing to look out for*

Peter assumes the role of leader among the Christians.

8. *Key Bible cross-reference*

Verses 17-21. See Joel 2:28-32.

9. *Key "by way of explanation"*

Verse 22, "accredited . . . by miracles, wonders, and signs." Jesus' miracles demonstrated that the expected Messiah had indeed arrived.

10. *Key "Quotable Quote"*

"No man is excluded from calling upon God, the gate of salvation is set open unto all men: neither is there any other thing which keepeth us back from entering in, save only our own unbelief."
John Calvin, commentating on Acts 2:21

Acts chapter 3

1. Before and after

Previous chapter: Chapter 2: The coming of the Holy Spirit and Peter's sermon

Following chapter: Chapter 4: Peter and John arrested, and Peter before the Sanhedrin

2. Analysis of chapter

A lame man healed by Peter and John. (1-11)

Peter's sermon to the Jews. (12-26)

3. Key verse

Verse 6: "Silver or gold I do not have, but what I have I give you. In the name of Jesus Christ of Nazareth, walk."

4. Key word / key phrase

Verse 6, "in the name of Jesus Christ of Nazareth, walk."

5. Key event / key person / key theme

Peter heals and preaches

6. Key thought

It is repentance that brings God's gift of forgiveness (verse 19), refreshment (verse 19) knowledge of Jesus (verse 20), and restoration (verse 21), but repentance involves a change of lifestyle (verse 26).

7. Key thing to look out for

Peter used every available opportunity to preach the gospel.

8. Key Bible cross-reference

Verse 13. See Exodus 3:15.

9. Key "by way of explanation"

Verse 24, "all the prophets from Samuel on." The prophecies of all the prophets from the time of Samuel all contained some important strand about the Messiah.

10. Key "Quotable Quote"

"If you are feeling tired and therefore in need of a spiritual tonic, go to the book of Acts."

D. Martyn Lloyd-Jones

Acts chapter 4

1. Before and after

Previous chapter: Chapter 3: Peter heals and preaches
Following chapter: Chapter 5: Ananias and Sapphira, miracles and persecution

2. Analysis of chapter

Peter and John imprisoned. (1-4)
The apostles boldly testify to Christ. (5-14)
Peter and John refuse to be silenced. (15-22)
The believers unite in prayer and praise. (23-31)
The believers share their possessions. (32-37)

3. Key verse

Verse 13: "When they saw the courage of Peter and John and realized that they were unschooled, ordinary men, they were astonished and they took note that these men had been with Jesus."

4. Key word / key phrase

Verse 12, "salvation is found in no one else."

5. Key event / key person / key theme

Peter before the Sanhedrin

6. Key thought

In the face of threats of punishments, the believers praised God and asked, not for release from danger, but for courage. See also 5:41.

7. Key thing to look out for

The characteristics of the early church.

8. Key Bible cross-reference

Verse 11. See Psalm 118:22.

9. Key "by way of explanation"

Verse 13, "courage." This is one of the characteristics of the first Christians. See 2:29; 4:29,31; 28:31.

10. Key "Quotable Quote"

"To witness to the gospel by word and life is the great calling of the ministry of the layperson."
Robert C. Jones, former National Director, Church Army, USA

Acts chapter 5

1. **Before and after**

   Previous chapter: Chapter 4: Peter and John arrested, and Peter before the Sanhedrin
   Following chapter: Chapter 6: Deacons appointed, and Stephen before the council

2. **Analysis of chapter**

   The death of Ananias and Sapphira. (1-11)
   The power which accompanied the preaching of the gospel. (12-16)
   The apostles imprisoned, but freed by an angel. (17-25)
   The apostles witness to Christ before the council. (26-33)
   The advice of Gamaliel, and the council let the apostles go. (34-42)

3. **Key verse**

   Verse 12: "The apostles performed many miraculous signs and wonders among the people."

4. **Key word / key phrase**

   Verse 3, "lied to the Holy Spirit."

5. **Key event / key person / key theme**

   Ananias and Sapphira

6. **Key thought**

   God's judgment comes to the early Christian fellowship.

7. **Key thing to look out for**

   Verse 42, for a summary of the message of the apostles.

8. **Key Bible cross-reference**

   Verse 19. See Genesis 16:7.

9. **Key "by way of explanation"**

   Verse 40, "flogged." This refers to the Jewish punishment of thirty-nine lashes. See 2 Corinthians 11:24.

10. **Key "Quotable Quote"**

    "After I have been wearied almost to death in preaching, writing and conversation, and going from place to place, God imparted new life to my soul, and enabled me to intercede with him for an hour and a half and two hours together."
    George Whitefield

Acts chapter 6

1. *Before and after*

Previous chapter: Chapter 5: Ananias and Sapphira, miracles and persecution

Following chapter: Chapter 7: Stephen's sermon and martyrdom

2. *Analysis of chapter*

The appointment of deacons. (1-7)

Stephen falsely accused of blasphemy. (8-15)

3. *Key verse*

Verse 11: "We have heard Stephen speak words of blasphemy against Moses and against God."

4. *Key word / key phrase*

Verse 7, "so the word of God spread."

5. *Key event / key person / key theme*

Deacons appointed

6. *Key thought*

Verses 13,14. There is a striking similarity between the changes brought against Jesus, and those brought against Stephen. He seems to have grasped the revolutionary newness of the Christian faith.

7. *Key thing to look out for*

The qualities needed for these "servants."

8. *Key Bible cross-reference*

Verse 3. See Exodus 18:21.

9. *Key "by way of explanation"*

Verse 6, "prayed and laid their hands on them." In the Old Testament people were commissioned for special tasks and had hands laid on them as a sign of God's blessing, Numbers 27:23. Prayer is seen to be vital here.

10. *Key "Quotable Quote"*

"Jesus Christ didn't commit the gospel to an advertising agency; he commissioned disciples."

Joseph Bayly

Acts chapter 7

1. Before and after

Previous chapter: Chapter 6: Deacons appointed, and Stephen before the council

Following chapter: Chapter 8: The expansion of the Church

2. Analysis of chapter

Stephen's defense. (1-50)

Stephen reproves the Jews for the death of Christ. (51-53)

The martyrdom of Stephen. (54-60)

3. Key verse

Verse 58: "Meanwhile, the witnesses laid their clothes at the feet of a young man named Saul."

4. Key word / key phrase

Verse 58, "began to stone him."

5. Key event / key person / key theme

Stephen's sermon and martyrdom

6. Key thought

Stephen's speech/sermon is a great summary of Old Testament salvation history.

7. Key thing to look out for

The first we hear of Saul (Paul) is in connection with the first Christian martyrdom.

8. Key Bible cross-reference

Verses 2-3. See Genesis 12:1.

9. Key "by way of explanation"

Verse 51, "uncircumcised hearts and ears." Stephen's hearers were all physically circumcised and proud to be Jews. But when Stephen pointed to the evil in their hearts they could not allow him to go on living.

10. Key "Quotable Quote"

"Solemn prayers, rapturous devotions, are but repeated hypocrisies unless the heart and mind be conformable to them."
William Law

Acts chapter 8

1. **Before and after**

    Previous chapter: Chapter 7: Stephen's sermon and martyrdom
    Following chapter: Chapter 9: Saul's conversion

2. **Analysis of chapter**

    Saul persecutes the Church. (1-4)
    Philip's success at Samaria. Simon the sorcerer baptized. (5-13)
    The hypocrisy of Simon detected. (14-25)
    Philip and the Ethiopian. (26-40)

3. **Key verse**

    Verse 4: "Those who had been scattered preached the word wherever they went."

4. **Key word / key phrase**

    Verses 15,17,19, "received the Holy Spirit."

5. **Key event / key person / key theme**

    The expansion of the Church

6. **Key thought**

    The spread of the Christian message was one positive result of persecution.

7. **Key thing to look out for**

    Philip's openness to the Holy Spirit was such that he could be led from a busy city mission to minister to one person on an inter-city highway.

8. **Key Bible cross-reference**

    Verses 32-33. See Isaiah 53:7,8.

9. **Key "by way of explanation"**

    Verse 30, "heard the man reading." In those days it was quite normal to read aloud, rather than read silently.

10. **Key "Quotable Quote"**

    "Assent to the truth of the Word is but an act of the understanding, which reprobates and devils may exercise. But justifying faith is a compounded habit, and hath its seat both in the understanding and will: and, therefore, called a believing 'with the heart' (Romans 10:10), yea, a believing 'with all the heart' (Acts 8:37)."
    William Gurnall

Acts chapter 9

1. Before and after

Previous chapter: Chapter 8: The expansion of the Church
Following chapter: Chapter 10: Peter and Cornelius

2. Analysis of chapter

The conversion of Saul. (1-22)
Saul is persecuted at Damascus, and goes to Jerusalem. (23-31)
Aeneas is healed. (32-35)
Dorcas is raised to life. (36-43)

3. Key verse

Verse 3: "As he neared Damascus on his journey, suddenly a light from heaven flashed around him."

4. Key word / key phrase

Verse 3, "a light from heaven flashed."

5. Key event / key person / key theme

Saul's conversion

6. Key thought

Saul's conversion is so pivotal that Luke records it three times. See also 22:3-16; 26:9-18.

7. Key thing to look out for

Paul's conversion illustrates perfectly that salvation is all due to God's grace.

8. Key Bible cross-reference

Verse 2. See Isaiah 17:1.

9. Key "by way of explanation"

Verse 10, "Ananias." He is only mentioned here and in 22:12. Like so many of God's faithful servants, his service for God went largely unrecorded.

10. Key "Quotable Quote"

"Entrance into heaven is not at the hour of death, but at the moment of conversion."
Benjamin Whichcote

Acts chapter 10

1. Before and after

Previous chapter: Chapter 9: Saul's conversion
Following chapter: Chapter 11: Peter defends his ministry, and the Antioch church

2. Analysis of chapter

Cornelius is told to send for Peter. (1-8)
Peter's vision. (9-18)
He goes to Cornelius. (19-33)
His teaching given to Cornelius. (34-43)
The gifts of the Holy Spirit poured out. (44-48)

3. Key verse

Verse 42: "He commanded us to preach to the people and to testify that he is the one whom God appointed as judge of the living and the dead."

4. Key word / key phrase

Verse 45, "even on the Gentiles."

5. Key event / key person / key theme

Peter and Cornelius

6. Key thought

The early Christians begin to learn that the gospel is not only for Jews.

7. Key thing to look out for

It is possible for the most dedicated Christian to be full of prejudice.

8. Key Bible cross-reference

Verse 34. See Deuteronomy 10:17.

9. Key "by way of explanation"

Verse 28, "God has shown me." Peter needed a vision to get his thinking in line with God's thinking about non-Jews. Now he saw that Jews and non-Jews were equal in God's sight.

10. Key "Quotable Quote"

"One filled with joy preaches without preaching."
Mother Teresa of Calcutta

Acts chapter 11

1. ### *Before and after*

   Previous chapter: Chapter 10: Peter and Cornelius
   Following chapter: Chapter 12: Herod's persecution

2. ### *Analysis of chapter*

   Peter's defense. (1-18)
   The success of the gospel at Antioch. (19-24)
   The disciples called Christians. Relief sent to Judea. (25-30)

3. ### *Key verse*

   Verse 15: "As I began to speak, the Holy Spirit came on them as he had come on us at the beginning."

4. ### *Key word / key phrase*

   Verse 4, "Peter . . . explained everything."

5. ### *Key event / key person / key theme*

   Peter defends his ministry

6. ### *Key thought*

   Verse 18 makes a convenient summary of the important step the early Christians had now taken about preaching the gospel.

7. ### *Key thing to look out for*

   Verse 29 shows how Christians should set about using their resources to help fellow-Christians.

8. ### *Key Bible cross-reference*

   Verse 1. See Hebrews 4:12.

9. ### *Key "by way of explanation"*

   Verse 18, "repentance unto life." All too often repentance is pictured as a negative turning away from sin without its integral second part being included: turning to Jesus for life.

10. ### *Key "Quotable Quote"*

    "It is a quality of the Kingdom of Christ that in it the repentance of sinners must always be preached."
    Martin Bucer

Acts chapter 12

1. Before and after

Previous chapter: Chapter 11: Peter defends his ministry, and the Antioch church

Following chapter: Chapter 13: First part of Paul's first missionary journey

2. Analysis of chapter

The martyrdom of James, and the imprisonment of Peter. (1-5)

He is delivered from prison by an angel. (6-11)

Peter departs, Herod's rage. (12-19)

The death of Herod. (20-25)

3. Key verse

Verse 11: "Now I know without a doubt that the Lord sent his angel and rescued me from Herod's clutches and from everything the Jewish people were anticipating."

4. Key word / key phrase

Verse 1, "King Herod arrested."

5. Key event / key person / key theme

Herod's persecution

6. Key thought

Miracles and prayer (verse 12) go together.

7. Key thing to look out for

It is hard not to laugh at the scene so graphically described by Luke.

8. Key Bible cross-reference

Verse 4. See Exodus 12:1-27.

9. Key "by way of explanation"

Verse 17, James, the Lord's brother, was now the leader of the church in Jerusalem.

10. Key "Quotable Quote"

"One can believe intellectually in the efficacy of prayer and never do any praying."

Catherine Marshall

Acts chapter 13

1. Before and after

Previous chapter: Chapter 12: Herod's persecution
Following chapter: Chapter 14: Second part of Paul's first missionary journey

2. Analysis of chapter

The mission of Paul and Barnabas. (1-3)
Elymas the sorcerer. (4-13)
Paul's teaching at Antioch. (14-41)
He preaches to the Gentiles, and is persecuted by the Jews. (42-52)

3. Key verse

Verse 12: "When the proconsul saw what had happened, he believed, for he was amazed at the teaching about the Lord."

4. Key word / key phrase

Verse 4, "sent on their way by the Holy Spirit."

5. Key event / key person / key theme

First part of Paul's first missionary journey

6. Key thought

Verses 29,30. The death and resurrection of Jesus formed the basis of early preaching.

7. Key thing to look out for

Verse 49. A wonderful portrait of the result of preaching the gospel. It is immediately followed by persecution from the Jews.

8. Key Bible cross-reference

Verse 17. See Exodus 1:7.

9. Key "by way of explanation"

Verse 46, "had to speak . . . to you first." Paul thought that he should preach to Jews first of all, as the gospel came from Jews and was first preached to them, and because he was a Jew himself. However, the Lord himself had commissioned Paul to go to the Gentiles (Acts 22:21).

10. Key "Quotable Quote"

"It is possible for the most obscure person in a church, with a heart right toward God, to exercise as much power for the evangelization of the world, as it is for those who stand in the most prominent positions."
John R. Mott

Acts chapter 14

1. Before and after

Previous chapter: Chapter 13: First part of Paul's first missionary journey
Following chapter: Chapter 15: The Jerusalem Council

2. Analysis of chapter

Paul and Barnabas at Iconium. (1-7)
A cripple healed at Lystra, and the attempt to sacrifice to Paul and Barnabas. (8-18)
Paul stoned at Lystra, and the churches visited again. (19-28)

3. Key verse

Verse 11: "The gods have come down to us in human form!"

4. Key word / key phrase

Verse 22, "many hardships."

5. Key event / key person / key theme

Second part of Paul's first missionary journey

6. Key thought

In their report to their home church, at the end of this first missionary journey, Paul and Barnabas emphasized that God was in control.

7. Key thing to look out for

Verse 22, Paul's honesty. In what way were his words strengthening?

8. Key Bible cross-reference

Verse 15. See Exodus 20:11.

9. Key "by way of explanation"

Verse 5, "stone them." Under the law this was the Jewish punishment for blasphemy.

10. Key "Quotable Quote"

"Lo, persecution and adversity for the truth's sake is God's scourge and God's rod and pertaineth unto all his children indifferently."
William Tyndale

Acts chapter 15

1. *Before and after*

Previous chapter: Chapter 14: Second part of Paul's first missionary journey
Following chapter: Chapter 16: First part of Paul's second missionary journey

2. *Analysis of chapter*

The dispute caused by false teachers. (1-6)
The council at Jerusalem. (7-21)
The letter from the council. (22-35)
Paul and Barnabas separate. (36-41)

3. *Key verse*

Verse 12: "The whole assembly became silent as they listened to Barnabas and Paul telling about the miraculous signs and wonders God had done among the Gentiles through them."

4. *Key word / key phrase*

Verse 6, "the apostles and elders met."

5. *Key event / key person / key theme*

The Jerusalem Council

6. *Key thought*

There is no difference between Jew and Gentile.

7. *Key thing to look out for*

Sharp differences arose between even the most missionary-minded of Christians. See verses 36-40.

8. *Key Bible cross-reference*

Verses 16-18. See Amos 9:11,12.

9. *Key "by way of explanation"*

The Council of Jerusalem was called to solve an urgent and serious disagreement: Did Gentile Christians have to become Jews, that is, be circumcised and obey the Jewish Law? Jews who held this view wanted to turn Christianity into a Jewish sect. The Council decided in favor of Paul and Peter.

10. *Key "Quotable Quote"*

"There is great force hidden in a gentle command."
George Herbert

Acts chapter 16

1. *Before and after*

> Previous chapter: Chapter 15: The Jerusalem Council
> Following chapter: Chapter 17: Second part of Paul's second missionary journey

2. *Analysis of chapter*

> Paul takes Timothy to be his assistant. (1-5)
> Paul proceeds to Macedonia, and the conversion of Lydia. (6-15)
> An evil spirit expelled, Paul and Silas scourged and imprisoned. (16-24)
> The conversion of the jailer at Philippi. (25-34)
> Paul and Silas released. (35-40)

3. *Key verse*

> Verse 14: "One of those listening was a woman named Lydia, a dealer in purple cloth from the city of Thyatira, who was a worshiper of God. The Lord opened her heart to respond to Paul's message."

4. *Key word / key phrase*

> Verse 1, "He came to Derbe."

5. *Key event / key person / key theme*

> First part of Paul's second missionary journey: from Asia Minor to Europe.

6. *Key thought*

> It is the Holy Spirit who is directing Paul.

7. *Key thing to look out for*

> Paul's and Silas' response to severe flogging, and unjust imprisonment.

8. *Key Bible cross-reference*

> Verse 14. See Revelation 1:11.

9. *Key "by way of explanation"*

> Verse 37, "without a trial." A Roman citizen could not be beaten in public. What is worse here is that the trial of Paul and Silas was also clearly contrary to Roman law. Verse 10: here for the first time, the story is told in the first person: "we". Luke has joined Paul, and is giving his own eyewitness account of events.

10. *Key "Quotable Quote"*

> "No human birth can compare to the supernatural birth of a child of God."
> J.M. Boice

Acts chapter 17

1. Before and after

Previous chapter: Chapter 16: First part of Paul's second missionary journey
Following chapter: Chapter 18: Paul's ministry in Corinth

2. Analysis of chapter

Paul at Thessalonica. (1-9)
The noble behavior of the Bereans. (10-15)
Paul at Athens. (16-21)
He preaches there. (22-31)
The scornful behavior of the Athenians. (32-34)

3. Key verse

Verse 5: "But the Jews were jealous; so they rounded up some bad characters from the marketplace, formed a mob and started a riot in the city."

4. Key word / key phrase

Verse 16, "Paul was greatly distressed."

5. Key event / key person / key theme

Second part of Paul's second missionary journey

6. Key thought

Verse 31, the proof of the truth of Christ is in the resurrection.

7. Key thing to look out for

Verse 11. The good characteristic displayed by the Bereans in this verse is a model for all time.

8. Key Bible cross-reference

Verses 24,25. See 1 Kings 8:27.

9. Key "by way of explanation"

In the time of Paul the Areopagus was a court which dealt with problems concerning religion and morals.

10. Key "Quotable Quote"

"Were you but as willing to get the knowledge of God and heavenly things as you are to know how to work in your trade, you would have set yourself to it before this day, and you would have spared no cost or pains till you had got it. But you account seven years little enough to learn your trade, and will not bestow one day in seven in diligent learning the matters of your salvation."
Richard Baxter

Acts chapter 18

1. *Before and after*

Previous chapter: Chapter 17: Second part of Paul's second missionary journey

Following chapter: Chapter 19: Paul's ministry in Ephesus

2. *Analysis of chapter*

Paul at Corinth, with Aquila and Priscilla. (1-6)

He continues to preach at Corinth. (7-11)

Paul before Gallio. (12-17)

He visits Jerusalem. (18-23)

Apollos teaches at Ephesus and in Achaia. (24-28)

3. *Key verse*

Verse 11: "So Paul stayed for a year and a half, teaching them the word of God."

4. *Key word / key phrase*

Verse 26, "they invited him to their home."

5. *Key event / key person / key theme*

Paul's ministry in Corinth

6. *Key thought*

Verses 5-7. It was not for lack of trying that Paul tried to convert the Jews.

7. *Key thing to look out for*

How encouraging Paul's vision must have been in the middle of all the persecution he received. See verse 9.

8. *Key Bible cross-reference*

Verse 18. See Numbers 6:18.

9. *Key "by way of explanation"*

Verse 11, "a year and a half." Paul stayed varying lengths of time in different places on his missionary travels. His year and a half stay in Corinth was one of the longer times he spent in one town.

10. *Key "Quotable Quote"*

"Christianity is a missionary religion, converting, advancing, aggressive, encompassing the world; a non-missionary Church is in the bands of death."
Friedrich Max Müller

Acts chapter 19

1. *Before and after*

Previous chapter: Chapter 18: Paul's ministry in Corinth
Following chapter: Chapter 20: Second part of Paul's third missionary journey

2. *Analysis of chapter*

Paul instructs the disciples of John at Ephesus. (1-7)
He teaches there. (8-12)
The Jewish exorcists disgraced. Some Ephesians burn their evil books. (13-20)
The storm of protest at Ephesus. (21-31)
The assembly appeased. (32-41)

3. *Key verse*

Verse 8: "Paul entered the synagogue and spoke boldly there for three months, arguing persuasively about the kingdom of God."

4. *Key word / key phrase*

Verse 23, "the Way."

5. *Key event / key person / key theme*

Paul's ministry in Ephesus

6. *Key thought*

Repentance is not enough. Christianity is made complete when the Holy Spirit is received following faith in Christ and his forgiveness.

7. *Key thing to look out for*

Demetrius the silversmith has not been the last person to viciously oppose Christianity in order to protect his commercial interests.

8. *Key Bible cross-reference*

Verse 4. See John 1:26,27.

9. *Key "by way of explanation"*

Ephesus was a wealthy and powerful city, "the treasure house of Asia." Paul's missionary strategy was to choose important centers with influence and links over a wide area.

10. *Key "Quotable Quote"*

"The Church is: a conspiracy of love for a dying world, a spy mission into enemy occupied territory ruled by the powers of evil, a prophet from God with the greatest news the world has ever heard, the most life changing and most revolutionary institution that has existed on earth."
Peter Kreeft

Acts chapter 20

1. Before and after

Previous chapter: Chapter 19: Paul's ministry in Ephesus
Following chapter: Chapter 21: Paul is arrested

2. Analysis of chapter

Paul's journeys. (1-6)
Eutychus restored to life. (7-12)
Paul travels toward Jerusalem. (13-16)
Paul's teaching to the elders of Ephesus. (17-27)
Their farewell. (28-38)

3. Key verse

Verse 7: "On the first day of the week we came together to break bread. Paul spoke to the people and, because he intended to leave the next day, kept on talking until midnight."

4. Key word / key phrase

Verse 28, "keep watch."

5. Key event / key person / key theme

Second part of Paul's third missionary journey

6. Key thought

Paul did not believe in ten-minute-long sermons.

7. Key thing to look out for

By God's grace Paul was able to turn Eutychus' tragic death into a triumph.

8. Key Bible cross-reference

Verse 24. See 2 Timothy 4:7.

9. Key "by way of explanation"

Verse 3, "a plot against him." This time the Jews thought that they would be able to finish Paul off. But God saved him through his last minute change of route.

10. Key "Quotable Quote"

"Wherever the missionary character of the doctrine of election is forgotten then God's people have betrayed their trust."
Leslie Newbigin

Acts chapter 21

1. Before and after

Previous chapter: Chapter 20: Second part of Paul's third missionary journey
Following chapter: Chapter 22: Paul's defense before the mob

2. Analysis of chapter

Paul's journey toward Jerusalem. (1-7)
Paul at Caesarea. The prophecy of Agabus, Paul at Jerusalem. (8-18)
He is persuaded to join in ceremonial observances. (19-26)
Being in danger from the Jews, he is rescued by the Romans. (27-40)

3. Key verse

Verse 12: "When we heard this, we and the people there pleaded with Paul not to go up to Jerusalem."

4. Key word / key phrase

Verse 33, "and arrested him."

5. Key event / key person / key theme

Paul is arrested

6. Key thought

The importance of discernment. Here, the Spirit warned of coming trials; the addition, "not to go," did not come from the Spirit. Paul was going under the compulsion of the Spirit (8:22).

7. Key thing to look out for

Paul's life was saved by Roman soldiers, stationed in the Fortress of Antonia at the northern end of the temple. Notice what the commander wanted (verse 34).

8. Key Bible cross-reference

Verses 23,24. See Numbers 6:13-21.

9. Key "by way of explanation"

Verse 18, "James." This James was Jesus' brother, the author of the New Testament letter bearing his name, and the leader of the Christians in Jerusalem.

10. Key "Quotable Quote"

"The Great Commission is far more than evangelism. The Great Commission is to make disciples."
Chuck Colson

Acts chapter 22

1. Before and after

Previous chapter: Chapter 21: Paul is arrested
Following chapter: Chapter 23: Plot to kill Paul

2. Analysis of chapter

Paul's account of his conversion. (1-11)
Paul directed to preach to the Gentiles. (12-21)
The anger of the Jews. Paul appeals to his Roman citizenship. (22-30)

3. Key verse

Verse 21: "Go; I will send you far away to the Gentiles."

4. Key word / key phrase

Verse 3, "I am a Jew."

5. Key event / key person / key theme

Paul's defense before the mob

6. Key thought

Verse 25. Paul used his God-given wits and his Roman citizenship to good effect.

7. Key thing to look out for

It seems that Paul never tired of telling his personal conversion story. His defense was to tell his story.

8. Key Bible cross-reference

Verse 2. See John 5:2.

9. Key "by way of explanation"

Verse 3, "brought up in this city." Although Paul was born in Tarsus, he was educated in Jerusalem and had the privilege of sitting at the feet of Gamaliel, the leading rabbi of the day.

10. Key "Quotable Quote"

"If my testimony makes anyone wish to emulate me, it is a mistaken testimony; it is not a witness to Jesus."
Oswald Chambers

Acts chapter 23

1. *Before and after*

Previous chapter: Chapter 22: Paul's defense before the mob
Following chapter: Chapter 24: Paul before Felix

2. *Analysis of chapter*

Paul's defense before the council of the Jews. (1-5)
Paul's defense. He receives a divine assurance that he will go to Rome. (6-11)
The Jews plot to kill Paul, Lysias sends him to Caesarea. (12-24)
Lysias's letter to Felix. (25-35)

3. *Key verse*

Verse 11: "Take courage! As you have testified about me in Jerusalem, so you must also testify in Rome."

4. *Key word / key phrase*

Verse 14, "until we have killed Paul."

5. *Key event / key person / key theme*

Plot to kill Paul

6. *Key thought*

The plot to kill Paul this time involved a solemn oath taken by those who wanted him dead.

7. *Key thing to look out for*

Had it not been for the quick thinking and courageous action of Paul's unnamed nephew Paul would have been killed.

8. *Key Bible cross-reference*

Verse 5. See Philippians 3:5.

9. *Key "by way of explanation"*

Verse 3, "whitewashed wall!" Paul was not paying any compliment here. Inside the well-painted tomb there were rotting corpses. Paul is calling the high priest Ananias a hypocrite to his face.

10. *Key "Quotable Quote"*

"The greatest mission field we face is not in some faraway land. It's barely across the street. The culture most lost to the gospel is our own—our children and neighbors."
Dwight Ozard

Acts chapter 24

1. *Before and after*

Previous chapter: Chapter 23: Plot to kill Paul
Following chapter: Chapter 25: Paul appeals to the Emperor

2. *Analysis of chapter*

The Tertullus' speech against Paul. (1-9)
Paul's defense before Felix. (10-21)
Felix trembles at Paul's arguments. (22-27)

3. *Key verse*

Verse 14: "I admit that I worship the God of our fathers as a follower of the Way, which they call a sect."

4. *Key word / key phrase*

Verse 27, "he left Paul in prison."

5. *Key event / key person / key theme*

Paul before Felix

6. *Key thought*

Verse 16. One of the sources of Paul's strength came from the fact that he had a clear conscience.

7. *Key thing to look out for*

What made Felix afraid?

8. *Key Bible cross-reference*

Verse 9. See 1 Thessalonians 2:16.

9. *Key "by way of explanation"*

Verse 5, "ringleader of a Nazarene sect." If this could be proved to be the case then Paul had broken the law. It was illegal to be the leader of a religious group, without the prior approval of the Romans.

10. *Key "Quotable Quote"*

"It is a crime against lost humanity to go in the name of Christ and missions just to do the social work and yet neglect calling men to repent and follow Christ with all their hearts."
K.P. Yohannan

Acts chapter 25

1. Before and after

Previous chapter: Chapter 24: Paul before Felix
Following chapter: Chapter 26: Paul is tried before Agrippa

2. Analysis of chapter

Paul before Festus, he appeals to Caesar. (1-12)
Festus confers with Agrippa about Paul. (13-27)

3. Key verse

Verse 10: "I am now standing before Caesar's court, where I ought to be tried. I have not done any wrong to the Jews, as you yourself know very well."

4. Key word / key phrase

Verse 12, "To Caesar you will go!"

5. Key event / key person / key theme

Paul appeals to the Emperor

6. Key thought

Verse 9. From this we can see that Paul was maliciously and falsely charged with heresy, sacrilege, and sedition. It is no wonder that he knew there would be no justice in Jerusalem.

7. Key thing to look out for

Verses 19,26. If it were not so tragic, Festus' bewilderment would be amusing.

8. Key Bible cross-reference

Verse 23. See 26:30.

9. Key "by way of explanation"

Verse 11, "I appeal to Caesar!" This meant appealing to Nero. As a Roman citizen Paul was claiming his rights. To appear before Caesar was to appear before the highest court in the empire.

10. Key "Quotable Quote"

"I hope no missionary will ever be as lonely as I have been."
Lottie Moon

Acts chapter 26

1. *Before and after*

Previous chapter: Chapter 25: Paul appeals to the Emperor
Following chapter: Chapter 27: Paul sails for Rome and is shipwrecked

2. *Analysis of chapter*

Paul's defense before Agrippa. (1-11)
His conversion and preaching to the Gentiles. (12-23)
Festus and Agrippa convinced of Paul's innocence. (24-32)

3. *Key verse*

Verse 13: "About noon, O king, as I was on the road, I saw a light from heaven, brighter than the sun, blazing around me and my companions."

4. *Key word / key phrase*

Verse 19, "not disobedient."

5. *Key event / key person / key theme*

Paul is tried before Agrippa

6. *Key thought*

Paul was accused of everything under the sun, including going mad.

7. *Key thing to look out for*

King Agrippa is put on the spot by Paul.

8. *Key Bible cross-reference*

Verse 23. See Isaiah 49:6.

9. *Key "by way of explanation"*

Verse 11, "I tried to force them to blaspheme." Paul, by his own admission here, in his pre-Christian days had tried to make Christians guilty of blasphemy so that they would be guilty of a capital offence.

10. *Key "Quotable Quote"*

"The missionary work of the non-professional missionary is essentially to live his daily life in Christ."
Roland Allen

Acts chapter 27

1. Before and after

Previous chapter: Chapter 26: Paul is tried before Agrippa
Following chapter: Chapter 28: Paul arrives in Rome to a two-year house arrest

2. Analysis of chapter

Paul's travels toward Rome. (1-11)
Paul and his companions endangered by a tempest. (12-20)
He receives God's assurance of safety. (21-29)
Paul encourages those with him. (30-38)
They are shipwrecked. (39-44)

3. Key verse

Verse 37: "Altogether there were 276 of us on board."

4. Key word / key phrase

Verse 41, "the ship struck a sandbar."

5. Key event / key person / key theme

Paul sails for Rome and is shipwrecked

6. Key thought

Paul showed that the more heavenly minded you are, the more earthly use you are.

7. Key thing to look out for

Had it not been for Paul, all the prisoners on the ship would have been killed.

8. Key Bible cross-reference

Verse 3. See Matthew 11:21.

9. Key "by way of explanation"

Verse 43, "the centurion wanted to spare Paul's life." The centurion ordered his soldiers not to kill any of the prisoners. Out of respect for Paul the centurion followed Paul's advice and not the instincts of his own soldiers. Paul was probably the most experienced traveler on the ship.

10. Key "Quotable Quote"

"There are no closed doors to the gospel, provided that, once you go through the door, you don't care whether or not you come back out."
Brother Andrew

Acts chapter 28

1. **Previous chapter**

   Chapter 27: Paul sails for Rome and is shipwrecked

2. **Analysis of chapter**

   Paul welcomed at Malta. (1-10)
   He arrives at Rome. (11-16)
   His meeting with the Jews. (17-22)
   Paul preaches to the Jews, and lives in Rome as a prisoner. (23-31)

3. **Key verse**

   Verse 31: "Boldly and without hindrance he preached the kingdom of God and taught about the Lord Jesus Christ."

4. **Key word / key phrase**

   Verse 30, "for two whole years."

5. **Key event / key person / key theme**

   Paul arrives in Rome to a two-year house arrest

6. **Key thought**

   The gospel is now being proclaimed in the heart of the empire.

7. **Key thing to look out for**

   Verse 3. The man who had taken command of the ship, now collects wood.

8. **Key Bible cross-reference**

   Verses 26,27. See Isaiah 6:9,10.

9. **Key "by way of explanation"**

   Verse 30, "two whole years." On reaching Rome Paul wasted no time in summoning the leading Jews in order to explain the kingdom of God to them.

10. **Key "Quotable Quote"**

    "Young man, if I thought I could win one more soul for Christ by standing on my head and beating a tambourine with my feet I would learn how to do it." William Booth, to Rudyard Kipling, after the latter had said how much he disliked tambourines.

Romans

Romans chapter 1

1. Following chapter

Chapter 2: God will be our judge

2. Analysis of chapter

The apostle's commission. (1-7)
Paul prays for the saints at Rome, and expresses his desire to see them. (8-15)
The gospel way of justification by faith, for Jews and Gentiles. (16,17)
The sins of the Gentiles. (18-32)

3. Key verse

Verse 16: "I am not ashamed of the gospel, because it is the power of God for the salvation of everyone who believes: first for the Jew, then for the Gentile."

4. Key word / key phrase

Verse 17, "a gospel of righteousness."

5. Key event / key person / key theme

Paul states his gospel

6. Key thought

Paul longed to meet up with the Christians in Rome.

7. Key thing to look out for

Paul's definition of the gospel.

8. Key Bible cross-reference

Verse 17. See Habakkuk 2:4.

9. Key "by way of explanation"

Verse 9, "gospel of his Son." For Paul this was identical with the gospel of God, see verse 1. The word "gospel" translates the Greek word *euangelian*, literally "good news."

10. Key "Quotable Quote"

"Romans 1:18 stands in its insistence that even in the most excellent men, however endowed with law, righteousness, wisdom, and all virtues, free will, their most excellent part, is nonetheless ungodly, and unrighteous, and merits God's wrath."
Martin Luther

Romans chapter 2

1. Before and after

Previous chapter: Chapter 1: Greetings, prayer, and theme

Following chapter: Chapter 3: Why the Jews did not believe, and righteousness described

2. Analysis of chapter

The Jews could not be justified by the Law of Moses, any more than the Gentiles by the law of nature. (1-16)

The sins of the Jews and all their vain confidence in their outward privileges. (17-29)

3. Key verse

Verse 12: "All who sin apart from the law will also perish apart from the law, and all who sin under the law will be judged by the law."

4. Key word / key phrase

Verse 2, "God's judgment."

5. Key event / key person / key theme

God will be our judge

6. Key thought

Verse 28. Paul's teaching about Jews who are not really Jews would have been hard for most Jews to swallow.

7. Key thing to look out for

What mattered for Paul was not the opinions of men, but to be praised by God.

8. Key Bible cross-reference

Verse 6. See Psalm 62:12.

9. Key "by way of explanation"

Verse 1, "no excuse." Like Jesus, Paul is saying that nobody has the right to pass judgment on anyone else. The Jews were especially guilty of despising anyone who did not keep the Law.

10. Key "Quotable Quote"

"For we account a man to be justified by faith alone, without the works of the law."

Martin Luther

Romans chapter 3

1. Before and after

Previous chapter: Chapter 2: God will be our judge
Following chapter: Chapter 4: Righteousness illustrated

2. Analysis of chapter

Objections answered. (1-8)
All humankind are sinners. (9-18)
Both Jews and Gentiles cannot be justified by their own deeds. (19,20)
The free grace of God through faith in the righteousness of Christ, yet the law
is not done away. (21-31)

3. Key verse

Verse 25: "God presented him as a sacrifice of atonement, through faith in his
blood."

4. Key word / key phrase

Verse 22, "righteousness from God."

5. Key event / key person / key theme

Why the Jews did not believe, and righteousness described

6. Key thought

The thought that nobody in God's sight is righteous is new to many people.

7. Key thing to look out for

The idea that righteousness comes through faith, and is a gift, goes against the
grain.

8. Key Bible cross-reference

Verse 14. See Psalm 10:7.

9. Key "by way of explanation"

Verse 18, "fear of God." This is reverence for God. It does not mean being
afraid of God, but standing in awe of God. Without such "fear of God"
godliness is impossible.

10. Key "Quotable Quote"

"The works of faith involve doing all that is commanded in Scripture. That is
why the Mosaic law is a "law of faith" (Romans 3:27; cf. 9:31f.). Every command
in the Bible should be understood as specifying an obedience which is
inspired from knowing that God has promised to be one's God."
Daniel Fuller

Romans chapter 4

1. *Before and after*

Previous chapter: Chapter 3: Why the Jews did not believe, and righteousness described
Following chapter: Chapter 5: Peace with God, and salvation from God's wrath

2. *Analysis of chapter*

The doctrine of justification by faith is shown by the case of Abraham. (1-12)
He received the promise through the righteousness of faith. (13-22)
And we are justified in the same way. (23-25)

3. *Key verse*

Verse 18: "Against all hope, Abraham in hope believed and so became the father of many nations."

4. *Key word / key phrase*

Verse 3, "it was credited to him as righteousness."

5. *Key event / key person / key theme*

Righteousness illustrated

6. *Key thought*

In verse 18, Abraham is said to have believed against all hope.

7. *Key thing to look out for*

Paul summarizes the point of Jesus' death and resurrection in verse 25.

8. *Key Bible cross-reference*

Verse 11. See Genesis 17:10.

9. *Key "by way of explanation"*

Verse 1, "Abraham, our forefather." Paul introduces Abraham, the patriarch of the Jewish nation, as all Jews looked up to him. But Paul uses him as the great example of somebody who was justified by faith.

10. *Key "Quotable Quote"*

"Justification by faith is the very heart of the gospel."
C.H. Spurgeon

Romans chapter 5

1. *Before and after*

Previous chapter: Chapter 4: Righteousness illustrated
Following chapter: Chapter 6: Sanctification and sin

2. *Analysis of chapter*

The results of justification through faith in the righteousness of Christ. (1-5)
That we are reconciled by his blood. (6-11)
The fall of Adam brought all humankind into sin and death. (12-14)
The grace of God, through the righteousness of Christ, has more power to
bring salvation, than Adam's sin had to bring misery, (15-19)
as grace increased all the more. (20,21)

3. *Key verse*

Verse 1: "Therefore, since we have been justified through faith, we have peace
with God through our Lord Jesus Christ."

4. *Key word / key phrase*

Verse 1, "we have peace with God."

5. *Key event / key person / key theme*

Peace with God, and salvation from God's wrath

6. *Key thought*

The whole point of Paul's teaching is to have peace with God, verse 1.

7. *Key thing to look out for*

Note how Paul contrasts Adam with Jesus from verse 12.

8. *Key Bible cross-reference*

Verse 12. See Genesis 3:6.

9. *Key "by way of explanation"*

Verse 14, "pattern." Through Adam sin spread to every person who is born.
Adam is said to be a "pattern" in the sense that his actions can be seen as
foreshadowing what Christ would do in reverse. That is, Jesus' one act
brought universal blessing, in place of Adam's universal sin.

10. *Key "Quotable Quote"*

"If we have peace with God and the peace of God, we will become
peacemakers."
Billy Graham

Romans chapter 6

1. *Before and after*

Previous chapter: Chapter 5: Peace with God, and salvation from God's wrath

Following chapter: Chapter 7: Sanctification and the Law

2. *Analysis of chapter*

Believers must die to sin, and live for God. (1,2)

This is urged by their Christian baptism and union with Christ. (3-10)

They are made alive to God. (11-15)

And are freed from the dominion of sin. (16-20)

The end of sin is death. (21-23)

3. *Key verse*

Verse 5: "If we have been united with him like this in his death, we will certainly also be united with him in his resurrection."

4. *Key word / key phrase*

Verse 23, "the wages of sin is death."

5. *Key event / key person / key theme*

Sanctification and sin

6. *Key thought*

"As soon as we are incorporated in Christ, we have the certitude that in the end we shall achieve victory in the fight." John Calvin, commentating on Romans 6:6.

7. *Key thing to look out for*

Paul says we are to count ourselves dead to sin.

8. *Key Bible cross-reference*

Verse 4. See Colossians 2:12.

9. *Key "by way of explanation"*

Verse 11, "count yourselves." The first step on the path of sanctification is to "count yourselves" dead to sin. Then do not let sin dominate your life, verse 12; and then offer yourself to God, verse 13.

10. *Key "Quotable Quote"*

"We are free from sin – yet we must battle against it."

Anders Nygren

Romans chapter 7

1. Before and after

Previous chapter: Chapter 6: Sanctification and sin
Following chapter: Chapter 8: Sanctification and the Holy Spirit

2. Analysis of chapter

Believers are united to Christ, that they may be fruitful. (1-6)
The use and excellence of the Law. (7-13)
The spiritual conflicts between corruption and grace in a believer. (14-25)

3. Key verse

Verse 7: "What shall we say, then? Is the law sin? Certainly not! Indeed I would not have known what sin was except through the law."

4. Key word / key phrase

Verse 7, "Is the law sin?"

5. Key event / key person / key theme

Sanctification and the Law

6. Key thought

Paul states that Christians need to struggle against sin.

7. Key thing to look out for

In his own great battle with sin Paul is jubilant because he was rescued by Jesus Christ.

8. Key Bible cross-reference

Verse 7. See Exodus 20:17.

9. Key "by way of explanation"

Verse 23, "another law." Paul states that there remains in a Christian "another law" which is always trying to tempt him away from Christ and from obeying God.

10. Key "Quotable Quote"

"The Law is a kind of mirror. When we look in the mirror we notice any dirty marks on our faces, so in the Law we are made aware first of our helplessness, then of our sin and finally the judgment."
John Calvin

Romans chapter 8

1. Before and after

Previous chapter: Chapter 7: Sanctification and the Law
Following chapter: Chapter 9: What about the Jews?

2. Analysis of chapter

The freedom of believers from condemnation. (1-9)
Their privileges as children of God. (10-17)
Their hope despite trials. (18-25)
Their assistance from the Spirit in prayer. (26,27)
Their interest in the love of God. (28-31)
Their final triumph, through Christ. (32-39)

3. Key verse

Verse 8: "Therefore, there is now no condemnation for those who are in Christ Jesus."

4. Key word / key phrase

Verse 1, "No condemnation."

5. Key event / key person / key theme

Sanctification and the Holy Spirit

6. Key thought

"We are free from death – yet we long for the redemption of our bodies."
Anders Nygren

7. Key thing to look out for

Note how the statement that Christians are no longer condemned by God is explained in detail in verses 2-17.

8. Key Bible cross-reference

Verse 36. See Psalm 44:22.

9. Key "by way of explanation"

Verse 2, "the law of the Spirit of life." In this phrase the word "law" means a controlling power. Paul uses it to refer to the power of the Holy Spirit. This is the power that deals with sin and death for the Christian.

10. Key "Quotable Quote"

"The essential contrast which Paul paints is between the weakness of the law and the power of the Spirit. For over against indwelling sin, which is the reason the law is unable to help us in our moral struggle (7:17, 20), Paul now sets the indwelling Spirit, who is both our liberator now from 'the law of sin and death' (8:2) and the guarantee of resurrection and eternal glory in the end (8:11,17,23)."
John R.W. Stott

Romans chapter 9

1. Before and after

Previous chapter: Chapter 8: Sanctification and the Holy Spirit
Following chapter: Chapter 10: Israel rejected Jesus and the prophets

2. Analysis of chapter

The apostle's concern that his countrymen were strangers to the gospel. (1-5)
The promises are made good to the spiritual seed of Abraham. (6-13)
Answers to objections against God's sovereignty in exercising mercy and justice. (14-24)
This sovereignty is in God's dealing both with Jews and Gentiles. (25-29)
The Jews seek justification, not by faith, but by the works of the law. (30-33)

3. Key verse

Verse 18: "Therefore God has mercy on whom he wants to have mercy, and he hardens whom he wants to harden."

4. Key word / key phrase

Verse 4, "the people of Israel."

5. Key event / key person / key theme

What about the Jews?

6. Key thought

Chapters 9-11 are a digression about the Jews.

7. Key thing to look out for

Everything about salvation depends on God's mercy.

8. Key Bible cross-reference

Verse 9. See Genesis 18:10.

9. Key "by way of explanation"

Verse 32, "not by faith." Paul is pointing out where Israel went wrong. She relied on her own "works" (deeds) rather than faith as she attempted to win God's favor.

10. Key "Quotable Quote"

"You cannot say that Luther invented the idea of justification by faith alone. Long before Luther it was taught by Augustine and Paul and Jesus and Moses. ... Luther merely restated what true Christians have understood for centuries, that justification is by faith alone."
John MacArthur, Jr.

Romans chapter 10

1. *Before and after*

Previous chapter: Chapter 9: What about the Jews?
Following chapter: Chapter 11: Israel's future and her restoration

2. *Analysis of chapter*

The apostle's earnest desire for the salvation of the Jews. (1-4)
The difference between the righteousness of the Law, and the righteousness of faith. (5-11)
The Gentiles stand on the same ground as the Jews, in justification and salvation. (12-17)
The Jews know this from Old Testament prophecies. (18-21)

3. *Key verse*

Verse 1: "Brothers, my heart's desire and prayer to God for the Israelites is that they may be saved."

4. *Key word / key phrase*

Verse 9, "Jesus is Lord."

5. *Key event / key person / key theme*

Israel rejected Jesus and the prophets

6. *Key thought*

Paul reveals his deep concern for the Jews.

7. *Key thing to look out for*

Note Paul's use of Old Testament quotations to back up his arguments.

8. *Key Bible cross-reference*

Verse 5. See Leviticus 18:5.

9. *Key "by way of explanation"*

Verse 15, "How beautiful are the feet of those who bring good news!" This quotation from Isaiah 52:7 refers to the people who told the exiles that they were about to be released from Babylon. Paul applies this to Christian preachers who bring good news about release from sin.

10. *Key "Quotable Quote"*

"The good news is that sin has been dealt with; that Jesus has suffered its penalty for us as our representative, so that we might never have to suffer it; and that therefore all who believe in him can look forward to heaven."
J.M. Boice

Romans chapter 11

1. ### *Before and after*

   Previous chapter: Chapter 10: Israel rejected Jesus and the prophets
   Following chapter: Chapter 12: Christian behavior in the Church and in the world

2. ### *Analysis of chapter*

   The rejection of the Jews is not universal. (1-10)
   God overruled their unbelief and made the Gentiles take part in the gospel privileges. (11-21)

3. ### *Key verse*

   Verse 6: "And if by grace, then it is no longer by works; if it were, grace would no longer be grace."

4. ### *Key word / key phrase*

   Verse 1, "Does God reject his people?"

5. ### *Key event / key person / key theme*

   Israel's future and her restoration

6. ### *Key thought*

   This chapter revolves around the kindness and severity of God, verse 22.

7. ### *Key thing to look out for*

   One day Israel will return to the Lord.

8. ### *Key Bible cross-reference*

   Verse 8. See Isaiah 29:10.

9. ### *Key "by way of explanation"*

   Verse 22, "kindness and sternness of God." Paul taught about both aspects of God's nature. Without his kindness he might appear to be a tyrant. Without his sternness he might appear to be an indulgent father.

10. ### *Key "Quotable Quote"*

    "It was not human beings who accomplished anything here [on the cross]; no, God alone did it. He came to human beings in infinite love. He judged what is human. And he granted grace beyond any merit."
    Dietrich Bonhoeffer

Romans chapter 12

1. *Before and after*

Previous chapter: Chapter 11: Israel's future and her restoration

Following chapter: Chapter 13: Christians, and the authorities, and their neighbors

2. *Analysis of chapter*

Believers are to dedicate themselves to God. (1,2)

To be humble, and faithfully to use their spiritual gifts. (3-8)

Exhortations about various duties. (9-16)

And to peaceful behavior toward all people. (17-21)

3. *Key verse*

Verse 2: "Do not conform any longer to the pattern of this world, but be transformed by the renewing of your mind."

4. *Key word / key phrase*

Verse 9, "cling to what is good."

5. *Key event / key person / key theme*

Christian behavior in the Church and in the world

6. *Key thought*

Christians are to be living sacrifices.

7. *Key thing to look out for*

Note that Christian behavior should be governed by love.

8. *Key Bible cross-reference*

Verse 16. See Proverbs 3:7.

9. *Key "by way of explanation"*

Verse 1, "living sacrifices." All Paul's readers were familiar with the Old Testament sacrificial system. Paul says Christians, in stark contrast to dead animal sacrifices, are to be "living sacrifices."

10. *Key "Quotable Quote"*

"All the fruits of the Spirit which we have are signs of grace, are summed up in charity, or Christian love; because this is the sum of all grace."

Jonathan Edwards

Romans chapter 13

1. *Before and after*

> Previous chapter: Chapter 12: Christian behavior in the Church and in the world
> Following chapter: Chapter 14: The principles of Christian freedom

2. *Analysis of chapter*

> The duty of subjection to the governing authorities. (1-7)
> Exhortations to mutual love. (8-10)
> To decent behavior and sobriety. (11-14)

3. *Key verse*

> Verse 7: "Give everyone what you owe him: If you owe taxes, pay taxes; if revenue, then revenue; if respect, then respect; if honor, then honor."

4. *Key word / key phrase*

> Verse 1, "the governing authorities."

5. *Key event / key person / key theme*

> Christians, the authorities, and neighbors

6. *Key thought*

> Paul teaches that the state authorities have been put in place by God.

7. *Key thing to look out for*

> Evil practices have no place in the Christian life.

8. *Key Bible cross-reference*

> Verse 9. See Exodus 20:13-15.

9. *Key "by way of explanation"*

> Verse 1, "governing authorities." Some Christians thought that they need not submit to pagan authorities since they only acknowledged Christ's authority. Paul teaches otherwise.

10. *Key "Quotable Quote"*

> "If the correction of unbridled despotism is the Lord's to avenge, let us not at once think that it is entrusted to us, to whom no command has been given except to obey and suffer."
> John Calvin

Romans chapter 14

1. **Before and after**

   Previous chapter: Chapter 13: Christians, the authorities, and neighbors
   Following chapter: Chapter 15: Paul's missionary plans

2. **Analysis of chapter**

   The Jewish converts cautioned against judging, and Gentile believers against despising Jews. (1-13)
   And the Gentiles told to take care not to give offense unnecessarily. (14-23)

3. **Key verse**

   Verse 1: "Accept him whose faith is weak, without passing judgment on disputable matters."

4. **Key word / key phrase**

   Verse 10, "what leads to peace."

5. **Key event / key person / key theme**

   The principles of Christian freedom

6. **Key thought**

   Look after the weaker brother.

7. **Key thing to look out for**

   Behave like a member of God's kingdom.

8. **Key Bible cross-reference**

   Verse 11. See Isaiah 45:23.

9. **Key "by way of explanation"**

   Verse 15. "your brother for whom Christ died." Christ died for those who are weak. If this is born in mind the strong Christian should not mind putting up with the weaker brothers and sisters.

10. **Key "Quotable Quote"**

    "To be a Christian is primarily to live in union with Jesus Christ, as a result of which baptism, belief and behavior slot naturally into place."
    John R.W. Stott

Romans chapter 15

1. Before and after

Previous chapter: Chapter 14: The principles of Christian freedom
Following chapter: Chapter 16: Paul greets his many friends in Rome

2. Analysis of chapter

How to behave toward the weak. (1-7)
Receive one another as brethren. (8-13)
The writing and preaching of the apostle. (14-21)
His intended journey. (22-29)
He requests their prayers. (30-33)

3. Key verse

Verse 7: "Accept one another, then, just as Christ accepted you, in order to bring praise to God."

4. Key word / key phrase

Verse 24, "when I go to Spain."

5. Key event / key person / key theme

Paul's missionary plans

6. Key thought

Be like Christ in the way you accept people.

7. Key thing to look out for

I hope to visit you soon.

8. Key Bible cross-reference

Verse 10. See Deuteronomy 32:43.

9. Key "by way of explanation"

Verse 17, "I glory." When Paul used this expression he was not attempting to boast about himself but rather about what Christ had achieved through him.

10. Key "Quotable Quote"

"Among the attributes of God, although they are all equal, mercy shines with even more brilliance than justice."
Miguel de Cervantes

Romans chapter 16

1. **Previous chapter**

    Chapter 15: Paul's missionary plans

2. **Analysis of chapter**

    The apostle recommends Phoebe to the Church at Rome, and greets several friends there. (1-16)
    Warns the Church against those who cause divisions. (17-20)
    Christian greetings. (21-24)
    The letter concludes by giving glory to God. (25-27)

3. **Key verse**

    Verse 3 "Greet Priscilla and Aquila, my fellow workers in Christ Jesus."

4. **Key word / key phrase**

    Verse 3, "Greet."

5. **Key event / key person / key theme**

    Paul greets his many friends in Rome

6. **Key thought**

    Note how many people Paul knew in Rome.

7. **Key thing to look out for**

    Verses 25-27. Paul's reasons for praising God.

8. **Key Bible cross-reference**

    Verse 23. See 2 Timothy 4:20.

9. **Key "by way of explanation"**

    Verse 25, "my gospel." Paul is not saying that he has a gospel that is different from the gospel every other Christian has. Rather Paul calls it "my" gospel as he received it by direct revelation. See Galatians 1:12.

10. **Key "Quotable Quote"**

    "The gospel is so simple that small children can understand it, and it is so profound that studies by the wisest theologians will never exhaust its riches."
    Charles Hodge

1 Corinthians and 2 Corinthians

1 Corinthians chapter 1

1. Following chapter

Chapter 2: True wisdom and the Spirit

2. Analysis chapter

A greeting and thanksgiving. (1-9)
Exhortation to brotherly love, and reproof for divisions. (10-16)
The teaching of a crucified Savior, which promotes the glory of God, (17-25)
and humbles all people before him. (26-31)

3. Key verse

Verse 25: "For the foolishness of God is wiser than man's wisdom, and the weakness of God is stronger than man's strength."

4. Key word

Verse 18, "cross."

5. Key event / key person / key theme

The disunity in the Church at Corinth

6. Key thought

Christ is preeminent and must be so in any fellowship if its abuses are to be corrected.

7. Key thing to look out for

The links and contrasts between wisdom and power.

8. Key Bible cross-reference

Verse 21. See Luke 10:21.

9. Key "by way of explanation"

Verse 23. Christ crucified was a "stumbling-block" to the Jews because they were not expecting a crucified Messiah, but a politically triumphant Messiah. Paul wrote this letter when we was coming to the end of his three years at Ephesus (16:5-9; Acts 20:31).

10. Key "Quotable Quote"

"Forbid it, Lord, that I should boast,
Save in the death of Christ my God.
All the vain things that charm me most
I sacrifice them to his blood."
Isaac Watts

1 Corinthians chapter 2

1. *Before and after*

Previous chapter: Chapter 1: Introduction and divisions
Following chapter: Chapter 3: The nature of ministers

2. *Analysis of chapter*

The simple way in which the apostle preached Christ crucified. (1-5)
The wisdom contained in this teaching. (6-9)
It cannot be known but by the Holy Spirit. (10-16)

3. *Key verse*

Verse 10: "The Spirit searches all things, even the deep things of God."

4. *Key word / key phrase*

Verse 13, "words taught by the Spirit."

5. *Key event / key person / key theme*

True wisdom and the Spirit

6. *Key thought*

God's wisdom comes from the Holy Spirit.

7. *Key thing to look out for*

Paul defines the spiritual person.

8. *Key Bible cross-reference*

Verse 9. See Isaiah 64:4.

9. *Key "by way of explanation"*

Verse 10, "Spirit searches all things." Because the Spirit understands the depths of God and his wonderful grace, he is able to reveal this to believers.

10. *Key "Quotable Quote"*

"For the message of the cross is the doctrine of salvation through the crucifixion of the Son of God as a sacrifice for human sins."
Charles Hodge

1 Corinthians chapter 3

1. Before and after

Previous chapter: Chapter 2: True wisdom and the Spirit
Following chapter: Chapter 4: Paul's ministry is misunderstood

2. Analysis of chapter

The Corinthians reproved for their divisions. (1-4)
The true servants of Christ can do nothing without him. (5-9)
He is the only foundation, and every one should take care how he builds on this. (10-15)
The churches of Christ should be pure and humble. (16,17)
And they should not boast because all they have comes from Christ. (18-23)

3. Key verse

Verse 11: "For no one can lay any foundation other than the one already laid, which is Jesus Christ."

4. Key word / key phrase

Verse 10, "an expert builder."

5. Key event / key person / key theme

The nature of ministers

6. Key thought

Paul hated Christian disunity.

7. Key thing to look out for

Only spiritual foundations will survive.

8. Key Bible cross-reference

Verse 20. See Hebrews 5:12,13.

9. Key "by way of explanation"

Verse 10, "I laid a foundation." Paul did this by preaching about Christ and his death.

10. Key "Quotable Quote"

"Next to the wicked lives of men, nothing is so great a disparagement and weakening to religion as the divisions of Christians."
John Tillotson

1 Corinthians chapter 4

1. *Before and after*

Previous chapter: Chapter 3: The nature of ministers
Following chapter: Chapter 5: Sexual immorality among Christians

2. *Analysis of chapter*

The true character of gospel ministers. (1-6)
Warns against despising the apostle. (7-13)
He tells them to view him as their spiritual father in Christ, and shows his concern for them. (14-21)

3. *Key verse*

Verse 4: "My conscience is clear, but that does not make me innocent. It is the Lord who judges me."

4. *Key word / key phrase*

Verse 4, "my conscience is clear."

5. *Key event / key person / key theme*

Paul's ministry is misunderstood

6. *Key thought*

Paul writes about his special relationship with the Corinthian Christians.

7. *Key thing to look out for*

When Christians had gone astray Paul never pulled his punches.

8. *Key Bible cross-reference*

Verse 12. See Acts 18:3.

9. *Key "by way of explanation"*

Verse 12, "we work hard with our own hands." By trade, Paul was a tentmaker. Acts 18:3.

10. *Key "Quotable Quote"*

"Set your own will entirely aside and strive to keep before your eyes your one and only goal, that is, the greater service and glory of God."
Ignatius of Loyola

1 Corinthians chapter 5

1. *Before and after*

Previous chapter: Chapter 4: Paul's ministry is misunderstood
Following chapter: Chapter 6: Taking a fellow-Christian to court, and sexual immorality

2. *Analysis of chapter*

The apostle blames the Corinthians for tolerating sexual immorality in their fellowship (1-8);
and tells them how to deal with this scandalous situation. (9-13)

3. *Key verse*

Verse 2: "And you are proud!"

4. *Key word / key phrase*

Verse 1, "a man has his father's wife."

5. *Key event / key person / key theme*

Sexual immorality among Christians

6. *Key thought*

"Your immorality knows no bounds."

7. *Key thing to look out for*

"Do not put up with wickedness in your fellowship."

8. *Key Bible cross-reference*

Verse 13. See Deuteronomy 13:5.

9. *Key "by way of explanation"*

Verse 1, "not . . . even among pagans." Paul was hitting out against incest among Christians. He points out that even pagans did not go in for this practice. Cicero said that incest was hardly ever found in Roman society.

10. *Key "Quotable Quote"*

"Satan fails to speak of the remorse, the futility, the loneliness, and the spiritual devastation which go hand in hand with immorality."
Billy Graham

1 Corinthians chapter 6

1. *Before and after*

Previous chapter: Chapter 5: Sexual immorality among Christians
Following chapter: Chapter 7: Counsel about marriage

2. *Analysis of chapter*

Warns against going to law before non-Christians. (1-8)
Sins which exclude one from the kingdom of God. (9-11)
Our bodies, which are the members of Christ, and temples of the Holy Spirit, must not be defiled. (12-20)

3. *Key verse*

Verse 11: "And that is what some of you were. But you were washed, you were sanctified, you were justified in the name of the Lord Jesus Christ and by the Spirit of our God."

4. *Key word / key phrase*

Verse 9, "Do not be deceived."

5. *Key event / key person / key theme*

Taking a fellow-Christian to court, and sexual immorality

6. *Key thought*

The whole person, spirit and body, belongs to Christ. The Christians are not to be under the control of any passion – emotional, or physical. Christ is their master.

7. *Key thing to look out for*

The reason why Christians must shun sexual immorality.

8. *Key Bible cross-reference*

Verse 16. See Genesis 2:24.

9. *Key "by way of explanation"*

Verse 19, "your body is a temple of the Holy Spirit." Christians should view their bodies as if they were sacred, lived in by God's Spirit. So their bodies should not indulge in sexual immorality."

10. *Key "Quotable Quote"*

"The monstrosity of sexual intercourse outside marriage is that those who indulge in it are trying to isolate one kind of union (the sexual) from all other kinds of union which were intended to go along with it and make up the total union."
C.S. Lewis

1 Corinthians chapter 7

1. Before and after

Previous chapter: Chapter 6: Taking a fellow-Christian to court, and sexual immorality

Following chapter: Chapter 8: Christian freedom, and the weaker Christian

2. Analysis of chapter

The apostle answers several questions about marriage. (1-9)

Married Christians should not seek to part from their unbelieving partners. (10-16)

Stay in the place you were in when the Lord called you. (17-24)

It is most desirable, because of the present crisis, for people to sit loose to this world. (25-35)

Great prudence should be used in marriage; it should be only in the Lord. (36-40)

3. Key verse

Verse 29: "What I mean, brothers, is that the time is short."

4. Key word / key phrase

Verse 3, "marital duty."

5. Key event / key person / key theme

Counsel about marriage

6. Key thought

Paul highlights the advantages of remaining single.

7. Key thing to look out for

Verse 35, Paul's underlying and controlling principle.

8. Key Bible cross-reference

Verses 10,11. See Luke 16:18.

9. Key "by way of explanation"

Verse 26, "present crisis." Paul's teaching is here colored by the "present crisis" which may refer to the evil society in which Christians are living. It is only because of this "present crisis" that Paul gives this teaching.

10. Key "Quotable Quote"

"Whenever anybody asks me a question about divorce, I refuse to answer it until I have first talked about two other subjects, namely, marriage and reconciliation."
John R.W. Stott

1 Corinthians chapter 8

1. *Before and after*

    Previous chapter: Chapter 7: Counsel about marriage
    Following chapter: Chapter 9: Paul's Christian freedom

2. *Analysis of chapter*

    The danger of having a wrong view of knowledge. (1-6)
    Take care not to upset weak Christians. (7-13)

3. *Key verse*

    Verse 1: "Knowledge puffs up, but love builds up."

4. *Key word / key phrase*

    Verse 9, "a stumbling block."

5. *Key event / key person / key theme*

    Christian freedom, and the weaker brother

6. *Key thought*

    When you sin against a fellow Christian you sin against Christ (verse 12).

7. *Key thing to look out for*

    The underlying principle to apply here comes in verse 1.

8. *Key Bible cross-reference*

    Verse 1. See 1 Corinthians 1:1.

9. *Key "by way of explanation"*

    Verse 1, "knowledge puffs up, but love builds up." Knowledge puffs up because it flatters our pride. Love builds up because it has the greatest good of the fellow Christian as the top priority.

10. *Key "Quotable Quote"*

    "Brotherly love is still the distinguishing badge of every true Christian."
    Matthew Henry

1 Corinthians chapter 9

1. *Before and after*

Previous chapter: Chapter 8: Christian freedom, and the weaker Christian
Following chapter: Chapter 10: The correct use of Christian freedom

2. *Analysis of chapter*

The apostle shows his authority, and asserts his right to be provided for. (1-14)
For the good of others he never insisted on this. (15-23)
He did all this, with care and diligence, to gain a crown that never fades. (24-27)

3. *Key verse*

Verse 14: "In the same way, the Lord has commanded that those who preach the gospel should receive their living from the gospel."

4. *Key word / key phrase*

Verse 1, "Am I not free?"

5. *Key event / key person / key theme*

Paul's Christian freedom

6. *Key thought*

Paul is forced to defend his own apostleship.

7. *Key thing to look out for*

Verse 22 summarizes Paul's policy toward fellow-Christians.

8. *Key Bible cross-reference*

Verse 9. See Deuteronomy 25:4.

9. *Key "by way of explanation"*

Verse 22, does not refer to letting go of principles, but shows Paul's deep sympathy, and intention always to come alongside people and feel with them where they are.

10. *Key "Quotable Quote"*

"The only right a Christian has is the right to give up his rights"
Oswald Chambers

1 Corinthians chapter 10

1. Before and after

Previous chapter: Chapter 9: Paul's Christian freedom
Following chapter: Chapter 11: Public prayer and disorder at the Lord's Supper

2. Analysis of chapter

Learn from the mistakes of the Israelites in the desert. (1-5)
Warns against all idolatrous, and other sinful practices. (6-14)
Taking part in idolatry cannot exist side by side with having fellowship with Christ. (15-22)
Everything we do is to be to the glory of God, and should not offend other peoples' consciences. (23-33)

3. Key verse

Verse 14: "Therefore, my dear friends, flee from idolatry."

4. Key word / key phrase

Verse 23, "not everything is beneficial."

5. Key event / key person / key theme

The correct use of Christian freedom

6. Key thought

An idol is anything that I instinctively turn to, to hold my life together and keep me going.

7. Key thing to look out for

By looking at the example of the Israelites, what do we learn not to do?

8. Key Bible cross-reference

Verse 26. See Psalm 24:1.

9. Key "by way of explanation"

Verse 31, "all for the glory of God." In chapters 8-10 Paul answers questions raised by the Corinthians. The basic principle in all these matters is that everything should be done for the glory of God, not for self-indulgence.

10. Key "Quotable Quote"

"Your days at the most cannot be very long, so use them to the best of your ability for the glory of God and the benefit of your generation."
William Booth

1 Corinthians chapter 11

1. ## Before and after

    Previous chapter: Chapter 10: The correct use of Christian freedom
    Following chapter: Chapter 12: The importance and correct use of spiritual gifts

2. ## Analysis of chapter

    The apostle, after an exhortation to follow him (1),
    corrects some abuses. (2-16)
    Also he rebukes their divisions, and disorderly celebrations of the Lord's Supper. (17-22)
    He reminds them of the nature and purpose of its institution. (23-26)
    And tells them the correct way to take part in this. (27-34)

3. ## Key verse

    Verse 1: "Follow my example, as I follow the example of Christ."

4. ## Key word / key phrase

    Verse 20, "when you come together."

5. ## Key event / key person / key theme

    Public prayer and disorder at the Lord's Supper

6. ## Key thought

    Verse 11, "In the Lord," men and women are partners, mutually dependant, and each must behave out of respect for the other in submission to God.

7. ## Key thing to look out for

    Why were so many feeble and ill?

8. ## Key Bible cross-reference

    Verse 7. See Genesis 1:26,27.

9. ## Key "by way of explanation"

    Verse 20, "not the Lord's Supper you eat." Their gluttony made a mockery of the Lord's Supper. For a woman to take off her head-covering was, in those days, a sign of sexual promiscuity. A shaved head was a sign of public disgrace.

10. ## Key "Quotable Quote"

    "The Lord's Supper (re)-presents the death of Christ and proclaims that death in and through the shared celebration."
    James D.G. Dunn

1 Corinthians chapter 12

1. *Before and after*

Previous chapter: Chapter 11: Public prayer and disorder at the Lord's Supper
Following chapter: Chapter 13: Paul's hymn on love

2. *Analysis of chapter*

The different uses of spiritual gifts are given. (1-11)
In the human body every part has its place and use. (12-26)
This is applied to the Church of Christ. (27-30)
There is something more excellent than spiritual gifts. (31)

3. *Key verse*

Verse 4: "There are different kinds of gifts, but the same Spirit."

4. *Key word / key phrase*

Verse 1, "about spiritual gifts."

5. *Key event / key person / key theme*

The importance and correct use of spiritual gifts

6. *Key thought*

Verse 27. Each Christian is a part of Christ's spiritual body. This is not a metaphor but is literally true.

7. *Key thing to look out for*

I am an organic part of Christ's body – what are the implications for me?

8. *Key Bible cross-reference*

Verse 28. See Ephesians 4:11

9. *Key "by way of explanation"*

Verse 7, "given for the common good." Some of the Corinthians had managed to misuse their God-given spiritual gifts. Paul corrects them by saying that all such gifts are not for personal indulgence, but for the "common good" of the Christian fellowship.

10. *Key "Quotable Quote"*

"What was special about the new dispensation was that, first of all, these gifts were not confined to any one group of people but extended to all – male and female, young and old. Secondly, these supernatural endowments were wonderfully diverse."
Charles Hodge

1 Corinthians chapter 13

1. Before and after

Previous chapter: Chapter 12: The importance and correct use of spiritual gifts

Following chapter: Chapter 14: Prophecy, tongues, and public worship

2. Analysis of chapter

The necessity and advantage of the grace of love. (1-3)

Its excellency is seen in its nature and in its effects (4-7);

and by its enduring characteristic. (8-13)

3. Key verse

Verse 13: "And now these three remain: faith, hope and love. But the greatest of these is love."

4. Key word / key phrase

Verse 13, "the greatest of these is love."

5. Key event / key person / key theme

Paul's hymn on love

6. Key thought

"All you need is love."

7. Key thing to look out for

Christian love is the antidote to all wrong thinking and wrong behavior.

8. Key Bible cross-reference

Verse l3. See Galatians 5:6.

9. Key "by way of explanation"

Verse 13, "the greatest of these is love." Love is even more important than spiritual gifts. For God is love, God gives us his love, and Christians are to show love to each other.

10. Key "Quotable Quote"

"Love seeketh not itself to please
Nor for itself hath any care,
But for another gives its ease
And builds a heaven in hell's despair."
William Blake

1 Corinthians chapter 14

1. Before and after

Previous chapter: Chapter 13: Paul's hymn on love
Following chapter: Chapter 15: Teaching about the resurrection

2. Analysis of chapter

Prophecy preferred to the gift of tongues. (1-5)
The uselessness of speaking in unknown languages. (6-14)
Exhortations to worship in a way that can be understood. (15-25)
The selfish display of gifts (26-33);
and women speaking in the Church. (34-40)

3. Key verse

Verse 12: "Since you are eager to have spiritual gifts, try to excel in gifts that build up the church."

4. Key word / key phrase

Verse 1, "eagerly desire spiritual gifts."

5. Key event / key person / key theme

Prophecy, tongues, and public worship

6. Key thought

Verse 1 gives the principle. The Greek verb translated "follow" means "pursue" – it suggests endeavor.

7. Key thing to look out for

Verse 12, "excel in gifts that build up the church." This is Paul's overriding consideration in connection with spiritual gifts. When you seek spiritual gifts seek those which will help the Christian fellowship.

8. Key Bible cross-reference

Verse 21. See Isaiah 28:11,12.

9. Key "by way of explanation"

"Prophecy" may be a prediction of future events. It also means seeing the will of God for specific needs in the immediate situation, and making that clear.

10. Key "Quotable Quote"

"The Spirit gives different Christians different gifts . . . but he works to produce the same fruit in all."
John R.W. Stott

1 Corinthians chapter 15

1. Before and after

Previous chapter: Chapter 14: Prophecy, tongues, and public worship
Following chapter: Chapter 16: Collecting for Jerusalem, and greetings

2. Analysis of chapter

The apostle testifies to the resurrection of Christ from the dead. (1-11)
He replies to those who deny the resurrection of the body. (12-19)
The resurrection of believers to eternal life. (20-34)
Objections against it answered. (35-50)
The mystery of the change that will occur to those living at Christ's second coming. (51-54)
The believer's triumph over death and the grave. An exhortation to be diligent. (55-58)

3. Key verse

Verse 58: "Therefore, my dear brothers, stand firm. Let nothing move you. Always give yourselves fully to the work of the Lord, because you know that your labor in the Lord is not in vain."

4. Key word / key phrase

Verse 4, "he was raised."

5. Key event / key person / key theme

Teaching about the resurrection

6. Key thought

Verse 56. Because Christ is raised the poison is taken out of death and Christians are made victorious.

7. Key thing to look out for

Paul gives pictures about the nature of the resurrection body.

8. Key Bible cross-reference

Verse 27. See Psalm 8:6.

9. Key "by way of explanation"

Verse 12, "Christ has been raised." Paul uses this verb "has been raised" seven times here to emphasize the certainty of Christ's bodily resurrection. See verses 4,12-14,16,17,20.

10. Key "Quotable Quote"

"Many Christians entirely disbelieve the resurrection; many fortify themselves with the horoscope; many adhere to superstitious observances, and to omens, and auguries."
John Chrysostom

1 Corinthians chapter 16

1. **Previous chapter**

    Chapter 15: Teaching about the resurrection

2. **Analysis of chapter**

    A collection for the poor at Jerusalem. (1-9)
    Timothy and Apollos commended. (10-12)
    Exhortation to be alert in faith and love. (13-18)
    Christian greetings. (19-24)

3. **Key verse**

    Verse 14: "Do everything in love."

4. **Key word / key phrase**

    Verse 2, "set aside a sum of money."

5. **Key event / key person / key theme**

    Collecting for Jerusalem, and greetings

6. **Key thought**

    Paul cannot trust the Corinthians even to welcome visiting Christian leaders.

7. **Key thing to look out for**

    Paul reiterates that they must do everything in love.

8. **Key Bible cross-reference**

    Verse 19. See Acts 18:2.

9. **Key "by way of explanation"**

    Verse 2, "set aside a sum of money in keeping with his income." This is to be done "on the first day of the week." The amount should be in proportion to one's means, that is, one's income. This money was to be used exclusively for the Lord's work.

10. **Key "Quotable Quote"**

    "The tithe can be a beginning way to acknowledge God as the owner of all things, but it is only a beginning and not an ending."
    Richard J. Foster

2 Corinthians chapter 1

1. ### Following chapter

    Chapter 2: Punishment and forgiveness

2. ### Analysis of chapter

    The apostle blesses God for comfort in, and deliverance from troubles. (1-11)
    He states his own and his fellow-laborers' integrity. (12-14)
    He tells them why he was not able to visit them. (15-24)

3. ### Key verse

    Verse 7: "And our hope for you is firm, because we know that just as you share in our sufferings, so also you share in our comfort."

4. ### Key word / key phrase

    Verse 4, "who comforts us."

5. ### Key event / key person / key theme

    The God of all comfort

6. ### Key thought

    It is in catastrophes and crises that we discover the mighty power of God.

7. ### Key thing to look out for

    "My actions stem from God's grace, not worldly considerations."

8. ### Key Bible cross-reference

    Verse 1. See Acts 18:1.

9. ### Key "by way of explanation"

    Verse 3, "the God of all comfort." When Christians are going through a time of suffering they are to remember to turn to God for comfort. When they comfort others they should do so with the comfort that they were comforted with.

10. ### Key "Quotable Quote"

    "The letters to the Corinthians reveal to us more of the personal character of the apostle than any of his other letters. They show him to us as a man, as a pastor, as a counselor, as in conflict not only with heretics, but with personal enemies. They reveal his wisdom, his zeal, his forbearance, his liberality of principle and practice in all matters not affecting salvation, his strictness in all matters of right and wrong, his humility, and perhaps above all, his unwearied activity and wonderful endurance."
    Charles Hodge

2 Corinthians chapter 2

1. Before and after

Previous chapter: Chapter 1: Giving thanks for God's comfort
Following chapter: Chapter 3: All ability is from God, and the superiority of the new covenant

2. Analysis of chapter

Reasons why the apostle did not come to Corinth. (1-4)
Instructions about restoring a repentant Christian. (5-11)
An account of his work and success in spreading the gospel of Christ. (12-17)

3. Key verse

Verse 14: "But thanks be to God, who always leads us in triumphal procession in Christ and through us spreads everywhere the fragrance of the knowledge of him"

4. Key word / key phrase

Verse 4, "great distress and anguish."

5. Key event / key person / key theme

Punishment and forgiveness

6. Key thought

Dealing with the Corinthians caused Paul pain.

7. Key thing to look out for

Paul emphasizes that he has been sent by God.

8. Key Bible cross-reference

Verses 12,13. See Acts 20:1.

9. Key "by way of explanation"

Verse 17, "we do not peddle the word of God for profit." Paul is attacking those false teachers who have wormed their way into the Corinthian Church and have taken the gullible for a ride.

10. Key "Quotable Quote"

"The Church authorities have excommunicated me for heresy, I excommunicate them in the name of the sacred truth of God. Christ will judge whose excommunication will stand."
Martin Luther

2 Corinthians chapter 3

1. *Before and after*

Previous chapter: Chapter 2: Punishment and forgiveness
Following chapter: Chapter 4: Paul's ministry, a most unlikely apostle, and Christian hope

2. *Analysis of chapter*

The preference of the gospel over the Law given by Moses. (1-11)
The preaching of the apostle and the power of the Holy Spirit. (12-18)

3. *Key verse*

Verse 15: "Even to this day when Moses is read, a veil covers their hearts."

4. *Key word / key phrase*

Verse 6, "he has made us competent."

5. *Key event / key person / key theme*

All ability is from God, and the superiority of the new covenant

6. *Key thought*

Paul claims that his capacity to serve God is God-given.

7. *Key thing to look out for*

Christians are to be increasingly transformed into Christ's likeness.

8. *Key Bible cross-reference*

Verse 6. See Jeremiah 31:31.

9. *Key "by way of explanation"*

Verse 3, "Are we beginning to commend ourselves again?" Paul is always having to justify himself before the accusing Corinthian Christians and the evil intentions of the false teachers in Corinth.

10. *Key "Quotable Quote"*

"The first service that one owes to others in the fellowship consists in listening to them."
Dietrich Bonhoeffer

2 Corinthians chapter 4

1. Before and after

Previous chapter: Chapter 3: All ability is from God, and the superiority of the new covenant
Following chapter: Chapter 5: Death and future glory

2. Analysis of chapter

The apostles worked with great diligence, sincerity, and faithfulness. (1-7)
They suffered a great deal on account of the gospel, but were also well-supported. (8-12)
Prospects of eternal glory keep believers from collapsing under troubles. (13-18)

3. Key verse

Verse 8: "We are hard pressed on every side, but not crushed; perplexed, but not in despair."

4. Key word / key phrase

Verse 1, "we have this ministry."

5. Key event / key person / key theme

Paul's ministry, a most unlikely apostle, and Christian hope

6. Key thought

People do not believe because they are blinded by Satan. The result of this darkness is tragic: they do not see the glory of Christ (verse 4).

7. Key thing to look out for

Paul explains why he does not lose heart.

8. Key Bible cross-reference

Verse 6. See Genesis 1:3.

9. Key "by way of explanation"

Verse 7, "we have this treasure in jars of clay." Treasures were kept is very ordinary looking jars. The gospel is the treasure. Paul is but a frail, unattractive jar of clay, keeping safe a great treasure.

10. Key "Quotable Quote"

"We cannot be content with an evangelism which does not lead to the drawing of converts into the Church, nor with a church order whose principle of cohesion is a superficial social camaraderie instead of a spiritual fellowship with the Father and with his Son, Jesus Christ."
John R.W. Stott

2 Corinthians chapter 5

1. Before and after

Previous chapter: Chapter 4: Paul's ministry, a most unlikely apostle, and Christian hope

Following chapter: Chapter 6: Reconciliation among Christians, and separation from unbelievers

2. Analysis of chapter

The apostle's hope and desire for heavenly glory. (1-8)

Why Paul had such concern for the Corinthians. (9-15)

The necessity of regeneration, and of reconciliation with God through Christ. (16-21)

3. Key verse

Verse 7: "We live by faith, not by sight."

4. Key word / key phrase

Verse 5, "what is to come."

5. Key event / key person / key theme

Death and future glory

6. Key thought

All Christians have two homes.

7. Key thing to look out for

"This is how you should look at people."

8. Key Bible cross-reference

Verse 10. See Romans 14:10.

9. Key "by way of explanation"

Verse 10, "appear before the judgment seat of Christ." This does not refer to a person being judged about whether he or she is a Christian. This is a different judgment when the value of what a Christian has done is on trial.

10. Key "Quotable Quote"

"Do something good for someone you like least, today."
Saint Anthony

2 Corinthians chapter 6

1. *Before and after*

Previous chapter: Chapter 5: Death and future glory
Following chapter: Chapter 7: Meeting Titus, and response to Paul's letter

2. *Analysis of chapter*

The apostle, with others, showed themselves to be faithful ministers of Christ, by their blameless life and behavior. (1-10)
On account of their affection for them they did not want them to have any fellowship with unbelievers and idolaters. (11-18)

3. *Key verse*

Verse 14: "Do not be yoked together with unbelievers."

4. *Key word / key phrase*

Verse 13, "open wide your hearts."

5. *Key event / key person / key theme*

Reconciliation among Christians, and separation from unbelievers

6. *Key thought*

"Do not become inextricably linked up with non-believers."

7. *Key thing to look out for*

The results of Paul's hardships.

8. *Key Bible cross-reference*

Verse 5. See Acts 16:23.

9. *Key "by way of explanation"*

Verse 14, "Do not be yoked together with unbelievers." Today, this verse is often applied to a Christian contemplating marriage with a non-Christian. In Paul's day it referred to the danger of aligning oneself with false teachers and their cancerous teaching.

10. *Key "Quotable Quote"*

"Whoever sheds a fervent tear for the hardships of his fellow man, heals his own wounds."
Basil the Great

2 Corinthians chapter 7

1. **Before and after**

   Previous chapter: Chapter 6: Reconciliation among Christians, and separation from unbelievers

   Following chapter: Chapter 8: Will you follow Macedonia's example in giving money?

2. **Analysis of chapter**

   An exhortation to be holy. (1-4)

   He rejoiced that their sorrow over their sins led to repentance. (5-11)

   And he rejoiced in the comfort they and Titus shared. (12-16)

3. **Key verse**

   Verse 6: "But God, who comforts the downcast, comforted us by the coming of Titus."

4. **Key word / key phrase**

   Verse 14, "Titus has proved to be true."

5. **Key event / key person / key theme**

   Meeting Titus, and response to Paul's letter

6. **Key thought**

   "Welcome us in your hearts."

7. **Key thing to look out for**

   God's promises should lead to a pure life.

8. **Key Bible cross-reference**

   Verse 5. See 2 Corinthians 2:13.

9. **Key "by way of explanation"**

   Verse 10, "godly sorrow . . . worldly sorrow." Paul points out that there is more than one kind of sorrow. Worldly sorrow after the consequences of sin leads only to death, but godly sorrow, which involves repentances, leads to life.

10. **Key "Quotable Quote"**

    "Earth has no sorrow that heaven cannot heal."

    Thomas Moore

2 Corinthians chapter 8

1. *Before and after*

Previous chapter: Chapter 7: Meeting Titus, and response to Paul's letter
Following chapter: Chapter 9: Giving money is a spiritual act

2. *Analysis of chapter*

The apostle urges them to be generous toward the poor saints. (1-6)
He underlines this by referring to their gifts, and by the love and grace of Christ. (7-9)
And by the willingness they had shown to do this good work. (10-15)
He commends Titus to them. (16-24)

3. *Key verse*

Verse 2: "Out of the most severe trial, their overflowing joy and their extreme poverty welled up in rich generosity."

4. *Key word / key phrase*

Verse 7, "grace of giving."

5. *Key event / key person / key theme*

Will you follow Macedonia's example in giving money?

6. *Key thought*

"Service is a great privilege."

7. *Key thing to look out for*

Verses 13-15 express an important principle

8. *Key Bible cross-reference*

Verses 1-4. See Romans 15:26.

9. *Key "by way of explanation"*

Verse 21, "For we are taking pains to do what is right." Paul had a clear conscience before God. He had not acted in a wrong way. But he was constantly being maligned. So he had to explain that he was always taking great care to do what was right, no matter what other people might accuse him of.

10. *Key "Quotable Quote"*

"Joy can be real only if people look upon their life as a service, and have a definite object in life outside themselves and their personal happiness."
Leo Tolstoy

2 Corinthians chapter 9

1. Before and after

Previous chapter: Chapter 8: Will you follow Macedonia's example in giving money?
Following chapter: Chapter 10: Discipline

2. Analysis of chapter

The reason for sending Titus to collect their gifts of money. (1-5)
The Corinthians should be cheerful in their giving. The apostle thanks God for his indescribable gift. (6-15)

3. Key verse

Verse 6: "Whoever sows sparingly will also reap sparingly, and whoever sows generously will also reap generously."

4. Key word / key phrase

Verse 6, "whoever sows generously."

5. Key event / key person / key theme

Giving money is a spiritual act

6. Key thought

"God is the greatest giver."

7. Key thing to look out for

"How to be a great giver."

8. Key Bible cross-reference

Verse 9. See Psalm 112:9.

9. Key "by way of explanation"

Verse 14, "the surpassing grace God has given you." Paul is trying to encourage the Corinthians to live with a generous spirit. Here he says that their concern for their fellow-Christians has not gone unnoticed, and that it is in itself a gift from God.

10. Key "Quotable Quote"

"Wesley's famous formula, 'Get all you can; save all you can; give all you can,' must be supplemented. It should read: get all you can; save all you can; freely use all you can within a properly disciplined spiritual life; and control all you can for the good of humankind and God's glory. Giving all you can would then naturally be a part of an overall wise stewardship."
Dallas Willard

2 Corinthians chapter 10

1. Before and after

Previous chapter: Chapter 9: Giving money is a spiritual act
Following chapter: Chapter 11: The apostle and his sufferings

2. Analysis of chapter

The apostle states his authority with meekness and humility. (1-6)
The apostle reasons with the Corinthians. (7-11)
The apostle seeks the glory of God, and to be approved by him. (12-18)

3. Key verse

Verse 4: "The weapons we fight with are not the weapons of the world. On the contrary, they have divine power to demolish strongholds."

4. Key word / key phrase

Verse 6, "every act of disobedience."

5. Key event / key person / key theme

Discipline

6. Key thought

If the great apostle Paul was so misunderstood in his own day it is hardly surprising that he continues to be maligned today.

7. Key thing to look out for

Paul's ministry is a war. How is victory to be won?

8. Key Bible cross-reference

Verse 17. See Jeremiah 9:24.

9. Key "by way of explanation"

Verse 5, "every thought . . . obedient to Christ." If this is accomplished then everything else in the Christian life will be better. For Christ needs to be Lord of our thinking.

10. Key "Quotable Quote"

"Christ is either Lord of all, or he is not Lord at all."
James Hudson Taylor

2 Corinthians chapter 11

1. Before and after

Previous chapter: Chapter 10: Discipline

Following chapter: Chapter 12: Boast about your weakness, and Paul's proposed third visit

2. Analysis of chapter

The apostle explains why he speaks about commending himself. (1-14)

He shows that he had freely preached the gospel. (5-15)

He explains what he was going to add in order to defend his own character. (16-21)

He gives an account of his work, concerns, sufferings, dangers, and deliverances. (22-33)

3. Key verse

Verse 14: "Satan himself masquerades as an angel of light."

4. Key word / key phrase

Verse 25, "three times I was shipwrecked."

5. Key event / key person / key theme

The apostle and his sufferings

6. Key thought

Love wants God's best for people. Therefore, as Paul does here, it exposes false claims.

7. Key thing to look out for

"Consider how I have been suffering for Christ."

8. Key Bible cross-reference

Verse 3. See Genesis 3:1-5.

9. Key "by way of explanation"

Verse 13, "masquerading as apostles of Christ." Those who claimed to be "super-apostles," verse 5, Paul now unmasks as being in the grip of "Satan." These false apostles were Jewish Christians (11:22), visitors to Corinth, who also spoke eloquently and criticized Paul. There is no clear indication of their teaching, but their behavior is certainly unchristian (e.g. 11:20).

10. Key "Quotable Quote"

"Suffering is one of the marks of the true Church."
Martin Luther

2 Corinthians chapter 12

1. *Before and after*

Previous chapter: Chapter 11: The apostle and his sufferings
Following chapter: Chapter 13: Examine yourselves, and greetings

2. *Analysis of chapter*

The apostle's revelations. (1-6)
They were to his spiritual advantage. (7-10)

3. *Key verse*

Verse 9: "Therefore I will boast all the more gladly about my weaknesses, so that Christ's power may rest on me."

4. *Key word / key phrase*

Verse 9, "my grace is sufficient."

5. *Key event / key person / key theme*

Boast about your weakness, and Paul's proposed third visit

6. *Key thought*

Paul has been deeply wronged.

7. *Key thing to look out for*

How does Paul show his love for the Corinthian Christians?

8. *Key Bible cross-reference*

Verse 2. See Romans 16:3.

9. *Key "by way of explanation"*

Verse 13, "I was never a burden to you." The Corinthians could not accuse Paul of sponging off them. He lived at his own expense. He did not accept any payment from the Corinthians. (See Acts 18:3.)

10. *Key "Quotable Quote"*

"This life is not righteousness, but growth in righteousness, not health but healing, not being but becoming, not rest but exercise. We are not yet what we shall be, but we are growing toward it; the process is not yet finished but it is going on. This is not the end of the road; all does not yet gleam in glory but all is being purified."
Martin Luther

2 Corinthians chapter 13

1. **Previous chapter**

   Chapter 12: Boast about your weakness, and Paul's proposed third visit

2. **Analysis of chapter**

   The apostle threatens obstinate offenders. (1-6)
   He prays for them to reform their ways. (7-10)
   He ends the letter with a greeting and blessing. (11-14)

3. **Key verse**

   Verse 11: "Aim for perfection."

4. **Key word / key phrase**

   Verse 5, "examine yourselves."

5. **Key event / key person / key theme**

   Examine yourselves, and greetings

6. **Key thought**

   "Give yourself a good spiritual check up."

7. **Key thing to look out for**

   "We are your servants."

8. **Key Bible cross-reference**

   Verse 1. See Deuteronomy 17:6.

9. **Key "by way of explanation"**

   Verse "Examine yourselves." The false teachers were always on the attack, falsely accusing Paul. Paul tells the Corinthian Christians that they should rather look into their own hearts and take their spiritual pulse.

10. **Key "Quotable Quote"**

    "We have fallen into the temptation of separating ministry from spirituality, service from prayer."
    Henri Nouwen

Galatians

Galatians chapter 1

1. **Following chapter**

   Chapter 2: Paul's authority and his gospel

2. **Analysis of chapter**

   The apostle Paul asserts his apostolic authority. (1-5)
   He reproves the Galatians for moving away from the gospel of Christ under the influence of evil teachers. (6-9)

3. **Key verse**

   Verse 6: "I am astonished that you are so quickly deserting the one who called you by the grace of Christ and are turning to a different gospel."

4. **Key word / key phrase**

   Verse 12, "by revelation from Jesus Christ."

5. **Key event / key person / key theme**

   Paul's credentials

6. **Key thought**

   The Christians in Galatia were turning away from the true gospel.

7. **Key thing to look out for**

   How does Paul show that his gospel is genuine?

8. **Key Bible cross-reference**

   Verse 13. See Acts 8:3.

9. **Key "by way of explanation"**

   Verse 8, "eternally condemned." Paul believes that it is so serious a sin to preach any gospel other than the true one that such people will be, and deserve to be, condemned by God forever.

10. **Key "Quotable Quote"**

    "We have no cause to be ashamed of the gospel of Christ; but the gospel of Christ may justly be ashamed of us."
    John Tillotson

Galatians chapter 2

1.   Before and after

Previous chapter: Chapter 1: Paul explains why he had authority to preach the gospel.

Following chapter: Chapter 3: Paul gives the content of the gospel

2.   Analysis chapter

The apostle declares he is an apostle of the Gentiles. (1-10)

He had publicly opposed Peter for telling Christians to adopt Jewish practices. (11-14)

3.   Key verse

Verse 16: "[we . . .] know that a man is not justified by observing the law, but by faith in Jesus Christ. So we, too, have put our faith in Christ Jesus that we may be justified by faith in Christ and not by observing the law, because by observing the law no one will be justified."

4.   Key word

Verse 16: "justified."

5.   Key event / key person / key theme

The arrival of "the men from James" leading to Peter's distancing himself from Paul, and Paul's confrontation of Peter.

6.   Key thought

Paul's complaint against Peter is summed up in verse 14. Peter's conduct in no longer eating with the Gentiles belied the truth of the gospel.

7.   Key thing to look out for

What led Peter to act as he did?

8.   Key biblical cross-reference

Verse 14. See Acts 15:10.

9.   Key "by way of explanation"

Verse 12, "Circumcision group." These are the "false brothers" of verse 4, Judaizers, who insisted that non-Jews who became followers of Jesus had to be circumcised and keep the Law of Moses. In other words, faith in Jesus was not enough to obtain salvation.

10.   Key "Quotable Quote"

"Paul taught that the Gentiles were justified by faith alone, without works of the law." Martin Luther

Galatians chapter 3

1. Before and after

Previous chapter: Chapter 2: Paul's authority and his gospel
Following chapter: Chapter 4: Salvation is through faith, not through obeying the Jewish Law

2. Analysis of chapter

The Galatians reproved for moving away from the great doctrine of justification alone, through faith in Christ. (1-5)
This doctrine is seen in the example of Abraham (6-9);
from the tenor of the Law and the severity of its curse (10-14);
from the covenant of promises, which the Law could not disannul. (15-18)
The law was a schoolmaster to lead them to Christ. (19-25)
Under the gospel true believers are all one in Christ. (26-29)

3. Key verse

Verse 6: "He believed God, and it was credited to him as righteousness."

4. Key word / key phrase

Verse 22, "through faith in Jesus Christ."

5. Key event / key person / key theme

Paul gives the content of the gospel

6. Key thought

"You have been taken for a ride."

7. Key thing to look out for

Verses 10-14 – the two gifts that come from faith in Christ.

8. Key Bible cross-reference

Verse 6. See Genesis 15:6.

9. Key "by way of explanation"

Verse 13, "hung on a tree." This was the pole on which criminals were crucified. Here it refers to the cross on which Jesus was crucified.

10. Key "Quotable Quote"

"Christ took away the curse of the law and the right which it had, so that even though you have sinned, even though you now have sin (for we must use the language of Scripture), yet you are saved. Our Samson has shattered the power of death, the power of sin, the gates of hell. This is what Paul means in Galatians 3:13. 'Christ redeemed us from the curse of the law, having become a curse for us.'"
Philip Melanchthon

Galatians chapter 4

1. *Before and after*

Previous chapter: Chapter 3: Paul gives the content of the gospel
Following chapter: Chapter 5: Paul's description of Christian freedom

2. *Analysis of chapter*

The folly of returning to legal observances for justification. (1-7)
The glad transformation made in the Gentile believers. (8-11)
The apostle argues against following false teachers. (12-18)
He expresses his earnest concern for them. (19,20)
And then explains the difference between what is to be expected from the Law, and from the gospel. (21-31)

3. *Key verse*

Verse 11: "I fear for you, that somehow I have wasted my efforts on you."

4. *Key word / key phrase*

Verse 7, "no longer a slave."

5. *Key event / key person / key theme*

Salvation is through faith, not through works of the Law

6. *Key thought*

"Do you want to become slaves again?"

7. *Key thing to look out for*

"Learn from Hagar and Sarah."

8. *Key Bible cross-reference*

Verse 27. See Isaiah 54:1.

9. *Key "by way of explanation"*

Verse 11, "wasted my efforts." If the Galatian Christians go back to keeping the Law, Paul feels that he will have wasted his breath teaching them about the gospel of grace which Jesus brought.

10. *Key "Quotable Quote"*

"It is one thing to have sin alarmed only by convictions, and another to have it crucified by converting grace. Many, because they have been troubled in conscience for their sins, think well of their case, miserably mistaking conviction for conversion."
Joseph Alliene

Galatians chapter 5

1. Before and after

Previous chapter: Chapter 4: Salvation is through faith, not through works of the law

Following chapter: Chapter 6: The gospel and service and separation from the world

2. Analysis of chapter

An earnest exhortation to stand firm in the freedom of the gospel. (1-12)

To beware of indulging a sinful temper. (13-15)

And to walk in the Spirit, and not to fulfill the evil desires of the flesh: the deeds of both are described. (16-26)

3. Key verse

Verse 7: "You were running a good race. Who cut in on you and kept you from obeying the truth?"

4. Key word / key phrase

Verse 16, "live by the Spirit."

5. Key event / key person / key theme

Paul's description of Christian freedom

6. Key thought

Christians are freed people. Note that Galatians 5:22,23 is a portrait of Christ.

7. Key thing to look out for

The fruit of sin is contrasted with the fruit of the Spirit.

8. Key Bible cross-reference

Verse 14. See Leviticus 19:18.

9. Key "by way of explanation"

Verse 22, "the fruit of the Spirit." This is not produced by keeping the Law. Discipline does help. But without the work of the Holy Spirit in a believer's life there will be no spiritual fruit.

10. Key "Quotable Quote"

"There are two freedoms – the false, where a man is free to do what he likes; the true, where a man is free to do what he ought."
Charles Kingsley

Galatians chapter 6

1. Previous chapter
Chapter 5: Paul's description of Christian freedom

2. Analysis of chapter
Exhortations to be meek, gentle, and humble. (1-5)
To be kind toward all people, especially to believers. (6-11)
The Galatians warned against the judaizing teachers. (12-15)
A solemn blessing. (16-18)

3. Key verse
Verse 7: "Do not be deceived: God cannot be mocked. A man reaps what he sows."

4. Key word / key phrase
Verse 2, "fulfill the law of Christ."

5. Key event / key person / key theme
The gospel and service and separation from the world

6. Key thought
"Be a burden-bearer."

7. Key thing to look out for
"I only want to boast in Jesus' death."

8. Key Bible cross-reference
Verse 15. See 1 Corinthians 7:19.

9. Key "by way of explanation"
Verse 12, "compel you to be circumcised." The "Judizers" thought that if Gentile converts to Christianity were circumcised in obedience to the Law, the Jews who wanted to persecute the Christians would be appeased. So they strongly advocated circumcision.

10. Key "Quotable Quote"
"It is not fitting, when one is in God's service, to have a gloomy face or a chilling look."
Francis of Assisi

Ephesians

Ephesians chapter 1

1. **Following chapter**

   Chapter 2: The resurrection life and unity

2. **Analysis of chapter**

   A greeting, and an account of saving blessings, prepared in God's eternal election, and bought by Christ's blood. (1-8)
   Open to Jews and Gentiles. (9-14)
   Prayer for spiritual enlightenment. (15-23)

3. **Key verse**

   Verse 4: "For he chose us in him before the creation of the world to be holy and blameless in his sight."

4. **Key word / key phrase**

   Verse 3, "every spiritual blessing."

5. **Key event / key person / key theme**

   Spiritual blessings in Christ

6. **Key thought**

   "This is your wonderful spiritual inheritance."

7. **Key thing to look out for**

   Nobody knows Jesus fully. Paul stresses the need to press on and know him more and more.

8. **Key Bible cross-reference**

   Verse 1. See Acts 18:19-21.

9. **Key "by way of explanation"**

   Verse 7, "In him we have redemption." The idea of redemption was not unfamiliar to the Ephesians who knew all about a ransom being paid as the price for redeeming a slave. Sinners were to be freed now that Christ had paid the ransom price for sin by his death on the cross.

10. **Key "Quotable Quote"**

    "The riches of the glory of his inheritance in the saints. Besides the heavenly inheritance prepared for the saints, there is a present inheritance in the saints; for grace is glory begun, and holiness is happiness in the bud. There is a glory in this inheritance, riches of glory, rendering the Christian more excellent and more truly honorable than all about him: and it is desirable to know this experimentally, to be acquainted with the principles, pleasures, and powers, of the spiritual and divine life."
    Matthew Henry

Ephesians chapter 2

1. *Before and after*

Previous chapter: Chapter 1: Greetings and prayer
Following chapter: Chapter 3: A revealed mystery

2. *Analysis of chapter*

The riches of God's grace toward men and women. This is seen in the dreadful state that they are naturally in, and by the happy change divine grace makes in them. (1-10)
The Ephesians called to reflect on their pre-Christian state. (11-13)
And the privileges and blessings of the gospel. (14-22)

3. *Key verse*

Verse 10: "For we are God's workmanship, created in Christ Jesus to do good works, which God prepared in advance for us to do."

4. *Key word / key phrase*

Verse 6, "God raised us up."

5. *Key event / key person / key theme*

The resurrection life and unity

6. *Key thought*

The fact that salvation is a gift, and is not dependent on who I am, or what I have achieved. This is utterly liberating.

7. *Key thing to look out for*

Verse 4, the reason why God saved us.

8. *Key Bible cross-reference*

Verse 17. See Isaiah 57:19.

9. *Key "by way of explanation"*

Verse 21, "joined together." Christians belong to Jesus. They are also linked up with all other followers of Jesus, and in this sense, are "joined together." Paul spells out the consequences of this.

10. *Key "Quotable Quote"*

"The work of redemption, including its purpose, method and result, could hardly be stated in clearer language than this."
Paton A. Gloag

Ephesians chapter 3

1. **Before and after**

   Previous chapter: Chapter 2: The resurrection life and unity
   Following chapter: Chapter 4: The nature of the Christian Church

2. **Analysis of chapter**

   The apostle states the scope of his ministry, and his qualifications and call for
   this. (1-7)
   God's wisdom has been made known. (8-13)
   He prays for the Ephesians. (14-19)
   And adds a thanksgiving. (20,21)

3. **Key verse**

   Verse 12: "In him and through faith in him we may approach God with
   freedom and confidence."

4. **Key word / key phrase**

   Verse 4, "insight into the mystery of Christ."

5. **Key event / key person / key theme**

   A revealed mystery

6. **Key thought**

   Paul never tires of calling himself a servant.

7. **Key thing to look out for**

   Paul tells the Ephesians what he prays for them.

8. **Key Bible cross-reference**

   Verses 4-6. See Colossians 1:26,27.

9. **Key "by way of explanation"**

   Verse 19, "surpasses knowledge." Paul is not saying that it is impossible to
   know anything about the Christian faith. But he is saying that it is so
   profound that nobody fully comprehends it.

10. **Key "Quotable Quote"**

    "Everything a theologian does in the Church contributes to the spread of the
    knowledge of God and the salvation of men."
    Martin Luther

Ephesians chapter 4

1. Before and after

Previous chapter: Chapter 3: A revealed mystery
Following chapter: Chapter 5: Challenging evil; wives and husbands

2. Analysis of chapter

Exhortations to be loving and united. (1-6)
To an awareness and use of spiritual gifts and graces. (7-16)
To purity and holiness. (17-24)
And to beware of the sins practiced by the heathen. (25-32)

3. Key verse

Verse 14: "Then we will no longer be infants, tossed back and forth by the waves, and blown here and there by every wind of teaching and by the cunning and craftiness of men in their deceitful scheming."

4. Key word / key phrase

Verse 16, "joined and held together."

5. Key event / key person / key theme

The nature of the Christian Church

6. Key thought

The gifts bestowed on us by the ascended Christ.

7. Key thing to look out for

What we are to put on and put off.

8. Key Bible cross-reference

Verse 8. See Psalm 68:18.

9. Key "by way of explanation"

Verse 17, "futility of their thinking." Non-Christians, no matter how clever they are, possess unenlightened minds. In this sense they will die in the "futility of their thinking." For any life without God is ultimately meaningless and far from being intellectually satisfying.

10. Key "Quotable Quote"

"No one can get anything out of life without God."
Meister Eckhart

Ephesians chapter 5

1. *Before and after*

Previous chapter: Chapter 4: The nature of the Christian Church
Following chapter: Chapter 6: Fighting the spiritual battle

2. *Analysis of chapter*

Exhortation to brotherly love. (1,2)
Warns against several sins. (3-14)
Instructions about living in a different way. (15-21)
The duties of wives and husbands are underlined by reference to the spiritual relationship between Christ and the Church. (22-33)

3. *Key verse*

Verse 11: "Have nothing to do with the fruitless deeds of darkness, but rather expose them."

4. *Key word / key phrase*

Verse 14, "wake up."

5. *Key event / key person / key theme*

Challenging evil; wives and husbands

6. *Key thought*

Christians are God's dearly loved children.

7. *Key thing to look out for*

Paul unpacks what it means to live as children of light.

8. *Key Bible cross-reference*

Verse 2. See Exodus 29:18.

9. *Key "by way of explanation"*

Verse 8, "darkness . . . light." Paul frequently uses such contrasts in his letters. Christians are to be full of light because God is light.

10. *Key "Quotable Quote"*

"Give light, and the darkness will disappear of itself."
Desiderius Erasmus

Ephesians chapter 6

1. *Previous chapter*

Chapter 5: Challenging evil; wives and husbands

2. *Analysis of chapter*

The duties of children and parents. (1-4)
The duties of servants and masters. (5-9)
All Christians are to put on spiritual armor against the enemy of their souls. (10-18)
The apostle seeks their prayers, and ends with his apostolic blessing. (19-24)

3. *Key verse*

Verse 11: "Put on the full armor of God so that you can take your stand against the devil's schemes."

4. *Key word / key phrase*

Verse 11, "Put on the full armor of God."

5. *Key event / key person / key theme*

Fighting the spiritual battle

6. *Key thought*

The Christian is able to obey, fight and win because of God's mighty power (verse 10).

7. *Key thing to look out for*

Note the power of God's armor.

8. *Key Bible cross-reference*

Verse 17. See Isaiah 59:17.

9. *Key "by way of explanation"*

Verse 12, "not against flesh and blood." Sometimes it must have seemed to Paul that he spent all his life fending off those who attacked him. But here Paul points to the source of such attacks and all evil. So he warns not so much about "flesh and blood" but about "the powers of the dark world."

10. *Key "Quotable Quote"*

"To remove warfare from a spiritual life is to render it unspiritual."
Watchman Nee

Philippians

Philippians chapter 1

1. **Following chapter**

    Chapter 2: Having Christ's mind

2. **Analysis of chapter**

    The apostle offers up thanksgivings and prayers, for the good work of grace in the Philippians. (1-7)
    He expresses his affection for them, and prays for them. (8-11)
    He tells them not to be upset at his sufferings. (12-20)
    He is prepared to glorify Christ by life, or death. (21-26)
    Instructions to live in a way which is worthy of the gospel. (27-30)

3. **Key verse**

    Verse 12: "Now I want you to know, brothers, that what has happened to me has really served to advance the gospel."

4. **Key word / key phrase**

    Verse 13, "I am in chains."

5. **Key event / key person / key theme**

    Paul writes from prison to thank God for the Philippians' partnership in the gospel.

6. **Key thought**

    Paul says that he may be in chains but the gospel is not.

7. **Key thing to look out for**

    What will be the result, for the Philippians, of conducting themselves in a manner worthy of the gospel (verse 27)?

8. **Key Bible cross-reference**

    Verse 1. See Acts 16:12.

9. **Key "by way of explanation"**

    Verse 17, "the former preach Christ out of selfish ambition." You might be forgiven for thinking that all who preach in Christ's name are good Christian preachers. But, no. Far from it, says Paul. Some preachers preach from jealousy and others from warped motives.

10. **Key "Quotable Quote"**

    "The whole point of the letter to the Philippians is: I do rejoice – do you rejoice?"
    J.A. Bengel

Philippians chapter 2

1. Before and after

Previous chapter: Chapter 1: Paul's present circumstances
Following chapter: Chapter 3: Knowing Christ

2. Analysis of chapter

Exhortations to a kind, humble spirit. (1-4)
The example of Christ. (5-11)
Diligence in the affairs of salvation, and to be examples to the world. (12-18)
The apostle's purpose in visiting Philippi. (19-30)

3. Key verse

Verse 3: "Do nothing out of selfish ambition or vain conceit, but in humility consider others better than yourselves."

4. Key word / key phrase

Verse 5, "your attitude."

5. Key event / key person / key theme

The attitude of Christ

6. Key thought

Paul sets out the example that all Christians should always follow.

7. Key thing to look out for

Verses 1-4 give four reasons for Christian love. Verses 5-11 give a further crowning reason.

8. Key Bible cross-reference

Verses 10,11. See Isaiah 45:23.

9. Key "by way of explanation"

Verse 7, "but made himself nothing." Literally this reads, "emptied himself." When Jesus came to this earth in human form he was still God and the only thing he emptied himself of was God's glory, which was only occasionally glimpsed in his life, during his transfiguration, for example. Verses 5-11 were probably an early Christian hymn.

10. Key "Quotable Quote"

"It's not great talents that God blesses, but great likeness to Jesus."
Robert Murray M'Cheyne

Philippians chapter 3

1. Before and after

Previous chapter: Chapter 2: Having Christ's mind
Following chapter: Chapter 4: Joy in contentment

2. Analysis of chapter

The apostle warns the Philippians against judaizing false teachers, and renounces his own former privileges. (1-11)
Expresses earnest desire to be found in Christ; also his pressing on toward perfection. (12-21)

3. Key verse

Verse 14: "I press on toward the goal to win the prize for which God has called me heavenward in Christ Jesus."

4. Key word / key phrase

Verse 10, "I rejoice greatly."

5. Key event / key person / key theme

Knowing Christ

6. Key thought

Note how Paul shows that he lived his life under the power of Jesus' resurrection.

7. Key thing to look out for

Even though Paul was at the end of his life he still pressed on to know Jesus better.

8. Key Bible cross-reference

Verse 5. See Acts 23:6.

9. Key "by way of explanation"

Verse 8, "knowing Christ Jesus my Lord." This was Paul's aim in his Christian life. This knowledge was more than an accumulation of facts, it was a daily experience.

10. Key "Quotable Quote"

"This is clear: He who does not know Christ does not know God hidden in suffering. Therefore he prefers works to suffering, glory to the cross, strength to weakness, wisdom to folly. These are the people whom the apostle calls 'enemies of the cross of Christ' (Philippians. 3:18) for they hate the cross and suffering and love works and the glory of works. Thus they call the good of the cross evil and the evil of a deed good. God can be found only in suffering and the cross."
Martin Luther

Philippians chapter 4

1. *Previous chapter*

Chapter 3: Knowing Christ

2. *Analysis of chapter*

The apostle exhorts the Philippians to stand firm in the Lord. (1)
Gives directions to some particular people, and to all in general. (2-9)
States that he is content no matter what happens to him. (10-19)
He concludes with prayer to God the Father, and his usual blessing. (20-23)

3. *Key verse*

Verse 4: "Rejoice in the Lord always. I will say it again: Rejoice!"

4. *Key word / key phrase*

Verse 4, "Rejoice in the Lord always."

5. *Key event / key person / key theme*

Joy in contentment

6. *Key thought*

Note how the theme of joy runs through this letter.

7. *Key thing to look out for*

In verse 13 Paul gives us the secret of his spiritual strength.

8. *Key Bible cross-reference*

Verse 18. See Exodus 29:18.

9. *Key "by way of explanation"*

Verse 13, "who gives me strength." As Paul lived his life in union with Jesus so he was given the necessary strength to cope with the constant pressures which assaulted him.

10. *Key "Quotable Quote"*

"A child of God should be a visible beatitude for joy and happiness, and a living doxology for gratitude and adoration."
C.H. Spurgeon

Colossians

Colossians chapter 1

1. **Following chapter**

   Chapter 2: Freedom in Jesus

2. **Analysis of chapter**

   The apostle Paul greets the Colossians, and blesses God for their faith, love, and hope. (1-8)
   Prays for their fruitfulness in spiritual knowledge. (9-14)
   Emphasizes the supremacy of Christ. (15-23)
   And shows how he is the apostle of the Gentiles. (24-29)

3. **Key verse**

   Verse 10: "And we pray this in order that you may live a life worthy of the Lord and may please him in every way."

4. **Key word / key phrase**

   Verse 18, "he might have the supremacy."

5. **Key event / key person / key theme**

   The supremacy of Christ

6. **Key thought**

   Paul links redemption with forgiveness of sins very clearly in verse 14.

7. **Key thing to look out for**

   For Paul, Christ was supreme over everything and everyone because he alone was God.

8. **Key Bible cross-reference**

   Verse 14. See Ephesians 1:7.

9. **Key "by way of explanation"**

   Verse 14, "In whom we have redemption." From verses like this the doctrine of substitutionary atonement flows.

10. **Key "Quotable Quote"**

    "When Christ is called the image of the invisible God (Colossians 1: 15), the expression is designed to remind us that we can have no knowledge of our salvation, until we behold God in Christ."
    John Calvin

Colossians chapter 2

1. Before and after

Previous chapter: Chapter 1: Greetings, prayer, and the pre-eminence of Christ
Following chapter: Chapter 3: Living the risen life with Christ

2. Analysis of chapter

The apostle expresses his love toward, and joy in the believers. (1-7)
He warns against the errors of heathen philosophy; also against Jewish traditions, and rites which had been fulfilled in Christ. (8-17)
Against worshiping angels; and against legal ordinances. (18-23)

3. Key verse

Verse 9: "For in Christ all the fullness of the Deity lives in bodily form."

4. Key word / key phrase

Verse 15, "disarmed the powers."

5. Key event / key person / key theme

Freedom in Jesus

6. Key thought

Paul stresses that for Christians all power comes as a result of the resurrection of Christ.

7. Key thing to look out for

Human regulations have no place for a person living his or her life in the Spirit.

8. Key Bible cross-reference

Verse 16. See Romans 14:1-6.

9. Key "by way of explanation"

Verse 9, "fullness of the Deity." This is one of the most important statements about the deity of Jesus made in the New Testament.

10. Key "Quotable Quote"

"God is best known in Christ; the sun is not seen but by the light of the sun."
William Bridge

Colossians chapter 3

1. Before and after

Previous chapter: Chapter 2: Freedom in Christ
Following chapter: Chapter 4: Prayer and wisdom, and personal greetings

2. Analysis of chapter

The Colossians are told to be heavenly-minded (1-4);
to put to death all corrupt desires (5-11);
to live in mutual love, forbearance, and forgiveness (12-17);
and as wives and husbands, children, parents, and servants, to live as servants of Christ. (18-25)

3. Key verse

Verse 12: "Therefore, as God's chosen people, holy and dearly loved, clothe yourselves with compassion, kindness, humility, gentleness and patience."

4. Key word / key phrase

Verse 1, "raised with Christ."

5. Key event / key person / key theme

Living the risen life with Christ

6. Key thought

For Paul, there was definitely a right way and a wrong way to live.

7. Key thing to look out for

Paul gives guidelines for Christian families.

8. Key Bible cross-reference

Verse 19. See 1 Peter 3:7.

9. Key "by way of explanation"

Verse 15, "peace of Christ." Christians are meant to be characterized, not by fighting and arguing, but by the peace that only Jesus can give. It is meant to rule them, in the sense that it governs all of their lives.

10. Key "Quotable Quote"

"There is only one permanent way to have the peace of soul that wells up in joy, contentment and happiness, and that is by repentance for sin and by personal faith in Jesus Christ as Savior."
Billy Graham

Colossians chapter 4

1. ### *Previous chapter*

   Chapter 3: Living the risen life with Jesus

2. ### *Analysis of chapter*

   Masters should act in a right and fair way toward their servants. (1)
   Christian people from every walk of life should persevere in prayer, and Christian prudence. (2-6)
   The apostle refers to others for an account of his affairs. (7-9)
   Sends greetings; and concludes with a blessing. (10-18)

3. ### *Key verse*

   Verse 14: "Our dear friend Luke, the doctor, and Demas send greetings."

4. ### *Key word / key phrase*

   Verses 3,4, "pray."

5. ### *Key event / key person / key theme*

   Prayer and wisdom, and personal greetings

6. ### *Key thought*

   Paul wanted to ensure that the Colossians did not think that prayer was an optional extra.

7. ### *Key thing to look out for*

   Verses 3 and 10 reveal that Paul is writing from his prison cell, but not with an imprisoned spirit.

8. ### *Key Bible cross-reference*

   Verse 12. See Colossians 1:7.

9. ### *Key "by way of explanation"*

   Verse 18, "I, Paul, write this greeting." As was quite usual in those days, Paul dictated his letters. But he often added a personal greeting at the end, in own hand, as here.

10. ### *Key "Quotable Quote"*

    "We must not talk about prayer, we must pray."
    Andrew Bonar

1 Thessalonians and
2 Thessalonians

1 Thessalonians chapter 1

1. **Following chapter**

   Chapter 2: Paul's foundation of the Church, and Satan's attack

2. **Analysis of chapter**

   The faith, love, and patience of the Thessalonians, are evident tokens of their election which was manifested in power when the gospel came to them. (1-5) Its powerful effects on their hearts and lives. (6-10)

3. **Key verse**

   Verse 3: "We continually remember before our God and Father your work produced by faith, your labor prompted by love, and your endurance inspired by hope in our Lord Jesus Christ."

4. **Key word / key phrase**

   Verse 7, "you became a model."

5. **Key event / key person / key theme**

   Thanksgiving for the faith of the Thessalonians

6. **Key thought**

   Paul links the Holy Spirit to conviction and power.

7. **Key thing to look out for**

   The Thessalonians are waiting for Jesus' return.

8. **Key Bible cross-reference**

   Verse 1. See Acts 17:1.

9. **Key "by way of explanation"**

   Verse 3, "faith ... love ... hope." Paul often linked these three Christian graces. See 5:8; Romans 5:2-5; 1 Corinthians 13:13; Galatians 5:5,6; Colossians 1:4,5. Paul's visit to Thessalonica is described in Acts 17:1-9. This was probably in the winter of AD 49/50.

10. **Key "Quotable Quote"**

    "The Christian hope is the hope which has seen everything and endured everything, and has still not despaired, because it believes in God."
    William Barclay

1 Thessalonians chapter 2

1. **Before and after**

    Previous chapter: Chapter 1: Paul commends their spiritual growth
    Following chapter: Chapter 3: Paul's great concern

2. **Analysis of chapter**

    The apostle reminds the Thessalonians of his preaching and behavior. (1-12)
    He reminds them of how they received the gospel as the word of God. (13-16)
    His joy on their account. (17-20)

3. **Key verse**

    Verse 10: "You are witnesses, and so is God, of how holy, righteous and blameless we were among you who believed."

4. **Key word / key phrase**

    Verse 2, "in spite of strong opposition."

5. **Key event / key person / key theme**

    Paul's foundation of the Church, and Satan's attack

6. **Key thought**

    The apostles' blameless conduct, sincerity and love in Thessalonica.

7. **Key thing to look out for**

    What do you find most challenging about the ministry of the apostles in Thessalonica?

8. **Key Bible cross-reference**

    Verse 14. See Acts 17:5.

9. **Key "by way of explanation"**

    Verse 9, "toil and hardship." Paul was never frightened of rolling up his sleeves and getting stuck in, unlike the Greeks, who looked down on manual labor.

10. **Key "Quotable Quote"**

    "Christian leadership . . . appears to break down into five main ingredients – clear vision, hard work, dogged perseverance, humble service and iron discipline."
    John R.W. Stott

1 Thessalonians chapter 3

1. *Before and after*

Previous chapter: Chapter 2: Paul's foundation of the Church, and Satan's attack

Following chapter: Chapter 4: Sexual morality, earning a living, and the dead

2. *Analysis of chapter*

The apostle sent Timothy to strengthen and comfort the Thessalonians (1-5)

He rejoiced at the good news about their faith and love. (6-10)

And for their increase in grace. (11-13)

3. *Key verse*

Verse 13: "May he strengthen your hearts so that you will be blameless and holy in the presence of our God and Father when our Lord Jesus comes with all his holy ones."

4. *Key word / key phrase*

Verse 12 "God's fellow-worker."

5. *Key event / key person / key theme*

Paul's intense love and care for his spiritual children.

6. *Key thought*

Verse 5, the power of the devil to tempt and harm young Christians.

7. *Key thing to look out for*

What does Paul specially pray for these persecuted Christians?

8. *Key Bible cross-reference*

Verse 3. See 2 Timothy 2:12.

9. *Key "by way of explanation"*

It is clear from these verses that Timothy met Paul in Athens, then returned to Thessalonica, joining Paul again in Corinth. This is a fuller account than the narrative in Acts 17:14-15 and 18:1-5.

10. *Key "Quotable Quote"*

"True patience grows with the growth of love."
Gregory the Great

1 Thessalonians chapter 4

1. *Before and after*

Previous chapter: Chapter 3: Paul's great concern
Following chapter: Chapter 5: The Day of the Lord, and holy living

2. *Analysis of chapter*

Exhortations to purity and holiness. (1-8)
To brotherly love, peaceful behavior, and diligence. (9-12)

3. *Key verse*

Verse 9: "Now about brotherly love we do not need to write to you, for you yourselves have been taught by God to love each other."

4. *Key word / key phrase*

Verse 16, "the dead in Christ will rise first."

5. *Key event / key person / key theme*

Sexual morality, earning a living, and the dead

6. *Key thought*

Christians please God by living holy, loving, peaceful, and productive lives.

7. *Key thing to look out for*

Verse 18. In what way are verses 13-17 an encouragement?

8. *Key Bible cross-reference*

Verses 15-17. See 1 Corinthians 15:51,52.

9. *Key "by way of explanation"*

Verses 13-18. Christians in Thessalonica seem to have been afraid that dead Christians would not experience the glory of the Second Coming. Paul corrects this view. "Clouds" are often a reference to the presence of the diving glory.

10. *Key "Quotable Quote"*

"Faith in Jesus without the expectation of Christ's *parousia* is a check that is never cashed, a promise that is not made in earnest."
Peter Lewis

1 Thessalonians chapter 5

1. **Previous chapter**

   Chapter 4: Sexual morality, earning a living, and the dead

2. **Analysis of chapter**

   The apostle tells the Christians to be ready for the coming of Christ which will come suddenly. (1-11)
   He gives instructions about several particular duties. (12-22)
   And concludes with prayer, greetings, and a blessing. (23-28)

3. **Key verse**

   Verse 17: "Pray continually."

4. **Key word / key phrase**

   Verse 2, "will come like a thief in the night."

5. **Key event / key person / key theme**

   The Day of the Lord, and holy living

6. **Key thought**

   Note how Paul contrasts light and darkness in this chapter.

7. **Key thing to look out for**

   Paul insists that evil must be avoided.

8. **Key Bible cross-reference**

   Verse 8. See Isaiah 59:17.

9. **Key "by way of explanation"**

   Verse 21, "Test everything." If the Christians Paul wrote to had not been so gullible he would not have had to issue so many warnings to them. All teaching had to be in line with the gospel of Jesus. That was the supreme test.

10. **Key "Quotable Quote"**

   "I do not think that in the last forty years I have lived one conscious hour that was not influenced by the thought of our Lord's return."
   Lord Shaftesbury

2 Thessalonians chapter 1

1. Following chapter

Chapter 2: Explanation about the Day of the Lord

2. Analysis of chapter

The apostle blesses God for the growing state of the love and patience of the Thessalonians. (1-4)
And encourages them to persevere despite all their sufferings for Christ. They are to keep his Second Coming again in mind. (5-12)

3. Key verse

Verse 8: "He will punish those who do not know God and do not obey the gospel of our Lord Jesus."

4. Key word / key phrase

Verse 3, "we ought always to thank God for you."

5. Key event / key person / key theme

Thanksgiving and prayer

6. Key thought

When Paul taught some aspect of the Christian faith he most often linked it to God's own nature.

7. Key thing to look out for

Here in verse 6 Paul says God is just and then he goes on to teach what flows from this.

8. Key Bible cross-reference

Verse 1. See Acts 17:1.

9. Key "by way of explanation"

Verse 6, "God is just." Because of God's justice he cannot ignore or wink at sin. God punishes sin, especially unrepentant sinners.

10. Key "Quotable Quote"

"The Lord is not only tender and merciful and full of compassion, but he is also the God of justice, holiness, and wrath."
Billy Graham

2 Thessalonians chapter 2

1. Before and after

Previous chapter: Chapter 1: Encouragement in persecution
Following chapter: Chapter 3: Pray for us, God is faithful, don't be idle

2. Analysis of chapter

Warns against the erroneous view that the time of Christ's coming is at hand.
There will first be a widespread rebellion against God from the faith, and a
revealing of the antichristian man of sin. (1-4)
His destruction, and the destruction of those who obey him. (5-12)
Encouragement that the Thessalonians will be kept safe from apostasy; an
exhortation to steadfastness, and prayer for them. (13-17)

3. Key verse

Verse 14: "He called you to this through our gospel, that you might share in
the glory of our Lord Jesus Christ."

4. Key word / key phrase

Verse 1, "Concerning the coming of our Lord."

5. Key event / key person / key theme

Explanation about the Day of the Lord

6. Key thought

Christians must stand firm.

7. Key thing to look out for

Verse 10. The lovers of evil have freely chosen their course of action.

8. Key Bible cross-reference

Verse 4. See Daniel 11:36.

9. Key "by way of explanation"

Verse 8, "the lawless one will be revealed, whom the Lord Jesus will
overthrow." The lawless one may seem to be mighty and strong but he will be
defeated by a mere "breath" from the mouth of Jesus. The "lawless one",
possibly the worst of the antichrists (1 John 2:18) will lead the rebellion against
God.

10. Key "Quotable Quote"

"When we fail to wait prayerfully for God's guidance and strength, we are
saying with our actions, if not our lips, that we do not need him."
Charles Hummel

2 Thessalonians chapter 3

1. *Previous chapter*

   Chapter 2: Explanation about the Day of the Lord

2. *Analysis of chapter*

   The apostle expresses confidence in the Thessalonians, and prays for them. (1-5)
   He urges them to steer clear of the lazy and of busybodies. (6-15)
   And concludes with a prayer for them, and a greeting. (16-18)

3. *Key verse*

   Verse 11: "We hear that some among you are idle. They are not busy; they are busybodies."

4. *Key word / key phrase*

   Verse 6, "every brother who is idle."

5. *Key event / key person / key theme*

   Pray for us, God is faithful, don't be idle

6. *Key thought*

   It was never beneath Paul to ask other Christians to pray for him.

7. *Key thing to look out for*

   Paul did not believe that idleness should have any place in the life of a Christian.

8. *Key Bible cross-reference*

   Verse 16. See Ruth 2:4.

9. *Key "by way of explanation"*

   Verse 11, "busybodies." One worse, in Paul's book, than the idle, were the busybodies. Perhaps because they had so much time on their hands they interfered with other people's lives.

10. *Key "Quotable Quote"*

    "Thou wilt never be spiritually minded and godly unless thou art silent concerning other men's matters and take full heed to thyself."
    Thomas à Kempis

1 Timothy and 2 Timothy

1 Timothy chapter 1

1. *Following chapter*

   Chapter 2: Praying in public, and women in public worship

2. *Analysis of chapter*

   The apostle greets Timothy. (1-4)
   The purpose of the Law given by Moses. (5-11)
   Paul's own conversion and call to be an apostle. (12-17)
   The obligation to maintain faith and a good conscience. (18-20)

3. *Key verse*

   Verse 6: "Some have wandered away from these and turned to meaningless talk."

4. *Key word / key phrase*

   Verse 7, "they do not know what they are talking about."

5. *Key event / key person / key theme*

   Beware of false teachers

6. *Key thought*

   Verse 4, "myths and endless genealogies." There are some things that are just best avoided. There is no need to delve into every heresy.

7. *Key thing to look out for*

   Verse 20, "handed over to Satan," possibly means excommunication – that is, put out of the church, into the world, where Satan rules.

8. *Key Bible cross-reference*

   Verse 2. See Acts 16:1.

9. *Key "by way of explanation"*

   Paul writes this letter to Timothy when Timothy has been left in charge of the church at Ephesus (1:3). His purpose is to advise and encourage "his true son in the faith" (1:2; 3:14,15).

10. *Key "Quotable Quote"*

    "For all the vigor of his polemic, St. Paul does not content himself with the denunciation of error, but finds the best defense against its insidious approaches in a closer adherence to the love of God and faith in Christ."
    F.F. Bruce

1 Timothy chapter 2

1. *Before and after*

   Previous chapter: Chapter 1: False teachers and correct Christian doctrine
   Following chapter: Chapter 3: Qualifications for Christian leadership

2. *Analysis of chapter*

   Pray for all people. (1-7)
   How men and women ought to behave. (8-15)

3. *Key verse*

   Verse 5: "For there is one God and one mediator between God and men, the man Christ Jesus."

4. *Key word / key phrase*

   Verse 1, "thanksgiving be made for everyone."

5. *Key event / key person / key theme*

   Praying in public, and women in public worship

6. *Key thought*

   God's purpose is that all people should lead peaceful, quiet and holy lives.

7. *Key thing to look out for*

   Verses 4-5 give the reason why it is very important to pray for everyone, without distinction.

8. *Key Bible cross-reference*

   Verse 7. See 2 Timothy 1:11.

9. *Key "by way of explanation"*

   Verses 11-14. Some say that Paul is expressing a ruling for all time, others that the underlying principles (humility, quietness, submission, obedience) may be expressed differently at different times in different cultures. Women are undeniably called to bear children and in doing this experience God's saving grace if they continue in the faith.

10. *Key "Quotable Quote"*

   "The marks of the Spirit's presence are biblical teaching, loving fellowship, living worship, and an ongoing, outgoing evangelism."
   John R.W. Stott

1 Timothy chapter 3

1. Before and after

Previous chapter: Chapter 2: Praying in public, and women in public worship

Following chapter: Chapter 4: False teachers

2. Analysis of chapter

The qualifications and behavior of gospel bishops. (1-7)

And of deacons and their wives. (8-13)

The reason for writing about these, and other church affairs. (14-16)

3. Key verse

Verse 1: "Here is a trustworthy saying: If anyone sets his heart on being an overseer, he desires a noble task."

4. Key word / key phrase

Verse 8, "deacons."

5. Key event / key person / key theme

Qualifications for Christian leadership

6. Key thought

Paul set high standards for anyone who aspires to be a deacon.

7. Key thing to look out for

In verse 15 Paul gives two descriptions of the Church.

8. Key Bible cross-reference

Verses 2-7. See Titus 1:6-9.

9. Key "by way of explanation"

Verse 8, "Deacons." "Deacon" means someone who serves. A deacon's job, according to Acts 6:1-6, included setting the elders free for their work of prayer and preaching. Apart from "overseers", who are also called elders, the job of a deacon is the only local Church office mentioned in the New Testament.

10. Key "Quotable Quote"

"According to the Scriptures the Spirit is the first and principal Leader."
Robert Barclay

1 Timothy chapter 4

1. *Before and after*

Previous chapter: Chapter 3: Qualifications for Christian leadership
Following chapter: Chapter 5: Church discipline

2. *Analysis of chapter*

Departures from the faith that have begun to appear. (1-5)
Several instructions, with reasons for carrying out various duties. (6-16)

3. *Key verse*

Verse 7: "Have nothing to do with godless myths and old wives' tales; rather, train yourself to be godly."

4. *Key word / key phrase*

Verse 2, "hypocritical liars."

5. *Key event / key person / key theme*

False teachers

6. *Key thought*

Verse 8, Godliness comes with practice.

7. *Key thing to look out for*

The error that has crept into the church is false asceticism. What is Paul's answer? (Note – food is not changed – the spirit of the person eating is changed.)

8. *Key Bible cross-reference*

Verse 1. See Acts 8:29.

9. *Key "by way of explanation"*

Verse 10, "Savior of all." Clearly it would be quite contrary to many other parts of biblical teaching to try to claim that this verse supports the idea of universalism. But what it does definitely say is that God is the Savior of all who go to him.

10. *Key "Quotable Quote"*

"You must not lose confidence in God because you lost confidence in your pastor. If our confidence in God had to depend upon our confidence in any human person, we would be on shifting sand."
Francis A. Schaeffer

1 Timothy chapter 5

1. Before and after

Previous chapter: Chapter 4: False teachers
Following chapter: Chapter 6: Having the correct attitude

2. Analysis of chapter

Instructions for older and younger men and women. (1,2)
Instructions to poor widows. (3-8)
Instructions about widows. (9-16)
The churches responsibility toward its overseers; Timothy's own health. (17-25)

3. Key verse

Verse 8: "If anyone does not provide for his relatives, and especially for his immediate family, he has denied the faith and is worse than an unbeliever."

4. Key word / key phrase

Verse 21, "keep these instructions."

5. Key event / key person / key theme

Church discipline

6. Key thought

Wisdom is needed when helping people.

7. Key thing to look out for

Which of these instructions are of particular relevance in your life?

8. Key Bible cross-reference

Verse 18. See Deuteronomy 25:4.

9. Key "by way of explanation"

Verse 23, "stop drinking water only." Paul's advice here should be thought of in connection with Paul's great concern for the physical and spiritual well-being of Timothy, rather than in connection with teaching about drinking or nor drinking alcohol.

10. Key "Quotable Quote"

"If your theology doesn't change your behavior, it will never change your destiny."
C.H. Spurgeon

1 Timothy chapter 6

1. Previous chapter

Chapter 5: Church discipline

2. Analysis of chapter

The duty of Christians toward believing, and other masters. (1-5)
The advantage of godliness with contentment. (6-10)
A solemn charge to Timothy to be faithful. (11-16)
The apostle repeats his warning to the rich, and closes with a blessing. (17-21)

3. Key verse

Verse 6: "But godliness with contentment is great gain."

4. Key word / key phrase

Verse 11, "pursue righteousness."

5. Key event / key person / key theme

Having the correct attitude

6. Key thought

Verse 10 is among the most misquoted verses in the Bible.

7. Key thing to look out for

What the rich are commanded to do.

8. Key Bible cross-reference

Verse 13. See John 18:37.

9. Key "by way of explanation"

Verse 20, "what has been entrusted to your care." Paul was very keen for
Timothy to appreciate the very great responsibility God had given him in
calling him to be a pastor.

10. Key "Quotable Quote"

"The pastoral charge consists in feeding the hungry, giving drink to the
thirsty, covering the naked, receiving guests, visiting the sick and those in
prison."
Robert Grosseteste, Letter, 1250

2 Timothy chapter 1

1. Following chapter

Chapter 2: Characteristics of a faithful minister

2. Analysis of chapter

Paul expresses great affection for Timothy. (1-5)
Exhorts him to improve his spiritual gifts. (6-14)
Tells him of many who deserted him; but speaks with affection of Onesiphorus. (15-18)

3. Key verse

Verse 7: "For God did not give us a spirit of timidity, but a spirit of power, of love and of self-discipline."

4. Key word / key phrase

Verse 8, "do not be ashamed."

5. Key event / key person / key theme

Be faithful to God

6. Key thought

The Christian life starts and finishes with grace.

7. Key thing to look out for

The instructions given to Timothy.

8. Key Bible cross-reference

Verse 2. See Acts 16:1.

9. Key "by way of explanation"

Verse 5, "your grandmother Lois." Paul reminds Timothy of the privilege he had to be born into a family that had a god-fearing grandmother, and mother who was a Christian. Verse 14, "the good deposit" is the gospel.

10. Key "Quotable Quote"

"Every Christian family ought to be, as it were, a little church consecrated to Christ, and wholly influenced and governed by his rules."
Jonathan Edwards

2 Timothy chapter 2

1. *Before and after*

Previous chapter: Chapter 1: Speaking as a spiritual father
Following chapter: Chapter 3: A snapshot of the last days

2. *Analysis of chapter*

The apostle exhorts Timothy to persevere with diligence, like a soldier, an athlete, and a farmer. (1-7)
Encouraging him by assurances of a happy result of his faithfulness. (8-13)
Warnings to shun quarrels and dangerous errors. (14-21)
Instructions to flee evil desires of youth, and to be zealous against error. Be kind to everyone. (22-26)

3. *Key verse*

Verse 10: "Therefore I endure everything for the sake of the elect, that they too may obtain the salvation that is in Christ Jesus, with eternal glory."

4. *Key word / key phrase*

Verse 16, "avoid godless chatter."

5. *Key event / key person / key theme*

Characteristics of a faithful minister

6. *Key thought*

In serving Christ, Timothy should use every ounce of energy he has.

7. *Key thing to look out for*

Paul knew the negative effect of quarrelling among Christians.

8. *Key Bible cross-reference*

Verse 19. See Numbers 16:5.

9. *Key "by way of explanation"*

Verse 10, "I endure everything for the sake of the elect." As far as Paul was concerned no suffering could be too great if it was going to help people to find salvation in Jesus.

10. *Key "Quotable Quote"*

"The leader should immerse himself in books that will further equip him for a higher quality of service and leadership in the kingdom of God."
J. Oswald Sanders

2 Timothy chapter 3

1. Before and after

Previous chapter: Chapter 2: Characteristics of a faithful minister
Following chapter: Chapter 4: Paul's impending martyrdom

2. Analysis of chapter

The apostle predicts the rise of dangerous enemies to the gospel. (1-9)
States how he is an example to Timothy. (10-13)
And exhorts him to continue in the teaching he had learned from the
Scriptures. (14-17)

3. Key verse

Verse 16: "All Scripture is God-breathed and is useful for teaching, rebuking,
correcting and training in righteousness."

4. Key word / key phrase

Verse 1, "terrible times in the last days."

5. Key event / key person / key theme

A snapshot of the last days

6. Key thought

"Do not be put off by godlessness."

7. Key thing to look out for

Paul warns that Christians are bound to face persecution for the name of
Jesus.

8. Key Bible cross-reference

Verse 8. See Exodus 7:11.

9. Key "by way of explanation"

Verse 16, "All Scripture is God-breathed." As not all of the New Testament had
been written at this stage, when Paul wrote these words he had the Old
Testament especially in mind. This is the part of the Bible which is so often
treated as irrelevant today.

10. Key "Quotable Quote"

"The Scriptures of the Old and New Testaments were given by inspiration of
God, and are the only sufficient, certain and authoritative rule of all saving
knowledge, faith, and obedience."
James Boyce

2 Timothy chapter 4

1. *Previous chapter*

   Chapter 3: A snapshot of the last days

2. *Analysis of chapter*

   The apostle solemnly charges Timothy to be diligent, even though many will not listen to sound teaching. (1-5)
   Reinforces this by mentioning his own impending martyrdom. (6-8)
   Asks him to visit him soon. (9-13)
   He mentions those who have deserted him; and expresses his faith about his own safe arrival in the heavenly kingdom. (14-18)
   Friendly greetings and his usual blessing. (19-22)

3. *Key verse*

   Verse 9: "Do your best to come to me quickly."

4. *Key word / key phrase*

   Verse 6, "poured out like a drink offering."

5. *Key event / key person / key theme*

   Paul's impending martyrdom

6. *Key thought*

   Verse 6. This is Paul's last will and testament to his beloved Timothy.

7. *Key thing to look out for*

   Verse 9. Christian friendship meant a great deal to Paul.

8. *Key Bible cross-reference*

   Verse 19. See Acts 18:2.

9. *Key "by way of explanation"*

   Verse 6, "I am already being poured out like a drink offering." Paul was expecting to be martyred at any time. Paul wrote this letter after his fourth missionary journey (not described in Acts). He was probably imprisoned in the Mamertine dungeon in Rome. The date was about 66/67 and Nero was the emperor.

10. *Key "Quotable Quote"*

    "It is not the pain but the purpose that makes the martyr."
    Augustine of Hippo

Titus

Titus chapter 1

1. Following chapter

Chapter 2: Sound teaching

2. Analysis of chapter

The apostle greets Titus. (1-4)
The qualifications of a faithful pastor. (5-9)
The evil spirit and practices of false teachers. (10-16)

3. Key verse

Verse 11: "They must be silenced, because they are ruining whole households by teaching things they ought not to teach – and that for the sake of dishonest gain."

4. Key word / key phrase

Verse 5, "I left you in Crete."

5. Key event / key person / key theme

Titus' work on the island of Crete

6. Key thought

Paul gives a check-list for all elders.

7. Key thing to look out for

Christians are not to be naïve, but to discern deceiving spirits (see also 1 Timothy 4:1).

8. Key Bible cross-reference

Verse 4. See 2 Timothy 4:10.

9. Key "by way of explanation"

Verse 12, "their own prophets." Paul is here referring to the poet Epimenides who was born in Knossos, a town in Crete. In Greek literature to "Cretanise" meant to tell a lie.

10. Key "Quotable Quote"

"The five tasks of pastoral care are:
to seek and to find all the lost;
to bring back those that are scattered;
to heal the wounded;
to strengthen the sickly;
to protect the healthy and to put them to pasture."
Martin Bucer

Titus chapter 2

1. ### *Before and after*

   Previous chapter: Chapter 1: Appoint elders
   Following chapter: Chapter 3: Keep up the good deeds

2. ### *Analysis of chapter*

   The duties which go hand in hand with sound teaching. (1-8)
   Believing servants must be obedient. (9,10)
   The grace of God. (11-15)

3. ### *Key verse*

   Verses 1,2,3,9, "Teach."

4. ### *Key word / key phrase*

   Verse 2, "teach."

5. ### *Key event / key person / key theme*

   Sound teaching

6. ### *Key thought*

   Different aspects of Christian teaching are relevant to different groups of people.

7. ### *Key thing to look out for*

   Verse 12, the teacher is himself taught.

8. ### *Key Bible cross-reference*

   Verse 14. See Psalm 130:8.

9. ### *Key "by way of explanation"*

   Verse 11, "grace of God." Paul could hardly put pen to paper without writing about the grace of God. This refers to God's love toward us shown in the death of Christ on the cross, so that those who believe in him might be forgiven.

10. ### *Key "Quotable Quote"*

    "Our office is a ministry of grace and salvation."
    Martin Luther

Titus chapter 3

1. Previous chapter

Chapter 2: Sound teaching

2. Analysis of chapter

Be obedient to rulers and authorities. (1-7)
Good deeds must be carried out, and useless disputes avoided. (8-11)
Instructions and exhortations. (12-15)

3. Key verse

Verse 9: "But avoid foolish controversies and genealogies and arguments and quarrels about the law, because these are unprofitable and useless."

4. Key word / key phrase

Verse 8, "devote themselves to doing what is good."

5. Key event / key person / key theme

Keep up the good deeds

6. Key thought

Rebirth is the work of the Holy Spirit.

7. Key thing to look out for

What must Titus avoid?

8. Key Bible cross-reference

Verse 13. See Acts 18:24.

9. Key "by way of explanation"

Verse 5, "saved us . . . because of his mercy." Paul stressed that personal salvation was a free gift from God and could never be earned. Thus he links "mercy" and "salvation" in this verse.

10. Key "Quotable Quote"

"As judgment is God's justice confronting moral iniquity, so mercy is the goodness of God confronting human suffering and guilt."
A.W. Tozer

Philemon

Philemon

1. *Take back your runaway slave*

2. *Analysis of chapter*

> The apostle's joy and praise for Philemon's steady faith in the Lord Jesus, and love for all the saints. (1-7)
> He presents Onesimus as a transformed person. The apostle promises to repay the value of whatever Onesimus has stolen. (8-22)
> Greetings and a blessing. (23-25)

3. *Key verse*

> Verse 14: "But I did not want to do anything without your consent, so that any favor you do will be spontaneous and not forced."

4. *Key word / key phrase*

> Verse 10, "I appeal to you."

5. *Key event / key person / key theme*

> Paul is pleading with Philemon to receive back his runaway slave.

6. *Key thought*

> Love (verse 8) and gratitude (verse 19) are to be Philemon's motives.

7. *Key thing to look out for*

> The reasons why Paul always thanks God for Philemon.

8. *Key Bible cross-reference*

> Verse 9. See Colossians 4:9.

9. *Key "by way of explanation"*

> Verse 11, "useless . . . useful." This is a play on the word "Onesimus" which means useful. He was useless. But now he, Onesimus, is living up to his name and is indeed useful. Onesimus and Tychicus are taking this letter to Colosse, along with Paul's letter to the Colossians (Colossians 4:16). Under Roman law the punishment for Onesimus, a runaway slave and a thief, was death.

10. *Key "Quotable Quote"*

> "Storm the throne of grace and persevere therein, and mercy will come down."
> John Wesley

Non-Pauline letters

Hebrews
James
1 Peter
2 Peter
1 John
2 John
3 John
Jude

Hebrews chapter 1

1. Following chapter

Chapter 2: God's program of salvation

2. Analysis of chapter

The supremacy of the Son of God in all his work. (1-3)
His superiority over all the holy angels. (4-14)

3. Key verse

Verse 3: "The Son is the radiance of God's glory and the exact representation of his being, sustaining all things by his powerful word."

4. Key word / key phrase

Verse 2, "spoken to us by his Son."

5. Key event / key person / key theme

Christ is superior to angels.

6. Key thought

Verse 3, "at the right hand," is the place of power; "sat down," indicates that Christ's work is finished. He is now ruling with God.

7. Key thing to look out for

Jesus is God's last word to humankind.

8. Key Bible cross-reference

Verse 5. See Psalm 2:7.

9. Key "by way of explanation"

The writer of the epistle is not known. Though the teaching is in harmony with Paul's the writing style and the emphases are not those of Paul. The writer was possibly Apollos (a name first suggested by Luther) or Barnabas.

10. Key "Quotable Quote"

"The great theme of the letter to the Hebrews is the finality of Jesus Christ."
John R.W. Stott

Hebrews chapter 2

1. Before and after

Previous chapter: Chapter 1: the pre-eminence of Jesus Christ
Following chapter: Chapter 3: Christ is superior to Moses

2. Analysis of chapter

Do not drift away from Christ and his gospel. (1-4)
His sufferings in no way lessen his pre-eminence. (5-9)
The reason for his sufferings. (10-18)

3. Key verse

Verse 4: "God also testified to it by signs, wonders and various miracles, and gifts of the Holy Spirit distributed according to his will."

4. Key word / key phrase

Verse 3, "such a great salvation."

5. Key event / key person / key theme

God's program of salvation

6. Key thought

Verse 10, Christ's coming to earth was completed when he went through suffering (the Greek verb "to perfect" means "to complete a process".)

7. Key thing to look out for

The reason why Jesus can help us in our temptations.

8. Key Bible cross-reference

Verses 6-8. See Psalm 8:4-6.

9. Key "by way of explanation"

Verse 13, "I will put my trust in him." This quotation from Isaiah 8:17 demonstrates complete trust in God. This was perfectly shown throughout the life and, pre-eminently, in the death, of Jesus.

10. Key "Quotable Quote"

"We will trust God to the extent we fear him; to the extent we stand in absolute awe and amazement at his great power and sovereign rule over all his creation."
Jerry Bridges

Hebrews chapter 3

1. *Before and after*

   Previous chapter: Chapter 2: God's program of salvation
   Following chapter: Chapter 4: The Christian's rest and Jesus the High Priest

2. *Analysis of chapter*

   Christ is superior to Moses. (1-6)
   The Hebrews are warned about the sin and danger of unbelief. (7-13)
   The necessity for faith in Christ, and to steadfastly follow him. (14-19)

3. *Key verse*

   Verse 5: "Moses was faithful as a servant in all God's house, testifying to what
   would be said in the future."

4. *Key word / key phrase*

   Verse 3, "worthy of greater honor than Moses."

5. *Key event / key person / key theme*

   Jesus is superior to Moses

6. *Key thought*

   Christians should concentrate on Christ.

7. *Key thing to look out for*

   The second series of warnings found in this letter.

8. *Key Bible cross-reference*

   Verse 2. See Numbers 12:7.

9. *Key "by way of explanation"*

   Verse 3, Jesus is the builder, and is therefore greater than Moses who is part of
   the building.

10. *Key "Quotable Quote"*

    "My salvation is not based on my faith; it is based on who Jesus Christ is."
    Josh McDowell

Hebrews chapter 4

1. Before and after

Previous chapter: Chapter 3: Jesus is superior to Moses
Following chapter: Chapter 5: Jesus the great High Priest

2. Analysis of chapter

Humble reverence is urged, so that none fall short of the promised rest through unbelief. (1-10)
Arguments and motives for faith and hope as we approach God. (11-16)

3. Key verse

Verse 1: "Therefore, since the promise of entering his rest still stands, let us be careful that none of you be found to have fallen short of it."

4. Key word / key phrase

Verse 10, "God's rest."

5. Key event / key person / key theme

The Christian's rest, and Jesus the High Priest.

6. Key thought

The Christian rests in the finished work of Christ. We don't have to labor to make ourselves right with God.

7. Key thing to look out for

The description of God's word. How can this help us?

8. Key Bible cross-reference

Verse 5. See Psalm 95:11.

9. Key "by way of explanation"

Verse 15, "tempted in every way, just as we are." Jesus' experience of temptation was the same as ours. It wasn't different because he was God.

10. Key "Quotable Quote"

"Sympathy with the sinner in his trial does not depend on the experience of sin, but on the experience of the temptation to sin, which only the sinless can know in its full intensity. He who falls yields before the last strain."
B.F. Westcott

Hebrews chapter 5

1. Before and after

Previous chapter: Chapter 4: The Christian's rest and Jesus the High Priest
Following chapter: Chapter 6: Christian maturity

2. Analysis of chapter

The ministry of a high priest is completely fulfilled in Christ. (1-10)
The Christian Hebrews reproved for their little progress in the knowledge of the gospel. (11-14)

3. Key verse

Verse 7: "During the days of Jesus' life on earth, he offered up prayers and petitions with loud cries and tears to the one who could save him from death, and he was heard because of his reverent submission."

4. Key word / key phrase

Verse 1, "Every high priest."

5. Key event / key person / key theme

Jesus the great High Priest

6. Key thought

Jesus was truly human (verses 7,8).

7. Key thing to look out for

Verses 13,14 give a definition of maturity. Mature Christians have understanding and wisdom.

8. Key Bible cross-reference

Verse 3. See Leviticus 9:7.

9. Key "by way of explanation"

Verse 14, "the mature." The writer to the Hebrews wants his readers to be among the mature who thrive on a spiritually solid diet. They should not be content to remain infantile in their spiritual understanding and knowledge.

10. Key "Quotable Quote"

"I've never met anyone who became instantly mature. It's a painstaking process that God takes us through, and it includes such things as waiting, failing, losing, and being misunderstood – each calling for extra doses of perseverance."
Charles Swindoll

Hebrews chapter 6

1. Before and after

Previous chapter: Chapter 5: Jesus the great High Priest
Following chapter: Chapter 7: Melchizedek

2. Analysis of chapter

The Hebrews are urged to go on to maturity in their Christian belief. The consequences of apostasy, or turning back, are described. (1-8)

The apostle encourages the Christians to persevere in faith and holiness. (9-20)

3. Key verse

Verse 10: "God is not unjust; he will not forget your work and the love you have shown him as you have helped his people and continue to help them."

4. Key word / key phrase

Verse 1, "Go on to maturity."

5. Key event / key person / key theme

Christian maturity

6. Key thought

Beware: this chapter contains the severest of warnings.

7. Key thing to look out for

Perseverance is the order of the day.

8. Key Bible cross-reference

Verse 19. See Leviticus 16:2.

9. Key "by way of explanation"

Verses 4-6 refer to people who have come under the influence of the Christian faith – and may be professing church-goers – but are not real Christians, but people whose basic inner relationship to God is unloving. Note that to love is omitted from the list in verses 4,5 (cf. verse 10).

10. Key "Quotable Quote"

"Faith is the Christian's foundation, hope is his anchor, death is his harbor, Christ is his pilot, and heaven is his country."
Jeremy Taylor

Hebrews chapter 7

1. *Before and after*

Previous chapter: Chapter 6: Christian maturity
Following chapter: Chapter 8: The new covenant

2. *Analysis of chapter*

The priesthood of Melchizedek and Christ are compared. (1-3)
Christ's priesthood is superior to the levitical priesthood. (4-10)
This is applied to Christ. (11-25)
The Church should be encouraged in their faith and hope from this. (26-28)

3. *Key verse*

Verse 27: "Unlike the other high priests, he does not need to offer sacrifices day after day, first for his own sins, and then for the sins of the people. He sacrificed for their sins once for all when he offered himself."

4. *Key word / key phrase*

Verse 1, "This Melchizedek."

5. *Key event / key person / key theme*

Melchizedek

6. *Key thought*

The mysterious Melchizedek is introduced (see Genesis 14:18-20).

7. *Key thing to look out for*

Jesus and Melchizedek are compared.

8. *Key Bible cross-reference*

Verse 21. See Psalm 110:4.

9. *Key "by way of explanation"*

Verse 1, "This Melchizedek was king . . . and priest." As both king and priest, Melchizedek prefigured these two ministries that particularly apply to Jesus.

10. *Key "Quotable Quote"*

"Christ has been too long locked up in the mass or in the Book: let him be your prophet, priest and king. Obey him."
George Fox

Hebrews chapter 8

1. *Before and after*

   Previous chapter: Chapter 7: Melchizedek
   Following chapter: Chapter 9: A superior sacrifice

2. *Analysis of chapter*

   Christ's priesthood is superior to Aaron's. (1-6)
   The superiority of the new covenant over the old covenant. (7-13)

3. *Key verse*

   Verse 13: "By calling this covenant "new," he has made the first one obsolete; and what is obsolete and aging will soon disappear."

4. *Key word / key phrase*

   Verse 8, "I will make a new covenant."

5. *Key event / key person / key theme*

   The new covenant

6. *Key thought*

   The limited value of the first covenant.

7. *Key thing to look out for*

   What was so special about the new covenant?

8. *Key Bible cross-reference*

   Verse 1. See Psalm 110:1.

9. *Key "by way of explanation"*

   Verse 8, "I will make a new covenant." This covenant will enable God's people to delight in doing his will, to have close fellowship with him, and to serve him with a renewed heart.

10. *Key "Quotable Quote"*

   "In the first covenant, works were required as the condition of life; in the second, they are required only as the signs of life."
   Thomas Watson

Hebrews chapter 9

1. Before and after

Previous chapter: Chapter 8: The new covenant
Following chapter: Chapter 10: The finality of Jesus' sacrifice

2. Analysis of chapter

The Jewish tabernacle and its worship. (1-5)
Its meaning is explained. (6-10)
The worship of the tabernacle is fulfilled in Christ. (11-22)
The necessity and power of Christ's priesthood and sacrifice. (23-28)

3. Key verse

Verse 5: "Above the ark were the cherubim of the Glory, overshadowing the atonement cover."

4. Key word / key phrase

Verse 28, "so Christ was sacrificed once to take away the sins of many people; and he will appear a second time, not to bear sin, but to bring salvation to those who are waiting for him."

5. Key event / key person / key theme

A superior sacrifice

6. Key thought

With the coming of Christ, the old sacrificial system is fulfilled and abolished.

7. Key thing to look out for

In what ways was the death of Christ superior to the old tabernacle rituals?

8. Key Bible cross-reference

Verse 7. See Leviticus 16:2-34.

9. Key "by way of explanation"

Verse 12, "once for all." In contrast to the daily and yearly sacrifices, Jesus' sacrifice of himself for the sins of the world happened just once, but is effective for all time. The "atonement cover" (verse 5) was a slab of gold on top of the ark on which blood was sprinkled once a year on the Day of Atonement.

10. Key "Quotable Quote"

"When Christ's hands were nailed to the cross, he also nailed your sins to the cross."
Bernard of Clairvaux

Hebrews chapter 10

1. Before and after

Previous chapter: Chapter 9: A superior sacrifice
Following chapter: Chapter 11: Examples of faith

2. Analysis of chapter

The insufficiency of sacrifices for taking away sin, and the necessity and power of the sacrifice of Christ. (1-18)
An argument for holy boldness in the believer's access to God through Jesus Christ, And for steadfastness in faith, and mutual love. (19-25)
The danger of apostasy. (26-31)
The sufferings of believers, and the need to persevere. (32-39)

3. Key verse

Verse 12: "But when this priest had offered for all time one sacrifice for sins, he sat down at the right hand of God."

4. Key word / key phrase

Verse 14, "he has made perfect."

5. Key event / key person / key theme

The finality of Jesus' sacrifice

6. Key thought

The curtain in the temple is identified with the body of Jesus.

7. Key thing to look out for

Christians are called to persevere in their faith.

8. Key Bible cross-reference

Verses 5-7. See Psalm 40:6-8.

9. Key "by way of explanation"

Verse 20, "the curtain, that is, his body." Mark 15:38 states that immediately after Jesus died on the cross the curtain which cut off the holy of holies in the temple from the holy place was "torn in two from top to bottom." The way into the very presence of God was now open to all.

10. Key "Quotable Quote"

"Let none therefore presume on past mercies, as if they were out of danger."
John Wesley

Hebrews chapter 11

1. Before and after

Previous chapter: Chapter 10: The finality of Jesus' sacrifice
Following chapter: Chapter 12: How to live by faith

2. Analysis of chapter

The nature and power of faith described. (1-3)
This is illustrated in the lives of different people, from Abel to Noah. (4-7)
By Abraham and his descendants. (8-19)
By Jacob, Joseph, Moses, the Israelites, and Rahab. (20-31)
By other Old Testament believers. (32-38)
Something better. (39,40)

3. Key verse

Verse 1: "Now faith is being sure of what we hope for and certain of what we do not see."

4. Key word / key phrase

Verse 4, "By faith."

5. Key event / key person / key theme

Examples of faith

6. Key thought

A galaxy of faithful Old Testament followers of God are detailed to encourage us in our faith.

7. Key thing to look out for

They all lived by faith in God, but this was expressed in a variety of ways.

8. Key Bible cross-reference

Verse 4. See Genesis 4:3-10.

9. Key "by way of explanation"

Verse 5, "By faith Enoch was taken from this life." Enoch was "translated" to heaven, as was Elijah. He did not experience death in the normal way. This he did, "by faith."

10. Key "Quotable Quote"

"Do not be troubled because you must live by faith, nor grow weary because hope is deferred. Your reward is certain; it is preserved for you in him who created all things."
Peter Chrysologus

Hebrews chapter 12

1. Before and after

Previous chapter: Chapter 11: Examples of faith
Following chapter: Chapter 13: An exhortation to love

2. Analysis of chapter

An exhortation to be constant and persevere, and the example of Christ is set out, and the gracious purpose of God in all the sufferings believers endured. (1-11)

Peace and holiness are commended, with warnings about despising spiritual blessings. (12-17)

The New Testament dispensation is shown to be much more excellent than the Old. (18-29)

3. Key verse

Verse 7: "Endure hardship as discipline; God is treating you as sons."

4. Key word / key phrase

Verse 2, "fix our eyes on Jesus."

5. Key event / key person / key theme

How to live by faith

6. Key thought

We can keep going with joyful, thankful and reverent hearts, because we are traveling to the glorious heavenly Jerusalem where Jesus is at the right hand of God.

7. Key thing to look out for

What view are Christians to take of hardship?

8. Key Bible cross-reference

Verse 20. See Exodus 19:12,13.

9. Key "by way of explanation"

Verse 1, "surrounded by such a great cloud of witnesses." The people listed in chapter 11 are now pictured as spectators in a great athletics arena. They encourage us in our pilgrimage and we are to toss off all unnecessary and sinful baggage for the race.

10. Key "Quotable Quote"

"True progress quietly and persistently moves along without notice."
Francis de Sales

Hebrews chapter 13

1. *Previous chapter*

Chapter 12: How to live by faith

2. *Analysis of chapter*

Exhortations about various duties, and the need to be content with God's providence. (1-6)
Respect the instructions of faithful pastors. Warnings against being led astray by false teaching. (7-15)
Further exhortations to duties that relate to God, to our neighbor, and to those set over us in the Lord. (16-21)
This letter should be taken seriously. (22-25)

3. *Key verse*

Verse 9: "Do not be carried away by all kinds of strange teachings."

4. *Key word / key phrase*

Verse 1, "Keep on loving each other."

5. *Key event / key person / key theme*

An exhortation to love

6. *Key thought*

"This world is not our home."

7. *Key thing to look out for*

Reasons why the Christian must not be afraid or discouraged.

8. *Key Bible cross-reference*

Verse 5. See Deuteronomy 31:6.

9. *Key "by way of explanation"*

Verse 9, "by grace, not by ceremonial foods." This verse states categorically that faith in Jesus has done away with any need to keep ceremonial food laws. Christians now life "by grace."

10. *Key "Quotable Quote"*

"Salvation is by grace through faith; yet we must work out our own salvation."
Richard J. Foster

James chapter 1

1. **Following chapter**

   Chapter 2: Faith and discrimination and good deeds

2. **Analysis of chapter**

   How to ask for God's help when suffering trials|, and how to behave in prosperous and in adverse circumstances. (1-11)
   Look on all evil as coming from ourselves, and all good from God. (12-18)
   The necessity of keeping a quick temper in check, and of receiving the word of God with meekness. (19-25)
   The difference between hypocrisy and real religion. (26,27)

3. **Key verse**

   Verse 2: "Consider it pure joy, my brothers, whenever you face trials of many kinds."

4. **Key word / key phrase**

   Verse 12, "perseveres under trial."

5. **Key event / key person / key theme**

   Overcoming temptation

6. **Key thought**

   Christians must do what God tells them to do. It is not enough merely to listen.

7. **Key thing to look out for**

   How does a Christian cope with trials?

8. **Key Bible cross-reference**

   Verse 1. See Matthew 13:55.

9. **Key "by way of explanation"**

   Verse 5, "wisdom." In the Bible, wisdom is practical. It means having insight into the principles by which God wants his people to live, and also knowing how they work out in the decisions and choices of everyday life. A breakdown of the principles is given in 3:17,18.

10. **Key "Quotable Quote"**

    "Though Satan instills his poison, and fans the flames of our corrupt desires within us, we are yet not carried by any external force to the commission of sin, but our own flesh entices us, and we willingly yield to its allurements."
    John Calvin

James chapter 2

1. Before and after

Previous chapter: Chapter 1: The test of faith
Following chapter: Chapter 3: Controlling the tongue and producing wisdom

2. Analysis of chapter

All professions of faith are vain, if they do not result in love and justice to others. (1-13)
The necessity of good works to demonstrate the sincerity of faith, which otherwise will be of no more benefit than the faith of devils. (14-26)

3. Key verse

Verse 5: "Listen, my dear brothers: Has not God chosen those who are poor in the eyes of the world to be rich in faith and to inherit the kingdom he promised those who love him?"

4. Key word / key phrase

Verse 1, "don't show favoritism."

5. Key event / key person / key theme

Faith and discrimination and good deeds

6. Key thought

"Love your neighbor" is the standard to live up to.

7. Key thing to look out for

The relationship between good deeds and faith.

8. Key Bible cross-reference

Verse 8. See Leviticus 19:18.

9. Key "by way of explanation"

Verse 8, "royal law." The law of love is here called the "royal law" for two reasons. First, love is the source of all law. Second, love is the supreme law and is superior to all other laws.

10. Key "Quotable Quote"

"Jesus said the first commandment is to love the Lord your God. The second is to love your neighbor as in fact you love yourself. He did not say as a third commandment to love yourself."
John R.W. Stott

James chapter 3

1. *Before and after*

Previous chapter: Chapter 2: Faith and discrimination and good deeds
Following chapter: Chapter 4: Humility and depending on God

2. *Analysis of chapter*

Warnings against proud behavior, and the harm done by an uncontrolled tongue. (1-12)
The superiority of heavenly wisdom especially when contrasted with worldly wisdom. (13-18)

3. *Key verse*

Verse 10: "Out of the same mouth come praise and cursing. My brothers, this should not be."

4. *Key word / key phrase*

Verse 9, "With the tongue."

5. *Key event / key person / key theme*

Controlling the tongue and producing wisdom

6. *Key thought*

How to gain victory over the tongue.

7. *Key thing to look out for*

Wisdom unpacked.

8. *Key Bible cross-reference*

Verse 9. See Genesis 1:26.

9. *Key "by way of explanation"*

Verse 6, "the tongue . . . is itself set on fire by hell." The tongue hurts the one who speaks, as well as those on the receiving end. "Hell itself" – all evil has its source in the devil.

10. *Key "Quotable Quote"*

"The proof that you have God's Spirit in your life is not that you speak in an unknown tongue, but that you know how to control the tongue that you do know about."
J. Sidlow Baxter

James chapter 4

1. Before and after

Previous chapter: Chapter 3: Controlling the tongue and producing wisdom
Following chapter: Chapter 5: The triumph of faith

2. Analysis of chapter

Here are warnings against corrupt affections, and love of this world, which are slights against God. (1-10)
Instructions not to do anything in life without constantly referring to God's will. (11-17)

3. Key verse

Verse 10: "Humble yourselves before the Lord, and he will lift you up."

4. Key word / key phrase

Verse 7, "submit . . . to God."

5. Key event / key person / key theme

Humility and depending on God

6. Key thought

Verse 7, Christians resist the devil by filling their minds with the power and presence of God.

7. Key thing to look out for

What sins marked the lives of the Christians to whom James was writing and what does James tell them to do to put things right?

8. Key Bible cross-reference

Verse 6. See Proverbs 3:34.

9. Key "by way of explanation"

Verse 8, "Wash your hands." In the Old Testament before a priest could enter God's presence in the tabernacle he had to wash his hands and feet as a sign of inner cleansing. So James's "wash your hands" in this verse corresponds to the words, "purify your hearts" which is in the same verse.

10. Key "Quotable Quote"

"God uses external circumstances to bring about internal purification."
Oswald Chambers

James chapter 5

1. **Previous chapter**

   Chapter 4: Humility and depending on God

2. **Analysis of chapter**

   God's judgments on rich unbelievers. (1-6)
   Be patient and meek under trials. (7-11)
   Warnings against swearing. Prayer in every situation. Christians should confess their sins to each other. (12-18)
   The happiness of being the means of the conversion of a sinner. (19,20)

3. **Key verse**

   Verse 13: "Is any one of you in trouble? He should pray. Is anyone happy? Let him sing songs of praise."

4. **Key word / key phrase**

   Verse 17, "he prayed earnestly."

5. **Key event / key person / key theme**

   The triumph of faith

6. **Key thought**

   The rich come under fire.

7. **Key thing to look out for**

   What to do when suffering comes.

8. **Key Bible cross-reference**

   Verse 20. See Proverbs 10:12.

9. **Key "by way of explanation"**

   Verse 9, "Don't grumble." The Bible is totally against the widespread practice of grumbling. Here, James is telling his readers not to grumble against their fellow-Christians.

10. **Key "Quotable Quote"**

    "At the earlier Methodist class meetings, members were expected every week to answer some extremely personal questions, such as the following: Have you experienced any particular temptations during the past week? How did you react or respond to those temptations? Is there anything you are trying to keep secret, and, if so, what? At this point, the modern Christian swallows hard! We are often coated with a thick layer of reserve and modesty which covers 'a multitude of sins' – usually our own. Significantly, James 5:16-20, the original context of that phrase, is the passage which urges, 'Confess your sins to one another, and pray for one another, that you may be healed.'"
    Michael Griffiths

1 Peter chapter 1

1. Following chapter

Chapter 2: Living stones, slaves of God, and the example of Jesus' suffering

2. Analysis of chapter

The apostle blesses God for his special benefits through Christ. (1-9)
Salvation by Christ foretold in ancient prophecy. (10-12)
All are exhorted to be holy. (13-16)
Obey the truth and love the brethren. (17-25)

3. Key verse

Verse 6: "In this you greatly rejoice, though now for a little while you may have had to suffer grief in all kinds of trials."

4. Key word / key phrase

Verse 3, "a living hope."

5. Key event / key person / key theme

The Christian hope

6. Key thought

Salvation was the theme of the Old Testament.

7. Key thing to look out for

All Christians are called to be holy. What help does this chapter give to the Christian who is traveling along "the highway of holiness" (Isaiah 35:8)?

8. Key Bible cross-reference

Verse 16. See Leviticus 11:44,45.

9. Key "by way of explanation"

Verse 16, "Be holy, because I am holy." This is a pivotal quotation from the Old Testament. To be holy means to be set apart, and in a Christian context this means to be separated from sin and to be dedicated to God.

10. Key "Quotable Quote"

"If we are born again of the Spirit of God, our one desire is a hunger and thirst after nothing less than holiness, the holiness of Jesus, and he will satisfy it."
Oswald Chambers

1 Peter chapter 2

1. *Before and after*

Previous chapter: Chapter 1: Hope and holiness
Following chapter: Chapter 3: How to suffer

2. *Analysis of chapter*

Desire to grow spiritually. (1-10)
Live good lives in this corrupt world. (11,12)
Submit to the authorities. (13-17)
Servants should submit to their masters. (18-25)

3. *Key verse*

Verse 2: "Like newborn babies, crave pure spiritual milk, so that by it you may grow up in your salvation."

4. *Key word / key phrase*

Verse 5, "like living stones."

5. *Key event / key person / key theme*

Living stones, slaves of God, and the example of Jesus' suffering

6. *Key thought*

Peter lists the things Christians need to get rid of so they can grow in the Christian life.

7. *Key thing to look out for*

Peter explains how Christians should be linked up with each other.

8. *Key Bible cross-reference*

Verse 3. See Psalm 34:8.

9. *Key "by way of explanation"*

Verse 9, "chosen people." Paul is by no means the only person to speak about election and predestination. Just as Israel was chosen by God in Old Testament times, (see Isaiah 43:10,20), so in the New Testament God's followers are said to be called, chosen, and elected by God himself.

10. *Key "Quotable Quote"*

"We were enemies of God through sin, and God had appointed the sinner to die. There must needs therefore have happened one of two things; either that God, in his truth, should destroy all men, or that in his loving-kindness he should cancel the sentence. But behold the wisdom of God; he preserved both the truth of his sentence, and the exercise of his loving-kindness. Christ took our sins 'in his body on the tree, that we by his death might die to sin, and live unto righteousness' (1 Peter 2:24)."
St. Cyril of Jerusalem

1 Peter chapter 3

1. Before and after

Previous chapter: Chapter 2: Living stones, slaves of God, and the example of Jesus' suffering

Following chapter: Chapter 4: Suffering as a Christian

2. Analysis of chapter

The duties of wives and husbands. (1-7)

Christians should be prepared to suffer for doing good. (8-22)

3. Key verse

Verse 8: "Finally, all of you, live in harmony with one another; be sympathetic, love as brothers, be compassionate and humble."

4. Key word / key phrase

Verse 14, "if you should suffer."

5. Key event / key person / key theme

How to suffer

6. Key thought

The gentle and quiet spirit should not only characterize wives (verse 4) – but all Christians (verses 8,15).

7. Key thing to look out for

What advice does Peter give about witnessing to non-Christians?

8. Key Bible cross-reference

Verse 6. See Genesis 18:12.

9. Key "by way of explanation"

There are different opinions about the meaning of verses 18-22; "spirits in prison" may mean angels who had rebelled against God, since "spirits" by itself never refers to human beings, but only to supernatural beings. "Preached" probably means "announced Christ's victory," rather than "evangelized."

10. Key "Quotable Quote"

"How is it that nobody has dreamed up any moral advances since Christ's teaching?"
Michael Green

1 Peter chapter 4

1. Before and after

Previous chapter: Chapter 3: How to suffer
Following chapter: Chapter 5: Submit to God

2. Analysis of chapter

Reflect on Christ's sufferings as you consider your own purity and holiness. (1-6)
The end of all things is a good reason to be sober, alert and prayerful. (7-11)
Suffer for being a Christian. (12-19)

3. Key verse

Verse 7: "The end of all things is near. Therefore be clear minded and self-controlled so that you can pray."

4. Key word / key phrase

Verse 13, "you participate in the sufferings of Christ."

5. Key event / key person / key theme

Suffering as a Christian

6. Key thought

"The end is near." (Christ's incarnation marked the beginning of "these last times" 1:20).

7. Key thing to look out for

Verse 11, the purpose and guiding principle of the Christian's actions.

8. Key Bible cross-reference

Verse 8. See Proverbs 10:12.

9. Key "by way of explanation"

Verse 4, "they heap abuse on you." Some fear that if they stand out in the crowd they will be made fun of. "Quite right," declares Peter. One reason you are likely to suffer is for steering clear of the wild and reckless living of the world.

10. Key "Quotable Quote"

"The Church is to develop a Christian counter-culture with its own distinctive goals, values, standards, and lifestyle – a realistic alternative to the contemporary technocracy which is marked by bondage, materialism, self-centeredness, and greed."
John R.W. Stott

1 Peter chapter 5

1. ## Previous chapter

   Chapter 4: Suffering as a Christian

2. ## Analysis of chapter

   Elders exhorted and encouraged. (1-4)
   Younger Christians are to submit to their elders, and to yield with humility and patience to God, and to be sober, alert, and steadfast in faith. (5-9)
   Prayers for their growth. (10-14)

3. ## Key verse

   Verse 7: "Cast all your anxiety on him because he cares for you."

4. ## Key word / key phrase

   Verse 6, "humble yourselves."

5. ## Key event / key person / key theme

   Submit to God

6. ## Key thought

   How to be a shepherd of God's flock.

7. ## Key thing to look out for

   How to beat the devil.

8. ## Key Bible cross-reference

   Verse 5. See Proverbs 3:34.

9. ## Key "by way of explanation"

   Verse 8, "alert." Peter knew what it was not to be alert when he fell asleep in the Garden of Gethsemane, Matthew 26:36-46.

10. ## Key "Quotable Quote"

    "Satan does not care what we do so long as we do not alert people to their sin. Our work is to wake people up."
    Catherine Booth

2 Peter chapter 1

1. *Following chapter*

   Chapter 2: False teachers condemned

2. *Analysis of chapter*

   Exhortations to make one's calling and election certain. (1-11)
   The apostle looks forward to his approaching death. (12-15)
   He confirms the truth of the gospel, and of Christ's coming as Judge. (16-21)

3. *Key verse*

   Verse 21: "For prophecy never had its origin in the will of man, but men spoke from God as they were carried along by the Holy Spirit."

4. *Key word / key phrase*

   Verse 10, "your calling and election."

5. *Key event / key person / key theme*

   The prerequisites for a fruitful Christian life.

6. *Key thought*

   God's power has given Christians all they need (verse 3) – but this has to be worked out in practical ways.

7. *Key thing to look out for*

   The vital importance of prophecy.

8. *Key Bible cross-reference*

   Verses 17,18. See Mark 9:2-7.

9. *Key "by way of explanation"*

   Verse 16, "cleverly invented stories." Peter denies that his teaching about Jesus has anything to do with fabricated stories. But Peter's words indicate that weird and wonderful stories purporting to be about Jesus were circulating in Peter's day. Peter was an eyewitness of the transfiguration (verses 16,17).

10. *Key "Quotable Quote"*

    "It is not the brains that matter most, but that which guides them – the character; the heart, generous qualities, progressive ideas."
    Feodor Dostoevesky

2 Peter chapter 2

1. Before and after

Previous chapter: Chapter 1: Cultivating a Christian character
Following chapter: Chapter 3: Confidence in Jesus' return

2. Analysis of chapter

Believers are warned against false teachers. These teachers will be punished. (1-9)
The wicked work of false teachers. (10-16)
They pretend to be free and pure. (17-22)

3. Key verse

Verse 1: "But there were also false prophets among the people, just as there will be false teachers among you."

4. Key word / key phrase

Verse 2, "there were also false prophets."

5. Key event / key person / key theme

False teachers condemned

6. Key thought

Peter describes the destruction false teachers bring in their wake.

7. Key thing to look out for

Peter's knock-out onslaught on false teachers.

8. Key Bible cross-reference

Verse 6. See Genesis 19:24.

9. Key "by way of explanation"

Verse 1: history is repeating itself, but how much worse these new false prophets are, in view of the fact that they have known Christ (verse 20).

10. Key "Quotable Quote"

"The soul which is possessed of this rich treasure of contentment, is like Noah in the ark, that can sing in the midst of a deluge."
Thomas Watson

2 Peter chapter 3

1. **Previous chapter**

   Chapter 2: False teachers condemned

2. **Analysis of chapter**

   Christ's final coming as Judge. (1-4)
   He will appear when he is not expected. The world will be destroyed by fire. (5-10)
   So we must be holy and stand firm in the faith. (11-18)

3. **Key verse**

   Verse 10: "But the day of the Lord will come like a thief."

4. **Key word / key phrase**

   Verse 3, "in the last days."

5. **Key event / key person / key theme**

   Confidence in Jesus' return

6. **Key thought**

   God's view of time differs from ours.

7. **Key thing to look out for**

   There is only one sure way not to be carried along by the evil world.

8. **Key Bible cross-reference**

   Verse 3. See Jude 18.

9. **Key "by way of explanation"**

   Verse 18. "knowledge." The false teachers were probably peddling an early form of Gnosticism, which taught that there was a "secret knowledge" not available to ordinary believers. In contrast, Peter says that Christians should be always growing in their knowledge of Jesus who is both their Lord and Savior. That is the only knowledge they need.

10. **Key "Quotable Quote"**

    "In Christ crucified is the true theology and the knowledge of God."
    Martin Luther

1 John chapter 1

1. **Following chapter**

   Chapter 2: Obeying and loving God, and dealing with heretics

2. **Analysis chapter**

   Christ is the Word of life. (1-4)
   To have fellowship with God holiness is essential. (5-10)

3. **Key verse**

   Verse 7: "But if we walk in the light, as he is in the light, we have fellowship with one another, and the blood of Jesus, his Son, purifies us from all sin."
   4. *Key word*
   "Fellowship" in verses 3, 6, 7.

5. **Key event / key person / key theme**

   John insists on the flesh and blood reality of the Incarnation.

6. **Key thought**

   Verse 8, some false teachers claimed they were above the ordinary laws of morality. John's answer is a categorical denial.

7. **Key thing to look out for**

   The ways in which John emphasizes that Jesus was a real human being.

8. **Key biblical cross-reference**

   Verse 1. See John 1:2.

9. **Key "by way of explanation"**

   See 2:19, "they went out from us." John is writing to answer the claims of false teaching which was probably an early form of Gnosticism. Gnostics believed they had secret knowledge which gave them enlightenment. They thought that matter was evil, and therefore denied that the Word was made flesh. Cerinthus, a heretical teacher in the time of John, taught that Christ only *seemed* to have a real body.

10. **Key "Quotable Quote"**

    "Thus we learn that we only make due progress in the knowledge of the Word of the Lord when we become really humbled and groan under the burden of our sins and learn to flee to God's mercy and find rest in nothing except his fatherly favor."
    John Calvin

1 John chapter 2

1. Before and after

Previous chapter: Chapter 1: Eyewitness and fellowship
Following chapter: Chapter 3: Being God's children and showing Christian love

2. Analysis of chapter

Christ's atonement helps in the battle against sin. (1,2)
Salvation results in obedience, and love for the brethren. (3-11)
Christians are spoken of as little children, young men, and fathers. (12-14)
All are warned against the love of this world, and against false teaching. (15-23)
They are encouraged to stand firm in faith and holiness. (24-29)

3. Key verse

Verse 9: "Anyone who claims to be in the light but hates his brother is still in the darkness."

4. Key word / key phrase

Verse 3, "obey his commands."

5. Key event / key person / key theme

Obeying and loving God, and dealing with heretics

6. Key thought

Here is an acid test for you: Do you hate any fellow-Christian?

7. Key thing to look out for

Here is another awkward question: Do you love aspects of the world's ways and values?

8. Key Bible cross-reference

Verse 7. See John 13:34.

9. Key "by way of explanation"

Verse 15, "the world" refers to any society where people live in opposition, or indifference, to God. It is characterized by sensuality, greed, and pride. It is ruled over by the devil.

10. Key "Quotable Quote"

"The corridors of the New Testament reverberate with dogmatic affirmations beginning 'We know,' 'We are sure,' 'We are confident.' If you question this, read the First Epistle of John in which verbs meaning 'to know' occur about forty times. They strike a note of joyful assurance which is sadly missing from many parts of the Church today and which needs to be recaptured."
John R.W. Stott

1 John chapter 3

1. Before and after

Previous chapter: Chapter 2: Obeying and loving God, and dealing with heretics

Following chapter: Chapter 4: Testing the spirits, and the proof of love

2. Analysis of chapter

The apostle states that the love of God makes believers his children. (1,2)

Live as God's children. (3-10)

Love for the brethren is a characteristic of genuine Christians. (11-15)

That love is described and seen by its actions. (16-21)

Grow in faith, love, and obedience. (22-24)

3. Key verse

Verse 11: "This is the message you heard from the beginning: We should love one another."

4. Key word / key phrase

Verse 11, "love one another."

5. Key event / key person / key theme

Living as God's children.

6. Key thought

To the question, "How can I keep going as a Christian?" John answers, "Remember how much God the Father has loved you."

7. Key thing to look out for

To the question, "What characteristics should I be displaying as a Christian?" John answers, "you should believe in Jesus Christ and you should be showing Christian love to your fellow-Christians" (verse 23).

8. Key Bible cross-reference

Verse 1: See John 1:12.

9. Key "by way of explanation"

Verse 17, "the love of God." The love that God pours into the hearts and lives of believers by the Holy Spirit enables Christians to love one another. To the question, "What is this love like?" John answers that it is exemplified in the life and death of Jesus Christ (verse 16).

10. Key "Quotable Quote"

"Fellowship is the sharing of the divine life and communion of the Father and the Son."

R.W. Orr

1 John chapter 4

1. Before and after

Previous chapter: Chapter 3: Being God's children and showing Christian love

Following chapter: Chapter 5: Grounds for assurance

2. Analysis of chapter

Believers warned against those who falsely claim to have God's Spirit. (1-6)

Brotherly love is encouraged. (7-21)

3. Key verse

Verse 13: "We know that we live in him and he in us, because he has given us of his Spirit."

4. Key word / key phrase

Verse 1, "test the spirits."

5. Key event / key person / key theme

Testing the spirits, and the proof of love

6. Key thought

"Don't believe everything you are told. Test the spirits."

7. Key thing to look out for

John's reasons for the pre-eminence of love.

8. Key Bible cross-reference

Verse 12. See John 1:18.

9. Key "by way of explanation"

Verse 6: "we" refers to the apostles (1:1-3). The tests of authenticity are: to acknowledge the pre-existence of Christ (he came); his humanity (in the flesh); his continuing reality (has come, i.e. he is still here verse 2); and to accept the witness of John and the other apostles.

10. Key "Quotable Quote"

"The proper Christian attitude to sin is not to deny it but to admit it, and then to receive the forgiveness which God has made possible and promises to us. If we confess our sins, acknowledging before God that we are sinners not only by nature (sin) but by practice also (our sins), God will both forgive us our sins and purify us from all unrighteousness (1 John. 1:9). In the first phrase sin is a debt which he remits and in the second a stain which he removes."
John R.W. Stott

1 John chapter 5

1. **Previous chapter**

   Chapter 4: Testing the spirits, and the proof of love

2. **Analysis of chapter**

   Brotherly love is the result of the new birth. (1-5)

   Jesus, the Son of God, is the true Messiah. (6-8)

   Eternal life is God's gift through Christ. (9-12)

   The assurance of God listening to and answering prayer. (13-17)

   The happy state of true believers, and a command to renounce all idolatry. (18-21)

3. **Key verse**

   Verse 13: "I write these things to you who believe in the name of the Son of God so that you may know that you have eternal life."

4. **Key word / key phrase**

   Verse 11, "God has given us eternal life."

5. **Key event / key person / key theme**

   Grounds for assurance

6. **Key thought**

   It is no good to know about Jesus, you must believe in him personally at first hand.

7. **Key thing to look out for**

   Verse 13, John's purpose in writing his letter.

8. **Key Bible cross-reference**

   Verse 11. See John 3:36.

9. **Key "by way of explanation"**

   Verses 18-20. John concludes with four great things that we know. First, we know we do not want to carry on sinning as before, verse 18; second, that we are God's children, verse 19; third, that the devil controls the world; and fourth, we know that our understanding comes from Jesus, verse 20. Verse 16, the sin that leads to death may be the deliberate and constant rejection of light.

10. **Key "Quotable Quote"**

    "Over and above your intelligent apprehension of it, over and above your intelligent and intellectual deduction of it, there is a direct and immediate assurance given by the Holy Ghost who sheds abroad the love of God in your heart. You are overwhelmed by it, it is poured out in your heart, and there is no uncertainty any more."

    D. Martyn Lloyd-Jones

2 John

1. ## Abiding in God's commands

2. ## Analysis of chapter

> The apostle greets the chosen lady and her children. (1-3)
> He states his joy in their faith and love. (4-6)
> He warns them against those who are out to deceive them. (7-11)
> His conclusion. (12,13)

3. ## Key verse

> Verse 7: "Many deceivers, who do not acknowledge Jesus Christ as coming in the flesh, have gone out into the world."

4. ## Key word / key phrase

> Verse 6, "you walk in love."

5. ## Key event / key person / key theme

> Faith and love

6. ## Key thought

> John links up truth, obedience, and love.

7. ## Key thing to look out for

> "Use your wits," says John, "don't have open house to your enemies."

8. ## Key Bible cross-reference

> Verse 5. See John 13:34.

9. ## Key "by way of explanation"

> Verse 10, "take him into your house." In those days it was usual for traveling Christian teachers to be given hospitality in Christian homes. Verse 1, "chosen lady" could refer to an individual or a church (see 1 Peter 5:13).

10. ## Key "Quotable Quote"

> "If a man be gracious and courteous to strangers, it shows he is a citizen of the world and that his heart is no island, cut off from other islands, but a continent that joins them."
> Francis Bacon

3 John

1. **Christian fellowship**

2. **Analysis of chapter**

    A warning against taking sides with Diotrephes, but a commendation for Demetrius, a man of excellent character. (9-12)
    He hopes to see Gaius soon. (13,14)

3. **Key verse**

    Verse 8: "We ought therefore to show hospitality to such men so that we may work together for the truth."

4. **Key word / key phrase**

    Verse 11, "do not imitate what is evil."

5. **Key event / key person / key theme**

    Imitate what is good

6. **Key thought**

    Genuine Christian teachers should never be cold-shouldered.

7. **Key thing to look out for**

    What are the qualities for which John praises Gaius?

8. **Key Bible cross-reference**

    Verse 1: See Acts 19:29.

9. **Key "by way of explanation"**

    Verse 6 "send them on their way," that is, with practical help – food, money, perhaps letters of introduction.

10. **Key "Quotable Quote"**

    "In the midst of the suffocating self-love of our modern and postmodern culture, the Bible is clear that our real hunger is to know the one true God revealed in its pages. Only in doing so will we satisfy our cravings for security and find the purpose for which we exist, hope, and be able to live free from slavery to self love."
    Scott J. Hafemann

Jude

1. **Defeating false teachers**

2. **Analysis of chapter**

> Greeting and warning of danger. (1-4)
> Danger from false teachers, and the punishment which will fall on them and their followers. (5-7)
> A dreadful description of these "dreamers". (8-16)
> Believers warned against being surprised that such deceivers are in their fellowship. (17-23)
> The letter ends with an encouraging doxology, or words of praise. (24,25)

3. **Key verse**

> Verse 24: "To him who is able to keep you from falling and to present you before his glorious presence without fault and with great joy."

4. **Key word / key phrase**

> Verse 24, "keep you from falling."

5. **Key event / key person / key theme**

> Persevere

6. **Key thought**

> Christians must be on the watch for immoral and godless men who have slipped unnoticed into the Christian fellowship.

7. **Key thing to look out for**

> Verses 20,21. Advice on how to withstand this evil teaching.

8. **Key Bible cross-reference**

> Verse 9. See Zechariah 3:2.

9. **Key "by way of explanation"**

> Verse 4, "a license for immorality." These perverse people argued that they could commit immorality with impunity as it was God's business to forgive them. Jude and 2 Peter are very similar, and it appears that one writer borrowed heavily from the other in order to counter similar false teachings. It is possible that the writer was Jude, the brother of Jesus.

10. **Key "Quotable Quote"**

> "When you shall see the wicked heresy, which is the army of Antichrist, standing in the holy places of the Church, then let those who are in Judea head for the mountains, that is, those who are Christians should head for the Scriptures. For the true Judea is Christendom, and the mountains are the Scriptures of the prophets and apostles."
> John Chrysostom

Revelation

Revelation chapter 1

1. Following chapter

Chapter 2: Letters to the first four of the seven churches

2. Analysis of chapter

The divine origin, the purpose, and the importance of this book. (1-3)
The apostle John greets the seven churches of Asia. (4-8)
Declares when, where, and how, the revelation was made to him. (9-11)
His vision, in which he saw Christ. (12-20)

3. Key verse

Verse 1: "The revelation of Jesus Christ, which God gave him to show his servants what must soon take place."

4. Key word / key phrase

Verse 1, "The revelation of Jesus Christ."

5. Key event / key person / key theme

John's vision

6. Key thought

In Revelation symbolism and metaphor are used to express God's final victory over all evil.

7. Key thing to look out for

Each aspect of the vision of Jesus is drawn from the Old Testament, notably Daniel 7. What is the overwhelming impression?

8. Key Bible cross-reference

Verse 4. See Exodus 3:14.

9. Key "by way of explanation"

Verse 8, "the Alpha and the Omega." This is the name given to Jesus. "Alpha" and "Omega" were the first and last letters of the Greek alphabet. Jesus rules everything, including history. The book may have been written about AD 95. John received this vision when he had been exiled to the Aegean island of Patmos.

10. Key "Quotable Quote"

"Christ is the Alpha and the Omega of the Bible, from the first verse in Genesis to the last verse in Revelation."
Octavius Winslow

Revelation chapter 2

1. Before and after

Previous chapter: Chapter 1: The revelation of Jesus
Following chapter: Chapter 3: The last three of the seven letters to the churches

2. Analysis of chapter

To the Church at Ephesus; (1-7)
To the Church at Smyrna; (8-11)
To the Church at Pergamos; (12-17)
To the Church at Thyatira. (18-29)

3. Key verse

Verse 10: "Be faithful, even to the point of death, and I will give you the crown of life."

4. Key word / key phrase

Verse 7, "he who has an ear, let him hear."

5. Key event / key person / key theme

Letters to the first four of the seven churches

6. Key thought

Verse 2, the early Christians had to test the authenticity of the teaching of those who professed to teach in the name of Christ.

7. Key thing to look out for

Note the different reasons why each church is commended.

8. Key Bible cross-reference

Verse 8. See Isaiah 44:6.

9. Key "by way of explanation"

Each letter follows a pattern: the risen Christ, with a title taken from the opening, speaks to the church. He describes the church, giving a specific message. The letter ends with a warning to listen, and an encouragement to those who conquer. The letters reveal the pressure the churches were under to conform to the society around them.

10. Key "Quotable Quote"

"It is a bad world, an incredibly bad world. But I have discovered in the midst of it a quiet and holy people who have learned a great secret. They have found a joy which is a thousand times better than any pleasure of our sinful life. They are despised and persecuted, but they care not. They have overcome the world. These people are the Christians – and I am one of them."
Cyprian

Revelation chapter 3

1. Before and after

Previous chapter: Chapter 2: Letters to the first four of the seven churches
Following chapter: Chapter 4: God's throne

2. Analysis of chapter

Letters to the Church at Sardis (1-6);
at Philadelphia (7-13);
and Laodicea. (14-22)

3. Key verse

Verse 20: "Here I am! I stand at the door and knock. If anyone hears my voice and opens the door, I will come in and eat with him, and he with me."

4. Key word / key phrase

Verses 1,8,15, "I know."

5. Key event / key person / key theme

The last three of the seven letters to the churches

6. Key thought

Verse 14. We can rely absolutely on the witness of Christ.

7. Key thing to look out for

Note the different reasons why the six churches are reprimanded.

8. Key Bible cross-reference

Verse 7. See Isaiah 22:22.

9. Key "by way of explanation"

Verse 9, "synagogue of Satan." This refers to the aggressive Jews who attacked the beliefs of the early Christians. Each message matches the situation of the church. Laodicea was the wealthiest city in Asia (verse 14). Its water supply was drawn from hot springs five miles to the south, and the water was tepid by the time it reached Laodicea.

10. Key "Quotable Quote"

"Blessed is the soul at whose door Christ stands and knocks. Our door is faith. That is the door by which Christ enters."
Ambrose of Milan

Revelation chapter 4

1. Before and after

Previous chapter: Chapter 3: The last three of the seven letters to the churches

Following chapter: Chapter 5: The sealed scroll

2. Analysis of chapter

A vision of God on his glorious throne, around which were twenty-four elders and four living creatures. (1-7)

Songs of worship. (8-11)

3. Key verse

Verse 6: "In the center, around the throne, were four living creatures, and they were covered with eyes, in front and in back."

4. Key word / key phrase

Verse 2, "a throne in heaven."

5. Key event / key person / key theme

God's throne

6. Key thought

The activity in heaven is worship.

7. Key thing to look out for

What are the overwhelming impressions that you receive from this account of worship in heaven?

8. Key Bible cross-reference

Verse 5. See Exodus 19:16.

9. Key "by way of explanation"

Verse 7. Compare this verse with the vision Ezekiel was given of four living creatures in Ezekiel 1:6,10, where each creature had four faces, that of a human, lion, ox, and eagle.

10. Key "Quotable Quote"

"Worship is a meeting at the center so that our lives are centered on God and not lived eccentrically. People who do not worship are swept into a vast restlessness."

Eugene H. Peterson

Revelation chapter 5

1. *Before and after*

Previous chapter: Chapter 4: God's throne
Following chapter: Chapter 6: Six seals opened

2. *Analysis of chapter*

A book sealed with seven seals, which could only be opened by Christ. (1-7)
All honor is given to him, as he is worthy to open the scroll. (8-14)

3. *Key verse*

Verse 6: "Then I saw a Lamb, looking as if it had been slain, standing in the center of the throne, encircled by the four living creatures and the elders."

4. *Key word / key phrase*

Verse 1, "sealed with seven seals."

5. *Key event / key person / key theme*

The scroll of destiny

6. *Key thought*

The Lamb is the only one worthy to open the scroll of destiny.

7. *Key thing to look out for*

The reason why the Lamb is worthy.

8. *Key Bible cross-reference*

Verse 5. See Genesis 49:9.

9. *Key "by way of explanation"*

The major framework of the book consist of a series of sevens (seven standing for completeness): seven churches; the seven seals, seven trumpets and seven bowls (chapters 2-16). The seals, trumpets and bowls describe judgments.

10. *Key "Quotable Quote"*

"The last book of the Bible takes the entire biblical revelation and reimages it in a compelling, persuasive, evangelistic vision which has brought perseverance, stamina, joy and discipline to Christians for centuries."
Eugene H. Peterson

Revelation chapter 6

1. **Before and after**

   Previous chapter: Chapter 5: The sealed scroll
   Following chapter: Chapter 7: Sealing and martyrs

2. **Analysis of chapter**

   The opening of the seals. The first, second, third, and fourth. (1-8)
   The fifth. (9-11)
   The sixth. (12-17)

3. **Key verse**

   Verse 11: "Then each of them was given a white robe, and they were told to
   wait a little longer, until the number of their fellow servants and brothers who
   were to be killed as they had been was completed."

4. **Key word / key phrase**

   Verse 1, "opened the first of the seven seals."

5. **Key event / key person / key theme**

   Six seals opened, revealing future events

6. **Key thought**

   The terror on the earth because of God's judgment.

7. **Key thing to look out for**

   Why had the martyrs been slain?

8. **Key Bible cross-reference**

   Verse 8. See Ezekiel 14:21. Four horses: see Zechariah 6.

9. **Key "by way of explanation"**

   The breaking of the first four seals brings in the four horsemen, with a deadly
   role to play. "The appearance of the horsemen marks 'the beginning of birth
   pangs" which herald the winding up of the first age (Mark 13:8)" (F.F. Bruce).

10. **Key "Quotable Quote"**

    "I tell you, brethren, if mercies and if judgments do not convert you, God has
    no other arrows in his quiver."
    Robert Murray M'Cheyne

Revelation chapter 7

1. Before and after

Previous chapter: Chapter 6: Six seals opened
Following chapter: Chapter 8: The seventh seal, the censer and the first four trumpets

2. Analysis of chapter

A pause between two great periods. (1-3)
The peace, happiness, and safety of the saints, as seen in an angel's sealing 144,000. (4-8)
A song of praise. (9-12)
The blessedness and glory of those that suffered martyrdom for Christ. (13-17)

3. Key verse

Verse 10: "And they cried out in a loud voice: 'Salvation belongs to our God, who sits on the throne, and to the Lamb.'"

4. Key word / key phrase

Verse 4, "144,000."

5. Key event / key person / key theme

Sealing and martyrs

6. Key thought

The "seal" is the Name and "Name" denotes character (14:1; 22:4). The people who belong to God are protected during the coming judgments.

7. Key thing to look out for

The description of the new age (15-17) (cf. Isaiah 40:11; 25:8; 40:10) when believers will serve God.

8. Key Bible cross-reference

Verse 1: See Jeremiah 49:36.

9. Key "by way of explanation"

Verse 4, "1444,000." This is a symbolic number and stands for faithful believers. It is a "great multitude" and consists of people from "every nation, tribe, people, and language," verse 9. Verse 1, the winds are the wins of judgment.

10. Key "Quotable Quote"

"It is the happiness of heaven to have God be all in all."
Jeremiah Burroughs

Revelation chapter 8

1. Before and after

Previous chapter: Chapter 7: Sealing and martyrs
Following chapter: Chapter 9: The fifth and sixth trumpet

2. Analysis of chapter

The seventh seal is opened and seven angels appear with seven trumpets, ready to proclaim God's purposes. (1,2)
Another angel throws down fire on the earth, which produces terrible storms of judgment. (3-5)
The seven angels prepare to sound their trumpets. (6)
Four sound them. (7-12)
Another angel announces greater woes to come. (13)

3. Key verse

Verse 2: "And I saw the seven angels who stand before God, and to them were given seven trumpets."

4. Key word / key phrase

Verse 1, "the seventh seal."

5. Key event / key person / key theme

The seventh seal, the censer, and the first four trumpets.

6. Key thought

Verse 1. In silent suspense heaven waits the final judgment, but the opening of the seventh seal introduces further judgments.

7. Key thing to look out for

The way in which all creation suffers as the result of human sin.

8. Key Bible cross-reference

Verse 7. See Exodus 9:23-25.

9. Key "by way of explanation"

Verse 2, "seven trumpets." In the Old Testament trumpets were used to herald some important event or to give instructions to troops in battle.

10. Key "Quotable Quote"

"God hath appointed a day, wherein he will judge the world by Jesus Christ, when every one shall receive according to his deeds; the wicked shall go into everlasting punishment; the righteous, into everlasting life."
Southern Baptist Theological Seminary

Revelation chapter 9

1. *Before and after*

Previous chapter: Chapter 8: The seventh seal, the censer and the first four trumpets
Following chapter: Chapter 10: The little scroll

2. *Analysis of chapter*

The fifth trumpet and the star falling from heaven; the opening of the bottomless pit, out of which come swarms of locusts. (1-12)
The sixth trumpet is followed by the freeing of four angels bound in the great river Euphrates. (13-21)

3. *Key verse*

Verse 11: "They had as king over them the angel of the Abyss, whose name in Hebrew is Abaddon, and in Greek, Apollyon."

4. *Key word / key phrase*

Verse 1, "the Abyss," (the dwelling-place of demons)

5. *Key event / key person / key theme*

The fifth and sixth trumpet

6. *Key thought*

These malign demon-horsemen released from the Abyss wreak hideous destruction (the fire, smoke and sulfur, verse 8, betray their origin).

7. *Key thing to look out for*

Even facing God's judgment some refused to repent (verse 20).

8. *Key Bible cross-reference*

Verse 2. See Genesis 19:28.

9. *Key "by way of explanation"*

Verse 1, "sounded his trumpet." The seven trumpets of chapters 8 – 9, and also of 11:15-19 announce the plagues. These are worse than the seals, but not as bad as the bowls. Verse 11, "Abaddon," and "Apollyon" both mean destruction.

10. *Key "Quotable Quote"*

"The law opens not nor makes visible God's grace and mercy, or the righteousness whereby we obtain everlasting life and salvation, but our sins, our weakness, death, God's wrath and judgment."
Martin Luther

Revelation chapter 10

1. *Before and after*

Previous chapter: Chapter 9: The fifth and sixth trumpet
Following chapter: Chapter 11: The two witnesses and the seventh trumpet

2. *Analysis of chapter*

The angel of the covenant presents a little open book, which is followed by seven thunders. (1-4)
At the end of the following prophecies, time should be no more. (5-7)
A voice directs the apostle to eat the book (8-10);
and tells him he must prophesy further. (11)

3. *Key verse*

Verse 11: "You must prophesy again about many peoples, nations, languages and kings."

4. *Key word / key phrase*

Verse 9, "the little scroll."

5. *Key event / key person / key theme*

The little scroll

6. *Key thought*

The contents of the scroll were sweet, because they were God's word, but bitter to digest because they concerned judgment (cf. Ezekiel 3:3,14).

7. *Key thing to look out for*

The contents of the scroll are given in Revelation 11:1-13.

8. *Key Bible cross-reference*

Verses 5-7. See Exodus 20:11.

9. *Key "by way of explanation"*

Verse 9, "Take it and eat it." John had to read, mark, learn and inwardly digest the contents of the scroll. See Psalm 119:103.

10. *Key "Quotable Quote"*

"Even if I were attempting to study the Scriptures and nothing else, from boyhood to decrepit old age, with the utmost leisure, the most unwearied zeal, and with talents greater than I possess, I would still be making progress in discovering their treasures."
Augustine of Hippo

Revelation chapter 11

1. Before and after

Previous chapter: Chapter 10: The little scroll
Following chapter: Chapter 12: The woman, war in heaven and on earth

2. Analysis of chapter

The state of the Church is represented by a temple which is measured. (1,2)
Two witnesses prophesy is sackcloth. (3-6)
They are killed, after which they arise and ascend to heaven. (7-14)
The seventh trumpet. (15-19)

3. Key verse

Verse 4: "These are the two olive trees and the two lamp stands that stand before the Lord of the earth"

4. Key word / key phrase

Verse 3, "my two witnesses."

5. Key event / key person / key theme

The two witnesses and the seventh trumpet

6. Key thought

It has been suggested that verses 1-4 refer to the literal Jerusalem temple and a period when its outer court was occupied by Rome (the 42 months). This historical event is moved into John's apocalyptic vision – the temple is now the people of God.

7. Key thing to look out for

The reasons for praising God.

8. Key Bible cross-reference

Verse 1. See Ezekiel 40:3.

9. Key "by way of explanation"

Verse 3, "1,260 days." In verse 2 there are said to be "42 months." The 1,260 days are made up of 30 days, that is 42x30=1,260. This period of time was a symbol (taken from Daniel) for a period of Gentile domination.

10. Key "Quotable Quote"

"Man's chief work is the praise of God."
Augustine of Hippo

Revelation chapter 12

1. *Before and after*

Previous chapter: Chapter 11: The two witnesses and the seventh trumpet
Following chapter: Chapter 13: The beast from the sea, and from the land

2. *Analysis of chapter*

A description of the messianic community and of Satan, represented by a woman and a great red dragon. (1-6)
Michael and his angels fight against the devil and his angels, who are defeated. (7-12)
The dragon persecutes the Church. (13,14)
His unsuccessful attempt to destroy her. He renews his war against her descendants. (14-17)

3. *Key verse*

Verse 9: "The great dragon was hurled down – that ancient serpent called the devil, or Satan, who leads the whole world astray. He was hurled to the earth, and his angels with him."

4. *Key word / key phrase*

Verse 1, "a woman clothed with the sun."

5. *Key event / key person / key theme*

The woman, war in heaven and on earth

6. *Key thought*

The victory of Christ and ruin of Satan (the dragon).

7. *Key thing to look out for*

The reason for the devil's fury (verse 12) and the believers' victory (verse 11).

8. *Key Bible cross-reference*

Verse 5. See Psalm 2:9.

9. *Key "by way of explanation"*

Verse 3. In the Old Testament dragons are used metaphorically to stand for God's enemies. The woman probably symbolizes the true Israel, out of which the Messiah came (verse 5).

10. *Key "Quotable Quote"*

"In the buzzing, booming confusion of good and evil, blessing and cursing, rest and conflict, St John discovers pattern and design. He hears rhythms. He discovers arrangement and proportion. He communicates an overpowering sense of an ending."
Eugene H. Peterson

Revelation chapter 13

1. Before and after

Previous chapter: Chapter 12: The woman, war in heaven and on earth
Following chapter: Chapter 14: The vision of the Lamb and of the harvest

2. Analysis of chapter

A wild beast rises out of the sea, to whom the dragon gives his power. (1-10)
Another beast, which has two horns like a lamb, but speaks as a dragon. (11-15)
It makes everyone worship its image, and receive its mark, as people who are given over to it. (16-18)

3. Key verse

Verse 6: "He opened his mouth to blaspheme God, and to slander his name and his dwelling place and those who live in heaven."

4. Key word / key phrase

Verse 1, "a beast coming out of the sea."

5. Key event / key person / key theme

The beast from the sea, and from the land

6. Key thought

The evil power of the beast out of the sea (perhaps the Roman Empire), and the beast out of the earth (may be the false prophet, 16:13). Today the beast might be said to represent totalitarian world power; and the prophet, false religion.

7. Key thing to look out for

The qualities needed by Christians (verses 10,18; also 14:12)

8. Key Bible cross-reference

Verses 1-7. See Daniel 7.

9. Key "by way of explanation"

Verse 13, "miraculous signs" do not always come from God and are not always intended to bring him glory, but rather, to deceive his followers. See Deuteronomy 13:1-3; Matthew 24:24.

10. Key "Quotable Quote"

"Nothing great was ever done without much enduring."
Catherine of Siena

Revelation chapter 14

1. Before and after

Previous chapter: Chapter 13: The beast from the sea, and from the land
Following chapter: Chapter 15: The victory song of the redeemed

2. Analysis of chapter

Those who remain faithful to Christ praise God. (1-5)
Three angels; one proclaiming the everlasting gospel; another, the downfall of Babylon; and a third, the dreadful wrath of God on the worshipers of the beast. The happy state of those who die in the Lord. (6-13)
A vision of Christ with a sickle, and of a harvest ready to be cut down. (14-16)
The symbol of a ripe grape harvest, trodden in the wine-press of God's wrath. (17-20)

3. Key verse

Verse 1: "Then I looked, and there before me was the Lamb, standing on Mount Zion, and with him 144,000 who had his name and his Father's name written on their foreheads."

4. Key word / key phrase

Verse 1, "the Lamb."

5. Key event / key person / key theme

The vision of the Lamb and of the harvest

6. Key thought

An interlude to encourage believers. There is victory and rest for those who remain faithful.

7. Key thing to look out for

Note what can be gleaned about the 144,000 (the true followers) verses 1-5. (Verse 4 probably symbolizes purity of heart.)

8. Key Bible cross-reference

Verse 1: See Ezekiel 9:4.

9. Key "by way of explanation"

Verse 10, "cup of wrath." In the Old Testament, God's wrath is often pictured as a cup full of wine which has to be drunk. See Psalm 75:8; Jeremiah 25:15.

10. Key "Quotable Quote"

"Jesus is our mouth, through which we speak to the Father; He is our eye, through which we see the Father; He is our right hand through which we offer ourselves to the Father. Unless He intercedes, there is no intercourse with God."
Ambrose

Revelation chapter 15

1. *Before and after*

Previous chapter: Chapter 14: The vision of the Lamb and of the harvest
Following chapter: Chapter 16: The bowls of God's anger

2. *Analysis of chapter*

A song of praise is sung by the Church. (1-4)
Seven angels with the seven plagues. To them one of the living creatures gives seven golden bowls full of God's wrath. (5-8)

3. *Key verse*

Verse 2: "And I saw what looked like a sea of glass mixed with fire and, standing beside the sea, those who had been victorious over the beast and his image and over the number of his name."

4. *Key word / key phrase*

Verse 3, "the song of the Lamb."

5. *Key event / key person / key theme*

The victory song of the redeemed

6. *Key thought*

After the song comes a further unfolding of God's purposes and judgment ("was opened" verse 5).

7. *Key thing to look out for*

What we are told here about the nature of God.

8. *Key Bible cross-reference*

Verse 5. See Exodus 38:21.

9. *Key "by way of explanation"*

Verse 3, "song of Moses." This is recorded in Exodus 15 and Deuteronomy 32. The song of Moses and the "song of the Lamb" both express God's triumph over his enemies. Verse 2. They were victorious because they did not worship the beast or let themselves be marked with his number (13:15-17).

10. *Key "Quotable Quote"*

"By engaging with the power of the devil, the fear of death, and the pains of hell, Christ gained the victory, and achieved a triumph, so that we now fear not in death those things which our Prince has destroyed."
John Calvin

Revelation chapter 16

1. *Before and after*

   Previous chapter: Chapter 15: The victory song of the redeemed
   Following chapter: Chapter 17: Overthrow of the great prostitute

2. *Analysis of chapter*

   The first bowl is poured out on the earth, the second on the sea, the third on the rivers and fountains. (1-7)
   The fourth on the sun, the fifth on the throne of the beast. (8-11)
   The sixth on the great river Euphrates. (12-16)
   And the seventh into the air, after which will follow the destruction of all antichristian enemies. (17-21)

3. *Key verse*

   Verse 16: "Then they gathered the kings together to the place that in Hebrew is called Armageddon."

4. *Key word / key phrase*

   Verse 1, "pour out the seven bowls."

5. *Key event / key person / key theme*

   The bowls of God's anger

6. *Key thought*

   These judgments are similar to the previous judgments but more severe because they affect the whole area.

7. *Key thing to look out for*

   "More terrible than the plagues themselves is the way in which those on whom they fall are but hardened in their impenitence." (F.F. Bruce)

8. *Key Bible cross-reference*

   Verse 10. See Exodus 10:21.

9. *Key "by way of explanation"*

   Verse 16, "Armageddon." This depicts the unspecified place where the final battle to overthrow evil will take place.

10. *Key "Quotable Quote"*

   "The existence of evil is not so much an obstacle to faith in God as a proof of God's existence, a challenge to turn toward that in which love triumphs over hatred, union over division, and eternal life over death."
   N.A. Berdyaev

Revelation chapter 17

1. Before and after

Previous chapter: Chapter 16: The bowls of God's anger
Following chapter: Chapter 18: Babylon's fall

2. Analysis of chapter

One of the angels who had the bowls explains the meaning of the previous vision of the antichristian beast that was to reign 1260 years, and then to be destroyed. (1-6)
The angel interprets the mystery of the woman, and the beast that had seven heads and ten horns. (7-18)

3. Key verse

Verse 17: "For God has put it into their hearts to accomplish his purpose by agreeing to give the beast their power to rule, until God's words are fulfilled."

4. Key word / key phrase

Verse 1, "punishment of the great prostitute."

5. Key event / key person / key theme

Overthrow of the great prostitute

6. Key thought

What effect do the descriptions of evil in this book have on us?

7. Key thing to look out for

How can we best fight evil and promote good?

8. Key Bible cross-reference

Verse 4. See Jeremiah 51:7.

9. Key "by way of explanation"

Verse 14, "Lord of lords and King of kings." In the middle of great evil God's power and sovereignty are reflected in this title of his. Verse 5, "Mystery," that is, the name is to be understood symbolically. In Revelation Babylon refers to Rome.

10. Key "Quotable Quote"

"People account it a great thing to have friendship and fellowship with an earthly king; how incomparably greater is the privilege of having fellowship and friendship with God, who is the King of kings, and the Lord of lords."
Tikhon of Zadonsk

Revelation chapter 18

1. Before and after

Previous chapter: Chapter 17: Overthrow of the great prostitute
Following chapter: Chapter 19: The marriage of the Lamb, and the rider on the white horse

2. Analysis of chapter

Another angel from heaven proclaims the fall of mystical Babylon. (1-3)
A voice from heaven admonishes the people of God in case they take part in her plagues. (4-8)
The lamentations over her. (9-19)
The Church called on to rejoice in her utter ruin. (20-24)

3. Key verse

Verse 1: "After this I saw another angel coming down from heaven. He had great authority, and the earth was illuminated by his splendor."

4. Key word / key phrase

Verse 2, "Fallen is Babylon."

5. Key event / key person / key theme

Babylon's fall

6. Key thought

Rome's great wealth came from exploitation of others and callous indifference to people's needs (verse 13).

7. Key thing to look out for

There are parallels between Rome and Western society. What can Christians do?

8. Key Bible cross-reference

Verse 11. See Ezekiel 27:31.

9. Key "by way of explanation"

Verse 2, "Fallen is Babylon." Babylon stands for any political system that opposes God. It stands for political power, decadence, and hatred of God's faithful followers. Here Babylon's fall is celebrated.

10. Key "Quotable Quote"

"To comment in detail on this severe and vivid poetry would be like trying to analyze every note in a piece of music: we wouldn't hear the tune. It is best simply to read it, perhaps aloud, and sense how tragic, how poignant, how catastrophic and inevitable is the collapse of a world power which overreaches itself."
Stephen Travis

Revelation chapter 19

1. Before and after

Previous chapter: Chapter 18: Babylon's fall
Following chapter: Chapter 20: Binding Satan and the reign of the martyrs,
Gog and Magog, and the final judgment

2. Analysis of chapter

Joy at God's victory over Babylon. (1-5)
The marriage of the Lamb. (6-10)
A vision of Christ going out to destroy the beast and his armies. (11-21)

3. Key verse

Verse 6: "Then I heard what sounded like a great multitude, like the roar of
rushing waters and like loud peals of thunder, shouting: "Hallelujah! For our
Lord God Almighty reigns.""

4. Key word / key phrase

Verse 7, "the wedding of the Lamb."

5. Key event / key person / key theme

The marriage of the Lamb, and the rider on the white horse

6. Key thought

These hymns of praise should be used in our own worship and prayers.

7. Key thing to look out for

What do verses 11-16 show about Christ?

8. Key Bible cross-reference

Verses 7-9. See Mark 2:19; 2 Corinthians 11:2; Ephesians 5:25-27.

9. Key "by way of explanation"

Verses 11-16 give a symbolic picture of Christ in his Second Coming. The
white horse is a symbol of victory. Verses 7-21 are a further reference to the
Battle of Armageddon (see 16:14-16).

10. Key "Quotable Quote"

"Praise is a soul in flower."
Thomas Watson

Revelation chapter 20

1. *Before and after*

Previous chapter: Chapter 19: The marriage of the Lamb, and the rider on the white horse
Following chapter: Chapter 21: The new Jerusalem

2. *Analysis of chapter*

Satan is bound and the martyrs reign. (1-6)
Satan set free. Gog and Magog. (7-10)
The last judgment. (11-15)

3. *Key verse*

Verse 1: "And I saw an angel coming down out of heaven, having the key to the Abyss and holding in his hand a great chain."

4. *Key word / key phrase*

Verse 2, "He seized the dragon."

5. *Key event / key person / key theme*

Binding Satan and the reign of the martyrs, Gog and Magog, and the final judgment

6. *Key thought*

Satan will finally be utterly defeated, and all humankind will be judged. This is a judgment of each individual.

7. *Key thing to look out for*

Verses 11-15, the scene is awesome in its grandeur and gravity. What is the basis of the judgment?

8. *Key Bible cross-reference*

Verses 11,12. See Daniel 7:9,10.

9. *Key "by way of explanation"*

Verse 4, "those who had been beheaded." This refers to Christian martyrs of all ages. Gog and Magog represent all the nations who make one final attack on God. Verse 2 "thousand years": the millennium. There are different views about the order of events, the meaning of the "thousand years" and "the first resurrection."

10. *Key "Quotable Quote"*

"In order to avoid lying to our interrogators or deceiving them, we freely go to our deaths confessing Christ."
Justin Martyr

Revelation chapter 21

1. Before and after

Previous chapter: Chapter 20: Binding Satan and the reign of the martyrs, Gog and Magog, and the final judgment
Following chapter: Chapter 22: The river of life

2. Analysis of chapter

A new heaven, and new earth: the new Jerusalem where God dwells, and all sorrow is banished from his people. (1-8)
Its heavenly origin, glory, and secure defense. (9-21)
More details about the new Jerusalem. (22-27)

3. Key verse

Verse 6: "It is done. I am the Alpha and the Omega, the Beginning and the End. To him who is thirsty I will give to drink without cost from the spring of the water of life."

4. Key word / key phrase

Verse 1, "a new heaven and a new earth."

5. Key event / key person / key theme

The new Jerusalem

6. Key thought

In the new Jerusalem God will be fully with his people. (To John a city was a place of community and happiness).

7. Key thing to look out for

What are the characteristics of the new Jerusalem?

8. Key Bible cross-reference

Verse 1. See Isaiah 65:17.

9. Key "by way of explanation"

Verse 4, "wipe every tear." In heaven, not only will tears be wiped away, but all reasons for crying will be a thing of the past. See 7:17; Isaiah 25:8. "No more sea," the Jews were afraid of the sea.

10. Key "Quotable Quote"

"Heaven is that state where we will always be with Jesus, and where nothing will separate us from him any more."
William Barclay

Revelation chapter 22

1. *Previous chapter*

Chapter 21: The new Jerusalem

2. *Analysis of chapter*

A description of the heavenly city, using the symbols of water and the tree of life, and of the throne of God and the Lamb. (1-5)
The truth and certain fulfillment of all the prophetic visions. The Holy Spirit, and the bride, the Church, issue their invitation, and say, "Come." (6-19)
The closing blessing. (20,21)

3. *Key verse*

Verse 8: "I, John, am the one who heard and saw these things. And when I had heard and seen them, I fell down to worship at the feet of the angel who had been showing them to me."

4. *Key word / key phrase*

Verse 1, "the river of the water of life."

5. *Key event / key person / key theme*

The river of life

6. *Key thought*

Jesus is coming.

7. *Key thing to look out for*

What does it mean for me to live in the light of Revelation 21 and 22?

8. *Key Bible cross-reference*

Verse 3. See Zechariah 14:11.

9. *Key "by way of explanation"*

Verse 2, "tree of life." The description of the tree of life in this chapter should be compared with Genesis 2:9; 3:22 and Ezekiel 47:12.

10. *Key "Quotable Quote"*

"I hope that the day is near at hand when the advent of the great God will appear, for all things everywhere are boiling, burning, moving, falling, sinking, groaning."
Martin Luther